POVERTY, MANPOWER, AND SOCIAL SECURITY

POVERTY, MANPOWER, AND SOCIAL SECURITY

Paul A. Brinker
The University of Oklahoma

Joseph J. Klos
Oklahoma State University

Austin Press
Educational Division of
Lone Star Publishers, Inc.
P.O. Box 9774
Austin, Texas 78766

Library of Congress Card Number: 75-13359
ISBN: 0-914872-07-9

Printed in the United States of America

The typestyles used in this book were Melior Roman and Italic and Spartan Demi-bold. Type was set in Austin, Texas by ON-LINE Computer Typesetting, Inc.

To Barbara and Marilyn (P.A.B.)
Frances and Frank (J.J.K.)

PREFACE

Economics textbooks on insecurity in the late 1930's concentrated on the problem of unemployment and the three major sections of the Social Security Act: unemployment insurance, old-age insurance, and public assistance. Patterns of economic insecurity changed with World War II and the post-war prosperity, but economic textbooks on insecurity did not change accordingly. Little work was done by economists on problems of low-wage industries or minority groups. Some have contended that until several years ago many economists were oblivious to the fact that there was widespread poverty in the United States. An attempt was made to remedy this gap in the first version (1968). Accordingly there was a chapter on the low-wage industry of agriculture and a discussion of such minority groups as Negroes, Mexican-Americans, American Indians, and Puerto Ricans. Extensive changes have been made in the second edition. Historical perspectives were given a fuller treatment as was welfare. The vast expansion of manpower programs in the 1960's called for an additional chapter in this section. Urban poverty was treated in more detail as was the War on Poverty program. Newer programs such as the negative income tax and others are also included in this work.

This second volume is divided into six main parts. Part I, Introduction, includes the first three chapters on historical perspectives, ideological perspectives, and poverty. Part II, Aging and Welfare (chapters 4 through 9), deals with problems of aging, the old age insurance program, and welfare. Also covered are private solutions to economic insecurity, such as life insurance. Part III, Problems of Disability and Health (chapters 10 through 14), covers problems of occupational disability, workmen's compensation and medical economic problems. Part IV, The Problem of Unemployment and Underemployment (chapters 15 through 20), deals with various types of unemployment and their remedies, unemployment insurance, and various private methods of alleviating unemployment such as the guaranteed annual wage. Part V, Problems of Low Income and Special Groups (chapters 21 through 25), includes the topics of rural and urban poverty along with poverty among such groups as blacks, Mexican Americans, American Indians, mainland Puerto Ricans, and families headed by women. Part VI, Solutions to Poverty (chapters 26 through 28), covers such topics as the minimum wage, the War on Poverty, the negative income tax, family allowances, and others.

We wish to thank Professor Robert J. Lampman of the University of Wisconsin who read the entire manuscript and made many valuable comments. We are also grateful for the following four professors who also read the manuscript in its entirety: Alexander Holmes and Marilyn Flowers of the University of Oklahoma and Ansel Sharp and Rudolph Trenton of Oklahoma State University. Also we are indebted to Mr. Alfred M. Skolnik of the Social Security Administration for his reading the chapter on workmen's compensation and to Mr. Skolnik, Patience Lauriat, and Jane Ceccarelli of the same agency for reading the chapters on the old age insurance program. Lastly we wish to thank our wives for the many aids given us on the manuscript.

P.A.B. and J.J.K.

CONTENTS

LIST OF FIGURES

LIST OF TABLES

PART I

INTRODUCTION

(HISTORICAL AND IDEOLOGICAL PERSPECTIVES AND POVERTY)

CHAPTER 1

HISTORICAL PERSPECTIVES

In attempting to earn a living, man has always been faced with a large number of economic problems. In most of the world today, per capita income is so low that many people do not have adequate food, clothing, and shelter. Fortunately, income is much higher in the United States than elsewhere. The median family income in the United States in 1973 was $12,051.[1] Many millions of Americans, however, live on much less than this amount. In this book we will be studying the poor and economically insecure people of the United States. Some of these people had an adequate income at one time, but have fallen into a lower income group because of a death, illness, an industrial accident, old age, or unemployment. Others in the poverty group never attained sufficient income to live well. Some in this group may be employed in low-wage industries or occupations. Many members of minority groups, such as blacks, persons of Spanish heritage, American Indians, as well as large numbers of whites have chronically low income.

PRIMITIVE SOCIETIES AND EARLY RELIGIONS

Early primitive societies gradually developed systems of social welfare. Anthropologists have pointed out that the purpose of the formation of such societies was not only to dominate weaker beings but also to provide for mutual protection and to promote the feeling of belonging. Mutual aid helped to promote security, but in some primitive societies the aged, the ill, or the otherwise handicapped were killed or abandoned as being too great a burden on the tribe. As tribes developed, a priesthood group arose, and this group often assumed leadership in protecting the helpless. Religion became a powerful force in dictating that charity be practiced. Practically all ancient religions preached charity either for the purpose of obtaining the grace of God, or out of a genuine feeling of pity.[2] From Venidad, a book of the ancient Zoroaster religion, we read: "The riches of the infinite God will be bestowed upon him who relieves the poor." A

---

[1]*Money Income of Families and Persons in the United States*, U.S. Department of Commerce, Bureau of the Census, Current Population Reports, Series P-60, No. 93, July 1974, Table 1.

[2]Walter A. Friedlander, *Introduction to Social Welfare* (Englewood Cliffs, N.J., Prentice-Hall, 1955), pp. 9-10.

Hindu epic has it that "he who giveth without stint food to a fatigued wayfarer, never seen before, obtaineth merit that is great."[3] Many societies in ancient and medieval times had proto-social welfare measures.

ANCIENT EGYPT

In ancient Egypt, as today, the way of life centered around the Nile. The Pharoah lived in great splendor and was entombed in splendor. But the life of the peasant, the laborer, and the slave was hard. They toiled in other men's fields, worked on the Pharoah's building projects, and died in misery.

Unification under a strong central government permitted a degree of organization of work not previously known.[4] Labor was conscripted to build and maintain dikes and canals, and the same conscripted labor built the Pharoah's great monuments. The central authority also saw to it that its labor had at least the bare minimum for existence, and provided for the storage of grain in the fat years to offset the shortages of the lean years. Such economic security as existed thus depended on the bounty of the Nile River and on the social organization brought about by a strong central government.

THE HEBREWS

Dictatorship, slavery, oppression, and mistreatment caused an obscure tribe, the Hebrews, to flee from the splendors of Egypt. From this obscure tribe much of the moral consciousness of the western world is derived. The Jewish Scriptures (the Christian "Old Testament") have exerted a tremendous impact on the thinking of the human race. One of its major themes is that of social injustice. Moses' anger and his act of slaying an Egyptian for oppressing a Hebrew[6] demonstrated his attitude toward injustice. Later a rule was laid down that if money were loaned to the poor, no interest should be charged.[7] Every seven years creditors released borrowers from all debts. At the same time a command was given: "Thou shalt surely open thy hand unto thy brother, to the needy, and to thy poor, in the land."[8] Even more stringent was the rule that every fifty years, the year of jubilee, the land had to be returned by creditors to their original

[3]Amos Warner, Mary Coolidge, and George Howard, *American Charities* (New York, Thomas Crowell Co., 1919), p. 5.

[4]Lionel Cassons and the editors of Time-Life Books, *Ancient Egypt*, Great Ages of Man series (New York, Time Incorporated, 1965), p. 12-31.

[5]*Ibid.*, p. 33.

[6]Exodus, 2:11-12.

[7]*Ibid.*, 22:25.

[8]Deuteronomy, 15:7.

owners. Any person who became poor and had to sell himself was permitted to do so only as a hired servant rather than a slave. He became free
during the year of jubilee.[9] In the book of Job we have an example of how
the wealthy patriarch should behave to those less fortunate than himself:

If I have withheld the poor from their desire, or have caused the eyes of the
widow to fail, or have eaten my morsel alone, and the fatherless hath not eaten
thereof;. . . If I have seen any perish for want of clothing, or that the needy had no
clothing . . . then let my shoulder fall from the shoulder blade and mine arm be
broken from the bone.[10]

And for all men there is Micah's "He hath showed thee, O man, what is
good; and what doth the Lord require of thee, but to do justly, and to love
mercy, and to walk humbly with thy God_"[11]

"Social Security" in ancient Israel was thus embodied in "the Law
and the Prophets" — commandments to the family to care for their own,
to provide for the sojourner, to be generous to the debtor, and be merciful
to the needy. Reality of course often fell short of the ideal, but the impact
on western civilization is almost beyond measure.

THE GREEKS

Western civilization was also much affected by Greek thought and
behavior. The thinking of Plato and of Aristotle are noteworthy, and
historians still inquire into the nature of Spartan and Athenian life. Sparta
and Athens represented opposing philosophies — military discipline on
the one hand and intellectual and political freedom on the other. In a
period when military concerns were paramount, Sparta became an armed
camp. Athens, on the other hand, had a superficial democracy. Every free
citizen could speak for himself, the population was small and intensely
civic-minded, and the rights of others were respected. Culture flourished.
But the "glory that was Greece" was a glory based on slavery. The citizens
could behave democratically because often over half the population was
in slavery. "With slaves to handle the daily chores and the routine work of
commerce and manufacturing, Athenian citizens were free to give their
time to public affairs."[13] A second group of underprivileged people in
Athens were women. A woman's place was in the home, and her main
social obligation was to remain silent.[14]

[9]Leviticus. 25:23-39.
[10]Job, 31:16-22.
[11]Micah, 6:8.
[12]C. M. Bowra and the editors of Time-Life Books, *Classical Greece*, Great Ages of Man
Series (New York, Time Incorporated, 1965).
[13]*Ibid.*, p. 94.
[14]*Ibid.*, p. 95.

Modern society has been profoundly affected by Ancient Greece, and especially by the thinking of Plato and Aristotle. Plato proposed an ideal society in which there were to be only three classes of people: the rulers, the soldiers, and the workers. His aristocractic leanings led him to believe that most of the people were incapable of ruling or profiting from education. In order that the rulers of the society would not become avaricious, he advocated communal living for this group. He also felt that wives and children should be common property to keep the rulers from pressing for material gain. Plato contended that extremes of wealth and poverty were harmful to a community, and that the ideal society should avoid both extremes.[15]

Aristotle, a pupil of Plato, rejected communism on grounds that communal property is not cared for properly. Futhermore, people enjoy products more if they are their own. Aristotle felt that communism would lead to much quarreling since those who worked hard would resent the lazy. Communism in wives and children was dismissed as weakening friendship and destroying love. However, Aristotle agreed with Plato's idea that there should be different classes of people in society. Aristotle was disdainful of manual labor, and like practically all other thinkers of his time, upheld the institution of slavery. He maintained that slaves were unable to guide themselves by reason. He held that great wealth on the one hand and poverty on the other were harmful; therefore, he put his faith in the middle class. Poverty, according to him, led to revolution and crime, whereas the desire for wealth caused even greater crimes in order to gratify passion or satisfy the desire for excess.

THE ROMANS

Rome, by the time of Christ, had supplanted Greece as the center of western civilization, and in doing so had absorbed much of Greek culture. Rome itself was a mighty empire from the time of Julius Caeser (100? — 44 B.C.) until at least 300 A.D. when the empire was clearly in decline. As a mighty empire, it established a *Pax Romana* throughout the Mediterranean area that permitted a level of civilization not previously recorded in human history.

Although there was nothing approaching an organized social insurance system, there were bits and pieces of social institutions that had a "social security" aspect. Among these may be mentioned a system of aid to orphans, free food and free entertainment for the poor, a system of inspection of housing and sanitation, and public doctors for the poor.

The Emperor Trajan (A.D. 54? - 117) is credited with setting up the system known as *alimenta*, a special fund equivalent to the imperial

---

[15]The material in Grecian and Roman thought is taken mainly from Emory S. Bogardus, *The Development of Social Thought* (New York, Longmans, 1950), Chapters 8-10.

budget for an entire year, and from which low-cost farm loans were made. The proceeds from the various loans were used to support orphans and the children of the poor — a sort of Roman Aid to Families with Dependent Children. Girls were granted smaller sums than boys, and illegitimate children less than legitimate. Yet all got some degree of support. The system was expanded by Trajan's successors and continued to operate for nearly 200 years.[16]

The patron-client relationship, which developed in Rome, has no modern counterpart. Large numbers of Romans above the plebian class were required to assume an obligation for the well-being of certain of their inferiors. It was a sort of mutual-assistance arrangement. By the time the Republic had evolved into an Empire, the patron-client relationship had become economic as well as social. Sometimes the patron provided his client with food or with money. If the client were out of work, this daily dole might be his only income.

Just how extensive this system was is not known, but "according to some accounts every Roman but the Emperor himself owed obeisance to someone higher, every Roman but the plebian owed assistance to someone lower."[17]Carried to the extreme no one but the slaves would have been engaged in productive activity. The decline and fall of Rome has sometimes been attributed to "bread and circuses," that is the giving of free grain to the poor, and admission of all comers without charge to theaters and circuses. More likely, however, the patron-client relationship was only a part-time activity, and patrician, plebian, and slave all rendered certain services.

CHRISTIANITY

The teachings of Jesus obviously have had an important impact on our civilization. The basic tenet of early Christian thought was that people should believe in a benevolent God who would grant them everlasting life in the hereafter. Also, "Thou shalt love thy neighbor as thyself."[18] Jesus himself practiced compassion by healing the sick, giving encouragement to those who were weary and heavy laden, and in feeding hungry multitudes. In his preaching He suggested that mercy be practiced. As good practices He specifically cited food to the hungry, water to the thirsty, lodging to strangers, clothing to the naked, and visitations to those who were sick or in prison. In relationships with other people, He suggested love for enemies, and reconciliation between those who have quarreled. If evil is done, Jesus recommended not reprisal but a turning of the cheek. If a person compels you to go a mile with him, Jesus suggested that

[16]Moses Hadas and the editors of Time-Life Books, *Imperial Rome*, Great Ages of Man series (New York, Time Incorporated, 1965), pp. 65-7.

[17]*Ibid.*

[18]*Matthew, 22:37-39.*

you go two miles. He added that you should give to those who ask or would borrow from you. This philosophy of love and the brotherhood of man may be summarized by what has come to be known as the Golden Rule: "And as ye would that men should do to you, do ye also to them likewise."[19]

Christianity, however, never spoke with a united voice on the matter of care for the poor. The letter of James emphasized the importance of good works:

If a brother or sister is ill-clad and in lack of daily food, and one of you says to them, Go in peace, be warmed and filled, without giving them the things needed for the body, what does it profit. So faith by itself, if it has no works, is dead.[20]

But the writings of Paul led to many interpretations. Parts of his letters emphasized love of fellow man, which should lead to good works; other passages emphasized the grace of God as the road to salvation:

For by grace you have been saved through faith; and this is not your own doing, it is the gift of God — not because of works, lest any man should boast.[21]

From this and similar passages some thought man's role was only passive — that salvation was a gift of God requiring no particular effort on man's part. Others taught that "good works" were necessary for salvation.

Subsequent Church fathers continued the controversy. St. Augustine (A.D. 354-430) put so much emphasis on the first commandment, belief in God, that no corollaries on welfare were worked out for this life.[22] The status quo was looked upon as ordained by God, and therefore nothing should be done to change society or alleviate the sufferings of the unfortunate. Earthly sufferings were temporary; salvation was eternal. At the other extreme eight centuries later was St. Francis of Assisi (1182-1226), who gave up a great wealth to live a life of poverty and of service to the poor.[23] The church and society were deeply moved by the teachings of St. Francis, and some credit his work with saving Christianity. Today there is little controversy within the Christian Church about doing good works. Christians, however, differ radically on whether and to what extent government should be involved in such programs.

---

[19]Luke, 6:31.

[20]The Letter of James, 2:15-17.

[21]The Letter of Paul to the Ephesians, 2:8-9.

[22]Bogardus, op. cit., pp. 170-171.

[23]James W. Thompson, An Economic and Social History of the Middle Ages (New York, Appleton-Century-Crofts, 1928), p. 694.

BYZANTIUM

The great Roman Empire eventually split into two parts, an eastern and western empire. The western empire fell to the barbarians, the east survived. Christianity had become the state religion in both areas, and when the west was overrun by the barbarians Christianity survived, and the barbarian or his descendants eventually became Christians themselves. Western Europe fragmented into hundreds of tiny states or principalities and the so-called "Dark Ages" descended on the West.

But the Eastern Roman Empire, centered around Constantinople and commonly known as Byzantium, persisted for eleven hundred years (330-1453 A.D.). Along with the Arabic regions Byzantium was the repository of civilization during the western dark ages. It was a society built partly on command, partly on religion, partly on tradition. The structure included Emperor or Empress, a military establishment, a church hierarchy, a guild system in industry and commerce, peasant farmers who were the backbone of the Empire, and as usual, many slaves. Life was of course harsh, the food supply was precarious, disease and pestilence were common, and military service was frequently required to turn back the barbarian. But despite all this Byzantium was a civilization which made an effort to provide for its poor.

Both government and the Church participated in such aid. The city had an ample supply of fresh water, available at street corners and in the public squares to everyone without charge, as was the system of public baths.[24] Government and Church provided medical and hospital care to all those who could not afford to pay. Records indicate that at times as many as 80,000 loaves of bread were distributed daily to the poor, and for those who were homeless, a haven existed at the monasteries.[25] Records also exist showing generous charitable activities by various Emperors and Empresses. Theodora, wife of Justinian is credited with equipping hospitals for the poor, and of converting an old palace into a home for destitute women.[26] Records of construction contracts also show that hospitals, homes for the aged, and homes for the infirm were frequent assignments for builders and architects.[27]

For the workers, the guild system was highly developed. Some 21 major guilds controlled the life and work of all artisans and tradesmen. Wages, hours, and quality of product were closely regulated. Each member of a guild could practice only his own trade, and the son generally succeeded the father in the same trade. In addition, the members of the guild

[24]Philip Sherrard and the editors of Time-Life Books, *Byzantium*, Great Ages of Man series (New York, Time Incorporated, 1966), pp. 36-37.

[25]*Ibid.*, p. 46.

[26]*Ibid.*, p. 57.

[27]*Ibid.*, p. 116.

were required to perform various unpaid public services, such as police work.[28]

THE MIDDLE AGES

While Byzantium flourished in Constantinople, chaos and despair set in in the West. The western Roman Empire fragmented into tiny duchies, principalities, bishoprics, and kingdoms. Trade collapsed due especially to piracy and to tariffs collected every few miles. A drastic population decline occurred in Rome and other major cities. Learning and literacy retreated to the monasteries. Certain areas, once farmed, reverted to forest. But eventually with the passage of centuries, the "low" middle ages turned to the "high" middle ages, and patterns of civilizations reappeared. These centered around church, manor, and guild.

From about 500 to 1000 A.D. the Church was the dominant organization in western Europe.[29] While much of church activity was directed toward maintenance of the status quo, and although the Church was often corrupt, an important part of its activity included aid and protection of the poor. Free food and free hospitalization, such as they were, were often provided. The Church insisted that the poor did not have to fast as much as the rich, and the Church forbade servile work on Sunday. For those endangered by secular authorities the Church provided sanctuary, endeavored to care for the aged and the helpless, and sought to mitigate violence by its teachings.[30] Some, however, have questioned whether or not the Church provided as much in porportion to its resources as did lay society.[31]

A second key medieval institution was the manor, headed by a lord and his family, and peopled by a few artisans and many serfs. Life was precarious. Disease and pestilence were common, famine was endemic, and petty warfare was almost continuous. Peasants willingly or grudgingly exchanged their freedom for serfdom, since as serfs they came under the lord's protection. They were bound to the lord for life, they must work on the lord's lands a certain number of days each week, and they must provide the lord with some of the produce of their own lands. In addition, a variety of taxes were commonly imposed on the serf: special charges might be levied on him when he took a wench in marriage, and the lord might strip his cottage when he died. In exchange, the lord and noble provided protection in time of war, knights were commonly hired to do the fighting, and food and clothing, if there were any surplus, might be provided to the serf and his family out of the lord's store.

[28]*Ibid.*, pp. 116-117.

[29]Anne Fremantle and the editors of Time-Life Books, *Age of Faith*, Great Ages of Man series (New York, Time Incorporated, 1965), p. 12.

[30]*Ibid.*, p. 36.

[31]Thompson, *op. cit.*, p. 684.

In the high middle ages (1000-1400 A.D.) the merchant and the craft guilds came into prominence in the West. Their prime purpose was economic, but they provided a type of "social security" as well. When the guildsman was sick, the guild appointed certain of the brethren to look after him. If old, or needy, or infirm, they were required to visit him regularly, to bring food and clothing, and to pray for his recovery. When he died they were required to pray for his soul. Guild funds were used to bail him out of jail, to pay his debts, to dowery his daughter, to finance his funeral, and to care for his widow.[32]

As the centuries wore on, and central governments began to be reestablished, government social welfare activities were resumed. In 13th century France, Louis IX, called Saint Louis, founded hospitals and asylums, and established homes for the blind and reformed prostitutes.[33] Legend has it that wherever he went he had people fed at public expense. Health ordinances began to be enacted in increasing numbers, some cities paid physicians to treat the poor, and Spain required physicians to make periodic examination of all citizens. The 13th and 14th centuries also saw the widespread development of hospitals, some taken over from the monasteries, some established directly by secular rulers.[34]

THE INCAS

Separate, so far as we know, from the development of civilization in western Europe, was the development of the great Inca civilization in the Andean Mountains. When the Spanish came in the 1500's the Inca civilization was probably the best governed country in the world. An excellent road system, a nationwide messenger service, and skilled engineering works such as agricultural terraces and canals were great physical accomplishments. A strong central government headed by the Inca gave organization, consistency, and continuity.

A nationwide "social security" system took care of the basic wants of all individuals.[35] Each year empire officials estimated the amount of land currently available, and alloted land on the basis of family size so that each family would raise enough food to feed itself.[36] The rest of the land, usually more than half of the total, was alloted to the state or used for the support of religion. Common people were required to cultivate the church and state lands before they worked on their own. The produce on the state lands went into a king's store out of which all state officials, soldiers, artisans and others were paid through a barter-credit arrangement. Out of

[32]Fremantle, *op. cit.*, p. 76.

[33]*Ibid.*, p. 147.

[34]*Ibid.*, p. 150.

[35]Jonathan Norton Leonard and the editors of Time-Life Books, *Ancient America*, Great Ages of Man series (New York, Time Incorporated, 1967), p. 10.

[36]*Ibid.*, pp. 106-7.

the king's store also, widows, the old, and the sick were cared for.[37] Part of the crop went into local storehouses to accumulate a surplus against possible future crop failures. And each family received an annual allowance of wool from state owned llama and alpaca herds from which the wife spun and wove clothing for the family.[38]

WELFARE IN ENGLAND

Since welfare law and practice in England were carried over to the American colonies, and after the Revolutionary War became law and practice in the United States, special attention is directed to the English developments. Early English practice was similar to that on the continent: Church, manor, and guild were the controlling institutions. Social welfare was provided mainly by the Church, and Church canon (law) provides us with much information. In the 12th, 13th and much of the 14th centuries, church canon was humane, but not blind to the fallibility of man. The destitute had a right to assistance, and those better off had a duty to provide it. "Poverty is not a kind of crime" and "A poor man is an honorable person" were basic tenets of the Church law.[39] The old and the sick, and the widows and orphans were singled out for special attention. But at the same time it was made clear that the able-bodied idler was not to be encouraged by handouts, but was to be "corrected" and urged to work. Even this was softened by the canonists who added that this held only if the person seeking assistance could find someone to employ him. The system was administered by the parish priest, and it was assumed that the priest knew who needed help and who did not.

Economic changes, however, set in, and in 1348 a great calamity occurred in the form of the Black Death (bubonic plague) which reduced the population in 1400 to perhaps half that of 1348. In consequence, the labor supply was greatly reduced, labor pressed for higher and higher wages, and some saw an opportunity for looting and violence. This resulted in a shift in attitudes toward the poor. Poverty now became a kind of crime and was formally linked to the problem of vagrancy.[40]

The changed attitude brought repressive legislation. In 1349, a Statute of Laborers was enacted which outlawed begging and required that dependent employees be required to work for their masters at the low wages existing before the coming of the Black Death. The Statute of Laborers, repressive as it was, marked the beginning of assumption of

[37]*Ibid.*, p. 89.

[38]*Ibid.*, p. 107.

[39]Blanche D. Coll, *Perspectives in Public Welfare*, U.S. Department of Health, Education and Welfare, Social and Rehabilitation Service, 1969, p. 2. See also Paul A. Kurzman, "Poor Relief in Medieval England: The Forgotton Chapter in the History of Social Welfare," *Child Welfare* Vol. 49 (October 1970), pp. 495-501.

[40]*Ibid.*, p. 4.

authority by secular government. A little known Statute of 1388, promulgated by Richard II, divided the poor into two classes, the deserving and the undeserving, or more specifically "beggars able to labour" and "beggars impotent to serve".[41] The former were to be punished, but the latter were to be given aid. Meanwhile, the statute books abounded in laws of ever-increasing severity and brutality.

Change came slowly. In 1530, the statute of Henry VIII made a clear distinction between vagrants who were to be punished and the impotent poor who were to be licensed by the local justice to beg. Begging solved nothing, however, and in 1536 Henry VIII enacted a statute providing for the voluntary collection of funds for the poor in the local parish. This approach also failed, since exhortation by the clergy was not effective. Repression continued. The law required that no mercy was to be shown the able-bodied unemployed. Such persons were "to be tied to the end of a cart naked and be beaten with whips through the same market-town or other place until his body be bloody by reason of such whipping."[42] After five years of experience with this law it was decided that penalties against idleness should be made even more stringent. For the second offense the upper part of the right ear was to be cut off, and the death penalty was assessed for continuing idleness. A later law in 1547 provided the idlers should be marked with a hot iron on the breast and enslaved for two years. If the person enslaved attempted to escape, he was to be branded on the forehead or cheek with the letter "S" and enslaved forever.[43]

ELIZABETHAN POOR LAWS

Punitive measures and reliance on voluntary contributions generally failed. It became increasingly obvious that responsibility for care of the poor would have to be shifted from the Church to secular agencies. During the reign of Queen Elizabeth (1558-1603) several such laws were enacted, the first in 1563. Each householder was to be compelled by law to make a weekly contribution based on the amount of his property and income. The law, however, relied on the clergy for the collection and was thus largely ineffective. So in 1572 Elizabeth enacted a statute setting up a secular "overseer of the poor" in each neighborhood with power to collect taxes and administer poor relief.[44] In the 1590's a severe depression set in, marked by famine, bread riots, and much unemployment. This situation led to the codification and modification of the Elizabethan Poor Laws during the years 1597 to 1601. Lawmakers then recognized the existence of large-scale involuntary unemployment.[45]

[41]Paul A. Kurzman, *op. cit.*, p. 499.
[42]Karl de Schweinitz, *England's Road to Social Security* (Philadelphia, University of Pennsylvania Press, 1943), p. 21.
[43]*Ibid.*, pp. 1-24.
[44]Paul A. Kurzman, *op. cit.*, p. 500.
[45]Blanche D. Coll, *op. cit.*, p. 5.

The Poor Law, which stood without major amendment for 233 years, distinguished three major categories of dependents: the vagrants, the involuntary unemployed, and the helpless.[46] The vagrant were to be forced to work or to be punished, largely as before, and much of the bad reputation of the Elizabethan Poor Law came from the brutal treatment of those deemed by authorities, with or without justification, to be vagrant. The involuntary unemployed were to be set to work on materials provided by the county or parish and located in "almshouses," or later on in "workhouses." This practice came to be called "indoor relief." The helpless, meaning the aged, the orphans, the sick, and the handicapped, were to be supplied with sustenance in their own homes. This aid was called "outdoor relief" (outside the almshouse). The law continued the authority to assess taxes for the support of the poor, and for local overseers to administer various types of aid. Parents were made legally liable for the support of their children and grandchildren, and children were liable for the care of their parents and grandparents. If parents were unable to care for the children, the parish might set them to work or bind them out as apprentices.[47]

Late in the 17th Century attitudes toward the poor hardened. The Protestant Reformation and especially Calvinism emphasized the virtues of industry, sobriety, and thrift. Wealth came to be regarded as a mark of virtue, and evidence of God's favor. Poverty came to be regarded as evidence of divine punishment for previous sin. In this situation amendments to the law were passed tending to make it more repressive. The Law of Settlement and Removal was enacted in 1662, which made it possible to have any poor person returned to his county or parish of origin.[48] Wealthy parishes did not want to pay taxes to support the poor who came in from elsewhere. As far as the poor were concerned, little was accomplished by returning them to their source, likely a low-income community. Yet the effort to do so illustrated the temper of the times as well as the shortsightedness of trying to provide for the poor on a purely local basis.

Complaints by taxpayers about the expense of both indoor and outdoor relief led to efforts to abolish outdoor relief and to eliminate almshouses in favor of "workhouses." The idea was that the county might be able to make a profit off the poor, either by operating a workhouse itself, or by contracting out to private parties the right to work the poor in exchange for their care. In 1722, Parliament passed a law which authorized such contracting. It also added that anyone who refused lodging and employment in such workhouses were to be denied any type of relief. The costs of relief were cut greatly by this act, for most of the poor attempted to remain out of the workhouses at all costs. The death rate in

---

[46]*Ibid.*, p. 6.
[47]*Ibid.*, p. 6.
[48]*Ibid.*, p. 7.

such workshops was exceptionally high both for children and the aged because the surroundings were crowded and unhealthful, and only a minimum of food was provided. The parishes in contracting out the workhouses attempted to pay as little money as possible, and the contractor attempted to make as much money as possible by providing little care for the poor.[49]

The "workhouse," as an effort to turn the almshouse into a profit making concern, was an economic failure; workhouses failed to break even. Yet by 1800 there were more than 4000 so-called workhouses with perhaps 100,000 inmates. As Sidney and Beatrice Webb pointed out, the workhouse had become by this time a shelter for social outcasts, in effect the almshouse with a different name. But there was a difference in attitude and purpose, as indicated by the fact that some almshouses evolved into hospitals, while some workhouses became jails, as is the case in several of our eastern states. Even when the workhouses proliferated, the basic and usual system of relief continued to be the relief of the poor in their homes (outdoor relief), sometimes in kind, but more often small money payments.[50]

The Napoleonic Wars brought steep rises in the cost of living, but wages did not rise nearly as fast. To offset the drop in the standard of living a number of parishes devised supplemental relief payments to the poor. Such payments were completely dissociated from employment in workhouses and were paid to the poor in their own homes. The new approach to relief began in 1795 and was called the "Speenhamland system" after the town, now a part of Newbury, in which it originated. This system, authorized by Parliament in 1796, allowed the supplementation of wages whenever they fell below a standard of subsistence as measured by the price of wheat. If the price of wheat, and thus of bread, were high, the supplement rose. If the price of wheat were low, the supplement was reduced. The size of the supplement also took into account the size of the family.[51]

In 1834, following widespread criticism of the poor law and of the Speenhamland system, Parliament enacted the Poor Law Reform of that year. The new law set as its objective the drastic reduction or elimination of all outdoor relief for the able-bodied.[52] Any help given should be less than the lowest wages earned by any independent laborer, and this was only to be in a well-regulated workhouse. The public and the Parliament had been led to believe that most recipients were able-bodied persons and their families, when in fact most were aged, disabled, dependent children,

---

[49]De Schweinitz, op. cit., pp. 1-24.

[50]Blanche D. Coll, op. cit., p. 8.

[51]Ibid., p. 10. See also Mark Blaug, "The Poor Law Reexamined," Journal of Economic History, XXIV (June 1964), pp. 231-232. See also Milton D. Spiezman, "Speenhamland: An Experiment in Guaranteed Income," Social Science Review, Vol. 40, No. 1 (March 1966), pp. 44-55.

[52]Blanche D. Coll, op. cit., pp. 10-15.

or sick. Other parts of the new Poor Law were directed at improving administration, and in this respect the "reform" may have been an improvement. But overall the so-called reform of 1834 was probably a backward step. The workhouse was used to terrorize the unemployed, and often the helpless as well. And the principle of "less eligibility," that is, paying less than the going wage, made little sense when applied to the aged, the disabled, and other helpless people. In any event, outdoor relief was not entirely eliminated. In 1844, there were 234,000 people in almshouses (or workhouses) as compared to 1.2 million receiving outdoor relief, and in 1850 there were 100,000 in almshouses and a million receiving relief. The system of poor relief was actually not drastically changed by the attempted reform. Local administrators were often aware of the lack of logic in trying to force all the poor into a workhouse, and outdoor relief in the home was often less expensive than indoor relief in the workhouse. Both indoor and outdoor relief continued.

TWENTIETH-CENTURY LEGISLATION

The system of workhouses and the crowding of all types of indigents together in unwholesome surroundings never provided an adequate solution to the problem of age or poverty. The main impetus to the elimination of the archaic system of social legislation came with the creation of a Royal Commission on the Poor Laws and Relief of Distress in 1905. Its report was published in 1909. Although sharply divergent viewpoints were expressed by the majority, who represented local relief officers and members of private charitable organizations, and the minority, composed of Fabians and Labor, the two groups were united on some important issues. Treatment was recommended over repression. Such new approaches as the creation of labor exchanges and abolition of child labor were recommended along with unemployment and invalidity insurance. Since the Liberals had returned to power in 1906, the time was ripe for sweeping changes in social legislation.[53] An Old Age Pensions Act was passed in 1909, along with an unemployment insurance system and a national health insurance program in 1911.

Since 1945 welfare services have been expanded. In 1945 a family allowance system was introduced. In 1946 the health insurance system was radically revamped to provide medical care for all residents (compulsory health insurance). A modernized system of child welfare services was introduced by the Children's Act of 1948. The premises of the welfare state were and are accepted by most members of British society. The term "welfare state" is used here in the narrow sense of denoting advocacy of social security and welfare programs rather than nationalization of industry.

[53]De Schweinitz, *op. cit.*, pp. 184-198.

WELFARE IN GERMANY

Attitudes and care of the aged and the poor have been more progressive in Germany than in England. In 1520 Martin Luther urged the abolition of begging. Instead he recommended that a "Common Chest" be created to provide food and money for the needy. Voluntary contributions were solicited to provide for the chest, but mandatory payments were also required. In addition to providing for the poor, the chest was used to pay the clergy, teachers, and other church officials. A number of towns adopted Luther's plans.[54] Later Frederick the Great, who ruled Prussia from 1740 to 1786, showed much concern for the welfare of his subjects. He said, "It is the business of a Sovereign, a great or small, to alleviate human misery." During his reign he carried out many acts to help the unfortunate.[55]

WELFARE IN HAMBURG

In the town of Hamburg in 1788 a plan was adopted and copied in Germany that was far ahead of welfare programs elsewhere. Funds were obtained by having each adult make weekly rounds in rotation among all the inhabitants. Physicians attended all who applied for relief to determine whether they could work. Those women and children who could work were employed in the spinning of flax. Men and boys were employed in such occupations as making rope, cleaning the streets, and repairing roads. A hospital was organized for the indigent aged and ill, and a number of doctors were recruited to provide treatment for those who could remain at home. Nurseries were arranged to care for children if the mothers were required to work, and allowances were provided to needy families. Children were not only paid for work, but an allowance was permitted for attendance at school.[56]

NINETEENTH CENTURY

Before there were Parliaments, a royal decree in Prussia in 1839 restricted the employment of children, and another decree in 1845 regulated excessive hours of work. Also many labor unions and benefit societies provided protection to more than two million members. More protection was provided for sickness and accidents than for old age. Modern Germany drew upon the prior progressive policies. Bismarck, for example, said, "It is the tradition of the dynasty which I serve that it takes the part of the

[54]*Ibid.*, pp. 36-38.
[55]W. Harbutt Dawson, *Social Insurance in Germany*, 1883-1911 (London, T. Fisher Unwin, 1912), p. 2.
[56]De Schweinitz, *op. cit.*, pp. 91-94.

weaker ones in the economic struggle."[57] Expediency also played a part in the formation of the legislation that was passed. Bismarck wanted to win the support of the working classes, and he favored doing so by passing social legislation. He also wished to contradict the socialist viewpoint that the state was merely an agency to suppress the masses and maintain capitalists in power. Accordingly, bills for old-age pensions were presented in the Reichstag in 1878 and for sickness and accident insurance in 1881. A sickness insurance bill was passed in 1883, an accident bill in 1884, and an old-age pension law in 1889.[58]

WELFARE IN THE UNITED STATES

Since most of our immigrants came from England, American ideas and programs for the aged and indigent followed the English system closely. Relief was handled on a local basis, and the conditions for obtaining assistance were made harsh to discourage any possibility of malingering. Whippings of beggars and driving them to other towns was practiced here as well as in England. In some cases, new immigrants lost their freedom when they became indentured servants to pay for their passage to America. Workhouses and almshouses in which all types of indigents were housed together became the main methods of caring for the aged and the poor.

Individualism became the dominant force in America, and little was done about the problem of insecurity. Fear of centralized authority has always been strong in the United States. It originated with the criticism against the English monarchy at the time of the American Revolution, and has been with us ever since. The abundance of resources in the United States and the successful working of our political democracy gave to our rural society the feeling that progress was automatic. All that people had to do to succeed was to work hard. Few security measures were needed, because people lived on farms and could provide security for their own relatives. Our thinking was also molded by the doctrine of predestination, which held that God had selected some for heaven and the remaining for hell. This doctrine left little room for charity toward unfortunates. Social legislation was not advocated, since eternal principles of justice were already in effect.

Gradually here in America, as in England, it was recognized that the almshouse system had many disadvantages. Instead of housing together such diverse groups as the handicapped, disabled, insane, sick, aged, orphans, criminals, and the deaf, dumb, and crippled, separate types of programs and care for each of the groups gradually became the practice. Virginia in 1769 founded an institution for the insane, and Kentucky in

[57]Dawson, op. cit., pp. 1-2.
[58]Ibid., pp. 12-21.

1822 founded two new institutions concurrently, one for the insane and another for the deaf and dumb.[59]

A system of outdoor relief began in 1883 in California when subsidies of $100 per year were provided for those living in public and private institutions and for the needy outside of institutions. The depressed condition of the State Treasury following the panic of 1894 caused a suspension of payments in 1895, which were not revived when good times returned. Gradually, however, our attitudes toward insecurity changed as we moved from a rural to an urban society. Urbanization brought with it a whole host of new problems such as unemployment, slums, and others which a *laissez-faire* doctrine was ill equipped to deal with. The fact that our people lived through two World Wars and a Great Depression shook the faith of those who maintained that progress would automatically come about. Instead, many people came to the realization that although progress was possible, it was something that had to be worked for. New institutions were needed to deal with new problems.[60]

Prior to the 1930's, the main social welfare legislation in the United States was workmen's compensation. This was solely state legislation that came into existence during the second decade of this century. Later, the basic Federal legislation passed was the Social Security Act of 1935. This act has three major programs: (1) unemployment insurance, (2) old-age insurance, and (3) assistance for the needy. In 1950 the permanently and totally disabled were covered under the Social Security Act. In 1960 medical payments for the needy were provided, and in 1965 under the Medicaid program such payments were later extended to all the needy. Also in that year the Medicare program (health insurance for most of the aged) was instituted. During the 1960's an attack was made upon distress in depressed areas. A Manpower and Development Training Act was passed to upgrade the skills of the unemployed and the poor. More federal aid was granted for education purposes. A "War on Poverty" program was instituted, and minority groups received the protection of civil rights legislation.

Today it is no longer held by most students of social welfare that poverty is mainly a matter of personal fault or personal inadequacy. This is not to deny that many kinds of personal inadequacy exist. Persons with low IQ's have an extremely difficult time in attempting to earn a living. People with higher IQ's may sometimes be slothful —lazy —but such personal inadequacy may be the fault of a poor environment. An inadequate diet and lack of medical care may cause sickness and a lack of energy, and may also be a cause of a low IQ in the offspring. Racial and other

[59]Josephine Chapin Brown, *Public Relief 1929-1939*   (New York, Holt, Rinehart & Winston, 1940), pp. 6-41.

[60]John Hogan and Francis Ianni, *American Social Insurance* (New York, Harper & Row), Chapter 4.

forms of discrimination may have a strongly discouraging effect upon the persons discriminated against. Identification of the poor goes a long way in an understanding of the poverty problem. If it is found that many are poor because of aging, illness, injury, unemployment, lack of education, or discrimination, then environmental changes may possibly reduce poverty.

Chapter 3 concentrates on the identification of those living in poverty and on an analysis of the causes of poverty. That chapter also calls attention to the categories of economic insecurity. Later chapters deal with the various programs which have been instituted to deal with poverty and insecurity, with the shortcomings of these programs, and with possible alternate programs which have been proposed. Proposed programs typically generate severe ideological arguments as to the direction the nation should take. Chapter 2, Ideological Perspectives, deals with these opposing attitudes.

Bibliography

Bogardus, Emory S., The Development of Social Thought (New York, Longman's, 1950).

Brown, Josephine Chapin, Public Relief, 1929-1939 (New York, Holt, Rinehart and Winston, 1940).

Coll, Blanche D., Perspectives in Public Welfare (Washington, U.S. Government Printing Office, 1969).

Dawson, W. Harbutt, Social Insurance in Germany (London, T. Fisher Unwin, 1912).

Friedlander, Walter A., Introduction to Social Welfare (Englewood Cliffs, N.J., Prentice-Hall, 1955).

Noss, John B., Man's Religions (New York, Macmillan, 1974).

de Schweinitz, Karl, England's Road to Social Security (Philadelphia, University of Pennsylvania Press, 1943).

Thompson, James W., An Economic and Social History of the Middle Ages (New York, Appleton-Century-Crofts, 1928).

Warner, Amos, Coolidge, Mary, and Howard, George, American Charities (New York, Thomas Crowell Co., 1919).

CHAPTER 2

IDEOLOGICAL PERSPECTIVES

ANTI-WELFARE STATISM — THE RADICAL RIGHT

In this chapter the term "welfare state" implies one in which the necessaries of life are provided to meet such exigencies as aging, premature death, disability, and others. In such a state, those without adequate opportunities are provided some. For example, a poor youth may be provided aid to go to college. The welfare state does not result in equality of opportunity. The son of a wealthy executive obviously has more opportunity than a poor youth provided college aid. The welfare state would make opportunity less unequal but not equal. As used here, the welfare state does not imply nationalization of industry or socialism, but merely protection against the exigencies cited above.

WORLD VIEW

The radical right has opposed the welfare state vigorously. Some of this group have made a fetish of our religious tradition. Many of them believe that the universe has purpose, and that this purpose is a reflection of the Judeo-Christian God's will and creation. They then argue that his ways are mysterious, and that evil is a necessary part of his plan, including disease, poverty, inequality, and even bestiality of man toward man. Since man cannot be trusted, creations of his, such as government, cannot be trusted either.

THE STATE

Much criticism of welfare by the radical right revolves around the growth of government. Because man is evil, the state is evil also. The state should be necessary simply to keep the peace among individual combatants. It can perform the useful function of protecting individual property rights, but this is about as far as it should go. The state is essentially artificial and evil, and because of the evil in man is also dangerous. The state should be drastically limited in function, and not even help the weak protect them-selves from the strong. The fewer functions of government, the better. Radical rightists often argue that they believe in a republican form of government, American constitutionalism, and western democracy; but, historically, they have usually opposed extension of suffrage, and some-times have favored limitation of representation by race, property, or superior education. In the United States radical rightists place great stress upon a strict interpretation of the constitution in terms of functions of government, upon separation of powers, a weak executive, and states' rights. All of these are favored in order to further a *laissez-faire* economic and social policy.

Milton Friedman, an economist, favors a limited and decentralized government on the ground that the great advances of civilization have come through individuals rather than centralized government. Individual achievements have been a product of genius, strongly held minority views, and a social climate permitting variety and diversity that cannot be duplicated by government. Friedman also fears that big government may lead to a curtailment of freedom. He opposes public housing on the ground that the number of dwelling units destroyed in the course of erect-ing public housing projects has been far larger than the number of new dwelling units constructed. He opposes the old-age and survivor's in-surance program on the ground that it involves a large-scale invasion into the lives of most people in the United States without any persuasive justification. He sees no reason why the young should subsidize the aged. Rather than requiring a compulsory purchase of old-age security through the government, Friedman would prefer that individuals be given the choice voluntarily as to whether they wish to purchase annuities or not.[1]

ABUSE OF WELFARE

Because of the belief that man is evil, neither those dispensing welfare nor those receiving it can be trusted. A number of investigations of abuse have been undertaken in a number of cities, and in some of these abuse was found. Most publicity was received from complaints of abuse in Newburgh, N.Y., a small town on the Hudson River (1961). A "Citizens Committee" report, authorized largely by City Manager Joseph Mitchell of Newburgh, for a time a John Birch society organizer, complained that Newburgh's relief rolls were loaded with "undesirable newcomers," mainly Southern Negro migrants who were engaging in widespread fraud to remain on relief. In order to protect Newburgh from such alleged

---

[1]Milton Friedman, *Capitalism and Freedom* (Chicago, University of Chicago Press, 1962).

abuses, a Newburgh plan was adopted. This plan was composed of a 13-point Welfare Code. Some of the points of the code follow. All able-bodied adult males on relief were to be assigned relief jobs. Voucher payments were substituted for cash payments. All those who refused jobs regardless of the type of employment were to be denied relief, as were those who quit a job voluntarily. Relief payments, except for the aged, blind, and disabled, were to be limited to three months in any one year. Payments were not to exceed that of the take-home pay of the lowest paid city employee with a family of comparable size. All applicants for relief who were new in the town were required to show evidence that their plans for coming to Newburgh involved a concrete offer of employment. Those on "general" relief and AFDC were required to pick up their voucher in police courts, where they were photographed and threatened with publication of their names. The same treatment was promised for those on other types of relief. Any mothers on relief because of illegitimate children were to be denied relief if they had any more illegitimate children. Foster-home care was to be provided for children whose home environment was not satisfactory.[2]

Both support and criticism were received on the Newburgh Plan. Senator Barry Goldwater described the plan "as refreshing as breathing fresh air of my native Arizona." A number of newspapers praised the action of Newburgh, whereas others criticized it. The *Richmond Times-Dispatch* editorialized against the "shiftless, slothful parasites who make careers of milking the public." On the other hand much criticism was directed at the Newburgh Plan by the National Association of Social Workers, the Child Welfare League of America, the American Public Welfare Association, the Citizens Committee for Children of New York, Catholic Charities of New York, the National Urban League, and the National Association for the Advancement of Colored People. Forty percent of the people on Newburgh's relief roles were nonwhites who had been largely agricultural workers, recruited in past years and left stranded. However, the costs to the city were found to be 13 percent of the city budget rather than the 30-33 percent, which officials of Newburgh had erroneously quoted. Furthermore, rather than 5 percent of the population receiving assistance as reported by Newburgh officials, the correct figure was 2.9 percent, which was the lowest percentage of people on relief among five upstate New York cities of comparable size. Only one able-bodied male could be found on relief, and not a single authenticated case of fraud had been uncovered in Newburgh.[3]

A temporary injunction was issued against the city of Newburgh, prohibiting it from putting into effect 12 of the 13 points of their code. The code was criticized by the National Association of Social Workers on a

[2]*Will the Newburgh Plan Work in Your City?* (New York, National Association of Social Workers, 1961), pp. 2-3.

[3]"What Happened in Newburgh?" *National Association of Social Workers News*, Vol. 70, No. 1 (November 1961), pp. 1,7-9.

number of grounds. The use of vouchers was criticized because it identified the recipient as being inferior. During the depression years, such vouchers had been abused by merchants who would cash them at a discount and pocket the difference. Cash payments have been used for years, because voucher payments have been viewed as unnecessary, punitive, and destructive to morale. The three-month limitation on relief payments was viewed as punitive and restrictive and not a solution to people without means of self-support who still must eat, be clothed, and have shelter. The requirement that to be eligible for relief the newcomer must have a bona-fide offer of employment was viewed as decreasing the mobility of labor, which would stunt our economic and social growth. The National Association of Social Workers identified the cause of many on relief as failure of Newburgh and other towns to solve the problem of hard-core unemployment. Its needle trades, resort employment, and function as a regional economic center had dwindled. It was recommended that Newburgh engage in a program of economic and social reawakening rather than a crackdown on its relief population. Attraction of industries, slum clearance, and public housing were suggested. It was further recommended that Newburgh adopt some of the more advanced welfare practices of Washington, D.C., San Francisco, and other towns which have attempted physical, social, and moral rehabilitation of those welfare recipients who need and can respond to such services.[4]

If and when abuse of welfare is found, improved administration should be able to eradicate it. Improved social services should be and have been able to reduce the numbers on welfare in many towns. Such recommendations from professional social workers have not received unanimous support, as may be seen from a statement issued by City Manager Mitchell of Newburgh. He maintained that he planned to use some "thought control" on social workers employed by the city and that in the future he would hire only workers without social work training.[5] Although abuses of relief have been found on a larger scale in towns other than Newburgh, the remedy suggested by liberals is improved administration rather than abolition of the program. An investigation in Washington, D.C. by a Senate committee found that 59.7 percent of Aid to Families with Dependent Children cases should have been ruled ineligible for relief.[6] A more recent finding in 1963 from a nationwide study found about 5 percent who should not have been receiving AFDC payments. Many radical rightists who have criticized welfare programs are really opposed to the entire welfare program. Having been outvoted on the welfare programs themselves, they devote their efforts to pointing out abuse of the programs. Abuse there has been and will be, but efficient administration should be able to reduce it to a minimum.

[4]*Will the Newburgh Plan Work in Your City?*, p. 4.
[5]"What Happened in Newburgh?" p. 8.

THE ELITE

A number of radical rightists have departed from Judeo-Christian thought and insist that the universe has no necessary meaning of a rational character, but is a struggle of all life for survival. The Nazi philosopher Rosenberg, the German philosopher Nietzsche, who argued that "God is dead," the social Darwinism of Herbert Spencer, and the notions of Stirner all reflect this attitude. Man is on his own as an individual because the universe makes no sense. Struggle is the essence not only of survival but the good life, and only strong or lucky men win. Selfishness and competition are the essence of the person. Success only goes to the cunning and strong. The good life and society come about by the contributions of the elite, the successful, and the strong. This group, exemplified in the writings of John Cowper Powys *(In Defense of Sensuality)* and Ayn Rand, insist that environment is not so important as heredity and sheer will, hard work, and "guts." Welfare is feared as a burden on the successful. Some radical rightists also assert that the high costs of welfare will result in such heavy taxation of private property as to eventually result in confiscation.[7]

INDIVIDUAL RESPONSIBILITY

Radical rightists are particularly fearful of the harmful effects of welfare upon the individual. Handouts by the government may destroy the incentive to work. An example is cited[8] in which a boy's incentive to go to college is destroyed simply because he gets along so well without it. There is little use in going to college, for without it the boy can earn $150 a week as an electrician. He works the 40-hour week, has paid vacations, has light work, and a union to protect him against discrimination. He has sufficient money to provide him a home, a car, the necessities of life and some luxuries for his family. Group insurance protects him against the problems of sickness and premature death, and his old age is taken care of by Social Security. Although a better position could be obtained by going to college, he would be less secure in this position. He would have to work longer hours and put in more effort as a professional worker. High taxes greatly reduce the extra income that he earns. In short, the advantages of college are not worth the effort.

Speaking of the effects of the welfare state on Britain, Charles Curran[9] points out that the welfare state there is built to working-class

---

[7]Barry Goldwater, *The Conscience of a Conservative* Shepherdsville, Ky., Victor, 1960), p. 62.

[8]Jesse Raley "Economic Puzzle," *American Mercury*, Vol. 88 (March, 1959), p. 91.

[9]Charles Curran, "The Old Order Cometh," *The Reporter* (May 28, 1959), pp. 28-31.

specifications. The British worker has demanded and obtained a noncompetitive society were "nobody need struggle to survive, where there is an assured livelihood for the weak, the slow, and the ungifted."[10] Although British workers are not dissatisfied with their lot, they don't show much enthusiasm for anything except mass amusements. Public housing is criticized by Curran on the ground that few meeting places have been erected to provide intellectual stimulation. The handouts of the welfare state have resulted in docility. Furthermore, freedom from responsibility creates an appetite for fantasy among the working class. The fantasy is shown in the worker's leisure-time tastes, his obsessional interest in television, and his appetite for football-pool gambling. The working man's newspapers are particularly deficient, for they stress personalities, entertainment, spectacle, sensual relations, and luxury. The basic criticism against the welfare state is that it has not generated an ethic. Christianity has been replaced by materialistic hedonism. About the only moral mortar of the welfare state is fear of the police. Although all the stock causes of crime have been removed — poverty, squalor, and illiteracy — the crime rate has soared to a record-breaking height. Like so many other conservatives, Curran suggests that the solution to the problem is moral regeneration. A basic question to be faced, however, is how this moral regeneration is to be effected.

Not only do welfare benefits have the disadvantage of conceding to the government the power to grant or withhold from the individual the necessities of life as the government sees fit, but also the responsibility of the individual to provide for his own needs and those of his family and neighbors is taken away.[11] The results are that the individual is transferred from "a dignified, self-reliant spiritual being into a dependent animal creature without his knowing it. There is no avoiding this damage to character under the welfare state."[12] In private charity, on the other hand, both donor and recipient know that charity is the product of humanitarian impulses, not something due to the receiver. Furthermore, the granting of private charity uplifts the donor, whereas there is no merit in forcing people to make a compulsory contribution through government programs when they may not want to do so.

Along similar lines, La Piere argues that the drive for security is malfunctional and that if continued may lead to disaster.[13] Rather than placing the blame on welfarism per se, La Piere criticizes the acceptance of the Freudian ethic. According to Freud, man is not born free; rather he is shackled with biological urges that in many instances must be suppressed to such an extent that the individual is in constant and grievous conflict with his society. The solution, according to Freudians, is to provide more

[10]Ibid., p. 28.
[11]Goldwater, op. cit., pp. 68-75.
[12]Ibid., p. 73.
[13]Richard La Piere, "The Apathetic Ethic," Saturday Review of Literature August 1, 1959), pp. 40-45.

security for individuals. But providing such security through psychoanalysts, permissive parents, progressive teachers, welfare workers, and others catering to the needs of individuals takes away from individual striving. Like many other conservatives, La Piere contends that all social progress is initiated by a few enterprising individuals who appear among the masses as evolutionary mutants, with inordinate faith in their own inborn ideas. If these individuals are suppressed and society destroys the individual will to succeed, society will stagnate.[14]

Edward Banfield contends that many of the welfare state proposals have not worked because they have been unable to improve lower class culture.[15] He particularly stresses the present-time orientation of the lower class that disables them from climbing from poverty. The theory of the failure to defer gratification by the poor has been criticized by S. M. Miller, Frank Riessman, and Arthur A. Seagull.[16] They point out that the rising consumer debt of the middle class shows little of a deferred gratification pattern (DGP). They quote a study which shows that there was little difference in the amounts middle and lower class students felt their parents had saved to give them a start in life. Also little difference was shown between what middle class and non-middle class students would do if $2,000 were given to them. They cite alternative explanations of why lower class students drop out of school earlier than middle class students. In rebuttal to the allegation that indulgence in sex is practiced more by lower-class youth, the authors point out that middle-class youth pet and masturbate more. The conclusion of the three authors, who cited other data as well, was that DGP was inadequate as the major variable in explanations of the behavior of the poor.

ANTI-WELFARE STATISM — THE RADICAL LEFT

Those on the radical left do not oppose welfare state programs per se. Historically, the radical left has been at the forefront in favoring Social Security and other welfare state programs. The basic criticism of the welfare state from the radical left viewpoint is that such a state will not solve the problems in society.

The radical leftists quote statistics to show that income inequality has not been lessening in recent years even with welfare state measures.

[14]Richard La Piere, *The Freudian Ethic* (New York, Duell, Sloan & Pierce, 1959).

[15]Edward C. Banfield, *The Unheavenly City Revisited* (Boston, Little, Brown and Co., 1974).

[16]S. M. Miller, Frank Riessman, and Arthur A. Seagull, "Poverty and Self-indulgence. A Critique of the Non-deferred Gratification Pattern," in Louis A. Ferman, Joyce L. Kornbluh, and Alan Haber, editors, *Poverty in America*, revised edition, (Ann Arbor, University of Michigan Press, 1971), pp. 416-432.

Gordon K. Lewis points out that England is still the class-ridden society it has always been. His criticism of this aspect of the welfare-state is as follows:

The welfare state is not the socialist commonwealth. England is still at bottom a class-ridden society, a Dickensian mixture of aristocratic remnants, plutocratic influence and middle-class sentiment. Professions such as the law and medicine, although not closed castes, still carry the marks of hereditary occupations. Institutions such as the Anglican Church continue to be bastions of social privilege and bishops, as a class, come overwhelmingly from a single social stratum trained in select schools like Marlborough and Merchant Taylors. The Diplomatic Service, despite the Eden reforms of 1943 and despite their proof, in the figure of Mr. Bevin, that a trade-union leader can become an outstanding Foreign Secretary, still resists effective democratization, and since 1945 only the occasional ambassador, Lord Halifax or Sir Oliver Franks, has been drawn from outside the ranks of the traditional career men. The sociology of the peerage shows that in its present state approximately three-quarters of its members come from the "public schools" and that, the creation of some one hundred new peers by Labor Cabinets since 1945 notwithstanding, an ennobled individual very rapidly acquires the conservative instincts of "noblesse oblige" and, in addition, sends his sons to Eton or Harrow and himself will seek out a business position rarely below the board-room level. It is also of interest to note that two of the major occupational sources of the class are ex-Army regular officers (39 percent of all peers) and lawyers (25 percent of new peers). Behind all this there lies the common source of a privileged educational system that has been substantially untouched by reform. For apart from the grotesque exclusiveness of the "public school," recent investigations of educational opportunity at both the grammar-school and university level suggest that, in the first place, a boy coming from a middle-class home has a greater chance of entering a grammar school than a boy from a working-class home and, secondly, the growing democratization of "Oxbridge" has meant, in terms of social attitudes, an assimilation of the working-class student into the value system of the traditional upper-class influence. The consequence, as Professor Pear has displayed in his fascinating study, is that English life is still pretty well dominated by a set of social prejudices and class differentiations based not so much upon graduations of income as upon the more subtle differences of speech, manners, dress, leisure pursuits, even modes of eating and drinking; and all of them defended in terms of a vague ideology of "Character" calculated to sustain the national habits of class separatism. Nor has this been seriously changed by the advent of new elites that, in themselves, are doing much to break down the more comic aspects of that separatism and to challenge the conservative spirit of the older professions, for although they are more hospitable to talent and ability they have not seriously challenged the basic society values and, indeed, themselves constitute covert elites profoundly disturbing to the principle of national community. The group-novel of C. P. Snow is a vast fictional footnote to that truth.

The welfare state has done little more than to enable the working classes to hold their own and thereby to keep just about in step with the general rise in wealth. It follows from this, as the third point, that the welfare state has not so much radically revised British social relationships as permitted the rise of a relatively larger minority of talented lower-class individuals into the strata above them. Public taxation has done little to eliminate the unearned income of the functionless shareholders of public companies, on the one hand, or the capital gains that have generated a new style of conspicuous consumption of the English rich, on the other, nor, even more important as a source of inegalitarianism, has it done much to reform a social value system wherein long and arduous work is often meanly rewarded and easy and satisfying work is generally well-paid.[17]

Gordon Lewis further points out that despite New Deal reforms, which he characterizes as basically the outcome of the distrust of the American gentleman class for a vulgar business society, the basic decisions of the American economy are still controlled by the corporate managerial class. It is they who determine the scale of operations, plant location, the commodities to be produced, the rate of capital expansion, and the amounts expended for research. The large powers held in the hands of the traditional rich and chief corporation executives are not affected by welfare legislation.

Professor Richard Titmuss, in evaluating a recent 15-years experience with the welfare state in Britain, states that larger gains have gone to the middle than lower classes. In view of the fact that lower-income persons move more frequently than upper-class persons, many of them become ineligible for private pensions. If one subscribes to the view as Titmuss does, that all society pays for such pensions, then the pensions of the rich are subsidized more heavily by the community than the pensions of the poor. For tax purposes, an upper-class person may deduct all of his ex-wives' maintanance allowances without any loss, but relief for mothers and children may be stopped if cohabitation is taking place. The lower classes are penalized for so-called immoral behavior, but the upper class is not. Also it has been found that higher-income groups make more use of the health service than lower-income groups. The former receive more specialist attention, occupy more of the beds in the better hospitals, and are more apt to obtain psychiatric care. Furthermore, the welfare state has not expanded the percentage of male undergraduates who are the sons of manual workers. Rather the percentage has dropped one percent. If subsidies to education are included, the father earning $60,000 a year receives 13 times more from the state than another father earning $1,500, in recognition of the dependent needs of childhood. Middle class

[17]Gordon K. Lewis, "Twentieth-Century Capitalism and Socialism: The Present State of the Anglo-American Debate," *Western Political Quarterly*, Vol. 12, 1959, pp. 101-103. Reprinted by permission of University of Utah, copyright owners.

families are also more heavily subsidized in housing. In conclusion, Titmuss feels that we should now concentrate on the problem of "ways of extending the welfare state to the poor."[18]

A further criticism of simply limiting reform to welfare legislation is that the goals of our present society are deficient. C. Wright Mills has pointed out in *The Power Elite* that our society has narrowed the meaning of success to big money and condemns failure as the chief vice. The emphasis on money inevitably produces the sharp operator and the shady deal. Furthermore, the goal of money does not produce men of conscience.

In the United States it has also been alleged that the welfare state has been directed mainly toward aiding the middle rather than lower classes.[19] Michael Harrington points out that agricultural parity payments have gone mainly to upper-income farmers. Much of the money for urban renewal has not provided housing for lower income groups. The poorest groups in our society, such as agricultural workers and domestic servants, are exempt from much of our social legislation. They are not covered under unemployment insurance laws and workmen's compensation laws, nor do they have collective bargaining rights under the National Labor Relations Act, as most other workers have. These observations by Mr. Harrington are irrefutable, although it is also true that some welfare payments, such as SSI, AFDC, and others, do go to low-income families. Nevertheless, Mr. Harrington is correct in maintaining that coverage under most of our welfare programs needs to be broadened to include some of the low income groups not now covered.

American Marxists, such as Paul Baran and Paul Sweezy,[20] raise their objection to the present system on the ground that inevitable surpluses arise in the monopolized industrial sector of the economy. These can only be used by creating an enormous military machine and engaging in highly inflated sales efforts in our society. Critics of Marxism argue that our   society is quite viable without military expenditures. Such expenditures were not needed when relatively full employment was reached in 1965, and such expenditures tended to weaken rather than aid the economy.

Another on the left who rejects the present system in the United States is Herbert Marcuse.[21] He places much emphasis on science as the most important reason for the essentially oppressive and destructive character of modern Western civilization. In criticizing Marcuse, Barrington Moore, Jr., points out that prior civilizations were also destructive

[18]Richard Titmuss, "The Role of Redistribution in Social Policy," *Social Security Bulletin*, Vol. 28, No. 6, (June 1965), pp. 14-20.

[19]Michael Harrington, *The Other America* (New York, Macmillan, 1962).

[20]Paul A. Baran and Paul M. Sweezy, *Monopoly Capital* (New York, Monthly Review Press, 1966). Paul A. Baran, *The Longer View* (New York, The Monthly Review Press, 1969).

[21]Herbert Marcuse, *Counterrevolution and Revolt*, (Boston, The Beacon Press, 1972).

before the advent of modern science and technology.[22] Furthermore, correct knowledge (the scientific approach) does not necessarily imply that the destructive component plays a serious role. Here Moore cites medicine as an example.

Erich Fromm criticized our present society from a mental health viewpoint.[23] He claims that an inequalitarian society causes severe personal problems, so much so that five percent of our population have complete nervous breakdowns and another 12 percent near breakdowns. He favors a planned economy blended with active participation from below.

David M. Gordon takes issue with the official statistics showing a reduction in the amount of poverty over the years.[24] However, in analyzing the statistical techniques he entirely disregards the in-kind payments to the poor in the form of food stamps, medical care, and housing subsidies. Gordon stresses the fact that it is relative poverty that needs to be eliminated rather than merely bringing the poor up to a minimum level. Here he cites statistics to the effect that there has been little change in the distribution of income since World War II. Radically changing the system would be necessary, in his opinion, to improve the relative position of the poor.

PRO-WELFARE STATISM

All liberals, many moderates, and some conservatives have supported welfare state measures for a number of years in almost all Western industrialized countries. In the United States, the main impetus toward the welfare state came during the liberal Democratic years of the 1930's and the early 1960's. However, during the more moderate Eisenhower period, a disability program was included with the OASDHI program. During the Nixon administration, the supplemental security income program placed a minimum under the incomes of the aged, disabled and blind that was much higher than in previous years. The Nixon administration also advocated a Family Allowance plan.

WORLD VIEW

The world view explained here is mainly that of liberals, although, as indicated above, many moderates and some conservatives support this view. Liberals in general take a hopeful view of life and the universe. They see the universe as having meaning, significance, and purpose, especially as related to the life of man. Sometimes, liberals follow the

[22]Barrington Moore, Jr., *Reflections of the Causes of Human Misery* (Boston, The Beacon Press, 1972), pp. 134-137.

[23]Erich Fromm, *Escape from Freedom* (New York, Avon Books, 1965).

[24]David M. Gordon, *Theories of Poverty and Underemployment* (Lexington, Mass., D. C. Heath and Co., 1972).

ideas of the Greeks and Roman Stoics; others follow in the Judeo-Christian religious tradition. Of immediate logical importance is the liberal position regarding man. Here it is maintained that man is significant, as a unique creature in the universe. The individual worth and dignity of man is affirmed. Man's character, behavior, and good or poor life are dependent in large measure upon both physical nature and social environment. Liberals are not pure environmentalists, but they do argue that man's personality is affected drastically by weather, food, and his social-institutional life. Some go further than others in this emphasis, but most claim that society cannot have good men, healthy men, or the good life under natural or social conditions of disease, poverty, and brutality. These conditions are dependent upon group or social action for continuance or removal. Liberals maintain that one man can rarely by himself overcome deserts, floods, slums, unemployment, malarial swamps, and the like. Especially do they argue that, in a highly industrialized society, the individual is influenced by a dependence upon social action to make for the good life.

Furthermore, liberals generally believe that man qua man is by nature sufficiently altruistic, generous, and compassionate to want to overcome bad conditions for others as well as himself, and is aesthetically motivated to dislike filth, disease, and disorder around him. And of more importance, men are sufficiently rational to see that they need to act together to accomplish these desired objectives even at the cost of individual effort and some sacrifice of immediate fulfillment of individual satisfaction.

This view of man is generally called the social or corporate and rational or benevolent view of man. It nowhere denies that men are not also individually fearful, selfish, capricious. It simply insists that the constructive aspects of personality can be fulfilled and utilized through mutual aid and cooperation, and that negative or destructive personal and social results of the situation can be reduced or even channeled to constructive ends.

THE STATE

Relative to the state, the liberal sees it not as an artificial or evil institution reflecting merely man's goodness or selfishness and tendency to violence, but as a natural institution like business or the family by which many social aims are accomplished beyond the capacity of the individual or other institutions. It is an institution that helps to integrate and create conditions of cooperation between the other institutions of society. The liberal does admit that the state is unique in monopolizing the power over the violent aspects of life (or insists that it should), but claims that this is desirable to bring justice, order and peace to society. Individual violence is reduced by channeling the violence through orderly processes under regular procedures. Thus state action reduces the sum total of violence that might exist if each person and group acted through primitive self-help.

The liberal argues, furthermore, that the functions of government are not of necessity limited to police and military protection. The liberal insists that in a highly complicated society the state function must extend to the integration of institutional life, because only the state can secure over-all effective results in certain areas. Most liberals in democratic countries with a social view of man do not believe that the state must "take on everything" and "own all property." When it comes to forms of government, most liberals are ardent democrats or parliamentarians who insist upon representative government, limitation of government under constitutional law, intellectual freedom, and one man-one vote, with universal adult suffrage, or government of and by, as well as for, the people.

The liberal tradition, then, rests upon a long line of thinkers from the Stoics, the Judeo-Christian religionists, the modern movement for republican government as exemplified in Great Britain, the United States, and other such countries, of present British and U.S. Constitutions, upon the Magna Charta, Petition of Rights, Declaration of Independence, Locke, Jefferson, Madison, Paine, the Chartists, Robert Owen, the two Mills, the Protestant social gospel movement of Rauschenbusch, Niebuhr, William Temple (the late Archbishop of York, who originated the term "welfare state"), the union movements in Great Britain and the United States, Dewey, Pound, the Progressive political movement in America, the speeches of Wilson and Franklin Roosevelt, and the bulk of sociological investigation in this day.

JUSTIFICATION FOR INCREASED GOVERNMENT INTERVENTION

Historically, classical liberalism has opposed the intervention of the state into the life of the nation. Abuses of government, typified by such monarchs as the Bourbons and Stuarts, certainly were apparent and needed rectifying. On the other hand, as the complexities of life have increased, more rather than less government intervention has become necessary. To cite an example from Professor Calvin Hoover that he describes as a well-worn cliche, municipal ordinances against keeping pigs were needed as soon as enough citizens congregated in one place to constitute a municipality. The curtailment of individual liberty of the swinekeepers was more than offset by the reduction of unpleasant odors to other citizens. Also, the state may perform some functions better than individuals. This was recognized long before Adam Smith, who listed national defense, justice, road, bridge and harbor construction, expansion of foreign trade, and education as proper functions of government. Since Smith's time the list of functions that government can do more efficiently has expanded considerably. Professor Hoover states that it is now commonplace to accept the proposition that social security inevitably provides more protection for the individual than he could obtain through his individual efforts. State intervention is also necessary to prevent economic depressions and inflation. The state has also been used to lessen the uninhibited conflict of the countervailing powers of labor and management to prevent injury to the public. Here state intervention may even go so far as to regulate both the internal and external affairs of corporations and labor unions. Increases in the costs of national defense and the fighting of wars have also expanded the powers of government.[25] Few would accept either the universal proposition that no government intervention (complete anarchism) would provide the best system for mankind, nor the opposite universal proposition that government is always superior to individual effort. Since no universals are available to us, the use of additional government intervention must be decided on a case-by-case basis.

In many instances in the past government spending has been too little. In 1943 heart disease killed more than half a million and disabled some 8-1/2 million persons in the United States. Yet in 1944 only $615,000 was spent for research on heart disease compared with the private expenditure of $31 million on advertising cigarettes. At the same time we spent almost nothing on cancer research, although it afflicted about 7 million people at that time. One company, on the other hand, spent $19 million to advertise soap.[26] The solution should not be to force people to consume what an enlightened person or group of persons believes they ought to, but rather conditions should be made available under which people may find out what they themselves want and recognize clearly the things which satisfy these wants. Increased governmental expenditures on heart, cancer, and other research have indicated a growing awareness of the needs in this direction. Table 2-1 indicates that social welfare expenditures have increased rapidly in recent years. However, in many areas they have not been sufficient to eradicate poverty.

EXCESSIVE GOVERNMENT CENTRALIZATION

In determining which level of government should administer welfare functions, most people would contend that the local government should be given preference provided that the more decentralized agency can ably perform the function. In an interesting book entitled *Beyond the Welfare State* Gunnar Myrdal writes of the future of welfare in the countries already having the welfare state.[27] He points out that a more responsible citizenship will result in eventually changing the welfare state from a

---

[25]Calvin E. Hoover, *The Economy, Liberty and the State* (Garden City, N.Y., Doubleday, 1961), pp. 356-359.
[26]Harry K. Girvetz, *From Wealth to Welfare* (Stanford, Stanford, 1950), p. 208.
[27]Gunnar Mrydal, *Beyond the Welfare State* (New Haven, Yale, 1960), Chapter VI.

TABLE 2-1: CIVILIAN PUBLIC SOCIAL WELFARE PROGRAMS IN RELATION TO GROSS NATIONAL PRODUCT, FISCAL YEARS, 1935-1973

Fiscal Year	Social Welfare Expenditures (in Billions)	Social Welfare Expenditures as Percentage of Gross National Product						
		Social Insurance	Public Aid	Health and Medical Services	Education	Other Welfare Services	Veterans' Programs	Total
1935-1936	7.4	0.5	4.4	0.9	3.1	0.1	0.6	9.6
1940-1941	9.1	1.1	3.2	0.7	2.6	0.1	0.5	8.2
1945-1946	11.8	1.3	0.6	0.5	1.8	0.1	1.5	5.8
1950-1951	23.6	1.5	0.8	0.8	2.5	0.2	1.8	7.6
1955-1956	34.6	2.6	0.8	0.7	3.0	0.2	1.1	8.4
1960-1961	57.9	4.4	0.9	0.9	3.9	0.2	1.0	11.5
1965-1966	87.6	4.5	1.0	1.0	4.5	0.4	0.9	12.3
1970-1971	171.9	6.5	2.1	1.1	5.6	0.5	1.0	17.0
1972-1973	215.2	7.0	2.3	1.0	5.3	0.5	1.1	17.5
1973-1974	241.7	7.3	2.5	1.0	5.4	0.5	1.0	18.0

Sources: Social Security Bulletin, various issues.

rather shallow, bureaucratic, strongly centralized, institutional machinery, manipulated by crafty organizational entrepreneurs and vested interests, into a more decentralized society in which individuals will take over functions formerly handled by the state. As an example, he points out that a law was passed in Sweden a little more than twenty years ago which forbade employers to discharge a woman for family reasons: because she became engaged, married, or had a child. The purpose of such a law was to prevent employers from substituting cheap, inexperienced help for more experienced, higher-paid women who had more seniority. Myrdal felt that the law was necessary then in order to force a change in an unwholesome prevailing custom of the time. At the present time, though, Myrdal believes that such a law could be repealed without risk, for public opinion is now more enlightened and would not condone the firing of a woman for the reasons given above. He foresees that a "welfare culture" more locally administered will come into existence within the structure of the welfare state.

For the United States, which has much less of a welfare state than western European countries, Myrdal points out that the process of national integration has still a considerable distance to go before it reaches the levels common to other western countries. Far more federal government legislation is needed. The weaker local and sectional community controls call for more direct state control through the courts and administration to enforce the general mores. In the long run, though, he feels that even in America, as more active citizen participation occurs on the local level, less centralized government control would be necessary.

MORE RESPONSIBLE GOVERNMENT

Professor Girvetz has analyzed methods by which governments, although expanding in function, may be made more responsive to the needs of the people. First, he lists the party system as necessary so that protest can be informed and organized. A multiparty system obviously is necessary for such protest rather than a single-party system. He also looks with favor upon such groups as the League of Women Voters, Americans for Democratic Action, the Committee for Economic Development, and the British Fabian Society to provide leadership in making the party system work and to make government more responsible to the people. He maintains that independent and powerful organization of workers is indispensable to democratic government. Labor needs protection not only against private managers but public supervisors as well. Those seeking monopoly power, such as totalitarian governments, dislike labor unions. Private groups who seek a monopoly of power, either covertly or openly, despise labor unions also. He thinks also that strong consumers' organizations are necessary to make governments responsible to the needs of the people, although he recognizes that in the United States consumer groups have been particularly weak and unorganized. Last but not least, he lists private enterprise as necessary to provide responsiveness of government. Such enterprise places a check on public enterprise. With the proper countervailing power, more rather than less freedom will result even though the power of the government increases.[28]

DANGERS OF INCREASED TAXATION

Some fear that increased taxes to cover the expanding government sector may prove the downfall of our society. A number of studies have been made on the effect of taxes on incentives. One study on the relation between the income tax and the relation to work concluded that highly progressive income taxes have not reduced incentives to work.[29] This study found that wage and salary employees have little choice in the amount of work they do. About the only choice available is whether to work at another job after working hours. Another study analyzed the impact of the federal income tax on labor force participation. The conclusion of this study was that the income tax has no effect on the size and composition of the labor force.[30]

Several studies have been made of the impact of taxes upon the work incentives of executives. Professor T. H. Sanders found that the economy has not lost a serious amount of executives' services due to taxes. He concluded that nonfinancial incentives outweigh financial incentives in motivating executives to work. The nonfinancial incentives of doing a good job, power, prestige, the sense of satisfaction of a responsible position, the sense of loyalty to an organization, and the organizational disciplines of the group, outweigh any negative incentives to reduce the amount of work due to high taxes.[31] Professor Dan Throop Smith concluded that executives' "day-to-day efforts and activities are in general not lessened by taxation."[32] Another study of the effects of high taxes on savings and investment shows little impairment from taxes. A number of ways are provided by which upper-income recipients avoid the full impact of the upper-bracket tax rates and are able to save large sums of money. Investment has not been unduly affected either. Some investors place their money in risky ventures to obtain capital gains, which are taxed much less than regular income. Owners and managers of business enterprises have continued to invest heavily also. A final conclusion from a

[28]Girvetz, op. cit., pp. 226-229.

[29]George F. Break, "Income Taxes and Incentives to Work: An Empirical Study," American Economic Review, Vol. 47 (1957), pp. 529-549.

[30]Clarence D. Long, "Impact of the Federal Income Tax on Labor Force Participation," Federal Tax Policy for Economic Growth and Stability (Washington, D.C., Joint Economic Committee, 1955), pp. 153-166.

[31]Thomas H. Sanders, Effects of Taxation on Executives (Cambridge, Harvard Business School, 1951).

[32]Dan Throop Smith, "Taxation and Executives," Proceedings of the National Tax Association, 1951 (Sacramento, Calif., 1952), p. 235.

number of studies by Harvard's Graduate School of Business was that current levels of tax rates will not cause serious long-run damage to the economy. The viewpoint that expenditures and taxes must be greatly reduced to preserve economic strength at home was not "substantiated by the facts."[33]

Much of our welfare program is financed through payroll taxes. These taxes are regressive rather than progressive. Their use should not hurt incentives to invest. In a more pessimistic vein, Professor Colin Clark contended that the critical point of taxation was 25 percent of national income. When taxation approached that level, various pressure groups will insist on deficits and other devices, which will result in inflation and an impairment of incentives. He cited statistical data, mainly from France, to support his position.[34] Few economists today would support the position of Professor Colin Clark. Even with high taxes, investment has been high, and taxation has already exceeded the critical 25 percent level without disastrous results. It is true, however, that the many suggestions for expanding welfare would tend to increase taxes even more. Ways and means will be needed to finance an even larger amount of government participation. Some have suggested that additional revenue could be obtained by closing some of the loopholes in our present laws. Some of the increases of government could be paid out of our increasing gross national product. Some of the countries of western Europe have substantially higher payroll taxes than we have. These countries have shown little ill effects from the higher taxes.

LIBERTY AND WELFARE

An important question to be answered is whether increased government intervention will result in the elimination of liberty. In Calvin Hoover's provocative book, *The Economy, Liberty, and the State,* he carefully analyzes the relation between the growth of the state and liberty. He concludes that for western Europe and the United States there has been no close correlation between the increasing amount of state intervention and the net limitation upon personal liberty. His findings, he says, seem to contradict the theory that extension of the power of the state is incompatible with the maintenance of personal liberty. He agrees that the expanding state did result in a serious curtailment of liberty under Nazi, Fascist, and Soviet regimes, but he sees no diminution of personal liberty in western Europe and the United States.

Hoover offers several reasons why personal liberty has not decreased in the latter countries. Of importance is his distinction between business liberty and personal liberty. A minimum wage law, for example, does

---

[33]J. Keith Butters, "Taxation, Incentives and Financial Capacity," *American Economic Review,* Supplement (May, 1954), p. 519.

[34]Colin Clark, "Public Finance and Changes in the Value of Money," *Economic Journal* (December, 1945), pp. 371-389.

limit the business liberty of an employer to pay less than the minimum, and acreage restrictions do limit the right of the farmer to plant as much as he wishes; yet such limitations are not considered as a loss of personal freedom of the type protected by the constitution, such as freedom of the press, speech, religion, protection against self-incrimination, and the like. Second, the intervention of the state generally appears only after the prior growth of power by some group. The purpose of the state intervention is to restrict too much power in the hands of one group. The National Labor Relations Act, for example, was passed primarily to give workers more power against the dominant corporate group. State intervention, then was felt to provide more individual liberty in protecting against corporations rather than restricting such liberty. Third, the state may intervene primarily to avoid a crisis. The intervention of the state during war to curtail wage or price increases may be viewed primarily as a protection against inflation rather than as an extension of state power.[35]

Hoover recognizes that the growth of the government in Russia has severely limited personal freedom. Furthermore, he doubts that a fully statized economy can be operated by a bureaucracy without the loss of personal liberty and representative government. In western Europe and the United States he thinks that it will be possible to maintain personal liberty even with some further expansion of government functions. He states that the further extension of state control is inevitable to ameliorate the economic status of lower-income groups and to keep our modern complex economy functioning at a tolerable level. Whether personal liberty will be maintained will depend on the restriction of government functions to those truly necessary, and to the maintenance of continuing popular control through elected representatives. The success of our economic system itself will be important in determining how much government intervention is necessary. The proper evolution of our institutions to maintain both high per capita income and liberty will depend fundamentally on the contradictory traits of tough-mindedness, goodwill, and responsibleness by those who supply the guidance to our system.[36]

INDIVIDUAL RESPONSIBILITY

Proponents of increased welfare have attempted to refute the argument that cradle-to-grave security will result in destroying individual responsibility. They maintain that improved and expanded welfare programs should increase rather than decrease responsibility. If a young person's opportunity to attend school is conditioned on the merit of his own work rather than the economic and social status of his parents, his responsibility should increase. Furthermore, forcing a child to grow up in a slum

[35]Hoover, *op. cit.*, pp. 330-337.
[36]*Ibid.*, pp. 341-377.

environment may seriously hinder the growth of a sense of responsibility. Clearing slum areas may provide a more conducive environment in which the person may assume more responsibility. Increased expenditures for education, housing, aging, and other welfare measures should also provide increased responsibility. Professor Girvetz maintains that the number of shiftless and lazy in our society has been grossly exaggerated mainly to relieve the remaining population of assuming responsibility for their care.[37] For those relatively few who are lazy or shiftless, the causes of such behavior are primarily due to lack of opportunity and a poor environment. Improving the environment through welfare measures should activate most persons to assume more of their responsibilities toward society. In short, welfare measures should increase responsibility rather than reduce it.

Summary

The radical right has vigorously opposed the welfare state. Some of this group follow a branch of Christianity which stresses evilness in man. Since man cannot be trusted, creations of his, such as government cannot be trusted either. Other non-Christian radical rightists claim that the great advances of civilization have come through individuals rather than centralized government. They therefore favor individualism over government programs. The radical right claims that welfare has been abused. This group claims that the lower classes are inferior because they are unable to defer present gratification. The radical right places much emphasis on a trust of elites and individual responsibility.

The radical left has supported Social Security and other welfare state programs. However, the radical left claims that the welfare state will not solve the various problems of society. This group has been critical that inequality of wealth has not been reduced in recent years. Class differentials and distinctions are still as great as ever. This group asserts that mental health and personal happiness will only be reached through a radically different organized society.

Pro welfare staters hold that our present society may improve the status of the poor through such government measures as income maintenance programs, improved education, housing, and employment. Improving the lot of the poor should make for a better society without any loss of personal freedom.

[37]Girvetz, op. cit., p. 233.

Bibliography

Banfield, Edward C., *The Unheavenly City Revisited* (Boston, Little, Brown and Co., 1974).

Baran, Paul A. and Paul M. Sweezy, *Monopoly Capital* (New York, Monthly Review Press, 1966).

Friedman, Milton, *Capitalism and Freedom* (Chicago, University of Chicago Press, 1962).

Fromm, Erich, *Escape from Freedom* (New York, Avon Books, 1965).

Gordon, David M., *Theories of Poverty and Underemployment* (Lexington, Mass., D. C. Heath and Co., 1972).

Harrington, Michael, *The Other America* (New York, MacMillan, 1962).

Hoover, Calvin E., *The Economy Liberty and the State* (Garden City, New York, Doubleday, 1961).

Marcuse, Herbert, *Counterrevolution and Revolt* (Boston, The Beacon Press, 1972).

Moore, Barrington, Jr., *Reflections on the Causes of Human Misery* (Boston, The Beacon Press, 1972).

Myrdal, Gunnar, *Beyond the Welfare State* (New Haven, Yale University Press, 1960).

Rand, Ayn, Ed., *Capitalism, the Unknown Ideal* (New York, New American Library, 1966).

Titmuss, Richard M., *Problems of Social Policy* (Westport, Conn., Greenwood Press, 1971).

CHAPTER 3

POVERTY, INEQUALITY, AND INSECURITY

Poverty, inequality, and insecurity are related but not identical problems. A wealthy person may be economically insecure without being bothered by inequality, and he is by definition not poor. At the other extreme, the entire population might be below the poverty level without feeling the indignities of inequality, and they might also be poor but secure. Generally, however, there is considerable overlap: those in poverty are also likely to be aware of inequalities, and to be insecure as well. The causes of inequality and of economic insecurity are also likely to be among the causes of poverty discussed below. Economic insecurity typically includes the hazards of old age retirement, the early death or loss of the family breadwinner, unemployment, and ill health and disability, all among the causes of poverty and inequality.

INCOME INEQUALITY

Median family income in the United States in 1973 was $12,051. This of course means that one-half the families received more, and one-half received less than that amount. In cumulative terms 6% of all families received less than $3,000, 15%, less than $5,000 and 24% less than $7,000 annual income. At the top of the scale about 35% of all families had incomes of $15,000 or more, while 9.3% had incomes of $25,000 or more.[1] Median income for whites in 1973 was $12,595 compared to $7,269 for Negroes and other races. In 1951 nonwhite income was only 53% of white income; in 1961, it was still 53; but in 1973 nonwhite income was 58% of that of whites. This is improvement, but it means that there still is a vast gulf between the median income of whites and nonwhites.

The extent of inequality can be more precisely shown by dividing the population into fifths or quintiles, as in Table 3-1, and showing the percentage of total income received by each fifth of the population. Thus the lowest fifth of the population received 4% of total income in 1972, while the highest fifth received 44%. The trend since 1929 may also be seen.

---

[1]Bureau of the Census, *Money Income in 1973 of Families and Persons in the United States*, Series P-60, No. 93, July 1974, Tables 1, 3 and 5.

Since 1929 income inequality has definitely decreased, the highest fifth having lost ground, the other four fifths having gained ground. In 1929, the top 5 percent received 30% of all income; in 1972, the top 5 percent received 17% of income. Most of the change, however, occurred between 1929 and 1947, there being but little change since 1947; since 1968 the degree of inequality has increased slightly.

Demographic and labor force characteristics shed additional light on income inequality. About 40% of the lowest quintile live in the South. Race is a factor: nationwide, in the lowest fifth, 79% are white and 21% are Negro and other races. Thirty percent of families in the lowest quintile are headed by a female. Thirty-five percent of lowest-quintile families have no income earner and 43% have only one. Source of income is also significant: in the lowest quintile, 26% of these families had "earnings only" and 39% had "earnings and income other than earnings," and the remaining 35 percent had neither (other than welfare).

By way of contrast, in the highest quintile only 5% are nonwhite; only 3% of such families are headed by a female; 45% of these families have two income earners and 31% have three or more; and 75% of such families had income from both earnings and income other than earnings. For those in the top five percent, 81% reported income from both earnings and income other than earnings. This reflects the concentration of ownership of income-producing wealth in the hands of the highest quintile. In recent years, public attention has shifted away from the problem of income inequality, and has focused on the problem of poverty.

POVERTY

In the United States, poverty, defined below, includes about 11% of the population, or around 23 million people. The poverty population includes disproportionate numbers of the aged and of dependent children, minority groups, residents of urban ghettos, residents of certain rural areas, and families headed by women. Statistics and classifications of poverty are given below, and while worthwhile, these tend to dehumanize the problem. Personal visits by the student to poverty homes will tend to be much more revealing. In lieu of such visits descriptions of actual cases as reported in Congressional hearings give an idea of the conditions in which some of our people live:

On an adjoining plantation we made another visit, one of the day's most pathetic. Mrs. Moore was living in relative comfort compared with Mary Lou Carsten, her nine children, and three grandchildren born of her daughter, not yet sixteen. When we entered the house, the woman, thirty years old but looking easily fifty, was sitting crosslegged on a bed with a faded red chenille bedspread draped over her legs. Although she must have been five feet nine inches tall, her flesh was so shrunken that she couldn't have weighed much more than 100 pounds. Her head,

TABLE 3-1

PERCENTAGE SHARE OF AGGREGATE INCOME RECEIVED BY EACH FIFTH OF FAMILIES RANKED BY INCOME, SELECTED YEARS

Quintiles	1929	1941	1947	1960	1968	1970	1972
Lowest Fifth	3.5%	4.1%	5.0%	4.9%	5.7%	5.5%	4.2%
Second Fifth	9.0	9.5	11.8	12.0	12.4	12.0	10.5
Third Fifth	13.8	15.3	17.0	17.6	17.7	17.4	16.8
Fourth Fifth	19.3	22.3	23.1	23.6	23.7	23.5	24.6
Highest Fifth	54.4	48.8	43.0	42.0	40.6	41.6	43.9
Top 5 Percent	30.0	24.0	17.2	16.8	14.0	14.4	17.0

Source: For 1929 and 1941, Edward C. Budd (ed), *Inequality and Poverty* (New York, W. W. Norton & Co., 1967), p. xiii; for 1947 and later years, Bureau of the Census, *Money Income in 1971 of Families and Persons in the United States*, Series P-60, No. 85, Table 13; and *Ibid., Consumer Income*, Series P-60, No. 89, July 1973, Table D, p. 3.

grotesque and large on her emaciated body, hung so heavily that she seemed barely able to hold it upright to say hello. Her voice was barely audible. Life had been drained out of her at thirty. We were told she had been sick, that doctors had been unable to determine the cause — and it seemed obvious that she was dying.

The stench in the house with only three rooms for thirteen people was sickening, especially in the room where the children sat clustered watching the inevitable TV. One little boy, in the fourth grade, sat isolated in a dimly lit corner of one room trying to do his lessons. The legs of the toddlers were bone-thin and bent, presumably from malnutrition. A baby, half-covered by a soiled sheet, was a mass of crawling flies.

This woman obviously could not work, nor were her children we saw old enough to do so even if there was work to be had. How did she live? She had no husband. Are you on welfare? "No", she said. They wouldn't let her have it because she had had babies by different men. She thought she was going to get a welfare check of $58 a month starting soon. The family's only income was what her 18-year-old son brought home working on a plantation — about $15 a week after expenses such as rent, light, medical bills, were deducted.

When we tried to make conversation with the little children, who squatted on the floor and toddled around the porch; they just looked at us with dulled eyes. As we left the woman on the bed raised her over-sized head and managed a half-pleading smile at the neighbor who had taken us there. "Seems I just can't get enough to eat these days," she murmured.[2]

Another case is taken from the testimony of Dr. Jack Geiger of the Tufts-Delta Health Center at Mound Bayou, Mississippi. Showing the Congressional committee a photograph of an emaciated 2-month old child under his project's care, Dr. Geiger said:

...He is not atypical. I have to assume that he is not premature and he is not dead. He is 2 months old in that picture and weighs 2 pounds less than when he was born. He had infectious diarrhea, dehydration, malnutrition, and anemia.

On the basis of all our data and our experience in the area let me tell you some more positive statements we can make about him. Even in that state, he is a lucky survivor. Our environment is such that many of his brothers and sisters literally die before they are born — The probability is good . . . that he was taken home to a deteriorating shack with a contaminated water supply, a sunshine privy, a crumbling ceiling, open windows, holes in the walls patched with newspaper, inadequate heat, to share an environment with three or four other people per room and countless flies, mosquitoes, roaches, and an occasional rat. In that environment, with the water supply, the probability is good that within the first

---

[2]"Nutrition and Human Needs: Hearings before the Select Committee on Nutrition and Human Needs of the U.S. Senate, 90th Congress." Testimony by National Council of Negro Women, Inc.: Workshops in Mississippi: A Report on Operation Daily Bread, October 1968, pp. 202-204.

week of his life he was ingesting some of his own excrement — or his brother's, or his neighbor's, or an animal's.[3]

A CLASSIFICATION OF THE POOR

The poor have been classified by S. M. Miller into four categories: (1) the stable poor; (2) the strained; (3) the copers; and (4) the unstable.[4] In essence the classification depends on whether or not the family is stable or unstable and on whether or not it is economically secure or insecure, as shown in Table 3-2.

TABLE 3-2

A CLASSIFICATION OF THE POOR

1. *The Stable Poor* economically secure stable family	2. *The Strained* economically secure unstable family
3. *The Copers* economically insecure stable family	4. *The Unstable* economically insecure unstable family

(1) *The stable poor* are made up mainly of the regularly employed, low-skilled, poorly paid stable families. The white rural Southern population makes up much of this group, although many Negro families are also represented here. Many of the aged poor also come under this classification. The children in this category are believed to have the best chance of being upwardly mobile.

(2) *The strained* have a secure economic position but the family is unstable, including unsettled young workers and alcoholic older workers. Many in this category are transitional — in the process of skidding into category four. Their children may also experience inter-generational skidding. On the other hand, children of immigrant families who are in this category have frequently been upwardly mobile.

(3) *The copers* get their name from the fact that while insecure, they still manage to cope with the situation. They have a rough time economically, but the family is intact. Many of the unemployed are found in this group, and correspondingly a considerable number of Negroes.

[3]*Promises to Keep: Housing Need and Federal Failure in Rural America*, Select Committee on Nutrition and Human Needs, U. S. Senate, 92nd Congress, 2nd Session, April 1972, p. 38.

[4]S. M. Miller, "The American Lower Class: A Typological Approach," *Social Research*, Vol. 31 (1964), pp. 1-22.

(4) *The unstable* combine economic insecurity with familial instability. In Miller's words, "The low-income class generally and the unstable in particular comprise a category of unskilled, irregular workers, broken and large families, and a residual bin of the aged, physically handicapped and mentally disturbed."[5] Newly urbanized Negroes, slum residents of ethnic groups, and long-term poor-white families are apt to be in this group. Illness, alcoholism, and inability to handle aggression, hostility, and dependence are common characteristics.

From the foregoing it is obvious that the poor are very diverse, ranging from those who are troubled mainly by low income to others with a complex of interrelated economic, social and psychological difficulties. Public policy, if it is to be appropriate, must ordinarily take into account the diversity and complexity of the problems of the poor.

DEFINITIONS OF POVERTY

Poverty has been described or defined in many different ways, but we will confine ourselves to three definitions, two of them economic, the other a noneconomic definition. The two economic definitions are (1) an absolute measure based on annual dollar income developed by the Social Security Administration and currently used by the Bureau of the Census, and (2) a relative measure developed by Victor Fuchs of the National Bureau of Economic Research. A noneconomic definition worthy of note is (3) the "social indicators definition," described by S. M. Miller, Martin Rein, Pamela Roby, and Bertram M. Gross. These three definitions of poverty are discussed in the three following sections.

BUREAU OF THE CENSUS' POVERTY THRESHOLDS

The Bureau of the Census currently makes use of a set of "poverty thresholds" developed by Mollie Orshansky and the Social Securiy Administration. In 1963 the Presidents' Council of Economic Advisors (CEA) estimated that any family of two or more with less than $3,000 annual income, and any single person living alone with less than $1,500 would be considered poor. The CEA estimate, however, did not take into account differences in sizes of families, differences between male and female-headed families, differences in the age of the family head, and differences in living expenses between farm and non-farm families. Mollie Orshansky,[6] making allowance for each of these variables, identified 248 separate family or single person situations but condensed these into 72

[5]*Ibid.*, p. 12.

[6]Mollie Orshansky, Division of Research and Statistics, Social Security Administration, "Counting the Poor: Another Look at the Poverty Profile," *Social Security Bulletin* (January 1965), pp. 3-29.

situations, and computed an appropriate poverty threshold for each one. A nonfarm family of two adults and two children needed $3,130 in 1963. Larger families, of course, needed more, smaller families less. A family of eight, two adults and six children needed $5,100 in 1963 to be at the poverty line. As the cost of living rises, the poverty lines or thresholds have been adjusted upward. Table 3-3 shows selected poverty standards for 1973.

TABLE 3-3

SELECTED POVERTY LEVEL THRESHOLDS IN 1973
BY SIZE OF FAMILY AND SEX OF HEAD,
BY FARM AND NON FARM RESIDENCE

	Nonfarm		Farm	
	Male Head*	Female Head*	Male Head*	Female Head*
Unrelated Individuals:	$2,350	$2,174	$1,951	$1,832
Under 65 years	2,395	2,215	2,035	1,883
65 years and over	2,151	2,123	1,829	1,804
All Families:				
2 Persons	2,904	2,847	2,439	2,346
Head under 65	2,999	2,908	2,546	2,455
Head 65 years and over	2,690	2,675	2,285	2,285
3 Persons	3,565	3,447	3,015	2,878
4 Persons	4,542	4,521	3,872	3,775
5 Persons	5,364	5,299	4,560	4,609
6 Persons	6,034	5,965	5,144	5,206
7 or more Persons	7,455	7,288	6,357	6,150

*For one person (i.e., unrelated individual), sex of the individual.

Source: Bureau of the Census, *Characteristics of Low Income Families*, Series P-60, No. 94, July 1974, Table 7.

In addition to the foregoing, the Census Bureau computes and publishes two variations of the poverty definition — one set at 75% of the official government standard and the other at 125% of this standard. Poverty defined at 75% of the official standard may be said to include only the "extremely poor," while the poverty level at 125% is commonly said to include the "near-poor." The near-poor include those whose situation is precarious since any major changes in their situation, accidents, chronic illness, natural disasters, or the birth of additional children, will be apt to reduce them from near-poor to below the poverty level. Taken as a whole the official poverty standard is a rather rigorous definition. The Department of Agriculture has estimated that only about 10% of persons spending the amounts allocated for food were actually able to get a nutritionally adequate diet.[7] Some take the position that the 125% level, the near-poor standard, more accurately reflects the true amount of poverty.

An offsetting consideration is that the official statistics do not consider nonmoney income such as food stamps, free medical care, and low rent in public housing. If these were counted the amount of poverty and the extent of inequality would be somewhat less.

A RELATIVE DEFINITION OF POVERTY

An alternate definition of poverty has been developed by Victor R. Fuchs of the National Bureau of Economic Research. He proposes that we define as poor "any family whose income is less than one-half the median family income."[8] Each year as median income rises the poverty line would be automatically reset at one-half (or some other fraction) of the new median. Thus as the level of living for the rest of the population rose, the poverty line would also rise. Victor Fuchs has calculated that for several recent years the percentage below the poverty line would range from about 19 to about 21%. (This conclusion follows from the "pear-shaped" distribution of income in the United States). One advantage claimed for this sort of definition is that it automatically adjusts the poverty line upward as the standard of living rises. Another advantage claimed is that the public policy focus would be shifted from the poverty problem to the problem of inequality of income and redistribution of income.

Different conclusions are reached as to whether or not poverty is being reduced depending on whether the absolute or relative definition is used. If an absolute definition is used there has been substantial reduction in poverty over the last several decades. Under the relative definition, little progress is being made in reducing poverty. The poverty definitions or indicators developed by the Social Security Administration and the Bureau of the Census are the most widely used in the United States today.

A NONECONOMIC DEFINITION OF POVERTY?

Some students of poverty, especially people in sociology, psychology, social work, and political science, believe that the definition of poverty should include more than the economic. They note that most definitions

---

[7]Mollie Orshansky, "How Poverty is Measured," *Monthly Labor Review* (February 1969), pp. 37-41.

[8]Victor R. Fuchs, National Bureau of Economic Research, "Redefining Poverty and Redistributing Income," *The Public Interest* (Summer 1967), pp. 89-94.

of poverty are stated in terms of current income, but they hold that income is only one of the dimensions of poverty and inequality. Besides a concern with current income, society should also be concerned with assets and basic services, which are economic, and with problems of *self-respect, status, opportunities for social mobility, and participation in many forms of decisions making.*[9] An increase in current income, these students argue, does not automatically lead to an increase in self-respect, status, social mobility, or participation. Therefore these dimensions are worthy of separate attention. Much of the income of the poor, such as public assistance payments, is demeaning, involving a loss of self-respect and status. Thus the satisfactions realized by the poor are believed to be disportionately low. For instance, $6000 of earned income may yield a family more than three times the satisfaction felt by a family with $2000 of assistance payments.

If poverty is to be redefined, we will need indexes of income stigma, and indicators of self-respect, status, opportunity, and participation. Such indicators can be developed, presumably based on questionnaires applied to a sample of the population. But these items will be more difficult to quantify. Indexes based on incomes are relatively easy to measure and to quantify, since income is objective and external in origin. The various social indicators, self-respect, etc., are to a large extent internal and subjective. Accordingly, while we can readily grant the desirability of a broader definition of poverty based on social indicators as well as income, at present, current dollar income adjusted each year for change in the cost of living is our best single indicator of the presence or absence of poverty.

WHAT CAUSES POVERTY?

Using the income criteria, about 23 million people, or 11.1% of the population, were below the poverty line in 1973. Why? What are the causes of poverty? If 11% were below the poverty line, 89% must have been above it. Why are some people above the poverty line, in many cases far above it? Or in other words, why do some people have enough income, or more than enough, while others have too little? The more some people work or the more property they have the more their income. And the higher the prices (that is, wages, rents, interest, and profits) they receive for each unit of work or of resources, the more their income. It follows that low income — or poverty — is related to the absence of, or too little, wage or resource income. People below the poverty line often own little or no property, often do not or cannot work, or if they do work they are paid very low wages. This is obvious enough, but it leads us to further questions:

[9]S. M. Miller, Martin Rein, Pamela Roby, and Bertram M. Gross, "Poverty, Inequality, and Conflict," *The Annals of the American Academy of Political and Social Science* (Septermber 1967), pp. 18-52.

Why do they engage in little or no work? Why do they own little or no property? And why, if they work, are they paid very low wages?

That many of the poor do not work is commonly known.[10] Related to this many believe that the poor are poor because they do not want to work, that they are lazy and incompetent, or that they are profligate and careless with their money. Others say that the poor are poor because they do not save and invest, or that they are morally inferior, that they breed excessive numbers of children who grow up to add to the poverty population, or that they are genetically inferior. Bumper stickers such as "I fight poverty; I work," typify the attitudes of many middle income people about the poor. Are these attitudes essentially correct? The first insight in to the causes of poverty rests on the identification of those living in poverty — that is the age, sex, race, occupation, and geography of the poverty population.

THE GEOGRAPHY OF POVERTY

Poverty is unevenly distributed over the United States. All states have some poverty, but the poverty rate is roughly twice as high in the South as in the rest of the country. The 1970 census showed that of the 27 million people in poverty in 1969, 12.4 million lived in the South. The poverty rate was 20.3% in the South, 10.1% in the Northeast, 10.8% in the North Central states, and 11.7% in the West. In the South itself the highest poverty rates occur in the East South Central States (Kentucky, Tennessee, Alabama, and Mississippi), and in the West South Central States (Arkansas, Louisiana, Oklahoma, and Texas). High poverty rates also exist in South Carolina, New Mexico, West Virginia, and North Carolina. In Table 3-4 the states are ranked in order of percent of persons below the poverty level. Separate columns show percent of families and percent of unrelated individuals below the poverty level. Within regions, rural areas have more poverty than urban areas, 18 percent compared to 12 percent.

UNRELATED INDIVIDUALS

Another group highly likely to be below the poverty line are "unrelated individuals." Unrelated individuals, as defined by the Census Bureau, are persons, 14 years and over, who are not living with any relatives. They may be living alone, or as part of a household including one or more other families or unrelated individuals, or residing in group quarters such as a

[10]Many of the poor do work. Data for 1973 indicate that 41.5% of heads of poor families are employed while another 5.5% were unemployed, and 53% were listed as "not in the labor force." The latter are mainly the aged, the disabled, or women with young children in their care. See *Characteristics of the Low Income Population*, Bureau of the Census, Series P-60, No. 94, Table 5, p. 8.

TABLE 3-4

POVERTY RATES BY STATES, FOR PERSONS, FAMILIES, AND UNRELATED INDIVIDUALS, UNITED STATES, 1969.

Percent Below The Poverty Level

State	Persons	Families	Unrelated Individuals
Mississippi	35.4%	28.9%	60.3%
Arkansas	27.8	22.8	58.0
Louisiana	26.3	21.5	52.8
Alabama	25.4	20.7	55.3
South Carolina	23.9	19.0	50.0
Kentucky	22.9	19.2	51.2
New Mexico	22.8	18.5	44.0
West Virginia	22.2	18.0	55.7
Tennessee	21.8	18.2	50.3
Georgia	20.7	16.7	45.8
North Carolina	20.3	16.3	47.5
Oklahoma	18.8	15.0	49.3
Texas	18.8	14.6	42.0
South Dakota	18.7	14.8	47.3
District of Columbia	17.0	12.7	24.4
Florida	16.4	12.7	38.5
North Dakota	15.7	12.4	42.1
Virginia	15.5	12.3	36.9
Arizona	15.3	11.5	36.7
Missouri	14.7	11.5	42.3
Montana	13.6	10.4	40.4
Maine	13.6	10.3	42.3
Idaho	13.2	10.9	42.3
Nebraska	13.1	10.1	40.5
Kansas	12.7	9.7	42.6
Alaska	12.6	9.3	25.9
Colorado	12.3	9.1	37.0
Vermont	12.1	9.1	40.2

Table 3-4 (continued)

Wyoming	11.7	9.3	36.7
Iowa	11.6	8.9	41.6
Oregon	11.5	8.6	37.9
Utah	11.4	9.1	44.7
California	11.1	8.4	27.3
New York	11.1	8.5	31.0
Rhode Island	11.0	8.5	40.7
Delaware	10.9	8.2	34.3
Minnesota	10.7	8.2	36.5
Pennsylvania	10.6	7.9	40.4
Illinois	10.2	7.7	33.4
Washington	10.2	7.6	33.8
Maryland	10.1	7.7	32.1
Ohio	10.0	7.6	37.4
Wisconsin	9.8	7.4	37.5
Indiana	9.7	7.4	37.9
Michigan	9.4	7.3	35.5
Hawaii	9.3	7.6	30.3
Nevada	9.1	7.0	25.9
New Hampshire	9.1	6.7	38.5
Massachusetts	8.6	6.2	31.6
New Jersey	8.1	6.1	31.2
Connecticut	7.2	5.3	28.6
United States	13.7	10.7	37.0

Source: *1970 U.S. Census, General Social and Economic Characteristics, United States Summary*, Table 182.

rooming house. They include a widow living by herself, or a lodger not related to anyone else in the household, or a servant living in an employer's household. Of the 23 million persons in poverty in 1973, 4.7 million were unrelated individuals. While the poverty rate for all persons was 11.1%, and 9.7% for all families, the poverty rate for unrelated individuals was an astonishing 25.6%.

The 1970 Census showed eight states (see Table 3-4) with more than 50% of unrelated individuals in poverty. For the United States as a whole the mean annual income of such persons was only $861. The mean income deficit, or shortage below the poverty level, was $952. In 1969, 37% of these people were in poverty, but only 13% were receiving public assistance. This problem is nationwide. In percentages of those receiving public assistance, the South outranks the rest of the nation, but the dollar amounts paid in the South are often quite low. Another aspect of the problem of unrelated individuals is that nearly half (48%) are persons aged 65 and over.

DEMOGRAPHIC CHARACTERISTICS

Demographic characteristics can indicate some of the causes of poverty, among them *old age*. Of all persons in families, 12% are below the poverty level, but for family members aged 65 and over, 17% are in poverty. Data for unrelated aged individuals (people not in families) show even more poverty, 51 percent. For the most part aged people are not in the labor force and, because of their age or ill health, or both, cannot reasonably be expected to work.[11]

Children also make up a disproportionate share of the poverty population. They also are not normally in the labor force, although some teenagers do have jobs, often part-time. About 16% of all children under 6 years of age are in families whose income is below the poverty line, 15% of those in ages 6 to 13, and 13% of those aged 14 to 17. The proportions of children in poverty are especially heavy in families headed by females. Under 6 years of age, 62% of the children are in poverty, while 54% of those aged 6 to 13, and 41% of those 14 to 17, are in poverty in female-headed families.[12] Neither the aged nor children under 16 can reasonably be expected to work, while children over age 16 may more profitably be in school.

Poverty is related to sex especially in the high incidence of poverty in *families with a female head*. The poverty rate for all persons in families with a male head is 9%; for all persons in families with a female head it is 33%. Similar percentages of course follow for the various age brackets. While the poverty rate for children under 6 years is 11% in families with a male head, it is 62% for such children with a female head.

For unrelated individuals, the poverty rate for all males is 30%; for all females, 42%. The same general pattern follows through the various age

---

[11]Data for this and following paragraphs are taken from the *1970 U. S. Census*, Detailed Characteristics, Table 259.

[12]*Ibid.*, p. 259.

categories. This only raises further questions: Why do females and especially families with a female head experience more poverty than do males?

As is commonly known, poverty is more prevalent among *blacks and persons of Spanish heritage* than among whites. For all persons in families the poverty rate among whites is 9%; for persons of Spanish heritage, 23%; and for blacks, 34%. Again this compels us to ask: Why do blacks and those of Spanish heritage suffer more poverty than do whites?

The larger the *number of children in the family* the more likely the family is to be in poverty. This of course follows largely from the fact that the poverty thresholds are adjusted for size of family. An annual income of $6,000 will be above the poverty level for a couple with one child, but below the poverty level for a couple with four or more children. Needs are greater for the large family than the small. Also, it is more difficult for the mother to work outside the home if the family has several small children. So need is higher and total family income may actually be smaller. Table 3-5 shows percent of families below the poverty level by number of

TABLE 3-5

PERCENTAGES OF FAMILIES WITH INCOME BELOW THE POVERTY LEVEL, BY SEX AND NUMBER OF CHILDREN, 1969

	All Families	Families with Male Head	Families with Female Head	
			Total	Widowed
All Families:	10.7	8.1	32.5	24.5
No related children under 18 years	9.2	8.6	14.5	16.5
With related children under 18 years	11.8	7.6	43.3	34.5
One related child	8.7	5.4	29.8	27.8
Two related children	8.7	5.4	38.5	30.8
Three related children	12.0	7.4	52.2	39.2
Four related children	16.8	11.1	62.8	49.3
Five related children	26.2	19.7	71.4	59.4
Six or more children	34.7	25.8	78.7	68.4

Source: *1970 U.S. Census, Detailed Characteristics,* Table 260.

TABLE 3-6

LABOR FORCE PARTICIPATION BY POOR FAMILY HEADS, BY AGE, SEX, AND RACE, 1969

Income Below the Poverty Level

	All Income Levels	Total Poor Population	Whites	Blacks	Spanish Heritage
All Family Heads	82.1%	48.0%	47.3%	50.0%	55.4%
Under 25 years	89.0	62.6	66.9	51.3	60.9
25-64 years	91.2	60.2	61.3	58.1	60.4
65 years and over	26.4	9.9	9.0	13.9	11.8
Male Head	85.3	54.5	52.8	83.1	70.5
Under 25 years	93.1	78.8	79.6	90.2	82.0
25-64 years	94.0	72.7	72.2	90.7	78.2
65 years and over	28.5	10.7	9.8	27.8	13.5
Female Head	55.7	34.7	32.6	52.7	44.3
With related children under 18	60.1	38.1	37.4	53.1	43.0
With related children under 6	51.6	35.1	34.3	47.5	34.5
Under 25	54.2	35.5	37.6	46.4	36.1
25-64 years	65.9	39.6	37.8	58.8	48.9
65 years and over	14.5	6.4	4.6	16.3	11.6

Source: *1970 U.S. Census, Detailed Characteristics, United States Summary,* Table 261.

children and by the sex of the family head. Small families, and especially small families with a male head, are least apt to be below the poverty line. But the larger the family in each column, the higher the poverty rate.

Degree of *labor force participation* is also a factor. As noted earlier many in the middle and upper income groups believe that the poor are poor because they do not work, or worse still because they do not want to work. Census data confirm that low-income people indeed do not participate in the labor force to the same extent as the general popuation. While 82% of all family heads are in the labor force, only 48% of low income heads are so classified. There are also the usual variations as to age, sex, and race, as shown in Table 3-6. About 55% of low-income male heads of families are in the labor force compared to 35% of low-income female heads. As to age, only about 10% of poverty family heads aged 65 and over were in the labor force, while 60 to 63% of younger low-income family heads were in the labor force. As to race, it is notable that higher percentages of poor blacks and of poor persons of Spanish heritage participated in the labor force to a greater extent than did poor whites. Black males were in the labor force almost to the same extent as males of all income levels. Black women and women of Spanish heritage in the low income brackets participated in the labor force to a greater extent than did white women.

The foregoing data do not prove that the poor do not work or do not want to work. In fact they tend to show the opposite. As Table 3-6 shows, sizeable percentages of the poor are in the labor force. But the income they earn is so low that they are still below the poverty line. The causes of their poverty then must lie in low hourly wages or low annual income, or high rates of unemployment. This compels us to ask: Why are their wages low, and why do they have high rates of unemployment?

The poor do in fact have high rates of unemployment, as may be seen in Table 3-7. Family heads of all income levels experienced only 2.5% unemployment in 1969, but the total poverty population experienced 8% unemployment. Variation again occurs according to age, sex, and race, with very heavy unemployment among the young, the female, the blacks and the persons of Spanish heritage. Unemployment is an obvious contributing factor to poverty.

Family income is closely correlated with number of weeks worked and the poverty rate is obviously higher among those who worked fewer hours. For instance, the poverty rate for a Negro family with a female head who worked 50-52 weeks was 28.7%, and rose gradually as fewer hours were worked until, for those who did not work at all, 72.4% were in poverty.[13]

The *occupations of the working poor* are generally those which traditionally have paid low wages. The most common occupations of male workers who were below the poverty level were farm laborers, private household workers, farmers, other common laborers, and service workers. In all of these occupations 10% or more of the workers were in poverty, ranging up to 31% for farm laborers and farm foremen. But virtually all occupations are represented in at least small amounts of poverty. Three percent of professional and technical workers, and 2.7% of nonfarm managers were found to be in poverty. Occupations of female workers in poverty are similar: farm laborers, private household workers, farmers, laundry employees, and service workers.[14] Pay in these jobs is notoriously low, and work is often irregular.

Lack of education, as measured by *years of educational attainment* is also associated with poverty. Overall for each race and sex, lack of educa-

[13]1970 U. S. Census, *Detailed Characteristics*, Table 262.
[14]1970 U. S. Census, *Low-Income Population*, Table 25.

TABLE 3-7

UNEMPLOYMENT RATES OF FAMILY HEADS OF ALL INCOME LEVELS AND OF POOR FAMILY HEADS IN THE LABOR FORCE BY AGE, SEX, AND RACE, 1969
(PERCENT OF THOSE IN THE LABOR FORCE)

Income Below the Poverty Level

	All Income Levels	Total Poor	Whites	Blacks	Spanish Heritage
		Population			
All Family Heads	2.6%	8.0%	7.6%	9.0%	10.2%
Under 25 years	4.0	10.3	8.8	15.4	11.0
25-64 years	2.4	7.7	7.5	8.3	10.1
65 years and over	4.1	6.5	6.1	7.8	10.4
Male Head	2.4	6.8	6.7	6.8	9.1
Under 25 years	3.6	7.9	7.5	9.6	9.3
25-64 years	2.2	6.6	6.6	6.4	9.0
65 years and over	4.0	6.4	5.8	8.3	10.3
Female Head	5.2	12.1	11.6	12.7	16.6
With related children under 18	6.1	12.4	11.8	13.1	16.8
With related children under 6	8.4	14.2	13.1	15.5	18.2
Under 25 years	10.6	19.1	15.4	25.3	23.3
25-64 years	4.8	11.2	11.1	11.3	15.8
65 years and Over	4.5	7.8	9.2	6.2	11.9

Source: *1970 U.S. Census, Detailed Characteristics, United States Summary*, Table 261.

tional attainment is strongly predictive of poverty. Caution of course must be exercised in this regard because of the circularity of causation. It may be that low educational attainment causes poverty, or it may be that poverty causes low educational attainment, or both. Schiller and others believe that causation is circular.[15]

[15]Bradley R. Schiller, *The Economics of Poverty and Discrimination* (Englewood Cliffs, New Jersey, Prentice Hall, 1973), pp. 98-105.

THE DECLINE OF POVERTY

During the 1930's in the midst of the worst depression in the 20th Century, President Roosevelt in a speech, said "I see before me one-third of a Nation ill-clothed, ill-housed, and ill-fed." Since then "one-third of the Nation in poverty" has been a sort of reference point from which progress has been made. Today about one-ninth of the nation is below the poverty level. The full employment associated with World War II helped many people pull themselves up out of poverty. After the war, except for intermittent short recessions, near full employment was maintained. In the decade from 1947 to 1957, Professor Lampman of Wisconsin found that poverty had been reduced from 28% to 19%. He noted other factors besides full employment contributing to the decline of poverty. One was that the number of rural families declined. The second was that workers

TABLE 3-8

NUMBER OF PERSONS BELOW THE LOW-INCOME LEVEL: 1960, 1965 AND 1970, AND PERCENT CHANGE, 1960-1970.

| | Numbers in Thousands | | | Percent Change |
	1960	1965	1970	1960-1970
Total, All Persons	39,851	33,185	25,420	−36.2%
Persons in Families, Total	34,925	23,809	20,330	−48.1
Family Heads, Total	8,243	6,721	5,260	−36.2
Non-Farm	6,649	5,841	4,822	−27.5
Farm	1,594	880	438	−72.5
Related Children, Under 18	17,288	14,388	10,235	−40.8
Other Family Members	9,394	7,249	4,835	−48.5
Unrelated Individuals 14 years and over	4,926	4,827	5,090	+ 3.3

Source: Bureau of the Census, Current Population Reports, Series P-60, Nos. 86 and 88.

shifted into higher-paid occupations. Third, workers moved into higher-paying industries. The improvement in income of the poor came from increasing the total income in the United States rather than redistributing income. In 1957, the lowest fifth of income receivers obtained 5 percent of all income. This was the same percentage that they received in the 1930's and in 1947. However, as Garvy and Denison point out, some redistribution may have occured. Older families, formerly living together with other spending units, now maintain separate households. Their income is lower since they have separated, and this pulls down the average of the bottom quartile.[16]

Tables 3-8 and 3-9 show the continuation in the decline of poverty during the decade of the Sixties. Absolute numbers of people and the percentage changes, 1960 to 1970, are shown in Table 3-8; annual percentages, by race, are shown in Table 3-9. The total number of persons in

TABLE 3-9

PERCENTAGES OF PERSONS BELOW THE POVERTY LEVEL, TOTAL, WHITE AND NEGRO AND OTHER RACES, 1959-1973

	All Persons	White	Negro and Other Races
1959	22.4%	18.1%	56.2%
1960	22.2	17.8	55.9
1961	21.9	17.4	56.1
1962	21.0	16.4	55.8
1963	19.5	15.3	51.0
1964	19.0	14.9	49.6
1965	17.3	13.3	42.1
1966	14.7	11.3	39.8
1967*	14.2	11.0	37.2
1968	12.8	10.0	33.5
1969**	12.1	9.5	31.0
1970	12.6	9.9	32.0
1971	12.5	9.9	30.9
1972	11.9	9.0	31.9
1973	11.1	8.4	29.6

*Data beginning with 1967 are based on revised methodology.
**Data beginning with 1969 are based on 1970 Census population controls and are therefore not strictly comparable with data for earlier years.

Source: Bureau of the Census, *Current Population Reports, Series P-60,* Nos. 86, 88, and 94.

---

[16]George Garvy, "Functional and Size Distribution of Income and Their Meaning," Papers and Proceedings of the 66th Annual Meeting of the American Economic Association, *American Economic Review,* Vol. XLIV (May, 1954), pp. 236-253. See also E. F. Denison, "Income Types and the Size Distribution: Relation to Functional Distribution and Factor Compensation," *Ibid.,* pp. 254-269.

poverty was reduced from around 40 million in 1960 to about 25 million in 1970, a decline of 36%. The largest percentage reduction, 72.5% occurred in poverty among farm family heads, reflecting a continuation of the departure of low-income families from the farm, and higher farm prices. The poverty level of nonfarm family heads was reduced much less — 27.5%. A notable exception to the reduction of poverty occurred among unrelated individuals where the total mount of poverty appears to have increased. Another exception, not shown in the table, is the population aged 65 and over, their poverty rate being 14% in 1959, but 15% in 1972.[17]

Table 3-9 shows the poverty estimates in annual percentages from 1959 through 1972. While 22% of the population was below the poverty level in 1959, by 1973 just over 11% were in poverty. The poverty rate for whites had been cut from 18% to 9%. The poverty rate for Negroes and other races was reduced from 56% to 30%. The percentage amount of reduction of nonwhites below the poverty level was greater than the reduction among whites, but there was obviously more room for improvement. The poverty rate among nonwhites is still over three times as great as that of whites.

A disturbing aspect of Table 3-9 is that the decline in poverty appears to have slowed. From 1959 through 1968 the poverty percentage for all persons went down an average of one point per year. From 1969 through 1973 the poverty percentage seems to have changed but little. If poverty is to be eradicated by 1985, a return to the rate of progress achieved during the mid-1960's will be necessary.

1974 POVERTY

Due to the recession of 1974, when GNP in constant dollars declined $18 billion or over three percent, the numbers in poverty increased from 22,973,000 to 24,260,000, an increase of 5.6 percent. In this recession, the number of whites in poverty increased 7.6 percent compared to only 1.1 percent for blacks. Due to the Supplemental Security Income program and increases in Social Security, the numbers of aged in poverty actually declined (1.4 percent). Concerning families, the percentages of families in poverty headed by women increased by 7.2 percent compared to a 4.6 percent in poor families headed by males. On the other hand, the percent of single males in poverty increased by 7.5 percent whereas the comparable figures for females was 1.0 percent.

ECONOMIC INSECURITY

While the problems of poverty and of income inequality are mainly a torment to low income groups, economic insecurity is a problem felt by all

[17]Bureau of the Census, Series P-60, No. 88, Table 1.

income levels. The very rich may fear the loss of their property and thus of their incomes. The middle-income family will wonder about possible loss of income due to sickness and disability, work accidents, unemployment, and termination of their income when they retire. The low income family suffers from all three problems: poverty, inequality, and insecurity.

Economic insecurity may conveniently be divided into four general categories involving in all cases a loss of income and in some cases unusual expenses. These four are: (1) old age retirement, (2) sickness and disability, (3) unemployment, and (4) loss of the family breadwinner. Each of these, and other poverty problems, and the various countermeasures developed by society to deal with them are discussed in the remaining chapters of the book.

Bibliography

Bagdikian, Ben. H., In the Midst of Plenty: A New Report on the Poor in America (New York, Signet Books, 1964).

Bell, Carolyn Shaw, The Economics of the Ghetto (New York, Pegasus, 1970).

Galloway, Lowell, Poverty in America (Columbus, Grid, 1973).

Gordon, Margaret S., ed., Poverty in America (San Francisco, Chandler, 1965).

Harrington, Michael, The Other America (New York, MacMillan, 1962).

Lampman, Robert J., Ends and Means of Reducing Poverty (Chicago, Markham, 1971).

Marmor, Theodore R., ed., Poverty Policy (Chicago, Aldine-Atherton, 1971).

Sackrey, Charles, The Political Economy of Urban Poverty (New York, W. W. Norton, 1973).

Schiller, Bradley R., The Economics of Poverty and Discrimination (Englewood Cliffs, Prentice-Hall, 1973).

Tussing, A. Dale, Poverty in a Dual Economy (New York, St. Martin's Press, 1975).

Will, Robert E., and Vatter, Harold G., eds. Poverty in Affluence (New York, Harcourt Brace & World, 1970).

PART II

AGING AND WELFARE

CHAPTER 4

PROBLEMS OF AGING

The number of those 65 and older in the United States has been increasing at a rate faster than the total population. Consequently the percentage of persons over 65 has been increasing. Table 4-1 compares the growth of total population with the population of those over 65.

Table 4-1 shows that the number of people over 65 will grow much larger in the near future. In 1940 more than 9 million of the population were 65 years of age or older, whereas by 1970 more than twice that number were 65 and older. The projection for the number of aged in the year 2000 is fairly accurate, because those who will reach the age of 65 have already been born.

A number of factors have contributed to the percentage increase of the aged.[1] For one thing, life expectancy has increased 18 years since 1900. Most of the gain in life expectancy has come because more young people remain alive, but older people do live several years longer than they formerly did. A second cause of an increased percentage of aged is the declining birthrate. In 1950 only 1 person out of 4 was under 15 years of age, whereas in 1900 one out of three was under 15. A third factor causing an increased percentage of the aged is that fewer immigrants are now coming to the United States. Since the immigrants were predominantly a younger group, the decline in their numbers has resulted in a larger percentage of those over 65.

DEPENDENCY RATIOS

The burden of support of nonworking groups in our society depends not only upon the number of aged not in the work force but the number of children as well. Table 4-2 cites the past and projected growth of those under 20 and those 65 and older.

With the high birth rate during World War II, dependency ratios increased but projections in Table 4-2 indicate a return to the declining dependency ratios. This table shows that the number of dependents is primarily a function of the number of children under 20 years of age. Dependency ratios for the aged will increase over the next few years, and the

---

[1]John J. Corson and John W. McConnell, *Economic Needs of Older People* (New York, Twentieth Century Fund, 1956), pp. 4-6.

TABLE 4-1

POPULATION GROWTH, 1870-2000

Year	Total Population	Population 65 Years of Age and Over	Percentage of Population Over 65
1870[1]	38,553,210	1,153,659	3
1900[1]	75,793,991	3,080,498	4
1940	131,669,275	9,019,314	7
1950[2]	151,132,000	12,269,000	8
1960[2]	179,935,391	16,207,237	9
1970[2]	204,800,000	20,156,000	10
Projections:			
2000[2][3]	278,599,000	28,839,000	10
2000[4]	247,974,000	28,051,000	10

[1]Excluding persons of unknown age

[2]Including armed forces overseas

[3]The fertility rate remains at its estimated 1970 level of 2,433 until 1980, and then moves gradually to 2,110 and remains there. An immigration of 400,000 per year is included

[4]The number of births held constant at the estimated 1971 fiscal year total of 3,732,000. No immigration.

Sources: Henry Sheldon, "Future Trends in Our Older Population," from Wilma Donahue and Clark Tibbits, eds., *The New Frontiers of Aging, (Ann Arbor, University of Michigan Press, 1957), Table IV, p. 74; reprinted by permission. U.S. Census of Population, 1960,* United States Summary, General Social and Economic Characteristics, PC (1) ICUS., U.S. Department of Commerce, Bureau of the Census, Table 65, p. 1-199; *Current Population Reports,* Series P-25, U.S. Department of Commerce, Bureau of the Census, various issues.

fact that more and more older people are retiring will place a heavier burden of support on those under 65. However, the children's dependency ratios have been decreasing, and this decrease coupled with increasing national income, should ease the burden of support of the aged somewhat.

ATTITUDES TOWARD THE AGED

Professor Leo W. Simmons, studying the role of the aged among 71 primitive tribes,[2] found almost without exception that these primitive tribes granted a great deal of prestige to the aged. Factors contributing to high prestige were the ownership of much private property, concentration of political power in restricted councils, the use of money, and the like. In matrilineal societies older women obtained a great deal of respect. Patrilineal societies, on the other hand, gave more prestige to men. Several factors tended to reduce the favor bestowed upon the aged. In more severe climates, where the aged might become more of a burden, less prestige was granted them. Also, when impermanency of residence caused a burden in moving the aged, less prestige was granted.

OLDER, RURAL ATTITUDES IN THE UNITED STATES

In the rural nineteenth century, aged grandparents usually enjoyed an honored and central position in our society. Frequently the boys stayed on the family farm until they became 21 years old. Then fathers attempted to help their sons establish a farm of their own nearby. Lack of modern transportation facilities prevented children from moving far away. On Sunday all of the children congregated for a day of social visiting with their parents. Cultural differences between the younger and older generations were small, and the tempo of social change was slow. The aged were honored, respected and esteemed. Furthermore, the extended family unit tended to be a self-sufficient social unit. Whenever the aged became enfeebled, shelter was provided by relatives, and the problem of feeding them was not particularly pressing on the farm.[3]

ATTITUDES TODAY

The shift from rural to urban living has considerably changed the cultural values attached to aging. At the turn of the century when American

---

[2]Leo W. Simmons, *The Role of the Aged in Primitive Society* (New Haven, Yale, 1945), pp. 50-81.

[3]Ernest W. Burgess, "The Older Generation and the Family," in Wilma T. Donahue and Clark Tibbitts, *The New Frontiers of Aging* (Ann Arbor, University of Michigan Press, 1957), pp. 158-171.

TABLE 4-2

DEPENDENCY RATIOS FOR THE UNITED STATES,
1870-2000

Year	Dependent Population Under 20[1]	Dependent Population 65 and Over[1]	Total Dependent Population
1870[2]	1,050	63	1,113
1900	863	79	942
1940	586	117	702
1950[3]	584	140	724
1960[3]	734	172	906
1970[3]	652	171	823
Projections:			
2000[3][4]	546	178	724
2000[3][5]	494	191	685

[1]Ratio of dependents to 1,000 nondependents (20-to-64 age group)
[2]Excluding persons of unknown age
[3]Including armed forces overseas
[4]The fertility rate remains at its estimated 1970 level of 2,433 until 1980, and then moves gradually to 2,110 and remains there. An immigration of 400,000 per year is included.
[5]The number of births held constant at the estimate 1971 fiscal year total of 3,732,000. No immigration.

Sources: Wilma Donahue and Clark Tibbitts, eds., *The New Frontiers of Aging*, (Ann Arbor, University of Michigan Press, 1957), Table IV, p. 74; reprinted by permission. *Current Population Reports*, Series P-25, U.S. Department of Commerce, Bureau of Census, various issues.

society was becoming urbanized, it became evident that the costs of rearing and educating children imposed an economic burden on the family rather than an economic advantage. Consequently, the birth rate began falling. Fewer children were available to support parents. Also improved educational facilities tended to give the younger generations cultural advantages that the older generation did not have. The result was that some of the younger group tended to look down upon their parents. One cultural goal of American society is that a young man should elevate himself above the social and economic position of his father. The son who surpasses his father then grants him less respect.

Whereas in rural society the care of an aged parent was no great economic burden on children, the burden becomes increasingly great in urban society. Food cannot be grown, but must be purchased. Housing may not be available for the aged.[4] In an urban society, the aged today tend to expect less and less help from children. A Cornell University study of 3,515 people aged 63 and 64 revealed that 89 percent did not expect to receive any financial aid from relatives, friends, or anyone else when they stopped working.[5] Another study in California found that only 29 percent of aged people receiving governmental old-age assistance felt that children should be required by law to support their parents.[6]

Other cultural values of American society are success in work and independence from others. Those not working or dependent on others are given less status. The problem is particularly acute among the aged, since youngsters may look forward to a period of independence and perhaps success, whereas most of the aged have passed their prime. Our society may be particularly harsh on the aged, because it keeps accurate records of chronological ages. In less developed societies, where no such records are kept, the aged person retires when physiological factors require it. In our society retirement may be mandatory even though the aged person can perform his job capably and wishes to continue working.[7]

THEORIES OF AGING

DISENGAGEMENT THEORY

One of the earlier theories of aging behavior developed by Cumming and Henry was that declining physical stamina results in the aged disengaging

---

[4]Ibid.

[5]The Study of Occupational Retirement, First Progress Report, Cornell University (Ithaca, Cornell University Press, 1953), p. 20.

[6]Floyd Bond et al., Our Needy Aged (New York, Holt, Rinehart and Winston, (1954), p. 299.

[7]Otto Pollak, Social Adjustment in Old Age, (New York Social Science Research Council, 1948), Bulletin No. 59, pp. 4-5.

from the activities of a society.[8] The disengagement theory was "intended to apply to the aging process in all societies, although the initiation of the process may vary from culture to culture, as may the pattern of the process itself." The process of disengagement was held to be intrinsic, that is, not affected by outside events and thus considered inevitable.

Cumming and Henry found that retirement and widowhood for women resulted in a lesser change in life than retirement for men. Women generally have closer relations with children and siblings than men have. Because most women's major function has been largely socio-emotional, they do not regret the loss of responsibility about domestic or working-world tasks the way men do about their work. Even men tend to adjust well. Although men face the three problems of loss of membership in a work group, loss of work, and loss of status identity, most adjust well, and succeed in solving these problems by enjoying the freedom of release from work and the opportunity to engage in recreation and other activities. Preoccupation with inner states and eventually the self-love of the very old aid in their adjustment.

A number of criticisms have been directed at the disengagement theory. Critics have pointed out that there is little disengagement among some primitive tribes.[10] Also in an Israeli kibbutz, little disengagement was found.[11] Neugarten, Havighurst, and Tobin maintain that the personality is quite crucial in determining whether disengagement occurs.[12] In a later article on disengagement, Elaine Cumming concedes that personality may have some impact on whether disengagement takes place, although she continues to subscribe to the disengagement theory.[13]

Streib and Schneider point out that although some of the aged disengage with regard to formal occupations, they may remain engaged in other spheres of life, such as interacting with children and grandchildren, visiting relatives, pursuing hobbies, traveling, and the like.[14] They are particularly critical of the formulation of disengagement theory by Ernest Damianopoulus who holds that abandonment of life's central roles, work for men, marriage and family for women, may result in crisis and loss of

[8]Elaine Cumming and William E. Henry, Growing Old: The Process of Disengagement (New York; Basic Books, 1961).

[9]Idem., p. 15.

[10]Daniel O. Cowgill and Lowell D. Holmes, eds., Aging and Modernization (New York, Appleton-Century-Crofts, 1972) pp. 12-13.

[11]Yonina Talmon, "Dimensions of Disengagement: Aging in Collective Settlements." Unpublished paper read at the International Gerontological Research Seminar, Markaryd, Sweden, 1963.

[12]Bernice L. Neugarten, Robert J. Havighurst, and Sheldon S. Tobin, "Personality and Patterns of Aging," in Bernice L. Neugarten, ed. Middle Age and Aging, (Chicago: University of Chicago Press, 1968) pp. 173-177. See Also Irving Rosow, Social Integration of the Aged, (New York: The Free Press, 1967) Chapter 4.

[13]Elaine Cumming, "Further Thoughts on the Theory of Disengagement," International Social Science Journal, Vol. 15 (1963) pp. 377-393.

[14]Gordon F. Streib and Clement J. Schneider, Retirement in American Society (Ithaca: Cornell University Press, 1971) p. 177.

morale unless different roles are available.[15] Streib and Schneider counter by arguing that disengaegment theorists incorrectly assume that work for most people is an interesting and stimulating experience. They are particularly critical of the claim that different roles are needed. They feel that the problem is to expand engagement in other on-going roles that have previously been practiced.

We may conclude that, with declining physical stamina, there is a tendency for most older people to disengage, particularly the older they get. However, the amount of disengagement varies from culture to culture and by class within cultures. The amount of disengagement will also vary according to the personality of the individuals involved. With retirement from work, other on-going roles may be expanded, as may be permitted by the health and personality variables of the individual.

THE AGED AS A SUB-CULTURE

Arnold Rose hypothesizes that the aged may lose some subcultural variations based on class, region, sex, and possibly even ethnic identification.[16] In turn, they are more likely to unite on the basis of age. He cites four influences which tend to keep the aged in contact with the larger society: (1) contacts with their family, (2) contacts with the mass media, (3) continued employment, perhaps on a part time basis, and (4) an attitude of active resistance toward aging. On the other hand, he cites a number of influences that may lead to the formation of an aged subculture in our society. Although some of the attributes of the status system carry over to the aged, the aged tend to place less emphasis on income than do younger persons. They confer more status on those within their own group who assume leadership in associations composed primarily of the aged. They place less value on sex. The roles of men and women tend to converge when the men remain at home and do some of the chores there. Their aspirations decline, and they begin to shift from independence to dependency. During the decade of the 1960's, Rose claims aging group-consciousness or aging group-identification greatly expanded the scope of the aging subculture. The growth of old-age clubs along with discussions of their common problems has aided in the growing group-consciousness. The growing number of aged also is a factor in promoting group-consciousness. Living alone more frequently has tended to separate generations.

The theory that the aged are forming a distinct subculture has been challenged by several scholars. Irving Rosow contends that because role losses inevitably affect more and more people it does not follow that clear

[15]Ernest Damianopoulus, "A Formal Statement of Disengagement Theory," in E. Cumming and W. E. Henry, Growing Old: The Process of Disengagement (New York, Basic Books, 1961) pp. 210-218.

[16]Arnold Rose, "The Subculture of the Aging: In Arnold Rose and Warren A. Peterson, eds., Older People and Their Social World, (Philadelphia: F. A. Davis Co., 1965), pp. 3-16.

normative prescriptions necessarily develop about their new situation of rolelessness.[17] He claims that role expectations tend to become open, loose, and flexible, and that there are almost no prescriptions about proper standards, and little consensus on appropriate or preferred conduct. The aged share in the general devaluation of the aged in our society. The aged also retain youthful self-images and deny that they are aged.

Gordon Streib has stated that it is just as plausible to argue that the aged are not a group in a true sociological sense as that they are. [18] They have little feeling of solidarity, consciousness of kind, or group spirit. They do not have any distinct culture traits nor do they usually operate as a distinct group. Streib claims that age is a less distinguishing group characteristic than sex, occupation, social class, and the like. The aged are not particularly attracted to organize and participate in groups. After analyzing factors which make for group identity. Streib finds little support for claiming a separate group identification. He concludes that the notion of the aged as a minority group does not increase understanding. It only obscures it.

Although it is true that most associations of the aged are with other aged persons, Bultena finds that this is not true of those 80 and over.[19] He concludes that the process of aging itself may be inimical in the oldest age group to the cultivation or perpetuation of subculture patterns.

MORALE

Some have claimed that disengagement or retirement results in lowered morale. However, in a longitudinal study conducted nationwide from Cornell University, Streib and Schneider conclude that retirement does not have the broad negative consequences for older people that had been expected.[20] Even though income was reduced, there was no significant increase in worry about money. There was no sharp decline in health, feelings of usefulness, or satisfaction in life after retirement.

Lemon, Bengston, and Peterson find no significant relationship between life satisfaction and activity with neighbors, relatives, formal

[17]Irving Rosow, op. cit., pp. 30-35.

[18]Gordon Streib, "Are the Aged a Minority Group," in Bernice Neugarten, ed. op. cit., pp. 35-46.

[19]Gordon L. Bultena, "Age-Grading in the Social Interaction of an Elderly Male Population," Journal of Gerontology, Vol. 23 (1968), pp. 539-543.

[20]Streib and Schneider, op. cit., 162-170. See also Robert J. Havighurst, "Retirement from Work to Play" in Eugene A. Friedman and Robert J. Havighurst, eds. The Meaning of Work and Retirement, (Chicago University of Chicago Press, 1954), pp. 191-192; Wayne E. Thompson and Gordon F. Streib, "Situation Determinants: Health and Economic Deprivation in Retirement," Journal of Social Issues, Vol. 14, No. 2, (1958) pp. 18-34; Richard Barfield and James Morgan, Early Retirement (Ann Arbor, University of Michigan Press, 1969), p. 4.

organization or solitary activity.[21] Their findings were not modified when such variables as age, sex, marital, and employment status were considered. They conclude that personality factors and availability of confidants were the important factors in good adjustment.

Another finding on morale has been that the aged in higher socioeconomic classes have higher morale than those lower on the scale.[22] In one such study, Arnold Rose concludes that the elderly in the future will be happier and less beset by problems than at present because there has been an upward movement in class structure.

Irving Rosow finds that morale may be affected by role loss.[23] Listing the four role losses as loss of employment, income, health, and spouse, Rosow finds that as more roles are lost, morale declines. One of his four, physical illness, has been found to be a critical antecedent of both isolation and mental illness.[24] Certain studies have shown a direct relationship between good personal adjustment and such indicators of religiosity as church membership, church attendance. Bible reading, belief in an afterlife, and religious faith.[25]

THE FAMILY

In recent years there has been a trend for the aged to live separately from their children or other relatives. In 1968, 81 percent of married couples, 67 percent of nonmarried men, and 60 percent of nonmarried women were not living with relatives.[26] The corresponding figures for 1952 were 69, 51 and 41 percent.[27] The higher the income of the aged, the less frequently they live with relatives. For a time the trend of moving from an extended to a nuclear family was viewed with alarm, because of the danger of isolating the aged. However, the evidence is substantial that the aged are not isolated and that there now exists a modified extended kin structure in American society to help meet the problem.[28] In the United States, for

[21]Bruce Lemon, Vern L. Bengston and James A. Peterson "Social Activity Theory of Aging," *Journal of Gerontology*, Vol. 27, No. 4 (1972), pp. 511-523.

[22]Arnold Rose, "Class Differences Among the Elderly: A Research Note," *Sociology and Social Research*, Vol. 50, (1965-1966) pp. 357-360.

[23]Irving Rosow, *Social Integration of the Aged*, (New York: The Free Press, 1967,) pp. 290-291.

[24]Marjorie Fiske Lowenthal, "Social Isolation and Mental Illness in Old Age," *American Sociological Review*, Vol. 20, No. 1 (1964), pp. 54-70. See also Marjorie F. Lowenthal and Paul L. Berkman, *Aging and Mental Disorder in San Francisco* (San Francisco: Jossey-Bass, Inc., 1967).

[25]David O. Moberg, "Religiosity in Qld Age," in Berncie L. Neugarten, ed., *op. cit.* pp. 497-508.

[26]Janet Murray, "Living Arrangement of People Aged 65 and Older," *Social Security Bulletin*, Vol. 34, No. 9, September, 1971, Table 1, p. 5.

[27]Lenore Epstein, "Living Arrangements and Income of the Aged," *Social Security Bulletin*, Vol. 26, No. 9, September, 1963, Table 5, p. 6.

[28]For six sources supporting this position, see Lillian E. Troll, "The Family of Later Life: A Decade Review," *Journal of Marriage and the Family*, Vol. 33, No. 2 (May, 1971), p. 264.

the aged with children, 84 percent had the nearest child less than an hour's distance from them.[29] Furthermore, 65 percent of the aged had seen at least one child during the day the interviewing took place or the day before. In addition, 60 percent of the aged said that they gave monetary help to children and 50 percent gave help to grandchildren (of those having grandchildren). A similar pattern was found for Denmark and Britain.

Although there is more mobility in society today, which may tend to isolate kinfolk, a trend has been noted for older parents past retirement age to move near their settled middle-aged children. Eventually there are more kin available to those who have moved to the new area than there are to those who stay behind.

A study of 70 middle class families with grandchildren who lived alone but near children shows that a majority of grandparents expressed satisfaction in their role as grandparents.[30] Some said that being near grandchildren made them feel young. Others were pleased to be able to help their grandchildren. Less than a third felt that being a grandparent had little of special significance for them.

LIVING ARRANGEMENTS AND HOUSING

If both aged members of a married couple remain alive, the problem of housing may not be an acute one, especially if the couple owns and has paid off the mortgage on their house. However, the couple may possibly desire smaller quarters. Space that had formerly been required for rearing a family is no longer necessary. When one member of the family dies, the problem of living quarters must be reconsidered. Six alternatives are available to the surviving member of the family.[31] The aged person can maintain a separate residence. The advantage of this type of arrangement is that it may prevent family friction with children or other relatives, and remaining in the same house gives continuity to the life that has been led before. A disadvantage of separate living accommodations is that it is expensive. Also, loneliness may become more of a problem, and eventually advanced old age may require some kind of care.

If the aged parent moves in with the adult children, expenses and loneliness are reduced. However, a number of problems arise. Not only may the children feel that there has been an intrusion in their lives, but the aged parent may also resent a lack of privacy. Housing arrangements

[29]Ethel Shanas, et. al., Old People in Three Industrial Societies (New York: Atherton Press, 1968), Table VII-28, p. 222.

[30]B. L. Neugarten and K. K. Weinstein, "The Changing American Grandparent, Journal of Marriage and the Family, Vol. 26, No. 2, (1964), pp. 199-204.

[31]Otto Pollak, The Social Aspects of Retirement (Homewood, Ill., Irwin, 1956) pp. 10-14.

may be congested. If the children have received more education than their parents, social distance between the two may cause less amicable living arrangements. Also, the high status of parenthood may be forfeited when it is necessary for an aged parent to live with children.

A third alternative is to move into an old-age colony, possibly in an area with a pleasant climate. Since moving to better oneself has become an accepted norm in our society, some of the aged do just this. Hotels catering to the aged also provide an alternate mode of living; however, little research has been done to evaluate the satisfactions and dissatisfactions of such a method of living. Yet another possibility is that two old people could live together. Such an arrangement would save on housing costs, and might possibly eliminate the loneliness of single living. Lastly, the aged could move into homes for the aged.

With many of the aged living alone, recent studies have shown that some of the aged needed various services to remain at home. In Britain, four percent of the aged living alone were receiving help with housework, but another six percent claimed that they needed but did not obtain such services. In Denmark the corresponding figures were 6 and 5 percent. Also, some of the aged were in need of "meals on wheels," shopping services, personal help with dressing or getting about the house, and limited nursing care. More of such services are being provided in Denmark and Britain than in the United States, although even in the former countries not all who wished for such services were getting them.[32] Providing a counseling service for the aged also may be beneficial.[33] Recently in the United States the federal government has appropriated small sums of money for local meals-on-wheels programs, but the program has been handicapped both by small appropriation and by having too few local voluntary groups to implement the program.

PUBLIC HOUSING

Since the income of many of the aged is particularly low, public housing programs have been inaugurated for the aged. Although our modern public housing program began with the Housing Act of 1949, no separate housing program for the aged was begun until the Housing Act of 1959. There has been less criticism of public housing for the aged than for

[32]Peter Twensend, "Welfare Services and the Family," in Ethel Shanas, et al., Older People in Three Industrial Societies (New York: Atherton Press, 1968), pp. 102-131.

[33]Jorome Kaplan, Caroline S. Ford, and Henry Wain, "Measuring the Impact of a Gerontological Counselling Service on a Medical Community," Journal of Gerontology, Vol. 21, (1966), pp. 27-30.

younger groups, since there is less vandalism among older people. Innovations in public housing for the aged have included space for health clinics, counselling and other services.[34]

RETIREMENT COMMUNITY LIVING

Some studies of retirement communities have found the residents as bored and disillusioned persons who lead shallow lives dominated by the hedonistic pursuit of happiness.[35] However, not all studies have arrived at such a conclusion.[36] High satisfaction was found in four planned retirement villages in Arizona.

INSTITUTIONAL LIVING

Between three and four percent of the aged in the United States live in an institutional setting. This is about the same percent as in Britain, but lower than Poland, Denmark and Israel, the latter two countries having between five and six percent living in institutions. An additional eight percent in the United States were at home bedfast and housebound, but this was a lower figure than in the other countries, where a high of 15 percent was reached in Israel.[37] Although institutionalization has been pictured as having destructive influences on the aged, Morton Lieberman concludes that the picture has been overdrawn.[38] He finds that many of the psychological effects are characteristic of the person prior to coming to an institution and are related in part to the reasons for being there.

Schrut studied 60 persons who lived in an institution that had both apartment-like dwellings and a central institutional home.[39] He found that those living in apartments, which were more like their previous living arrangements, showed less anxiety about their health and less fear or preoccupation with death than those living in the more central institutional home.

Another such study showed no significant difference in self-esteem

[34]*Annual Report to the Senate Special Committee on Aging: 1972 Highlights*, United States Department of Housing and Urban Development, 1972, p. 23. For an example of high satisfaction of the aged living in public housing, see Frances Merchant Carp, *A Future for the Aged: Victoria Plaza and Its Residents* (Austin, University of Texas Press, 1966).

[35]C. Davis, "Death in Sun City," *Esquire*, Vol. 133 (Oct., 1966), pp. 135-l37; M. C. Paulson "Are All the Days Balmy in Retirement Cities," *National Observer*, (Oct. 2, 1967), p. 24; J.H. Peck, *Let's Rejoin the Human Race*,(Englewood Cliffs, New Jersey, Prentice Hall, 1963); C. Trillon "Wake Up and Live," *New Yorker*, Vol. 40 (April 4, 1964).

[36]Gordon Bultena and Vivian Wood, "The American Retirement Community: Bane or Blessing" *Journal of Gerontology*, Vol. 24, (1969) pp. 209-217.

[37]Ethel Shanas, "Measuring the Home-Health Needs of the Aged in Five Countries," *Journal of Gerontology*, Vol. 26 (1971) pp. 37-40.

[38] Morton A. Leiberman, "Institutionalization of the Aged: Effects on Behavior," *Journal of Gerontology*, Vol. 24 (1969) pp. 330-340.

[39]S. D. Schrut, "Attitudes Toward Old Age and Death," *Mental Hygiene*, Vol. 42 (1958) pp. 259-266.

between those in a retirement home and those about to enter the same home.[40] The amount and quality of interaction was found to explain changes in self-esteem. The conclusion from this study was that institutionalization does not necessarily have detrimental effects on older persons.

A Ralph Nader study group of nursing homes reported "heart-rending tragedies."[41] This group quoted the Social Security Administration to the effect that 80 percent of the nursing homes that received public tax dollars did not meet minimal Federal standards. The Nader group was particularly critical of the Social Security Administration for ignoring standards altogether rather than instituting a massive drive to help the nursing homes to come up to standards. Lack of a high quality nursing home staff was pointed out. Lack of safety equipment existed in some homes along with poor administration of drugs, too permissive medical experiments, and too frequent use of kickbacks on drugs.

EMPLOYMENT OF THE AGED

In January of 1975 there were 1.9 million men in the labor force aged 65 and over (21 percent of the aged men) compared with almost one million women (8 percent).[42] Men earning higher pay are more prone to keep working than those in less skilled jobs.[43] There has been a trend over the years for larger and larger percentages of older men to retire rather than work. In 1890, for example, 69 percent of older men were in the labor force. Today many who continue to work do so on a part-time basis. The option given under the Social Security Act to retire early at age 62 on a reduced pension has induced more people to retire at the earlier age. Ill health has induced much of the earlier retirement,[44] and so has unemployment.[45]

With pensions becoming more adequate it is probable that in the future more and more persons will retire earlier than at present. In 1965, the United Automobile Workers Unions negotiated a contract providing

[40]Nancy A. Anderson, "Effects on Institutionalization on Self-Esteem," *Journal of Gerontology*, Vol. 22 (1967), pp. 313-317.

[41]Claire Townsend, ed., *Old Age: The Last Segregation*, (New York, Bantam Books, 1971).

[42]*Employment and Earnings*, U. S. Department of Labor, Vol. 19, No. 9 (Feb. 1975), Table A-4, pp. 30-31.

[43]Lenore A. Epstein and Janet H. Murray, "Employment and Retirement," in Bernice L. Neugarten, ed., *op. cit.*, p. 354.

[44]Richard Barfield and James Morgan, *Early Retirement: The Decision and the Experience* (Ann Arbor, University of Michigan Press, 1969).

[45]A study of early retirees under the Social Security system showed that 45 percent retired for health reasons and 27 percent retired due to job related conditions such as compulsory retirement (12 percent), a discontinuance of the job (11 percent), or dissatisfaction with their job (4 percent). Another 17 percent simply wanted to retire. See Virginia Reno, "Why Men Stop Working At or Before 65: Findings from the Survey of New Beneficiaries," *Social Security Bulletin*, Vol. 34 (June, 1971), p. 3.

for as much as $400 a month in pensions for those aged 60 to 65. A questionnaire was sent to those retiring early. The most frequent reason for retiring given by 47 percent was an adequate retirement income. The next largest percentage retired because of poor health (24 percent), followed by 19 percent who wanted more free time, 6 percent who were dissatisfied with their jobs, and three percent who didn't like their boss or the people on the job.[46]

Although the trend has been toward earlier retirement, some persons prefer work to leisure. Such persons have been handicapped in the past by employers setting age deadlines on hiring. A former Secretary of Labor, Willard Wirtz, testified in 1967 that a Department of Labor study showed that half of all private job openings were barred to applicants over 55, a quarter to those over 45, and almost all to those over 65.[47]

In order to promote employment of the aged, President Kennedy issued an executive order in 1963 outlawing discrimination against the aged in federal employment and President Johnson in 1964 followed with another order outlawing discrimination against the aged on federal contracts. A number of states also have such laws. Congress in 1967 passed the Age Discrimination in Employment Act. This Act applied to most employers of 25 or more persons, but federal, state and local government employees are excluded. The prohibitions of the law do not apply if the differentiation due to age is caused by a bona fide seniority system or a pension plan, but neither of these may be a subterfuge to evade the purposes of the Act. Back pay may be received if illegal discrimination has been found. The Act is enforced by the Secretary of Labor. In fiscal 1972, there were 6,067 establishments investigated for violation of the Act. Of these 2,185 were found not in compliance. Almost half of the noncompliance violations dealt with illegal advertising by employers, over a third dealt with employers refusing to hire, 16 percent concerned promotional bars, and less than 10 percent were discharge cases.[48]

Solutions to more employment for the aged desiring work include, beside fair employment laws, improved counseling and placement, more flexible retirement plans, gradual retirement, and new employment opportunities. Labor unions for years have protected the rights of older workers through seniority, antidiscrimination clauses, job adjustment clauses, retraining, and others. Some unions have provided for early retirement for workers, whereas others have negotiated clauses outlawing compulsory retirement. Many unions have negotiated pension plans, and a few, such as the United Automobile Workers Union, have opened

[46]A. William Pollman, "Early Retirement: A comparison of Poor Health to Other Retirement Factors," *Journal of Gerontology*, Vol. 26, No. 1, (1971), pp. 41-45.

[47]Testimony of Willard Wirtz, *Hearings Before the Subcommittee on Labor of the Committee of Labor and Public Welfare*, United States Senate, 90th Congress, 1st Session on S 839 and S 788, May 15-17, 1967, p. 37.

[48]*Age Discrimination in Employment Act of 1967* (Washington: U. S. Department of Labor, Employment Standards Division, 1970) Table 4, p. 18.

some senior citizens centers. Others, like the Industrial Union of Electrical Workers, have organized retired workers' clubs.[49] In several instances, employment has been promoted by the aged themselves, in having retired entrepreneurs organize firms to provide employment for the aged desiring work.[50]

INCOME OF THE AGED

SOURCES OF INCOME

Table 4-3 shows from what sources the aged receive their income. Over half the income of nonmarried aged men and women was obtained from retirement benefits and almost half of married couples' income was from the same source. Such benefits, mainly OASDHI (Social Security) benefits, constituted the largest single source of income for both the married and non-married aged. However, a sizable percentage of the income of married aged was derived from earnings (39 percent).

AMOUNT OF INCOME

A detailed breakdown of income of the aged is shown in Table 4-4.

The earnings of those working full time are much higher than those not working, but only a minority of the aged are engaged in full-time work. Even with government assistance, the income of the aged is quite low. Attention is particularly invited to the large percentages of both men and women with less than $1,000 income. Studies show that income of the aged is particularly low among the nonwhite and farm aged. One study showed that in 1969, 50 percent of Negroes 65 and over were living in poverty compared with 23 percent of all whites the same age.[51] Farm aged are also quite poor, as are the aged living in the poorer states of the United States [52]

[49]For a summary of union aids for older workers, see Ewan Calgue, Balraj Palli, and Leo Kramer, The Aging Worker and the Union (New York: Praeger Publishers, 1971).

[50]For a description of several plans, see Paul A. Brinker, Economic Insecurity and Social Security (New York: Appleton-Century-Crofts, 1968), p. 41.

[51]Current Population Reports: Consumer Income Series, p. 60, No. 76 U. S. Department of Commerce, Bureau of the Census (Dec., 1970), Table 4, p. 40.

[52]Ibid., Series P-60, No. 46, Table 3, p. 12 and Lenore Epstein, "State Variations in Income of the Aged." Social Security Bulletin, Vol. 26, No. 1 (January 1963), Table 1, p. 4.

TABLE 4-3
INCOME SHARES: PERCENTAGE DISTRIBUTION OF MONEY INCOME BY SOURCE FOR AGED UNITS (65 AND OVER), 1967.

Source of money income	All Units	Married Couples	Nonmarried persons		
			Total	Men	Women
Number (in thousands)					
Total	16,779	5,989	9,789	2,356	7,434
Reporting on income	12,177	4,474	7,779	1,954	5,816
Percent of income	100	100	100	100	100
Earnings	29	39	15	17	14
Retirement benefits	46	42	51	56	48
OASDHI	34	30	40	40	39
Other public pensions	7	6	8	10	7
Private group pensions	5	6	3	6	2
Veterans' benefits	3	3	4	5	4
Public Assistance	4	2	7	5	8
Income from assets	15	13	18	14	19
Personal contributions[1]	1	(2)	1	(2)	2
Other Sources	3	2	4	2	4

[1] Contributions by relatives or friends not in household.
[2] 0.5 percent or less

Sources: Lenore Bixby, "Income of People Aged 65 and Over," *Social Security Bulletin*, Vol. 33, No. 4, 1970. Table 3, p. 11.

TABLE 4-4
INCOME SIZE BY OASDHI BENEFICIARY[1] STATUS:
PERCENTAGE DISTRIBUTION OF AGED UNITS (65 AND OVER)
BY MONEY INCOME CLASS, 1967

Total Money Income	All Units		Married Couples		Non-married persons					
					Total		Men		Women	
	Benefi-ciary	Non Benefi-ciary	Benefi-ciary	Non Benefi-ciary	Benefi-ciary	Non Benefi-ciary	Benefi-ciary	Non Benefi-ciary	Benefi-ciary	Non Benefi-ciary
Number (In thousands):										
Total	12,446	2,146	4,913	720	7,533	1,426	1,928	302	5,605	1,125
Reporting on Income	9,676	1,638	3,692	485	5,984	1,153	1,613	247	4,371	907
Percent of Units	100	100	100	100	100	100	100	100	100	100
Less than $1,000	17	30	3	5	26	42	18	28	30	46
1,000-1,499	20	20	7	4	28	26	23	24	29	26
1,500-1,999	16	8	12	6	18	8	20	5	17	9
2,000-2,499	12	8	13	6	11	8	15	16	9	6
2,500-2,999	8	3	11	4	5	3	7	7	4	2
3,000-3,499	6	3	11	6	4	2	5	2	3	2
3,500-3,999	5	2	9	4	2	2	3	3	2	1
4,000-4,999	6	6	12	11	2	3	4	3	2	3
5,000-7,499	6	8	14	19	2	4	3	6	2	2
7,500-9,999	2	7	5	20	1	2	1	4	1	1
10,000-14,999	1	2	3	7	1	1	(2)	1	1	1
15,000 or more	1	2	1	7	(2)	(2)	(2)	1	(2)	(2)
Median Income	$1,904	$1,490	$3,109	$5,218	$1,412	$1,068	$1,742	$1,322	$1,207	$1,032

[1] Excludes beneficiaries who received their first benefit in February 1967 or later, transitionally insured, and special age-72 beneficiaries.
[2] 0.5 percent or less.

Source: Lenore Bixby, "Income of People Aged 65 and Over," Social Security Bulletin, Vol. 33, No. 4, 1970, Table 4, p. 12.

ADEQUACY OF INCOME

Data for 1972 indicate that there were 3.7 million aged persons living in poverty.[53] Other data demonstrating the meager economic resources of the aged show that many of those over 65 held few financial assets.[54] Amendments to the Social Security Act in 1972, effective January 1, 1974, should make aged income more adequate.

PROBLEMS OF PREMATURE DEATH

Statistics show that a surprisingly large percentage of males die early in life. Table 4-5 shows that 32 percent of white males aged 20 will not live to age 65. White females live somewhat longer. Nonwhites have a lower life expectancy than whites, again with males dying sooner than females.

TABLE 4-5

Percentage Surviving to Age 65 and Average Life
Life Expectancy, at specified ages for
white males, 1969

Present Age	Percentage Surviving to age 65	Average Life Expectancy (in years)	Average Life Expectancy Beyond age 65 (in years)
20	68	50.1	5.1
30	69	41.0	6.0
40	71	31.9	6.9
50	75	23.3	8.3
60	87	16.0	11.0

Source: *Vital Statistics of the United States*, 1969, Vol. II, U.S. Department of Health, Education and Welfare, Part A, Table 5-1, p. 5-4.

[53]*Consumer Income: Characteristics of Low-Income Population, 1972* U. S. Bureau of the Census, Series P-60, No. 91, December, 1973, Table I, p. 9.

[54]From the *1968 Survey of the Aged* it was found that half the married couples who reported had less than $12,000 in such financial assets as money in banks or credit left with insurance or other institutions, and stocks or bonds. The corresponding figure for non-married persons was that two-thirds had less than $1,500. See Janet Murray, "Homeownership and Financial Assets Findings from the 1968 Survey of the Aged," *Social Security Bulletin*, Vol. 35, No. 8 (Aug., 1972) p. 3.

Depending on the age at which death occurs, a number of problems are created. If the prematurely deceased male has young children, the mother is faced with the dual task of not only supporting the children but taking care of them as well. Generally women earn less income than men, and probably the death of the male breadwinner results in a lower standard of living for the family. If the surviving wife comes from a working-class family, very probably she will not be prepared for a skilled or clerical occupation. She is then forced into unskilled work at extremely low pay. Private life insurance may help appreciably. Also, under the Social Security Act, survivors insurance is now made available along with aid to dependent children benefits. Even with those aids, the death of the breadwinner generally causes a decided drop in the standard of living of the remaining members of the family.

Summary

The number of people over 65 will grow much larger in the future. The problem of supporting them should not prove insurmountable, given a rising gross national product, and provided that family size is controlled sufficiently so that not too many children need to be supported.

The American culture with its stress on activity and work tends to downgrade the aged as a group. Several theories of aging have been promulgated in the recent past. One is that the aged tend to disengage. The amount of disengagement will depend on personality and class variables. Others have suggested that the aged will tend to develop a subculture of their own, but there is no consensus of viewpoint on this theory.

In general, morale of the aged in American society tends to be good. Personality, substitute roles, class, role loss, ill health, and religion all have an impact on morale. There has been a trend toward more and more of the aged to retire from work, although a minority still want to remain in the workforce. Retirement of the aged has caused serious income problems that have only recently been recognized by American society. The major support for those aged not working has been the Social Security OASDHI program.

The aged experience more health problems than younger groups, and they also have less income with which to buy health care. Recognition of the problem has caused Congress to legislate specifically for the health care of the aged (to be discussed in chapters 12 and 13).

Bibliography

Barfield, Richard and James Morgan, *Early Retirement: The Decision and Experience* (Ann Arbor, University of Michigan Press, 1969).

Cowgill, Daniel O. and Lowell D. Holmes, ed's, *Aging and Modernization* (New York, Appleton-Century-Crofts, 1972).

Cumming, Elaine and William E. Henry, *Growing Old: The Process of Disengagement* (New York, Basic Books, 1961).

Neugarten, Bernice L., *Middle Age and Aging* (Chicago, University of Chicago Press, 1968).

Rose, Arnold and Warren A. Peterson, ed's, *Older People and Their Social World* (Philadelphia, F. A. Davis Co., 1965).

Rosow, Irving, *Social Integration of the Aged* (New York, The Free Press, 1967).

Shanas, Ethel, *et. al.*, *Old People in Three Industrial Societies* (New York, Atherton Press, 1968).

Streib, Gordon F. and Clement J. Schneider, *Retirement in American Society* (Ithaca, Cornell University Press, 1971).

Townsend, Claire, ed., *Old Age: The Last Segregation* (New York, Bantam Books, 1971).

CHAPTER 5

OLD AGE INSURANCE: HISTORY, ADMINISTRATION, COVERAGE AND ELIGIBILITY

OLD-AGE PENSIONS ABROAD

GERMANY

The first industrial country to pass an old-age pension law for its citizens was Germany. In the 1880's, Chancellor Otto von Bismarck, the arch-conservative "Iron Chancellor," fearing the rising political power of the Socialists, secured the enactment in the Reichstag of a number of reforms, among them sickness insurance in 1883, workmen's compensation in 1884, and old-age pensions in 1889.[1] Taxes were assessed against both employers and employees, and the government contributed to the fund out of general revenues, so that by 1911 a type of "tripartite" financing, involving employee, employer, and the general taxpayer, was in effect.[2]

Under the original law of 1889, old-age pensions were claimable at age 70 even if the worker continued working. Later, that age limit was lowered to 65, and pensions could be received even at 60 provided the worker had been unemployed for at least a year.[3]

Survivors' benefits to widows and dependent children were added by amendments in 1911. However, the social insurance schemes were extremely hard hit by the inflation of the early 1920's. Benefits became less and less adequate as the cost of living rose, and the value of the assets of the programs was destroyed. The depression of the thirties also caused difficulties. Because of reduced contributions, benefits had to be reduced

---

[1]W. Harbutt Dawson, *Social Insurance in Germany*, 1883-1911 (London, T. Fisher Unwin, 1912), p. 212.

[2]C. A. Kulp, Social Insurance Coordination: *An Analysis of German and British Organization* (Washington, Social Science Research Council, 1938), p. 212.

[3]Sakman, *et. al.*, "An Outline of Foreign Social Insurance and Assistance Laws," Bureau Report No. 5, Washington, D.C., Foreign Security Agency, Social Security Board, Bureau of Research and Statistics (1940), pp. 10-11.

and the government had to increase its share of the cost.[4] In 1938 the government paid about 40 percent of the old-age-invalidity pensions from general revenues.[5] Following World War II the programs were reorganized and expanded.

West Germany today has a comprehensive social insurance system including (1) old age, disability, and survivors insurance, (2) sickness and maternity insurance, (3) work injury insurance, (4) unemployment insurance, and (5) a universal family allowance. The old-age insurance program covers employed persons, with separate but identical provisions for wage earners and salaried employees, and special systems for miners, public employees, self-employed artisans, and self-employed farmers. Financing is tripartite; the insured person pays 9% of his wages or salaries subject to maximum earnings, the tax on the employer's payroll is 9%, and the government contributes an annual subsidy of about 15% of the total cost of the system. The maximum earnings for contribution purposes are two times the national average earnings for the past three years. The old-age pension is payable at age 65 or at age 60 if unemployed for one year. The insured person must have paid in at least 180 months of contributions in order to qualify. The old-age pension amount is 1.5% of worker's assessed wages multipled by the number of years he has been insured. There are also dependents, survivors, and invalidity pensions related to the old-age pension amount.

ENGLAND

In England the effort to secure the enactment of an old-age pension law persisted for over 140 years before it finally succeeded. As early as 1772, a bill providing for old-age annuities paid by local government passed the House of Commons but was defeated in the House of Lords. A nationwide compulsory old-age and disability insurance law was advocated in 1786. During the 1800's the campaign continued sporadically but without success. In the 1870's the campaign to provide some sort of compulsory government insurance intensified. A clergyman of the Church of England, the Reverend William Blackley, led the campaign, and the English give him much credit for eventual success. Finally, in 1908, an Old Age Pension Act, financed solely by the government,[7] was enacted, and in 1911 unemployment and health insurance were added.

In 1925, a contributory pension system was enacted to supplement the government financed system. Equal benefits were paid at 65 to all those contributing to the system regardless of size of earnings. At age 70

---

[4]Kulp, op. cit., p. 71.
[5]Ibid., p. 119.
[6]Social Security Programs Throughout the World, 1973, Washington, D.C., U.S. Department of Health, Education and Welfare, Social Security Administration (1973), pp. 80-81.
[7]Encyclopaedia Britannica, Eleventh Edition, Vol. XX, 1911, pp. 64-66.

the non-contributory system became applicable, and a means test remained in effect for those 70 and over. Under the contributory system, pensions were also paid to widows, dependent children, and orphans of those who had paid into the fund.[8]

The Beveridge Report, issued in 1943, made suggestions for wholesale improvements in the British Social security system. After the war the Labour Party was returned to power and extensive changes were made, including the beginning of a family allowance program in 1945 and the National Health Service in 1946. Additional changes became law in 1959. The system of all workers paying the same tax and receiving the same benefit was modified. Graduated benefit amounts were added on top of the previously existing flat benefit amounts.[9]

Legislation enacted in 1965, 1966, 1969, and 1970 embody the provisions under which national insurance pensions are currently paid. Like Germany, England has old age and invalidity, sickness and maternity, work injury, and unemployment insurance as well as a National Health Service and a universal public system of family allowances. Employer-employee contributions plus sizeable government subsidies out of the general revenue finance several programs. In 1973, most programs paid a minimum benefit of £6.75 a week plus graduated amounts depending on total employee contributions paid in.[10]

OTHER COUNTRIES

Many countries preceded the United States in providing old age pensions, as may be seen by scanning the dates when these countries adopted a program: Germany, 1889; Denmark, 1891; New Zealand, 1898; Austria, 1906; Great Britain, 1908; Australia, 1908; Iceland, 1909; France, 1910, Luxemburg, 1911; Romania, 1912; The Netherlands, 1913; Sweden, 1913; Spain, 1919; Uruguary, 1919; U.S.S.R., 1922; Belgium, 1924; Bulgaria, 1924; Chile, 1924; Czechoslavakia, 1924; Hungary, 1928; South Africa, 1928; Poland, 1933; and Greece, 1934.[11]

Old Age pensions of some sort now exist in most of the countries of the world, with expansion continuing. In 1940, 33 countries; in 1949, 44 countries; and in 1958, 58 countries had old age pension programs, most of these also providing invalidity (permanent disability) and survivors benefits as well. By 1973, of the 142 independent countries in the world, 105 had some such program. Nearly every year a new program is enacted somewhere in the world, and each year important amendments are made to many existing programs. All countries in Europe, and most in North, South, and Central America have such programs. Considerable expansion

[8]Kulp, op. cit., pp. 145-156.
[9]"New Graduated Retirement Benefits in Great Britain", Social Security Bulletin, Vol. 22 (September, 1959), pp. 4-9.
[10]Social Security Programs Throughout the World, 1973, op. cit., pp. 232-233.
[11]Ibid., pp. 1-253.

is now occurring in Africa, where 39 of 41, and in Asia and Oceania, where 30 of 42 countries had programs of some sort in 1973.

HISTORY OF OLD-AGE PENSIONS IN THE UNITED STATES

EARLY HISTORY

In colonial America and in the early United States, the indigent aged were put into the same institutions with all other groups who were unable to take care of themselves. During and following this period, care for the aged, as for other groups, was provided by local communities. Almshouses were the accepted method of care, although some communities on occasion gave "outdoor" relief—aid to the family in cash or in kind in their own home.

Not until the twentieth century were more comprehensive plans for the aged introduced. Arizona in 1914, Alaska in 1915, and Montana, Nevada and Pennsylvania in 1923, enacted old-age pension laws. It is interesting to note that most of these acts were passed in western states and were popularized as "Pioneer Pension" laws. None of these laws, however, effectively provided for the aged. Some laws, as in Arizona and Pennsylvania, were declared unconstitutional, and others depended entirely on county financing, which was often not provided. A more workable type of law was passed in California in 1929. This law was mandatory, and required that both the state and the county contribute money for pensions for the aged. Before 1935, seven other states adopted laws similar to California's.[13]

One major group who received old-age pensions were soldiers and sailors. By 1910, all but six states had granted old-age pensions to Civil War veterans, and after World War I thirty states made provision for aged veterans of that war.[14] For many years the federal government also had a pension program for veterans. Patriotism and the voting power of veterans groups were sufficient to provide security for at least one group in America.

IMPACT OF THE GREAT DEPRESSION

The main impetus to the passage of federal old-age pensions and other social legislation came from the Great Depression of the 1930's. Private

[12]Ibid.

[13]Harvey Lebrun, "Evolution of the American Pension System", Sociology and Social Research, Vol. 20 (1935-1936), pp. 453-462.

[14]Anne H. Geddes, Trends in Relief Expenditures, 1910-1935, Research Monograph X, Washington, D.C., Works Progress Administration (1937), p. 3

charities were swamped as more and more people applied for relief. Local governments, traditionally the main providers of relief, were faced with larger and larger relief loads, but at the same time revenues were decreasing, for many people were forced to default on their property taxes. A few states attempted to step into the breach, but their taxing abilities were limited also. Borrowing from banks became necessary, but neither local nor state governments had sufficient resources to borrow on any large scale, and many such governments had already borrowed up to their statutory or constitutional limits. Some state constitutions did not permit them to handle the problem of relief at all.[15] As the depression deepened and more and more were thrown out of work, the only government capable of preventing starvation and hunger on a mass basis was the federal government.

FEDERAL ACTION PRIOR TO 1935

As early as 1907 a bill was introduced in Congress to provide for old-age pensions for all elderly people in need of assistance. Four years later another bill was introduced calling for $4 a week pensions for all those over 60 years of age who had an income of less than $10 a week. These measures, however, failed of enactment, and with the coming of World War I, Congress turned its attention to the prosecution of the war and to international affairs. In the 1920's, since the level of business activity was generally high, a conservative reaction set in, and Congress paid little attention to the problems of the needy. It was not until the onslaught of the Great Depression that the federal government took any action, and the action then taken was directed toward the relief of the needy of any age. In 1932 Congress created a Reconstruction Finance Corporation with authority to lend $300 million to the states and localities for relief purposes. When Franklin D. Roosevelt assumed office in March of 1933, practically all of this money had been lent out. In that year the Federal Emergency Relief Administration was created, followed at intervals by other programs such as the Civil Works Administration, the Public Works Administration, the Civilian Conservation Corps, the Works Progress Administration and the National Youth Administration. The great proliferation of temporary measures led to the feeling that something more permanent should be created to provide for such emergencies beforehand. This added weight to the argument that a federal insurance program should be instituted.[16]

[15]Lewis Meriam, *Relief and Social Security* (Washington, Brookings Institution, 1946), pp. 10-11.

[16]Maxwell Stewart, *Social Security* (New York, Norton, 1937), pp. 89-90, 111.

COMMITTEE ON ECONOMIC SECURITY

After several bills on old-age pensions and unemployment insurance had been introduced in Congress, President Roosevelt appointed, in June 1934, by executive order, the Committee on Economic Security. This committee was composed mainly of cabinet level officials with the Secretary of Labor as Chairman. In the same executive order the President created an Advisory Council to the Committee on Economic Security. This council was composed of 23 experts on social insurance from the fields of industry, labor, and social work. An Executive Director (Edwin E. Witte of the University of Wisconsin) was chosen to implement the executive order, and a Technical Board was also created to help with the program.[17] The completed reports of the staff members comprised more than a dozen large volumes of typewritten material.[18] The Advisory Council submitted its report on December 18, 1934, and the Committee on Economic Security its report on January 15, 1935.[19] After a hearing in both houses of Congress, the Social Security Bill was introduced.

Supporting data for an old-age pension program showed that many of our aged were without economic resources. In Connecticut, for example, it was found in 1932 that 49 percent of the aged there had income of less than $300 per year, and that more than 33 percent had no income of any kind. Other studies in New York and Massachusetts revealed that from 23 to 65 percent of the aged had incomes of less than $300 annually, and less than $5000 in property.[20] Almshouses were rejected as a solution to the problems of the aged. Shocking deficiencies had been found in this type of care. Such houses still suffered from having too many diverse groups of disabled all thrown together with too little financial resources to provide adequate care.

The Committee on Economic Security formulated a plan which provided for two programs for the aged. One, an insurance program, would provide payments as a matter of right to wage-earners who would contribute to the system. The other was an old-age assistance program, which would cover only those in need and would be financed from general tax revenues.

[17]Edwin E. Witte, *The Development of the Social Security Act* (Madison, Wisconsin, University of Wisconsin Press, 1962). p. 9.

[18]*Ibid.*, p. 40.

[19]Grace Abbott, *From Relief to Social Security* (Chicago, University of Chicago Press, 1941), pp. 199-200.

[20]*Social Security in America*, pp. 149-199.

CONGRESSIONAL ACTION ON THE
SOCIAL SECURITY BILL

At the Congressional hearings on the bill, few appearances were made by employers. Representatives of the United States Chamber of Commerce and the National Retail Dry Goods Association spoke in favor of the program although some amendments were suggested by the former. The bill was attacked by the National Association of Manufacturers, the Illinois Manufacturers' Association, and the Ohio Manufacturers' Association. The latter organization violently attacked the bill. However, at the time of the Congressional hearings, employer groups in general knew so little about the bill that no decisive stand was taken. Later, such groups were aroused by opponents of the measure and sent many letters and telegrams of protest to their Congressmen.[21]

Meanwhile, in California Dr. Francis E. Townsend of Long Beach proposed what came to be known as the Townsend Plan, and organized a nationwide movement to support his plan. He suggested that pensions of $200 per month be paid to all aged persons without applying a means test of any kind. The program was to be financed by a 2% gross transactions tax. Estimates by economists indicated that the income from the tax would fall far short of enough to pay the $200 per month pensions. Also the $200 a month benefit seemed unduly high in relation to the incomes of many workers at that time. In any event, conservatives both in and out of Congress were frightened by the Townsend Plan and by the strength of the lobbying in its behalf.

The Social Security Bill went first to the Ways and Means Committee in the House of Representatives. Few members of the Committee were sympathetic to the bill, and some went to the President with the advice that the old-age insurance provision of the bill could not be passed. Roosevelt, however, insisted that the insurance program was an important part of the bill, and that the essential features must remain intact. Edwin Witte maintained that the firm stand taken by the President saved the old age insurance program.[22] The impression of serious opposition to the bill and no real support was counteracted by Secretary of Labor Perkins, who secured the signatures of 50 prominent people in favor of the bill. This support of the bill, plus that of President Roosevelt, plus the conservatives' fear of the Townsend Plan, enabled the bill to be passed by a 371 to 33 vote in the House. In the Senate the conference committee deadlocked for an entire month on the Clark amendment, which would have exempted people covered by private retirement systems from the plan provided that the annuities paid were as high as that to be paid by the Federal government. The Roosevelt administration vigorously opposed the Clark amendment on the ground that industry would insure the better

[21]Witte, op. cit., pp. 88-91.
[22]Witte, op. cit., pp. 91-95.

risks and leave an adverse selection for the government.[23] The conference committee finally agreed to strike the amendment, and the Social Security Act passed the Senate by a vote of 76 to 7. The historical measure was signed into law by President Roosevelt on August 14, 1935, and the Supreme Court upheld the constitutionality of the law by an 8 to 1 vote in 1937.[24]

ADMINISTRATION

For a number of reasons, federal administration, rather than administration by the states, was adopted for the old-age insurance program. For the other two major sections of the Social Security Act, unemployment insurance and public assistance, administration was left in the hands of state agencies, subject to loose federal guidelines. A purely federal system for old-age insurance was favored because it would be easier to administer. Identical legal provisions and administrative procedures nationwide should make for less complexity and lower costs. Actuarily, a federal system is more sound since estimates of total population can be made more easily.[25]

The old-age insurance program is administered by the Social Security Administration, which is part of the Department of Health, Education, and Welfare. The Social Security Administration has offices throughout the country. The purposes of these offices are to supply information on the program and to process claims. Each worker has a social security number which is used to keep a record of earnings upon which benefits are based. These records are kept at the central office of the Social Security Administration in Baltimore, Maryland. A beneficiary has the right to challenge a decision on his pension. A referee hears and makes a decision on the case. Further appeal is made to the Appeals Council of the Social Security Administration, and then to the Federal courts.

The consensus is that the old-age and survivors insurance program has been administered efficiently. In recent years the administrative problems imposed on the Social Security Administration have been intensified by a variety of amendments to OASI and by the enactment of new programs such as Medicare, benefits for victims of "black lung" disease, and "supplemental security income." The agency has met the challenge by considerable modernization of methods including computer controlled record keeping, automated claim processing, the use of multifont optical scanners, teletype linkage of Social Security offices, and the microfilming

[23]Joseph P. Harris, "The Social Security Program of the United States," *Political Science Review*, Vol. 30, No. 3 (June, 1936), pp. 456-482.

[24]Victor Christgau, "Old-Age and Survivors Insurance After Twenty Years", *Social Security Bulletin*, August 1955, pp. 12-17.

[25]Social Security Board, *Social Security in America*, Washington, D.C., Government Printing Office (1937), pp. 200-201.

of data.[26] Administrative expenses for OASI for fiscal year 1971-72 were $582 million or 1.7% of cash benefit payments, which that year amounted to $35.5 billion.[27] Since 1953 administrative expenses have increased in dollar amount but have declined as a percentage of contributions and of benefit payments. In recent years the percentages have been 2% or less.[28] Little criticism has been heard about the administration of the old-age insurance program.

COVERAGE UNDER THE OLD-AGE INSURANCE PROGRAM

The Social Security Act of 1935 covered less than 60 percent of the civilian work force in the United States.[29] The largest excluded group was the self-employed, who numbered betwen 10 and 11 million people in 1940. This figure included farm operators and farm tenants. The next largest excluded group was 4 to 5 million hired farm laborers, followed by about 3.5 million state and local government employees and a smaller number of federal employees. The other two large exempted groups were domestic workers (about 2.5 million) and about 800,000 employees working for nonprofit organizations.[30] A major reason for excluding these groups was the fear that the administrative problems of covering them would be insurmountable.

Since such a large percentage of the aged were not covered under the insurance program, Congress created a second program, called old-age assistance (OAA), to provide pensions for those in need and drawing little or nothing under the insurance program. Until 1953 more old people received payments from the old-age assistance program than pensions from the old-age insurance program. As more and more people were covered under the insurance program, it became the larger program.

In 1939 a minor change was made to cover those working people who had already reached the age of 65. Under the original act of 1935, workers already over 65 were not taxed and could not quality for benefits. Major increases in coverage came in amendments to the Social Security Act in 1950, 1954, and 1956.

[26]Jack S. Futterman, "Administrative Developments in the Social Security Program Since 1965," *Social Security Bulletin*, Vol. 35, No. 4 (April 1972), pp. 3-9.

[27]*Social Security Bulletin*, Vol. 36, No. 6 (june 1973), Table M-5, p. 37.

[28]Robert J. Meyers, "Administrative Expenses of the Social Security Program," *Social Security Bulletin*, Vol. 32, No. 9 (September 1969), pp. 20-27.

[29]"A Report to the Secretary of Health, Education, and Welfare on Extension of Old Age and Survivors Insurance to Additional Groups of Current Workers," Washington, D.C., Consultants on Social Security (1953), p. 2.

[30]*Social Security Yearbook*, 1942, Washington, D.C., p. 115.

SELF-EMPLOYED

The largest excluded group, the self-employed, had been excluded for administrative reasons. Experience under the act had shown that records for many millions of small employers could be kept accurately. Since this was so, it was reasoned that the self-employed could be covered also, and they were in 1950. In 1954, self-employed farmers were covered, in 1956 dentists and lawyers were covered, and in 1965 medical doctors were also covered. Today the only self-employed who are not covered are those who have net earnings of less than $400 a year.

A higher tax was placed on the self-employed than on employees, since the self-employed have no employer from whom matching contributions can be collected. Actuaries argued that the tax on the self-employed should be twice as high as that collected from the employee in order to equal the combined employer-employee contributions. The self-employed wanted to pay only the same percentages as was being collected from the employee alone. Congress compromised by setting the tax on the self-employed at one and one-half times the amount paid by the employee. Later increases in taxes have narrowed the difference between the amount paid by the self-employed and the employee alone. In 1975 the tax rate paid by the self-employed was 7.9% compared to 5.85% paid by the employees and matched by an equal 5.85% paid by the employer on the payroll.

HIRED FARM LABOR

By 1950 a number of arguments were presented for covering farm employees. The problem of administering the system to small employers had been successfully solved. Also, at least 16 other countries had successfully covered farm workers in government old-age pension programs.[31] In addition, it was found that poorer states had more people on welfare, since farm hands were not covered under the insurance program. In Mississippi, for example, only 2 out of 10 workers in 1940 were in covered employment compared with 7 out of 10 in Rhode Island.[32] Also, it was found that agricultural workers from time to time were employed in covered employment, but earned too little to qualify for benefits. Thus, even though hired farm laborers have been one of the poorest groups in the nation, they had to pay social security taxes from which they received no benefit. For example, 46 percent of a sample of migratory workers in the five states of New Jersey, Michigan, Virginia, North Carolina, and Kentucky had earned wages in covered employment and thus paid social

[31]Wilbur J. Cohen, "Foreign Experience in Social Insurance Countries for Agricultural and Domestic Workers," Social Security Bulletin, Vol. 8 (February, 1945), p. 5.

[32]"Equality of Rights to Social Security," Social Security Bulletin, Vol. 10 (November, 1947), p. 20.

security taxes. Yet only 10 to 15 percent of these workers were eligible to draw social security benefits.[33]

The arguments for hired farm labor coverage proved persuasive, and regularly employed farm workers were covered under the OASDHI program in 1950. Coverage was further broadened in 1954 and changed in 1956. As of the latter date all hired farm laborers were covered who earn $150 or more a year from one employer or who work for one employer on 20 or more days for cash pay computed on a time rather than piece-rate basis. The amendments also provided that a crew leader may be considered an employer. At the present time almost all farm workers are covered except those working for only short periods of time.

GOVERNMENT EMPLOYEES

State and local government employees were originally excluded from the Social Security Act because of the constitutional difficulty of the federal authority taxing state and local governments. Beginning in 1951, the constitutional difficulty was circumvented by providing a type of optional coverage. State and local government employees who were not under a retirement system of their own were covered provided the state or local governments gave their consent. Under the 1954 amendments, state and local government employees already covered under retirement systems were given the option of federal coverage provided that the state or local government and the employees both approved. By 1965 about 70% of state, county, and local employees were covered under the OASDHI program.[34] Several anomalous situations now exist concerning state coverage. In all but 20 states, coverage is available only by means of a referendum among any retirement system group. The remaining 20 states, which are named in the law,[35] may use the referendum or an alternative system whereby coverage is extended to only those members of a retirement system or group who desire such coverage, but only provided that all employees who later become employed will automatically be covered under OASDHI. A different set of rules applies to the coverage of policemen and firemen. In 21 states named in the law policemen and firemen in a separate retirement system can be covered if the state so desires. In the remaining states firemen, but not policemen, can be covered if the governor of the state certifies that the overall benefit protection of the fireman

[33]Fred Safier, Walter Quinn, and Edward I. Fitzgerald, "The Agricultural Worker in Employment Covered by Federal Old-Age and Survivors Insurance," Social Security Bulletin, Vol. 4 (July, 1941), pp. 11-14.

[34]"Report of the Advisory Council on Social Security: The Status of the Social Security Program and Recommendations for Its Improvement," Social Security Bulletin, Vol. 28 (March 1965), p. 37. See also, "State and Local Government Employment Covered Under OASDHI," Social Security Bulletin, Vol. 34, No. 4 (April 1971), pp. 34-36.

[35]Compilation of the Social Security Laws, House of Representatives, 93rd Congress, 1st Session, Document No. 93-117, Vol. 1 (Washington, U. S. Government Printing Office, 1973), pp. 144-163.

would be improved by coverage. In addition, a favorable referendum for firemen is required.

Federal government employees generally are not covered by old-age and survivors insurance since they are under the separate Civil Service Retirement System. In 1951, any Federal employee not under another retirement system was included under OASDHI. Members of the uniformed services, who in effect are "employees" of the Federal government, are also covered for social security purposes.

DOMESTIC WORKERS

Domestic workers had been covered under the 1935 act if they were employed by hotels, restaurants, or other business establishments, but household domestic employees were excluded from coverage. Since it had been found that the OASDHI program could successfully be applied to small employers, in 1950 it was decided to cover about one million of the 1.8 million household workers who were more regularly employed.[36] Coverage was slightly broadened in 1954 to include 100,000 to 200,000 more domestic workers.[37] To qualify for coverage today, a domestic employee must earn $50 a quarter from a single employer.

NONPROFIT ORGANIZATIONS

Originally, nonprofit organizations had been excluded because such organizations had not been subject to taxation. In 1950 it was provided that if a nonprofit organization wished to be covered, and if two-thirds of the employees voted for coverage, those voting for coverage plus all new employees would be covered under the act. Since the votes were overwhelmingly in favor of coverage, Congress deleted the two-thirds vote requirement in 1960.

The problem of separation of church and state created a knotty problem on coverage of clergymen and members of religious orders. This problem was solved in 1954 when this group was given the option on an individual basis to join the program or not. However, to elect coverage, a clergyman was required to file a waiver certificate within the second year in which he had earnings of $400 or more after 1954. Congress extended the date on several occasions because a number of clergymen who had originally rejected coverage requested another opportunity to be covered. This section of the law was improved in 1967 when it was provided that all clergymen would be covered unless they specifically rejected coverage

[36]George H. Leibowitz, "Old Age and Survivors Insurance Coverage Under the 1950 Amendments," *Social Security Bulletin,* Vol. 13 (December, 1950), p. 7.

[37]"A Report to the Secretary of Health, Education, and Welfare on Extension of Old Age and Survivors Insurance to Additional Groups of Current Workers," p. 14.

for religious reasons. A further change occurred in 1972 when the amendments of that year provided that members of a religious order who had taken a vow of poverty (they had previously been excluded) could be covered as employees if the order made an irrevocable election of coverage for its entire membership and its lay employees.[38]

PRESENT COVERAGE

Table 5-1 shows the increase in coverage from 1940 through 1972. Not quite 90% of those now working in paid employment are covered under the OASDHI program. Of the 8.6 million listed as not covered in 1972, 2.3 million are covered by the federal civil service retirement program, and an additional 2.9 million are covered by state and local systems but not by OASDHI.[39] The latter make up the major part of those listed in the table as "Permitted, but not Covered." Most of the remaining workers not covered by OASDHI are persons who work irregularly and who do not meet the relatively low earnings test required for coverage. Part-time domestic workers, part-time farm laborers, and self-employed people with very low earnings fall in this group. Others not covered include some state and local goverment employees who are not covered under such systems, and employees of non-profit organizations, who (or their organization) have elected not to be covered. If the 5.2 million who are covered by federal, state, or local systems, but not by OASDHI, are added to the 74.9 million who are covered by OASDHI, then 95.9% of paid employment is covered by some sort of public system.

ELIGIBILITY

In 1935 rather severe work requirements had to be met for eligibility in the OASDHI program. Not only had a worker to earn $2,000 in wages but he also had to be employed in five separate calendar years. The 1939 amendments substantially lessened the requirements for coverage. Even with the more lenient eligibility requirements, the Advisory Council to the Social Security Board in 1948 pointed out that standards were still so stringent that only about 20 percent of the population aged 65 and over were either insured or receiving benefits. The eligibility requirements have been amended and liberalized a number of times since then. Eligibility now depends on whether the applicant has "fully insured" or "currently insured" status, which in turn depends upon the applicants' "quarters of coverage."

A quarter of coverage, for most kinds of employment, is a calendar

[38]Robert M. Ball, "Social Security Amendments of 1972: Summary and Legislative History," *Social Security Bulletin* Vol. 36, No. 3, (March 1973), p. 18.
[39]*Social Security Bulletin, Annual Statistical Supplement*, 1972, Table 5 and Table 22.

TABLE 5-1

PERSONS IN PAID EMPLOYMENT AND COVERAGE STATUS UNDER OASDHI, SELECTED YEARS

(in millions, except for percentages)

	1940	1950	1960	1970	1972
Total Paid Employment	46.4	60.0	67.5	80.6	83.5
Total Covered:					
Number	26.8	38.7	59.4	72.1	74.9
Percent of Paid Employment	57.8%	64.5%	88.0%	89.5%	89.6%
Wage and Salary	26.8	38.7	52.6	66.2	68.9
Self-Employed			6.8	5.9	6.0
Total Not Covered:	19.6	21.3	8.1	8.5	8.6
Federal Civilian	0.9	1.7	2.0	2.5	2.3
Nonfarm Self-Employed	5.2	6.2	1.3	0.9	0.9
Domestic Service	2.3	2.0	0.9	0.5	0.5
Other	11.2	11.4	1.3	1.2	1.2
Permitted, but not Covered			2.6	3.4	3.7

Source: *Social Security Bulletin, Annual Statistical Supplement, 1972*, Table 25.

quarter in which a worker is paid $50 or more in wages in employment covered by the law. People in self-employment who have net earnings of $400 or more in a year get four quarters of coverage for that year. Farm workers get one quarter of coverage for each $100 of cash wages paid during the year. In all cases the maximum number of quarters earned per year is four.

FULLY INSURED

To be fully insured a worker must have at least one quarter of coverage for each year elapsing after 1950, or, for younger workers, one quarter of coverage for each year after the year in which the worker attained age 21. Years are counted until the year in which the worker reaches age 62. Thus a worker who retired in 1975 needed 24 quarters for fully insured status; one retiring in 1981 will need 30 quarters; and one retiring in 1991 will need 40 quarters.[40] If a person dies before reaching age 62, the count stops with the year before the one in which the person dies. In cases of early death the worker must have had at least six quarters of coverage. The maximum number of quarters needed for fully insured status is 40; with 40 quarters of coverage a worker is said to be "permanently insured." Quarters of coverage earned any time after 1936 may be counted against the number of years after 1950. Quarters of coverage earned after a worker is 62 can also be counted if necessary to achieve fully insured status.

A special "transitional insured" status was created by the 1965 amendments and subsequent amendments. This status provides benefits to workers who reached 72 before 1969. The minimum number of quarters of coverage is three and varies with the worker's age or the age of his widow. The 1966 amendments created "special age 72" benefits under which individuals who reached that age before 1968 can qualify even though they had no quarters of coverage. Beginning in June, 1974, the benefit amount was $64.40 for both the transitionally insured and the "special-age 72" benefits. Other governmental pensions, public assistance, or Supplemental Security Income will reduce or eliminate the special-age 72 benefits, but do not affect benefits paid to the transitionally insured.[41]

CURRENTLY INSURED

To be "currently insured" a worker must have at least six quarters of coverage in the 13-quarter period ending in the quarter in which he or she

[40]*1973 Social Security and Medicare Explained* (Chicago, Commerce Clearing House, Inc., 1972), pp. 83-85.
[41]*Ibid.*, pp. 85-90.

becomes entitled to old-age benefits, disability benefits, or dies. Currently insured status is especially important in providing protection for certain survivors of workers who die young and who for many reasons may not have achieved fully insured status.[42]

"DISABILITY FREEZE"

Since eligibility to benefits depends on quarters of coverage in paid employment, it was in earlier years possible that a worker might fail to qualify because of a period of total disability. Accordingly in 1954 the law was amended to provide a "disability freeze," meaning in effect that certain quarters or years when a worker is totally disabled are "frozen," that is, not counted in determining the number of quarters of coverage needed for a person to be fully or currently insured. The disability freeze also applies in the calculation of the benefit amount. The effect of the disability freeze is to enable some people who have periods of disability to remain eligible for benefits and to prevent the erosion of the size of their benefits because of the disability.[43]

INSURED STATUS REQUIRED

To qualify for Social Security benefits either fully insured status, or currently insured status, is required for the various types of benefits. Disabled workers, discussed in a later chapter, are subject to a more stringent requirement. The following shows the insurance status requirements for various categories of beneficiaries:

Beneficiary Category	Insured Status Required of Worker
Retired worker	Fully insured
Disabled worker	Fully insured and insured for disability
Dependents of retired worker (Old-age and disability): Wife, Divorced Wife, Husband, Child, or Grandchild	Fully insured
Survivor of worker: Widow, Widower, Divorced Wife, or Parent	Fully insured
Widowed Mother, or Surviving Divorced Mother	Fully or currently insured
Child or Grandchild	Fully or currently insured
Lump sum payment beneficiary	Fully or currently insured

[42]*Ibid.*, pp. 91.
[43]*Ibid.*, pp. 113.

THE AGE REQUIREMENT

In 1935 it was provided that pensions would be paid to those covered workers who retired at age 65. In 1956 women workers and wives were permitted to receive benefits if they retired at age 62 rather than 65 but at permanently lower benefits than they would receive if they had retired at age 65. The same provision was made applicable to men by amendments in 1961. Those who favored reducing the retirement age to 62 argued that people who lose their jobs at a higher age have a more difficult time finding a new one. Although it is true that seniority rights and other considerations cause less elderly people to be laid off, once unemployment is experienced it tends to be of long duration. The reduction in age did not cost the system any additional expense, for the reduction in benefit amount was sufficient to offset the age reduction.

A study from 1962 through 1965 showed that about half the men and two-thirds of the women workers awarded retirement benefits under social security programs were under 65. A study of the early retirees showed that a majority of those claiming benefits at age 62 were prompted to do so either by unemployment or the need to supplement earnings that were characteristically low or had dropped off substantially. The Advisory Council on Social Security in 1965 expressed concern over the low pensions of this group since they are actuarially reduced.[44]

THE RETIREMENT TEST

All governmental pension programs must designate whether pensions will automatically be paid whenever age 65 or some other age is reached, or whether a pension should be received only when income decreases due to retirement from the work force. A few countries grant pensions regardless of retirement, but most countries, including the United States, have a retirement test. The original provisions of the Social Security Act prohibited an old-age recipient from earning any money in covered employment. The law has been modified a number of times since 1935 to permit more and more earnings. At the present time, a person aged 72 and over may earn any amount he wishes and still draw OASDHI benefits. For those below that age, earnings up to $2760 per year have no effect on benefits. If the worker makes over $2760 a year, the total amount payable to the worker and his family who are drawing benefits based on his account are reduced by one-half the amount over $2760. For instance, if a worker's annual earnings amount to $3000 his total annual benefits will be reduced by $120 (one-half of $3000 minus $2760). A worker whose earnings record would entitle him to a benefit of $200 per month ($2400 per year), but whose annual earnings were $7560, would receive no

[44]Lenore A. Epstein, "Early Retirement and Work-Life Experience", *Social Security Bulletin*, Vol. 29, No. 2 (March, 1966), pp. 3-10.

benefits. But there is no reduction in any month in which the worker earns less than $230 even though his annual earnings exceed $2760.

The retirement test applies only to earnings in employment or self-employment. Interest and dividends, rents and royalties, insurance endowments, veterans pensions, capital gains, and gifts and inheritances do not result in the loss of Social Security benefits. If it is argued old-age retirement benefits exist to make up for low incomes at retirement, then the unequal treatment of employment income and property income cannot be justified. However, since employees and the self-employed have been taxed and thus contributed to the system, Congress felt that the system should be viewed more as an annuity and that benefits be paid regardless of the amount of property income. Furthermore, people would be less likely to save if their dividend or interest income would disqualify them from Social Security.

Several arguments may be cited in favor of paying pensions regardless of whether the worker retires. Private annuities are paid under this type of arrangement. Also, some production is lost if recipients are forced to retire from the work force. Some of the aged may wish to continue working, and perhaps their desires should be given due consideration. Lastly, although paying pensions at 65 regardless of earnings would cost more, wealthier nations may be able to afford such payments.

Weighty arguments can be mustered for maintaining the retirement test. If pensions were paid regardless of retirement, perhaps some persons would be less likely to retire. In depression times, the failure to retire may cause unemployment problems for younger people who should have replaced the aged. If the earnings test were eliminated entirely, the payroll taxes would have to rise one percent, according to an estimate of the chief actuary of the Social Security Administration.[45] If it were decided that it was possible to increase the payroll tax by one percent, there might be more justification for raising benefits in general rather than abolishing the retirement test. Also, if a major goal of the program is to aid in replacing income lost through retirement, the retirement test should be continued.[46]

Summary

Other countries adopted a system of old-age pensions much earlier than the United States. Germany passed such a law in 1889, and England followed in 1908. Although pension programs abroad have had to weather the severe stresses of inflation and depression, they have been gradually improved and strengthened. Such laws have become integral parts of

[45]Robert J. Myers, "Earnings Test Under Old-Age, Survivors, and Disability Insurance, Basis, Background, and Experience," *Social Security Bulletin*, Vol. 27, No. 5 (May 1964), p. 12.

[46]. For a more comprehensive treatment of applying a retirement test, see Eveline Burns, *Social Security and Public Policy* (New York, McGraw-Hill, 1956), Chapter 6.

Western civilization and are spreading to the rest of the world as well. Changes in legislation over the years have been to broaden and strengthen the social security system rather than weaken or abolish it.

The OASDHI program is one of the few security programs in the United States that is administered solely by the federal government. Administrative expenses of the program are quite low, and the administration of the program has been efficient.

In the United States, prior to the twentieth century, the English practice was followed by dispensing relief on a local basis and providing a harsh system so as to discourage malingering. Prior to the Social Security Act of 1935 several states provided a system of old-age pensions, but few of the programs were adequately financed, and pensions were quite low. The Great Depression hastened passage of a national security system in the United States. Our basic law was passed in 1935. Opposition to an old-age insurance system was intense in some quarters, but strong support from President Roosevelt and leading citizens was sufficient to ensure passage of the Act.

When the Social Security Act was first passed, less than 60 percent of the civilian work force was covered under it. The major exclusions were the self-employed, agricultural workers, government employees, domestic employees, and employees of nonprofit organizations. Since 1935 the trend has been to cover most of the excluded groups so that today about 90 percent of the work force is covered under the insurance program of the Social Security Act, and an additional 5% covered by separate public employee retirement systems.

Eligibility under the OASDHI program is determined on the basis of past earnings. Over the years eligibility requirements have been eased to permit more coverage under the program. The age of retirement was set at 65 years of age in 1935 and has remained at that age, although persons may now retire on a reduced benefit at age 62. Some debate has arisen over whether persons should be required to retire to receive an old-age insurance benefit. Those 72 years of age and older do not have to retire. Others below this age must retire, but over the years they have been permitted to earn an increasingly larger income.

CHAPTER 6

OLD AGE INSURANCE:
BENEFITS AND TAXATION

Today's complex tax and benefit structure results from simple beginnings in 1935 and the year by year attempts to improve the program. Inadequacy of benefits, and in many cases the nonexistence of benefits, led to substantial changes in the law. In early years certain decisions had to be made which helped to determine what we have today. After reviewing the evolution of benefits and the policy issues which had to be decided, the chapter describes present day benefit determination. The latter part of the chapter deals with social security taxes and reserves, and with developing problems in the old age and survivors insurance system.

EVOLUTION OF THE BENEFIT STRUCTURE

FLAT VS. GRADUATED BENEFITS

A basic issue which had to be decided at the very outset was whether to pay the same benefit to all recipients or to graduate benefits according to wages earned. A few countries have adopted the flat grant system, but most countries vary benefits according to past wages. The flat grant system has a distinct advantage in being simple to administer, but it has serious disadvantages as well.[1] Middle and upper income people tend to argue that such a system is inequitable. Basing benefits on past earnings has the advantage of maintaining higher incomes for those who have earned more. High-wage recipients lose more income when they retire, and therefore it is felt that more benefits should be provided for them, especially since these groups have paid more taxes into the program. Some justify a differential in benefits on the ground that those who produce more are entitled to higher current wages and to higher retirement benefits as well. After weighing all the arguments, Congress decided in 1935 to vary benefits according to past earnings.

But if benefits are based on past earnings there is the problem that

---

[1]Eveline Burns, *Social Security and Public Policy* (New York, McGraw-Hill, 1956), pp. 38-39.

low-income workers earn so little that a pension based on their earnings would be totally inadequate. For this reason the benefit formula adopted favored low-income recipients in two ways. The formula itself was weighted in favor of low-wage earners, and minimum benefit amounts were prescribed.

MINIMUM BENEFITS

In 1935 the minimum benefit was set at $10 a month. By 1974 this figure had been raised to $93.80 per month for a worker retiring at 65 and $75.10 for a worker retiring at age 62. In addition, the 1972 law, amended in December, 1973, provided for a new type of minimum benefit based on the number of years the worker had worked in covered employment. This provides a minimum benefit of $9.00 multiplied by the number of years over 10 that the worker has worked for the system.[2]

MAXIMUM BENEFITS

The law also provided for maximum benefit amounts as a corollary of weighting the formula in favor of low income groups. The maximum primary insurance amount in the original act was $85 a month, but this figure has been raised several times since. In 1974 the maximum was $469, but no one could actually qualify for that amount since several years of contributions at the maximum tax base are necessary. It is in fact no longer possible to state a fixed maximum amount since the 1972 amendments established a cost-of-living escalator, discussed below.[3]

DEPENDENTS' BENEFITS

A major change in type of benefits came in 1939 when it was decided to pay pensions not only to retired workers but to their dependents as well. A wife aged 65 or over was made eligible to receive a benefit in addition to that received by the retired worker, as were children under 18. In 1950 a wife under age 65 with a child under age 18 in her care was made eligible for dependent's benefits. In the same year, it was provided that dependent husbands could draw benefits on the basis of the work record of the wife.[4]

In 1956 an amendment provided that a retired worker's wife could receive dependents' benefits at age 62 instead of 65, but only on condition that the benefit would be permanently reduced. The 1956 amendment

[2]1974 *Social Security and Medicare Explained*, op. cit., para. 509.6.
[3]1974 *Social Security and Medicare Explained*, op. cit., para. 521.
[4]Naomi Riches, "Women Workers and Their Dependents Under the 1950 Amendments," *Social Security Bulletin*, Vol. 14 (August, 1951), p. 11.

also provided that any disabled child over 18 could receive dependent benefits provided that he had been disabled prior to age 18.[5]

In 1965 the age limit for benefits for dependent children was raised from 18 to 22 provided the dependent was continuing as a full time student. Also aided by the 1965 amendments were divorced women. A divorced woman who had been married to her spouse for 20 years or more could now receive dependent benefits on her former husband's amount at age 62, if she is not remarried. Previously the law required that the husband must have been contributing to her support when he became entitled to social security benefits, but the support requirements were removed by the 1972 amendments. The 1972 amendments also provided for dependents' benefits for grandchildren where the worker is providing at least half the support for the child and where the child's natural or adoptive parents or stepparents were disabled or not alive.[6]

SURVIVORS' BENEFITS

Another important addition in type of benefit came in 1939 with the payment of survivors' benefits to widows 65 and over, children under 18, widows under 65 provided there were children under 18 present, and dependent parents over 65 provided that the deceased worker was not survived by a widow or child who was eligible for benefits. Since 1939, further amendments have liberalized eligibility for survivors' benefits. In the 1950 act, dependent widowers 65 and over were made eligible. Divorced surviving wives were made eligible in the same year provided that an eligible child was present in the home. In 1956 widows or parents were made eligible for payments at age 62 instead of 65, and disabled children over 18 were granted survivors' benefits provided they had become disabled before 18. Amendments in 1958 made it possible to pay benefits to surviving dependent parents even though benefits were also being paid to the widow or children under 18.

In 1965 a widow became entitled to benefits at age 60 rather than 62, but at reduced amounts. Also if a widow could have qualified for benefits and had remarried after reaching age 60 she was eligible for whichever benefit is larger: either one-half the retirement benefit of her former husband or a wife's benefit based on the earnings of her present husband. A problem still exists here, however, since a widow at age 65 can now receive 100% of her deceased husband's primary insurance amount, so widows often have a dis-incentive to remarry. In 1967, widows, dependent widowers, and surviving divorced wives, if they are disabled, were permitted to obtain benefits beginning at age 50, but at reduced amounts. And the 1972 amendments authorized grandchildren to receive survivors'

---

[5]Charles I. Schottland, "Social Security Amendments of 1956: A Summary and Legislative History," *Social Security Bulletin*, Vol. 19, No. 9 (September 1956), pp. 3-15; 31.

[6]Robert M. Ball, "Social Security Amendments of 1972: Summary and Legislative History," *Social Security Bulletin*, Vol. 36, No. 3 (March 1973), p. 17.

benefits under the limited conditions where the natural or adoptive parents were either not living or were disabled at the time the grandparents became entitled to benefits or died. In cases where a child is entitled to benefits on more than one worker's record, benefits will be based on the work record which will provide him with the highest amount.[7]

The magnitude of the face value of survivors' benefits is often overlooked in discussions about social security. One authority estimated that in 1939 the face value of such benefits was equal to the face value of all private life insurance written in the United States, and that such was still true in 1966.[8]

LUMP SUM PAYMENTS

The lump sum payment is a specialized kind of survivors' benefit payable after the death of the worker and designed to help with burial expenses. If there is no widow or widower this payment is made to whomever pays the burial expenses, or to the funeral director. Over the years lump-sum payments have been substantially curtailed. The 1939 law provided for lump-sum payments equal to six times the primary insurance amount. This figure was cut to three times the primary insurance amount in 1950. A further restriction came in 1954, when the maximum lump-sum payment was limited to $255. Since the minimum primary insurance amount multiplied by three now exceeds $255, the lump sum payment is $255 in every case. Cuts in the lump-sum payment are in contrast to the increase in monthly benefits for retired workers. Such cuts are anomalous in view of increasing burial costs. If lump-sum payments are looked upon as aid in burial expenses, then they should increase in line with the increased costs experienced at death.

COMPUTATION OF THE BENEFIT AMOUNT

In the previous chapter it was seen that *eligibility* for benefits depends on the attainment of either "fully insured" or "currently insured" status, achieved by a sufficient number of "quarters of coverage." If the worker is determined to be eligible, the next question which then arises is the computation of the actual benefit amount for the retired worker, the disabled worker, the dependents, and for survivors. The basic benefit is the amount paid to the worker who retires at age 65; this is called the *primary insurance amount* (PIA). The primary insurance amount depends in turn

[7]*1974 Social Security and Medicare Explained, op. cit.,* para. 514.
[8]Arthur Altmeyer, *Formative Years of Social Security* (Madison, Wisconsin, University of Wisconsin Press, 1966), p. 102.

upon the workers' *average monthly wage* (AMW), or for self-employed people the average monthly earnings (AME). The expression "average monthly wage" is used herein, but this should be understood to include the earnings of the self-employed.[9]

AVERAGE MONTHLY WAGE

The basic idea of an average monthly wage is relatively simple, being the total taxed income divided by the total number of months of work. A somewhat more complex but more accurate definition is that:

$$AMW = \frac{\text{total taxed wages plus taxed self-employment income in benefit computation years}}{\text{number of benefit computation years x 12}}$$

Prior to 1975 the average monthly wage was computed somewhat more advantageously for women than for men. Beginning in 1975 the computation is made in the same way for both sexes, as follows:

First determine the number of years to be used. For older people who were 21 or over in 1950, this is the number of years after 1950 and before the year in which the individual died or reached age 62. For younger people the count of years starts with the year after the year in which the individual reached 21, and continues through the year before reaching 62, or death if earlier. Years in which a worker was determined to be disabled during all or part of the year are not counted. Secondly, deduct five years from the total, but the deduction must not reduce the number of years to less than two. Total years minus five is the workers' "benefit computation years." The worker is permitted to deduct the five years in which his earnings were lowest, and any years of disability are not counted. This has the effect of raising his average monthly wage.

Third, total taxed earnings in benefit computation years must be added. This cannot be more than the annual income amounts on which taxes are levied in years since 1950, shown in Table 6-1. If the worker made less than these amounts he must of course add in only the actual earnings for that year. Any self-employment income credited in any year after 1950 is also counted, and if the worker had both wages and self-employment income, his average monthly wage is figured on the basis of combined earnings subject to the upper limits shown in Table 6-1. His total taxed earnings are then divided by the number of months in his benefit computation

---

[9]The benefit computation detail given herein should not be regarded as exhaustive. Certain minor details are omitted for reasons of space. A potential beneficiary should consult his local Social Security office or visiting representative, as he must in any case when he is applying for benefits.

years, always a multiple of twelve. The result will be the worker's average monthly wage (reduced to even multiples of $1).[10]

TABLE 6-1

MAXIMUM TAXABLE EARNINGS, BY YEAR

1951-1954	$ 3,600
1955-1958	4,200
1959-1965	4,800
1966-1967	6,600
1968-1971	7,800
1972	9,000
1973	10,800
1974	13,200
1975	14,100
1976	15,300

Source: *1974 Social Security and Medicare Explained* (Chicago, Commerce Clearing House, Inc., 1974), para. 508.2.

PRIMARY INSURANCE AMOUNT

The primary insurance amount (PIA) is found by applying a table or formula written into the law to the average monthly wage. The formula has been changed at least ten times since 1935. Tables are computed on the basis of the law's formula and in actual practice the primary insurance amount is found by locating the worker's average monthly wage in the left hand column of the table and finding the appropriate PIA on that line. For workers who retire exactly at age 65 their "old-age insurance benefit" is the same as their PIA. The primary insurance amount is the basis for computing most other benefit amounts. Reduced benefits for those who retire before age 65, dependents' benefits, and survivors' benefits are all computed as some fraction of the PIA.[11]

Except in the case of reduced benefits, discussed below, the following *dependents* receive 50% of the retired or disabled worker's PIA:

1. Wife at age 65.
2. Wife, if under 65 and she has an entitled child in her care.
3. Divorced wife at age 65, if they had been married at least 20 years, and she is not currently remarried.
4. Husband at age 65 if he had been receiving at least half of his support from his wife.
5. Child, if under age 18, or under 22 if a full-time student, or after 18 if disabled before 18.

[10] *1974 Social Security and Medicare Explained*, op. cit., para. 508.
[11] *Ibid.*, para. 509.

6. Grandchild if (a) the child's natural or adoptive parents were either not living or were disabled at the time the grandparent became entitled, or if (b) the child was legally adopted after the death of the grandparent by the grandparent's surviving spouse.

Some *survivors* may receive 100% of the worker's PIA. These include a:

1. Widow who first becomes entitled at age 65 or after, provided the husband had not been receiving a reduced amount.
2. Surviving divorced wife, similar to the widow, but she must have been married to the deceased individual at least 20 years, and must not be currently remarried. If a subsequent marriage terminates, her entitlement resumes.
3. Widower who first becomes entitled at age 65 or after, provided the wife had not been receiving a reduced amount, and provided the widower had been receiving at least half his support from his wife.

If the widow, surviving divorced wife, or widower were receiving benefits on the basis of a reduced old-age benefit, the survivor's benefit may not be larger than (a) the reduced amount previously received by the insured worker or (b) 82-1/2% of the basic PIA. If there is only one dependent surviving parent, the benefit is 82-1/2% of the PIA. If there are two dependent surviving parents, each receives 75% of the PIA. The following survivors also receive 75% of the PIA:

1. The surviving mother who has an eligible child in her care.
2. The surviving divorced mother, subject to the limiting circumstances applying to the surviving divorced wife.
3. Each surviving child, subject to family maximum amounts.
4. The surviving grandchild, subject to the limiting circumstances applying to a dependent grandchild.[12]

REDUCED BENEFITS

Retired workers, wives, widows, divorced wives, widowers, husbands (and disabled people in some cases), may elect to take a reduced benefit in order to begin receiving benefits before age 65. In each case the benefit is actuarially reduced to take account of the longer period over which it will normally be paid. This provides an element of flexibility in the law so that people who find themselves in differing circumstances can choose a course which seems best to them. One study of those aged 62 through 64 who had stopped work indicated that 54% stopped for reasons of health, 17% because they wanted to retire, 13% because their job had been discontinued, 4% because they were "dissatisfied," 3% because of compulsory retirement, and the remainder for miscellaneous other reasons.[13] The amount of the reduction of benefits is based on the number

[12]*Ibid.*, para. 511-518.
[13]Virginia Reno, "Why Men Stop Working at or Before Age 65; Findings From the Survey of New Beneficiaries," *Social Security Bulletin*, Vol. 34, No. 6 (June 1971), pp. 3-17.

of months before age 65 that the person elects to begin receiving benefits. For a worker, who may retire as early as age 62, the reduction is 5/9th of 1% of the PIA times the number of months before age 65. If he retired exactly at age 62 the reduction amounts to 20%. For the widow or widower, who may retire as early as age 60, the reduction is 19/40ths of 1% times the number of months before age 65. If the widow retires exactly at age 60 her benefits are reduced by 28-1/2%. For dependent wives or husbands, who may elect to begin receiving benefits at age 62, the reduction is 25/36ths of 1% times the number of months before age 65. If the dependent takes benefits exactly at age 62 the reduction is 25%. (Still another formula applies to disabled widows or widowers who may begin receiving benefits as early as age 50). The reduced benefit is ordinarily a permanently reduced amount. However, if the person earns income between the start of election of benefits and age 65, and if the retirement test causes him to lose benefits for some of the intervening months, his benefits will be recalculated at age 65.[14]

INCREMENT FOR DELAYED RETIREMENT

The 1972 amendments provided for an increase in a worker's old-age benefit of one percent for each year (one-twelfth of 1% per month) between the ages of 65 and 72 that he does not receive benefits either because he continued working or he had not become entitled. The worker who continues to work until age 72 would receive a 7% increase, but the increase applies only to the old-age benefit, not to dependents or survivors benefits.[15]

This increase is modest compared to the increments provided in many other countries. Some countries provide no increment as did the United States before 1972, but among those that do, some representative increments are: Argentina, 5% for each year that pension is deferred, maximum increment, 25%; Chile, 10% for each 150 weeks of contributions after a pension has been awarded; Costa Rica, 0.5% for each month of deferment after age 60; Czechoslovakia, 4% per year for years of work and deferred benefits; Denmark, 6% increase in pension if deferred 3 years, and 10% if 5 years; France, 5% of earnings per year for deferral after age 60; Iceland, up to a maximum increment of 67% for five years deferral; Israel, 5% for each year retirement is postponed; Mexico, 2% of earnings per year of work after age 65; Sweden, increase of 0.6% per month for deferral between ages 67 and 70; United Kingdom, £0.06 a week for each nine weeks of contributions after pensionable age; and Venezuela, 5% per year after pensionable age.[16] The increments provided in most laws outside the United States appear to range from 3% to 6% for each year of

---

[14]1974 *Social Security and Medicare Explained, op. cit.,* para. 507.1.
[15]*Ibid.,* para. 509.5.
[16]*Social Security Programs Throughout the World, 1973, op. cit.*

deferred retirement. Since most people do not live for 20 years after age 65, a 5% increment for each year of deferred benefits appears reasonable.

AUTOMATIC BENEFIT "ESCALATOR"

The 1972 and 1973 amendments provided for periodic increases in benefits whenever there has been an increase in the Consumer Price Index of 3% or more. If in the first calendar quarter of the year the cost-of-living is found to be 3% or more greater than the same quarter in the prior year or the most recent quarter in which a legislated benefit increase occurred, benefits will be increased by the same percentage. However, there can be no cost-of-living adjustment if in the prior year Congress legislated an increase in benefits or if in the prior year such an increase became effective. Under special provisions, a cost-of-living increase went into effect in June, 1975. The first automatic adjustment in the taxable wage base became effective in January, 1975. This also automatically provided higher average monthly wages, higher primary insurance amounts, and higher maximum family benefit amounts.[17]

Juanita Kreps has suggested that Social Security benefits should also include an annual improvement factor for increases in the standard of living. As per capita GNP rises, the aged, whose benefits are based on earnings when real incomes are much lower, will receive a declining share of the rising product of society. Suppose, for instance, that in decade A, median family incomes were $10,000, while the median family social security benefit were $5,000. Then suppose that in decade B, median family income in constant dollars had risen to $20,000. The social security benefit would still be $5,000 in constant dollars as provided by the cost-of-living escalator. The standard of living of the aged would then be only 25% of the median instead of 50% as it had been in decade A. Kreps suggests that an adjustment should be made in benefits to allow the aged to maintain the same relative standard of living.[18]

ADEQUACY OF BENEFITS

The low level of benefits has been a problem since the inception of the program. In the early years recipients of old-age assistance generally received more than beneficiaries of old-age insurance. Between 1939 and 1950, Congress twice increased OAA benefits, but did not change the formula to improve OASDHI. The result was that by June of 1948, a single male under the OASDHI program received $18.94 monthly compared

[17]*Social Security and Medicare Explained,* op. cit., para. 208 and para. 509.7.
[18]See Juanita Kreps, *Lifetime Allocations of Work and Income: Essays in the Economics of Aging* (Durham, North Carolina, Duke University Press, 1971).

with \$35.46 under OAA. For couples the amounts received were respectively \$26.39 and \$53.15.[19] Anomalously, those who were being taxed under the OASDHI program were receiving about half of the benefits of old-age assistance beneficiaries who were paying no direct social security tax. The need for larger pensions became so urgent that a number of labor unions in 1949 and 1950 concentrated on obtaining larger pensions as their number one issue in bargaining negotiations. The success of many unions in obtaining pensions financed solely by corporations influenced business groups finally to support larger social security benefits. The old-age insurance program financed by both employers and employees was less expensive to corporations than private pension plans financed solely by them.

Since 1950 benefit amounts have been increased very substantially, as shown in Table 6-2. While benefit increases have been partly negated by inflation, benefits have, on the whole, increased more rapidly than the cost of living. In the five year interval, 1950-1955, the benefit increase was almost four times that of the cost-of-living. In the next three five-year intervals the percentage benefit increase was generally about twice that of the rise in the consumer price index. Further benefit increases occured in 1973, an 11% increase went into effect in 1974, and an 8% increase was made in 1975.

Benefit amounts alone are still ordinarily not enough to raise many workers above the poverty level. Fortunately, most beneficiaries have other sources of income. The 1968 Survey of the Aged indicated that about 26% of beneficiaries have some income from earnings, 15% have private pensions and annuities, 11% draw veterans benefits, 8% receive some income from public assistance, and 52% have income from assets. Some families receive several forms of income; other families perhaps only one. The same study showed that income shares of all aged OASDHI beneficiaries, by source, are as follows: OASDHI benefits 42%; earnings, 22%; income from assets, 16%; other public and private pensions, 10%; veterans benefits, 4%; public assistance, 3%; and other sources, 3%.[20]

Whether or not benefits are now "adequate" depends largely on each person's definition of adequacy. In 1973, 16.3% of all persons aged 65 and over were below the poverty level. If benefits are termed adequate for those above the poverty level, and inadequate for those below, a substantial social problem still exists involving 3.3 million aged persons.[21]

[19]Bureau of Old Age and Survivors Insurance, "Public Assistance Supplementation of the Income of Old-Age and Survivors Insurance Beneficiaries," *Social Security Bulletin*, Vol. 12 (October, 1949), pp. 10-13.

[20]Lenore E. Bixby, "Income of People Aged 65 and Older: Overview from the 1968 Survey of the Aged," *Social Security Bulletin*, Vol. 33, No. 4 (April 1970), pp. 3-25. See also, Lenore E.Bixby and Virginia Reno, "Second Pensions Among Newly Entitled Workers: Survey of New Beneficiaries," *Social Security Bulletin*, Vol. 34, No. 11 (November 1971), pp. 3-7.

[21]*Characteristics of the Low Income Population: 1973* (Advance Report), Bureau of the Census, Current Population Reports, Consumer Income, Series P-60, No. 94, Table 3.

TAXATION

Old-age pensions obviously cost billions of dollars. In fiscal year 1974 the OASDHI program paid out $47.8 billion to aged workers, their dependents and survivors, $6.2 billion to disabled workers, their dependents and survivors, and an additional $10.7 billion for health insurance for the aged. This was about $9 billion more than was paid out in the previous year, and large annual increases are continuing. The federal government is thus faced with the important problem of financing such a program.

Any government program may be financed either by taxation, borrowing, or the creation of new money. Whichever method is used, there is a transfer in the use of resources. If finance is by taxation, the use of resources (goods and services) is transferred from the taxpayer to the recipient of the social security benefits. Financing by the creation of new money, either by the printing press or by the Federal Reserve and the banking system, may cause inflation. Such financing transfers the use of

TABLE 6-2

AVERAGE OASDHI CASH BENEFITS FOR RETIRED WORKERS AND THE CONSUMER PRICE INDEX, SELECTED YEARS

	Benefits		*Price*	
Year	*Retired Workers*	*Percent Increase in Five-Year Interval*	*Consumer Price Index, 1967-100*	*Percent Increase in Five-Year Interval*
1950	$ 43.86		72.1	
1955	61.90	41.1%	80.2	11.2%
1960	74.04	19.6	88.7	10.6
1965	83.92	13.3	94.5	6.5
1970	118.10	40.7	116.3	23.1
1971	132.17		121.3	
1972	161.97		125.3	
1973	166.42		133.1	
1974[1]	187.11		151.9	

[1]Data for September, 1974.

Source: *Social Security Bulletin*, Vol. 36, No. 6 (June 1973), Tables M-13 and M-31; and *Ibid.*, Vol. 38, No. 1 (January 1975), Table M-13 and M-40.

resources from who ever is hurt by inflation to the social security beneficiaries. Borrowing is more complex, depending on to whom the government sells bonds. If bonds are sold to the general public, the short run effect is similar to taxation. If bonds are sold to the banking system, and are then purchased by the Federal Reserve System, the effect is to create new money, and is therefore inflationary. The government must be careful not to create too much new money; otherwise a runaway inflation will occur. In such an inflation, all liquid assets tend to become worthless. Accordingly, money creation is not ordinarily regarded as a rational way of financing a social insurance program, and borrowing to pay benefits can perhaps be justified only in dire emergency. Governments the world over endeavor to rely on some type of taxation to finance benefits.

Any type of tax, whether income, sales, payroll, property, or whatever, could be used to finance a social security program. Most countries in the world have relied on payroll taxes upon both employees and employers or on "tripartite" financing, involving supplements out of the general revenues. In 1971, information on the tax systems of 101 countries with some form of old age program indicated that 46 had tripartite financing, 40 had joint employer-employee financing, 7 had financing by government general revenues only, and the rest had a mixture of other arrangements. In the 86 countries with either tripartite or joint employer-employee financing, 54 countries collected the largest share from the employer. In 24 countries the employer-employee contributions were the same. Only three countries collected the largest amounts directly from the employee, while general revenues provided the largest share in the remainder.[22] The United States is among the 24 countries relying on equal employer-employee contributions, with no subsidy from the general revenues.

RECENT CHANGES IN TAXATION

The basic system of employer-employee payroll taxes, plus special taxes on the self-employed, remains in effect, but there have been important amendments in recent years. Table 6-3 shows the tax rates currently provided in the law, from 1974 through 1985. Tax rates are scheduled to rise due to the scheduled increase in the tax to finance hospital insurance. The Social Security tax rate on the employer and on the employee is scheduled to remain at 4.95% until the year 2010 (plus rising rates for hospital insurance), and the rate on the self-employed is fixed at 7.0%. Congress has, however, frequently changed the tax rate in the past, so these tax rates are apt to be changed long before 1985.

With a tax rate of 5.85% (inclusive of the hospital rate) levied on a tax base (in 1976) of $15,300 employees making that amount or more have

[22]*Social Security Programs Throughout the World, 1971, op. cit.,* pp. 1-249.

TABLE 6-3

SOCIAL SECURITY CONTRIBUTION RATES, 1974-1985

Year	Social Security Rate	Hospital Insurance Rate	Combined Rate
Employer and Employee Rates (each):			
1974-1977	4.95%	0.90%	5.85%
1978-1980	4.95	1.10	6.05
1981-1985	4.95	1.35	6.30
Self-Employment Taxes:			
1974-1977	7.0%	0.90%	7.90%
1978-1980	7.0	1.10	8.10
1981-1985	7.0	1.35	8.35

Source: *1974 Social Security and Medicare Explained,* par. 201, 202.

$895.05 withheld from their wages. This is matched by an equal amount paid by the employer for a total of $1,790.10 paid per year per employee. Employees earning less than $15,300 will of course pay correspondingly smaller amounts. Self-employed people making $15,300 or more per year pay $1,208.70.

AUTOMATIC ADJUSTMENTS IN THE TAXABLE WAGE BASE

The 1972 amendments provided for adjustments in the tax base whenever automatic increases in benefits occur. If the cost-of-living, as measured by the Consumers Price Index increases by 3.0% or more in a one-year period, or in the period since the most recent legislated increase, benefits, as noted before, will be increased by a corresponding percentage. Whenever such a benefit increase goes into effect in June, the Secretary of Health, Education, and Welfare is directed to determine the increase in the taxable wage base which will go into effect the following January. The law provides a ratio to be used for this determination, subject to the proviso that the annual wage base will be some multiple of $300.[23] The first such upward adjustment went into effect in January, 1975, when the taxable wage base became $14,100, and the second such increase occurred in January, 1976, when the base became $15,300.

[23]*1974 Social Security and Medicare Explained, op. cit.,* para. 208.

THE TAX ON EMPLOYEES

A number of advantages exist for placing a payroll tax on an employee's pay. A major advantage is that the worker then feels that he is entitled to a pension as a matter of right since he is being taxed. Also there is protection against excessive liberalization of benefits, since workers realize that any increase in benefits must be paid out of the increased taxes they pay. A payroll tax on employees has some disadvantages, also. Unlike the personal income tax, taxes must be paid on the first $15,300 earned (1976); there is no exemption of $750 for each dependent, nor are there any deductions for medical costs, and the like. In the absence of such deductions, low income earners must bear a heavy burden. The tax is clearly regressive, because the present 5.85% must be paid on the first $15,300 earned, but not on additional income. A person earning $15,300 pays 5.85% of his wages, but a person earning $30,600 pays a tax of only 2.925% of his wages. Offsetting the disadvantage of the higher tax rate to low wage earners is the fact that the benefit formula is weighted in favor of low-income groups. As to the incidence of the payroll tax on employees, it is generally agreed that the employee must pay the tax himself. It may be argued that the workers will attempt to force the employer to pay higher wages to pay for the tax, but if workers had such strong bargaining power they would have attempted to get higher wages before the imposition of the tax.[24]

THE TAX ON EMPLOYERS

A tax equal to that collected from employees is paid by each employer at the same rate (5.85%) on the first $15,300 of payroll per employee. The total tax paid is thus 11.7%. It is widely believed by workers and by the general public that the burden of the employer tax falls on the employer. Economists, however, point out that most if not all of the tax on the employer is shifted either forward to consumers in the form of higher prices, or backward to the workers themselves in the form of lower wages.[25] Since consumers are wage or salary personnel, workers in general bear the burden of the tax whichever way it is shifted.

John A. Brittain's analysis indicates that most of the tax is shifted backward to the workers in the form of lower cash wages. In addition, Brittain points out that the tax for unemployment compensation is also shifted to the employees, so that some workers, especially those making $4,200 or less, are bearing a combined tax of about 13% on their pay.[26] For

[24]Ida C. Merriam, *Social Security Financing*, Bureau Report No. 17, Washington, D.C., Social Security Administration, Division of Research and Statistics, 1953, pp. 16-17.

[25]See for instance Joseph A. Pechman, Henry J. Aaron, and Michael K. Taussig, *Social Security, Perspectives for Reform* (Washington, The Brookings Institution, 1968), Chapter VIII, pp. 173-213; and John A. Brittain, *The Payroll Tax for Social Security* (Washington, The Brookings Institution, 1972).

[26]Brittain, *op. cit.*, pp. 95-96.

workers earning more than $15,300, the percentage of the tax on their total income is less and less as their income rises. The combined employee-employer payroll tax is thus not only severely regressive but also falls most heavily on those making less than $4,200, that is the working poor who are below the poverty line. Collecting such taxes from those who are in poverty is clearly inconsistent with the national effort to eliminate poverty.

EVALUATION OF THE PAYROLL TAX

Arguments in favor of the payroll tax include the fact that it does give the workers a feeling that they have paid for the program and the fact that the tax has been able to bring in large amounts of revenue. But the fact the tax is regressive and that the largest percentages are collected from the poor cannot be glossed over. Some experts, including officials of the Social Security Administration, the Advisory Council on Social Security, and others including Brittain and Pechman, et al., have recommended at one time or another that the government should bear part of the cost of the OASDHI program out of general revenues. One Advisory Council, for example, recommended obtaining one-third from a payroll tax on employees, one-third from a payroll tax on employers, and one-third from the general revenues of the government.[27] This recommendation rests on the premise that federal government revenues are mainly derived from the progressive income tax.

Other proposals are that personal exemptions such as those in effect for the federal income tax be made applicable to the OASDHI and the unemployment insurance payroll taxes. Were this the case much of the burden on the working poor would be relieved. To offset the revenue loss it is sometimes proposed that the ceiling on taxable earnings be eliminated. If the tax applied to all earnings it would be more nearly a proportionate tax. But a regressive element would still remain since much of the income of upper income groups is derived from property, not from current earnings. A subsidy out of the federal general revenues, mainly derived from the progressive income tax, is again suggested. If personal exemptions were in effect, if the social security tax applied to total earned income, and if there were a subsidy out of the general revenues, the regressivity of social security taxes could be largely eliminated.[28]

[27]J. S. Parker, "Financial Policy in Old-Age and Survivors Insurance, 1935-50," *Social Security Bulletin*, Vol. 14 (June, 1951), pp. 3-10.
[28]See especially Brittain's Chapter V, "Proposals for Reform."

RESERVES

THE SOCIAL SECURITY TRUST FUND

The social security trust fund is actually four separate trust funds. There is the original old age reserve account (1935), now called the old-age and survivors insurance trust fund, created by the 1939 legislation. There is a separate disability insurance trust fund, which began operation in 1956; a hospital insurance trust fund, 1966; and a supplementary medical insurance trust fund, also 1966. The latter three funds were kept separate from the old-age and survivors insurance fund because some in Congress feared that unexpected expenses in the new programs might jeopardize the cash benefits for OASI.

In the early decades of the operation of the OASI trust fund there was much controversy over the projected size of reserves, how the fund should be operated, where the funds should be invested, what the impact on the economy was, and other questions. Some of the early framers of the 1935 legislation envisaged a full actuarial reserve — a reserve large enough to meet all accrued liabilities if the plan were terminated. Congress soon backed away from this idea. Some feared the deflationary effects of accumulating a large reserve, and a sharp recession in 1938 in the midst of the Great Depression contributed to these fears. Accordingly, Congress kept the OASI tax at a low 1% each on both the employer and the employee on the first $3,000 of annual income instead of allowing scheduled increases to go into effect. The tax was not raised to 1.5% until 1950, although the inflationary period during World War II would have been an ideal time to accumulate a larger reserve. The opponents of a large reserve, however, prevailed. Secretary of Treasury Morgenthau suggested that the system only accumulate sufficient reserves to be three times as large as annual benefits. During the war, increased earnings caused social security tax collections to increase much faster than benefits so that the reserve became about six times as large as benefits. But the idea of the full actuarial reserve was abandoned.[29]

The present reserve has sometimes been called a "contingency reserve," and sometimes a "pay-as-you-go" operation. Under a pay-as-you-go plan, annual tax collections would equal annual benefit payments. In particular months the Treasury might have a surplus in the OASI account, and in other months the balance might be negative. Such negative balances would be financed by short-term borrowing. With a contingency reserve the amount in the trust fund would be kept at some chosen small

[29]References on social security reserves include: Seymour Harris, *The Economics of Social Security* (New York, McGraw-Hill, 1941), Chaps. 1-12; J. S. Parker, *Social Security Reserves* Washington, D.C., American Council on Public Affairs, 1942); Burns, *op. cit.*, Chap. 10; Raymond H. Manning, *Financing Social Security* (Washington, D.C., Library of Congress, Legislative Reference Service, 1946), pp. 41-61; and Merriam, *op. cit.*, pp. 30-45.

TABLE 6-4

**STATUS OF THE OLD-AGE AND SURVIVORS INSURANCE
TRUST FUND SELECTED FISCAL YEARS (in millions of dollars)**

Fiscal Year	Contribution Income	Cash Benefit Payments	Total Assets	Total Assets as a Multiple of: Contribution Income	Cash Benefits
1939-40	$ 550	$ 16	$ 1,745	3.17	116.33
1944-45	1,310	240	6,613	5.05	27.67
1949-50	2,106	727	12,892	6.12	17.73
1954-55	5,087	4,333	21,141	4.16	4.88
1959-60	9,843	10,270	20,829	2.12	2.03
1964-65	15,857	15,226	20,180	1.27	1.33
1969-70	29,955	26,267	32,616	1.09	1.24
1972-73	41,319	42,170	36,416	0.88	0.86
1973-74	48,455	47,849	37,867	0.78	0.79

Source: *Social Security Bulletin*, Vol. 38, No. 1, (January 1, 1975), Table M-5.

multiple of annual benefit payments. In recent years, Congress has directed that the reserve should be at least 75% of one year's benefits. The present reserve, which meets this test, may thus be called a contingency reserve, but it is not far removed from a pay-as-you-go operation.

Table 6-4 shows the contribution income, cash benefits paid, and total assets in the OASI trust fund in selected fiscal years. During the first 17 years of its existence the trust fund grew steadily until by 1954 it reached $20.6 billion. Then for the next 12 years total assets in the fund fluctuated between $18 and $22 billion, and in 1966 the total was again $20.6 billion. Thereafter, the trust fund again began to grow, and currently stands in excess of $38 billion. But, as may be seen from Table 6-4, the current assets of the trust fund are now smaller than annual contribution and benefit payments. As a multiple of either contribution income, or cash benefits, the trust fund has declined from over four in 1955 to less than one in 1973. If there were no current income the trust fund would be exhausted in less than one year.

A TRUST FUND DEFICIT?

Although the Old Age and Survivors Insurance Trust Fund had a balance of about $38 billion in 1975, which may seem to be an enormous sum of money, worry is developing that the Fund will soon begin to shrink and will eventually (unless changes are made) be exhausted. Independent actuarial studies have recently called into question the assumptions made by the Social Security Administration's actuaries. Roger Kaplan, Roman Weil and Robert J. Myers all hold that the assumptions used by the SSA to estimate income in relation to benefits have been overly optimistic. Kaplan and Weil hold that social security taxes will need to be 50 to 75% higher than current levels to support future benefits.[30] Robert J. Myers, the Social Security Administration's chief actuary from 1947 to 1970, also believes that the bureau's projections have been too optimistic.[31]

Three general factors appear to be mainly responsible for the projected deficit. The first is the automatic adjustment of benefits to offset the effect of inflation as provided by the 1972 amendments. This proviso will cause workers to draw monthly benefits which are a substantially greater proportion of their earnings than has been the case in the past. Assuming that prices will rise, for workers retiring in 1974 the "replacement ratio" (the worker's primary insurance amount as a percentage of his taxable earnings in his last working year) for a worker earning the maximum taxable amount during his lifetime was about 29%. Present law will cause the replacement ratio to gradually increase. By 2050 the top

---

[30]*Wall Street Journal*, "A Long Look at the SSS," July 15, 1974, p. 10.

[31]Richard Egan, "Is It Social Insecurity?" *The National Observer*, October 26, 1974, p. 1; p. 21.

wage earner would have a replacement ratio of about 38%, and median and low income workers will experience corresponding increases in their replacement ratios.[32]

A second factor is the current decline in the birth rate. Since Americans are having fewer and fewer children than ever before, in the future the worker-beneficiary ratio will eventually decline. This means that there will be relatively fewer workers to pay the taxes which finance benefits. Today there are about 3.2 workers for every beneficiary; by 2010 the ratio will be about 2.9; and by 2025 the ratio will drop to 2.3.[33] Furthermore if the SSA's fertility rate assumptions are overly optimistic, the difficulty will be even greater. For 1974 the actual fertility rate (the average number of lifetime births per woman) was in fact slightly lower, at 1.87, than SSA's projected 1.938.

A third factor is that the Social Security Administration's economic assumptions are open to doubt. The Administration has projected that there will be a sustained annual 2 percent gain in real wages. Such an increase would go far to finance higher benefits in the future. Critics, however, argue that the American economy has undergone a fundamental change so that real wages are no longer increasing. Geoffry N. Calvert, an actuary, points out that real wages have decreased in certain years since 1966.[34] If real wages rise by 1% per year in the future, instead of the projected 2%, the deficit in the Social Security system will increase.

ALTERNATIVE SOLUTIONS TO THE PROJECTED DEFICIT

If the above pessimistic analysis does in fact turn out to be correct, what are the possible remedies_ Several solutions immediately suggest themselves, most of them unpleasant: (1) if the present projected benefits remain in effect, an increase in taxes (or new taxes) over and above those already provided for is one possibility; (2) benefits could be scaled down to fit the existing structure of taxation; (3) the retirement age could be raised from 65 to 66, 67, or 68; (4) a subsidy could be provided out of the Treasury's general revenues; or (5) some combination of two or more of the above. The subsidy proposal is generally strongly opposed by some conservatives who favor the present regressive tax structure and who argue that a subsidy "would convert the system into an outright welfare program."[35] Liberals, however, who deplore the regressivity of the present system of employer-employee payroll taxes are more likely to favor

[32]Ibid., p. 21.
[33]Ibid.
[34]Ibid.
[35]"Social Security: Promising Too Much to Too Many?" U.S. News and World Report, July 15, 1974, pp. 26-30.

such a subsidy. They would argue, as does Brittain and others, that the system should be financed by a subsidy out of the general revenues. If in fact a deficit does develop, and if it is argued that the regressivity of Social Security taxes should be reduced, a subsidy out of the general revenues appears to be the preferable course of action.

RECENT CRITICISMS

Periodically, various allegations are made that the "social security system is a fraud," or that the "system is bankrupt," or that it is a "bad deal for young workers," or that social security will return "less than half" as much as would be returned by private insurance. A recent series of newspaper articles written by Warren Shore of the staff of *Chicago Today* appeared in many newspapers throughout the country in June 1974, repeating many of the above statements.[36] Mr. Shore made such statements as Social Security can "wipe out your chances for a secure future," that Social Security "is steadily tearing down" the financial future of the young worker; that "Social Security has not done any of what it set out to do," that the system now takes so much out of a paycheck that "saving is discouraged;" and many other similar statements.

Some of the criticisms have at least some foundation in fact, such as the criticism that retirement benefits may be lost between ages 65 and 72 because of income from employment or self-employment. This argument was discussed in an earlier section. If all are to receive benefits beginning at age 65 or earlier, tax collections will have to be adjusted upward. Actuaries can compute the required tax adjustments. Mr. Shore's criticism at this point would result in higher taxes on younger workers. Another criticism turns on the fact that workers with incomes equal to the maximum taxable amount pay as much in social security taxes as do upper income groups. As Brittain and others have noted, this inequality can be corrected by greatly increasing the taxes on upper income groups, or by a subsidy to the system paid out of general revenues.

Other statements made by Shore appear to be without substantiation. Statements to the effect that private insurers could offer much better benefits are allegations without facts. No private insurance company today returns benefits in the same ratio to cost as does Social Security. Administrative and selling costs in private insurance are consistently higher than in Social Security. Sometimes critics of Social Security seem to forget that current Social Security taxes are used to pay many benefits besides retirement, to wit: payments to dependents; to survivors and their dependents; to the disabled and their dependents and survivors; and "Part A" Medicare benefits.

[36]See for instance *The Dallas Morning News*, June 9-13, 1974.

Statements to the effect that Social Security is a "bad deal" for the young also ignore the fact that if the young were not paying Social Security taxes — that is, if there were no Social Security system, the young would have to be providing support for their aged parents and grandparents. Otherwise the aged would be in abject poverty, as was indeed the case before OASDHI existed. The young can of course expect that when they reach retirement age others younger than they will be paying Social Security taxes to finance their benefits. Only if the system were abolished would the young currently paying taxes fail to get future benefits. But the abolition of the system is for political purposes highly unlikely. No political party dares to suggest the termination of the system, and this fact alone guarantees future benefits.

Summary

The old-age and survivors insurance system pays benefits graduated according to previous earnings, but weighted in favor of low income groups. Additional benefits are paid to dependents and survivors. The trend has been to cover more people and to pay higher benefits, although benefits alone still do not provide an adequate level of living.

Benefits are based on the worker's average monthly wage. A formula or table is used to convert the average monthly wage to a primary insurance amount, which is the basic amount paid to a worker who retires at age 65. If he retires earlier he must take a reduced amount. Dependents and survivors benefits are based on the primary insurance amount.

Payroll taxes on both employers and employees have been used to finance the system since its inception. These taxes have been very productive of revenue, but they have been criticized by many because they are regressive, falling most heavily on low income workers.

Although the trust fund appears to be large, it is far short of an actuarial reserve. Recent analysis indicates that the trust fund may soon begin to contract and eventually be exhausted. For this reason, and also because the payroll taxes are regressive, many economists have suggested that the government pay a subsidy to the system out of the general revenues. Such a subsidy would reduce the regressivity of the total tax structure and also help to avoid a future deficit in the trust fund.

Bibliography (Chapters 5 and 6)

Altmeyer, Arthur, *Formative Years of Social Security* (Madison, University of Wisconsin Press, 1966).

Brennan, Michael, Taft, Philip, and Schupak, Mark, *The Economics of Age* (New York, Norton, 1967).

Burns, Eveline M., *Social Security and Public Policy* (New York, McGraw-Hill, 1956).

Haber, William, and Cohen, Wilbur J., eds., *Social Security: Programs, Problems, and Policies* (Homewood, Ill., Irwin, 1960).

Harris, Seymour, *The Economics of Social Security* (New York, McGraw-Hill, 1941).

Hogan, John D., and Ianni, Francis A. J., *American Social Legislation* (New York, Harper, 1956).

Jenkins, Shirley, Ed., *Social Security in International Perspective; essays in honor of Eveline M. Burns* (New York, Columbia University Press, 1969).

Kreps, Juanita, *Lifetime Allocations of Work and Income: Essays in the Economics of Aging* (Durham, North Carolina, Duke University Press, 1971).

Meriam, Lewis, *Relief and Social Security* (Washington, Brookings Institution, 1946).

Pechman, Joseph A., Aaron, Henry J., and Taussig, Michael K., *Social Security Perspectives for Reform* (Washington, Brookings Institution, 1968).

Turnbull, John G., Williams, C. Arthur, Jr., Cheit, Earl F., *Economic and Social Security* (New York, Harper, 1956).

Wilcox, Clair, *Toward Social Welfare* (Homewood, Illinois, Irwin, 1969).

Witte, Edwin E., *Social Security Perspectives* (Madison, University of Wisconsin Press, 1962).

Witte, Edwin E., *The Development of the Social Security Act* (Madison, University of Wisconsin Press, 1962).

CHAPTER 7

PUBLIC ASSISTANCE: AID
TO FAMILIES WITH
DEPENDENT CHILDREN

Public assistance programs are discussed in Chapters 7 and 8. Chapter 7 discusses the role and function of public assistance programs and gives a brief general overview of public assistance in the United States as it existed before the enactment of Supplemental Security Income. It then deals with the Aid to Families with Dependent Children (AFDC) program and with the difficulties and controversies associated with this program. Chapter 8 deals with the Supplemental Security Income program, general assistance and the food programs.

The role of public assistance and the relation between social insurance and public assistance were noted by the 1971 Advisory Council on Social Security in the following passage:[1]

The Council recognizes the widespread agreement that social insurance is preferable to public assistance as a method of income maintenance, and the Council fully concurs in that agreement. The preference for social insurance, though, has led to strong pressures to have it assume an increasingly larger role in income maintenance by providing substantial benefits, regardless of the extent to which the insured worker was covered by the program.

Social insurance cannot and should not be expected to do the whole job of income maintenance. Any program that bases benefit amounts on earnings from work in covered employment and not on the needs of the individual will in some cases require supplementation through public assistance or private means. Responsibility for meeting individual needs in our society continues to remain largely with the individual and with private efforts by him and on his behalf; but to the extent that these efforts and social insurance are inadequate, final responsibility for meeting individual need must rest with public assistance. Assistance is designed to back-stop social insurance programs and private efforts to maintain income when earnings stop. Whenever other measures are insufficient, it is the responsibility of public assistance to assure that people have enough to eat, a place to live, clothes to wear, medical attention, and the other essentials of living.

The Council recognizes that there is a need for a public assistance program

---

[1]"Reports of the 1971 Advisory Council on Social Security," *Social Security Bulletin*, Vol. 34, No. 6 (June 1971), pp. 17-19.

which will allow people to receive payments sufficient to meet their needs and to receive such payments with dignity.

. . . All members of the Council agree, however, that the present public assistance programs require a thorough overhaul in order to improve their adequacy, their equity, and their efficiency.

The Council believes that improvements in public assistance programs will reduce pressures to distort the contributory social insurance program. An adequate public assistance program would make it unnecessary for social security to perform functions that are not appropriate to a wage-related program. . . .

Two major differences exist between public assistance and social insurance. In the case of public assistance, *need* must be shown to qualify for benefits, but social insurance benefits are paid as a matter of right to eligible workers. Second, public assistance is *financed by general revenues*, either by the federal government alone, or on a matching basis with the states, or by state and local general revenues, whereas social insurance programs are usually financed by payroll taxes on both employers and employees.

Prior to the enactment of the Supplemental Security Income program in 1972, several separate federal-state categorical assistance programs existed. These had been provided for by the Social Security Act of 1935 and included Old Age Assistance (OAA), Aid to the Blind (AB), Aid to Families with Dependent Children (AFDC), and Aid to the Permanently and Totally Disabled (APTD), which was added by amendment in 1950. OAA, AB, and APTD have been replaced by the Supplemental Security Income program. AFDC still exists as a separate categorical federal-state program. In addition General Assistance (GA), a lineal descendant of the old Elizabethan Poor Law, still exists in a majority of states. Medical Assistance, commonly called Medicaid, is actually an assistance program, but discussion of it is deferred to one of the chapters on health.

Table 7-1 shows the number of recipients of the various assistance programs and the average monthly payment for each program in selected years. Table 7-2 shows total annual expenditures for the same years. As may be seen, general assistance and old-age assistance were once the largest programs, but now AFDC is by far the largest. In 1973, nearly 11 million persons, or about 74% of all public assistance recipients, received AFDC payments. Average monthly payments to AFDC recipients are, however, the smallest of the public assistance programs. Of total expenditures in 1973, about 63% went to AFDC recipients, about 15% went to the needy aged, and about 14% went to the disabled. In 1972, effective in 1974, Congress enacted a new program called Supplemental Security Income (SSI) which replaced the adult assistance programs (OAA, AB, and APTD). In addition, there have been many proposals to alter or replace AFDC, so a thorough examination of this program is in order.

TABLE 7-1
PUBLIC ASSISTANCE: NUMBER OF RECIPIENTS AND AVERAGE MONTHLY PAYMENTS, SELECTED YEARS
Number of Recipients (Thousands)

Year	Old-Age Assistance	Aid to the Blind	Aid to the Permanently and Totally Disabled	Aid to Families With Dependent Children	General Assistance[1]
December:					
1940	2,070	73		1,222	3,618
1950	2,786	98	69	2,233	866
1955	2,538	104	241	2,192	743
1960	2,305	107	369	3,073	1,244
1965	2,087	85	557	4,396	677
1970	2,082	81	935	9,659	1,056
1971	2,024	80	1,068	10,653	982
1972	1,934	80	1,168	11,065	864
1973	1,820	78	1,275	10,814	708
Average Monthly Payment: Per Recipient					
1940	$20.25	$ 25.35		$ 9.85	$ 8.30
1950	43.05	46.00	$ 44.10	20.85	22.25
1955	50.05	55.55	48.75	23.50	23.30
1960	58.90	67.45	56.15	22.35	24.85
1965	63.10	81.35	66.50	32.85	31.65
1970	77.65	104.35	97.65	49.65	57.85
1971	77.50	106.50	102.25	52.30	64.80
1972	80.00	112.85	106.10	53.95	72.20
1973	76.16	112.00	109.73	56.95	79.75

[1]Data incomplete

Source: *Social Security Bulletin*, Vol. 37, No. 6 (June 1974), Table M-25.

TABLE 7-2

PUBLIC ASSISTANCE: TOTAL PAYMENTS
(in millions of dollars)

Year	Total	Old Age Assistance	Aid to the Blind	Aid to the Permanently and Totally Disabled	Aid to Families With Dependent Children	General Assistance[1]
1940	$ 1,020	$ 472	$ 22	$ —	$ 133	$392
1950	2,354	1,454	53	8	547	293
1955	2,517	1,488	68	135	612	214
1960	3,263	1,626	86	236	994	320
1965	3,996	1,594	77	417	1,644	261
1970	8,429	1,866	97	976	4,857	632
1971	10,197	1,919	101	1,185	6,230	761
1972	11,152	1,894	105	1,393	7,020	741
1973	11,357	1,743	104	1,610	7,211	688

[1]Data incomplete.

Source: *Social Security Bulletin*, Vol. 3, No. 6 (June 1974), Table M-26.

AID TO FAMILIES WITH DEPENDENT CHILDREN (AFDC)

HISTORY AND EVOLUTION OF AFDC

"Mother's Aid" laws were first enacted in Missouri and Illinois in 1911. As originally conceived such laws were intended to help a widowed mother care for her dependent children. The idea was to keep the family together if possible, and to reduce the number of children placed in orphan's homes. Over the years a few more states enacted such programs but with the coming of the Great Depression most states and localities neared bankruptcy. Accordingly when the Social Security Act was passed in 1935 a system of matching grants to the states was instituted. The program was called Aid to Dependent Children, since the payments were normally made on behalf of the children and not to adults. Later, the law was amended to provide for matching grants to the needy adult caring for the children, and within a few years the name of the program became Aid to Families with Dependent Children.

With the passage of time the program was expanded to cover children whose dependency was due to the incapacity or disability of one or both parents, and also to include dependent children in families where the father was absent from the home due to divorce, separation, desertion, or imprisonment, and where the father was unknown. In 1961 the program was further extended to include children of parents who were unemployed, but only 24 states and the District of Columbia have elected to pay benefits to unemployed parents. Today AFDC is predominately a program to care for dependent children whose father is absent from the home. In Table 7-3 it will be seen that cases where the father is dead make up only a little over 4% of the total. The father was incapacitated in about 10% of the cases, and unemployed in another 6%. Absence of the father from the home accounted for 76% of the cases in 1971. Table 7-4 shows AFDC families by status of the mother.

The evolution in the nature of AFDC is due to a number of factors. Two of the reasons seem beneficial. The percentage of orphans has declined because the proportion of fathers who die while their children are young has declined remarkably in the past 60 years. Improved medical care and nutrition have significantly reduced the percentages of "half" and "full" orphans. Another factor is the OASDHI program. In December, 1973, 2,912,000 children of deceased workers, 1,161,000 children of disabled workers, and 614,000 children of retired workers were drawing such benefits. In the same month 548,000 widowed mothers under age 60 were drawing OASDHI benefits. Were it not for the OASDHI program many of these would be on AFDC, or in cases where the family has been awarded AFDC to supplement small social security benefits, the AFDC would

TABLE 7-3

AFDC FAMILIES, BY STATUS OF THE FATHER WITH RESPECT TO THE FAMILY, 1971

Status of the Father	Percent of Families	
Dead	4.3%	
Incapacitated	9.8	
Unemployed or Employed Part Time	6.1	
Enrolled in work or training program		2.2
Awaiting enrollment after referral to WIN		1.2
Neither enrolled nor awaiting enrollment		2.7
Absent from the Home:	76.2	
Divorced		14.2
Legally separated		2.9
Separated without court decree		12.9
Deserted		15.2
Not married to mother		27.7
In prison		2.1
Other reasons		1.2
Other Status:	3.6	
Step-father case		2.6
Children deprived of support or care of mother		0.9
Unknown		0.1
Total	100.0	

Source: U.S. Department of Health, Education, and Welfare, *Findings of the 1971 AFDC Study, Part I. Demographic and Program Characteristics*, Table 15.

TABLE 7-4

AFDC FAMILIES, BY STATUS OF THE MOTHER, 1971

Status of the Mother		*Percent*
Mother in the home	92.8	
Employed: full-time		8.3%
part-time		5.6
Enrolled in work or training program		4.1
Awaiting enrollment after referral to WIN		2.2
Physically or mentally incapacitated		11.3
No marketable skills or suitable employment not available		7.6
Needed in home full-time time as home-maker		37.1
Actively seeking work		5.3
Not actively seeking work		11.3
Mother not in the home	7.0	
Dead		1.9
Deserted		2.9
In mental institution		0.2
In other medical institution		0.1
Absent for another reason		1.9
Unknown	0.1	
Total	99.9	

Source: U.S. Department of Health, Education, and Welfare, *Findings of the 1971 AFDC Study, Part I. Demographic and Program Characteristics*, NCSS Report AFDC-1, December 1971, Table 21.

need to be larger. So the decline in percentage of orphans drawing AFDC is partly due to favorable changes.

The larger percentages drawing AFDC because the father is absent from the home can hardly be said to be favorable. Divorce, desertion, separation, and illegitimacy rates are higher than 40 years ago and this seems to account for part of the rise in AFDC rates. This has led to severe criticism of the program. It is said that the program is making family instability and illegitimacy more likely and is in fact subsidizing them. This may not be true, but it is widely believed. Even if it is so, a social dilemma exists. The children involved are in no way at fault. Society can hardly stand by without helping its needy future citizens no matter what the conduct of the parents involved. Many proposals have been made in this regard but all of them involve severe economic or social costs.

Another criticism is of a racist nature. In 1971, 45.4% of the recipient children were white, while 45.6% were black. Yet blacks make up only about 11% of the total population. Critics then attribute the cost of the AFDC program to the instability of the Negro family, or to the improvidence of Negro fathers, or other worse remarks. But such critics appear to forget much of American history, and that it is in the public interest to eliminate discrimination against Negroes in education, jobs, housing, and other aspects of social life. The real villain in this situation appears to be not the AFDC program, but past and present discrimination against minority groups which creates the situation in which these groups need more help.

RECENT RAPID GROWTH OF AFDC

The recent rapid growth of AFDC has added to the criticisms. AFDC now has about 11 million recipients, including about 8 million children and 3 million adults. Between 1968 and 1972, the AFDC rolls shot upward. In 1969 over 1 million, in 1970 over 2 million, and in 1971 another 1 million new recipients were added to the program. In 1972 growth slowed to about 400,000 new recipients, while in 1973 and 1974 the number of recipients declined slightly. Dollar expenditures rose correspondingly. Whereas the program cost approximately $1 billion in 1960, total expenditures exceeded $7.9 billion in 1974.

There are a number of explanations why AFDC has grown. Although the birth rate has declined in recent years, there has been a substantial increase in the total number of families and of children in the population. Also, as noted above, there has been an increase in the proportion of families headed by women and in the rate of illegitimacy. The change in eligibility rules permitting families with an unemployed father to qualify caused a minor expansion in the rolls. Others have attributed the large increase mainly to the large migration from the South to the North where welfare programs are more accessible.[2]

There have been several U. S. Supreme Court decisions which have removed obstacles to eligibility to benefits.[3] Three of these cases seem especially significant. In 1968 in *King v. Smith* (392 U.S. 309) the court struck down the "man-in-the-house" rule under which many states had denied benefits. In 1969 in *Shapiro v. Thompson* (394 U.S. 618) the court declared unconstitutional any state durational residence requirements. And in 1971, in *Graham v. Richardson* (403 U.S. 365), the court ruled out a state plan requiring citizenship in the United States or a period of years' residence as an alternative. Previously, many states had had a one-year residence requirement. Now a family must ordinarily establish residence, but no time interval need elapse before they become eligible for benefits. In a similar ruling, not directly involving AFDC, the Supreme Court in February 1974 struck down Arizona's one-year residency requirement for indigent medical and hospital care.

Some also credit (or blame) the National Welfare Rights Organization (NWRO) for the expansion of the numbers on AFDC. This group functions somewhat in the fashion of a labor union in behalf of welfare clients. Its leader, George Wiley, has borrowed many of the tactics which were successful for Samuel Gompers, founder of the AF of L. Instead of dissipating their efforts in seeking a wide range of goals, they have concentrated on getting more welfare benefits, now. While they have not been particularly effective as a lobbying group, they have been effective on a local level, especially in large cities. Many times poor people are unaware of their rights or do not know how to cope with the welfare bureaucracy in the local office. The NWRO has served as an effective intercessor. While their total membership is only a tiny fraction of the welfare population, they are well-organized and single-minded. Their 1968 activities in New York City may be taken as an illustration. New York's rules already provided for special grants to welfare recipients for certain standard nonrecurring needs, such as household equipment, but this provision was almost never called to the attention of clients. The NWRO began to alert clients to their rights which led to an escalation in demands for special grants. Large additional sums had to be paid out "to make the power structure live by their own rules."[4] While taxpayers may resent even the existence of an organization of welfare clients, virtually every interest group in the United States has its own association or union.

[2]Edward V. Sparer, in a joint statement on behalf of the Columbia University School of Social Work, Mobilization for Youth, and Project on Social Welfare Law of New York University School of Law, *Social Security Amendments of 1967*, Hearings before the Committee on Finance, U. S. Senate, 90th Congress, 1st Session, on H.R. 12080, Part 3 (Sept. 20-26, 1967), pp. 1761-1771.

[3]Irene Lurie, "Legislative, Administrative, and Judicial changes in the AFDC program, 1967-71," *Studies in Public Welfare, Paper No. 5 (Part 2), Issues in Welfare Administration: Intergovernmental Relationships, Joint Economic Committee*, 93d Congress, 1st Session, pp. 69-108. See especially pp. 104-107.

[4]Gilbert Y. Steiner, *The State of Welfare* (Washington, D.C., The Brookings Institution, 1971). See especially his Chapter 8, "Organizing Welfare Clients," pp. 280-313.

None can deny the right to insist on adherence to existing law. Their tactics have generally been those of non-violent confrontation, peaceful picketing and publicity, and education of welfare people as to their rights under the law. Accordingly, the success of this group must be considered one of the factors related to the rapid expansion of AFDC rolls and costs.

AFDC BENEFITS FOR UNEMPLOYED FATHERS

In 1961 a new approach was taken to the problem of the deserting father. Previously, some states had made elaborate efforts to find deserting fathers and force them to support their families. Efforts of this type, however, often turned out to be more expensive than AFDC payments to the family, and enthusiasm for this approach waned when this fact became apparent. Other critics charged that part of the problem of desertion was due to certain provisions in the AFDC program itself. To be eligible for AFDC, it was required originally that the father either not be present or be ill. Under such an arrangement a premium was placed upon the father deserting. Much criticism has been directed at circumstances in which the father supposedly separates from the mother but continues to remain at home, or comes home at odd hours when the social worker will not find him. If aid could be given to families in which the father is unemployed or earns only small amounts, he would be less inclined to desert. In May, 1961, the Social Security Act was amended to provide that families with unemployed fathers could become eligible for AFDC payments. This came to be known as AFDC-U, the U representing unemployed father. Unfortunately, only 24 states and the District of Columbia implemented this amendment. Suggestions that Congress make this provision mandatory on the states have not prevailed. Even for those states covering unemployed fathers, state definitions of unemployment have varied so much that coverage has varied also. To provide more uniformity in coverage, the 1967 amendments gave a more precise definition of unemployment which, in several respects, narrowed coverage considerably. An unemployed father may not be covered under AFDC in any month in which unemployment compensation is received, regardless of whether the unemployment compensation is substantially less than the AFDC payment. Also, the unemployed father must have worked at least 6 of 13 quarters ending within one year before the application for aid. Since coverage of unemployed fathers under AFDC is so small, we may conclude that the welfare laws still place a premium on the desertion of the father. In addition, some fathers, even though employed, earn so little that they, too, can increase their family income via AFDC benefits through desertion. How much desertion actually occurs because of the lack of benefits for the unemployed is difficult to say, since motives for desertion tend to be complex.

EFFORTS TO SLOW THE GROWTH OF AFDC

STATE EFFORTS

The non-welfare public is periodically much exercised about the "welfare problem," meaning especially the rapid growth of AFDC. Accordingly, state legislatures and the Congress in virtually every session consider, and sometimes enact, new amendments, intended, usually without success, to slow the growth of AFDC. State efforts sometimes take the form of restrictive or punitive rules designed to keep people off the AFDC rolls whether they are needy or not. State law or state or local officials may decide that some are ineligible because of "deviant behavior," thus imposing their own standards of behavior on others. A wide variety of such state or local practices have existed in the past, many of them of doubtful legality.[5]

Sometimes states, when they find themselves short of funds, reduce the benefits of all recipients by some percentage or dollar amount. Other state practices in the past have included a total stoppage of welfare payments during months when various fruits or vegetables were ready to be harvested. Some states have attempted to deny benefits to alcoholics or drug addicts, and to others convicted of various crimes. The dilemma obviously is that while society may not approve of the behavior of parents, the children are innocent victims and cutting off benefits to such families tends to punish the children more than it does the parents.

FEDERAL EFFORTS

The federal government, as guided by legislation enacted by Congress, has endeavored to slow the growth of AFDC by somewhat more enlightened methods. These include the social service and rehabilitation approach of 1962, the work and training emphasis in 1967, the "welfare freeze" of the same year, the "day-care" approach in recent years, and other amendments.

The Public Welfare Amendments of 1962 embodied the attempt to shift the emphasis from cash benefits to rehabilitation and social services. Where previous law had provided 50% federal financing, the new law authorized 75% federal financing of state social service activities. The law also specified that no AFDC case worker was to have more than 60 cases. The idea was that skilled, intensive, personal case work with a limited number of families could transform the recipient into a productive, self-supporting, taxpaying member of society. To reflect the new emphasis the federal agency in charge of public assistance became the Social and

---

[5]See for instance the statement of Edward V. Sparer, op. cit., p. 1767.

Rehabilitation Service. Unfortunately, however, the trained personnel to effectively carry out the intent of the law simply did not exist. The most highly trained social workers often work for private agencies where salaries are higher. States often must rely on whomever they can find, trained or untrained. One state, Mississippi, actually dropped its social services in AFDC after 1965 because the 60 case-worker rule was adding to the states' costs even though the state received 75% federal funds. In other states the program was carried out by a "constantly shifting group of untrained workers."[6] The social service approach cannot be said to have failed; it is more accurate to say that it never had a fair test. Winifred Bell and others offered evidence in 1962 of situations in which the added costs of intensive social work were more than offset by the reductions in the welfare rolls, so that money was actually saved.[7] In one of the projects the added costs came to $124,000 and the savings from removing families from the rolls were $256,000. Unfortunately, however, limited local successes were overwhelmed by large increases in the welfare rolls elsewhere.

Disappointment with the lack of statistical evidence of reduction of the AFDC rolls as the results of the 1962 amendments led Congress to try again in 1967. This involved more attention to the "day-care" idea, new emphasis on work and training projects, some attempts to reduce the disincentive to work, and the "welfare freeze." The welfare freeze embodied in the 1967 amendments can be disposed of briefly. Congress imposed an upper limit on the extent of federal matching for AFDC cases attributable to desertion or illegitimacy. Using January, 1967, as a base, no increase in the proportion of children under age 21 receiving AFDC because of the absence of the parent from the home was to be allowed. The freeze never actually went into effect. Both Presidents Johnson and Nixon agreed to delay its imposition, and in 1969 Congress repealed the freeze. A storm of opposition had greeted the freeze idea. Had it gone into effect it would have had the effect of punishing helpless deserted and illegitimate children, or it would have required a large increase in expenditures by the states which the states felt they could not bear. Some members of Congress later admitted they had not realized the extent to which the freeze would have imposed an intolerable burden on state budgets.[8]

The work and training provisions of the 1967 amendments required all states to set up work and training programs for welfare recipients by July 1, 1969. State welfare agencies were directed to determine which

[6]Steiner, op. cit. See especially Chapter 2, "Tireless Tinkering with Dependent Families," pp. 31-74.

[7]Winifred Bell, "The Practical Value of Social Work Services: Preliminary Report on 10 Demonstration Projects in Public Assistance," reported in Public Welfare Amendments of 1962, Hearings before the Committee on Ways and Means, House of Representatives, 87th Congress, 2nd Session, on H.R. 10032 (February 7-13, 1962), pp. 410-415.

[8]Steiner, op. cit., pp. 44-50.

people were appropriate for referral to the program. These may not include (1) children under age 16 or going to school; (2) any person with illness, incapacity, advanced age, or remoteness from a project; or (3) persons whose continued presence in the home is required because of the illness or incapacity of another member of the household. All other persons are referred to the nearest Department of Labor public employment office. These offices are directed to move as many as possible directly into employment. This assumes that job openings are available and that the referee has a useable skill. If there is no job, and no marketable skill, training is the next recourse. All those found suitable receive training appropriate to their needs, and payments of up to $30 per month above their regular welfare payments are made. These features caused the program to be called the work-incentive program (WIN). If there is no job, and if the person is not deemed suitable for training, the employment office is directed to make arrangements for special public works projects with public agencies or nonprofit private agencies.

The degree of success of the WIN program relative to the size of AFDC appears to be small. Though expanding, the largest annual first time enrollment through fiscal year 1972 was 121,000.[9] Successful completers, that is persons who were employed three to six months after being placed, have ranged from 20% to 30%. Dropouts from WIN without good cause average 21% of terminees.[10] Results of the program are sensitive to cyclical economic conditions.

Overall, WIN has so far been a small program relative to the size of AFDC, and what success WIN has had has been more than overwhelmed by the rapid rise of the AFDC rolls. But disappointment with WIN is very closely related to what people expected of it at the outset. Those who expected that all AFDC mothers would be put to work were obviously grossly unrealistic and doomed to disappointment from the first. Those who were aware of the complexities of the problems of AFDC families, of ill health, mental difficulties, lack of skills, lack of education and the like, and aware of the problems of appropriate manpower training were not disappointed. They tended to look upon WIN as a worthwhile program.

Another major effort of the 1967 amendments was the renewed attention to day-care facilities. If welfare mothers are to go to work or be trained for work, provisions of some sort must be made for the care of their preschool age children, and in many cases, depending on working hours, for older children before or after school. The 1962 amendments had authorized some funds for day-care facilities, but not much emphasis was

[9]U. S. Department of Labor, *Manpower Report of the President*, March 1973, Table F-1, p. 227.

[10]For additional data on difficulties with the WIN program, see *Studies in Public Welfare, Paper No. 3, The Effectiveness of Manpower Training Programs: A Review of Research on the Impact on the Poor,* Joint Economic Committee, 92nd Congress, 2d Session, November 20, 1972, pp. 6-8 and 50-56.

then placed on day-care, and very little federal money was ever appropriated under the 1962 authorization. In 1967 Congress again turned its attention to day-care, and in 1969 President Nixon proposed an escalated day-care effort. Adequate day-care is an obvious corollary of a work and training program for AFDC mothers, but there are many difficulties and controversies, especially involving the high cost of day-care.

The 1967 amendments also endeavored to reduce the disincentive effects of AFDC payments. There had been much criticism of the method of determining family need, especially the treatment of earned income. If the state reduced the assistance payment by $1 for each $1 of additional earned income, it was in effect applying a tax rate of 100% on income from working. Previous law had permitted the states to disregard small amounts of earned income in determining need. The new amendments required the states to disregard all earned income of any child receiving AFDC if the person is a full-time student or a part-time student who is not a full-time employee. Most important, however, was the further requirement that the state must disregard the first $30 plus one-third of the remainder of total monthly earned income of all other individuals whose needs are included in determining the family assistance payment. This was an improvement over the previous 100% tax on work income, but after the first $30 per month it is still a "tax" of 66 2/3% on additional income from working. Only welfare people and the extremely wealthy are subjected to such tax rates.

ILLEGITIMACY AND AFDC

The family is perhaps society's most basic institution and any threat to its stability is widely viewed with alarm. Rising rates of illegitimacy and any tendency by the AFDC program to encourage illegitimacy cause deep concern among much of the general population. Critics commonly charge that AFDC causes illegitimacy and family break-ups. As noted in Table 7-3 the 1971 study found that in 28 percent of the families the father was "not married to the mother." This was about the same percentage found in the 1969 study and about 1% point higher than found by the 1967 study. A 1960 study by the Bureau of Public Assistance found that the rate of illegitimacy was rising; that the rate was higher among women in their twenties than among teen-agers; that among non-whites the rate was ten times that among whites; that the rate was higher in southern states than elsewhere; and was highest in the large cities. The study listed four causes of increased illegitimacy: (1) failure to integrate nonwhite and other groups into the accepted American culture pattern; (2) increasing premarital relations; (3) changing patterns of life due to threat of war and annihilation, the practice of going steady, more employment of women, and the increasing mobility in life; and (4) improvement in health which permits more women to have children.[11]

Evidence in that study and in subsequent studies throws doubt on the proposition that women have illegitimate children simply to draw AFDC benefits. In 1960 only 13 percent of illegitimate children were drawing such benefits. Many of the AFDC mothers were working, usually in jobs with low pay, which indicates that they did not have illegitimate children simply to withdraw from the work force. Most families did not and do not remain on the AFDC rolls for long periods of time. In the 1971 study, 68% of the families had been on AFDC less than three years, and only 6% had been on the rolls 10 years or more. Also, 57% of AFDC families have no illegitimate children; 22% have one; 10% have two; 5% have three; and only 6% have four or more.[12] In view of the relatively small benefits and the added responsibility of more children requiring low income to be spread thinner, the 1960 study concluded it was highly doubtful that AFDC encouraged women to have illegitimate children. Later data showed that during the time families are on AFDC, the incidence of illegitimacy is less than that of the general public.

All sorts of suggestions have been advanced for attempting to reduce illegitimacy among AFDC mothers. Some have suggested that the mother be required to submit to compulsory sterilization in order to qualify for aid. This suggestion is usually dismissed as cruel, inhumane, and probably unconstitutional. Another common proposal is to exclude some illegitimate children from the program, particularly if they are second or additional illegitimate children. Some states have passed such laws, but they have been either vetoed by the governor or declared unconstitutional. The Social Security Administration has threatened the state with loss of federal financial participation in the program on the grounds that such a law would contravene the rights of persons to equal protection of the law under the Fourteenth Amendment to the Constitution. By this action, the federal government is not condoning immorality; it is simply insisting that children in need be provided for regardless of whether they are born in or out of wedlock. To deny aid on such grounds would simply punish an already disadvantaged child for the shortcomings of the parents.

A third suggestion is that aid be denied on the basis of the "unsuitability of the home." Such a criterion is not used in the Social Security Act, but, in 1971, 18 states required "that the home be suitable" or similar wording. A few of the states have simply denied assistance without any assurance that a plan is being worked out for a suitable upbringing of the child. In other states attempts are made to improve the home, and as a last

[11]Illegitimacy and Its Impact on the Aid to Dependent Children Program, U. S. Department of Health, Education and Welfare, Bureau of Public Assistance, 1960, pp. 1-82.

[12]Findings of the 1971 AFDC Study, Part I, Demographic and Program Characteristics, U. S. Department of Health, Education and Welfare, NCSS Report AFDC-1, December 22, 1971, Tables 12 and 32.

resort some provide for court authority to remove the child from the home. Removal of very many illegitimate children from their mother would be expensive to implement. Lack of sufficient adoptive parents for nonwhite children would make the construction of a large number of institutions for children necessary.

Another suggestion that has aroused controversy is that public aid funds be used to pay for birth control information and devices desired by clients. In 1967 the Social Security amendments required states to offer family planning services on a voluntary basis to all appropriate AFDC recipients. Proponents argue that extensive family planning services will result in fewer illegitimate children. Opponents, on the other hand, argue that promiscuity will be encouraged. Catholic groups have opposed the measure on the ground that it is a deviation from previous governmental neutrality on birth control. A more extensive change occured with the U. S. Supreme Court decision in January, 1973 (*Jane Roe v. Henry Wade*), setting aside virtually all state laws forbidding abortion.[13] Catholic and some Protestant groups are also opposed to this decision. Whether or not birth control information, the pill and other devices, or the legalization of abortion have noticeable effect on the number of children on AFDC remains to be seen. In recent years the national birth rate has declined sharply, but this may be due to economic or other motives, and the impact of the declining birthrate on AFDC is not yet clear.

The law and the public attitude toward the illegitimate child are becoming more sympathetic. For many centuries English and American law of bastardy restricted the rights of the illegitimate child. Originally the bastard was nobody's son, not even his mother's. The bastard had no right of inheritance, and few other rights. In 1576, English law required the parents to support their bastard children, but the motive was not so much to benefit the child as to relieve the state of the welfare burden. In recent years the term "bastard" has gradually been supplanted by "illegitimate" or "child born out of wedlock." Many European countries and some Latin American countries now grant substantially equal rights to illegitimate children. Some states in the United States, among them Arizona and Oregon, have abolished the concept of illegitimacy, and others have moved toward equality.[14] In 1968, the U. S. Supreme Court held that discrimination on the basis of illegitimacy is unconstitutional.[15]

CURRENT AFDC PROGRAM DATA

Table 7-5 shows the range of average cash payments per family and per recipient in July 1973. Family payments ranged from a low of $52.49 in

13*New York Times,* January 23, 1973, pp. 1 and 20.
14Harry D. Krause, "Why Bastard, Wherefore Base?" *The Annals of The American Academy of Political and Social Science,* Vol. 383 (May, 1969), pp. 8-70.
15*Levy v. Louisiana,* 391 U.S. 68 (1968) and *Glona v. American Guarantee & Liability Insurance Co.,* 391 U.S. 73 (1968).

Mississippi to a high of $286.22 in New York. Generally most southern and some midwestern states pay below average benefits, while most eastern, northern and far-western states pay above average benefits. On a per recipient basis, payments averaged $53.98 for the whole United States, substantially less than for the adult category programs (OAA, AB, APTD). These figures reflect the belief that children need less than do adults, which in turn is reflected in the federal formula for AFDC recipients. The government pays $15 of the first $18 of the average monthly payment per recipient and 50 to 65% of the next $14, depending on the state's per capita income. If this formula is used, the state must pay all of any amount above $32 per month. Instead of this formula, states may elect to use the "federal medical assistance formula" which ranges from 50% to 83%, depending on the state's per capita income. The latter formula was used by 33 states in 1971.

TABLE 7-5

AFDC AVERAGE CASH PAYMENTS, PER FAMILY AND PER RECIPIENT, JULY 1973

Average Per Family:

Average Payment[1]	Number of States	Average Payment[1]	Number of States
Less than $100.00	6	$160.00—$189.99	6
100.00—119.99	6	190.00— 210.99	9
120.00—139.99	8	220.00— 249.99	8
140.00—159.99	7	250.00— 289.99	4

U.S. Average: $187.28

Average Per Recipient:

Average Payment[1]	Number of States	Average Payment[1]	Number of States
Less than $20.00	2	$50.00—$59.99	6
20.00—29.99	4	60.00— 69.99	12
30.00—39.99	11	70.00— 79.99	5
40.00—49.99	12	80.00— 89.99	2

U.S. Average: $53.98

[1]Does not include vendor payments for medical care.
Source: U.S. Department of Health, Education, and Welfare, *Public Assistance Statistics,* July, 1973, NCSS Report A-2, Table 7.

Table 7-6 shows recipient rates for AFDC in the ten highest and ten lowest jurisdictions. As will be seen, the recipient rates are highest in southern states and in states with great urban aggregations. Generally, the plains and mountain states have the lowest recipient rates. High recipient rates tend to reflect high need, an above-average minority group population, and greater effort by some states than others. Low recipient rates reflect the opposite, including in some states a low assistance effort, often taking the form of restrictive provisions in state legislation designed to keep people off the AFDC rolls.

In 1971, three-fourths of AFDC families lived in metropolitan areas. As to race, 48% of the families were white, 43% were black, 6.5% unknown, and 2%, other. The size of AFDC families is decreasing slowly with 54% of the families having only one or two children. Marital breakup (45%) remains the primary reason for absence of the father, and "not married to mother" (28%) is the second most important reason. About 14% of the mothers are working either full time or part time, and 4% were enrolled in a work or training program. Children of the mothers who are working or being trained were cared for as follows: 42% in their own homes, 39% in someone else's home, and 7% in a group care center. Only 3% of AFDC mothers had any college education, and only 19% were high school graduates. Education of the father is mostly unknown, 57%, but only 2.5% are known to have any college education, and only 9% are known to be high school graduates.

Birthplace of the mother gives some indication of migration of the AFDC family. Overall, 52% of recipients were drawing benefits in the state of their birth. About 90% of Mississippi recipient mothers were born in Mississippi, but at the other extreme only 32.5% of California recipient mothers were born in that state. One-third of Illinois' recipient mothers were born in east-south central states; 32% of Maryland's were born in South Atlantic states; and 25% of New York's recipient mothers were born in Puerto Rico. Eighty-one percent of AFDC families had been provided one or more social services during the past one year. As to Department of Agriculture food programs, 53% participated in the food stamp plan and 15% received donated food.[16]

[16]U. S. Department of Health, Education and Welfare, *Findings of the 1971 AFDC Study, Part I. Demographic and Program Characteristics.* See also *Part II. Financial Characteristics,* and *Part III. National Cross-Tabulations; AFDC: Selected Statistical Data on Families Aided and Program Operations,* NCSS Report H-4, June 1971. There are also similar reports on earlier studies conducted by the Department in 1961, 1967, and 1969. The reader is also directed to *Studies in Public Welfare,* a series of papers published by the Subcommittee on Fiscal Policy of the Joint Economic Committee, Joint Committee Print, 93d Congress, 1st and 2d Sessions, 1972 and 1973.

TABLE 7-6

RECIPIENTS OF AFDC MONEY PAYMENTS, TEN JURISDICTIONS WITH HIGHEST, TEN WITH LOWEST RATIOS, JUNE 1973
(per 1000 population)

Ten Highest Jurisdictions		Ten Lowest Jurisdictions	
District of Columbia	141.3	South Dakota	31.7
Puerto Rico	93.8	New Hampshire	30.2
Mississippi	79.7	North Carolina	29.2
Georgia	71.4	Montana	28.7
Louisiana	69.9	Iowa	28.0
Illinois	68.7	Nebraska	25.8
New York	67.2	Idaho	25.5
California	67.1	Nevada	25.4
Maine	66.8	North Dakota	22.9
Michigan	65.0	Wyoming	20.3

U.S. Average 51.7

Source: U.S. Department of Health, Education, and Welfare, *Public Assistance Statistics*, July 1973, NCSS Report A-2, Table 13.

Summary

Public assistance programs serve as a supplement to social insurance programs, such as OASDHI. Since the insurance programs are based on a previous work and earnings record, and since many of the aged, blind, disabled or dependent children will not have and in many cases cannot have a work record, assistance programs of some sort continue to be necessary.

The Aid to Families with Dependent Children program is the largest and most intensely criticized assistance program. Efforts to rehabilitate these families by social services, or to train the adults for gainful employment, have helped, but beneficial effects from these efforts tend to be obscured by the continued rise in numbers of AFDC recipients. Many proposals continue to be made for drastic changes in AFDC.

CHAPTER 8

PUBLIC ASSISTANCE: SUPPLEMENTAL SECURITY INCOME AND THE FOOD PROGRAMS

OLD AGE ASSISTANCE

The federal-state Old Age Assistance program paid cash benefits to needy persons aged 65 and over. The program was administered by each state separately but was financed on a matching basis, with a majority of the funds coming from the federal government. In 1973 the federal payment was $31 of the first $37, and 50% to 65% of the next $38, depending on the state's per capita income. If a state desired to pay larger benefits, it must pay all of any amount above $75 per month. States, however, were permitted to use an optional formula called the "Federal medical assistance percentage," under which federal funds varied from 50% to 83%, depending on the state's per capita income. Thirty-three states made use of the latter formula in 1973.[1]

Even though weighted in favor of low income states, the formulas still worked a hardship on low income states, since they had a higher percentage of their people on assistance and a lower taxpaying ability. The proportion of people on OAA varied considerably from state to state. For instance, the recipient rate per 1,000 population in June, 1973, was 35.9 in Mississippi, 30.6 in Alabama, and 28.4 in Arkansas, compared to only 2.4 in Maryland, 2.3 in Connecticut, and 2.0 in Utah.[2]

Another difficulty with the program was the wide variation in benefit amounts from one state to another. In June, 1973, payments varied from $52 per month in South Carolina to $171 in New Hampshire.[3] In that month the average payment in the whole United States was about $79 per month, far below the poverty threshold. But about two-thirds of OAA recipients also received at least small benefits from OASDHI. In addition,

---

[1]U. S. Department of Health, Education and Welfare, *Characteristics of State Public Assistance Plans Under the Social Security Act*, Public Assistance Report No. 50, 1971 Edition, p. 134. In this chapter, the programs for the aged, the blind, and the disabled are discussed separately, although in 1973, 19 states operated a combined adult categories program called Aid to the Aged, Blind, and Disabled (OASBD).

[2]U. S. Department of Health, Education and Welfare, *Public Assistance Statistics*, July, 1973, NCSS Report A-2, Table 13.

[3]*Ibid.*, June 1973, Table 4.

they were eligible for either Medicare or Medicaid, and some were also buying food stamps at less than their face value. Yet in 1973, 3.4 million aged persons, or 16.3% of the total aged population, were below the poverty level. Tables 7-1 and 7-2 (previous chapter) show program data for old age assistance.

PUBLIC AND PRIVATE PROGRAMS FOR THE BLIND

Estimates of the number of blind in the United States vary between 292,000[4] and 430,000.[5] In addition there are an estimated 1,240,000 persons who are severely visually handicapped and cannot read newspaper print with the aid of correcting glasses. Of this number, about 1,100,000 were 45 years of age or older.[6]

History records a wide variety of measures to aid the blind, ranging from special state schools, federally subsidized books and apparatus for the blind, and federal and state funds to pay tuition and purchase books and supplies for blind students unable to pay their own way. The blind also are permitted a double exemption on the federal income tax. In addition private groups, such as the Lion's Club, maintain eye banks to make corneal transplants. Under the Randolph-Shepard Act of 1936, as amended, blind persons are authorized to operate vending stands in federal and other buildings. Under the Bankhead Act of 1920, the blind are also eligible for federally subsidized vocational rehabilitation.

AID TO THE BLIND (AB)

The major program for the blind, which covered more blind people than any other program, was the assistance program under the Social Security Act. It was financed by matching federal with state money, using the same formula, or formulas, used under OAA. In August, 1973, about 78,000 recipients received AB payments. Recipient rates were higher in southern states than in the north central or northwestern states, since blindness is more prevalent in the South. The average payment in August was $112.18, but payments varied considerably from state to state.

Since 1962, the blind are aided by amendments exempting certain income in determining eligibility. The 1965 amendments required that a state must disregard the first $85 per month of earned income, plus one-half of all the rest. This requirement amounted to a zero "tax" on their

[4]Kenneth Trouern-Trend, *Blindness in the United States*, National Institute of Neurological Diseases and Blindness, November, 1968, p. 5.

[5]Irving P. Schloss,"Legislation for the Aging," *The New Outlook for the Blind*, Vol. 65, No. 2 (February 1971), pp. 51-55. See also Samuel Finestone, *et. al., Social Casework and Blindness* (New York, American Foundation for the Blind, 1960), p. 147; and Barbara C. Coughlan, "Future Directions of Government Programs," *The New Outlook for the Blind*, Vol. 65, No. 7 (September 1971).

[6]Irving P. Schloss, *op. cit.*

first $85 per month and a 50% "negative income tax" on additional earned income. AB recipients actually have very little other income. In 1970 their total nonassistance income averaged only $45.62 per month, of which only $11.65 came from earnings and $27.11 came from OASDI cash benefits. Only 7% of all AB recipients had any income from earnings, while 34% had income from OASDI. Only 19% participated in the food stamp plan and 13% received donated food. Only 2% of recipients received any payments, direct or indirect, from other programs such as housing or vocational rehabilitation.[7]

AID TO THE PERMANENTLY AND TOTALLY DISABLED (APTD)

The APTD program was enacted to 1950 to supplement the Aid to the Blind program, since it was recognized that there are many forms of disability other than blindness. All states except Nevada had an APTD program in 1973. Annual expenditures in the whole United States were approximately $1.6 billion in 1973, making this the third largest assistance program behind AFDC and OAA.

The general requirements set forth in the Social Security Act for OAA and AB also applied to APTD. The federal contribution formulas were the same. Each state set its own definition of disability. In general, the impairment could be either mental or physical, had to be verified by medical findings, must not be likely to be improved by therapy, and could apply to either a wage earner or a homemaker. The disability determination had to be made by a team of specialists, including a doctor, social worker, and in some states, a vocational rehabilitation counselor. Factors such as age, training, experience, and social setting could be considered in making the disability determination. Some states required that the recipient accept recommended corrective treatment and/or referral to training offered by vocational rehabilitation services before being eligible for assistance.[8]

Like other federal-state assistance programs, the benefits varied widely from state to state. While the United States average in September 1973 was $108.48, benefits ranged from $60 in Louisiana to $181 in Massachusetts. Recipients were also eligible for vendor payments for medical care in addition to these cash benefits.

The U. S. Department of Health, Education, and Welfare, conducted nationwide surveys of the recipients of APTD in 1962 and again in 1970.[9]

[7]U. S. Department of Health, Education and Welfare, *Findings of the 1970 AB Study, Part II, Financial Circumstances, NCSS Report AB-2,* December 1972, Tables 79-102.

[8]U. S. Department of Health, Education and Welfare, *Social Security Programs in the United States,* pp. 102-103.

[9]U. S. Department of Health, Education and Welfare, *Characteristics of Recipients of Aid to the Permanently and Totally Disabled, Findings of the 1962 Survey: State Tables,* June 1964; U. S. Department of Health, Education and Welfare, *1962 Study of APTD Reci-*

Some of the findings of the 1970 study include the following. Fifty-nine percent of the recipients were found to be between age 50 and 65. Sixty-five percent were white, 29% were black. A high proportion, 37%, had never married. Fifty-six percent were living in the state of their birth, and 24% had been born in a southern state but had moved to another state. Fifty-one percent had less than an eighth-grade education, only 9.4% had finished high school, and only 3.2% had any years in college. Ninety percent had not completed a vocational training course. Twenty-eight percent had never been employed and only 1.8% were currently employed, either part time or full time. These statistics may be disconcerting, but they are not surprising, since these people have been found by their respective states to be totally and permanently disabled. More than half of the recipients had two or more disabling conditions.[10]

SUPPLEMENTAL SECURITY INCOME (SSI)

Widespread criticism of the various welfare programs, especially criticism of AFDC, led Congress and the President to consider various other alternative programs. In 1969 and again in 1971, President Nixon proposed a Family Assistance Plan (FAP) to replace AFDC and to include certain of the working poor. His proposal had some of the aspects of a "negative income tax," discussed in the final chapter. Others have proposed alternate types of guaranteed annual incomes, which generally contain negative income tax features as well. The Family Assistance Plan was twice passed by the House of Representatives, but each time failed of enactment in the Senate, where a coalition of conservatives who thought the program went too far and of liberals who thought the program did not go far enough combined to defeat the bill.

Meanwhile Governor Rockefeller of New York, and others, were proposing that all assistance programs be federalized. They argued that this would eliminate many of the problems associated with state administered programs, such as the wide range in benefits from state to state, problems of migration and residency, wide ranges in recipient rates due to harsh legislation or to stringent administration in some states, relative's responsibility laws, property liens and the like. Since the FAP proposal was under active consideration, separate legislation was introduced in 1970 to provide for a new federalized adult categories program covering the aged, the blind, and the disabled. After considerable legislative

pients: *National Cross-Tabulations,* January 1967; and U. S. Department of Health, Education and Welfare, *Findings of the 1970 APTD Study, Part I. Demographic and Program Characteristics NCSS Report APTD-1,* September 1972.

[10]U. S. Department of Health, Education and Welfare, *Findings of the 1970 APTD Study, Part I, Demographic and Program Characteristics,* NCSS Report APTD-1, SEptember 1972, Table 45.

maneuvering, the legislation was enacted by the Congress late in October 1972, and was signed into law by the President as Public Law 92-603.[11]

The new legislation repealed the previously existing federal-state program of aid to the aged, the blind, and the permanently and totally disabled (except in Puerto Rico, the Virgin Islands, and Guam), and established by amendment of Title XVI of the Social Security Act the new program known as the Supplemental Security Income. The law was further amended in the summer of 1973, and in December of 1973, but went into effect as amended on January 1, 1974. It established a basic payment (subject to deductions) of $146 per month for an individual and $219 a month for a couple, generally applicable to all persons previously receiving benefits under OAA, AB, or APTD, and such additional aged, blind, or disabled people that may be found eligible. States were authorized to supplement the federal amounts if they choose to do so, and any state supplementation is disregarded in computing the federal amount.

Eligibility includes the aged 65 or over; the blind with vision no better than 20/200 with correcting lens, or so-called "tunnel" vision, meaning a visual field of 20 degrees or less; and the disabled, meaning those with a mental or physical impairment which prevents the person from doing any substantial work and which is expected to last at least 12 months or result in death. The recipient may be either a U. S. citizen, or an alien lawfully admitted for permanent residence, or aliens who are permanent residents and are lawfully here "under color of law" in accordance with the Immigration and Nationality Act. Inmates of public institutions are not eligible for SSI, except for persons in public or private health facilities who are receiving Medicaid benefits, in which case their SSI payment is reduced. Disabled and blind persons are referred to state agencies for possible rehabilitation, and they must not unreasonably refuse such services. Disabled addicts and alcoholics are referred to appropriate agencies for treatment and are ineligible for payments if they fail to accept such treatment or to comply with the terms and requirements of the treatment. SSI payments are not made directly to the alcoholic or drug addict, but to a representative payee on his behalf.[12]

Resources owned may limit eligibility. An individual with "countable" resources worth more than $1,500, and a couple whose countable resources exceed $2,250, are not eligible. The family home, personal effects, and household goods of a reasonable value are not regarded as countable resources. The portion of the retail value of a car which exceeds $1,200 may be counted, but no part of the value of a car used in transportation to a job or to a place for regular medical treatment is counted. Life insurance policies up to a face value of $1,500 per person are

[11]"Social Security Amendments of 1972: Summary and Legislative History," *op. cit.,* pp. 3-25.

[12]The material in this section is based on Department of Health, Education and Welfare Publication No. (SSA) 74-11015, *Introducing Supplemental Security Income,* November 1973. See also *Supplemental Security Income Program,* Hearings before the Committee on Finance, U. S. Senate, 93d Congress, 1st Session, June 19, 1973.

not counted. Persons whose assets exceed these limits by small amounts will be permitted to sell their assets in order to qualify, but the administration may require the repayment out of the proceeds of the sale of any SSI received pending sale.

Income received from other sources may also limit eligibility. For this purpose certain income is "countable;" certain other income has no affect on SSI payments. Persons who have countable quarterly income of $438 ($146 a month) and couples who have countable quarterly income of $657 ($219 a month) are not eligible. Computations are made on the basis of calendar quarters. If a person is eligible for a payment for a full quarter, the amount is paid in three equal monthly payments.

The following are *not* included in determining countable income: (1) any regular cash payment by a state or locality which is based on need and which is a supplement to SSI, (2) the first $60 per quarter ($20 a month) of earned or unearned income, such as social security benefits, annuities, rent, interest, and the like, (3) the next $195 per quarter ($65 per month) of earned income (wages or earnings from self-employment) plus one-half of the earned income over $195, or over $255 per quarter if there is no unearned income. Miscellaneous other income is not countable, such as: limited earnings of a child attending school; irregular or infrequent earned income of $30 or less in a calendar quarter; irregular or infrequent unearned income of $60 or less in a quarter; or home-grown produce consumed by the individual and his family.

The "tax" rate is thus zero on any supplement based on need paid by the state. It is also zero on the first $20 per month of other unearned income, and zero on the first $65 per month of income from earnings. Above $65 per month the tax rate is 50% on income from earnings. On unearned income such as OASDHI benefits above $20 per month, the tax rate is 100%. This is similar to the previously existing provisions in the Aid to the Blind program, but is an improvement since it now applies to the aged and the disabled.

SSI *payments* are subject to periodic cost-of-living adjustments. Effective in July, 1975, payments to recipients were adjusted upward to a maximum of $473.10 per quarter for an individual, payable in three monthly checks of $157.70. For a couple the quarterly payments were adjusted upward to $709.80, payable in three monthly checks of $236.60. Most recipients who have earned or unearned income will receive less. If, for instance, a single person is receiving an OASDHI payment of $360 per quarter ($120 per month) and no other income of any kind, the first $60 is ignored, so countable income is $300. The basic quarterly amount is $473.10. The countable income of $300 is deducted leaving a remainder of $173.10. The person would then receive a SSI payment of $57.70 per month. His total monthly income would be $120 (OASDHI) plus $57.70 (SSI) or $177.70.

Any state, if it chooses to do so, may pay a supplement over and above the federal SSI payment, and such state supplement is not countable income in figuring SSI so long as it is paid on a regular basis and is based on need. If the state chooses to administer its own supplement it must pay all of its own administrative costs. States, however, may enter into an agreement with the federal government under which the federal government will administer the state supplement. In this case the federal government assumes all the administrative cost and also guarantees the state against any increase in cost over its 1972 expenditures for OAA, AB, and APTD. The objective of these provisions is to encourage, as much as possible, a single national administrative system in place of the "more than 1,150 state and county welfare programs of cash assistance to the needy. . . ."[13]

In addition to the above optional supplementation, amendments enacted during the summer of 1973 require a type of mandatory supplementation by the state. This was designed to protect recipients who were on the rolls in December, 1973, against a reduction in income in January, 1974. In order to be eligible for federal matching funds for Medicaid, each state (except Texas) must agree to maintain the income of its December, 1973, OAA, AB, and APTD recipients at the December 1973 level. If the state chooses, the federal government will administer the mandatory supplementation as well as the optional supplementation. By September 1974, 33 states had chosen to let the federal government administer their supplementary payments, and 18 states had elected state administration. Generally the states with large populations chose federal administration.

Congress put the administration of the new program in the hands of the Social Security Administration, partly because of their very good record in administering OASDHI, but on logical grounds as well. The great majority of people eligible for SSI were already receiving at least small retirement, or survivor, or disability benefits, so the Social Security Administration already has earnings and other records on most recipients. But the administration of this program will be more difficult than OASDHI. In the case of old age insurance, the administration simply determined eligibility, computed the benefit amount, and wrote monthly checks to the beneficiary, subject only to the test of retirement. There are no property limitations in OASDHI, and no attention is paid to income other than income from employment or self-employment. Under SSI, however, property and other income must be considered. This is a considerably more complex undertaking.

[13]Statement of Caspar W. Weinberger, Secretary of the Department of Health, Education and Welfare, in the Hearings before the Committee on Finance, cited above, p. 2.

CURRENT SSI OPERATIONS

In December 1973, the last month in which the old federal-state assistance programs operated, 3,173,000 persons (1,820,000 aged; 78,000 blind; and 1,275,000 disabled) received such assistance benefits. By January 1975, 4,046,600 persons were receiving SSI. This included 2,308,100 aged persons, 74,500 blind, and 1,664,000 disabled.[14] The total number of persons receiving SSI payments was thus 27.5% greater than the number receiving comparable public assistance benefits in December, 1973.

Average benefits under the new program are somewhat higher than those which were paid under the old federal-state assistance programs. In states with federally-administered state supplementation, combined federal and state payments to the aged ranged from $64 in Indiana to $139 in Massachusetts. Previously, those states had paid $57 and $121, respectively, under OAA. Payments to the disabled under SSI ranged from $98 in Kansas to $208 in Massachusetts. Previously those states had paid $79 and $156, respectively, to the disabled under APTD. While benefits are higher than under the old assistance programs, it is apparent that considerable state-to-state variation still exists.

EVALUATION OF SUPPLEMENTAL SECURITY INCOME

The Supplemental Security Income program is a considerable improvement over the previous federal-state categorical assistance programs. By instituting a nationwide program directed by the federal government, most of the shortcomings of the state programs can be avoided. Benefit and eligibility rules are now the same throughout the country. State procedures which had denied benefits to needy people in some states are bypassed. A type of "negative income tax" arrangement is in effect so that the welfare recipient is no longer subjected to a "100% tax" if he finds a job. Another advantage is that the program is administered by the Social Security Administration so that the stigma of being on welfare is avoided. The latter, however, depends on how the recipients themselves view the program.

Some criticims can be made of Supplemental Security Income. There is both optional and mandatory supplementation of SSI by the states. States are required to supplement SSI if the SSI benefit is less than the payments made by the states in December 1973. States may also add an optional amount as each state sees fit. Thus, there is still variation in benefits from state to state, although somewhat less than before. Another

[14]*Social Security Bulletin*, Vol. 37, No. 6 (June 1974), Table M-27; and *Ibid.*, Vol. 38, No. 5 (May 1975), Tables M-22 and M-30.

shortfall of the program is that it did nothing about the Aid to Families with Dependent Children program, which is by far the largest welfare program.

GENERAL ASSISTANCE (GA)

General assistance may be thought of as a residual program under which a person who cannot qualify under any one of the categorical assistances may be able to get aid. A person or family may be in need without being under 18, or over 65, or blind, or permanently and totally disabled. The breadwinner of the family may be unemployed but ineligible to receive unemployment compensation either because he was not covered in the first place or because he has exhausted his unemployment benefits without having found a job. Or he may be sick or disabled without meeting the SSI test for permanent and total disability.

General assistance is actually the oldest of all public assistance, being the United States remnant of the old Elizabethan Poor Law of 1601. In most states it was the only form of public relief until around and after 1900, when the categorical assistances discussed above began to come into existence. During the Great Depression of the 1930's, general assistance was an enormously large program, at one time providing benefits in cash or in kind to about 6 million families. After the establishment of federal grants-in-aid to the categorical assistances, and especially with the prosperity associated with World War II, general assistance declined to its present residual role. It is now in a sense a back-up program to unemployment compensation. As may be seen in Table 7-1, general assistance rises in recession years and declines in years with a high level of employment. In December 1974, the states reported 586,000 cases with 855,000 recipients.

The federal government does not participate in general assistance in any way; the program is entirely a state, or local, or state-local one. The lack of federal financial participation tends to cause some states to slight this program. They tend to put their limited state funds into programs where $1 of state money may attract a dollar or more of federal money. Other states which do try to meet the needs of their general assistance cases find the program burdensome. For both reasons, general assistance payments tend to be quite low. In November 1974, only three states paid as much as $120 per month and 15 states paid less than $40 per month.[15]

As is true of the other assistance programs, recipient rates vary widely from state to state. Data on recipients are not very reliable since the program is operated only on a local basis in some states, and information often is not reported to the state or to the Department of Health, Education, and Welfare. In June 1973, the recipient rate for the United

[15]Social Security Bulletin, Vol. 38, No. 5 (May 1975), Table M-33, p. 64.

States as a whole was put at 3.6 per 1,000 population. Hawaii's rate at 18.1 and Rhode Island's rate at 13.0 were the two highest. In several southern, mountain, and plains states, the recipient rate was either very low or unreported.[16]

FOOD PROGRAMS

Despite the fact that the United States has the highest per capita income of any large nation in the world, several million poor people suffer from malnutrition and from diseases related to malnutrition, and occasionally some Americans literally starve to death.[17] Testimony before the Senate Select Committee on Nutrition and Human Needs in 1969 showed that black children (and many white children) often receive about half of needed calories, and that worms often reduce even this inadequate nutrition. Also it was found that the premature birth rate among the poor was three times that of the well-to-do, and that large numbers of prematurely born infants grow to maturity with intellectual capacity significantly below normal.

A variety of steps have been taken by the federal government to provide food for the hungry. These include surplus commodity distribution, the food stamp program, the school lunch and school breakfast program, day care and summer feeding programs, the Women, Infants, and Children program, and a feeding program for the elderly. The largest programs are the food stamp program and the school lunch program. Surplus commodity distribution is being phased out. The Women, Infants, and Children's program is a new program under which needy pregnant women, new mothers, and their infants and small children are given free foods on a regular basis over and above their food stamp allotment. The other programs are relatively small but are being expanded, and are important to a limited number of recipients.[18]

SURPLUS COMMODITY DISTRIBUTION

During the Great Depression of the 1930's, Congress authorized the Department of Agriculture to buy surplus farm commodities and make them available to state welfare and other agencies for distribution to needy families. The motive was probably as much, or more, to aid the farmers as it was to feed the hungry, but for this reason the program enjoyed

[16]U. S. Department of Health, Education and Welfare, *Public Assistance Statistics*, July 1973, NCSS Report A-2, Table 13.

[17]Nick Kotz, *Let Them Eat Promises*, (Englewood Cliffs, N.J. Prentice-Hall, 1969). Kotz summarized a number of studies made of the hunger problem. See, for instance, pp. 37-38, 111-112, 121-122, 195-197, and 251-256.

[18]For an extensive discussion of federal food programs see the *Food Rights Handbook* (August 1974), prepared by The Children's Foundation, Washington, D.C.

widespread political support. Reflecting the farm relief motive, only commodities which were in surplus were distributed to the poor. As a consequence the poor often received only a few commodities, such as flour, cornmeal, rice, and lard, far from a balanced diet. Presidents Kennedy and Johnson gradually expanded the program until 22 commodities were being distributed in 1968. However, many counties throughout the nation did not participate in the program, and, of those that did, many distributed considerably less than 22 commodities.[19] Over the years many billions of pounds of food were distributed. In 1965 alone, 1.1 billion pounds were distributed, worth about $470 million.[20] In recent years, however, Congress has opted in favor of the food stamp program, and direct commodity distribution was terminated in 1975.

THE FOOD STAMP PROGRAM

Food stamps have become by far the largest food distribution program. The idea was first tried in 1939 when the needy were given 50 cents' worth of blue stamps free for every dollar's worth of orange stamps purchased. The orange stamps could be spent on any food product, but the blue stamps could only be used to purchase surplus foods. The plan did appear to increase food consumption by needy families, but it was discontinued in 1943.

President Kennedy reinstituted food stamps on a trial basis, in 1961, in eight depressed counties. The program was given statutory authority by the Food Stamp Act of 1964, and was reformed and broadened by the Food Stamp Act of 1971 (Public Law 91-671). The program grew only slowly during the 1960's. Even by fiscal year 1967 only $115 million was appropriated, and by 1969 the food stamp supplement was still only $250 million. In the 1970's, however, rapid growth set in, when expenditures reached $610 million in fiscal 1970, $2.2 billion in 1972, about $3 billion in fiscal 1974, and a projected $4 billion for fiscal 1975. Correspondingly, the number of people participating in the food stamp program grew slowly in the 1960's, but rapidly in the 1970's. As late as 1969, only 3.2 million people received food stamps, but by January 1974 there were about 14.5 million recipients, and about 17 million in January 1975. Early in 1975 the Ford Administration was endeavoring to cut back on the program.

The applicant generally must apply at a county welfare office, where if eligible he receives an "Authorization to Purchase." He must usually buy his monthly quota of stamps (at a reduced price) at a local postoffice. He then uses the stamps to purchase whatever foods he desires at a partic-

---

[19]See Gilbert Steiner, The State of Welfare, (Washington, D.C., The Brookings Institute, 1971), especially his Chapter 6, "Stamps for the Hungry."

[20]Budget of the United States, fiscal year ending June 30, 1967, Washington, D.C., Bureau of the Budget, p. 136.

ipating grocery store. Stores usually participate, since the banks accept the cancelled food stamps as money and then are reimbursed by the U. S. Treasury.

The program works on a household basis.[21] The dollar amount of food stamps the household can get is based on the size of the household. The amount the household must pay is graduated according to the household's income after certain deductions. Households with no income or with large deductions can get food stamps free. People who are receiving public assistance are automatically eligible. Many working families not on assistance but with low incomes or large expenses qualify. The unemployed, married students, and workers on strike may also qualify. The latter two groups were made ineligible by the Act of 1971, but the Supreme Court in November 1972 ruled that those provisions violated the equal protection clause of the constitution, so students and strikers are again eligible.[22] Families whose income is above the maximum allowable may sometimes also qualify if they have very large expenses, such as catastrophic illness or severe loss due to storms or floods.

One argument made in favor of the food stamp program is that it bears some resemblance to the "negative income tax" idea, since very low income people are eligible for a basic grant and since the subsidy declines as income increases.[23] For instance, a family of four with a net monthly income of $30 or less can get $154 worth of food stamps free (January 1975). As income rises by $10 per month, the family must generally pay $3 more for the same amount of stamps, depending on tables published periodically by the Department of Agriculture. Where this arrangement prevails, the "negative income tax" rate is 30%.

Another argument made in favor of the program is that participants have a much larger selection of foods than was possible under the commodity distribution program. A third claim is that it eliminates the need for a separate warehousing system operated by welfare authorities to distribute food; the participants simply buy their foods from the regular grocery stores.

Difficulties with the food stamp program include a low participation rate. For the United States as a whole only about 40% of those eligible are currently receiving food stamps, and in many counties the problem is much worse. In 1973, the Select Committee on Nutrition and Human Needs designated 263 of our 3,042 counties as "hunger counties."[24] A

[21]Guide to the Food Stamp Program (New York, Food Research and Action Center, October 1974).

[22]Studies in Public Welfare, Paper No. 8, "Income-Tested Social Benefits in New York: Adequacy, Incentives, and Equity," Subcommittee on Fiscal Policy of the Joint Economic Committee, 93d Congress, 1st Session, July 8, 1973, pp. 37-38.

[23]"Changing the Welfare Concept," Business Week, No. 2354 (October 26, 1974), pp. 121-122.

[24]Hunger 1973 and Press Reaction, Select Committee on Nutrition and Human Needs, United States Senate, 93d Congress, 1st Session, November 1973.

"hunger county" was defined as one which had 25 per cent or more of its population below the poverty line and had 33% or less of its poor participating in a federal food program. Another statistic obtained from 40 states by the same group showed that 1,062 counties provided a federal food program to 33 percent or less of their poor. Another problem is that inflation, especially the rapid rise in food prices, has tended to outrun the upward adjustments periodically made by the Department of Agriculture.[25] Still another difficulty is that families often do not have the cash to purchase stamps. The problem has been partly alleviated by providing free stamps for the very poor, and by permitting a family to buy a reduced percentage of stamps twice a month instead of all or nothing once a month. Another problem is that many people seem to be embarrassed or demeaned by the use of food stamps rather than money. Due to all the problems associated with administering a food stamp program, the Citizens Board of Inquiry into Hunger and Malnutrition in the United States recommended in a published report on *Hunger U.S.A. Revisited* that food assistance programs be replaced with adequate cash grants.[26]

SCHOOL LUNCH AND BREAKFAST PROGRAMS

Another program to increase food consumption and also improve the health of children was provided by the National School Lunch Act of 1946. The Food and Nutrition Service of the U. S. Department of Agriculture provides both federal funds and surplus commodities to participating state education agencies for distribution to public and private schools.[27] Funds are distributed on a matching basis with the lowest income states receiving the larger federal subsidies. All school lunches are subsidized to a limited extent, but children from low income families can be provided either free lunches or reduced price lunches, depending on family size and income. In 1972, 7.9 million children received free or reduced price lunches.

The Child Nutrition Act of 1966 started the National School Breakfast Program.[28] The program is similar to the school lunch program, except that in many communities the breakfast program is operated by a church or community action agency. Children who are eligible for the school lunch program are also eligible for breakfasts. The program especially benefits AFDC families where the mother has an early morn-

[25]All food programs are administered on the federal level by the Food and Nutrition Service of the U. S. Department of Agriculture. On the state and local levels, the administering agency is normally the public welfare agency.

[26]For a critique of administrative problems, see Robert Greenstein, "Why Six Million Poor Southerners Can't be Fed," *New South*, Vol. 28, No. 1, 1973.

[27]*Studies in Public Welfare, Paper No. 8, op. cit.*, pp. 47-51.

[28]*Food Rights Handbook, op. cit.*, pp. 4-5.

ing job and where the children had previously been coming to school without breakfast. Shortcomings in both programs exist partly due to the fact that some older schools in ghetto areas and also in poor rural areas do not have lunch facilities, so not all eligible children are provided for. Another difficulty is the stigma attached to participation in the program.

COMMON PROBLEMS OF ASSISTANCE PROGRAMS

ELIGIBILITY

The question of eligibility is one of the major problems in assistance programs. Payments should be made only to the "needy," but in order to certify only those in need, a "means" or "needs" test is required in AFDC, in the SSI program, and in the Food Stamp program. The income of the applicant and sometimes the amount of his property must be determined. This requirement demands much more investigation into individual affairs than is necessary in OASDHI, where payments are automatically received at a certain age provided the aged person retires. In effect, the assistance applicant must take a pauper's oath admitting that he has insufficient income or property to support himself. A means test is looked upon as demeaning, but legislators generally regard such a test necessary to properly administer an assistance program. Others, however, have taken the position that the means test could be much simplified, perhaps a simple declaration on the part of the applicant to be followed by spot-checking by the case worker.[29]

Property limitations exist in all states in AFDC, in General Assistance, in the Supplemental Security Income program, and in the food stamp program. In the AFDC program, states use a wide variety of limits, including various overall dollar limits on all property, or separate limits for real and personal property, or in a few cases limits only on real property but not on personal property.[30] Ownership of a home of modest value is normally permitted, but ownership of real property other than the home is severely limited and often is disqualifying. All states permit the ownership of various amounts of personal property. A majority of states disqualify an applicant who is found to have transferred his property in order to qualify for assistance.

---

[29]Ellen Winston and Gladys O. White, "Simplifying Need Determination in Public Assistance," *Welfare in Review*, Vol. 5, No. 8 (October 1967), pp. 1-5; and Linda Winiecke, "Self-Determination of Need for Social Services Among OAA Recipients," *Welfare in Review*, Vol. 9, No. 4 (July-August 1971), pp. 1-6.

[30]For details on each state, see *Characteristics of State Public Assistance Plans*, Public Assistance Report No. 50, 1971 Edition, *op. cit.*

RESIDENCE REQUIREMENTS

Residence requirements have been set aside by the Supreme Court (*Shapiro v. Thompson*, 394 U.S. 618, 1969). Previously 42 states in the OAA program, 39 states in AB, 40 states in APTD, and 39 states in AFDC had such requirements. Often the residence requirements were five of the last nine years and one year immediately preceding application for assistance. The court decided that a residence requirement violates the equal protection clause, and was "invidious discrimination" against the plaintiffs. The decision permitted the states to require residence, but not to impose any time requirement. A few states passed new legislation attempting to establish durational residence requirements, but the Court struck them down in 1972.[31] The Supplemental Security Income program, since it is nationwide, has no residence requirement, except that aliens who have entered the United States illegally are not eligible. In the AFDC program, states paying above average benefits still worry about an influx of applicants from other states.

THE INCENTIVE PROBLEM

The incentive problem is present in all welfare programs to some extent, but it is believed to be most serious in the AFDC program. Not many people in the other assistance categories can be expected to work. The median age of OAA recipients in 1970 was 75.5 years, and for spouses, 71 years. The permanently and totally disabled are by definition not able to work. The blind are similarly handicapped. A small fraction of the disabled and the blind may be rehabilitated and trained, but past experience does not indicate that the welfare rolls will be significantly reduced by these methods. In the AFDC program, 8 million are children who might better be in school than at work. So the incentive problem comes down largely to the 3 million adult recipients of AFDC, the large majority of whom are the welfare mothers. Even here, society must decide whether it prefers that the mother should be at work or at home caring for the children. If society decides they should be at work, then expensive basic education, vocational training, job placement, and day-care facilities for the children are needed.

Previously, there was disincentive to work because most states, after a low dollar limit was reached, deducted one dollar from the welfare check for each one dollar of income from work, or a "tax" of 100%. These laws have been modified to ignore the first $30 per month of income from work and 1/3 of income over $30. But even this amounts to a 66-2/3% tax on working; some lower percentage, perhaps 30 or 40 percent, would be preferable.

[31]Irene Lurie, "Legislative, administrative, and Judicial Changes in the AFDC Program, 1967-71," *Studies in Public Welfare*, Paper No. 5 (Part 2), Subcommittee on Fiscal Policy, Joint Economic Committee, 93d Congress, 1st Session, pp. 69-108.

THE MULTIPLICITY OF PROGRAMS

A more serious and complex type of difficulty exists due to the presence of several coexisting government programs.[32] Besides AFDC, a family might be eligible for one or several other benefits. Some families may be receiving small survivor benefits from OASDHI. All or nearly all are eligible for Medicaid. Some, perhaps half the families, will be purchasing food stamps, and others will be participating in the school lunch program. A small number may be in public housing. Others will be receiving social services of one kind or another.

For some of these programs, all families below a certain annual income are eligible; all above that amount are ineligible. Thus, what has come to be called a "notch" may exist. For instance, if families with income below $5,000 are eligible for a certain program which yields the family annual benefits of, say, $500, an increase of income from $4,990 to $5,010 may leave the family worse off by $480. The loss of income is the notch, and such situations are apt to have strong disincentive effects. Notches can be avoided if a complex graduated scale is set up so that as income rises, program benefits decline slowly. The food stamp program is set up in this fashion. Notches are also introduced when eligibility to one program is tied to receipt of benefits in another. This is the case with the assistance programs and Medicaid. So long as the family is eligible for cash assistance it is also fully eligible for Medicaid. If the family earns enough to become ineligible for AFDC, Medicaid and other benefits may be lost, so the earnings increase must be quite large to make up for the loss of Medicaid.

The multiplicity of programs is also apt to generate equity problems. There are differences in size of the benefit package from one state to another, and differences from one family situation to another. There is also the problem that the total amount of benefits where the family head is not working may be as large as the income where the head is working. This, of course, generates severe resentment on equity grounds by the working family toward the welfare family.[33]

ADMINISTRATIVE PROBLEMS

The administration of the various public assistance programs is of staggering complexity. Any single assistance program taken alone is apt to be difficult to administer. But the difficulties are multiplied by the existence

---

[32]James R. Storey, *Studies in Public Welfare, Paper No. 1, Public Income Transfer Programs: The Incidence of Multiple Benefits and the Issues Raised by Their Receipt*, Subcommittee on Fiscal Policy, Joint Economic Committee, 92d Congress, 2d Session, April 10, 1972.

[33]*Ibid.*, pp. 11-18.

of several overlapping types of benefits (cash payments, social services, Medicaid, OASDHI, food stamps, veterans benefits, housing programs, school lunch programs, etc.)[34] Some are administered on the state level, some by local agencies, some by the federal government. One office may not know what the other is doing, and the applicant is disadvantaged by being required to go from one agency to another. Different offices of the same agency, or different personnel within a particular large office, may apply the same policy differently. Turnover of welfare agency personnel in New York City has been estimated at 61% per year. Pay is relatively low, there is little time for training new workers, regulations frequently change, and sometimes disappointed clients threaten, abuse, or actually harm office personnel.[35]

Underpayments, overpayments, and outright fraud are always possible, but precisely how much of each occurs is not known. Studies of error and ineligibility have yielded widely varying results:

New York City's 1969-70 quality control program measured ineligibility rates at 0.9 percent for the adult categories and 1.6 percent for AFDC; in contrast, the Comptroller concluded that "a conservative estimate of the actual rates of ineligibility within the (New York City) caseload at any given point of time" was 2.5 percent for the adult categories and 7 percent for AFDC. The Comptroller General of the United States estimated that in late 1968 and early 1969, 10.7 percent of New York City's AFDC families were ineligible, an additional 34.1 percent received overpayments, and an additional 14.9 percent were underpaid.[36]

Sharon Galm, author of Paper No. 5 (Part 1), *Studies in Public Welfare*, cited above, concluded as follows:

Public assistance programs are not being managed efficiently, for they cannot be. The present welfare system may have worked well in the small communities of the past, where welfare recipients were few and caseworkers knew everyone in town. But, in today's large cities, where anonymity is the rule, welfare administrators who attempt to comply with all provisions of the law face an impossible task.

Unmanageable welfare programs do not serve the Nation well. Delays in processing applications, rules too complex for recipients to understand, and eligibility conditions which encourage family dissolution wreak havoc in the

---

[34]*Problems in Administration of Public Welfare Programs*, Hearings before the Subcommittee on Fiscal Policy, Joint Economic Committee, 92d Congress, 2d Session, Part 1, March 20; April 11-13, 1972; See also *Studies in Public Welfare, Paper No. 5 (Part I), Issues in Welfare Administration: Welfare — An Administrative Nightmare*, Subcommittee on Fiscal Policy, Joint Economic Committee, 92d Congress, 2d Session, December 31, 1972, and *Studies in Public Welfare, Paper No. 5 (Part 2), Issues in Welfare Administration: Intergovernmental Relationships*, Subcommittee on Fiscal Policy, Joint Economic Committee, 93d Congress, 1st Session, March 12, 1973.

[35]*Problems in Administration of Public Welfare Programs, op. cit.*, pp. 91-271.

[36]*Studies in Public Welfare, Paper No. 5 (Part I), op. cit.*, p. 36.

lives of the poor. Dysfunction in the welfare system also has profound consequences for taxpayers. . . . Welfare recipients not only drain public funds, but
also represent lost production, lost income, and lost taxes paid. Thus, unmanageable welfare programs betray the needy and violate the public trust.

As long as welfare programs are fragmented and incompatible, they cannot
function smoothly. As long as eligibility conditions are unverifiable, intangible,
or inordinately complex, they cannot be properly enforced. As long as employment and support collection services confront perverse incentives and lack supporting incentives and opportunities, they will remain starved for staff. As long
as welfare programs are conducive to error and fraud and not amenable to their
detection, redress, or prevention, welfare payments will be misdirected.

To solve the problems in welfare administration, a hunt-and-peck method of
legislating will not work. In fact, legislative tinkering may be counterproductive,
for keeping welfare law in a constant state of flux tends to paralyze welfare administration. As New York's welfare director said, "(We) do not have the luxury
of continuing to tamper with the system on a piecemeal basis." To achieve administrative control, comprehensive, carefully planned legislative reform is
needed. . . .[37]

Summary

Assistance programs are intended to supplement social insurance payments, especially in cases where need can be shown. Previously, there
were three separate federal-state programs, OAA, AB, and APTD, under
which the needy aged, blind, or disabled might draw benefits. These have
now been federalized into a new Supplemental Security Income (SSI) administered by the Social Security Administration and financed almost entirely by the federal government. There is, however, mandatory supplementation by the states so as to "hold harmless" any beneficiary who previously received larger benefits under the earlier federal-state programs.
States may also make additional supplements on an optional basis. In a
majority of states the supplementary payments are administered by the
federal government.

General assistance is a small state or local program under which the
needy may be able to receive benefits if they are not eligible for any other
type of assistance. Since no federal funds are available, many states make
only extremely small general assistance payments.

Food programs, especially the food stamp program, have expanded
considerably in recent years, but many of those eligible are still not
receiving such benefits. Several supplementary food programs, such as
the school lunch program and the new program for Mothers, Infants, and
Children, help to relieve hunger and improve health.

[37]*Ibid.*, pp. 42-43.

Administration of public assistance programs tends to be very difficult, and these problems are complicated by possible recipient participation in several programs at once. Because of these overlaps, difficult "notch" and equity problems are introduced.

Bibliography (Chapters 7 and 8)

Barth, Michael C., Carcagno, George J., and Palmer, John L., *Toward an Effective Income Support System: Problems Prospects and Choices* (Madison, Institute for Research on Poverty, University of Wisconsin, 1974).

Blechman, Barry M., Gramlich, Edward M., and Hartman, Robert W., *Setting National Priorities: The 1976 Budget* (Washington, The Brookings Institution, 1975).

Donovan, John C., *The Politics of Poverty,* 2nd ed. (New York, The Bobbs-Merrill Co., 1973).

Goodwin, Leonard, *Do the Poor Want to Work* (Washington, The Brookings Institution, 1972).

Kershaw, Joseph A., *Government Against Poverty* (Chicago, Markham Publishing Company, 1970).

Levitan, Sar A., Rein, Martin, and Marwick, David, *Work and Welfare Go Together* (Baltimore, Johns Hopkins University Press, 1972).

Lubove, Roy, *Poverty and Social Welfare in the United States* (New York, Holt, Rinehart and Winston, 1972).

Steiner, Gilbert Y., *The State of Welfare* (Washington, The Brookings Institution, 1971).

Studies in Public Welfare, Papers 1 through 12, Subcommittee on Fiscal Policy of the Joint Economic Committee, 93d Congress, Joint Committee Print (Washington, U. S. Government Printing Office, 1972 and 1973).

CHAPTER 9

PRIVATE METHODS OF PROTECTION AGAINST OLD AGE AND DEATH

Social Security records show that the average monthly benefit received by a widowed mother in January, 1975, was $134, and the average benefit received by a surviving child was $127. Since most men prefer that their families have a larger income than this amount, millions of families buy private insurance to provide additional security against premature death. Private insurance also helps the widow pay the expenses of the funeral and last illness, and perhaps adds a capital amount to her assets. Before the existence of OASDHI, private insurance was one of the few protections available. Now that Social Security has been in existence long enough to be a mature program, Social Security is usually thought of as the basic protection, and private insurance is thought of as a method of supplementing Social Security.

INDIVIDUAL LIFE INSURANCE

Insurance is based on the laws of probability, or on what is called the law of large numbers. The life or death of any one individual is highly unpredictable, but the number per 1,000 in a certain age group who will die each year can be predicted with considerable accuracy. Mortality tables show a person's chances by age and sex for each possible age. Life insurance premiums can thus be calculated for each age group with great accuracy. In effect a large number of people pay a small premium each year to provide for the payment of a larger sum to the beneficiaries of the few who die in that year. For any one year the risk is thus spread out over the group. Or a single family may think of insurance as spreading out its loss over a large number of years.

Since 1900 the total value of life insurance in the United States has grown enormously, from about $7.5 billion to $1.6 trillion in 1972. By far the most important types of insurance are *ordinary life* and *group life*, making up 52.1% and 38.7%, respectively of the face value of policies. *Industrial life insurance*, making up only 2.5% of the total, is a type issued in small amounts and sold to industrial workers. Premiums are collected weekly or monthly at the policyholder's home. Administrative costs are high and this type of insurance is growing very slowly. *Credit life* insurance on the other hand is growing rapidly, now making up 6.7% of the total. This sort of insurance is normally sold in connection with debt, and is designed to pay the balance of a loan if the borrower should die.

TYPES OF ORDINARY LIFE INSURANCE

Life insurance companies sell many types of ordinary life policies, but for convenience these may be grouped into four main categories: term, straight life, limited-payment life, and endowment insurance. Term insurance provides protection for a limited period of time only, most frequently one to five years. There is no savings element in term insurance. If the insured does not die within the specified time, the policy terminates, and no cash value or other payments are made by the insurance company. Term insurance may be renewed after each five year period, but the policy becomes more and more expensive as a person ages. On the other hand, it is the least expensive type of insurance when the breadwinner of the family is relatively young.

The type of insurance sold most frequently is straight life insurance, this type making up about 45% of all ordinary life insurance in force in the United States in 1970. Straight life insurance is part protection, part savings. In the early years of a policy, it is almost entirely protection. In the later years it becomes more and more savings, until at maturity (age 100), it is entirely savings. Under straight life insurance, payments are made regularly throughout the life of the insured, and at death the beneficiaries collect.

A third type of insurance frequently sold is limited payment life, this type making up about 11% of all ordinary life insurance in force in 1970. Premium payments are made for only a limited number of years, usually 20, but perhaps 30, or some other number of years. Thereafter the policy is paid up, and no further premiums are required.

Endowment insurance makes up about 5% of the total of ordinary life insurance in force. It provides that the beneficiaries receive the face value of the policy if the insured dies before a specified length of time. If the insured does not die within this length of time, then he receives the face value of the policy.

INSURANCE PROGRAMMING

Insurance is still often bought in a haphazard manner. An agent may approach a prospect and urge him to buy a policy without much regard to the individual's needs. More scientific methods of analysis, often called insurance programming,[1] are available. The better insurance agents are

[1]For a detailed analysis of insurance programming see William J. Casey, *Life Insurance Desk Book*, 2nd ed. (New York, Institute for Business Planning, 1965), pp. 73-98.

now well trained, and have been taught to analyze the individual needs of their clients. First of all, the asset and income needs of the family, after their breadwinner has deceased, must be estimated. Needs are highly individual and will vary greatly from family to family. A family with a mortgage on a house needs different protection than one that has already completed payments. Mortgage insurance, a type of decreasing term insurance, is appropriate for the family with the large mortgage.

Expenses during the last illness and burial costs must be met also. Since such expenses are not recurring, they may be covered by term insurance. The more regular expenses of the family will vary according to how many children there are in the family, and their ages. As children grow older, more income is needed to provide for them. The peak costs come during the late teens and early twenties if a college education is provided. Thereafter the children probably will be independent, and the income needs of the widow should be much less.

In insurance programming the income potential of the family must be considered. Some families are able to accumulate sufficient savings to make investments. Income should be available from these investments. Survivors benefits under the Social Security program will provide additional income. Insurance programming has led to increasing sales of family policies and family income policies which combine whole life insurance and various amounts of term insurance depending on estimated family needs.

GROUP LIFE INSURANCE

This type of life insurance originated much later than individual life insurance. The date usually given for the beginning of large-scale group life insurance is 1912, when Montgomery Ward signed a contract with the Equitable Life Assurance Society. Group life insurance has grown by leaps and bounds since its inception. Growth has been particularly fast since 1950, when there was about $48 billion of group life. By 1972, thirteen times as much, or about $631 billion was in force. In 1950, group life made up about 20.4% of total life insurance, in 1960, about 30%, and in 1972, about 39%.[2]

Group insurance is normally issued to the employer for the benefit of the employees, and is usually one-year renewable term insurance. Normally all members of a group are covered without a medical examination. Sometimes the entire cost of the insurance is paid by the employer, and sometimes there is joint employer-employee sharing of the cost. If the employees pay for a portion of the cost, they generally are given the option of whether to join.

---

[2]*Life Insurance Fact Book, 1973,* (New York, Institute of Life Insurance), p. 25.

Group insurance has a number of advantages that account for its prodigious growth.[3] The fact that eligibility is automatic is quite clearly an advantage to those who are unable to pass a physical examination. Also insurance companies sometimes refuse to sell term insurance to individuals engaged in certain occupations, yet in almost all of these industries group insurance is sold. The fact that young people are entering employment and old people leaving helps the cost record if retired personnel are not covered under the plan. Mortality experience has demonstrated that the costs of death are no higher in group policies than they are for death under individual life insurance policies.

A second advantage of group life insurance is that it is low cost insurance. The fact that one policy is sold covering many people cuts selling costs. Administrative costs are also lower. Expenses of medical examinations are saved, along with the costs of individual inspection reports. Term insurance is the lowest-cost type of insurance, and group term insurance is even cheaper than individual term insurance, since there are fewer selling, administrative, and medical costs.

Several disadvantages of group life insurance may be noted.[4] Many workers complain about the temporary nature of the insurance; they do not obtain any benefits if they retire because of illness or old age. Most group insurance does carry a conversion privilege which permits the insured to convert to another type of insurance without a physical examination. But the cost of insurance is then computed at the current age of the worker, which makes the premium much higher. Relatively few workers exercise the conversion privilege.

A fundamental criticism of group insurance is that it fails to consider the individual needs of the workers. Insurance programming is not practiced under group insurance, and coverage which fits one family may not fit another. This disadvantage of group insurance is of such importance that it probably will not replace the need for individual insurance.

EVALUATION OF PRIVATE LIFE INSURANCE

By 1969, 86% of men and 74% of women had some type of life insurance. In the 45-54 group, 92% of heads of households owned some life insurance, while 67% of families with heads 65 or over had one or more policies. By income, families with an annual income in the $10,000 to $20,000 range were the most frequently insured, with 95% having life insurance. Under the $5,000 level, 70% had at least one family member insured.[5] The wide range in size of policies makes an average almost

[3]Davis W. Gregg, *An Analysis of Group Life Insurance*, 3rd ed. (Philadelphia, University of Pennsylvania Press, 1962), pp. 18-19. See also Elvin F. Donaldson and John F. Pfahl, *Personal Finance*, 5th ed. (New York, The Ronald Press Company, 1971), pp. 276-280.

[4]Davis W. Gregg, *op. cit.*, pp. 22-23.

[5]*Life Insurance Fact Book, op. cit.*, pp. 13-14. A national survey of life insurance holdings was conducted in 1969 for the Institute of Life Insurance.

meaningless, but for what it is worth, life insurance per family amounted to $22,900 at the end of 1972. This would be equal to about 24 months of total disposable personal income per family at that time. Survivors' benefits under OASDHI add to the family's income security after the death of the breadwinner, but the amounts available are small for low income families. Also some families have no life insurance at all, including 30% of the families whose income is under the $5,000 level. Death of the breadwinner in a low income family may force the survivors to resort to public assistance.

ANNUITIES AND PENSION PLANS

Annuities and pension plans provide protection just opposite to that of life insurance. They protect against the risk of living too long rather than dying too soon. The term "annuity" itself means an annual payment, but as applied to insurance, it means payments after a certain age has been reached. Annuities were slow to grow in the United States. In 1920 annuity premiums were only about one-half of 1% of life insurance premiums. The major impetus to annuities came from the Great Depression of the 1930's. Stocks purchased during the 1920's lost most of their value, and many corporate bonds went into default. But few insurance companies failed, and since the cost-of-living fell, the real value of annuities increased. Those who had purchased annuities appeared to be both wise and fortunate. Rapid growth of annuity and pension plans occurred from about 1934 on. By the end of 1972 about 2 million people had individual annuities, about 12.4 million were in pension plans funded with life insurance companies, and about 25 million people were covered by private pension plans not funded with life insurance companies.

INDIVIDUAL ANNUITIES

Individual annuities have grown more slowly than have group annuities. There are about 2 million individual annuity contracts in force with United States life insurance companies, and an additional 600,000 ordinary life insurance contracts which have been converted into "supplementary contracts" making current payments similar to annuities. The main advantage of an annuity is safety of the dollar amount. The return to the annuitant tends to approximate that from other types of liquid savings. The main disadvantage of the annuity, however, is inflation. The purchasing power of a fixed annuity (and of any other liquid asset), erodes each year at the current rate of inflation.

GROUP ANNUITIES AND PRIVATE PENSION PLANS

Group annuity and pension plans have grown more rapidly than have the individual annuities. The enactment of the Social Security Act in 1935 publicized retirement income, and thereafter group annuity and private plans began to spread. World War II provided an impetus to group plans when wages were frozen, for it was ruled that certain fringe benefits such as new pension programs would be permitted. Also, during World War II, the excess profits tax was so high that a group pension plan could be inaugurated out of profits at a very small net cost. After the war, social security benefits were increasing only very slowly, causing labor unions to attempt to obtain larger pension through collective bargaining. They were helped in this respect by a National Labor Relations Board decision in 1948 in the Inland Steel Case in which it was ruled that employers must bargain on pensions. Price and wage controls from 1971 to 1974 renewed the emphasis on bargaining for fringe benefits.

A great variety of group annuity and private pension plans exist, and there are many ways of classifying such plans. One classification deals with methods of finance. Plans in which the employees help pay the cost are called "contributory." Plans in which the employer pays the full cost are "noncontributory." In 1960 about 75% of the plans were noncontributory, and by 1970 80% were noncontributory.[6] Arguments in favor of the contributory plans are that the additional income from workers should enable larger pensions to be paid. Also workers will have more interest in the program if they participate in financing. Greater worker awareness of the cost of increasing benefits would help to keep benefits within reasonable limits. Arguments in favor of noncontributory pensions are that workers pay for them anyway in the form of higher price of products or in smaller wage increases. The employer will usually have a freer hand in administering the program if he bears the entire cost. Also, of importance is the fact that the employer's payments are deductible as a business cost whereas worker's payments are not.[7]

Pension plans may also be classified as to whether they are single-employer or multi-employer. Another classification is on the basis of whether or not the plan is vested. Pension vesting is the granting to the worker of an irrevocable right to receive the pension benefits earned through his employment, the benefits usually starting at a specified retirement age. By 1970 more than three-fourths of covered workers were in plans that had vesting provisions.[8] Vesting is increasing at a faster pace in the multi-employer plans and in the noncontributory plans. Other

[6]Harry E. Davis and Arnold Strasser, "Private Pension Plans, 1960 to 1969 — An Overview," *Monthly Labor Review*, Vol. 93, Pt. 2 (July 1970), pp. 45-56.
[7]Dan McGill, *Fundamentals of Private Pensions* (Homewood, Ill., Irwin, 1955), pp. 65-66.
[8]Davis and Strasser, *op. cit.*, pp. 45-46.

classifications of plans can be made on the basis of age at retirement, mandatory *vs.* optional retirement, length of service required, retirement benefit formulas, types of industry covered, geography, and the like.[9] Yet another classification is on the basis of funding: group annuities *funded* with private insurance companies, and private pension plans *not funded* with insurance companies.

GROUP ANNUITIES FUNDED WITH LIFE INSURANCE COMPANIES

At the end of 1972 about 9.4 million people were covered by group annuities funded with life insurance companies, and an additional 3 million were covered by other arrangements.[10] Also growing steadily are the self-administered pension plans, but recent criticism of the latter has led to renewed emphasis on group annuities financed through insurance companies. Group annuities have the same sort of cost advantage as does group life insurance. Selling and administrative costs are noticeably lower. The group annuity, however, is subject to the same problem which plagues the individual annuity, that is, the loss of purchasing power due to inflation.

The two major types of group annuity are the *deferred annuity* and *deposit administration*. Under a deferred annuity plan the insurance company purchases a unit of deferred annuity each time a premium is received, and the sum of these benefits is paid as monthly income upon retirement. Under a deposit administration program, all the money received by the insurance company is placed in a common fund, and when the employee retires, money is withdrawn from the fund to buy an annuity for that individual. About four times as many people (7.5 million) are covered by deposit administration plans than by deferred annuities (1.8 million).[11]

Deposit administration plans allow the employer more flexibility in funding the plan, but they may be riskier from the worker's point of view. The employer may suspend premium payments for a time, or he may reduce or increase contributions within the limits set by the insurance companies' underwriting rules. Under deposit administration plans, the

[9]For a more detailed discussion of the many aspects of pension plans see, among others, the Davis and Strasser article cited above; for a thorough discussion of vesting, see Dan M. McGill, *Preservation of Pension Benefit Rights* (Homewood, Ill., Richard D. Irwin, Inc., 1972) and Dan M. McGill, *Fulfilling Pension Expectations* (Homewood, Ill., Richard D. Irwin Inc., 1962). For a more general discussion of policy issues, see *The Debate on Private Pension* (Washington, D.C., American Enterprise Institute, 1968); for a discussion of private pensions in England, see Gordon A. Hosking, *Pension Schemes and Retirement Benefits* (London, Sweet and Maxwell, 1968); and for regulation abroad, see Frank M. Kleiler, "Regulation of Private Pension Plans in Europe," *Monthly Labor Review*, Vol. 94, Pt. 1 (April 1971), pp. 33-39.

[10]*Life Insurance Fact Book, 1973, op. cit.,* p. 40.

[11]*Life Insurance Fact Book, 1973,* pp. 39-40.

insurance company cannot guarantee an exact pension until the annuity is bought at the time of the retirement of the worker.

To combat the difficulties caused by persistent inflation the "variable annuity" has been introduced. Some of these are sold on an individual basis, but most are group contracts. Most of the large companies now sell such annuities and many of the smaller companies are going along with the trend. The variable annuity is usually based on the prices of the common stocks in which the funds have been invested, or it may be based on a cost-of-living index.[12]

PRIVATE PENSION PLANS NOT FUNDED WITH INSURANCE COMPANIES

There are about two and one-half times as many employees covered under self-administered plans as under plans administered by life insurance companies. Corporations, unions, and others who set up funds, attempt to save money by administering their own private pension plans. One saving is in taxes. Money set aside as pension reserves is nontaxable, but insurance companies must pay taxes on their premium income. Another saving is the avoidance of the selling commissions associated with private insurance. Certain expenses, however, cannot be avoided. If reserves are accumulated under self-administered plans (as they should be), the funds are generally held by a trustee, often a commercial bank trust department, and fees must be paid to the trustee. Another expense which cannot (or should not) be avoided is that of paying an actuary to advise the corporation or union on costs of the program. Generally some expenses are saved by self-administering, but the worker's pension may not be as safe as it would be if administered by an insurance company.

Labor unions were among the early organizers of private pension plans, several of which came into existence before 1900. Benefits were usually limited to death, disability, and homes for aged members. In 1908, the International Typographical Union established a pension plan and they were followed by plans set up by railroad, construction, electrical workers and other unions before 1930. These funds had assets of $11.5 million in 1929, but they were quickly exhausted during the Great Depression of the 1930's, and few were paying any benefits by 1940.

Beginning in the 1940's unions shifted their efforts from self-financing to obtaining employer support in providing pension payments to retired workers. Early plans were commonly restricted to the employees of a single company, and today most plans are still single-employer plans. However in some unionized industries with many small employers it was more economical to have an area or nation-wide plan administered by the

[12]Donaldson and Pfahl, op. cit., pp. 724-729.

union. Such is often the case in the construction industry and in the garment trades. Here the benefits are usually financed entirely by employer contributions, but the funds are administered and the level of benefits determined solely by the union. Also some giant industries now have multi-employer funds.

The Taft-Hartley Act, passed in 1947, required that all plans subsequently established which involved negotiated employer contributions be administered jointly by employers and employees. Today the great majority of multi-employer funds are jointly administered. The Federal Welfare and Pension Plans Disclosure Act of 1958 required the filing of certain reports which are valuable sources of data,[13] but until 1974 there was little federal regulation of private pension plans.

A great diversity of benefit formulas exist. Usually benefits are computed in one of the three ways: (1) Benefits may be a uniform flat amount, such as $100 per month, after a specified minimum age and number of years of service; (2) benefits may be related to years of service alone, such as $5 per month for each year of service; or (3) benefits may be related to years of service and level of earnings, such as 1% of monthly earnings for each year of service. Plans also vary according to other provisions such as minimum and maximum amounts, and treatment of social security benefits.[14]

Benefit amounts, given the above methods of computation, are naturally closely related to both length of employment and earnings. According to a 1969-70 survey, men with 40 or more years of service and annual earnings of $10,000 or more had a median annual private pension of $4,620, while men with less than 20 years of service and earnings of less than $6,000 annually had a median pension of only $650. Highest benefits went to professional and managerial people in transportation, public utilities, and finance, and the lowest benefits went to unskilled and semiskilled workers in mining, construction, and service industries. Pensions for women were less than half those for men, reflecting differences in amount of earnings and length of service between the sexes.[15] Race was also a factor. The median pension for a white man was $2,130, while that for blacks and other races was $1,230.[16]

The number of workers covered by private pension plans is not precisely known but is estimated to be between 24 and 31 million.[17] A number of factors tend to lead to overstatement of coverage. An unknown

[13]H. Robert Bartell, Jr., and Elizabeth T. Simpson, *Pension Funds of Multiemployer Industrial Groups, Unions and Nonprofit Organizations,* Occasional Paper 105 (New York, National Bureau of Economic Research, 1968), pp. 1-3. See also Phillip Cagan, *The Effect of Pension Plans on Aggregate Saving: Evidence from a Sample Survey,* Occasional Paper 95 (New York, NBER, 1965), and Daniel M. Holland *Private Pension Funds: Projected Growth,* Occasional Paper 97 (New York, NBER, 1966).

[14]Walter W. Kolodrubetz, "Private Retirement Benefits and Relationships to Earnings: Survey of New Beneficiaries," *Social Security Bulletin,* Vol. 36, No. 5 (May 1973), pp. 16-37.

[15]*Ibid.,* pp. 17-20.

[16]*Ibid.,* p. 31.

[17]"Pensions: The Reformation Begins," *Newsweek,* Vol. LXXXVII, NO. 13 (September 24, 1973), pp. 98; 100.

amount of duplication exists where workers may be covered by both an insured plan and a noninsured plan, or by a multi-employer plan as well as a union sponsored plan. Another source of double counting lies in the fact that some workers have entitlement to vested pensions from previous employers. And a wide margin for error should be allowed for estimated coverage of small employers and groups.[18] It may be that the lower estimates are more accurate than the higher.

Contributions into the programs continue to increase rapidly. Table 9-1 shows contributions and other program data for both insured and noninsured plans in selected years. It will be noted that employers pay the great preponderance of contributions, and that the percent paid by the employers is increasing. In 1950 the employers' share was 84%; in 1972 it was over 91%.

EVALUATION OF PRIVATE PENSION PLANS

Protection against loss of income at old age is now provided from three main sources: government social security payments, private pension plans, and individual savings. For most people, individual savings cannot be safely relied upon, because only people in the highest income brackets are able to save much. Also persistent inflation erodes the values of liquid savings and of fixed annuities. The viewpoint expressed here is that Social Security should carry the largest share of the burden.

Pension benefits plus social security are now approaching an adequate minimum, especially for those who happen to be represented by strong labor unions or who happen to work for employers who have pension systems. The median pension payment in 1973 was about $2,100 per year, double that of ten years earlier. Average social security payments have risen to about $2,000 annually for a single person and $3,300 for a couple, again about double that of a decade earlier.[19] Certain collective bargaining contracts recently negotiated are even more generous. General Electric, dealing with a coalition of 14 unions, agreed to retirement at age 62 with pensions based on a range of $6.50 to $9.50 a month for each year worked.[20] Anheuser-Busch in an even more generous settlement agreed to a plan under which employees with 15 years seniority can retire at age 60 with full pay for the next five years. At age 65 the retirees will then receive $12 a month for every year of service plus social security.[21] But these are the exceptions.

[18]Walter W. Kolodrubetz, "Employee-Benefit Plans, 1971," *Social Security Bulletin*, Vol. 36, No. 4 (April 1973), pp. 17-33.

[19]Ralph E. Winter, "The Golden Years: Retirees Live Better As Private Pensions, Social Security Rise," *Wall Street Journal*, January 23, 1974, pp. 1; 14.

[20]"Why GE Buckled on Pension Costs," *Business Week*, No. 2284 (June 16, 1973), pp. 92; 96.

[21]"Brewers Establish a Pension Landmark," *Business Week*, No. 2285 (June 23, 1973), p. 28.

TABLE 9-1

PRIVATE PENSION AND DEFERRED PROFIT-SHARING PLANS: CONTRIBUTIONS, BENEFICIARIES, BENEFIT PAYMENTS, AND RESERVES, SELECTED YEARS

	1950	1960	1970	1972
Employer Contributions, Total (million)	$1,750	$4,710	$12,580	$16,940
Insured Plans	720	1,190	2,860	4,200
Noninsured Plans	1,030	3,520	9,720	12,740
Employee Contributions, Total (million)	$ 330	$ 780	$ 1,420	$ 1,600
Insured Plans	200	300	350	400
Noninsured Plans	130	480	1,070	1,200
Number of Beneficiaries, Total (thousands)	450	1,780	4,720	5,500
Insured Plans	150	540	1,220	1,350
Noninsured Plans	300	1,240	3,500	4,200
Amount of Benefit Payments, Total (million)	370	1,720	7,360	10,000
Insured Plans	80	390	1,330	1,700
Noninsured Plans	290	1,330	6,030	8,300
Reserves, Total (billions)	$ 12.1	$ 52.0	$ 137.1	$ 167.8
Insured Plans	5.6	18.8	40.1	50.3
Noninsured Plans	6.5	33.1	97.0	117.5

Source: *Social Security Bulletin*, Vol. 37, No. 5 (May 1974), Table 6, P. 21.

The major disadvantage of relying on private pensions is that large numbers of workers are not covered. There are over 72 million wage and salary workers in the nonfarm labor force, so (depending on various coverage estimates) between 41 and 48 million workers have no private pension coverage. Workers in small, non-union establishments are unlikely to be covered. Only two-fifths of employees in the trade and service industries are covered. Workers in establishments where the pay is low, even if unionized, are usually not covered. Short-term and part-time employees are almost never covered. And, depending on the company, low-paid office workers are often not covered, even if the non-office workers are covered.[22]

Private pensions probably increase the degree of inequality of income distribution. They mainly cover the better paid unionized workers and middle and upper income white-collar workers, managers and professionals. The cost of these pensions is likely passed on in part to the general public in the form of higher prices of the goods and services produced. Or it is borne in part by the general taxpayer who must pay more taxes to make up for tax revenues not collected from employers who have pension plans.[23] So the general taxpayer is paying higher taxes, and low income people are paying higher prices to finance the private pensions of middle and upper income groups.

Another possible detrimental effect of private pension plans is that they may impede the mobility of labor. The impact of pension plans on mobility cannot be easily measured since so many other factors affect mobility. Seniority in layoff, chances for promotion with seniority, longer vacations with pay, and home and community attachments make workers reluctant to move. The overall turnover figure in manufacturing in this country in 1972 was about 4% per month,[24] but this figure conceals a higher turnover of younger workers and a lower turnover of older workers. It is probably true that private pensions slow down the mobility of older workers.

Also of importance is the problem that pension plans make employers reluctant to hire older workers. A company would not want to hire a man at age 64, only to have to pay him a pension a year later. Employers protect themselves on this score by requiring that a number of years be worked before becoming eligible for a pension. For instance, a plan may provide that workers can retire at age 60 or over with 10 or more years of service, with compulsory retirement at age 65. But in this case employers are reluctant to hire workers from about age 48 through 55.

[22]Emerson Beier, "Incidence of Private Retirement Plans," *Monthly Labor Review*, Vol. 94, Pt. 2 (July 1971), pp. 37-40.

[23]Statements of Ralph Nader and Karen Ferguson, Public Interest Research Group, Washington, D.C., *Welfare and Pension Plan Legislation*, Hearings before the General Subcommittee on Labor, of the Committee on Education and Labor, House of Representatives, 93d Congress, 1st Session, pp. 243-249. See also the statement of Robert D. Paul, President, Martin E. Segal Co., pp. 55-59.

[24]*Manpower Report of the President* (Washington, D.C., U. S. Government Printing Office, March 1973), Table C-10, p. 199.

Workers over 55 are effectively excluded from participating in the plan. Many plans also discourage retired workers from taking a job with another company. Often the pension will be reduced or suspended if the worker takes another job, especially with a competing company.[25]

Another disadvantage of private pension plans is that many workers who appear to be covered do not in fact qualify for a pension. More than three-fourths of covered workers are in plans that provide for vesting, that is, the achievement of a nonforfeitable right to a pension benefit. To gain this right there are age, length of service, or a combination of age and service requirements, so vesting varies greatly from one plan to the next. Often 10 or more years of service with the same employer are required, at which point partial vesting is achieved. For each additional year of work for that employer, the vested amount is increased by some percentage. Many workers, including managers and professionals, change jobs frequently, and thus may never achieve a vested right.[26]

Furthermore, vesting often does not guarantee that a pension will be paid. If a company closes a plant, or merges with another company, or goes into bankruptcy, or simply discovers that it cannot meet its pension obligations, the worker may get nothing, or a fraction of what he expected. If the fund is administered by a union, there is sometimes outright fraud. Union officials in both the Teamsters and United Mine Workers unions, for instance, have plundered their respective pension funds.[27] This has led to demands for vigorous regulation by the federal government, including full funding and requirements that administration be by third parties, such as insurance companies or commercial bank trust departments.

Also there have been proposals that pension plans, in addition to being fully funded and fully vested, should also be "fully portable." "Portability" means that a worker would carry his vested rights with him from job to job and eventually convert them into a single pension. Probably some sort of federal agency would serve as a pension-credit clearinghouse.[28] When a worker changed jobs he would not have to start over. That is, he would not have to work another 10 years for a second or subsequent employer before achieving vested status. Others have proposed that federal law should mandate that *all* non-agricultural employers be required to provide a fully funded, fully vested, and fully portable pension plan. It is argued that this would meet not only the problems of workers who change jobs, but also the inequity involved in the noncoverage of an estimated 41 to 48 million workers.[29] Currently a

[25]Harry E. Davis, "Pension Provisions Affecting the Employment of Older Workers," *Monthly Labor Review*, Vol. 96, Pt. 1 (April 1973), pp. 41-45.

[26]*Welfare and Pension Plan Legislation*, Hearings, *op. cit.* Statement of Dr. Robert W. Chairns, Executive Director, American Chemical Society, pp. 133-138.

[27]"Pensions: The Reformation Begins," *op. cit.*, p. 98.

[28]*The Debate on Private Pensions* (Washington, D.C., American Enterprise Institute, March, 1968), p. 4.

[29]Statement of Robert D. Paul, *op. cit.*, p. 57.

movement is underway in Europe to make private pensions compulsory. The British Parliament recently decided that companies lacking pension plans must launch them by 1975, and similar legislation is pending in Switzerland.[30]

Another set of problems has to do with the amount, quality, and use of pension fund reserves. The amount of reserves has grown greatly, and by the end of 1972, reserves were estimated at around $170 billion for both the insured and noninsured plans.[31] Reserves are still growing in total amount, but the rate of growth has slowed somewhat as the amount of benefit pay-out increases. Moreover, the total amount of reserves conceals problems with particular funds. Studies made by the Pension Research Council and by the Bureau of Labor Statistics indicate that a majority of plans are in good shape.[32] Around half the plans studied had assets equal to or greater than their liabilities. This is usually true of plans which had been in existence for a number of years. But new plans and small-employer plans do not appear so firmly established. And some of the giant plans including the coal mining industry funds and the two huge Teamster union funds appear to have low benefit-security ratios. Also the assets in some funds are questionable. In one fund, 70% of the assets consisted of unpaid employer contributions past due for up to six years. Others list securities of questionable value, including some without verifiable market value. At the other extreme most of the plans funded with the larger insurance companies appear to be quite sound.

THE PENSION REFORM ACT OF 1974

After years of public complaint about difficulties with private pensions and after almost as many years of Congressional hearings, Congress passed the Pension Reform Act of 1974 (P.L. 93-406), and President Ford signed it into law on Labor Day. The law is very detailed and complex, running to 203 pages of fine print.[33] The major provision of the act are as follows:

Federal regulation is established over all new private pension plans set up in 1975 or thereafter, and over all old plans already in existence beginning in January 1976. Generally all private plans affecting interstate commerce will be covered, but federal, state, or local government plans, and most church operated plans are not covered.[34] Primary administrative

---

[30]"Multinationals: Money Men Ride the Pension Fund Boom," *Business Week*, No. 2316 (February 2, 1974), p. 32.

[31]"Pensions: The Reformation Begins," *op. cit.*, p. 98.

[32]Murray W. Latimer, "Benefit Security in Private Pension Plans — A Review Article," *Monthly Labor Review* Vol. 93, Pt. 1 (May 1970), pp. 47-50.

[33]*Pension Reform Act of 1974, Law and Explanation* (Chicago, Commerce Clearing House, Inc., September 1974), pp. 111-314.

[34]*Explanation of Pension Reform Act of 1974* (Chicago, Commerce Clearing House, Inc., 1974), para. 109.

responsibility is assigned to the Internal Revenue Service, and a Pension Benefit Guarantee Corporation is established in the Department of Labor. Information in reports made to the IRS and to the Labor Department will be shared with the Social Security Administration for the publication of reports beginning in 1979.[35]

The law contains extensive regulations dealing with plan participation. Generally, new employees cannot be required to wait more than one year before beginning to participate in a plan. Employees under age 25, however, can be required to wait until that age before their participation begins. Also, if a plan provides for 100 percent vesting after three years, the plan can require a three year waiting period. Further, "defined benefit"[36] plans may exclude those who are within five years of normal retirement age when they commence work. Seasonal employees, defined as those who work less than 1,000 hours in a 12-month period, can be excluded. Under previously existing internal revenue codes, plans must meet 70 percent or 80 percent coverage requirements and may not discriminate in favor of officers, shareholders, or highly paid employees as to benefits or contributions.[37]

To deal with the problem that employees all too often received little or no benefits, the law requires that all covered plans provide for complete vesting of all accrued benefits derived from employer contributions. A plan may adopt any one of three alternative vesting schedules: (1) Under the "five-to-fifteen year rule," the employee's benefits must be at least 25% vested after five years of service, 50% vested after 10 years, and 100% vested after 15 years of service; or (2) under the "ten-year rule," the plan must provide that benefits are 100% vested after ten years of service; or (3) under the "rule of 45," whenever the employee's age plus his years of service totals 45 he must be at least 50% vested, graduating up to 100% vested when the employee has 10 or more years of service and the sum of his age and years of service equals or exceed 55.[38] The foregoing vesting schedules apply only to benefits derived from the employer's contribution to the plan; benefits derived from the employee's own contributions must be 100% vested at all times.

Further, the law established funding requirements to insure the financing of benefits. In order to be eligible to take pension contributions as tax deductions, the employer's minimum annual contribution to a defined benefit plan must cover the total normal cost of funding the plan plus amortization of past service costs. For old plans already in existence, past service liabilities may be amortized over a maximum of 40 years. Past service costs of new plans may be amortized over a maximum of 30 years.

---

[35]*Ibid.*, para. 901-922.

[36]In a "defined benefit" plan, the amount of the benefit is established in the plan; in a "defined contributions" plan, the employer's contribution is established, but the amount of the employee's benefits are not.

[37]*Explanation of Pension Reform Act of 1974, op. cit.*, para. 101-106.

[38]*Ibid.*, para. 201.

Failure to meet the required funding standards will subject the employer to an excise tax of five percent of the accumulated funding deficiency, and if not corrected within 90 days after notice by the Internal Revenue Service the excise tax becomes 100% of the funding deficiency.[39]

To protect the worker against possible loss of benefits arising from complete or partial termination of a plan, all plans are required to obtain plan termination insurance from a new Pension Benefit Guarantee Corporation (PBGC) established in the Department of Labor. In the first year of operations, each plan must pay a premium of $1 per participant per year for single-employer plans, and 50 cents per participant in multi-employer plans. In later years, an option provides for somewhat lower premium rates. If a plan is terminated, the PBGC will pay benefits to the worker limited to the lesser of (a) 100% of average wages during an individual's highest paid five years of participation in the plan, or (b) $750 per month. These limits will be adjusted upward for cost-of-living increases according to similar changes made in Social Security contributions and benefits. A solvent employer would be liable to reimburse the PBGC for any pension amounts paid by it, but the liability may not exceed 30 percent of the employer's net worth.

The act also requires that employees receive clearly written descriptions of their pension plans and have access to supporting financial statements. Reports must be filed with the Secretary of Labor, beginning in 1975. In addition, various fiduciary standards are imposed on officials managing the funds.

EVALUATION OF PENSION REFORM ACT

The new legislation appears to be a substantial improvement over the previously existing situation. Eventually private pension plans will be "fully funded and fully vested" for the longer term employees. Some difficulties appear to remain for those whose work is irregular or seasonal and for those who change jobs frequently. The law does not provide "portability." Also, the law does nothing for the many millions of workers in companies or industries where there is no private pension plan. New plans may be set up in some of these industries, but some argue that the new law may discourage the inauguration of new plans. There is also some fear that the law creates vast new liabilities for many companies.[40] This is especially true in companies or industries whose plans had been grossly underfinanced in the past.

---

[39]*Ibid.*, para. 301; 302; 333.
[40]"The Hidden Corporate Debt," *Business Week*, No. 2345 (August 24, 1974), pp. 46-47; See also "Workers, Bosses Alike Face Many Unknowns in New Pension Law," *Wall Street Journal*, August 28, 1974, p. 1.

Summary

Since people generally desire greater protection for their families than is provided by Social Security alone, most men take out life insurance policies. Life insurance provides protection against the loss of income by dying. There are several types of life insurance, such as straight life, term insurance, endowments and the like. The advantages and disadvantages of each must be analyzed to determine the best buy for each individual person. In recent years, insurance programming has been adopted to fit the needs of insurance to the individual person. Many corporations also provide life insurance for their employees through group life insurance policies. Although group policies are cheaper than individual life policies, they do have a major disadvantage of not tailoring the policy to the needs of the particular individual. In recent years, life insurance sales have grown by leaps and bounds, but it is mostly wealthier individuals who have adequate amounts of insurance. The typical family has insufficient insurance to provide for more than a year or two of additional income. To provide adequate defense against the exigency of the death of the bread-winner, it is suggested that protection be provided along several fronts. Adequate Social Security payments plus adequate life insurance plus adequate education of the widow should provide ample protection against the danger of premature death. Unfortunately, many of our people, especially in the lower income brackets, do not have adequate protection now.

Annuities and private pension plans provide protection against the risk of living too long. Many people buy individual annuities which enables them to supplement their income in old age. Others benefit from group annuities administered by life insurance companies. The largest number of private pensions are provided through self-administered corporate pension plans or by plans administered by unions. Such pensions supplement the payments provided by Social Security. Persons having such pension have considerably more income than those who do not have them. The result has been that some of our aged have much larger income at retirement than others. As yet, the people of the United States have been unable to devise a plan whereby all the aged have an adequate income.

Bibliography

Barfield, Richard, and Morgan, James, *Early Retirement, The Decision and the Experience* (Ann Arbor, Michigan, The University of Michigan, 1969).

Bartell, Jr., H. Robert, and Simpson, Elizabeth T., *Pension Funds of Multi-employer Industrial Groups, Unions and Nonprofit Organizations*, Occasional Paper No. 105 (New York, National Bureau of Economic Research, 1968).

Belth, Joseph M., *Life Insurance, A Consumer's Handbook* (Bloomington, Ind., Indiana University Press, 1973).

Black, Jr., Kenneth, *Life Insurance*, 6th ed. (New York, Appleton-Century-Crofts, 1966).

Blanchard, Fessenden S., *Making the Most of Your Retirement* (New York, Doubleday, 1963).

Burgess, Ernest W., *Aging in Western Societies* (Chicago, University of Chicago Press, 1960).

Casey, William J., *Life Insurance Desk Book* (New York Institute for Business Planning, Inc., 1965).

Donaldson, Edwin F., and Pfahl, John K., *Personal Finance*, 5th ed. (New York, The Ronald Press Company, 1971).

Hasking, Gordon A., *Pension Schemes and Retirement Benefits*, 3rd ed. (London, Sweet and Maxwell, 1968).

Magee, John H., *Life Insurance* (Homewood, Ill., Richard D. Irwin, Inc., 1958).

McGill, Dan M., *Fulfilling Pension Expectations* (Homewood, Ill., Richard D. Irwin, Inc., 1962).

McGill, Dan M., *Life Insurance*, Rev. ed. (Homewood, Ill, Richard D. Irwin, Inc., 1967).

McGill, Dan M., *Preservation of Pension Benefit Rights* (Homewood, Ill., Richard D. Irwin, Inc., 1972).

Melone, Joseph J., *Collectively Bargained Multi-Employer Pension Plans* (Homewood, Ill., Richard D. Irwin, Inc., 1963).

Nader, Ralph, and Blackwell, Kate, *You and Your Pension* (New York, Grossman Publishers, 1973).

Patterson, Edwin W., *Legal Protection of Private Pension Expectations* (Homewood, Ill., Richard D. Irwin, Inc., 1960).

PART III

PROBLEMS OF DISABILITY AND HEALTH

CHAPTER 10

PROBLEMS OF OCCUPATIONAL DISABILITY, SAFETY, AND REHABILITATION

OCCUPATIONAL DISABILITY

The 1970 Census counted 112 million people aged 18 to 64, and of these 12 million, or nearly 11 percent, reported some type of disability, either partial or complete. Over 7 million reported some sort of partial disability and not quite 5 million reported complete work disability. Duration of disability varied from less than 6 months to 10 years or more, as may be seen in Table 10-1. Obviously, loss to the worker and his family is more severe if the disability is complete and if it is of long duration or permanent. Disability may be classified according to whether it is temporary or permanent, and as to whether it is partial or total. Thus, in order of increasing severity there is: temporary partial disability, temporary total disability,

TABLE 10-1

PERSONS AGE 18 TO 64 WITH PARTIAL OR COMPLETE WORK
DISABILITY, BY DURATION, 1969

	Partial Work Disability (thousands)	Complete Work Disability (thousands)
Less than 6 months	663	405
6 to 11 months	490	318
1 to 2 years	1,076	796
3 to 4 years	1,081	803
5 to 9 years	1,217	975
10 years or more	2,633	1,633
Total	7,160	4,931

Source: U. S. Census, 1970, *Persons with Work Disability*, Table 1.

permanent partial disability, and permanent total disability. Temporary partial disability may be so mild as to occasion no loss of work time, and usually no statistics are shown for it. Temporary total disability is normally severe enough to cause one or more days of lost work time, and the next two are permanent. A fifth possibility is, of course, death. Permanent total disability, however, may be more burdensome on the surviving members of the family than death, especially where the disabled person requires constant attention for years on end.

The incidence of disability rises with age. Whereas only 6 percent of the population aged 18 to 34 had a work disability, 20 percent of those aged 55 to 59, and 26 percent aged 60 to 64 reported disability. Disability for the younger person, however, may be a more serious matter, since there are many more years before retirement, and there may be young children to raise. Disability also varies somewhat by race: 10 percent of whites aged 18-64 reported disability compared to 14 percent of nonwhites. And the women tend to be somewhat less disabled (10 percent) than do men (12 percent).[1]

As would be expected, disability has a severe effect on family income. In 1969 where the head of the family aged 18 to 64 had no work disability the average family income was $11,864. If the family head had only a partial disability, family income averaged $10,359. But where the famly head had a complete work disability, average income from all sources was only $5,136.[2] Some families have small work incomes; some get disability checks from social security, and some receive public assistance or other aid.

NUMBER OF WORK INJURIES PER YEAR

The number of industrial injuries in the United States is far larger than most people would suspect. Table 10-2 shows that over 2 million workmen receive disabling injuries each year. The great majority of these are temporary total disabilities involving at least one day's lost work time. The more serious injuries causing permanent disability or death are not so numerous, but these result in very burdensome economic difficulties for the worker or his family.

FREQUENCY AND SEVERITY RATES

Frequency and severity rates have been developed to help pinpoint industries and occupations which are accident prone. The frequency rate measures the number of disabling injuries per million employee-hours worked. A disabling injury is one which causes the loss of at least one

---

[1] U. S. Census, 1970, *Persons with Work Disability*, Tables 1 and 6.
[2] *Ibid.*, Table 10.

TABLE 10-2

ESTIMATED NUMBER OF DISABLING WORK INJURIES,
ALL INDUSTRIES, 1940-1973

Year	Temporary Total Disabilities	Permanent Disabilities	Injuries Resulting in Death	All Disabling Injuries
1940	1,782,000	89,600	18,100	1,889,700
1945	1,913,900	89,900	16,500	2,020,300
1950	1,851,600	84,900	15,500	1,952,000
1955	1,834,000	81,800	14,200	1,930,000
1960	1,854,000	82,200	13,800	1,950,000
1965	2,000,900	85,000	14,100	2,100,000
1970	2,095,700	90,000	14,300	2,200,000
1973	2,395,800	90,000	14,200	2,500,000

Source: *Handbook of Labor Statistics*, 1950, Bulletin No. 1016, U. S. Department of Labor, Bureau of Labor Statistics, Table G-2, p. 178; *Monthly Labor Review*, Vol. 79 (1956), p. 439; Vol. 85 (1962), p. 410; *Accident Facts*, 1966 (Chicago, National Safety Council), pp. 23-39; and *Accident Facts*, 1974 edition, pp. 23-39.

day's work time. The severity rate is the number of days of disability resulting from disabling work injuries for each million employee-hours worked. Some industries have a low frequency rate but a high severity rate; others have the opposite. Some, for instance mining and logging, have both a high frequency rate and a high severity rate. Certain selected industries are shown in Table 10-3. All of these have above average frequency and severity rates.

COSTS OF INDUSTRIAL INJURIES

Accidents occur more frequently among the young and middle-aged and among lower-income wage earners because of the type of work involved. Usually those injured tend to have a larger number of dependents than others in our society.

[3]Harold M. Somers and Anne R. Somers, *Workmen's Compensation* (New York, Wiley, 1954), p. 10.

TABLE 10-3

INDUSTRIES WITH HIGH WORK-INJURY RATES, 1970
(in order of severity)

	Frequency[1]	Severity[2]
Coal mining and preparation	41.6	7,792
Lead-zinc mining and milling	56.8	6,980
Logging camps and logging	42.4	6,157
Local government fire protection	41.7	4,349
Heavy construction	35.7	3,624
Sawmills and planing mills	35.5	3,478
Concrete brick and block	35.8	3,179
Local government refuse collection and disposal	63.9	2,598
Local government police	45.6	2,521
Roofing and sheet metal work	43.0	2,218
Meat packing plants	46.9	1,194
Average, all manufacturing	15.2	759

[1]Injury-frequency rate is the number of disabling work injuries for each million employee-hours worked.

[2]Injury-severity rate is the number of days of disability resulting from disabling work injuries for each million employee-hours worked.

Source: *Handbook of Labor Statistics*, 1972, U. S. Department of Labor, Bureau of Labor Statistics, Table 163.

The economic burden of industrial accidents and diseases lies partly on workers, partly on employers, and partly on society in general. Although workers are partially compensated for losses due to industrial accidents and diseases, much of the economic burden still lies directly on them. Benefits paid under the workmen's compensation laws (next chapter) are often only a minor fraction of the worker's previous wage, and an even smaller fraction of the present value of his total loss.[4] The National Safety Council estimated work accidents costs in 1968 to be about $9 billion, yet in that year only $2.35 billion were paid in benefits.[5]

Employers, too, are faced with heavy costs due to industrial accidents. They must pay the premium costs for workmen's compensation insurance, and sizeable sums must often be paid for damages under employers' liability actions. Indirect costs to employers include loss of time by experienced workers and damage to machinery and other property. Estimates indicate that the indirect cost is several times that of the direct cost. Lastly, society as a whole suffers from lost production, and from the costs of caring for impoverished families, court costs, and costs of administering a program for the injured.[6]

OCCUPATIONAL DISEASES

Many industries are faced not only with accident problems but with occupational disease problems as well. While precise national data are lacking, well known occupational diseases include lead poisoning, common in lead smelting and refining, paint manufacturing, printing, and pottery glazing. Some industries no longer use lead, and in others effective means of control have been developed. Radioactive substances, including radium and uranium, are sources of burn and poisoning. Dust from various processes is a source of much trouble including silicosis, pneumoconiosis, and asbestosis. Motion, pressure, shock, vibration, extreme temperatures, excessive noise and intensive lights are all occupational hazards. Over 13,000 toxic substances are now listed by the National Institute of Occupational Safety and Health.[7]

OCCUPATIONAL SAFETY AND HEALTH

Toward the end of the nineteenth century, the growth of large-scale industry tended to depersonalize production. Employers could not know each worker personally. The heavy immigration at that time permitted the employment of masses of "Wops," "Bohunks," "Polocks," and others who were regarded then as second-class citizens. These factors, coupled with the increased mechanization of industry, the long work day, and

[4]Monroe Berkowitz, "Workmen's Compensation Income Benefits: Their Adequacy and Equity," Supplemental Studies for the National Commission on State Workmen's Compensation Laws, Volume I (Washington, Government Printing Office, 1973), pp. 189-274.

[5]Accident Facts, 1970 Edition (Chicago, National Safety Council), p. 25.

[6]Somers and Somers, op. cit., pp. 9-15.

[7]James C. Hyatt, "U. S. Inspection Unit Finds Itself Caught in Critical Cross Fire," Wall Street Journal, August 20, 1974, pp. 1; 14.

child labor, resulted in an extremely high accident rate. In one year, ending June 30, 1907, 4,534 workers were killed in the railroad industry alone, and in the same year 2,534 men also lost their lives in the bituminous coal industry.[8] With the high cost of both industrial accidents and diseases, it was inevitable that sooner or later society would attempt to improve the wretched conditions. Both the number of accidents and their severity have decreased since the early years of the twentieth century. But since 1958 the frequency rate but not the severity of accidents in all manufacturing has been increasing.[9]

SAFETY AND STATE GOVERNMENT

In 1877, Massachusetts passed the first state law requiring safety standards. In 1911, Wisconsin enacted a law which empowered its Industrial Commission to ascertain and prescribe safety standards, devices, and safeguards to enforce their use. Within a few years a number of other states passed similar legislation.[10] But the legislation has often been ineffective. A handful of states, among them California and New York, eventually established programs which were given qualified approval by safety experts. But unfortunately most states "have failed miserably to put the principles into practice."[11] Many state programs "can only be described as a sham; they are weak, underfunded, and staffed by political hacks who don't even pretend to enforce their inadequate regulations."[12] Another weakness has been the failure to inspect small firms even though typically they are most in need of safety improvements.

SAFETY AND THE FEDERAL GOVERNMENT

The failure or inadequacy of state regulation, the recent tendency for the accident frequency rate to rise, and the growing awareness of the problem of occupational diseases gradually brought the federal government into the field. Since 1936 at least ten pieces of legislation have been enacted which have some bearing on occupational safety and health. (See Table 10-4.) Many of these, however, dealt primarily with wages, hours, and other working conditions, and often only incidentally with work safety.

Legislation such as the Walsh-Healy Act of 1936, the Service Contract Act of 1965, and the Contract Work Hours and Safety Standards Act

---

[8]Somers and Somers, op. cit., pp. 7-9.

[9]Handbook of Labor Statistics, 1972, op. cit., Table 163. The frequency rate in all manufacturing in 1958 was 11.4; by 1970 it had risen to 15.

[10]Ibid., p. 369.

[11]Dan Cordtz, "Safety on the Job Becomes a Major Job for Management," Fortune, Vol. 86, No. 5 (November 1972), pp. 112-117; 162ff.

[12]Ibid., p. 114.

TABLE 10-4

FEDERAL SAFETY LEGISLATION

Title of Legislation	Date
Walsh-Healey Public Contracts Act	1936
Fair Labor Standards Act	1938
Longshore Safety Amendment	1958
Radiation Hazards Act	1959
Migrant Health Act	1962
Farm Labor Contractor Registration Act	1963
Service Contract Act	1965
Federal Metal and Nonmetallic Mine Safety Act	1966
Contract Work Hours and Safety Standards Act	1969
Federal Coal Mine and Safety Act	1969
Occupational Safety and Health Act	1970

Source: *Federal Labor Laws and Programs*, U. S. Department of Labor
Employment Standards Administration, Bulletin 262, September 1971, pp. 79-127.

of 1969 authorizes the Secretary of Labor to establish safety standards to be included in Federal contracts let to private bidders. In accepting a contract the contractor agrees to abide by the established standards. The Secretary may study, inspect, hold hearings, issue orders with respect to violations, and secure injunctions in U.S. District Courts when necessary. In some circumstances involving willful or gross violations, the Secretary is authorized to debar contractors from the award of new government contracts for a period of three years.[13]

Significant pieces of legislation applying to mining were enacted in 1966 and 1969. The Federal Metal and Nonmetallic Mine Safety Act was passed in the earlier year, and the Federal Coal Mine Health and Safety Act was passed in 1969. The 1966 act provided for federal enforcement of mandatory health and safety standards where the state plan is found to be satisfactory. Federal standards are published in the Federal Register and are effective one year after publication. The act requires that each under-

[13]*Federal Labor Laws and Programs*, U. S. Department of Labor, Employment Standards Administration, Bulletin 262, September 1971, pp. 94-96; 101-106.

ground mine be inspected at least once a year. The Bureau of Mines in the Department of the Interior administers this act.

Publicity about pneumoconiosis, commonly called black-lung disease, and a rash of coal mine disasters led to the Federal Coal Mine Health and Safety Act of 1969. This provided for the payment of monthly benefits to miners disabled by, or to the widows of miners who died of, black-lung disease. It also provided for mandatory health and safety standards and for frequent inspections by the Bureau of Mines.

OCCUPATIONAL SAFETY AND HEALTH ACT OF 1970

General safety legislation, first proposed by President Johnson and urged also by President Nixon, was enacted in December, 1970. This law covers every employer engaged in a business affecting interstate commerce. The only employers specifically not covered are those covered under other federal legislation such as the Coal Mine Health and Safety Act. Administration and enforcement of the act is vested in the Occupational Safety and Health Administration (OSHA) under the Secretary of Labor. Appeals from actions of the OSHA go to an independent quasi-judicial board, the Occupational Safety and Health Review Commission, whose three members are appointed by the President. Research and related functions are vested in the Secretary of Health, Education, and Labor whose functions are carried out by the National Institute for Occupational Safety and Health (NIOSH).[14]

The act authorizes the administrators to establish occupational safety and health standards partly by ordering into effect previously existing private standards, such as those issued by the National Fire Protection Association, or new standards developed by NIOSH. Temporary emergency standards can be established immediately upon publication in the National Register. Any person adversely affected by a standard may challenge its validity by petitioning a U.S. Court of Appeals within 60 days of its promulgation.

Any employee or his representative may request an inspection of the work site by sending a signed written notice to the Department of Labor. Inspectors may enter establishments at any reasonable time without giving prior notice to the employer. If a safety violation is found the employer is issued a written citation describing the violation and fixing a

---

[14]*Ibid.*, pp. 109-120. See also Dan Cordtz, *op. cit.*, "What are the Provisions of the New Safety Act?" *Safety Standards*, March-April 1971, pp. 5-10; "HEW Establishes New National Institute," *Safety Standards*, July-August, 1971, pp. 8-9; "States Plan for Job Safety and Health," *Safety Standards*, March-April, 1972, pp. 21-24; Phyllis E. Lehman, "Two Years of OSHA," *Job Safety and Health*, Vol. 1, No. 6 (May 1973), pp. 3-7; "To Conquer Occupational Diseases," *Job Safety and Health*, Vol. 1, No. 7 (June 1973), pp. 3-7; and "Why Voluntary Compliance?" *Job Safety and Health*, Vol. 1, No. 11 (October 1973), pp. 22-24.

reasonable time for its abatement. Thereafter the Labor Department notifies the employer of any penalty to be assessed. The employer has 15 days within which to notify the Department that he wishes to contest the citation or proposed penalty. A contest by the employer normally leads to a hearing before the Occupational Safety and Health Review Commission. The commission may affirm, modify, or vacate the citation or proposed penalty. Review of Commission orders may be obtained by appeal to a U.S. Court of Appeals.

Willful or repeated violations of the Act's requirements may incur penalties of up to $10,000 for each violation. "Serious violations," meaning those in which there is a substantial probability that death or serious physical harm could result, carry mandatory monetary penalties of up to $1,000 for each violation, and may be assessed for up to that amount for each day the violation persists. In cases where an imminent danger exists which could reasonably be expected to cause death or serious physical harm before the danger can be eliminated, the Secretary of Labor is authorized to seek a restraining order in a U.S. District Court, in effect stopping a particular operation until the danger can be abated.

Another aspect of the act is the encouragement of state administration and enforcement of their occupational safety and health laws. Federal preemption of the field is specifically disclaimed. If the state has a program in operation which is approved by the Secretary of Labor, regulation is left to the state. States may get 90 percent federal matching funds to develop their new programs, and thereafter may receive grants of 50 percent of the cost of operating their programs. The state plan must conform to a list of federal standards in order to be approved.[15] The Secretary is required to make a continuing evaluation of the way a state plan is carried out and to withdraw approval whenever the state plan is found unsatisfactory.

Employers are required to keep records of work-related deaths, injuries, and illnesses, and to make reports as required by the Secretary of Labor. The Secretaries of Labor and of HEW are directed to collect, compile, and analyze statistics on work injuries and illnesses. If an approved state plan is in operation, statistics will be collected through the state agency.

Virtually all states are endeavoring to set up approved state plans,[16] and by January, 1974, OSHA had approved 23 state programs covering 30 million workers.[17] Small businesses generally prefer regulation by state authorities if there is to be regulation. Labor unions have been skeptical of the effectiveness of state regulation, and past experience confirms their

---

[15]Federal Labor Laws and Programs, op. cit., pp. 115-116.
[16]James F. Foster, "State Plan for Job Safety and Health," Safety Standards, March-April, 1972, pp. 21-24.
[17]"OSHA News Briefs," Job Safety and Health, Vol. 2, No. 3 (March 1974), p. 2.

judgment. Some national corporations are now indicating their preference for uniform national standards, even if enforcement is turned back to the states.[18]

EVALUATION

The Occupational Safety and Health Act has been met by considerable criticism especially from small businessmen, who sometimes complain that "OSHA is going to put me out of business." Some call it the "most dangerous piece of legislation for American business since the Wagner Act." Within organized labor, some have praised the law, also comparing it to the Wagner Act, while another union official spoke of "mismanagement, a conscious disregard for workers rights, a callous view of human life, and policies favoring the industries the act was designed to regulate."[19] Early criticism has been ascribed to the difficulties of putting a new program into effect, a lack of qualified inspectors, some "bureaucratic bungling," the largeness of the effort underway, the lack of modern safety standards for many operations, and some need for amendment of the new law to allow companies to secure from OSHA pre-inspection evaluation and advice. Criticism from small businessmen is not surprising since much of the need for improvement lies in the small business area, and some small businesses had never before had a thorough safety inspection.

On the whole, however, the act appears to be a significant step forward. The administrative machinery is now largely in place. From April 1971 through August 1974, OSHA made 172,000 inspections and issued 115,000 citations.[20] There has been emphasis on education and voluntary compliance, but the act has real teeth behind the voluntary compliance. New statistics on job accidents and diseases are slowly becoming available. A possible threat to the success of the act lies in the behavior of the states and of federal enforcement. If state performance is allowed to return to previous low standards, the act will be effectively negated.

REHABILITATION

In spite of the utilization of best practices, accidents are still bound to occur. In the early history of mankind, inhumanity to man was apparent in the treatment of the crippled. Accidents or deformities were ruled to be

---

[18]Dan Cordtz, op. cit., p. 168.

[19]Phyllis E. Lehman, op. cit., p. 3.

[20]Alexander J. Reis, "An Assessment of Three Years of OSHA: Labor Department View," an address at the Industrial Relations Research Association meeting, San Francisco, December 28, 1974, p. 2.

the curse of devils, and abandonment to beggary and ridicule was the rule rather than the exception. Eventually, the more humane teachings of Christianity plus the growth of democracy resulted in improved treatment. Today modern medicine and adult education can accomplish a great deal in rehabilitating the disabled.

As used in this section "rehabilitation" means both vocational and medical rehabilitation. It also covers both the rehabilitation of those injured on the job and rehabilitation of persons with non-job connected disabilities. The disabilities involved may be physical, mental, or social. A social disability is a situation where it is believed that societal conditions have caused a person to develop attitudes and personality characteristics that render him unable to work effectively. Often totally disabled persons have a combination of physical, mental and social problems. In this connection, rehabilitation often deals with hard-to-employ groups, such as drug addicts, alcoholics, criminals, the emotionally ill, and the mentally retarded.

PUBLIC REHABILITATION: LEGISLATIVE HISTORY

The first state vocational rehabilitation law was enacted by Massachusetts in 1918. National legislation came in 1920 when along with the separate program for veterans Congress passed an Industrial Rehabilitation Act. Several Congressmen had pointed out that industrial disabilities were eight times as numerous as armed forces disabilities. The new act provided for federal grants to the states to help finance vocational rehabilitation of persons handicapped by physical defect or deformity, whether congenital or acquired by accident, injury, or disease.[22] Massachusetts amended her law in 1921 to conform with the federal legislation, and other states slowly enacted rehabilitation laws also.

Very little money was appropriated during the 1920's and 1930's. The Social Security Act of 1935 included a provision for permanent authorization by congress for annual appropriations of $2 million per year, increased by the 1939 amendments to $3 1/2 million annually. By 1943 only 210,000 persons had been rehabilitated. In 1943, the Barden-LaFollette Act expanded the program to include the rehabilitation of the blind and mentally disabled. Broadened services were authorized for medical and hospital care, maintenance and transportation, and tools and equipment. An amendment in 1954 made matching grants available for state construction of rehabilitation centers. Matching grants were also authorized for

[21]W. Scott Allan, *Rehabilitation: A Community Challenge* (New York, Wiley, 1958), pp. 2-3.

[22]Kathaleen C. Arneson, "Legislative Perspective," *Rehabilitation Record*, May-June 1970, pp. 27-31.

research on new methods and techniques. Annual grants to the states were increased to $23 million.

Legislation in the 1960's included the welfare amendments of 1962, 1965, and 1967 which endeavored to make rehabilitation an integral part of welfare programs. These acts liberalized federal matching grants, put renewed emphasis on the improvement of workshops and rehabilitation centers, and on the construction of new facilities, and included a mandate to the state to expand services to all persons in need of and eligible for rehabilitation by 1975.

The 1968 amendments further broadened the scope of rehabilitation by authorizing vocational evaluation and work adjustment to the disadvantaged, whether or not disabled.[23] Another significant piece of legislation in 1968 was the Architectural Barriers bill under which federal financing is made available to encourage the building of ramps and the removal of barriers so that handicapped people, especially people in wheelchairs, may have easier access to public facilities.[24]

The Social Security Amendments of 1972, besides instituting the Supplemental Security Income (SSI) program, also made some changes in vocational rehabilitation for those judged suitable for such services and mandates acceptance of the services if offered. It is estimated that up to 20 percent or about 200,000 of the blind and the disabled who receive SSI will be referred for rehabilitation. Of those perhaps 100,000 will be accepted for rehabilitation services.[25]

The Rehabilitation Act of 1973 reflected a compromise after three years of stormy struggle between those in Congress who wished to expand rehabilitation, and those in the Nixon Administration who desired to limit the role of the federal government.[26] The new law authorizes $1,546 million over 2 years for grants to the states. The federal share of funds may not exceed 90 percent, but the nonfederal share may be in cash or in kind. The state plan must expand, improve, and give priority to programs for the most severely handicapped. The law directs client participation in developing a rehabilitation plan for him. Existing research, demonstration, and training programs are continued. The law also prohibits discrimination against the handicapped in any federal program operated with federal funds, and directs the Secretary of Labor to require all federal contractors to take affirmative action to promote the employment of the handicapped.[27]

---

[23]Ibid., p. 30.

[24]Joseph Hunt, "A Decade of Progress," *Journal of Rehabilitation*, National Rehabilitation Association, Vol. 35 (Jan.-Feb. 1969), pp. 9-11.

[25]John W. Dalaplaine, "Income Maintenance and Rehab for the Blind," *Rehabilitation Record*, May-June 1973, pp. 34-35.

[26] Kathaleen C. Arneson, "The Rehabilitation Act of 1973," *Social and Rehabilitation Record*, Vol. 1 (January 1974), pp. 6-9.

[27]Ibid., p. 9.

REHABILITATION CENTERS AND
SHELTERED WORKSHOPS

Fifty-four states and territories now have active rehabilitation programs. As recently as 1965, five states had no rehabilitation facilities, and in others very little rehabilitation was actually accomplished. Under the impetus of the 1965 amendments, the total number of rehabilitation centers has expanded considerably in recent years. Facilities are commonly associated with state university hospitals and other large municipal medical facilities. Goods and services provided include: medical programs; corrective surgery or therapeutic treatment; prosthetic and orthoptic devices; maintenance, not exceeding the estimated cost of subsistence; occupational licenses, tools, equipment, and initial stocks and supplies; transportation in connection with other rehabilitation services; and other goods and services necessary to render a handicapped person employable.[28]

State agencies provide a substantial portion of the services through their own facilities, but also contract out parts of the work to other public and private rehabilitation facilities, including "sheltered workshops." A rehabilitation center becomes a sheltered workshop whenever the U.S. Department of Labor issues to it a certification of exemption from the requirement to pay minimum wages.[29] The sheltered workshop is designed to provide employment for handicapped people who cannot work competitively but who do have capabilities for partial self-support. Sometimes it is a half-way house providing a period of adjustment and work experience before moving to a job, completely independent of the rehabilitation program. In other cases it may be the individual's only chance for a permanent job. Sometimes it is necessary to redesign the job, tools, and machinery to fit the capabilities of the worker.[30]

Sweden and the Netherlands have developed the sheltered workshop idea to a greater extent than has the United States. In Sweden there are three types of subsidies for such groups: grants-in-aid for construction; subsidies for the initial purchase of equipment; and client wage subsidies. Usually the workshops are operated by a municipality or county although some are privately sponsored. The program is part of the Swedish full employment program under which a distinctly lower level of unemployment than that in the United States has been achieved.[31]

[28]State Vocational Rehabilitation Agency Fact Sheet Booklet, U. S. Department of Health, Education and Welfare, Rehabilitation Services Administration, 1971, p. 1.

[29]Edward A. Rossit and Earl A. Graybeal, "Sheltered Workshop Certification," Journal of Rehabilitation, Vol. 37 (May-June 1971), pp. 30-31. See also C. Ray Asfsahl, "Sheltered Workshop Management," Journal of Rehabilitation, Vol. 37 (Sept.-Oct., 1971), pp. 17-19; 40.

[30]Jesse H. Oswalt and Murl Wayne Parker, "VR Viewed By An Industrial Engineer," Ibid., (March-April, 1971), pp. 17-19. See also Louis E. Davis, "Reconstructuring Jobs," Manpower, February 1970, pp. 3-6.

[31]John R. Kimberly, "Sheltered Workshops in Sweden," Rehabilitation Record, March-April, 1972, pp. 35-38.

REHABILITATION AND WORKMEN'S COMPENSATION

Barriers to adequate rehabilitation include numerous deficiencies in state workmen's compensation legislation. There is a growing awareness that the end goal of workmen's compensation should be rehabilitation of disabled workmen. But state laws and administrative rules sometimes militate against rehabilitation. Some state programs require that a disability must be static or fixed before the case may be accepted. Others have required that the entire process of litigation must be completed before commencing rehabilitation. In January, 1972, 18 states had various limits on the kinds of medical rehabilitation for which the state would pay.[32]

Another difficulty is that the worker may fear that his workmen's compensation benefits may stop if he undertakes rehabilitation. If this is the case he will have less incentive to try to rehabilitate himself. A growing number of states now provide for full workmen's compensation benefits while the worker undergoes rehabilitation, but several still do not.[33] Even this type of provision is not entirely adequate, for a workman may incur other expenses during rehabilitation, such as travel, maintenance away from home, plus tuition and equipment costs. Additional states are endeavoring to improve their laws in this regard. Several of the states have also experimented with a requirement that workmen's compensation payments be suspended if the worker, without good cause, refuses to undergo rehabilitation.

HIRING THE HANDICAPPED

Despite prolonged advertising campaigns urging employers to "hire the handicapped," many employers are reluctant or unwilling to do so. In a 1960 study covering 1,221 employers engaged in manufacturing in six states, nearly 60 percent of the employers were unwilling to hire workers with certain physical impairments.[34] Of the six types of disabilities for which the survey checked, employers were most reluctant to hire persons with epilepsy or lung and back ailments, and were least reluctant to hire persons with eye disabilities, limb or other orthopedic disabilities, or heart trouble.

[32]Louise B. Russell and Carl J. Schramm, "Three Issues in Compensation Medical Care," Supplementatl Studies for the National Commission on State Workmen's Compensation Laws, Vol. II, op. cit., p. 284. See also Earl F. Cheit, Injury and Recovery in the Course of Employment (New York, Wiley, 1961), pp. 298-299.

[33]See Florence C. Johnson, "Changes in Workmen's Compensation in 1971," Monthly Labor Review, January 1972, pp. 51-55; "Changes in Workmen's Compensation Laws in 1972," Monthly Labor Review, January 1973, pp. 45-49; and "Changes in Workmen's Compensation Laws in 1973," Monthly Labor Review, January 1974, pp. 32-38.

[34]Lloyd W. Larson, "Workmen's Compensation Laws and the Employment of the Handicapped," Monthly Labor Review, Vol. 85, No. 2 (Feb. 1962), pp. 145-148.

A 1970 study of 108 companies in Minnesota showed similar results. Employers were questioned to determine their degree of willingness to hire ten types of handicapped people for four types of jobs, production, management, clerical, or sales. Generally employers were quite reluctant to hire the blind, the deaf, the epileptic, the mentally retarded, and those with back ailments. They were more willing to hire those with diabetes or peptic ulcer, and those who had lost one arm or leg. They were more favorable toward placing the handicapped in production or clerical work than in management or sales.[35]

Often the handicapped person can, in fact, work as effectively as regular workers. Numerous studies have shown that handicapped people on the average have performed as well as their nonhandicapped counterparts.[36] Often they are so appreciative of having a job that their absentee and turnover rate is lower than that of other workers, while productivity and injury rates are about the same.

HARD-TO-EMPLOY GROUPS

Certain groups including the emotionally ill, the mentally retarded, public offenders, drug addicts, alcoholics, and others, may be classified as "hard-to-employ." Each of these categories varies substantially from the others, and there is great individual variation within a particular group. Also, many individuals fall into two or more of the above categories, perhaps using alcohol and drugs, and being a public offender as well as emotionally disturbed. Because there are severe employment problems— some can hardly be rehabilitated at all, others only partially rehabilitated—and because employers are reluctant to hire individuals who bear the labels, they are classed as "hard-to-employ."[37]

---

[35]C. Arthur Williams, Jr., "Is Hiring the Handicapped Good Business," *Journal of Rehabilitation*, Vol. 38 (March-April, 1972), pp. 30-34.

[36]*Ibid.*, p. 30.

[37]For those who desire to pursue the problems of particular "hard-to-employ" groups, the following references are suggested: Thomas Kelly and Gregory March, "Rehabilitating the Alcoholics," *Rehabilitation Record*, (Sept.-Oct. 1971), pp. 23-24; "Dealing with the Drinking Problem," *Manpower*, Vol. 2 (Dec. 1970), pp. 3-4; Phillip Mason, "Drug Users and Jobs," *Manpower*, Vol. 5 (Feb. 1973), pp. 15-20; Lloyd Feldman, "Retardation, Poverty and Jobs," *Manpower*, Vol. 1 (Sept. 1969), pp. 30-32; Janet K. Brown, "Mental Patients Work Back Into Society," *Manpower*, Vol. 2 (Feb. 1970), pp. 23-25; "Working Back to Mental Health," *Manpower*, Vol. 5 (Jan. 1973), pp. 23-26; John J. Galvin, "Training Correctional Manpower," *Manpower*, Vol. 3 (Jan. 1971), pp. 14-17; George A. Pownall, "Employment Problems of Released Prisoners," *Manpower*, Vol. 3 (Jan. 1971), pp. 26-30; Clyde E. Sullivan, "Changes in Correction: Show or Substance," *Manpower*, Vol. 3 (Jan. 1971), pp. 2-7; Clyde E. Sullivan, "From Jail to Community," *Rehabilitation Record*, Jan.-Feb. 1969, pp. 1-4; Patricia Marshall, "Criminal Records and Public Jobs," *Manpower*, Vol. 3 (Dec. 1971), pp. 3-7; "Prison Jaycees: Forging the Missing Link," *Manpower*, Vol. 4 (March 1972), pp. 15-19; Barry S. Bader, "Opening Public Jobs to the Disadvantaged," *Manpower*, Vol. 4 (April 1972), pp. 9-13; and Delores Board, "Pointing Parolees Toward the Mainstream," *Manpower*, Vol. 5 (October 1973), pp. 10-12.

In 1970. Congress passed a Comprehensive Alcohol Abuse and Alcoholism Prevention, Treatment, and Rehabilitation Act (Public Law 19-616). This Act created a National Institute on Alcohol Abuse and Alcoholism to administer formula grants to the states, and contracts and project grants for the prevention and treatment of alcohol abuse and alcoholism, and for the rehabiltation of the victims of this disease. An HEW publication in 1971 on "Alcohol and Health" reported that there were nine million abusers of alcohol, or alcoholics, in the United States. Alcoholism plays a major role in half of our highway fatalities, and an even higher ratio among young people. Alcoholism was estimated to cause a loss of $10 billion in work time, $2 billion in health and public welfare cost, and $3 billion in property damage each year. In 1973, the Federal government allocated $30 million to states, in addition to a somewhat larger amount for community projects. Among special projects were a drinking driver program, one for federal employees and American Indians, and taking over alcohol projects formerly funded through the Office of Economic Opportunity.

EVALUATION OF REHABILITATION

To summarize, the success of rehabilitation will depend on the quality of medical care, the adequacy of rehabilitation centers, the solving of workmen's compensation problems, the willingness of employers to rehire injured workmen, and their willingness to hire the "hard-to-employ." Some progress has been made in recent years in improving the rehabilitation program in the United States, but still further progress is needed. The quality of medical care needs upgrading, and the number of rehabilitation centers needs expanding. More of the injured need to go through a rehabilitation program. Better interrelation between workmen's compensation and rehabilitation is necessary. Lastly, more employers need to get over the fear of hiring handicapped workers. In some European countries, employers are required to hire a certain percentage of their workers from a total handicapped group.[38] Here in America, it is hoped that a more voluntary system will adequately solve the problem.

OCCUPATIONAL DISABILITY AND THE LAW

In the early years of the factory system no laws existed to protect or help the injured workmen.[39] In order to obtain damages from an employer,

[38]Allan, op. cit., p. 110.

[39]For a brief history of the development of the law from which most of the material in this section was taken, see Somers and Somers, op. cit., Chapter 2.

worker had to sue in court and win. If the worker was killed by the accident, no remedy of any kind was available by law, because the injured workmen was required to do the suing. In court an injured workman had to base his case on the common law of negligence or tort liability. The common law was based on the assumption that someone was at fault in each accident. Whoever it was had to pay the damages. If it was the employer, he paid; but if the worker or a fellow worker was at fault, then no damages could be collected.

At law the employer had three defenses. First, he could maintain that the worker himself was a contributing cause to the accident (contributory negligence). Second, he could maintain that a fellow employee was the cause of the accident, and absolve himself from the cost (fellow-servant rule). As an example of this type of case, it was held in England in 1837 that a butcher boy's helper was not entitled to damages from his employer because the injury was due to the butcher boy's overloading a van. The third defense was that if the work was somewhat dangerous, the workman should have known this when he accepted employment. Having accepted a job, he assumed the risks of any injuries that might occur (assumption of risk). In a 1924 case in New York, a girl sued because she had contracted tuberculosis when working in a damp, unsanitary, unventilated cellar of a candy manufacturer. The judge denied her damages on the ground that the girl was fully aware of the conditions under which she worked. In short, the injured workman had little redress under the common law. If he sued, he probably would lose his job. Then, the case itself might cost the workman a great deal of money. The defenses available to the employer were so powerful that the workman did not stand much chance of winning. One student of the subject found that workers obtained no legal relief in seven out of eight cases.[40]

EMPLOYERS' LIABILITY LAWS

The failure of the common law to provide adequate protection for injured workmen resulted in a number of state statutes being passed. These were called Employer's Liability laws. Some of these laws prohibited the employer from forcing an employee to sign a contract to relieve the employer of all liability for accidents at work. By 1908, 27 states had passed such laws. Other modifications of the common law permitted the right of suit in death case (41 jurisdictions). Other laws in almost all states restricted the defenses of the employer — particularly the fellow-servant rule.

In spite of the laws giving injured workmen more rights, employers' liability statutes did not provide adequate protection. In the first several

[40]E. H. Downey, *Workmen's Compensation* (New York, Macmillan, 1924), p. 144.

decades of this century, 40 investigatory bodies were appointed to investigate the problem of industrial accidents. Almost all the bodies recommended that the common law and employers' liability statutes be replaced by a system of workmen's compensation. Under employers' liability laws, one study from three states showed, no compensation was received at all in almost one third of the cases and $1,000 and over was obtained in less than 10 percent of the cases.[41] Another study showed that nine of the largest liability insurance companies paid on only one claim out of eight in the period from 1906-1908.[42] Furthermore, 30 to 50 percent had to be deducted from awards to pay the legal fees for injured workmen. John R. Commons found that of $1 million paid to liability insurance companies in 1911, only $300,000 was received by injured workmen.[43]

Several other difficulties may be noted with employers' liability laws. Court cases took quite long to settle. In Ohio an average time of three years per case elapsed before final awards were rendered. In Illinois the same length of time elapsed before damages were actually received. Another criticism was that the awards received varied quite inconsistently. Whereas one worker might obtain as much as $2,700 for the loss of an eye, another less fortunate worker would recieve as little as $290.[44] Finally, few employers adopted safety methods. Court awards were so few and so small that they had little financial incentive to do so.

With such a serious indictment employers's liablity laws, it was not long until the various states began passing workmen's compensation laws.These are discussed in the next chapter.

Summary

Many work injuries occur each year in the United States. The frequency and severity of accidents vary considerably from one industry to another. The costs of industrial accidents are enormous and are borne by the injured and by society as a cost of production. Occupational diseases cost additional sums. A number of groups have been interested in safety — private groups, labor unions, insurance companies, and governments. Such groups are also interested in the rehabilitation of injured workmen. Because handicapped workers perform well, and because rehabilitation of the injured is less expensive than welfare payments, rehabilitation program are worthwhile. Rehabilitation has been handicapped by a lack of adequate medical care, too few rehabilitation centers, a reluctance to undertake rehabilitation because of workmen's compensation payments,

---

[41]I. M. Rubinow, Social Insurance (New York, Holt, Rinehart % Winston, 1913), pp. 93-95.

[42]Somers and Somers, op. cit., p. 23.

[43]John R. Commons, Labor and Administration (New York, Macmillan, 1913), p. 395.

[44]H. A. Millis and R. E. Montgomery, Labor's Risks and Social Insurance (New York, McGraw-Hill, 1938), p. 193.

and the failure of employers to hire the handicapped. Improvement in all these areas is possible.

In the early days of the factory system, workers had to sue if they were injured, since no laws protected them. Certain legal defenses of the employer made it extremely difficult for workers to collect damages. At the beginning of the twentieth century, employers' liability law were passed which restricted the defenses of employers. Because of the costs and delays under employers' liability laws, such laws have been superseded by workmen's compensation laws. Failure to provide adequate coverage under workmen's compensation means that large numbers of injured workers must still take their chances under less adequate employers' liability laws.

Bibliography

Allan, W. Scott, *Rehabilitation: A Community Challenge* (New York, Wiley, 1958).

Berkowitz, Monroe, ed., *Rehabilitating the Disabled Worker* (Washington, Vocational Rehabilitation Administration, 1963).

_____, *Workmen's Compensation: The New Jersey Experience* (New Brunswick, Rutgers University Press, 1960).

Blake, Roland P., *Industrial Safety*, 3rd ed. (Englewood Cliffs, New Jersey, Prentice-Hall, 1963).

Cheit, Earl F., *Injury and Recovery in the Course of Employment* (New York, Wiley, 1958).

_____, and Margaret Gordon, eds., *Occupational Disability and Public Policy* (New York, Wiley, 1963).

Feinberg, Lawrence B., and English, R. William, *Rehabilitation in the Inner City* (Syracuse, Syracuse University, 1970).

Oberman, C. Esco, *A History of Vocational Rehabilitation in the United States* (Minneapolis, Denison, 1965).

Roth, Julius A. and Eddy, Elizabeth M., *Rehabilitation for the Unwanted* (New York, Atherton Press, 1967).

Wright, George N., and Trotter, Ann Beck, *Rehabilitation Research* (Madison, University of Wisconsin, 1968).

CHAPTER 11

WORKMEN'S COMPENSATION

The failure of employers' liability laws resulted in the enactment of a number of workmen's compensation laws by state legislatures in the first two decades of this century. These laws attempted to correct the major deficiencies under the common law and employers' liability laws. Workmen's compensation laws were based on the premise that payment should be made to injured workmen regardless of who was at fault in causing the accident. Industrial accidents were simply a part of the cost of producing goods and services. Employers were required to assume the risks of these costs, as well as any other costs of production. Another purpose of workmen's compensation was to eliminate delay and unnecessary costs of litigation. Payments were to be awarded by separate workmen's compensation boards to speed procedure. Benefits were fixed for each type of injury so that, it was thought, there would be little need to litigate, particularly since the common law defenses of employers were made inapplicable. Employers would not have an interest in delaying cases in the hope that such delays would encourage employees to settle for less. The amounts were fixed, so that there was little to gain by delay.

Drafters of workmen's compensation laws also hoped that since employers would be required to pay, strong incentives would be provided for more safety. In order to lessen the costs of insuring, it was felt that employers would make every effort to improve safety. Some of the early state laws recognized the importance of safety by including it in the title of the law. In Massachusetts, for example, the law was titled: "An Act Relative to the Payment of Employees for Personal Injuries Received in the Course of the Employment and to the Prevention of Such Injuries."[1] Although the safety movement preceded passage of workmen's compensation laws, there is no question that such laws gave a strong impetus toward promoting more and better safety. Merit rating, basing premiums on past records of accidents, gave a direct incentive to reduce accidents, and gradually employers began to see the advantages of improved safety on its own merits. Today the importance of safety is so well recognized that most large employers would adopt the best type of safety practices regardless of whether workmen's compensation laws were in existence or not. There is doubt today that merit rating has any appreciable effect on

---

[1]Arthur H. Reede, *Adequacy of Workmen's Compensation* (Cambridge, Mass., Harvard, 1947), p. 321.

204

industrial safety, but it will probably continue to exist as a device to reduce rates for larger companies. The coverage of occupational diseases also stimulated the growth of industrial hygiene. Workmen's compensation can take part of the credit for the reduction in accidents and deaths, and the elimination or reduction of the incidence of many occupational diseases.

The first workmen's compensation laws provided only for cash benefits. There was little medical care for the injured, and the concept of rehabilitation was not an original part of such laws. With the development of workmen's compensation after World War I, it was recognized that medical care and rehabilitation should be made an important part of the program. Medical benefits were expanded, and rehabilitation has become the keystone to the whole program, at least in theory.[2]

The first workmen's compensation law was passed to cover Prussian railroads in 1838. The first nationwide law came in Germany in 1884. Thereafter one nation after another in Europe introduced some type of workmen's compensation legislation. By 1973, 125 countries had some sort of work injury law. In the United States, thanks to President Theodore Roosevelt, a federal compensation law was passed in 1908 to cover Civil Service employees. The next year Montana passed such a law for its coal miners, but it was declared unconstitutional. Between 1910 and 1915, 30 states passed workmen's compensation laws, but a number of these were declared unconstitutional. In order to make such laws constitutional, some states either amended their constitutions or provided that the employer could elect to be covered under the law. By 1917, most of the legal problems on election had been settled by the United States Supreme Court, which ruled in three different cases that workmen's compensation laws were legal regardless of whether they were mandatory or provided for exclusive state insurance funds. Shortly after the Supreme Court decisions, nine other states passed workmen's compensation laws so that by 1920 all states but six, concentrated in the South, had such laws. The last state to pass such a law was Mississippi in 1948. Today, there are 58 workmen's compensation jurisdictions — the 50 states, the District of Columbia, Puerto Rico, Virgin Islands, American Samoa, Guam, The Trust Territory of the Pacific Islands, and two federal acts covering federal employees and longshoremen.

COVERAGE

Even though coverage of workers under workmen's compensation laws has been expanding over the years, it is far from complete today. A number of industries are not covered. The railroad industry and seamen are

[2]Harold M. Somers and Anne R. Somers, *Workmen's Compensation* (New York, Wiley, 1954), pp. 26-28.

covered under two separate federal employers' liability laws. The workers in both industries feel that benefits are higher under these laws, and therefore they have opposed being covered under workmen's compensation.[3]

Those most frequently exempt from coverage are agricultural workers, domestic workers, casual labor, employees in small firms, and state and local government employees. A minority of states do not have a compulsory coverage law, and a slight loss of coverage results here. In 12 states, the workmen's compensation law applies only to hazardous or extra-hazardous industries. Coverage in these states is much less than elsewhere. A few states limit the type of occupational diseases covered, although all states now cover some such diseases.

Certain eligibility requirements tend to limit the coverage of injured workmen under certain circumstances. In order to be covered under workmen's compensation acts, the injury must occur "out of and in the course of employment." Much legal debate has ensued over whether accidents have indeed so occurred. In general, injuries occurring on the way to or from work are not covered, but sometimes workers are covered if they are riding in special buses furnished by the employer. Liberal courts tend to cover workers dressing on the employer's premises, and workers injured through the horseplay of others. Usually injuries due to natural causes, such as frostbite, heat prostration and the like, are covered only if the job requires unusual exposure. Under these circumstances most lightning cases would not be covered.

If a worker has engaged in misconduct, benefits are either denied entirely or reduced. Self-inflicted injuries, and injuries resulting from intoxication, are generally not compensable. Some states refuse payment to workers who fail to use safety appliances. Little is known about what percentage of accidents is not covered because of not "arising out of and in the course of employment."

To summarize on coverage and eligibility, in 1915 about 41 percent of all eligible workers were covered under workmen's compensation laws.[4] This figure rose to 84 percent by 1972. Southern and Southwestern states have less coverage than other states. Although labor unions and other groups have lobbied for improved coverage, their strength has not been sufficient to obtain full coverage, particularly in the states that are not as yet heavily industrialized. Since most authorities conclude that workmen's compensation laws are superior to employers' liability laws, they have recommended more coverage under workmen's compensation laws.

[3]Earl F. Cheit. Injury and Recovery in the Course of Employment (New York. Wiley. 1961). Chaps. 7, 8.
[4]Reede. op. cit., Table 3. p. 17.

BENEFITS

Benefits under workmen's compensation are of three types. Cash payments are made to aid workers to continue to support their families while incapacitated. Secondly, medical payments are provided for the cost of medical care. Thirdly, rehabilitation payments are also made (see previous chapter). The cash payments are divided into four types of payments depending on the severity of the accident. For those killed in industry, death benefits are paid. For those permanently incapacitated, permanent total disability payments are made. For those losing limbs or suffering other permanent damage to parts of their bodies, permanent partial disability payments are made. The remaining injuries, which do not result in the permanent loss of a member, are called temporary total disabilities.

DEATH BENEFITS

Approximately 14,000 deaths occur each year in industry. The social loss could be computed as the present discounted value of the total earnings that the victim would have earned during his remaining work years minus the cost of his maintenance during this period. It would be expected, then, that death benefits would be less than permanent total disability payments, since there are no costs of supporting the injured workmen. Many states, however, pay the same benefits in death cases as in permanent total disability injuries. Benefits if based on need should also vary with the number of dependents that remain to be supported.[5] Quite clearly, a widow with four minor children is in need of more economic support than a widow who has no children.

Adequacy of compensation for death varies considerably, depending on the state involved. Some states come close to approaching an adequate benefit; others fall considerably short. Most of the states vary payment according to the number of dependents, but a minority do not. The trend over the years has been toward coverage for dependents.

Presumably, need would dictate that payments be continued until death of the widow, or remarriage, or until children reach at least the age of 18. In 1940, only six jurisdictions had such coverage; by 1973, however, only 19 jurisdictions limited such benefits.

FORMULA FOR DEATH BENEFITS

Most jurisdictions base payments on a percentage of wages earned by the worker before his injury. The most typical percentage provided for a widow with children is 66-2/3 percent of wages with the next most frequent percentage being 60 percent. The figure has risen from 50 percent in

[5]*Ibid.*, p. 66.

1915, but many states place maximum limits on weekly payments so that many dependents receive much less than 66-2/3, of wages. Fourteen jurisdictions have a maximum weekly benefit of less than $60, the lowest of these being Mississippi ($40). Eight of the states providing for a maximum below $60 are border or southern states. The maximums in other jurisdictions are much higher. The highest is Arizona, with a weekly maximum of $153.85.

Another important restriction of death benefits is absolute limits on the total amounts of money paid. Thirteen states have such a limitation (December, 1973).[6] In order to protect the low-wage family, all jurisdictions except two have a minimum weekly benefit. The minimums range from $5 a week in two jurisdictions to $75 in the most liberal state.

ADEQUACY OF DEATH BENEFITS

The inclusion of survivors' benefits under the Social Security Act have made death benefits much more adequate. The National Commission on State Workmen's Compensation Laws found as of 1971 that only 13 of 51 jurisdictions provided for less than 60 percent of wage loss when both workmen's compensation and Social Security were added together. For the unlucky few widows who could draw only workmen's compensation, 41 of the 51 jurisdictions provided for less than 40 percent of the wage loss.[7]

Since OASDHI has been expanding, some have contended that all payments for the problem of premature death could be made through OASDHI and thus workmen's compensation for such tragedies could be abolished. Several arguments may be made, though, on the side of retaining workmen's compensation. Sir William Beveridge argued for the continuation of workmen's compensation on the grounds that it provided benefits to compensate for hazardous work, along with economic incentives for improved safety. It also offered the only justification for limiting liability under the common law.[8]

The 1965 amendments to the Social Security Act limited disability payments so that a disabled worker may not receive more in monthly benefits from both Social Security and workmen's compensation combined than 80 percent of the average monthly earnings credited to his Social Security before he became disabled. Amendments to the Social Security Act in 1967 stipulated that in computing average earnings, worker's earnings in excess of the annual amount taxable under Social Security could be included. No change was made which would restrict

[6]Alfred M. Skolnik and Daniel N. Price. "Workmen's Compensation Under Scrutiny." Social Security Bulletin, Vol. 37. No. 10 (Oct. 1974). p. 14.

[7]C. Arthur Williams and Peter S. Barth. directors. Compendium on Workmen's Compensation (Washington. Government Printing Office 1973). p. 142.

[8]Sir William Beveridge. Social Insurance and Allied Services (New York. Macmillan. 1942). pp. 39-40.

concurrent payment of survivors' benefits and death benefits under workmen's compensation.

PERMANENT TOTAL DISABILITY BENEFITS

The same type of formula is used in permanent total disabilities as other injuries. That is, percentage of wages is paid subject to certain maximum and minimum weekly amounts. The duration of these payments is limited in 19 of the 50 states although recommendations from the Department of Labor and the Model Act call for payments throughout life or for the period of the disability. In 11 states, the largest amount of money that a totally disabled worker can receive in benefits is less than $25,000, an amount less than the average American worker earns in four years of full-time work.[9]

The National Commission on State Workmen's Compensation Laws recently computed the wage loss of a 35-year-old craftsman with a wife and two dependent children who was earning $8,590 at the time of his disability. The Commission found that 31 states paid less than 60 percent of the wage loss and 21 more beneficient jurisdictions paid between 60 and 80 percent. Their figures included both workmen's compensation and Social Security. Only 16 of the 50 states paid maximum weekly benefits for a family of four that was equal to or greater than the national poverty figure.[10]

A study in Oklahoma of children of the severely disabled showed that serious injury not only affects the workers themselves, but a lack of income precludes many of their children from obtaining further education.[11] The income of the workers dropped on the average from $6,000 to $3,800 after the injury, even though some of the wives went to work. Of 43 children reaching college age after the injury, only six enrolled in college. The federal government provides monthly college allowances for children of veterans who either were killed in action or suffer a service connected total disability. As yet, no such benefits have been included under workmen's compensation.

The value of workmen's compensation benefits is eroded by inflation. Also, if the benefit formula is tied to past wages, the injured workmen are not permitted to share in the productivity gains of the future. To provide more adequate benefits, the National Commission on State Workmen's Compensation Laws recommended that permanent total benefits be paid not as a percent of the injured workman's wage but as a percent of the state's average weekly wage. On the other hand, the Commission was

[9]*The Report of the National Commission on State Workmen's Compensation Laws*, (Washington. Government. Printing Office. 1972). p. 65.

[10]C. Arthur Williams and Peter S. Barth. op. cit., p. 126.

[11]Paul A. Brinker and E. Wayne Murdock. "Children of the Severely Injured." *Journal of Human Resources*, Vol. 8.(1973),pp. 242-248.

critical of too liberal benefits in a few states that were paying permanent total disability payments to some who retained substantial wage earning capacity.

PERMANENT PARTIAL INJURIES

Permanent partial injuries are divided into what are called scheduled and nonscheduled injuries. The scheduled injuries provide for a specific amount of payment for a specific loss, such as $15,000 for the loss of the arm at the shoulder. The nonscheduled injuries are compensated as a percentage of wages for a limited period. Vast differences and inconsistencies in payments exist between the states. Some states pay more for the loss of an arm than a foot, whereas others pay just the opposite. For the loss of an arm at the shoulder, six states provide $25,000 and over (1972), whereas 7 states pay under $10,000. Most states pay more for the loss of an arm than a leg, although the healing period is longer for loss of a leg and earnings are impaired more. Apparently most of the states were misled into thinking about machine operations when they granted larger benefits for the loss of an arm. In such cases, losses of arms would result in a greater loss of earning power than the loss of a leg. However, most losses of legs occur in mining, lumbering, construction and transportation, all industries in which the loss of a leg has tended to bar future employment.

When workmen's compensation laws were first passed, permanent partial benefits were predominantly based on loss of earnings. Most of the states later adopted a flat-rate disability schedule because they feared that paying workers according to the loss of earning power would tend to discourage workers from finding better jobs. Later, California experimented with a different basis for permanent partial benefits. Both occupation and age were considered in computing benefits. A worker who lost a finger in an occupation in which the use of a finger was vital to the work would suffer much more economic loss than another worker whose loss of a finger was immaterial to his occupation. Age also was considered a factor. The assumption was made that the loss of recuperative powers of an older man should call for more compensation, even though an injured younger man would be handicapped for a longer period of time. Some 75 pages of schedules were needed to compare the various injuries by occupation and ages. Although some inequities have been found within the system, a number of authorities feel that the California system provides for more equitable permanent partial benefits than other states.[12]

The National Commission on State Workmen's Compensation Laws (1972) found that there were more variations among states and more divergence between statutes and practices for permanent partial benefits than other types of workmen's compensation benefits. The Commission recommended that consideration be given to two types of permanent partial benefits. One would be based on impairment (loss of a limb, for example) even though no wage loss was incurred. The rationale here was that the impairment results in losses entirely unrelated to possible lost remuneration. The impairment may result in lifetime effects on the personality and normal activities of the worker. The second type of benefit would be paid both because of the impairment and the loss of wages.

Most permanent partial cases result in minor rather than major limb loss. About 87 percent of such cases are classified as minor rather than major. Four states pay 30 percent or more of their total workmen's compensation benefits on such claims, whereas five other states pay less than 10 percent. Unfortunately, permanent partial benefits are much less adequate for those severely injured than those experiencing minor loss.

TEMPORARY TOTAL DISABILITY

Most industrial injuries (95 percent) result in no permanent injury to the workman, but are of a temporary nature only. On the average, these injuries result in only several weeks of disability. A California sample shows that 9 percent of the temporary total injuries cause the loss of only one day of work, and 44 percent do not extend beyond seven days. Almost three-fourths of the injuries are healed within 21 days, and only 6 percent of these injuries last beyond six months.[13]

Most of the states pay a percentage of wage as a benefit, usually 66-2/3's percent of wages. But, in 1971, 18 states set the maximum weekly benefit at $60 or less. When workmen's compensation laws were first passed, the weekly maximums had been only slightly below the average weekly wage in manufacturing, which was $11.22. That weekly maximums have not kept pace with averages can be seen by noting that average weekly manufacturing wages in 1971 for the median of the 18 states was $134. Two states had a maximum benefit set as low as 33 percent of their average weekly wages in manufacturing. The maximum benefits fell below the poverty level ($79.56 per week) in 33 out of 52 jurisdictions. However, some improvement has been made since 1961 in paying larger benefits. In that year a single worker with 3 weeks' disability received 37 percent of his pay compared with 46 percent in 1973.[14]

[12]Reede. op. cit., pp. 121-122.

[13]Cheit. op. cit., p. 151 and Table 2.1. p. 29; Dorothy McCamman and A. M. Skolnik, "Workmen's Compensation: Measures of Accomplishment," Social Security Bulletin, Vol. 17. No. 3 (March. 1954). p. 8; "Workmen's Compensation Injury Table." Proceedings of the Casualty Actuarial Society, Vol. XLII. p. 140.

[14]Alfred M. Skolnik and Daniel N. Price. "Workmen's Compensation Under Scrutiny." Social Security Bulletin, Vol. 37. No. 10. Oct. 1974. pp. 3-25.

MEDICAL BENEFITS

When workmen's compensation laws were first passed, they provided only for cash payments to compensate for loss of wages. Shortly after passage of such laws, it became apparent that more cognizance should be taken of medical care in the program. Gradually more medical benefits were introduced into the laws until by 1962 the number of jurisdictions limiting benefits was only 15. Since then eleven additional states provided for unlimited benefits for physical disabilities so that by 1974 only four of the 54 jurisdictions limited such benefits. Additionally, six have more limitations on medical care for occupational diseases than for injuries. Some of the states which limit medical care provide that a patient cannot receive further medical benefits if no such benefits are paid during a stipulated period, such as two years. Such a requirement obviously excludes treatment in cases where the effects of a work-related injury or disease return after a period of time. Eighteen states also limit medical care by providing that the services of certain types of medical practitioners will not be paid for, such as psychiatrists, psychologists, chiropractors, occupational therapists and the like.[15] The National Council on State Workmen's Compensation Laws, among others, has recommended that full medical benefits be provided in all states. The additional costs of providing complete medical benefits would not be large.

One of the problems involved in medical care is who should choose the doctor. If the employer or insurance company has the right to choose the doctor, there is the danger that the doctor might favor the employer in determining the amount of injury. Too many favorable decisions in favor of the employee might cause the employer or insurance company to dismiss the doctor. Where the company doctor passes on the medical determination, it is contended that the state agency sees only a one-sided picture. It is almost the same as granting a company the right to choose the attorney to defend the injured workman. On the other hand, permitting the workman the free choice of a doctor may be criticized, also. In such cases, the physician may be inclined to report more serious damage in order that the workman may receive a larger award. Conflicting reports, depending upon whom the physician represents, were shown in a study of court cases by Professor Sam Barton in Texas.[16]

In early workmen's compensation laws, few states gave the worker the right to choose his own physician. Gradually, this right has expanded until in 1972, 25 states either permit the injured worker the free choice of a physician or choice from a panel. Some of the states using the panel system allow the employer to choose the panel, whereas in others the workmen's compensation board selects it. From Professor Barton's study

[15]C. Arthur Williams and Peter S. Barth. op. cit., Table 10.4. p. 148.
[16]Sam B. Barton. How Texas Cares for Her Injured Workers (Denton. Tex., North Texas State College. 1956). pp. 37-40.

of Texas cases and a survey of the literature, he maintained that the method of selecting a doctor is one of the major issues in workmen's compensation. Although the National Commission on State Workmen's Laws found little difference in payments between employer-choice and employee-choice states, they found a 10 percent higher use of specialists in the employee-choice states. The Commission in 1972 recommended that the worker be permitted the initial selection of his physician, either from among all licensed physicians in the state, or from a panel of physicians selected or approved by the workmen's compensation agency.[17]

In order to insure adequate medical care, the U. S. Department of Labor has recommended that the workmen's compensation agencies supervise the delivery of medical care. As of 1972 only 26 have such a provision in their law. Such a medical-rehabilitation agency should be able to order carriers or employers to provide necessary medical care, to limit payments for medical and rehabilitation services to usual and customary levels, and, when appropriate, to require patients to seek consultation or change the form and source of treatment.

REHABILITATION BENEFITS

A total of 27 of the 50 states provide for special maintenance benefits during the period of rehabilitation. The number of such states totaled only 7 in 1946. The National Commission on State Workmen's Compensation Laws (1972) recommended that workmen's compensation agencies be authorized to provide for such benefit. The maintenance benefits would be in addition to the worker's other benefits. The Commission found that workmen's compensation agencies were not doing a good job of assuring that workers with work-related disabilities were helped to recover lost abilities. At the present time, the costs of vocational rehabilitation are borne mainly by the general taxpayer. The Commission suggested that employers finance the cost of such rehabilitation for two reasons. One was that since the firm was the source of the cause, it should pay. The other was that state departments of vocational rehabilitation have been less than consistent in attending to the occupationally disabled.

Sometimes workmen's compensation payments have inhibited workers from seeking rehabilitation. One suggestion here is to provide that if a worker refuses rehabilitation, the benefit should be cut to the amount the worker would have obtained after rehabilitation. A more stringent control would be to deny all benefits if the worker refuses rehabilitation.

[17]C. Arthur Williams and Peter S. Barth. op. cit., pp. 153-155.

SECOND INJURY FUNDS

In order to aid in the reemployment of the injured, all but three states have some form of second injury (or subsequent-injury) funds. Under these funds, a worker who comes to work with only one eye, and then loses his good eye, is paid compensation for total disability. The employer is charged only for the loss of one eye, and the second injury fund pays the remainder. The states may obtain money for the second injury fund in death cases when the victims leave no surviving dependents. However, insufficient money is generally obtained from this source so that an assessment of employers in proportion to benefits may be made. Even though almost all states have second-injury funds, most of the states limit the number of specified covered disabilities. Only 20 states provide for the broader coverage on all types of prior impairments, as recommended by the United States Department of Labor.

BENEFITS — CONCLUSION

In analyzing adequacy of benefits, duplicating benefits from other programs must be considered. It is possible for an injured workman to draw benefits from Social Security, public assistance, private disability plans (probably only a third provide offsets to workmen's compensation benefits), group life insurance, and individual insurance policies. One study of the overlap concluded that the overlap was not large.[18] One reason was that public assistance, for example, will not be paid if income from other sources is too large.

The National Commission on State Workmen's Laws concluded that workmen's compensation benefits were too low. They recommended a payment of 66-2/3's percent of the worker's gross weekly wage, subject to a maximum of 66-2/3's in 1973 and 100 percent in 1975 of the state's average wage. Since workmen's compensation costs are only a small part of payroll costs, the Commission estimated that payroll costs would not rise as much as two percent in any state, and for 33 of them the added cost would be less than 1.249 percent of payrolls.

Data for 1972 show that workmen's compensation benefits increased to $4.0 billion from $3.56 billion a year earlier — a 13 percent increase. However, most of the increase was due to black lung payments.[19]

[18]C. Arthur Williams, Jr. and Peter S. Barth, op. cit., p. 43.
[19]Alfred M. Skolnik and Daniel N. Price, "Workmen's Compensation Under Scrutiny," Social Security Bulletin, Vol. 37, No. 10 (October, 1974), pp. 8-9.

INSURANCE PROBLEMS UNDER WORKMEN'S COMPENSATION

There are a number of different ways that employers may insure the costs of workmen's compensation. Large employers may self-insure if they satisfy all the state requirements, such as posting bond or depositing securities. Only six jurisdictions do not permit employers to self-insure. About 10 percent of all benefit outlays are made by self-insurance (1971).

In 18 jurisdictions, the states have a state fund with which employers may insure. Of these 18 jurisdictions, six provide for exclusive state funds; that is, employers may insure only with the exclusive state fund, and may not take out private insurance. In the other 12 of the 18 jurisdictions having state funds, the funds are competitive, that is, employers may either insure through the state fund or through a private insurance company. In all the other jurisdictions there is no state fund, so that employers must insure through private insurance companies, or possibly self-insure.

The amount of workmen's compensation insurance sold has increased steadily over the years. For almost three decades, private insurance companies have been responsible for more than 60 percent of benefit outlays, although this percentage dropped in 1971 to 58 percent, due to payment of black lung benefits that have been incorporated into state fund figures. Over the years, competitive state funds have increased their sales at the expense of monopolistic state funds, and stock companies have lost business, on a percentage basis, to the mutuals. The estimated cost of workmen's compensation insurance exceeded $5 billion in 1971, and represented about $1.13 per $100 of covered payrolls, the same proportion as in 1970, but higher than $1.07, the cost in the three years prior to 1970.

MERIT RATING

In order to reward a good safety record and encourage safety, rates are modified by merit rating. Since merit rating is impractical for very small risks, it is not applied to employers paying premiums of less than $750 for at least two years. It thus excludes about 80 percent of firms, but since experience rated firms are large, merit rating applies to about 80 percent of all insured employees. In a few states, merit rating is based upon the amount of safety practices put into operation. In most states, this system of merit rating has been superseded by prospective experience rating, in which the actual experience rating over a given period, usually one to three years, is compared with the average of the classification to which the employer belongs. Another method, more attractive to large companies, is retrospective rating, in which an employer is tentatively rated, and then the final premium is adopted after the year of experience. About 30 percent of all workmen's compensation premiums are paid by employers who use retrospective rating. In order to provide more stimulus to reduce accidents via merit rating, the Commission suggested that current eligibility requirements for experience rating be reduced for those having annual premiums of $500 rather than the current figure of $750. The Commission also recommended that an employer's favorable experience with injuries be more equitably reflected in individual employer insurance charges.

PROFITABILITY OF WORKMEN'S COMPENSATION

In 1972, for example, nonparticipating stock companies showed a 5.3 percent net gain ratio over premiums charged, compared with 13.4 percent for mutual companies.[20] In general, the losses incurred as a percentage of premiums have been about the same for stock and mutual companies. The greater profitability of mutual companies comes from fewer expenses incurred. Most of the differences in expenses is due to selling costs.[21] Stock companies generally pay a commission to agents on each policy sold, whereas mutual companies usually pay their salesmen a salary. Mutual companies have also engaged in more selective underwriting over the years. The poorer net gain experience of the stock companies explains why they have been doing a smaller percentage of the business.

STATE VERSUS PRIVATE INSURANCE

The percentage of business written by state funds has remained relatively constant since 1917 even though the costs of state funds are lower than private insurance companies. State funds have fewer selling costs than private companies. In weighing the merits of state funds versus private insurance, services rendered must also be evaluated. In this regard, some of the state funds have not rated too well. Lack of adequate personnel standards and low salaries have been typical of a number of state funds. Some state funds have also been slow in paying claims. Safety work by many states has been inferior to that of the better private carriers. On the other hand, some private insurance companies have been criticized for being

[20]Alfred Skolnik, "Twenty-Five Years of Workmen's Compensation Statistics," *Social Security Bulletin*, Vol. 29, No. 10 (October, 1966), Table 9, p. 22.

[21]*Ibid.*; Reede, *op. cit.*, pp. 251-260. In a later publication, Professor Reede stated that he felt that commission scales were higher than warranted. Especially was this true on renewal commissions, in which the agent's services are likely to be somewhat less valuable than when the policy was first written. See Arthur H. Reede, "Workmen's Compensation Reform," in *Proceedings of a Conference on Workmen's Compensation, 2nd Annual Conference on Business Insurance, Oregon State University (June 1964)*, pp. 43-53.

unwilling to assume high risks. A problem of this kind becomes quite grave if no state fund is available with which the employer may insure. One possible solution here is to require the companies to assume a specific proportion of the poor risks.[22]

Attempting to analyze the merits of state funds versus private insurance is difficult. Perhaps the safest generalization is that some state funds have operated efficiently, as have some private insurance companies. On the other hand, other state funds and other private insurance companies have operated inefficiently.[23] Self-insurance is the cheapest way of assuming compensation liability. There has been a slight trend toward more self-insurance since 1960, but such a method is only available to large and financially sound firms.

ADMINISTRATION OF WORKMEN'S COMPENSATION

COURT ADMINISTRATION

Alabama, Louisiana, New Mexico, Tennessee, and Wyoming have no separate machinery for administering their workmen's compensation program. In these states, if the parties fail to agree on a settlement, they may go to court. Practically all studies of court administration of workmen's compensation laws have been critical of it. Specialized agencies should be better able to administer workmen's compensation than a court. In recognition of this weakness, four of the five states using court administration now have assigned limited responsibilities to an administrative agency to improve administration.

STATE ADMINISTRATIVE AGENCIES

A more acceptable method of administering workmen's compensation is through state administering agencies. Either the agencies are a part of the State Department of Labor (23 jurisdictions), or they are an independent state agency (27 jurisdictions).[24] Since workmen's compensation is one type of labor legislation, a number of jurisdictions have placed the administration of such laws under their Department of Labor. This form of administration has been criticized on the ground that the State Department of Labor may not be completely unbiased. For this reason, a majority of jurisdictions prefer to have a separate agency.

---

[22]Somers and Somers, op. cit., pp. 132-134.
[23]Reede, op. cit., pp. 237-238. 259-260. 304-316.
[24]C. Arthur Williams and Peter S. Barth. op. cit., Table 14-1. pp. 216-217.

As in many phases of governmental activity, the state workmen's compensation agencies have had a difficult time of properly administering workmen's compensation because of lack of funds. In Texas, for example, funds provided for administration were so small that they amounted to only $30 on the average for each case processed.[25] In view of the reluctance of many state legislatures to appropriate sufficient money, 21 states (1972) impose some administrative costs upon insurance companies and self-insurers.[26] That such a device is bringing in more money may be seen by the fact that those states making such assessments received in income in 1972 an average of $3.20 per $100 of benefits disbursed compared with $1.60 per $100 for states not making such an assessment.[27]

Lack of sufficient income has meant that in many states salaries have been too low to attract high quality personnel. Besides the salary problem, the lack of Civil Service regulations has resulted in a large turnover of personnel with every new administration. Fortunately, more and more states are adopting Civil Service procedures to aid in maintaining a more efficient work force.

PROCESSING CASES

The estimated time of making payments after the injury in the United States is one month, although some of the more efficient jurisdictions are able to make payments within one or two weeks. The one-month average is an improvement over the early days of workmen's compensation, when the average time of payment was more than two months.[28]

Court cases naturally take longer. In Texas, one study showed the elapsed time from the injury to settlement of a court case was ten months.[29] In Rhode Island, it commonly takes from 15 months to two years for hearing and trial cases. The further the case is appealed, obviously, the longer it takes to settle. Another criticism of court handling of workmen's compensation cases applies to those jurisdictions that permit "trial de novo." Under this arrangement, the courts are not confined to the function of settling the legal issues involved, but they redetermine the facts in the case rather than accepting them from the state administering agency. The International Association of Industrial Accident Boards and Commission (IAIABC), and the National Commission on State Workmen's Compensation Laws favor a resolution against court determination of the facts.

[25]Barton. op. cit., p. 64.
[26]Analysis of Workmen's Compensation Laws, 1972 edition. Washington. U. S. Chamber of Commerce. pp. 41-42.
[27]Alfred M. Skolnik and Daniel N. Price. op. cit., p. 24.
[28]Somers and Somers. op. cit., p. 155.
[29]Barton. op. cit., p. 35.

In spite of the weakness of trial de novo, such appeal does provide additional protection to workers. At least, this was the finding of Professor Sam Barton in a study of 145 Texas cases.[30]

LITIGATION PROBLEMS

It had been hoped when workmen's compensation was first introduced that litigation would be reduced considerably. It was expected that payments would be automatically determined without recourse to expensive litigation. In practice, workmen's compenation has not eliminated extensive use of attorneys. In Oklahoma, for example, labor unions specifically advise all injured workmen to hire an attorney for their own protection. On the opposing side, insurance companies and self-insurers employ some 5,000 attorneys to work primarily on workmen's compensation cases.[31] One major issue causing litigation revolves around whether the disability is due to employment, and thus covered under the law. Hernias, occupational diseases, and other borderline types of cases cause much litigation. The other major litigation issue is the determination of the extent of disability.[32] It is generally expected that the amount of litigation will remain large.

Attorneys' fees constitute another problem. Fees tend to vary from 1/10 to 1/3 of benefits and sometimes more.[33] Where fees are some fraction of benefit awards, attorneys are encouraged to engage in litigation. Another problem concerning attorney fees involves the questions of who should pay them. Some have suggested that the states should shift the fees to employers in cases where he or the insurer has acted in an unjustified manner.[34]

LUMP-SUM PAYMENTS

In administering workmen's compensation, most states permit benefits to be paid in a lump sum rather than in the form of a weekly benefit. When such a payment is made, the employer or insurance carrier usually is released from any further payment. A number of arguments can be advanced in favor of lump-sum payments, which account for its popularity. First of all, the case can be settled quickly without going to a hearing and thus save legal time and expense. Workers receive cash immediately, and, in general, money today is considered more important than money

[30]Ibid., pp. 24-31, 72.

[31]Somers and Somers, op. cit., p. 180.

[32]For an analysis of these problems, see Arthur Williams and Peter S. Barth, op. cit., Chapter 12.

[33]Ibid., p. 184.

[34]Cheit, op. cit., p. 268. For a similar position, see James O'Brien, AFL-CIO, "Lawyers' Fees and Workmen's Compensation," Trial, Vol. 9, No. 5, (Sept.-Oct., 1973), pp. 42-43.

received later. Some of the money may be used for investment purposes or enable the injured workman to open a busines . One study has been made of the use of funds by those obtaining lump-sum benefits. This study found only 14 percent of the funds were for investment or rehabilitation purposes.[35]

In weighing the advantages and disadvantages of lump-sum payments, most authorities are of the opinion that the disadvantage outweigh the advantages. The IAIABC has suggested that the lump-sum payments should be used only in cases in which they would facilitate the rehabilitation of of the worker, and that they should not be used for capital enrichment or the convenience of either the claimant's lawyer or the company or insurance carrier. The IAIABC has recommended that a better alternative to lump-sum payments would be to increase weekly benefits.[36] In spite of the serious disadvantages, the lump-sum payment is widely used.[37] The IAIABC has further recommended that employers or insurance carriers should not be released from additional liability. That agency suggested that a state should have the right at any time to reopen a case, because sometimes damage from an accident or occupational disease may not manifest itself until years later. Only a few states, however, have adopted this recommendation.

RECORD KEEPING

One criticism of workmen's compensation administration has been that the record keeping and statistical analysis in most states has been extremely poor. The dearth of statistics has handicapped the successful operation of workmen's compensation. In a few jurisdictions, analysis of length of time before payment has provided administrators with an incentive to maintain or improve on the average. Records of amounts paid on certain type of injuries should also prove of value for future settlements. An analysis of workmen's compensation statistics in 1959 confirmed the same findings of a quarter of a century ago that record keeping in workmen's compensation needed substantial improvement.[38] For a number of years, few states ever adopted standards proposed for adequate record keeping. Hopefully, this problem has been solved now by the Occupational Safety and Health Act of 1970, which requires that standardized and adequate records be kept.

[35]Cheit. op. cit., p. 276.
[36]Discussion of Industrial Accidents and Diseases. Bulletin 105 (Washington. D.C.. U. S. Department of Labor Standards 1949). pp. 283-284.
[37]Somers and Somers. op. cit., p. 161.
[38]Cheit. op. cit., p. 252.

COST OF ADMINISTRATION

The costs of administering workmen's compensation are quite high. In 1971 the proportion of premium benefit as a percent of premium costs was 60.8 percent. This was a slightly higher figure than that of 58.4 percent in 1970. The loss ratio for private companies in 1971 was 51.5 percent compared with 71.2 percent for state insurance funds. Administrative costs were much lower in Ontario, which reported that such expenses were 7.5 percent of receipts. In Ontario the fund is an exclusive state fund, and court review has been outlawed.[39]

INSOLVENCY OF FIRMS OR CARRIERS

Injured workers may lose their compensation because of the insolvency of the carrier, or insolvent or noncomplying employers. To provide for payment, the National Commission on State Workmen's Compensation Laws recommended that each state provide benefits to workers who face a loss of benefits for such reasons.

POSSIBLE FEDERAL ADMINISTRATION

Owing to the many weaknesses in state workmen's compensation laws, the AFL-CIO for a number of years has advocated that a federally administered law be passed governing all the states. This suggestion has received little support in Congress. Failing this, the only alternative is to improve the laws in the 58 jurisdictions. Such revisions are difficult, particularly in those states which workers are unorganized and have no real lobby. In such states, workmen's compensation laws probably will not be improved substantially in the near future. However, the National Commission on State Workmen's Compensation Laws in 1972 felt that there were sufficient advantages to state administration so that federal administration should not be implemented. They added that if the most essential of their recommendations were not met by 1975, Federal mandates should be included to guarantee compliance. Fortunately, the total costs of workmen's compensation average only one percent of payrolls, so that improvements may be made without too heavy an additional cost burden. However, the lack of political power of blue-collar workers in a number of states will make improvements of workmen's compensation difficult in those states.

[39]Somers and Somers, op. cit., pp. 193-196, 309-317.

TRENDS IN OTHER COUNTRIES

To better evaluate workmen's compensation in the United States, the National Commission on State Workmen's Compensation Laws made a study of such laws in other countries: The United Kingdom, West Germany, Russia, Netherlands, Japan, India, and Israel.[40] Several trends were noted. One was a growing reliance upon social insurance. Another was the extension of coverage to other than employed persons. A third was the coverage of workers when the injury arose out of employment rather than in the course of employment. A fourth was pronounced emphasis on rehabilitation. Lastly, special courts were used to adjudicate and review appeals to take advantage of personnel having a specialized knowledge in the field.

Summary

Workmen's Compensation laws were passed beginning in 1908 in the United States, after it had been found that employers liability laws had failed to solve industrial accident problems. Exclusion from coverage of such groups as agricultural workers and employees of small employers has resulted in about one of every seven workers not being covered under workmen's compensation laws.

Benefits payments are least adequate for those more severely injured. Over the years, workmen's compensation has been paying a smaller and smaller percentage of the injured worker's wage. Workmen's compensation benefits have tended to impede rehabilitation on occasion and experts have been working on how cash payments can best promote rather than impede rehabilitation. Yet to be completely solved is the problem of some persons receiving payments both under OASDHI and Workmen's Compensation.

In general, workmen's compensation has not been administered well in theUnited States. When workmen's compensation was first adopted, it was thought that cases would be settled with little or no need for attorneys and litigation. In practice, litigation continues at a high rate. The IAIABC has recommended that a state should have the right to reopen a case at any time, but few states have adopted this proposal. With all these weaknesses in workmen's compensation administration, the cost of administering this program is much higher than for other security programs.

---

[40]C. Arthur Williams and Peter S. Barth, *op. cit.*, Chapter 6.

Bibliography

Berkowitz, Monroe, Workmen's Compensation: *The New Jersey Experience* (New Brunswick, N.J., Rutgers, 1960).

Barton, Sam B., *How Texas Cared for Her Injured Workers* (Denton, Tex., North State College, 1956).

Earl Cheit, *Injury and Recovery in the Course of Employment* (New York, Wiley, 1961).

Gill, Inez *Workmen's Compensation in New Mexico* (Santa Fe, Legislative Council Service 1955).

Reede, Arthur H. Adequacy of Workmen's Compensation (Cambridge, Mass, Harvard, 1947)

Report of the National Commission on State Workmen's Compensation Laws (Washington, Government Printing Office, 1972).

Somers, Harold M. and Anne R. Somers, *Workmen's Compensation* (New York, Wiley, 1954).

William C. Arthur and Peter S. Barth, directors, *Compendium on Workmen's Compensation* (Washington, Government Printing Office, 1973).

CHAPTER 12

HEALTH PROBLEMS IN THE UNITED STATES

NATIONAL HEALTH EXPENDITURES

In fiscal year 1974, the people of the United States spent over $104 billion for health purposes. This amounted to $485 per person per year and was 7.7% of the Gross National Product. Health expenditures are rising at a rate of 9 to 12 percent each year, so that in 1975 health expenditures were estimated at about $114 billion. Between 1965 and 1974, health expenditures more than doubled; from 1960 to 1974 they quadrupled; and they were almost nine times as large in 1974 as in 1950 (Table 12-1). This was due partly to inflation and partly to population increase, but after both of these are allowed for, health expenditures in terms of per capita constant dollars nearly tripled between 1950 and 1974. Average per capita utilization of health services and supplies has been rising, and there has been a rising level and scope of services resulting from the development of new techniques, new drugs, and improved treatment processes.[1] By 1974 about 60% of the expenses were paid through private arrangements, 40% through public agencies. This marks a substantial shift since 1929, when payments were nearly 87% private.

In addition to the foregoing figures dealing with health expenditures, another part of the cost is loss of earnings due to disability, partial or total. The 1970 census data indicate that the partially disabled suffered an income loss of about $5.4 billion, while the income loss of the totally disabled was about $9.4 billion.[2] Thus in 1969 the loss of income was at least $13.8 billion. Allowing for about 30% inflation from 1969 through 1974, the net loss of income in 1974 may be placed conservatively at $19 billion. This added to the $104 billion of direct expenditures for medical care gives a health cost of $123 billion in 1974.[3]

Current health expenditures may be seen in Table 12-2, showing national health expenditures by type. It will be seen that hospital care ab-

[1]"National Health Expenditures, Fiscal Year 1973," *Research and Statistics Note*, No. 24, U. S. Department of Health, Education and Welfare, December 27, 1973. See also Nancy L. Worthington, "National Health Expenditure, 1929-1974," *Social Security Bulletin*, Vol. 38 (February 1975), pp. 3-20.
[2]1970 Census of Population, *Persons with Work Disability*, Table 10, p. 111.
[3]See also Daniel N. Price, "Cash Benefits for Short-Term Sickness, 1948-72," *Social Security Bulletin*, Vol. 37 (January 1974), pp. 19-30. Mr. Price estimates the income loss for short term illness in 1972 to be $19.4 billion, offset by $6.6 billion of cash benefits.

sorbed the most money, 39.2%, followed by physicians' services, 18.2%. Other large expenditures went for drugs and drug sundries, dentists' services, construction, and nursing home care.

TABLE 12-1

NATIONAL HEALTH EXPENDITURES, TOTAL, PERCENT OF GNP, AND PERCENT PRIVATE, PERCENT PUBLIC
(Selected Fiscal Years)

	Amount (Millions)	Per Capita	Percent of GNP	Percent Private	Percent Public
1929	$ 3,589	$ 29.16	3.6%	86.7%	13.3%
1940	3,863	28.83	4.1	79.8	20.2
1950	12,028	78.35	4.6	74.5	25.5
1960	25,856	141.63	5.2	75.3	24.7
1965	38,892	197.81	5.9	75.5	24.5
1970	68,058	328.17	7.1	62.9	37.1
1974	104,239	485.36	7.7	60.4	39.6

Source: *Social Security Bulletin*, February 1975, p. 5; and "National Health Expenditures, Fiscal Year 1973," *Research and Statistics Note No. 24*, U. S. Department of Health, Education and Welfare, December 27, 1972.

TABLE 12-2

NATIONAL HEALTH EXPENDITURES BY TYPE, FISCAL YEAR 1974

	Amount (millions)	Percent
Total	$104,239	100.0
Hospital care	40,900	39.2
Physicians' services	19,000	18.2
Dentists' services	6,200	5.9
Other professional services	1,990	1.9
Drug and drug sundries	9,695	9.3
Eyeglasses and appliances	2,153	2.1
Nursing-home care	7,450	7.1
Expenses for prepayment and administration	4,224	4.1
Government public health activites	2,126	2.0
Other health services	3,445	3.3
Research	2,684	2.6
Construction	4,372	4.2

Source: *Social Security Bulletin*, February 1975, p. 9.

THE HEALTH CARE COST PROBLEM

Large and persistent increases in health care costs are occurring, and medical costs are rising more rapidly than most other costs. The consumer price index for all items (1967=base 100) in September, 1974, stood at 152, while that for medical care was 155. Hospital costs have risen much more sharply, the index for a semi-private room being 209.6 and rising, and operating room charges were 211.4 and rising. The index for physicians' fees was 155.9; for dentists' fees, 150.5; and laboratory tests, 142.1.[4]

The rapid increases can be explained in terms of supply and demand. While the supply of medical personnel and facilities has increased slowly, demand has increased more rapidly. The demand for medical care appears to be "income elastic," that is, as national income rises, the demand for medical care rises more rapidly. Also, the enactment in 1965 of the Medicare and Medicaid programs added substantially to the demand, while supply has been slow to respond. It is frequently said that the government added to the health care cost problem by adding to the demand, while doing very little to add to the supply. It follows that future government programs need to be more concerned about adding to supply of medical personnel and facilities whenever new programs are enacted which will add to demand.

Another aspect of the health care cost problem is its uneven occurrence. At any one time some families have little or no medical expense; others will have very large, perhaps catastrophic expenses. For a single family, there may be several years on end with only minor expenses, but then a year or years in which medical expenses are enormous. Some type of insurance, either private or public, is therefore sensible. Health costs tend to be unpredictable for the individual, but predictable for large numbers such as the entire population. Appropriate premiums can therefore be calculated, so that the family pays a smaller certain amount each year instead of facing the prospect of a catastrophic loss in a particular year.

MEDICAL PROBLEMS AMONG LOW-INCOME GROUPS

Practically all studies of medical care show deficiencies of care among low-income groups. On such measures as number of untreated conditions, number of dental caries, and general level of nutrition, low-income persons are in poorer health than persons with higher income.[5] Statistics, such as number of diagnosed conditions, probably understate the disparity between low-income and other groups, since low income people make lower use of physicians. Low-income persons frequently hold jobs

[4]*Social Security Bulletin*, Vol. 37 (December 1974), Table M-38, p. 76.
[5]*Health Characteristics of Low-Income Persons*, U.S. Department of Health, Education and Welfare, Public Health Service, Series 10, No. 74, July 1972, pp. 1-2.

which do not have sick leave, and they are apt to try to continue to work rather than lose a day's pay. Also, low-income persons tend to have less access to medical care, and the quality and range of services is much lower than those available to persons with more money. Fewer services exist in the immediate residential area of low-income persons. The ratio of doctors to the population is much lower in the central cities than in the suburbs. Often low-income persons make use of hospital emergency rooms and public clinics for health care, and are apt to be treated by different persons at each visit.[6]

Contrary to what might be expected, poor people have somewhat more hospital admissions and stay for longer periods on the average than those of higher income.[7] But this reflects the fact that they are more seriously ill before they obtain admission to the hospital. Also they have had little or no preventive medical care, and little or no early treatment of a disease when it might be curable. Longer hospital stays are thus a consequence of poor prior medical care. In the hospital the low-income person is apt to be placed in a crowded ward, to be treated more impersonally, and with less regard for the patient's feelings and dignity.

A related problem is that there is apt to be a distance between the poor and the professionals who provide them services. This contributes to poor communication and mutual dissatisfaction between professionals and low-income clients. Similarly, the poor are apt to have greater difficulty in dealing with complicated bureaucratic organizations, and ironically bureaucratic procedures are most noticeable in the public clinics, the form of medical care specifically developed for the poor.[8]

MEDICAL CARE IN RURAL AREAS

All studies of medical care in the United States show deficiencies in medical care in rural areas. Fewer farm residents visit a doctor than urban residents. While people in standard metropolitan statistical areas (SMSA) visited doctors 4.6 times per person during 1969-70, farm people made only 3.2 visits. Rural people are particularly deficient in obtaining prenatal and postnatal care, general checkups and immunizations. Dental care is also lacking among rural people. While people in SMSA's averaged 1.8 visits to the dentist per year, rural nonfarm people had 1.2 visits and rural farm people 1.1 visits. By region, the rural South still has less medical care than the urban South, and southern states generally have lower medical care ratios than other regions.[9]

[6]Mary W. Herman, "The Poor: Their Medical Needs and Health Services," *The Annals of the American Academy of Political and Social Science, The Nation's Health: Some Issues,* Vol. 399 (January 1972), pp. 12-21.

[7]*Ibid.,* p. 18.

[8]Mary W. Herman, *op. cit.,* pp. 20-21; see also Irving Leveson, "The Challenge of Health Services for the Poor," *The Annals, op. cit.,* pp. 22-29.

[9]*Vital and Health Statistics, Health Characteristics by Geographic Region, Large Metropolitan Areas, and Other Places of Residence,* Public Health Service, Series 10, No. 86, January 1974, pp. 11-14.

One of the problems of medical care in rural areas is that lower incomes there tend to inhibit doctors and dentists from locating there. States with high per capita income tend to have higher doctor and dentist population ratios than do low-income rural states. In 1970 for the whole United States there were 171 physicians per 100,000 resident population. States such as New York (238) and Massachusetts (211) were considerably above average. These contrast with Alabama (89), Arkansas (93), Mississippi (83), and South Carolina (91). In addition the American Medical Association notes that there are 140 counties in the United States with a total population of half-million with no doctors at all.[10] Nationwide, it is estimated that there are 5,000 small communities in the United States without a doctor.[11] The disparity is less when considering only general practitioners. Specialists tend to locate in the larger cities and are associated with the larger hospitals. But the distance to the larger cities does prevent many rural people from getting adequate hospital care. Compared to the national average of 47 dentists per 100,000 resident population, the District of Columbia has 86 and New York 68. On the other hand, Mississippi has only 26, South Carolina 27, and Alabama and Arkansas 30.[12] Both doctors and dentists in rural areas tend to be much older than they are in metropolitan areas.

MEDICAL PROBLEMS OF THE AGED

Our population aged 65 and over has increased enormously since 1900. Most of the increase in the aged population has come through a reduction in the death rate in early years. A much higher percentage of our young people can expect to reach age 65, but death rates rise geometrically with age. Those reaching 65 now live somewhat longer than those who reached this age in 1900, but there has been more improvement for females than for males. The old, of course, experience more illness than the young. The young have more acute conditions, but they recover more quickly, so that the old have slightly more days of restricted activity due to acute conditions than do people of all ages.[13] The situation for chronic illness is much worse. Only 0.7 percent of those under 17 years of age are restricted in activity due to chronic conditions, whereas 42.3 percent of those aged 65 and over are. About 46 percent of males aged 65 and over and 40 percent of females are so restricted.[14]

As would be expected, the greater amount of chronic illness causes the aged to use hospital facilities much more frequently and for longer

[10]Lester Velie. "The Shocking Truth About Our Children's Health Care." *Reader's Digest*, Vol. 104 (May 1974). p. 171.

[11]Aubrey C. McTaggart. *The Health Care Dilemma* (Boston. Holbrook Press. 1971). p. 8.

[12]*Statistical Abstract of the United States*, 1972. Table 102. p. 70.

[13]"Current Estimates from the Health Interview Survey. 1972." *Vital and Health Statistics*, Series 10. No. 85. p. 12.

[14]"Limitation of Activity Due to Chronic Conditions." *op. cit.*, Table 1. p. 17.

periods of time than those in lower age groups. Because of the nature of their illnesses the hospital costs of the aged per day are estimated to be about 2-1/2 times that of those who are younger.[15] Unfortunately, the aged have fewer economic resources to meet these higher costs. These problems have been compounded because the cost of medical care has been rising rapidly in recent years. The enactment of the Medicare program in 1965 (discussed in the next chapter) substantially eased the burden on the aged, although some problems of medical care for the aged still remain.

LACK OF PREVENTIVE MEDICINE

One of the major criticisms that has been leveled against the present fee-for-service medical system is that too little preventive medicine is practiced. In the past, probably because of the fees involved, most people went to doctors only after they became ill. The major effort was on cure rather than prevention.

Early diagnosis plays an important part in preventive medicine. Many diseases can be successfully cured if treatment begins early. Late discovery of a disease such as cancer often means that the patient cannot be cured. All screening examination studies have shown that many people have diseases of which they are unaware. For example, in cancer tests for women, it is found that of every 1,000 women examined, about eight of them will have cancer, carcinoma of the cervix, either in its earlier stages or in a later stage. Other tests show that about 5-1/2 persons per 1,000 will have a previously unknown diabetes.[16] Other studies reveal that medical examinations uncover much illness that is not being treated. If all American people would receive regular periodic medical examinations, disease would be greatly reduced. Most people as yet do not obtain periodic examinations. Until they do, Americans will not be as healthy as they could be.

HOSPITAL FACILITIES

The number of hospitals in the United States was slow to grow; by 1873, when the first census of hospitals was taken, only 178 hospitals were listed. Thereafter, the construction of hospitals occurred at a rapid rate so that by 1928, the total number of hospitals reached 6,852. The depression and World War II caused a virtual halt in the construction of new hospitals. By 1946, we had 572 fewer general hospitals than we had in 1928,

[15]*Bulletin*, Health Information Foundation, February 1960.

[16]Testimony of Dr. John Porterfield, Deputy Surgeon, Public Health Service, *Health Needs of the Aged and Aging*, Hearing Before the Subcommittee on Problems of the Aged and Aging, The Committee on Labor and Public Welfare, U. S. Senate, 86th Congress, 2nd Session (April 1960), p. 37.

although the number of hospital beds increased by 61 percent over this same period. A comprehensive study of hospital needs was made in 1944 by the Commission of Hospital Care, an organization sponsored by the American Hospital Association and the U. S. Public Health Service. Their conclusion as to the lack of adequate hospital facilities aided in obtaining federal aid for hospital construction in 1946 (the Hill-Burton Act).[17]

The number of hospitals has increased by about five percent since 1950, while the number of beds has increased by about 11 percent. But the number of beds per 1,000 population has declined since 1950 from 9.6 to 7.9 in 1970. There has been a substantial decline in hospitals operated for profit, and a corresponding increase in numbers of hospitals owned by local governments and by private nonprofit organizations, especially churches.

The location of the hospitals is a source of concern. The bigger and better hospitals are located in the larger metropolitan areas, but this means that rural areas often have no hospital facilities. The impact of this is at least partly offset by better roads and highways. Another problem is that the new hospitals tend to be built in suburban areas, while the hospitals in the central city are apt to be old and decaying. As a consequence, not only the remote rural areas, but also the residents of the urban ghettos are apt to have only limited access to hospitals.

Another problem stems from population changes. The declining birth rate has led to empty pediatric and obstetrical beds across the nation while there are insufficient beds for the chronically ill. Many of the chronically ill could be cared for in quality nursing homes, "extended care facilities," but, while there are large numbers of nursing homes, many do not meet the standards established by Medicare. Thus, the aged who might otherwise be cared for in a nursing home at less expense remain in costly hospital rooms.[18]

A lack of coordination in the whole hospital system leads to a different type of problem, the duplication of facilities beyond real need. Hospital administrators, like administrators everywhere, tend to be empire-builders. Each large hospital endeavors to provide specialty care for a wide variety of ailments. As a consequence, there is a needless duplication of facilities. In the state of New York the Governor's Committee on Hospital Costs noted that 38 hospitals had facilities for open-heart surgery. Yet in a one year period there was no open-heart surgery in six hospitals, and less than ten operations in seven others. Only one hospital out of 38 met the requirement of one operation per week needed to maintain the proficiency of the heart surgery team.[19] Area wide planning and controls

[17]Leslie Morgan Abbe and Anna Mae Bovey, The Nation's Health Facilities: Ten Years of the Hill-Burton Hospital and Medical Facilities Program, 1946-56. Publication No. 616. Washington, D.C., U. S. Department of Health, Education and Welfare, Public Health Service (1960), pp. 11-12.
[18]Aubrey C. McTaggart, op. cit., p. 74.
[19]Ibid.

obviously could reduce or eliminate this sort of problem, but there will be resistance from ambitious empire-builders.

SHORTAGE OF MEDICAL PERSONNEL

Whether or not there actually is a shortage of medical personnel is a matter of some controversy. To an ill person trying to find a new physician in a hurry, or to a remote community trying to attract at least one doctor, the answer seems obvious. To Harry Schwartz, who has written extensively in defense of American medicine as it is, there is no shortage, and he raises the possibility that there may even be a surplus of physicians by 1980.[20]

The physician-population ratio may be taken as one indication. In 1880 there were 163 doctors per 100,000 population; by 1929 the figure had dropped to 125. Thereafter a reverse set in and by 1950 there were 149 doctors per 100,000 population. During the next ten years the ratio was virtually unchanged, and stood at 148 in 1960. During the 1960's, however, the number of physicians rose substantially and the 1970 figure was put at 171.[21] The 1972 Manpower Report to the President estimated that by 1980 there will be 440,000 physicians in the United States. If the population reaches 235 million by 1980, the ratio will reach 187 per 100,000. The increase during the 1960's, continuing in the 1970's, came from two sources. The number of graduates of medical schools has gradually increased, as has the number of foreign doctors. In 1970 there were about 9,400 graduates of medical schools, and the Manpower Report expects the number to rise to about 14,000 per year by 1979-80. Foreign physicians are emigrating to the United States at a rate of from 3,000 to 5,000 per year, and this of course adds to the supply of physicians.[22] If the above data prove to be correct, the doctor shortage may be eased by 1980. But shortages in rural areas and in urban ghettos persist.

Economic analysis has sometimes supported the charge that there is a doctor shortage contrived by the American Medical Association to raise doctors' incomes. The Friedman-Kuznets study published in 1954 indicated that doctors' earnings were greater than the amounts justified by cost plus a normal profit.[23] They studied five independent professions, using data from 1929 to 1936, and concluded that there was supply restriction. In their words, "limitations on the number of persons in a position to enter the professions must be considered the basic reasons for the

[20]Harry Schwartz. *The Case for American Medicine* (New York. David McKary Company. 1972). See especially Chapter III. "The Doctor Shortage." pp. 59-87. See also Harry Schwartz. "Health Care in America: A Heretical Diagnosis." *Saturday Review*, Vol. 54. Pt. 2 (August 1. 1971). pp. 14-17; 55.

[21]*Statistical Abstract of the United States, 1972*, Table 101. p. 70.

[22]*Ibid.*, p. 69.

[23]Milton Friedman and Simon Kuznets. *Income From Independent Professional Practice* (New York. National Bureau of Economic Research. 1954). pp. 95-173.

difference between extra returns and extra costs. . . ."[24] They further pointed out that large numbers of young people cannot enter the profession because they cannot make the necessary capital investment.

Others have cited this study to support the charge that the American Medical Association has deliberately restricted entry in order to raise physicians' incomes.[25] But there are dissenters from this point of view. H. Gregg Lewis, in updating the Friedman-Kuznets study, reversed some of their conclusions, holding that the doctor shortage and high incomes for physicians reflect a strong increase in relative demand for physician's services.[26] In brief, the demand for physician's services is "income elastic," that is, a rise in the gross national product leads to a more than proportionate rise in the demand. This fact is consistent with the data shown in Table 12-2. Health expenditures are in fact making up a larger and larger percentage of GNP as GNP rises.

But the fact that demand has increased rapidly does not prove that there is no physician shortage, nor does it prove that the AMA has not restricted entry into the medical profession.[27] Increasing demand and supply restriction may occur simultaneously. Lynch, who has updated earlier studies, finds that there is a physician shortage in the sense that physician's income exceeds normal profit, but that the AMA is not the immediate cause. Two of his conclusions are as follows:

(1) There is a shortage and it has become worse since the middle 1950's — or, if we had enough physicians in the middle 1950's, then we have too few now. (2) The immediate cause of the shortage was not the restrictionist policies of the AMA, but the increased demand or willingness to pay on the part of the public.[28]

Similar analysis is applicable to dentists, nurses, and other medical personnel. As to the dentist population ratio, it is remarkably constant. The ratio per 100,000 resident population was 57 in 1950, 56 in 1960, and 58 in 1970. The nurse-population ratio, on the other hand, appears to be improving. In 1950 the ratio was 249 per 100,000 resident population; in 1960, 282; and in 1970, 345. Again, the ratios vary widely from state to state, the south generally being short of medical personnel, and the north and east having high ratios. Rural areas and urban ghettos generally have low ratios, while high-income suburban metropolitan areas have high

[24]*Ibid.*, p. 94.

[25]Reuben A. Kessel, "Price Discrimination in Medicine," *Journal of Law and Economics*, Vol. 1 (October 1958). See also Elton Rayack, *Professional Power and American Medicine* (Cleveland, World Publishing, 1967), and Tibor Scitovsky, "The Trend of Professional Earnings," *American Economic Review*, Vol. 56 (March 1966), p. 38.

[26]H. Gregg Lewis, *Unionism and Relative Wages in the United States* (Chicago, University of Chicago Press, 1963).

[27]Michael Lynch, "The Physician Shortage," The Economists' Mirror," *The Annals of the American Academy of Political and Social Science*, Vol. 399 (January 1972), pp. 82-88.

[28]*Ibid.*, p. 88.

rates. The income motive appears to be the determining factor. The country is also short of many types of paramedical workers.[29]

THE QUALITY OF MEDICAL CARE

Many people complain about the poor quality of American medical care. Others say that care in America is the best on earth. Generally you and I as medical laymen are hardly competent to judge whether or not our medical care is good or bad. For the most part, we have to rely on the doctors themselves for judgment about the quality of medical care. Unfortunately, doctors and dentists and other groups as well are reluctant to speak ill of their fellow professionals. But some bits of evidence can be weighed.

One bit of evidence has to do with unnecessary surgery. One study estimated that there were two million unnecessary operations in the United States each year.[30] Since it is impossible for a doctor to be right in every diagnosis, the Joint Commission for Accreditation of Hospitals allows a ten percent error in surgical matters. But in a five-hospital survey it was found that only 63% of the surgery was justified in one hospital, as compared to 86% in the best of the five.[31] One of the most distinguished surgeons in the world once complained that about one-half of his work consisted of attempts to correct the bad results of surgery undertaken by doctors inadequately trained in the field.[32] Generally, the fee-for-service method of payment in the United States and health insurance itself put a premium on complicated surgery. If a doctor practices good preventive medicine, he collects only small fees. But if drastic surgery is performed, the fee is large. Often such surgery is necessary and probably a sizeable majority of doctors do not recommend surgery simply to collect fees. But some doctors apparently do respond to the economic incentive.[33]

The lack of sufficient medical personnel may have a direct bearing on the quality of medical care. Since doctors work extremely long hours, time spent for research and study of new medical developments necessarily is limited. One intensive study made of 88 general practitioners in North Carolina by the University of North Carolina Division of Health Affairs and the Rockefeller Foundation found that 39 of the physicians (44 percent) were doing relatively poor work. Their major weakness was that they lacked fundamental clinical medical knowledge and skill, as

---

[29]See Herman M. Sturm. "Technological Developments and Their Effects Upon Health Manpower." *Monthly Labor Review*, Vol. 90, No. 1 (January, 1967), Table 3, p. 7.

[30]Martin L. Gross. *The Doctors* (New York: Random House. 1966). pp. 189-211.

[31]V. N. Slee. "Streamlining the Tissue Committee." *Bulletin, American College of Surgeons*, Nov.-Dec. 1959, p. 519.

[32]"Quality as Well as Quantity of Medical Care." *Group Health Institute of 1959*, Proceedings of the Group Health Association of America, p. 116.

[33]Selig Greenberg, *The Troubled Calling* (New York, Macmillan, 1965), pp. 211-217. See also Roul Tunley, *The American Health Scandal* (New York, Harper & Row, 1966), pp. 45-47.

evidenced by limited history-taking, physical examination, and the use of laboratory aids to diagnose. Many of the doctors were relying mainly on digests put out by drug companies, because they could not keep up with the professional study of literature.[34]

Another bit of evidence concerning the quality of medical care is the growing number of malpractice suits.[35] Most patients are reluctant to sue their own physician, and few do so where there is a close personal relationship. But with the growing trend toward impersonal and very costly care, more patients are bringing suit. Only a few cases ever reach court, and in those that do it is difficult to get a judgment in favor of the patient. Testimony of expert witnesses is needed, and few physicians are willing to testify against their fellow physicians. Occasionally, very large judgments are returned against the doctor. If this becomes more common, doctors will likely endeavor to raise their fees to all patients in order to cover possible judgments against themselves.

The United States is the only major country where until recently we have acted as if we thought that medical care is a privilege. In most of the rest of the world it is regarded as a right. Matters of privilege generally boil down to finances. Those who can afford it ordinarily do get good medical care; those who cannot may or may not get good care. Our philosophy in this matter is gradually shifting to that prevailing in the rest of the world. The enactment in 1965 of Medicare and Medicaid is evidence of the recognition that the aged and poor have a right to better medical care.

PUBLIC HEALTH PROGRAMS

What might be called public health programs have existed since ancient times.[36] Greek civilizations placed a high degree of importance on personal hygiene, but the weak, ill, and crippled were either ignored or destroyed. Roman civilization was known to have supervised public bars, houses of ill fame, and weights and measures. Many streets were paved, and a system of drainage installed. Garbage and rubbish were regularly removed. Aqueducts and tunnels were constructed to provided a relatively safe water supply.

During the Dark Ages, little public health was practiced. People seldom bathed, and there was an utter disregard for sanitation. Refuse and waste were allowed to accumulate in and around dwellings. During the

---

[34]O. L. Peterson, et. al., "An Analytical Study of North Carolina General Practice, 1953-54." *Journal of Medical Education* (December 1956), Part 2, p. 47.

[35]Aubrey C. McTaggart. op. cit., pp. 12-13.

[36]This section on the history of public health has been drawn mainly from John J. Hanlon. *Principles of Public Health Administration*, 3rd ed. (St. Louis. C. B. Mosby Co.. 1960). Chap. 2.

fourteenth century the Black Death in the form of bubonic plague deci-
mated whole countries. As a first halting step to the control of diseases a
number of ports banned entry of infected ships or quarantined those who
were ill. The spread of leprosy was eventually checked by rigid segregation of those having the disease, so that it was largely eradicated from
Europe by the sixteenth century.

As late as the nineteenth century in many areas good public practices
were at a minimum. One writer, Edwin Chadwick, noted that more than
one-half of the children of the working classes died before their fifth
birthday. In England a National Vaccination Board was established in
1837, and in 1848 a General Board of Health was created for the entire
country. In the United States, city health departments were in evidence in
Baltimore as early as 1798 and in Charleston, South Carolina, and Philadelphia shortly thereafter. The first efforts in public health were directed
at the control of such diseases as typhoid fever, cholera, smallpox, and
yellow fever. Around 1870 the states began organizing state departments
of public health.

FEDERAL PROGRAMS

A Marine Hospital Service Act was passed in 1798 to provide medical and
hospital care for sick and disabled seamen. In 1878, the first port quaran-
tine act was passed to prevent the spread of epidemic diseases. Gradually
the number of hospitals for seamen expanded until today 12 hospitals are
in existence for this group. These hospitals are administered by the
United States Public Health Service, which was created in 1902, and took
its present name in 1912. A leprosy hospital was constructed in 1917, and
a federal venereal disease program inaugurated in 1918. In 1921, the
federal government began supporting maternal and children's health, and
in 1929, three federal hospitals were constructed for drug addicts. By 1935,
the total federal budget for health service, however, amounted to only $10
million annually.

With the passage of the Social Security Act in 1935, federal public
health expenditures began to expand as did state and local spending. By
fiscal year 1974, total public health expenditures (federal, state and local)
reached $37.4 billion, the largest amount being spent for Medicare ($11.3
billion) and the next largest amount for Medicaid ($11.2 billion). Spending
for general hospital and medical care ($5.0 billion), veterans hospitals and
medical care ($2.8 billion), Defense Department ($2.7 billion) followed in
that order.[37]

[37]Nancy L. Worthington, "National Health Expenditures, 1929-1972," *Social Security Bulletin*, Vol. 38, No. 2 (February 1975), p. 10.

STATE PUBLIC HEALTH PROGRAMS

Each of the states has a Department of Public Health. The main function of these departments is to promote the establishment of full-time local health departments. Financial aid is sometimes provided to local health departments. Direct services are often provided in the form of mobile chest X rays, dental clinics, venereal disease clinics, plus activities connected with sanitary engineering, laboratory services, and statistical services. As in most other programs, some states provide relatively complete services, whereas others do not. Almost all state Departments of Public Health provide for control over general communicable diseases and tuberculosis, and programs for control of mosquitoes and rodents. Most participate in research and educational programs for cancer, heart disease, and other ailments. Other common services include maternal and child health programs, occupational health services, laboratory services, and vital statistics. On the other hand, many of the state departments do little or nothing in regard to arthritis, diabetes, and other diseases.[38]

LOCAL PUBLIC HEALTH PROGRAMS

On the local level, the largest single budget item is for public nursing, for which about half of all local public health funds are spent. The figure is somewhat lower, about 35 percent, in the larger local health units. Public health nurses provide nursing care in homes, aid in the treatment of patients, and guide individuals with social and emotional difficulties to the appropriate community agencies. In addition, public health nurses collaborate with other professions in fostering community health programs and in education in public health.[39] For many indigents, the local public health office provides a limited source of low-cost medical care.

In the area of environmental health, vast strides have been made over the years to improve the purity of our water supplies, install sewerage systems, pasteurize milk, and remove garbage and refuse. In spite of these improvements, much still remains to be done. Some communities are still without water works systems, and others without sewer systems. Adequate facilities are particularly deficient in rural areas. The goal of having all milk pasteurized has not been reached either. Air pollution problems remain severe in most industrial areas of the nation, and efforts are being made to control automobile exhaust emissions. The cost of controlling air pollution is likely to be immense, but this should be compared with the cost of not controlling air pollution. The development of DDT and other pesticides has made possible the control of mosquitoes, flies, and other harmful insects, but the pesticides themselves are in many cases health hazards.

[38]Hanlon. *op. cit.*, pp. 346-351.
[39]*Ibid.*, Chap. 18.

In the past, a good deal of public health has been directed toward control of communicable diseases. Diseases such as smallpox, typhoid fever, and yellow fever have been reduced to minimum proportions in the United States. In spite of the obvious merits of compulsory vaccination, less than half the states require it, another twenty allow local jurisdiction to make the decision, while seven states have laws prohibiting or restricting compulsory vaccination.[40] The success of the polio vaccines demonstrates what can be done, but even in this case it is difficult to get more than about 80 percent of those under age 20 vaccinated.

With the reduction in importance of the communicable diseases, public health groups have been turning their attention to the chronic diseases which are becoming relatively more important. Some of the more progressive public health units have been conducting mass screening tests on all who will volunteer in an effort to find previously undetected disease. Commonly such programs discover diabetes, tuberculosis, glaucoma, and other diseases, many of which can be cured or controlled.

In the past, public health programs were vigorously opposed as being socialistic and unneeded. More recently, such groups as the American Medical Association have taken a more favorable attitude toward public health. It has been realized that the indigent are unlikely to be able to obtain adequate medical care through private medicine. If these groups could obtain care through public health departments, then the American Medical Association maintains that all persons could have access to medical care. In spite of the changed attitude of the American Medical Association, public health groups are still short of funds and personnel to carry out adequately all their suggested functions. In realizing that public health should function on a broader scale, some state and local groups have been expanding their expenditures in this field. However, most of the increase has come in a few states — New York, California, Pennsylvania, Ohio, and New Jersey.

IMPROVED MEDICAL FACILITIES AND PERSONNEL

THE HILL-BURTON ACT

In order to help alleviate hospital shortages, Congress passed the Hill-Burton Act in 1946. Important amendments were enacted in 1954, 1964, and in 1970. Under the act, as amended, Congress has appropriated varying amounts ranging from a low of $65 million in 1954 to a high of $270

---

[40]*Ibid.*, pp. 551-553.

million in 1967. The appropriation for 1972 was $194.9 million.[41] The money is appropriated to the states on the basis of a matching formula which considers per capita income and population. The original act required that the sponsor contribute two dollars for every one dollar of federal money. Since needs were greater in the poorer states, under these arrangements the poorer states had to raise larger sums of money than the wealthier states. In 1949, the law was amended to permit the federal government to contribute from one-third up to a maximum of two-thirds, depending on the per-capita income of the state. Under this arrangement, the neediest states have constructed about three times as many beds per person as the wealthier states.[42]

Because of the deterioration of hospital facilities in poverty areas, a further change in the formula was made in 1970. The amendments of that year, enacted over President Nixon's veto, authorized the federal share to be increased up to 90 percent of the project cost for "(1) facilities providing service for persons in rural or urban poverty areas, or for (2) projects offering potential for reducing health care costs through shared services, interfacility cooperation or through free-standing outpatient facilities."[43] The amendments of that year also: increased the authorization of funds to $400 million per year; provided for $500 million per year in loan guarantees for construction and modernization of health facilities; authorized an interest rate subsidy so that rates would be three percent less than prevailing market rates; provided for the assignment of priority to areas of relatively small financial resources; and added neighborhood health centers to the list of facilities eligible for federal funds.

Most Hill-Burton funds have been used for construction or modernization of general hospitals (71%). Lesser amounts have been used for long term care facilities (14%); outpatient facilities (5.5%); rehabilitation facilities, (3.6%); public health centers, (2.7%); and minor amounts for mental and tuberculosis hospitals and for state health laboratories. Through fiscal year 1971, Hill-Burton funds had provided $3.7 billion, matched by $9.1 billion of state and local funds, for a total of $12.8 billion in construction. About 59% of the funds have been used for voluntary nonprofit facilities; 41% for public facilities, mainly local-government.

In the early years the focus was on the construction of hospitals in rural areas where none existed. In recent years the emphasis has shifted to modernizing obsolete facilities in urban areas. Altogether about 45% of Hill-Burton projects and over half of the inpatient-care beds provided by the program are in standard metropolitan statistical areas, two-thirds of these in the central city. For all projects the program has shifted away

[41]*Hill-Burton Program Progress Report, July 1, 1947-June 30, 1971*, U. S. Department of Health. Education and Welfare. Health Services and Mental Health Administration. 1972. p. 13.
[42]Paul A. Brinker and Burley Walker. Jr.. "The Hill-Burton Act: 1948-1954." *Review of Economics and Statistics*, Vol. 44 (1962). p. 210.
[43]*Hill-Burton Program Progress Report, July 1, 1947-June 30, 1971*, op. cit., p. 4.

from the construction of new facilities toward the modernization of existing facilities. In 1948, 80% of the funds for general hospitals were for new facilities; by 1971, 96.5% of such funds were for modernization.[44]

To a degree not often true of federal health programs the Hill-Burton program came near to fulfilling its original objectives. Over the years, however, the nature of hospital needs changed. The out-migration of population from rural areas made surplus many of the small hospitals constructed under the original objectives. The unexpected decline in the birthrate has led to a surplus of obstetrical beds in many areas. The spread of the third-party payment coverage for hospital costs (private insurance, Medicare, and Medicaid) made it possible for many institutions to go directly to capital markets for funds, thus circumventing Hill-Burton controls on the distribution of facilities. But at the same time, facilities for the poor and the near-poor were deteriorating badly, especially in the central city. There is also a lack of ambulatory facilities in the inner city, and considerable reluctance on the part of lenders to supply funds for central city facilities. The Hill-Burton program has gradually changed in the direction of meeting these latter needs.[45]

HEALTH PROFESSIONS EDUCATIONAL ASSISTANCE ACT (1963)

In order to encourage the training of additional medical personnel, the Health Professions Educational Assistance Act was passed in 1963. This act provided that the federal government appropriate matching grants of $105 million over a three-year period for the construction of new teaching facilities for the training of physicians, pharmacists, optometrists, podiatrists, nurses, and professional public health personnel. Also $35 million was appropriated to assist in the construction of new teaching facilities for the training of dentists, and the same amount of money was appropriated for the replacement or rehabilitation of existing facilities for the training of all the above listed medical personnel. The amount of the federal grant is determined by the Surgeon General, but may not exceed 66.7 percent for new facilities, 50 percent for other facilities, and 75 percent for public health facilities.

Additional aid for medical education appears to be in order. Large sums of money are needed to finance four years of college, four years of medical school and one or more years of internship or residency. Systems of scholarships and low-interest loans are recommended to aid medical and dental students, especially students from low- or middle-income families. The medical schools themselves are chronically short of funds. They must continually update their facilities as technology changes, and

[44]*Ibid.*, Chart 3. p. 33.
[45]*Hill-Burton Hospital Survey and Construction Act*, Committee on Labor and Public Welfare. U. S. Senate. 93rd Congress. 1st Session. Committee Print. June 1973. pp. 17-18.

they must pay their teaching personnel salaries sufficient to induce the best doctors to devote at least part of their time to teaching. Present medical schools need to be expanded, and a steadily rising number of medical students must be recruited. Larger private and governmental appropriations will be necessary to ensure an adequate supply of physicians in the future.

NURSES TRAINING ACT (1964)

In order to encourage additional training for nurses, Congress in 1964 passed the Nurses Training Act. This act provided matching grants of $5 million for fiscal 1966 and $10 million for the next three fiscal years to construct new facilities for collegiate schools of nursing, or the replacement or rehabilitation of existing facilities for associate degree or diploma schools of nursing. The amount of the grant is determined by the Surgeon General, but may not exceed two thirds of the cost of new facilities and one-half of the cost of other facilities. A loan was also created for those taking nurses training, with a limit of $1,000 per student for the academic year.

OTHER LEGISLATION

Much other legislation, some major, some minor, pertaining to health care has been enacted. Major legislation is dealt with in the next chapter. Much of the other legislation had to do with authorizing the Public Health Service to conduct research on various chronic deseases, and various aids to education. These include: the National Mental Health Act of 1946; the National Heart Act of 1948; the National Dental Research Act of 1948; an act in 1950 authorizing research in arthritis, rheumatism, multiple sclerosis, cerebral palsy, epilepsy, and other diseases; a National Health Survey Act in 1956; the Health Research Facilities Act of 1956, amended in 1965; the National Library of Medicine Act in 1956; the International Health Research Act of 1960; the Community Health Services and Facilities Act of 1962; the Heart Disease, Cancer, and Stroke Amendments of 1965; the Comprehensive Health Planning and Public Health Services Amendments of 1966; the Allied Health Professions Personnel Training Act of 1966; the Partnership for Health Amendments of 1967; the Health Manpower Act of 1968; and the Health Services Amendments of 1968.[46] Subsequent legislation authorizing Health Maintenance Organization (HMO) and Professional Standards Review Organizations (PSRO) will be discussed in a later chapter.

[46]*Compilation of Selected Public Health Laws*, Senate Committee on Labor and Public Welfare and the House Committee on Interstate and Foreign Commerce. 1st Session. Joint Committee Print. February 1969. pp. 487-489.

Summary

This chapter has been concerned with the weaknesses of present medical care in the United States. A balanced picture of medical care should include the strengths of the American medical system as well as the weaknesses. Certainly over the past 100 years great improvements have been made in medical care. The death rate has been lowered, and people are living longer. Certain diseases, such as diphtheria, smallpox, and many others, have been controlled. The Salk and Sabin vaccines have greatly reduced the amount of poliomyelitis. Good medical schools exist, and they are turning out a gradually increasing number of graduates. Professional meetings, conferences and clinical clubs help to disseminate new research findings. High quality medical publications are available to all doctors.

In spite of rapid advances made in medical care, weaknesses still persist. While many acute illnesses have been largely conquered, the chronic illnesses have not been. A larger research effort is needed in this area. Too little medical care is being provided low income groups, the aged, and rural inhabitants. Too little preventive medicine is being practiced. There are too few nursing homes in the United States. The quality of care in some nursing homes is not what it ought to be. There are not enough doctors, dentists, nurses, and other paramedical workers.

The Public Health Service was the first public attempt to supplement private medicine in the United States. Much valuable research activity, preventive medicine, and help for local indigents is provided through this service. The Hill-Burton program was largely successful in reducing the hospital shortage in rural areas, but need has changed causing the program to be redirected toward aiding hospital construction and modernization in the central city. Other legislation has been directed toward easing the health manpower shortage, but a continuing effort is needed in this area.

Bibliography

Edwards, Marvin H., *Hazardous To Your Health* (New Rochelle, N.Y., Arlington House, 1972).

Fuchs, Victor R., *Health, Economics and Social Choice* (New York, Basic Books, 1975)

Gerber, Alex, *The Gerber Report* (New York, David McKay Company, 1971).

Greenberg, Selig, *The Quality of Mercy* (New York, Atheneum, 1971).

Hanlon, John J., *Principles of Public Health Administration*, 3rd ed., (St. Louis, C. V. Mosby Co., 1960).

Kennedy, Edward M., *In Critical Condition* (New York, Simon and Schuster, 1972).

McTaggart, Aubrey C., *The Health Care Dilemma* (Boston, Holbrook Press, 1971).

Ribicoff, Abraham, *The American Medical Machine* (New York, Saturday Review Press, 1972).

Schwartz, Harry, *The Case for American Medicine* (New York, David McKay Company, 1972).

Strickland, Stephen P., *U. S. Health Care* (New York, Universe Books, 1972).

Tunley, Roul, *The American Health Scandal* (New York, Harper & Row, 1966).

CHAPTER 13

DISABILITY INSURANCE, MEDICARE, AND MEDICAID

TEMPORARY DISABILITY: PRIVATE ARRANGEMENTS

Temporary ill health is of a less serious nature than permanent and total disability. Nevertheless, a person who loses two or three weeks to six months or more of pay because of illness may face grave economic hardship. For 1972 it was estimated that the income loss from short-term occupational illness was $19.4 billion, offset by $6.6 billion of cash benefits from statutory and non-statutory arrangements.[1] About 49 million people, or two-thirds of all private and public wage and salary workers, have some kind of formal protection against loss of earnings when temporarily ill. This includes those covered under statutory programs and those covered by voluntary plans.

The two major forms of voluntary plans are insurance, including self-insurance, and sick leave. Voluntary insurance plans covered an estimated 17 million workers in 1972. These plans generally provide one-half to two-thirds wage replacement after a waiting period of 3 to 7 days. Duration of benefits sometimes varies by length of work experience but more commonly is some fixed maximum ranging from 13 to 26 weeks. In 1972, insurance companies collected $3.4 billion in premiums and paid out $2.0 billion in benefits. Benefits were thus 59% of premium payments.[2]

Sick leave, the other major private arrangement, is commonly paid as full replacement of earnings without a waiting period for a maximum of 5 to 15 days per year. Formal sick leave plans covered about 16 million workers in private industry and in government in 1972. The estimated dollar amount of sick leave was more than $3.8 billion, the majority of which (67%) was paid to government workers. Almost all Federal workers are entitled to sick leave and perhaps 90 percent of full-time state and local government employees have this protection. Exclusive sick leave plans, mainly governmental, replaced 77% of the income loss of covered workers. Workers in private industry received $1.3 billion in formal sick leave plans in 1972. In addition many companies pay sick leave at the option of the employer and these are not included in the above statistics.[3]

---

[1]Daniel N. Price, "Cash Benefits for Short-Term Sickness, 1948-72," *Social Security Bulletin*, Vol. 37 (January 1974), pp. 19-30.
[2]*Ibid.*, p. 23.
[3]*Ibid.*, pp. 24-25.

TEMPORARY DISABILITY INSURANCE

Temporary disability insurance (TDI) laws exist in five states: Rhode Island (1942), California (1946), New Jersey (1948), New York (1949), and Hawaii (1969). Puerto Rico also has a law (1968), and the railroad industry is covered nationwide under a federal law (1946). All of the laws, except that in New York, are closely related to unemployment insurance, with similar coverage, benefits and administration. The New York program is more closely allied to that state's workmen's compensation law.

California, Puerto Rico and Rhode Island provide one program of benefits without regard to whether workers are employed, unemployed, or in noncovered employment when their disability begins. Hawaii, New Jersey and New York provide two systems of disability benefits, one for the individuals who suffer disability when employed, and another for persons who become disabled while unemployed. The similarities and differences in the six state laws are discussed below.[4]

COVERAGE AND ELIGIBILITY

Coverage is similar but not identical to that in each state's unemployment insurance laws. Generally, all people employed in industry and commerce are covered, while people employed in agriculture, government, domestic service, nonprofit, family and self-employment are generally not covered. There is limited coverage of agricultural workers in California, Hawaii, and Puerto Rico.

To be eligible for disability payments, a worker must prove that he or she is unable to work due to some physical or mental illness. Normally medical certification from an attending physician is required, except that in California, Hawaii, and Puerto Rico certification from an authorized religious practitioner will be accepted. Prolonged illness necessitates a renewed certification. Disability claims, together with the certification, are normally filed by mail. If a claimant is dissatisfied with the determination made on his claim he may make appeal to appropriate appeal bodies in each state.

Most states specify a base period such as one year or some other period of time as a foundation for eligibility. During his base period the worker must have worked a certain minimum number of weeks or have earned a certain minimum dollar amount. If a worker's claim is approved he becomes eligible for benefits during a period of time specified in state

---

[4]This section is based mainly on Section 600, "Temporary Disability Insurance Coordinated with Unemployment Insurance," in *Comparison of State Unemployment Insurance Laws*, U. S. Department of Labor, Manpower Administration, January 1972, with revision to January 1974, pp. 6-1 to 6-17.

law, usually the next 52 consecutive calendar weeks. Benefit payments, however, may not exceed a maximum of 26 weeks in any one benefit period, and the maximum may be less than 26 weeks, depending on the amount of work or wages in the base period. The worker receives benefits only during the period when he is ill, which might be only two or three weeks.

DISQUALIFICATIONS

A number of disqualification and noneligibility provisions have been written into the laws. Generally, the worker must be disabled, and he may be declared ineligible if he voluntarily withdrew from the labor force for reasons other than disability. In some states a disabled claimant who had been participating in a labor dispute is ineligible. Intentional self-inflicted injuries, and attempts to obtain benefits through fraud, are disqualifications. Generally, any conduct which would disqualify the worker under the states' unemployment insurance law will also disqualify him for TDI. Similarly, receipt of unemployment insurance benefits precludes receipt of TDI.

Receipt of workmen's compensation benefits ordinarily makes the worker ineligible for TDI, but the difference will be paid in most states if the TDI benefit is larger than the workmen's compensation benefit. In New Jersey and New York receipt of workmen's compensation payments precludes TDI payments. Other types of income, such as wages, employer pensions, and old-age and survivors insurance benefits, may affect eligibility or be disqualifying. If the employer continues to pay wages or part of regular wages, the disability benefit may be eliminated or reduced so that the combined total is not more than the previous regular wage. If a worker begins to draw an employee pension or social security retirement benefits he is generally presumed to have withdrawn from the labor force.

BENEFITS

Benefits are normally computed as some fraction of the worker's previous earnings in his base period. State law may specify some percentage such as 50 percent of his average weekly wage, or state law may include a schedule or table showing the benefit amount associated with previous earnings. Often, however, the actual benefits received will be less than the benefit amount indicated by the percentage specified in the law. All states specify a maximum amount which may not be exceeded. The maximums range from $68 per week in Rhode Island to $119 in California. Highly paid workers will be limited to the maximums; workers with lower wages may get less, depending on the state formula. Minimums are also written into the laws, ranging from $10 to $25. Actual benefit amounts (average) in 1971 ranged from $49 per week in Puerto Rico to $71 in New York.[5]

All six programs have a waiting period of seven consecutive days. The waiting week is noncompensable in all cases except in New Jersey, where the week becomes compensable after benefits have been paid for three weeks. A noncompensable waiting period reduces program and administrative costs.[6]

TYPE OF FUND AND FINANCING

In five of the six states the program may be funded either through a state fund or with private insurance companies, and in some cases by self-insurance. In Rhode Island all contributions are paid into a pooled state fund and all benefits are paid from that fund. In California, New Jersey and Puerto Rico coverage through an insurance company may be substituted for coverage by the state plan. Private coverage must be approved by the state agency and must generally provide contributions at least as favorable as may be obtained through the state fund.

All six TDI programs are financed either partly or wholly by taxes on employees. In California and in Rhode Island the taxes fall almost entirely on employees. In New Jersey, New York, Hawaii, and Puerto Rico the taxes fall on both the employee and the employer. The tax on the employer is likely to be shifted either forward to the consumer or backward to the worker.

EVALUATION

Temporary disability insurance has been the slowest to expand of all types of social insurance. The method of financing these programs, usually through taxes on employees, has not been particularly popular with workers. Early concern about possible abuse of disability insurance has generally not been borne out by experience. The requirement that illness must be medically verified has tended to limit abuse. Also the state fund, the private insurance company, and the employer himself in the case of self-insurance, are "contrary interests" who endeavor to limit abuse in their own self-interest. Most private carriers do not consider benefit abuse as a serious overall problem.[7]

[5]Social Security Bulletin, Annual Statistical Supplement, 1971, Table 23, p. 45.
[6]Ibid.
[7]John S. Sickley, "The Impact of a State Disability Act on Insurance Companies: A Study of the California Experience," Research Monograph No. 71 (Columbus, Ohio State University, Bureau of Business Research, 1954). See also Margaret Dahm, "Temporary Disability Insurance in the United States," International Labour Review, Vol. 78 (1958), pp. 568-570.

The overall extent of protection against income loss due to short term disability remains quite limited. About one-third of the work force has no protection of any kind. Only about 34 percent of the income loss is made up by all programs, private or public, in existence.[8] In the TDI program, while the formulas call for benefits that replace one-half to two-thirds of the wage loss, in actual practice the proportion of wage loss replaced is about one-fourth. Increases in maximum limits in state laws lag behind the rate of inflation. Provisions limiting duration of benefits have not been liberalized for many years. And 45 states have no TDI programs.

PERMANENT DISABILITY INSURANCE

Permanent disability may result from a number of causes such as the major chronic illnesses, or from severe industrial, automobile, home, and other accidents. Often such disability occurs many years before age 62, when the worker becomes eligible to draw social security retirement benefits. Illness so serious that it permanently deprives the worker of his job obviously creates severe economic distress.

DISABILITY UNDER OASDHI

The first regulation of the permanently and totally disabled under the regular Social Security program came in 1954 with the "disability freeze" amendment to the Social Security Act. This amendment provides that in computing a worker's average monthly wage to determine his retirement benefits, the years of permanent and total disability can be disregarded. Disregarding such years has the effect of raising the worker's average monthly wage and thus his benefits.

In 1956, it was decided to add benefits for the permanently and totally disabled to the OASI program, thus making it OASDI. Coverage was restricted to those aged 50 and over. A tax of 0.25 each on both the employer and the employee was levied, and a separate disability trust fund was established. After a few years experience it was found that malingering was only a minor problem, and the disability trust fund began accumulating a surplus. In 1960, the age 50 requirement was eliminated so that workers of any age who qualified could draw benefits if permanently and totally disabled. Such disability is a serious matter at any age, but it is even more disastrous for a younger worker who is apt to have young children in his care.

In order to finance the broadened disability program, the tax rate was raised in 1965, 1967, and 1969, and eventually to 0.55 percent each on both

[8]Daniel N. Price, op. cit., pp. 26-27.

employer and employee. The rate is scheduled to rise to 0.575 percent in 1978. The tax base is the same as that for OASI ($15,300 in 1976), subject to upward adjustment as the Cost of Living Index changes. The tax rate for self-employed people was 0.795 percent in 1976 on the same tax base, and the rate is scheduled to rise to 0.84 percent in 1978.[9] The disability insurance trust fund has grown intermittently since 1956, and in December, 1974 stood at $8.1 billion, up $0.2 billion over the previous year.[10] The disability trust fund and the current tax rates appear to be adequate.

DISABILITY BENEFITS

To qualify for disability benefits under OASDHI, a disabled worker must not only be fully insured but must also have had a total of five years (20 quarters) out of the last ten years (40 quarters) in covered employment. The 1967 amendments lowered the eligibility requirements for those under 31 by providing that they could qualify if they were covered in one-half of the quarters after age 21 and the time they were disabled, but the number of covered quarters must not be less than six. The 1972 amendments provided that a blind worker need only be fully insured (must have as many calendar quarters of coverage as the number of years elapsed after age 21). The amendments of that year also lowered the waiting period from six months to five months. Benefits continue until the disability ends, or the individual dies, or reaches age 65 and becomes eligible for old age benefits.

Payments to disabled workers equal 100 percent of the primary insurance amount paid to a retired Social Security beneficiary. In January, 1975, disabled workers received an average payment of $106; wives and husbands, $62; and the children, $56. Benefits awarded to the newly disabled were somewhat larger, being for a worker, $219; for wives and husbands, $64; and for the children, $62.[11] In January, 1975, 3.9 million people were receiving disability benefits under OASDHI. This included 2.2 million disabled workers, 0.4 million wives and husbands, and 1.3 million children.

At the same time about 1.7 million disabled people were receiving benefits from the Supplemental Security Income program on the basis of their disability. Many of these had not qualified under the insurance program, or were receiving so little income from it that they were eligible for assistance. Another 485 thousand people (miners, widows, and dependents) were drawing benefits, payable from general revenues of the Treasury, for black-lung disease (pneumoconiosis), under terms of the Federal Coal Mine Health and Safety Act of 1969.[12]

[9]*Social Security Bulletin*, Annual Statistical Supplement, 1971, p. 24.
[10]*Social Security Bulletin*, Vol. 38 (May 1975), Table M-6, p. 43.
[11]*Ibid.*, Table M-13, p. 50.
[12]*Ibid.*, Table M-23, p. 58 and Table M-35, p. 66.

DISABILITY DEFINED

For purposes of the "disability freeze," disability means (1) any medically determinable physical or mental impairment that can be expected to result in death, or has lasted or can be expected to last for a continuous period of not less than 12 months, and that renders an individual unable to engage in any substantial gainful activity, or (2) blindness. For both benefits and "freeze" purposes an individual is deemed disabled only if his impairment is of such severity that he is not only unable to do his previous work, but cannot, considering his age, education, and experience do any other substantial gainful work. Whether or not any work exists in the national economy, or whether any work exists in the area in which he lives, or whether a specific job vacancy exists for him, or whether he would be hired if he applied for work is not to be considered.[13]

The disability determination is made by an agency of the state government, usually the state Office of Vocational Rehabilitation. The purpose of this provision is to put the disability applicant into immediate contact with the rehabilitation agency. If he is in fact found to be disabled, and certified as such so that benefits can begin, he will also be considered for rehabilitation by that agency.

REHABILITATION AND TRIAL WORK PERIODS

Rehabilitation provides hope for the disabled for a return to productive status in society, but too much should not be expected of it. In 1965, only about 2.5% of total worker applicants actually undertook rehabilitation. Only about one applicant in ten showed enough promise of successful rehabilitation to be referred to the state agency. Of those referred only about one in four was actually accepted for such services.[14] Most totally disabled people are generally not good candidates for rehabilitation. This is further indicated by the reasons why disability benefits are terminated, to wit, mainly death and conversion to old age benefits at age 65. Only about two percent make medical recovery, and some of the recoveries occur without the aid of rehabilitation agencies.[15] Often, those who do recover or are rehabilitated have difficulty finding jobs. Thus rehabilitation must not be thought of as a cure-all for the problems of the totally disabled.

Congress has from time to time added amendments to the law to encourage a higher level of rehabilitation. One amendment provides that

[13]*1974 Social Security and Medicare Explained* (Chicago, Commerce Clearing House, Inc., 1974), para. 510.1.

[14]Ralph Treitel, "Financing of Disability Beneficiary Rehabilitation," *Social Security Bulletin*, Vol. 32 (April 1969), pp. 29-34.

[15]Jack Schmulowitz, "Recovery and Benefit Termination: Program Experience of Disabled-Worker Beneficiaries," *Social Security Bulletin*, No. 36 (June 1973), pp. 3-15.

benefits may be denied to the disabled person in any month in which the individual refuses, without good cause, to accept rehabilitation services. Another amendment provides for a "trial work period" as an incentive for personal rehabilitation efforts. A disabled person may work for as many as nine months without affecting his right to benefits, provided his disability does not cease during that period. During this period, the work done may not be used as proof that disability has ceased. After nine months work, which need not be consecutive, work done is evidence of cessation of disability. However, benefits will continue for an additional three months, so it is possible for benefits to continue for a total 12 months after the individual has returned to work.[16] This provision helps to reduce the reluctance of the disabled person to return to work.

There has also been some reluctance on the part of state agencies to accept rehabilitation cases, especially where the agency is short of funds. To deal with this problem, the 1965 amendments provided that the cost of rehabilitation services would be payable out of the disability trust fund, provided that reimbursement in any year may not exceed one percent of the total amount of disability funds dispensed in the previous year. The 1972 amendments raised this to one and one-half percent.

DISABILITY BENEFITS AND WORKMEN'S COMPENSATION

In some cases where a worker is disabled by an industrial accident or disease he or she may be eligible for benefits under state or federal workmen's compensation legislation as well as under OASDHI. A reduction is made in the social security disability benefit, except where the state is reducing the workmen's compensation benefit because of the federal disability law. Total benefits paid under the two programs may not exceed 80% of the *higher* of (a) the workers average monthly wage used for computing social security benefits; or (b) his actual average monthly earnings during the five consecutive years after 1950 when his earnings were highest; or (c) his actual average monthly earnings in his one best year in the five-year period immediately preceding the year in which he became disabled. In no case are total benefits reduced below the total for which the worker is eligible under social security.[17]

EVALUATION

One persistent criticism of permanent disability benefits under Social Security has been that the disabled were not provided any help with their medical expenses. After intermittent debate for several years, Congress in

---

[16]*1974 Social Security Bulletin and Medicare Explained, op. cit.,* para. 510.5.
[17]*Ibid.,* para. 510.8.

1972 extended hospital insurance protection under Medicare to disabled workers under OASDHI and to those under the railroad disability program (as well as to certain other disabled persons).[18] However the disabled worker must have been entitled to disability benefits for 24 consecutive months before becoming entitled to Medicare. Such benefits began in July 1973. Early experience indicates lower-than-anticipated expenses for the care of the disabled.[19]

Other criticisms of the disability provisions have been directed at the severe definition of disability and its severe administration. Still others have criticized the five-month waiting period as working an undue hardship on the disabled, especially where the worker is not entitled to workmen's compensation or in the forty-five states where there is no temporary disability insurance program. However, it should be noted that if the definition is liberalized or the waiting period is shortened, additional thousands will be able to quality for longer periods of time, and if so, tax rates will need to be raised in order to maintain the financial integrity of the program.

MEDICARE

In 1965, amendments to the Social Security Act provided for medical care for the aged under the insurance program. OASDI then became OASDHI. Additional important amendments were made in 1967 and in 1972, and minor amendments were made in 1969 and 1971. The following legal provisions and data are those prevailing under the 1972 amendments. Essentially Medicare is a two-part program. What is generally called "Part A Medicare" is compulsory, is financed by social security taxes, and provides for hospital insurance and a wide range of other benefits.[20] "Part B Medicare" is optional with the aged, is financed by monthly contributions by the aged themselves matched by federal funds taken from general revenues, and provides various surgical, medical, and related benefits. To over-simplify, Part A is similar to Blue Cross which provides hospitalization benefits, while Part B is similar to Blue Shield which provides surgical and other benefits.

ELIGIBILITY FOR PART A BENEFITS

Generally all people aged 65 and over who are entitled to regular social security or railroad retirement benefits are also eligible for hospital in-

---

[18]*1974 Social Security and Medicare Explained, op. cit.*, para. 605.5.

[19]Jonathan Spivak, "Social Security Financially Hurt by Dip in Births," *Wall Street Journal*, June 4, 1974, p. 2.

[20]The expressions "Part A" and "Part B" come from Title XVIII of the Social Security Act. Hospital insurance and related benefits are in Part A; medical insurance and related benefits are found in Part B.

surance and related benefits.[21] All people who were 65 years of age before 1968 were automatically covered, and others with as little as three quarters of coverage were eligible under "transitional entitlement." Younger people will need quarters of coverage as under old age insurance. Anyone born in 1929 or later will need 40 quarters of coverage. Some of those who are not covered, such as federal workers and their dependents are covered under a different law, the Federal Employees Health Benefits Act of 1959. Aliens, certain convicts, and those who somehow never accumulated quarters of coverage are the few who have no protection. They can voluntarily enroll for hospital insurance coverage provided they pay a premium of $36 per month. Altogether about 20.9 million persons aged 65 and over were covered by Part A in 1971,[22] and coverage is estimated to reach 22 million in 1975.

PART A BENEFITS

Medicare pays for most hospital charges up to a maximum of 90 days during a "spell of illness." The patient must pay for the first $104 and a charge of $26 a day beginning with the 61st day of hospitalization. In addition, each person has a lifetime reserve (which may be used only once) of 60 days after the first 90 days, but the person must pay $52 per day during the lifetime reserve. Covered costs include those for a semi-private room, or for a private room if the doctor certifies that it is medically required. Regular hospital nursing services, drugs and supplies, and diagnostic services furnished to inpatients are covered.[23]

After three consecutive days in a hospital, Part A covers post-hospital care in a "skilled nursing facility" for up to 100 days during a spell of illness. The patient pays a charge of $13 per day after the 20th day of care. To qualify for care in such a facility the patient must be admitted to the facility for further treatment of a condition for which he had been hospitalized, and he must be admitted within 14 days after discharge from the hospital. To qualify as a "skilled nursing facility," a rather rigorous set of standards must be met. Generally, 24-hour nursing service must be available, physicians must be available on a regular basis, policies of the facilities must be developed and supervised by at least one physician, the facility must maintain clinical records on all patients, and several other standards must be met. The standards are such that most ordinary nursing homes do not qualify, and as a result some areas have no convenient certified skilled nursing facility.[24]

[21]1974 Social Security and Medicare Explained, op. cit., para. 605-605.5.

[22]Medicare, 1971, Section a, Enrollment, U. S. Department of Health, Education and Welfare, Social Security Administration, April 1973, p. ix.

[23]Ibid., para. 609-611.

[24]While there are about 6,750 hospitals participating in Medicare, there are only about 4,000 certified skilled nursing facilities. Certified home health agencies number about 2,200, and there are about 3,000 certified independent laboratories. See Health Insurance Statistics, U. S. Department of Health, Education and Welfare, Social Security Administration, DHEW Pub. No. (SSA) 75-11702, May 16, 1975.

Part A also covers up to 100 home-health visits during a spell of sickness and within one year after discharge from a hospital or skilled nursing facility. The home-visit plan must be established by a doctor and carried out by para-medical personnel. Included are such services as intermittent nursing care, and physical, occupational, and speech therapy.

The purpose of many of the foregoing provisions is to prevent overuse of hospital facilities. The dollar charges levied against the patient while he is in a hospital or skilled nursing facility are of this nature. The 90-day limit has this effect also. The existence of skilled nursing facilities and the provision for home-health visit are intended to give the doctor an alternative to indefinite hospitalization of the patient.

In fiscal year 1974 there were 8.3 million claims approved for payment and $7.0 billion paid out for these bills. Hospitals accounted for most

TABLE 13-1

MEDICARE, PART A: NUMBER OF CLAIMS APPROVED FOR PAYMENTS, AMOUNTS, BY TYPE OF BENEFIT, 1968-1974

Total:	1968	1970	1972	Fiscal 1974
Number of Claims Paid (thousands)	7,854	7,409	7,064	8,382
Amounts Reimbursed (millions)	$3,947	$4,787	$5,532	$7,046
Inpatient Hospital:				
Number of Claims Paid (thousands)	5,954	6,239	6,354	7,365
Amount Reimbursed (millions)	$3,557	$4,518	$5,373	$6,807
Per Claim	$ 597	$ 724	$ 846	$ 924
Home Health:				
Number of Claims Paid (thousands)	510	561	402	587
Amount Reimbursed (millions)	$ 38	$ 46	$ 37	$ 59
Per Claim	$ 74	$ 82	$ 91	$ 100
Skilled Nursing Facility:				
Number of Claims Paid (thousands)	1,018	609	308	431
Amount Reimbursed (millions)	$ 348	$ 223	$ 123	$ 181
Per Claim	$ 342	$ 366	$ 298	$ 419

Source: *Social Security Bulletin*, Vol. 36 (November 1973), Table M-19, p. 55; and *Ibid.*, Vol. 38 (May 1975), Table M-18, p. 54.

of these, there being 7.3 million bills and $6.8 billion reimbursed to hospitals. (See Table 13-1.) The average hospital claim came to $1,219, of which $924, or 76 percent, was paid. There were only 431,000 nursing facility claims and only 587,000 home-health claims.[25]

"PART B" BENEFITS

Medical insurance, or Part B, benefits are available to all resident citizens 65 and over, whether or not eligible for social security or railroad benefits. In the early years of the program, enrollment was voluntary during certain designated enrollment periods. The 1972 amendments provided that most retirees drawing benefits would be automatically covered unless they specifically declined coverage. About 20 million persons were covered by Part B in 1971,[26] and coverage is estimated at about 21.6 million for 1975. Under Part B the patient must pay the first $60, called the "deductible," of covered expenses in the calendar year. Thereafter the Federal Government will pay 80% of the reasonable charges for any covered services during the rest of the year.

Covered services include doctors services, a wide variety of medical and other health services, and home health services. Doctors services include surgery, home, office, and institutional calls. Dentists are included only for dental surgery. Optometrists are included only for establishing the medical necessity of prosthetic lenses. The 1972 amendments provided for payments to chiropractors only for spinal conditions demonstrated to exist by X-ray. A wide variety of medical services and appliances are covered. These include: X-rays and laboratory tests; radiation therapy; splints and casts; ironlungs, oxygen tents, and other appliances for use in the home; artificial legs, arms, and eyes; and other physical and speech therapy furnished to outpatients. Home-health services provide for 100 visits a year without a requirement of previous hospitalization.[27]

In 1974, Part B paid out $3.2 billion to pay the major part of over 67 million medical bills. Physicians received $2.6 billion of that amount. (See Table 13-2). Outpatient hospital and independent laboratory charges made up most of the remainder. Altogether, the program reimbursed 73 percent of total medical charges.[28]

FINANCING MEDICARE

Part A benefits are financed by part of the regular OASDHI taxes. Under current law the tax rate for 1974-1977 is 0.90% each on both the employer

[25]Social Security Bulletin, Vol. 36 (November 1973), Tables M-19 and M-20, pp. 55-56, and Ibid., Vol. 38 (Mary 1975), Tables M-18 and M-19, pp. 54-55.
[26]Medicare, 1971, op. cit., p. ix.
[27]1974 Social Security and Medicare Explained, op. cit., para. 631-653.
[28]Social Security Bulletin, Vol. 38 (May 1975), Tables M-20 and M-21, pp. 56-57.

TABLE 13-2

MEDICARE, PART B: NUMBER OF REINBURSED BILLS AND
AMOUNTS REIMBURSED, 1968-1974

	1968	1970	1972	1974
Total:				
All Services (thousands)	31,444	39,695	51,754	67,237
Amount Reimbursed (millions)	$1,342	$1,750	$2,227	$3,154
Physicians Services (thousands)	25,627	32,850	42,164	53,597
Amount Reimbursed (millions)	$1,220	$1,573	$1,975	$2,647
Home Health Services (thousands)	495	430	278	472
Amount Reimbursed (millions)	$22	$23	$15	$38
Outpatient Hospital Services (thousands)	3,499	4,031	5,688	7,924
Amount Reimbursed (millions)	$44	$85	$136	$299
Independent Laboratory Services (thousands)	434	665	1,278	1,835
Amount Reimbursed (millions)	$6	$9	$17	$26
All Other Services (thousands)	1,312	1,715	2,306	3,215
Amount Reimbursed (millions)	$45	$61	$83	$137

Source: *Social Security Bulletin*, Vol. 35 (May 1972). Table M-20, p. 50: and *Ibid.*, Vol. 38 (May 1975). Table M-20, p. 56.

and the employee on the first $15,300 of annual income, subject to adjust-
ment as the cost-of-living index changes. In 1978, the rate is scheduled to
rise to 1.10% each. The self-employed pay the same rate as the employee.
This means that twice as much money is collected to support benefits for
each worker as is collected to pay benefits for each self-employed person.
Part B benefits are paid by monthly premiums from the aged themselves,
normally deducted from their social security retirement checks. The rate
for fiscal year 1975 was $6.70 a month. These funds are matched by an
equal amount paid by the federal government out of the general revenues.

These monies are maintained by the U.S. Treasury in two separate
trust funds, a "hospital insurance trust fund" for Part A, and a "supplementary medical insurance trust fund" for Part B. In December, 1974 the
hospital trust fund had total assets of $9.1 billion, while the Part B trust
fund had only $1.5 billion. The hospital trust fund has slowly increased
and generally appears to be adequate. The Part B trust fund is less adequate but has been increasing in recent years from a low of only $57 million
in 1970.[29] A large trust fund for either Part A or Part B is not considered
necessary. Benefits each year are paid out of tax collections that year.
Trouble, however, could occur in a prolonged period of above-average
unemployment causing tax collections to fall. If necessary, the Federal
government could resort to deficit spending and money creation to
replenish the funds, but as a general rule the trust funds are expected to
maintain a contingency reserve.

FISCAL INTERMEDIARIES

Prior to the enactment of Medicare in 1965 there was much opposition
from doctors and others who did not want "federal interference" in medical practice. Also private insurance companies feared the loss of some of
their health insurance business. To overcome the opposition of both
groups, the law provided that both Part A and Part B would be handled
through private carriers. Generally, the doctor or hospital provides the
service and then bills the appropriate private carrier. The carrier determines the amount to be compensated and makes the payments. The carrier is then periodically compensated by the Social Security Administration.

The Social Security Administration has selected twelve intermediaries under Part A, five of which operate on a nationwide basis,[30] and
seven which are local. The Blue Cross Association is the principal Part A
fiscal intermediary, subcontracting its intermediary functions to 74 individual Blue Cross plans throughout the United States. At the end of

[29]*Social Security Bulletin*, Vol. 38 (May 1975), Tables M-7 and M-8, pp. 44-45.
[30]*1974 Social Security and Medicare Explained, op. cit.*, para. 696. The five nationwide
intermediaries are Aetna Life and Casualty Co., the Blue Cross Association, Mutual of
Omaha, Prudential Insurance Co., and Travelers Insurance Co.

1971, Blue Cross was the intermediary for about 91% of about 6,750 hospitals participating in Medicare.[31] Under Part B, the Social Security Administration has selected carriers on a state-wide basis, and sometimes on a part-of-state basis. Generally the doctor submits the claim to the appropriate carrier, such as Blue Shield, but if the doctor does not desire to do so, the patient bills the carrier.[32]

PROFESSIONAL STANDARDS REVIEW ORGANIZATIONS (PSRO'S)

The original Medicare law provided for Utilization Review Committees to be established for each participating hospital or extended care facility. The committees generally include two or more physicians, normally those with no financial interest in the hospital or nursing facility. Reviews are made of admissions, services provided, and duration of stay of Medicare patients with a view of preventing overuse of facilities. If the committee finds that further stay in the hospital is not medically necessary, Medicare payments may be cut off.[33]

The Utilization Review Committees were widely criticized as varying from good to ineffective. Accordingly, the 1972 amendments authorized new review mechanisms known as Professional Standards Review Organizations. Some 203 PSRO's have been established throughout the country on an area basis, sometimes only one per state in sparsely populated areas.[34] Generally there are a minimum of 300 physicians in a PSRO area. The basic idea of the PSRO is peer-review. The doctors in each area will review the quality of care in that area. At first the PSRO will concentrate on hospital care, later extending to nursing homes and mental hospitals. A PSRO may petition the Secretary of Health, Education, and Welfare to apply peer-review to treatment in doctors offices. The law applies to patients whose bills are paid by government programs, including Medicare, Medicaid, and maternal health and child welfare.

Criticism of the new PSRO's comes from two sources, the doctor's themselves and from consumer advocates. Some doctors are very resentful of the idea of being checked on by their fellow doctors. The Association of American Physicians and Surgeons has filed suit asking that the law be declared unconstitutional. The American Medical Association has vacillated, partly because some members support the idea, some oppose. Consumer groups have complained that there is no user representation on

[31]*Problems Associated With Reimbursements to Hospitals for Services Furnished Under Medicare*, Social Security Administration, Department of Health, Education and Welfare, August 3, 1972, p. 7.

[32]The patient can determine his paying agent from *Your Medicare Handbook*, DHEW Publication No. (SSA) 73-10050, which is issued to all Medicare beneficiaries.

[33]*1974 Social Security and Medicare Explained, op. cit.*, para. 668.

[34]James G. Driscoll, "Is Your Doctor Good?" *The National Observer*, May 4, 1974, pp. 1; 18.

the PSRO, and that consumers have no way of knowing which doctor is practicing poor or dangerous medicine.[35]

EVALUATION

Generally Medicare has worked quite well. There have been criticisms, but most of these have dealt with details or with gaps in the benefits provided. Some have complained about the deductibles which the patient must pay before benefits start, and others have pointed out that the deductibles complicate the administration of the program. The deductibles, however, serve to reduce the tax cost of the program and probably help check overuse of the facilities. However, many people have taken out private health insurance which cover the deductibles in Medicare, and where this occurs the financial disincentive to use facilities is circumvented.

Another criticism is that two separate arrangements, Parts A and B, are not actually necessary. The entire list of benefits under both parts could be financed by Social Security taxes, thus eliminating the enrollment problem in Part B and relieving the aged of the premium expense of that part.

MEDICAID

As was stated earlier, medical care was provided in the 1950's for public assistance recipients by vendor payments, i.e., payments made by the state to doctors and hospitals for services rendered to welfare clients. This program was expanded to "medically needy" aged people not on welfare—by the Kerr-Mills Act in 1960. The 1965 amendments introduced what is now called the Medicaid program, in effect expanding the Kerr-Mills idea to all ages and categories of needy people. Those receiving categorical assistance (OAA, AB, AFDC, or APTD) automatically qualified for medical aid. Those needy persons not on assistance who fit into one of the above assistance categories and cannot pay for it are also eligible. Coverage is mandatory for those who were receiving OAA, AB, and APTD on January 1, 1972. It is optional with the state for those who became newly eligible under the Supplementary Security Income (SSI) program enacted in 1972.

MEDICAL BENEFITS

Services provided may be comprehensive or may be rather limited, depending on how the state chooses to operate within the options provided

35*Ibid.*, p. 18.

by federal law. Federal law provides a comprehensive list of 17 services that a state Medicaid plan may provide. It then specified five services which the state must provide, or as an option, the state must provide any seven of the first 16 services listed in the law. Most state plans do endeavor to provide the basic five which are: inpatient hospital services, outpatient hospital services, laboratory and X-ray services, skilled nursing home services, and physician's services. Under the seven of 16 option, if either inpatient hospital care or skilled nursing facility services are provided, the state must also provide physician's services. Other benefits or services which the state may provide at its option include home health care, private duty nursing, clinic services, dental services, physical therapy, prescribed drugs, dentures, prosthetic devices, and eyeglasses, intermediate care facility services, and others.

Most Medicaid money goes for inpatient hospital services and nursing home care. Data for November, 1973, showed those two services receiving 34.5 percent and 34.2 percent respectively of the total. Other significant amounts went for physicians services (10.9%), prescribed drugs (7.0%), outpatient hospital services (2.8%), dental care (2.7%), and other (7.9%).[36]

FEDERAL-STATE FINANCIAL ARRANGEMENTS

The federal government provides matching funds to the states on a formula basis to help each state operate its Medicaid program. Subject to various limitations, the federal government pays to the state a part, known as the "federal medical assistance percentage" of the state's Medicaid expenditures.[37] The federal percentage ranges between 50 and 83 percent depending on the per capita income of the state. The higher the state's per capita income the less the federal percentage, except that the federal percentage may not be less than 50%. In 1974-75 the percentage was 50% in the 13 wealthiest states. The lower the states per capita income the higher the federal percentage, up to 83%. In 1974-75 the highest percentage paid was 80.55 percent paid to Mississippi. All states are paid at a rate of 75 percent to compensate the state's professional medical personnel and staff and 50 percent for general administration. The 1972 amendments authorized 90 percent federal funds to aid the states in developing mechanized claims processing, information, and cost determination systems. The amendments of that year also authorized 90 percent federal funds to assist the states in furnishing family planning services and supplies.

[36]*Medical Assistance (Medicaid) Financed Under Title XIX of the Social Security Act,* NCSS Report B-1, August 1974, Table 13.
[37]*1974 Social Security and Medicare Explained, op. cit.,* para. 769.

CURRENT MEDICAID DATA

All states except Arizona now participate in the federal-state Medicaid program. Arizona makes some medical vendor payments to assist recipients out of state funds. Puerto Rico, the Virgin Islands, Guam, and the District of Columbia also have federal-state programs in effect. In 1974 about $11.2 billion was expended for medical vendor payments, about $11.1 billion under Medicaid and another $107 million by states and localities for general assistance recipients.

Medicaid operates very differently from state to state, some states providing much more care than others. Generally, the northern industrial states paid the highest average amounts, while lower amounts are often paid in southern states. New York's average payment was almost five times as great as that in New Hampshire. There is also wide variation among the states as to recipient rates per 1,000 population, the recipient rate in New York being seven times that in Wyoming. A low recipient ratio ordinarily does not indicate a low amount of sickness in a particular state; it more commonly indicates degree of severity of eligibility provisions in the state law and severity of administration.

Per capita spending also varies widely from state to state, being nearly 14 times a large in New York as in New Hampshire in May 1973. Per capita spending tends to reflect both need and state effort. Wealthy states with large ghetto populations are apt to have high per capita spending. On the other hand, needs are apt to be great in low-income states also, but such states are often unable or unwilling to spend large amounts for assistance. The data indicate the shortcomings of state administration of such programs.

EVALUATION

The Medicaid program has brought medical care to many of the poor who previously found it financially out of reach. The program may be criticized, however, on several accounts. It is an assistance program and the person must be needy in order to qualify. Some people who need care may shun the program because of the demeaning aspects of a means test.

Economically the program tends to redistribute services from the general taxpayer to the welfare recipient. Since doctors and hospitals render the services and are paid by the state program, the program redistributes funds from the general taxpayer to doctors and hospitals. In many cases, physicians and hospitals were formerly providing free care to welfare recipients, but are now being paid. Thus much of the financial benefit goes to the medical vendor.

Another obvious difficulty with the program is its administration by the states. The programs vary widely from state to state. If a person happens to live in New York the benefits are relatively generous. If he lives in certain southern, plains, or mountain states, he may not be eligible at all, or if eligible will receive only very limited benefits.

Summary

Temporary Disability Insurance provides protection against loss of income due to short-term illness in five states, Puerto Rico, and in the railroad industry. Since New York, New Jersey, and California are among the five states, about one-fourth of the total U.S. labor force has protection under TDI laws. In other states many are voluntarily protected by private insurance and by sick leave plans. But much of the population remains unprotected against this hazard.

Permanent disability insurance is provided under OASDHI. Benefits are not payable unless disability has lasted five months and is expected to last 12 months or more or to result in death. Permanently disabled people under 65 are eligible for benefits under Medicare only after they have been disabled for 24 months. Altogether, about 3.5 million people are receiving benefits under this program.

Medicare for those aged 65 and over came into existence under the 1965 amendments to the Social Security Act. There are actually two programs, one providing hospital and related benefits and the other providing medical and other services. About 21 million people are covered by hospital benefits and about 20 million by the medical insurance benefits. About 76 percent of hospital costs, and about 73 percent of medical charges, are being reimbursed.

Medicaid is a federal-state assistance program paying various proportions of the medical and hospital bills of the needy. Generally, all those who are recipients of cash assistance payments are eligible, and certain others not receiving cash payments but who are deemed "medically needy" are also eligible. The program varies widely from state to state, depending upon provisions of the state law and severity of administration.

CHAPTER 14

PRIVATE AND GOVERNMENTAL HEALTH INSURANCE AND GROUP MEDICINE: CURRENT PROGRAMS AND PROPOSALS

PRIVATE HEALTH INSURANCE

Private health insurance may be divided for convenience into (1) private insurance company arrangements, (2) Blue Cross and Blue Shield plans, and (3) independent (group) health insurance plans. In the United States the first private company organized specifically to sell health insurance was founded in 1847. Frequent rail and steamboat accidents led to the formation of an accident insurance company in 1850. By 1900, 47 American companies were issuing accident insurance. The accident policies eventually were expanded to cover loss of income due to a limited number of diseases such as typhus, typhoid, scarlet fever, smallpox and others. These policies normally had a seven-day waiting period, and benefits were limited to 26 consecutive weeks. Only loss of income was covered; there was no protection against hospital, surgical, or other medical expenses.[1]

BLUE CROSS AND BLUE SHIELD

The beginning of Blue Cross plans (nonprofit hospital insurance) in the United States is usually traced to an experiment tried in 1929 when school teachers in Dallas made an agreement with the Baylor University Hospital whereby teachers were to receive three weeks of hospital care in return for paying $3 per semester. The plan proved successful. With the deepening of the depression in the early 1930's, many hospitals became hard pressed for operating funds. A number of them attempted to obtain financing by using the Baylor plan. The first city-wide plan was put into operation in Sacramento, California, in July, 1932, and shortly thereafter plans were instituted in Newark, St. Paul, and elsewhere.

[1] *73-74 Source Book of Health Insurance Data*, (New York, Health Insurance Institute), pp. 7-8.

In 1936 a Commission on Hospital Service was created by the American Hospital Association to serve as a clearinghouse for such plans. The Blue Cross system was officially organized in 1937 when the commission, later called the Blue Cross Association, began to approve plans that met their standards. Gradually, Blue Cross plans expanded until today there are about 74 locally autonomous Blue Cross associations throughout the nation. These associations cover a state or part of a state, and, with the exception of North Carolina, these plans do not compete with one another. Hospitals have been the main organizers of Blue Cross associations. Members on the boards of directors of these associations represent the hospitals, the medical profession, and the public.

Blue Shield plans specialize mainly in providing surgical benefits rather than hospital benefits, as Blue Cross does. About 70 locally autonomous Blue Shield plans have been organized, and have received approval for operation by the National Association of Blue Shield Plans, governed by 11 directors, three of whom are appointed by the American Medical Association. A local medical society usually has been the organizer of a local group, and most of the plans are underwritten by participating physicians.

COMMERCIAL INSURANCE COMPANIES

At first, private insurance companies showed little interest, but Blue Cross and Blue Shield showed that there was consumer demand for such protection, so private companies began to sell hospital and surgical insurance. Initially, the private companies sold only group insurance, but later individual policies were sold.[2] With the passage of time, additional types of health insurance were offered, including major medical expense insurance, comprehensive major medical, or single plan insurance, and dental expense insurance. Early insurance often covered only the family breadwinner, but most plans today also cover the spouse and children.

INDEPENDENT OR GROUP PRACTICE PLANS

Other prepayment plans or arrangements are sponsored or operated by community-consumer groups, employer-employee groups, private group clinics, dental service corporations, and vision service corporations. The community-consumer groups include group practice plans, such as the Kaiser plans on the West Coast and the Health Insurance Plan of Greater New York. Such plans have often met opposition from organized medicine, but because of their innovative ideas have had a significant im-

[2]Louis S. Reed, "Private Insurance in the United States: An Overview," *Social Security Bulletin*, Vol. 28, No. 12 (December 1965), pp. 3-5.

pact on the thinking of the public and of the medical profession. Other independent plans have grown out of post-war collective bargaining and
frequently have led to group practice arrangements also. Some are financed by joint employer-employee contributions, but for tax reasons
sole financing by the employer is becoming more common. Still other independent plans include those centered around a local clinic, and other
groups similar to, but separate from, Blue Cross and Blue Shield. Group
practice plans and Health Maintenance Organizations will be discussed at
greater length in a separate section below.

COVERAGE

The extent of coverage by private health insurance is not precisely
known. The data used here are those published annually by the Health Insurance Institute, but the data published by the Social Security Administration generally run about 10 percent less.[3] In 1972 it was estimated that
181.6 million, or about 90 percent of the resident civilian population, had
some form of hospitalization.[4] Additional data is shown in Tables 14-1
and 14-2.

TABLE 14-1

NUMBER OF PERSONS WITH PRIVATE
HEALTH INSURANCE COVERAGE,
BY TYPE OF COVERAGE, 1950-1972
(millions)

	1950	1960	1970	1972
Hospital Expense	76.6	130.0	175.4	181.6
Surgical Expense	54.2	117.3	162.7	166.3
Regular Medical Expense	21.6	86.9	140.7	143.0
Major Medical Expense	—	27.4	78.2	79.9
Dental Expense	—	—	6.6	8.9

Source: 73-74 Source Book of Health Insurance Data, Health Insurance
Institute, 1974, p. 19.

[3]Both sets of data must take into account survey and reporting errors, duplication of
coverage, and unknown amounts of coverage such as that for persons in institutions. For a
discussion of the difficulties of health insurance data gathering see Marjorie Smith Mueller,
"Private Health Insurance in 1971: Health Care Services, Enrollment, and Finances," Social
Security Bulletin, Vol. 36 (February 1973), pp. 7-8.
[4]73-74 Source Book of Health Insurance Data, op. cit., p. 19.

TABLE 14-2

HEALTH INSURANCE COVERAGE BY TYPE OF EXPENSE
AND TYPE OF INSURER, 1972
(millions)

	Hospital Expense	Surgical Expense	Regular Medical Expense	Major Medical Expense
All Insurers	181.6	166.3	143.0	—
All Insurance Companies	115.0	102.8	78.4	79.9
Group Policies	83.8	85.3	72.2	73.9
Individual and				
Family Policies	49.9	32.5	14.9	6.0
Blue Cross, Blue Shield, and				
Medical Society Plans	79.6	71.0	66.6	—
Other Plans	8.6	10.9	9.8	—
(Duplication)	(40.3)	(33.4)	(20.5)	—

Source: *73-74 Source Book of Health Insurance Data*, Health Insurance
Institute, 1974, pp. 20-24.

Of total hospitalization coverage in 1972, insurance companies protected about 63 percent, Blue Cross and Blue Shield and other medical
society plans protected 44 percent, and independent plans covered
another 5 percent. The total exceeds 100 percent because of duplication of
coverage. Since 1960 coverage by insurance companies has increased by
about 50 percent; coverage by Blue Cross and similar plans has increased
by 37 percent; and the independent plans have grown by 54 percent.[5]
Coverage by Blue Cross and Blue Shield was slowed during the 1960's
because the same rates for persons of all ages were charged, including
those over 65, even though the expenses of covering the aged are estimated to be 2-1/2 times as high as those under 65. Private insurance companies took advantage of this situation by offering policies which covered
only those under 65 at somewhat lower rates than Blue Cross. Often Blue
Cross was left only with the high cost customers, which forced them to
raise their rates still higher. Faced with this situation, some of the Blue
groups modified their same-rate-for-all policy. The enactment of the
Medicare program in 1965 in effect rescued Blue Cross, since a large majority of participating hospitals have designated Blue Cross as their fiscal
intermediary.

[5]*Ibid.*, p. 20.

BENEFITS AND PREMIUMS

A total of $21 billion in health insurance benefits was paid by private insuring organizations in the United States during 1972, triple the amount paid in 1962. Insurance companies normally make indemnity payments to the insured person to meet some part of his covered expenses. Blue Cross and Blue Shield normally pay directly to the hospital or physician for services they have rendered. In 1972 insurance companies paid $8.6 billion in benefits toward hospital, surgical, and other medical costs, (plus another $2 billion paid for income loss due to disability), while Blue Cross and Blue Shield and other similar plans paid out $10.4 billion.[6]

Total health insurance premium receipts in 1972 were about $25.7 billion, of which $14.3 billion were received by insurance companies, and $11.4 billion received by Blue Cross and Blue Shield, and similar plans. As can be seen, the Blue Cross and Blue Shield plans return a higher percen-

TABLE 14-3

HEALTH INSURANCE OPERATING EXPENSES AS PERCENT OF
PREMIUM INCOME AND PER ENROLLEE, 1973

	Operating Expense	
	As Percent of Premium Income	Per Enrollee (dollars)
Blue Cross	5.2%	$ 5.49
Blue Shield	11.5	5.59
Insurance Companies:		
Group policies	13.0	13.88
Individual policies	47.0	25.16
Independent Plans	7.6	11.05

Source: Marjorie Smith Mueller, "Private Health Insurance in 1973: A Review of Coverage, Enrollment and Financial Experience," *Social Security Bulletin*, Vol. 38 (February 1975), p. 35.

[6]*Ibid.*, pp. 35-42.

tage of the premium dollar to the enrollee than do the private insurance companies. Blue Cross and Blue Shield are nonprofit organizations, and also have a more centralized administrative structure than do the large number of big and little insurance companies. Table 14-3 shows data on operating expense as a percent of premium income and operating expense per enrollee in 1973. Individual insurance with a private insurance company is obviously an expensive proposition.

ARGUMENTS FOR PRIVATE INSURANCE

A number of arguments may be presented to support the position that private insurance provides the best solution to our medical problems. The fact that private insurance has expanded so rapidly has been cited as evidence of its success in meeting the problem of paying for health care. In 1940, only 12 million people had health insurance in this country. By 1960 the number had climbed to 130 million, and by 1972 the figure had reached 182 million. The fact that the insurance has been bought voluntarily rather than compulsorily is extolled as providing the individual with the freedom of choice to purchase as he sees fit. Also, the great variety of plans throughout the country has been cited as providing valuable experimentation to determine better types of protection.

CRITICISMS OF PRIVATE INSURANCE

A basic criticism of private health insurance (or of any such insurance) is that it results in the overuse of hospital or other facilities. If the marginal cost of additional health care is entirely paid by insurance, there is little incentive on the part of the consumer to curtail his usage. In such circumstances, the doctor and the hospital may cooperate with the patient at the expense of the insurer. Also, if a person has hospitalization insurance, but not other kinds of health care insurance, he or she is apt to insist on treatment in a hospital when it might not be needed. Facilities may thus be overused or usage distorted.

Another basic criticism of private health insurance is that many millions, mostly the poorer groups in our society, do not have health insurance. These people, it is contended, need insurance even more than do middle and upper income groups. Hospital insurance is owned by 182 million people, and 166 million have surgical coverage. But fewer, about 80 million, have major medical expense coverage. Dental insurance reaches only about 9 million people.[7] Typical major medical plans do not pay for the first $100, $200, or $500 of expenses. They pay 75 to 80 percent of the remaining bills, with maximum limits frequently of $10,000, $25,000, or $50,000. Regular medical plans without major medical

---

[7]*Source Book of Health Insurance Data, op. cit.*, p. 19.

coverage usually provide some limited number of days of hospitalization, such as 60, 90, or 120 days. The policies that provide for longer coverage must be read with extreme care. Important illnesses, such as heart disease, cancer, and mental illness, may be excluded. Many Blue Cross contracts do not provide payment for mental illness, tuberculosis, alcoholism, drug addiction, and self-imposed injuries.

The failure to provide comprehensive care and to cover all people has resulted in insurance paying only 40.9 percent of all consumer medical care costs in 1973. Although 75 percent of all consumer hospital costs were paid for by insurance, only 49 percent of all doctors' bills, and only 7 percent of other types of care were paid for through insurance. Of total national expenditures for personal health care ($86 billion in 1973), private insurance met 25 percent; 36.4 percent came from direct out-of-pocket payments by consumers; 37 percent was met by public funds; and 1.4 percent came from philanthropy.[8]

A criticism of the nonprofit plans is that they have been unduly under the control of hospitals and doctors. In 1964, 43 percent of the governing boards of Blue Cross were hospital representatives, another 16 percent were medical personnel, and only 32 percent of the personnel were from other walks of life. On Blue Shield governing boards, 63 percent were physicians, 6 percent were hospital representatives, and the remaining were public representatives, some of whom were plan executives who were on the board of trustees of the plan.[9] Critics contend that the interest of hospitals and physicians are overrepresented and that consumer interests are underrepresented. As the program matures and the medical profession realizes that its interests are being adequately protected, there may be more nonphysician participation at the policy-making level of Blue Shield.[10]

Another criticism of the Blue Shield insurance is that it pays surgical fees only and does not pay for routine office calls. Actually, only about 10 percent of physicians' services are performed in hospitals. Some claim that office calls are generally small amounts, and that the insurance principle cannot be used. A study of this problem was made by the Health Information Foundation — National Opinion Research Center. This group found that costs of out-of-hospital services are almost as unevenly distributed among families as hospital costs. Such costs were heavier than surgery costs. More families incurred over $200 per year for physicians' services than for surgery.[11] In view of the obvious costs, some proponents

[8]Marjorie Smith Mueller, "Private Health Insurance in 1973," *Social Security Bulletin*, Vol. 38 (February 1975), p. 37.
[9]Reed, *op. cit.*, pp. 8, 10.
[10]Charles G. Hayden, "An Evaluation of Blue Shield Plans," *Building America's Health*, Vol. 4, p. 54.
[11]Harold M. Somers and Anne R. Somers, *Doctors, Patients, and Health Insurance* (Washington, D.C., The Brookings Institution 1961), p. 380.

of private insurance suggest that it be sold to provide for payments of visits to the doctor's office after the second or third call. Some insurance of this type is now in existence.

Proponents of private insurance have argued for it on the grounds that it permits experimentation. Critics reply that experimentation has already shown that what is needed is comprehensive care. Anything less than that is unsatisfactory and may simply result in inequality of benefits for various people. New health care arrangement need not preclude further experimentation. Moreover, the existence of many types of arrangements throughout the world provides for continuing experimentation on an international basis.

Current private insurance arrangements may also be criticized as being regressive in effect. If low and middle income people pay the same amount for insurance as the wealthy, then they are paying a much higher percentage of their income for medical care than are the wealthy. Private insurance is thus regressive. A few voluntary programs do attempt to lighten the burden on low income families by having a graduated rate based on income. But if this is carried very far, wealthy people will elect not to be covered, thus causing the risk to be spread among fewer people at higher cost to low and middle income families.

GROUP PRACTICE PLANS

A major alternative to our traditional individual practice, fee-for-service medical care is prepaid group practice. Such plans as the Health Insurance Plan of Greater New York (HIP), the Kaiser Foundation Medical Care Program, and the Group Health Cooperative of Puget Sound fall into this category. Anne R. Somers lists the essential ingredients as follows:

1. prepayment, usually by monthly dues;
2. group practice;
3. a unified medical center, including both hospital and satellite clinics;
4. voluntary enrollment, based on the choice of two or more different kinds of health plans;
5. payment of physicians and hospitals on the basis of capitation or fixed fees per time period for each enrollee, regardless of the amount of care provided; and
6. coverage of the full spectrum of comprehensive care, starting with prevention.[12]

[12]Anne R. Somers, Health Care in Transition: Directions for the Future (Chicago, Hospital Research and Educational Trust, 1971) pp. 51-52.

Group practice, as defined by the U. S. Public Health Service, is a group of three or more physicians practicing two or more specialties who pool their income.[13] Generally the number of physicians is much larger than three, and an organizational structure handles the finances, provides the facilities, and supervises the provision of basic and supplemental medical care. The organization views its responsibility as the provision of health care; it is not just a conduit of medical expense dollars. It assumes the responsibility for the cost and for the quality of medical care. And full use is made of computer capability and other modern managerial tools.[14]

The larger groups, their date of organization, and their memberships in 1972, were the Group Health Association (Washington, D.C. 1937), 85,000; the Kaiser Foundation Health Plan (1942), 3.6 million in six area plans; the Group Health Cooperative of Puget Sound (Seattle, 1947), 173,000; and the Health Insurance Plan of Greater New York (1947), 740,000. Other significant groups include the Ross-Loos Medical Clinic (Los Angeles, 1929), and the Community Health Association of Detroit.

THE HEALTH MAINTENANCE ORGANIZATION ACT OF 1973

In recent years, prepaid group plans have come to be called "health maintenance organizations," or HMOs. Prior to 1972 it was difficult for Medicare recipients to participate in group medicine plans, so the Social Security Amendments of that year included a provision that such beneficiaries could choose to receive their covered health-care services from an HMO, and the organization would be reimbursed on a capitation basis for all Medicare services.[15] Then in December, 1973, the Health Maintenance Organization Act was enacted and signed by the President. The act has a number of provisions designed to bring about the more rapid expansion of HMOs. Among other provisions, the act commits the federal government to a limited trial-period support of HMOs,[16] by authorizing a total appropriation of $375 million over a five-year period. Funds for 1974-1976 are earmarked for feasibility studies, planning, and initial development. For 1977, $85 million is authorized only for initial development, with some funds earmarked for research and evaluation each year.

Another significant provision is that all companies employing 25 or more people are required to offer their employees membership in an HMO, provided a qualified one is available in the area, as an alternative to the company's existing medical insurance plan. To make HMOs more

[13]Aubrey C. McTaggart, op. cit., p. 190.
[14]Somers, op. cit., p. 52.
[15]Independent Health Insurance Plans in 1972, Preliminary Estimates, Research and Statistics Note No. 11, U. S. Department of Health, Education and Welfare, May 3, 1974, p. 2.
[16]Health Maintenance Organization Act of 1973, Research and Statistics Note, No. 5, Ibid., March 12, 1974, pp. 1-8.

widespread, the legislation supersedes legal barriers in about 20 states where prepaid group plans had been restricted or prohibited.[17]

A number of Blue Cross plans and at least 20 insurance companies are aiding the growth of HMOs as sponsors, administrators, marketers, and as reinsurers. Some industrial concerns are starting HMOs for their own employees, and others have agreed to provide some start-up money for groups for their employees sponsored by others. There were less than 50 HMOs in the United States when President Nixon first proposed the bill in February 1971, and 128 when the bill was signed in December 1973. Most of these, however, will have to be modified and improved in order to qualify as HMOs under the details of the new law.

The "medical foundation" type of HMO is also likely to expand. Under this arrangement, run entirely by the doctors themselves, there is central record keeping and financing, but no hospital to build or buy. A group of doctors join in an association which accepts prepayment for comprehensive services for patients who sign up. The association contracts with existing hospitals and other facilities to provide necessary services, and arranges for quality review as required. Such foundations are popular in California where many doctors started them to head off loss of patients to the Kaiser Plan.[18]

ADVANTAGES OF PREPAID GROUP MEDICINE

Prepaid group practice has a number of advantages. Both general practitioners and specialists should be able to see more patients. The general practitioner sends more of the patients along to specialists, and thus has more time for his remaining patients. The specialist obtains the advantage of having his case-load already worked up, studied, and diagnosed. Also, when doctors work in a group, they may pool their equipment although more and more doctors in solo practice are also doing this. Patients obtain the advantage of seeing specialists more frequently and thus should receive a higher quality medical care.

Another advantage of group practices is that the records of each patient are kept in a master record file. Under solo practice, the general practitioner would have one set of records and the specialist another. Another advantage is that the doctors may arrange their schedules so that they have more time off. Physicians may rotate on the weekend and take vacations without any loss of patients or pay. They are also protected against illnesses of their own, for their pay continues while they are ill. The medical group arranges that a physician be available for 24 hours of the

[17]"A Revolutionary Plan to Keep People Healthy," Business Week, No. 2313 (January 12, 1974), pp. 58-60.

[18]Ibid., p. 60. For more detailed discussion of this type of organization, see Richard H. Egdahl, M.D., "Foundations for Medical Care," New England Journal of Medicine, Vol. 288 (March 8, 1973), pp. 491-498.

day, seven days a week. Under this type of arrangement, patients feel less embarrassed about calling a doctor during the night or on weekends. Lastly, the physicians benefit from group practice by using the group conference technique. Frequent consultations on complicated cases redound to the advantage of both the patient and physicians. As one student put it, "Doctors sometimes do need, and usually respond well, to the realization that their work is observable and observed."[19]

Prepaid group insurance results in more preventive medicine being practiced. It is to the advantage of the physicians to keep their patients well in order to reduce the number of visits. Medical groups provide health information to subscribers, health lectures on pertinent topics, and may provide classes for expectant mothers and seminars on child psychology for parents. The fact that members do not have to pay for each call has encouraged more preventive medicine and has reduced the usage of hospitals. Data for 1970 show that hospitalization of people covered by the Federal Employees Health Benefits program, a type of group practice, was only 433 hospital days per 1,000 covered persons. This compares with 482 days for those covered by individual practice; 936 days for those covered by Blue Cross-Blue Shield; and 1,076 covered by those under the Aetna Life Insurance plan.[20]

DISADVANTAGES OF PREPAID GROUP MEDICINE

Comprehensive group practice has not been without its critics. The American Medical Association, although it has recently softened its opposition, has long been critical of prepaid group practice. It pointed out that the successful plans have generally had middle income subscribers, and that HMOs are not likely to work either in poor ghetto areas or in remote rural settings. The indigent and the medically indigent will continue to need help from the Medicaid program. The AMA also advances the argument that group practice creates an incentive to under-treat and under-hospitalize the patient.[21]

Proponents of fee-for-service medicine fear that the prepaid plan detracts from the personal physician-patient relationship, although those in favor of the prepaid plan contend that their own plan improves physician-patient relations. Patients no longer have to fear that the physician is suggesting an operation just to make money from the patient. Proponents of group practice also point out that the general practitioner may continue his private practice during office hours, along with seeing patients who are members of the group plan.

[19]Alan Gregg, *Challenges to Contemporary Medicine* (New York, Columbia, 1956), p. 61.

[20]Mueller, *op. cit.*, p. 13.

[21]John R. Kernodle, M.D., "HMOs: Can They Maintain Health?" *Wall Street Journal*, August 8, 1973, p. 14.

Those favoring prepaid group practice hail it as being the best solution to medical problems, superior to private insurance plans and to national health insurance. Proponents of national health insurance, on the other hand, contend that while prepaid group practice plans are an improvement over private insurance, they still do not give the coverage of compulsory plans. Group practice plans still cover only a minor fraction of the United States population, mostly people on the east and west coasts, and like private insurance, certain kinds of medical care expense are not covered.

NATIONAL HEALTH INSURANCE

A system of national health insurance generally requires that the government levy a tax on people in order to pay for medical services. Many countries use the payroll tax, although some countries simply finance the scheme from general revenues. The types of medical services provided, such as hospitalization, physicians' services, drugs and the like, must all be spelled out in the program.

In order to provide as much freedom as possible, physicians are usually given the opportunity either to enroll in the system or not as they wish. Patients, too, are given the freedom to select doctors of their choice. They may go to a doctor who is not registered in the program if they are willing to pay private fees. Since the medical costs of registered physicians are paid for by the program and charges from nonregistered physicians are not, most people go to a doctor who is registered. Consequently, most of the doctors have little choice but to join the system.

A maximum number of patients is set for each doctor. Under some national health insurance systems in the world, doctors are free to treat additional private patients, but other countries forbid this practice. Doctors are given the privilege of deciding whether they will accept patients who have requested their services. Payment to the doctor is generally based on a flat sum per person per year (capitation system). It would be possible to pay the doctor for each visit, such as is done for dentists' services under the British national health service. Usually, though, payment is made per person registered, rather than per doctor's visit. There are several reasons for using the flat sum per person. Obviously, there is less paper work involved. Furthermore, some contend that there would be a tendency under the fee-for-service system for doctors to suggest more frequent treatment than necessary since the government would be paying for it. Problems would arise from doctors who abuse the system, even though they would be in a small minority. For these and other reasons, most national health insurance systems have abolished the fee-for-service system.

The fact that payments are made by the government according to the number of patients registering with the doctor makes national health insurance somewhat different from a socialized medicine program. Under the latter, all doctors would be employees of the government. Under national health insurance, they are not employees of the government, but simply receive capitation fees.

The first public sickness insurance program was established in Germany in 1883. Several other countries enacted programs before 1900, others by 1911, and several more before 1950. In 1973, about 70 countries had some type of sickness and maternity benefit program. An additional 15 nations had maternity insurance only, and 9 others offer limited medical benefits. Virtually all countries in Europe have either a national health service or national health insurance. All but five of the nations in the western hemisphere have some sort of program. Several countries in the Middle East and in the Orient have programs, and some of the newly independent nations in Africa are establishing programs.[22]

ARGUMENTS FOR NATIONAL HEALTH INSURANCE

A number of weighty arguments can be made in favor of national health insurance. Proponents of this type of medicine contend that everyone should have access to medical care regardless of income. They point out that making medical care available should result in people having more periodic examinations, which should tend to reduce the amount of illness. The emphasis of the medical profession should be to keep people well (preventive medicine), rather than only attempting to cure people after they become ill. If people regularly avail themselves of periodic examinations under compulsory health insurance, or under any type of medical practice, there is little doubt that the incidence of disease would be reduced.

Proponents of national health insurance also point out that most of the modern countries of the world have such a system. Of all of the countries that have introduced a national health program, none has ever rescinded it. If the system were unworkable, it would be abolished. The fact that all the countries having it still keep it is cited as evidence of the success of national health insurance.

[22]*Social Security Programs Throughout the World*, 1973, U. S. Department of Health, Education and Welfare, Social Security Administration, Research Report No. 44, pp. xvi-xviii. A few representative dates of enactment are as follows: Germany, 1883; Austria, 1888; Hungary, 1891; Sweden, 1891; Denmark, 1892; Belgium, 1894; Norway, 1909; United Kingdom, 1911; Switzerland, 1911; Australia, 1912; Netherlands, 1913; Poland, 1920; Japan, 1922; Chile, 1924; Spain, 1929; Argentina, 1934; Brazil, 1936; New Zealand, 1938; Venezuela, 1940; Mexico, 1942; Columbia, 1946; India, 1948; Israel, 1953; Uruguay, 1958; Finland, 1963; and Canada, 1966.

Proponents of national health insurance are critical of private health insurance, although they would agree that it is superior to having no insurance at all. Their major objections revolve around lack of comprehensive coverage. Such groups as the poor, the aged, rural people, and others, are underrepresented. These are the very groups who need an insurance program more than those who have it. Then, too, the types of medical coverage are not broad enough to suit proponents of national health insurance. They would prefer that doctor's calls and services of physicians be covered for everyone in the country under a national system.

ARGUMENTS AGAINST NATIONAL HEALTH INSURANCE

In spite of the weighty arguments in favor of national health insurance, many people in the United States are strongly opposed to it. The American Medical Association and the medical profession in general are bitterly opposed to compulsory health insurance. These groups extoll the benefits of voluntary health insurance, and point out that with more and more people voluntarily buying health insurance there is no need for a compulsory program. Granted that the lower-income groups do not have sufficient health insurance, they argue that these groups could be provided medical care under an expanded public health program. Opponents of national health insurance fear that the personal relationships between doctor and patient might be severed, although there is little evidence of this happening in countries that have adopted such insurance. According to opponents, placing doctors on a fixed annual fee would destroy the incentive of doctors. However, there would be some incentive remaining in that a doctor would have to be competent enough to attract people to agree to have him serve them. Opponents, however, still feel that insufficient incentive is provided under this system.

The medical profession is particularly disturbed that the compulsory system would result in the government determining the income of doctors. If, for example, the government decided that each doctor could serve a maximum of 1,000 people for an annual fee of $20 per person, the maximum income that a general practitioner could receive from the government would be $20,000 annually. If the annual fee were raised to $30, then the annual government income of doctors would be $30,000. The annual income of doctors would depend mainly on what the government would decide to pay. Since the members of the medical profession already earn high income, they would prefer that the present system of medical care continue, and that the government have nothing to do with the amount that physicians earn.

Other arguments against national health insurance are that too many people would abuse the system since there would be no concurrent outlay. Under these circumstances, too many people might avail themselves of the services of physicians and hospital care. Unlimited demands would be made on a doctor's time with only limited payment in return. Britain and other countries having compulsory insurance, however, have been able to keep this problem under control. It is also alleged that too much red tape would be involved in such a system. Even under voluntary insurance, physicians must now fill in more forms than they had before the introduction of insurance. Still more would need filling out if everyone were under an insurance program. Offsetting the additional paper work would be the fact that doctors would no longer have to send bills to people.

NATIONAL HEALTH INSURANCE PROPOSALS

Proposals for a system of national health insurance in the United States were first made not long after Germany adopted its system in 1883. Further attention was paid to the issue after Great Britain set up such a program in 1911. In a sense a type of health insurance was adopted by many states in the form of workmen's compensation legislation. Many states enacted such laws during the period 1911-1915. Such legislation covered only job-connected accidents and diseases, and a strong movement got underway to adopt insurance for non-job-connected accidents and diseases. The American Medical Association and other groups actively opposed such legislation. When the United States went to war against Germany in 1917, health insurance was labeled "Made in Germany" and was defeated.

During the 1920's the issue languished, but with the coming of the Great Depression a renewed attempt was made to enact health insurance. In 1934 the Committee on Economic Security recommended that it be adopted along with other economic security programs. But in order to secure the passage of the Social Security Act in 1935, health insurance was dropped from the bill. After World War II, President Truman pressed for the passage of comprehensive health insurance as embodied in the Wagner-Murray-Dingell Bill, but the measure again fell short of enactment. President Eisenhower showed little interest in health insurance, but finally in 1965 President Johnson secured the passage of the Medicare and Medicaid bills.

CURRENT PROPOSALS

A large number of alternatives are currently under consideration; in 1974 at least sixteen bills were introduced in both houses of Congress. They ranged all the way from minor tax credit proposals to comprehensive federalized programs. Four major proposals may be taken as illustrative: (1) the Kennedy-Griffiths Health Security Bill; (2) the Nixon-Ford Administration's program, (3) the Long-Ribicoff proposal, and (4) the Kennedy-Mills proposals.

In 1971, Senator Kennedy and Rep. Griffiths proposed a Health Security Bill which never passed that would have covered virtually all medical costs including office visits, dental care for children, and a wide range of other health services. The system was to be financed by Social Security payroll taxes plus Federal subsidies out of the general revenues. The system would be administered by a federal agency and most private insurance would be displaced. The annual cost of this proposal has been variously estimated at from $35 to $60 billion per year.[23]

The proposals made by the Nixon and Ford Administrations differed from the Kennedy proposals, especially in the role played by private insurance. Under the Nixon-Ford proposals, all employers would be required to carry insurance generally with a private company or with Blue Cross and Blue Shield. The bill would specify a wide range of benefits including hospital and doctor bills, prescription drugs, certain preventive services, prenatal and maternity care, benefits for children, and nursing home and psychiatric care up to an annual limit. States would contract with private insurance companies to provide the same benefits for the unemployed and for low-income families. The elderly would continue to receive Medicare. The program would be financed by a payroll tax with the employer paying 75 percent of the total. The estimated annual cost was put at about $37 billion.

The proposal advanced by Senators Long and Ribicoff would offer only "catastrophic illness" insurance, plus improvements in the existing Medicare and Medicaid programs. Benefits would begin only when the patient had incurred $2,000 in expenses, or been hospitalized for 60 days. Thereafter, the patient would pay 20 percent of doctor bills and $21 per day for hospitalization up to $1,000. Thus the program would pay for all expenses above a total of $3,000. Joint employer-employee payroll taxes would finance the program. Estimated annual cost was put at $9 billion per year.

In April, 1974, Senator Kennedy joined with Congressman Wilbur Mills in a new proposal similar in many respects to the administration's bill. The scope of benefits would be very similar. The family deductible amount would be smaller and no family would pay more than $1,000 out-of-pocket per year. While the Nixon proposal would largely permit private insurance companies to manage and finance the program, under the Kennedy-Mills proposals private insurance would serve only as fiscal intermediaries as under the Medicare program. A payroll tax of 4 percent on earnings up to $20,000 with employers paying 3 percent, employees 1 percent, would finance the program. The administration and the Kennedy-Mills proposals are thus not far apart.

[23]"National Health Insurance is the Way," Business Week, No. 2315 (January 26, 1974), pp. 70-71, and "Insuring the National Health," Newsweek, Vol. 83 (June 3, 1974), pp. 73-74.

Summary

Large numbers of Americans now have some form of private health insurance either with private companies, Blue Cross and Blue Shield, or with various independent plans. About 182 million have hospital insurance, but only lesser numbers have other forms of health insurance. Many of the people who need protection the most have little or no insurance. In 1973 private insurance paid for only 25 percent of total national personal health care costs.

Group practice plans have often been urged as an alternative to solo practice. Many believe the group practice can provide high quality care at lower cost and can emphasize preventive medicine to a greater extent than is likely under solo practice. The Health Maintenance Organization Act of 1973 is likely to provide further stimulus to the growth of group plans.

All major industrial nations of the world except the United States have some form of national health insurance or socialized medicine. A wide variety of health insurance proposals are under active consideration in the United States. Most observers agree that some sort of national health insurance will be enacted in the near future.

Bibliography

Bowers, John Z., and Purcell, Elizabeth (eds.), *National Health Services* (New York, The Josiah Macy, Jr. Foundation, 1973).

Burns, Eveline M., *Health Services for Tomorrow* (New York, Dunellen, 1973).

Cater, Douglas, and Lee, Phillip R., *Politics of Health* (New York, Medcom, 1972).

Eckstein, Harry, *The English Health Service* (Cambridge, Harvard, 1958).

Faulkner, Edwin J., *Health Insurance* (New York, McGraw-Hill, 1960).

Forsyth, Gordon, *Doctors and State Medicine* (Philadelphia, Lippincott, 1966).

Gemmill, Paul F., *Britain's Search for Health* (Philadelphia, University of Pennsylvania, 1962).

Gerber, Alex, *The Gerber Report* (New York, David McKary, 1971).

Lindsey, Almont, *Socialized Medicine in England and Wales* (Chapel Hill, University of North Carolina, 1962).

McTaggart, Ambrey C., *The Health Care Dilemma* (Boston, Holbrook, 1971).

Owen, David, *A Unified Health Service* (London, Pergamon, 1968).

Somers, Anne R., *Health Care in Transition: Directions for the Future* (Chicago, Hospital Research and Educational Trust, 1971).

PART IV

THE PROBLEM OF UNEMPLOYMENT AND UNDEREMPLOYMENT

CHAPTER 15

UNEMPLOYMENT, UNDEREMPLOYMENT, AND MANPOWER PROGRAMS

Prior to the Industrial Revolution, unemployment presented few problems to mankind. In economies that were primarily agrarian, workers could remain on the land all year, and at least share in the food grown there. A basic threat to security came with famines and failure to grow the necessary crops, but at least people were employed in the attempt to produce goods. As more and more people moved into towns and cities, unemployment became one of the major problems faced by urban civilization. This was true because nations experienced periodic panics or reductions in business. During these periods goods could not be sold, and it became unprofitable to retain laborers. With layoffs came grave problems because workers no longer were living on farms and growing their own food. They were thrown on their own resources until rehired, but unfortunately many had meager resources.

THE MEASUREMENT OF UNEMPLOYMENT

One of the first steps necessary before the unemployment problem can be adequately attacked is to obtain statistics on the amount and duration of unemployment. In the United States several sets of statistics on unemployment are available, but the most frequently cited statistics are those of the Bureau of the Census, which publishes monthly estimates of unemployment. It compiles its figures of the total number of unemployed in the country each month from a sample of 50,000 addresses. In this probability sample, representative of the entire civilian noninstitutional population, the census divides the population into three groups: the employed, the unemployed, and those not in the work force. The census defines as employed those who are aged 16 years and over who during a specified week (1) work full or part time for pay or profit; (2) work without pay in a family enterprise (farm or business) at least 15 hours; or (3) have a job but do not work because of illness, vacation, labor-management dispute, or bad weather. The census considers a person unemployed if he or she is 16 years or over and is not working but is seeking a job during a specified week. Persons on layoff or waiting to begin a new job (within 30 days) need not meet these job-seeking requirements to be classified as unemployed. Table 15-1 shows the annual statistics compiled by the Bureau of Census from 1947 to 1973.

TABLE 15-1: Unemployed Persons 16 Years and Over and Unemployment Rates by Sex and Color, 1947-73

Year and month	Number unemployed (thousands)									Unemployment rate								
	Total			White			Negro and other races			Total			White			Negro and other races		
	Total	Males	Fe-males	Total	Males	Fe-males	Total	Males	Fe-males	Total	Males	Fe-males	Total	Males	Fe-males	Total	Males	Fe-males
1947	2,311	1,692	619							3.9	4.0	3.7						
1948	2,276	1,559	717							3.8	3.6	4.1	3.5	3.4	3.8	5.9	5.8	6.1
1949	3,637	2,572	1,065							5.9	5.9	6.0	5.6	5.6	5.7	8.9	9.6	7.9
1950	3,288	2,239	1,049							5.3	5.1	5.7	4.9	4.7	5.3	9.0	9.4	8.4
1951	2,055	1,221	834							3.3	2.8	4.4	3.1	2.6	4.2	5.3	4.9	6.1
1952	1,883	1,185	698							3.0	2.8	3.6	2.8	2.5	3.3	5.4	5.2	5.7
1953	1,834	1,202	632							2.9	2.8	3.3	2.7	2.5	3.1	4.5	4.8	4.1
1954	3,532	2,344	1,188	2,860	1,913	947	674	431	243	5.5	5.3	6.0	5.0	4.8	5.6	9.9	10.3	9.3
1955	2,852	1,854	998	2,248	1,475	773	601	376	225	4.4	4.2	4.9	3.9	3.7	4.3	8.7	8.8	8.4
1956	2,750	1,711	1,039	2,162	1,368	794	592	345	247	4.1	3.8	4.8	3.6	3.4	4.2	8.3	7.9	8.9
1957	2,859	1,841	1,018	2,289	1,478	811	569	363	206	4.3	4.1	4.7	3.8	3.6	4.3	7.9	8.3	7.3
1958	4,602	3,098	1,504	3,679	2,488	1,191	925	611	314	6.8	6.8	6.8	6.1	6.1	6.2	12.6	13.8	10.8
1959	3,740	2,420	1,320	2,947	1,904	1,044	794	518	276	5.5	5.3	5.9	4.8	4.6	5.3	10.7	11.5	9.4
1960	3,852	2,486	1,366	3,063	1,987	1,076	787	497	290	5.5	5.4	5.9	4.9	4.8	5.3	10.2	10.7	9.4
1961	4,714	2,997	1,717	3,742	2,398	1,344	970	599	371	6.7	6.4	7.2	6.0	5.7	6.5	12.4	12.8	11.8
1962	3,911	2,423	1,488	3,052	1,915	1,137	859	508	351	5.5	5.2	6.2	4.9	4.6	5.5	10.9	10.9	11.0
1963	4,070	2,472	1,598	3,208	1,976	1,232	864	496	368	5.7	5.2	6.5	5.0	4.7	5.8	10.8	10.5	11.2
1964	3,786	2,205	1,581	2,999	1,779	1,220	786	426	360	5.2	4.6	6.2	4.6	4.1	5.5	9.6	8.9	10.6
1965	3,366	1,914	1,452	2,691	1,556	1,135	676	359	317	4.5	4.0	5.5	4.1	3.6	5.0	8.1	7.4	9.2
1966	2,875	1,551	1,324	2,253	1,240	1,013	621	311	310	3.8	3.2	4.8	3.3	2.8	4.3	7.3	6.3	8.6
1967	2,975	1,508	1,468	2,338	1,208	1,130	638	299	338	3.8	3.1	5.2	3.4	2.7	4.6	7.4	6.0	9.1
1968	2,817	1,419	1,397	2,226	1,142	1,084	590	277	313	3.6	2.9	4.8	3.2	2.6	4.3	6.7	5.6	8.3
1969	2,831	1,403	1,428	2,261	1,137	1,124	570	266	304	3.5	2.8	4.7	3.1	2.5	4.2	6.4	5.3	7.8
1970	4,088	2,235	1,853	3,337	1,856	1,480	752	379	373	4.9	4.4	5.9	4.5	4.0	5.4	8.2	7.3	9.3
1971	4,993	2,776	2,217	4,074	2,302	1,772	919	474	445	5.9	5.3	6.9	5.4	4.9	6.3	9.9	9.1	10.8
1972	4,840	2,635	2,205	3,884	2,160	1,724	956	475	482	5.6	4.9	6.6	5.0	4.5	5.9	10.0	8.9	11.3
1973	4,304	2,240	2,064	3,411	1,818	1,593	894	423	471	4.9	4.1	6.0	4.3	3.7	5.3	8.9	7.6	10.5

Source: Handbook of Labor Statistics, 1974, Table 60, p. 144.

CRITICISM OF EMPLOYMENT STATISTICS

Criticisms have been made that the official census statistics tend to both overestimate and underestimate the number of unemployed. Those maintaining that the figures tend to exaggerate the problem point out that the major social problem arises only for the male unemployed group from ages 25-65. The problem of unemployment among women, it is alleged, can largely be forgotten, since most women are not heads of family nor primarily breadwinners in the family. Unemployment, to such women, supposedly is not a major problem for they can always fall back on the earnings of their husbands. Similarly, unemployment among youth does not present a serious problem, for youth can depend on their parents for support. Those 65 years of age or over can draw either their old-age pension or old-age assistance. If only the male unemployed aged 25-64 are counted, the unemployment statistics would be much lower. For example, in 1971 when unemployment was recorded at 4,993,000 only 1,379,000 (28 percent) were males aged 25 through 64.

On the other hand, it must be pointed out that many women are the heads of households and the only support for their families. Similarly, many males below the age of 25 have families to support. In many instances, the earnings of a second person in the family are essential to economic well-being. Moreover, many married women who are unemployed also have unemployed husbands. Of 929,000 married women unemployed in 1961, 171,000, or 18 percent, had husbands who were also unemployed.[1] Unemployment among secondary workers (not the primary breadwinners) may therefore result in a serious exhaustion of family economic resources.[2]

Those who criticize the official unemployment statistics as being too small suggest that a number of changes be made to count the number of unemployed more accurately.[3] The census classifies people as employed even though they work as little as one hour during the survey week. In 1971, there were 2,440,000 nonagricultural workers who worked 35 hours or less even though they wanted full-time work.

Some people drop out of the work force entirely after a futile search for a job. If jobs were available, this group would accept them. These people are not counted as unemployed; if they were, the unemployment figures would be higher. Unemployment of this type is frequently referred to as hidden unemployment. Data has been gathered on the amount of hidden unemployment since 1967 on a regular basis through the Current Population Survey. From 1967 through 1972, the amount of hidden

[1]Ewan Clague, "Adequacy of Unemployment Data for Government Uses," *Monthly Labor Review*, Vol. 55 (1962), pp. 128-129.

[2]Robert L. Stein, "Married Women and the Level of Unemployment," *Monthly Labor Review*, Vol. 84 (1961), p. 870.

[3]Stanley Lebergott, "Measuring Unemployment," *Review of Economics and Statistics*, Vol. 36 (1954), pp. 397-398.

unemployment varied from a low of 574,000 in 1969 to a high of 765,000 in 1972.[4] The discouraged workers experiencing hidden unemployment were divided into two groups, those who were discouraged because of job-market factors as contrasted to personal factors. Included in job-market factors were persons who had looked for a job but could not find it, or thought that no jobs were available. Personal factors were that employers thought the worker too young or too old, that they lacked education, skills, or training, or had other personal handicaps. The job-market factors accounted for 54.2 percent of all hidden unemployment in 1969 before the 1969-1970 recession, but for 70.6 percent of the hidden unemployment in 1972, when the effects of the recession were still being felt in the labor market.

Of the 765,000 persons classified in 1972 as discouraged workers, only about 70,000, or less than one-tenth, were men aged 25 to 59. Blacks have a heavy representation of discouraged workers. Most of the discouraged workers say they plan to actively seek work within the next 12 months so that they have not permanently given up on the job market. In short, hidden unemployment is a relatively small percentage of total unemployment and is concentrated mainly among those in the secondary labor force.

In measuring unemployment, the Manpower Administration of the United States Department of Labor breaks down the statistics into 150 major employment centers according to the adequacy of their labor supply. The following table shows the classifications used.

With the recession in 1974, statistics showed that the number of areas in group F increased from 1 to 2 from June, 1973 to June, 1974. On the latter date, both Ponce in Puerto Rico and Flint, Michigan, had an F rating, whereas on the earlier date, only Ponce had this rating. During the same period the E ratings rose from two to three. In the latter period, Atlantic City, Tacoma, Wash., and Mayaguez, Puerto Rico, had an E rating, whereas a year before only Mayaguez and Lowell, Mass., had such a rating.

These data do not measure poverty in the slums. For such a measurement, the Department of Labor in 1966 devised a new index called the

[4]Paul O. Flaim, "Discouraged Workers and Changes in Unemployment," *Monthly Labor Review*, Vol. 96. No. 3 (March 1973), pp. 8-16. For studies showing econometric measurements of hidden unemployment and the problems with them, see N. J. Simler and Alfred Tella, "Labor Reserve and the Phillips Curve," *Review of Economics and Statistics*, Vol. 50. No. 1 (February 1968), pp. 32-49; Wayne Vroman, "The Labor Force Reserve: A Re-Estimate;" *Review of Economics and Statistics*, Vol. 52. No. 2 (October 1970); A. D. Butler and G. O. Demopoulos, "Labor Force Behavior in the Full Employment Economy," *Industrial and Labor Relations Review*, Vol. 25, No. 3 (April 1970), pp. 379-393; Larry Sawers, "Urban Poverty and Labor Force Participation: Note," *American Economic Review*, Vol. 62. No. 3 (May 1972), pp. 414-421; Joseph L. Gastwirth, "Estimating the Number of 'Hidden Unemployed,'" *Monthly Labor Review*, Vol. 96. No. 3 (March 1973), pp. 17-26; and Jacob Mincer, "Determining Who Are the 'Hidden Unemployed,'" *Monthly Labor Review*, Vol. 96, No. 3 (March 1973), pp. 27-30.

TABLE 15-2

CLASSIFICATION OF THE 150 LABOR MARKET AREAS

Labor Supply Category	Percentage of Unemployment[a]	Description
Group A	Less than 1.5	Overall labor shortage
Group B	1.5 to 2.9	Low Unemployment
Group C	3.0 to 5.9	Moderate Unemployment
Group B	6.0 to 8.9	Substantial Unemployment
Group E	9.0 to 11.9	Substantial Unemployment
Group F	12.0 or more	Substantial Unemployment

[a]Based on area's total work force

Source: *Area Trends in Employment and Unemployment*, Washington, U. S. Department of Labor, Manpower Administration, May 1973, p. 5.

subemployment index. In order to meet this definition one of the following criteria had to be met:[5]

1. Persons unemployed according to the conventional definition of unemployment.
2. Those working part time but wanting full time work.
3. Heads of households and other members under 65 working full time but earning poverty wages.
4. Half the men 20 to 64 who are not in the work-force.
5. An estimate of the men presumed living in an area and belonging to one of the four other groups, but who are not to be found.

The data for the sub-employed compared with the unemployment in the slum areas is shown in Figure 15-1. Quite obviously all of these areas showed high rates of subemployment. The ten areas had a subemployment rate of 34 percent. Unfortunately, data for subemployment is not gathered on a regular basis, so that it is not possible to determine whether conditions in these areas are improving or not. Releasing subemployment figures regularly might be embarassing to the political groups in power, and to local Chambers of Commerce.

[5]Barbara Field, "The Subemployment Index-A New Measure," *Conference Board Record*, Vol. 5, No. 7 (July 1968), pp. 26-29.

Figure 15-1

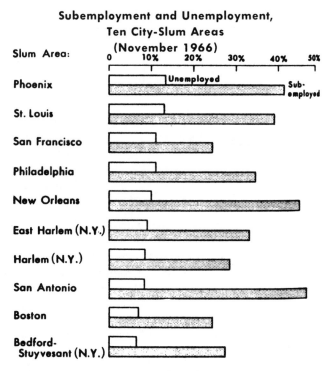

Subemployment and Unemployment,
Ten City-Slum Areas
(November 1966)

Sources: A series of pamphlets entitled *Subemployment in the Slums of*
(Boston, New Orleans, New York, Philadelphia, Phoenix, St. Louis, San
Antonio, San Francisco), U.S. Department of Labor, March 1967.

DURATION OF UNEMPLOYMENT

The main casualties of unemployment are those who are unable to find
jobs for a number of months or even years. The Great Depression of the
1930's caused much more long-term unemployment than the less severe
postwar recessions. As late as April, 1940, two-thirds of the unemployed
had been without jobs for more than three months. In the post World War
II period, the long-term unemployed, defined as being unemployed 15
weeks and over, have been a relatively small percentage of those
employed. In 1969, for example, while there was an unemployment rate
of 3.5 percent, only 0.5 percent were long-term unemployed. Yet when
recessions occur the percentage of those unemployed for a longer period
of time increases. When the rate of unemployment reached 5.9 percent in
1971, those unemployed for 15 weeks or more rose to 1.4 percent of the
civilian labor force. Persons under 24 have longer spells of unemployment
than those 25 to 44. From age 45 on, the unemployed have a more difficult
time finding jobs. Minority groups also experience longer unemployment
than whites.

TABLE 15-3

Major Unemployment Indicators, 1948-73

Year and month	All civilian workers	Men, 20 years and over	Women, 20 years and over	Both sexes, 16 to 19 years	White	Negro and other races	House-hold heads	Married men	Full-time workers	Part-time workers	Un-employed 15 weeks and over[1]	State insured[2]	Labor force time lost[3]
1948	3.8	3.2	3.6	9.2	3.5	5.9	.....	.....	.....	.....	0.5	3.1	.....
1949	5.9	5.4	5.3	13.4	5.6	8.9	.....	.....	.....	.....	1.1	6.0	.....
1950	5.3	4.7	5.1	12.2	4.9	9.0	.....	.....	.....	.....	1.3	4.8	.....
1951	3.3	2.5	4.0	8.2	3.1	5.3	.....	.....	.....	.....	.5	3.0	.....
1952	3.0	2.4	3.2	8.5	2.8	5.4	.....	.....	.....	.....	.4	3.0	.....
1953	2.9	2.5	2.9	7.6	2.7	4.5	.....	.....	.....	.....	.3	2.8	.....
1954	5.5	4.9	5.5	12.6	5.0	9.9	.....	.....	.....	.....	1.3	5.1	.....
1955	4.4	3.8	4.4	11.0	3.9	8.7	.....	2.8	.....	.....	1.1	3.5	4.8
1956	4.1	3.4	4.2	11.1	3.6	8.3	.....	2.6	.....	.....	.8	3.4	5.1
1957	4.3	3.6	4.1	11.6	3.8	7.9	.....	2.8	.....	.....	.8	3.7	5.3
1958	6.8	6.2	6.1	15.9	6.1	12.6	.....	5.1	.....	.....	2.1	6.3	8.1
1959	5.5	4.7	5.2	14.6	4.8	10.7	.....	3.6	.....	.....	1.5	4.4	6.6
1960	5.5	4.7	5.1	14.7	4.9	10.2	.....	3.7	.....	.....	1.4	4.8	6.7
1961	6.7	5.7	6.3	16.8	6.0	12.4	.....	4.6	.....	.....	2.2	5.7	8.0
1962	5.5	4.6	5.4	14.7	4.9	10.9	.....	3.6	.....	.....	1.6	4.4	6.7
1963	5.7	4.5	5.4	17.2	5.0	10.8	3.7	3.4	5.5	7.3	1.5	4.3	6.4
1964	5.2	3.9	5.2	16.2	4.6	9.6	3.3	2.8	4.9	7.2	1.3	3.7	5.8
1965	4.5	3.2	4.5	14.8	4.1	8.1	2.8	2.4	4.2	6.7	1.0	3.0	5.0
1966	3.8	2.5	3.8	12.8	3.3	7.3	2.2	1.9	3.5	6.2	.7	2.4	4.2
1967	3.8	2.3	4.2	12.9	3.4	7.4	2.1	1.8	3.4	6.9	.6	2.5	4.2
1968	3.6	2.2	3.8	12.7	3.2	6.7	1.9	1.6	3.1	6.5	.5	2.2	4.0
1969	3.5	2.1	3.7	12.2	3.1	6.4	1.8	1.5	3.1	6.2	.5	2.2	3.9
1970	4.9	3.5	4.8	15.2	4.5	8.2	2.9	2.6	4.5	7.6	.8	3.4	5.3
1971	5.9	4.4	5.7	16.9	5.4	9.9	3.7	3.2	5.5	8.7	1.4	4.0	6.4
1972	5.6	4.0	5.4	16.2	5.0	10.0	3.3	2.8	5.1	8.6	1.3	3.5	6.0
1973	4.9	3.2	4.8	14.5	4.3	8.9	2.9	2.3	4.3	7.9	.9	2.8	5.2

[1] Unemployment rate calculated as a percent of civilian labor force.

[2] Insured unemployment under state programs—unemployment rate calculated as a percent of average covered employment. As is the case with other data presented in this table, data relate to the week containing the 12th of the month.

[3] Man-hours lost by the unemployed and persons on part-time for economic reasons as a percent of potentially available labor force man-hours.

Source: *Handbook of Labor Statistics, 1974,* Table 59, p. 143.

MAJOR UNEMPLOYMENT INDICATORS

Statistics that break down employment according to sex, age, color, marital status, industry and occupation are published regularly. Some of the aspects of unemployment are shown in Table 15-3. The data from this table show that younger women tend to experience a higher rate of unemployment than those who are older. Minority groups have a rate of unemployment that is almost twice as high as that for whites. Part-time workers also have higher rate of unemployment than full-time workers. Those aged 16 to 19 have a much higher rate of unemployment than those who are older. With unemployment concentrated in the above groups, Martin Feldstein found that even during 1971, a year of relatively large unemployment, only 46 percent of the unemployed had involuntarily lost their previous jobs.[6] The remainder were those who voluntarily left their jobs, were reentering the labor force, or had never worked before. In the more favorable employment market year of 1969 only 36 percent of the unemployed had involuntarily lost their jobs.

Certain industries also experience more unemployment than others. By major industry groups, the following have unemployment rates above average: agriculture, manufacturing, wholesale and retail trade. Those having a smaller percentage of unemployment are mining (since 1966); transportation; finance, insurance, and real estate; service industries; and government. In January, 1975, the construction industry had the highest rate of unemployment, 15.0 percent, compared with 8.2 for the national average and 3.4 percent for government, the lowest of all groups. Broken down by occupations, those having a rate of unemployment above average are laborers, service workers, and operatives. Those below average are professional workers, managers, clerical workers, salesworkers, craftsmen and private household workers.

COMPARATIVE RATES OF UNEMPLOYMENT IN VARIOUS COUNTRIES

In the Great Depression, practically all countries experienced large amounts of unemployment. Today the rate of unemployment is lower, but varies among countries. The rates for the United States are higher than for most western European countries. Several explanations have been given for the differential rates.[7] Demographic factors were disregarded as a cause of the differential rate of unemployment, because the

[6]Martin Feldstein, Lowering the Permanent Rate of Unemployment (Washington, Joint Economic Committee, 1973), pp. 11-12.

[7]Robert J. Myers and John H. Chandler, "Toward Explaining International Unemployment Rates," Monthly Labor Review, Vol. 85 (1962), pp. 969-974.

labor force grew in some of the other countries faster than in the United States. A more rapid rate of industrial expansion was an important reason for the smaller amount of unemployment elsewhere. Another factor is that some countries with low unemployment provide more legal protection for workers. In Italy, the worker's right to his job is safeguarded both by law and by union contracts. In Germany, France, and Great Britain, both private employers and the state, itself a large employer, feel a high degree of responsibility for employment, and continue to provide employment even when sales decline. In Japan, appointment to a regular job assumes employment until retirement. Monthly salaries replace hourly wages.

THE DISADVANTAGED

Several theories have been advanced to explain the high unemployment and underemployment of disadvantaged people. Three such theories are discussed below: (1) the culture of poverty, (2) a psychological theory, and (3) a dual labor market theory.

THE CULTURE OF POVERTY

Oscar Lewis has developed the theory that many of the poor are disadvantaged because they have fallen into a "culture of poverty."[8] This culture might best be described as one of alienation or hopelessness that conditions will ever improve. Lewis described the culture of poverty in terms of some seventy traits. On the level of the individual, the major characteristics of the culture are strong feelings of marginality, of hopelessness or dependence, and of inferiority. On the family level the major traits are an absence of childhood, early initiation into sex, free unions or consensual marriages, a relatively high incidence of abandonment of wives and children, a trend toward female or mother-centered families, strong predisposition to authoritarianism, and a verbal emphasis upon family solidarity that is only rarely achieved because of sibling rivalry, and competition for limited goods and maternal affection. At the local community level, those living in a culture of poverty have poor housing, overcrowdedness, and gregariousness, but little organization beyond the level of the nuclear and extended family. Lewis pointed out that his concept dealt with class rather than race since many of the slum dwellers in Mex-

[8]Oscar Lewis, *Five Families*, (New York, Basic Books, 1959; The Children of Sanchez (New York, Random House, 1961; *Pedro Martinez; A Mexican Peasant and His Family, 1964)*; "The Culture of Poverty," *Scientific American*, Vol. 215, No. 4, (1966), pp. 19-25; *La Vida* (New York, Random House, 1966); and *A Study of Slum Culture; Backgrounds for La Vida* (New York, Random House, 1968).

ico City and San Juan do not constitute a distinct ethnic or racial group and thus do not suffer from racial discrimination.

Lewis claimed that the culture of poverty was passed on from generation to generation and so perpetuated itself. Slum children learn the basic values and attitudes of the culture of poverty by the time they are six or seven and are not psychologically geared to take advantage of rising income.

In looking at poverty in the United States, Lewis estimated that only about 20 percent of the poor were living in the culture of poverty. The groups in the United States falling into the culture of poverty were some very low income Negroes, Mexicans, Puerto Ricans, American Indians and Southern poor whites.

As to solutions to the problem, Lewis claimed that curing the culture of poverty may be more difficult than curing poverty itself, because the culture of poverty constituted a whole way of life for many of the poor. In the United States, he held, an improved standard of living along with aiding the poor climb into the middle class, possibly by psychiatric treatment and social work, would be helpful. In underdeveloped countries, there are so many more poor that psychiatrists could hardly begin to cope with the problem. Here, creating basic structural changes in society, by redistributing wealth and organizing the poor, might be helpful in abolishing some of the basic characteristics of the culture of poverty, even though poverty itself might not be banished.

CRITICISMS OF THE CULTURE OF POVERTY

Lewis' concept of the culture of poverty aroused considerable discussion and criticism in professional circles.[9] Anthony Leeds pointed out that Lewis held two inconsistent positions at the same time. Lewis claimed that the culture of poverty was transmitted through a social system passed down by the family although at the same time his description of the culture of poverty was in terms of traits, which are independent elements that should be transmissable to anyone, regardless of culture.[10] Leeds conceded that isolated families do pass down along family lines their particular form of adaptation to their environment, but he claimed that it is not necessary to postulate a culture to account for such behavior. Instead, the continuity of behavior can be explained in psychosocial states of the

[9]Charles Valentine, *Culture and Poverty* (Chicago, University of Chicago Press, 1968); see also a series of reviews on this book in *Current Anthropology*, Vol. 10 No.'s 2 & 3, (April-June, 1969), pp. 181-200; and Eleanor Burke Leacock, ed., *The Culture of Poverty* (New York, Simon and Schuster, 1971).

[10]Anthony Leeds, "The Concept of the 'Culture of Poverty:' Conceptual, Logical, and Empirical Problems, with Perspectives from Brazil and Peru," in Eleanor Burke Leacock, ed., *op. cit.*, pp. 226-284.

family, external barriers imposed on the families, and structural isolation from learning situations. Here, Herbert Gans makes a contribution by asserting that empirically it is difficult to say whether the culture of poverty is a direct or indirect cause of continuing poverty, for it would be necessary to know how people would react to better economic conditions.[11] According to Gans, those who use the culture concept tend to see behavioral patterns and their supporting norms as resistant to change simply because they are culture. This concept of culture really is ahistorical, since it is obvious that cultures do change.

Among other criticism, Eleanor Leacock pointed out that many psychologists do not hold to the view that the "value-attitude system" is set by the age of six or seven.[12] Although conceding that some of the individual's personality takes shape in the early years, she cited Jerome Kagan to the effect that profound developments take place in personality between the ages of six and ten.[13]

A number of Lewis' critics were quite hostile to the public policy implications of the culture of poverty theory. In holding that behavior of the poor was dysfunctional, the policy proposals for eradicating poverty tend to concentrate on the behavior of the poor. The critics maintained that behavior of the middle and upper classes may be more crucial in explaining poverty than adaptations of the poor. On this point, Lewis conceded that "in the long run the self-perpetuating facets are relatively minor and unimportant as compared to the basic structure of the larger society."[14] At the same time, he still held that if basic improvements were made in society, a large number of families would have many social and psychological problems for which special services would be necessary.

Leonard Goodwin found that commitment to the work ethic was high in all groups, both black and white, even among long-term welfare recipients.[15] Black men, however, whether on or off welfare were much less confident of their ability to succeed even compared with white males on welfare. From this and other studies, Goodwin concluded that the plight of the poor cannot be blamed on deviant goals or a deviant psychology, as Lewis has contended. Instead the poor differ from the affluent because of their different experiences of success and failure in the world. He cited a number of studies to the effect that the poor face discriminatory barriers to advancement in education and in occupation. He suggested that the

[11]Herbert Gans, "Culture and Class in the Study of Poverty," in Daniel P. Moynihan, On Understanding Poverty (New York, Basic Books, 1969).

[12]Eleanor Leacock, ed., op. cit., p. 13.

[13]Jerome Kagan and Howard Moss, Birth to Maturity (New York, Wiley and Sons), 1962.

[14]"Culture and Poverty: Critique and Counter-Proposals," Current Anthropology, Vol. 10, No's 2 & 3, 1969, p. 192.

[15]Leonard Goodwin, Do the Poor Want to Work (Washington, Brookings Institute, 1972).

discriminatory barriers be removed, and that a guaranteed income be provided. to reduce the cost of failure.

In conclusion, there is no question that some of the poor have difficulty holding better jobs when offered them. Some personal rehabilitation may be necessary for this group. On the other hand, a greater effort upon the part of the middle and upper classes to provide a better institutional framework holds the most potential for improving the lot of the poor.

PSYCHOLOGICAL THEORY OF UNEMPLOYMENT

Some psychologists, like the Tiffanys and others, have pointed to a lack of positive self-esteem and problems of interpersonal incompetence as a cause of unemployment and underemployment.[16] Some disadvantaged persons are "work inhibited" because of psychological disabilities. Many people lose jobs because of interpersonal problems. Some of these people do not have manifest psychiatric disorders but are occupationally maladjusted. They fail in an interaction situation. To avoid further unpleasantness at the work place, they may exhibit too much aggressiveness, or they may simply solve their problem by running away from the workplace and quit. After quitting, they become further isolated socially and may become inept in job-seeking.

In the area of training, Tiffany and others have suggested a shift in the focus from skill training to personal and interpersonal training. Counselors may build self-esteem by giving social recognition and objective rewards to the disadvantaged. Counselors must make every effort to reinforce their clients' behavior when the latter make honest attempts to resolve interpersonal difficulties without running away from the situation. Role-playing may also help. Here the job-hopper could play the role of a steady worker. Sensitivity training may aid also in improving interpersonal relationships.

THE DUAL LABOR MARKET THEORY

Attitudes toward work must be analyzed within the framework of the types of labor markets that exist. Michael J. Piore has argued that the labor market is divided into a primary and secondary market.[17] The primary market is characterized by high wages, good working conditions,

---

[16]Donald W. Tiffany, James R. Cowan, and Phyllis M. Tiffany, *The Unemployed: A Social-Psychological Portrait (Englewood Cliffs, N.J., Prentice-Hall Co., 1970)*.

[17]Michael J. Piore, "On-the-Job Training in a Dual Labor Market" in Arnold R. Weber, et. al. (ed's.), *Public-Private Manpower Policies*, Madison, Wisconsin; Industrial Relations Research Association, 1969 and "Manpower Policy" in Samuel Beer, et. al., The State and the Poor (Boston: Winthrop Public Co., 1970), pp. 53-83.

stability of employment, chance of advancement, equity, and due process in the administration of work rules. In contrast to these favorable characteristics, the secondary labor market has low wages and few fringe benefits, poor working conditions, high labor turnover, little chance of advancement, and often arbitrary and capricious supervision. Piore claims that the distinctions between workers in the two sectors parallel those between jobs. That is, workers in the secondary sector, relative to those in the primary sector, exhibit greater turnover, higher rates of lateness and absenteeism, more insubordination, and engage more freely in petty theft and pilferage. Secondary employment lacks the organized social life found in many primary establishments which foster such activities as athletic teams, dances, picnics and cafeterias. On the contrary, workers in the secondary market rely upon the street rather than the workplace for social satisfaction.

Dual labor market theory obviously has different public policy implications than Lewis's culture of poverty theory. Doeringer and Piore contend that the central goal of public policy should be to overcome the barriers which confine the disadvantaged to the secondary labor market.[18] Expanding aggregate demand will help to place some of the disadvantaged in the primary labor market, but more disadvantaged workers may be helped at a lower real cost if direct efforts are made to facilitate the movement of workers out of the secondary sector. Secondary jobs should be converted into primary jobs. Various types of public policies may be needed, depending on the various types of workers in the secondary market. English language instruction and literacy training may help some, as will special health and child-care services. Penalties for earning money should be lessened in the welfare program. Discrimination should be lessened for blacks in schools, housing, and employment. Longshoring and unskilled construction work have already moved a considerable way toward decasualization, and in some cities, household and office cleaning firms have emerged which use sophisticated equipment and a regular work force. Minimum wages could be raised to make the labor market more satisfactory to the workers. Also, social legislation could be amended to cover more disadvantaged workers.

David M. Gordon comprehensively analyzed the secondary labor market theory and contrasted it with more orthodox theory.[19] He concluded that the secondary labor market theory was more valid than more orthodox theory. However, he was critical of secondary labor market theory for not taking class concepts more into consideration. Writing from a radical perspective, Gordon criticized Bennett Harrison's suggestion that the public employment service could aid secondary workers on the

[18]Peter B. Doeringer and Michael J. Piore, *Internal Labor Markets and Manpower Analysis*, (Lexington, D.C. Heath, 1971).

[19]David M. Gordon, *Theories of Poverty and Underemployment* (Lexington Mass., D.C. Heath, 1972). He cites a list of secondary labor market studies on p. 44.

ground that it is not in the interests of the capitalist class to ameliorate the conditions of the poor.

MANPOWER PROGRAMS

EUROPEAN PROGRAMS

In devising remedies, Great Britain and West Germany place much emphasis on a quota system for employment of the hard-to-employ. Germany has a better record than Great Britain in employing the hard-to-employ even though its law covers a more severely disabled group. Reubens attributes the better German record to a tighter labor market and greater government pressure on employers to hire these people. The quota system has the disadvantage of placing less emphasis on training, but it does provide employment.

Other countries having quotas were France and Italy. As contrasted to the above countries, neither the Netherlands nor Sweden have quotas. Instead, these two countries put more emphasis on sheltered workshops and public work programs. In these countries public works have not been considered personally degrading. Also, their public works have not been troubled with high costs due to inefficiency, corruption, leakage of funds, competitive and overlapping of agencies, and the choice of inappropriate or private benefit projects. Sweden also has been active in providing training programs for its unemployed. Sweden has trained much larger percentages of the unemployed than has the United States.[20]

U. S. PROGRAMS — MANPOWER DEVELOPMENT AND TRAINING ACT — INSTITUTIONAL TRAINING

A number of states inaugurated training programs for the unemployed beginning in 1957. The federal government sponsored a small program under the Area Redevelopment Act of 1961. The program was expanded under the Manpower Development and Training Act (MDTA) in 1962. The original thrust of the program was to train those already technologically unemployed, for example, coal miners in Appalachia and textile workers in New England. When the threat of widespread technological unemployment did not materialize in the 1960's, the MDTA program began concentrating on groups discriminated against and persons who were poorly equipped to function successfully in the free labor market.

[20]Beatrice Reubens, *The Hard to Employ, European Programs*, (New York, Columbia University Press, 1970).

Originally, the act called for 52 weeks of training to be financed by the federal government but administered by the states. The equivalent of average unemployment insurance benefits was paid to trainees to provide support for them while in training.

Experience gained under the act resulted in amendments to it. To aid those unable to read and write, a 20-week basic education period was added to the 52-week training period in 1963. Due to the inadequacy of payments to trainees of the average state unemployment benefit, the states were permitted in 1963 to raise benefits on an individual basis, depending on need, to as much as $10 weekly over the unemployment benefit. In 1965, the permissable training period was raised from 52 to 104 weeks, and a 10 percent matching fund was required from the states. Lack of adequate medical care resulted in amendments in 1966 which provided for physical examinations and minor medical care. Older worker programs were instituted, as was an experimental program for inmates of correctional institutions. The eligibility requirement for participation was reduced from two years attachment to the labor force to one. Also, in that year, 20 percent of the federal funds were reserved for administrative discretion and thus provided more flexibility in the program. The 1968 amendments gave states more control over the use of funds.

A peak in enrollment was reached in 1966 (177,500), and since then has fluctuated from between 130,000 and 155,600. Data on race shows a relatively high percentage of Negroes and Spanish speaking persons in the program.

When the MDTA program first started, enrollees were channeled into single occupation classes. Later, multi-occupational experiments were conducted which eventually developed into both multi-occupational classes and skill centers. The skills centers have the advantage of permitting enrollees to enter training at any time during the year, receive training in several related occupations, train at their own pace, and complete training at various skill levels of an occupation.[21] Skill centers must provide a large number of services to be certified. In addition to training, the skills centers must provide basic and remedial education, employment and personal counseling, placement of trainees and follow-up of center graduates. In addition, other supportive services, such as prevocational orientation, access to child care, and assistance with housing and transportation are provided. In 1973 there were 70 skills centers operating throughtout the country.

In spite of the obvious advantages of skills center training, several weaknesses may be noted.[22] The skills centers have been handicapped by erratic financing and budgeting procedures. Also, too frequent use of low level courses such as food service, building maintenance, and sewing

[21]Garth Mangum and John Walsh, *A Decade of Manpower Development and Training* (Salt Lake City. Olympus Publishing Company. 1973). p. 53.
[22]*Ibid.*, pp. 62-81.

courses have been provided the most disadvantaged, some of whom have found themselves in jobs that they could have obtained without entering training. Another weakness has been that some of the housing for the skills centers has been substandard, and much of the equipment is obsolete or worn-out. Also, the supportive services lack sufficient funding. Results are that illness is a major cause of dropouts. Also, only about 30 percent of the child care needs of recipients is being met. Separate skills centers have the additional disadvantage of fostering segregated education. To eliminate this weakness, several areas have begun to integrate skills centers with nonsegregated community colleges. Administratively, the skills centers and the community colleges are separate, but having a center at the college enables more of the disadvantaged to be served on an integrated basis.

Single operating classes enroll about 50 percent of MDTA trainees compared with 23 percent for multi-occupational centers, 17 percent for skills centers, and 10 percent by individual referrals to existing schools. In individual referrals most of the existing schools require a high school diploma and the same requirement as other students for admittance. Existing schools are used to place the less disadvantaged MDTA enrollees.[23]

In a study of MDTA institutional training in 14 areas from 1969 to 1971, it was found that 72 percent of the slots were in the following occupations: clerical, welding, automotive, health occupations, and the metal machine trades. These were the areas, according to Mangum and Walsh, where MDTA training was most successful. On the other hand, they were critical that four groups of occupations with substantial skill content were not covered by MDTA training: electricity and electronics occupations, bookkeeping and accounting occupations, keypunch operators, and wholesale sales occupations.

ON THE JOB TRAINING

An alternative to institutional MDTA training has been MDTA on-the-job training (OJT), now called the JOP (Jobs-Optional) program. A major advantage of on-the-job training is that jobs are available to the workers after they have successfully completed training. An added advantage of the JOP program is that it is less costly to the government, since the employers pay part of the costs of training. One study of MDTA-OJT training from 1964 to 1966 in 24 SMSA's found relatively high benefit-cost ratios for most areas.[24] The largest benefit-cost ratios were found in areas that had larger percentages of nonwhites as trainees. Expanding areas were found to have higher ratios than places experiencing less growth. By

[23]*Evaluation of the MDTA Institutional Individual Referral Program, Final Report* (Salt Lake City: Olympus Research Corporation, June, 1972.

[24]Dale B. Rasmussen, *Determinants of Rates of Return to Investment in On-the-Job Training*, Ph.D. dissertation Southern Methodist University, 1969.

1969 the enrollment under OJT and the Jobs program (to be discussed below) exceeded that of the institutional MDTA program.

EVALUATION OF MDTA AND OJT

Corri Azzi has been critical of the OJT program.[25] In a study of two manufacturers, he found that they were receiving training subsidies even though there was a tight labor market and they would have hired employees anyway.

A recent Social Security analysis showed that MDTA enrollees experienced earning gains which were less than a control group who had not undertaken training. Mangum and Walsh, though, point out that since the enrollees were better off than those who started but failed to finish training, it was difficult to explain why the completers fell behind those taking no training. They contend that the six factors used for comparison with the control group may have been too few to adequately compare the groups. Factors such as education, family background, and residence were not used as controls.

Due to the relatively poor showing of MDTA training it has been suggested that the program be discontinued. On the other hand, others recommend that it could be improved by providing better equipment and services. An improved manpower analysis could aid in providing training for occupations where there is more need and the pay is good.

JOBS PROGRAM

In order to reach the more disadvantaged for on-the-job training, the National Alliance of Businessmen (NAB) set up 50 local offices throughout the country. All additional training costs above normal were to be financed by the federal government. These costs have been running about $3,000 per trainee. Less than 100,000 persons annually have been initially enrolled with federal financing since the beginning of the program. However, NAB reports that many firms have begun hiring the disadvantaged without applying for the federal subsidy. If nonsubsidized trainees are included, the figure cited above would more than double. Most of the workers hired under this program have been Negroes. There have only been a few jobs openings in the clerical and sales areas. High participation industries include communications; electric, gas, and sanitary services; electrical equipment and supplies; retail food stores; aerospace com-

[25]Corry F. Azzi, *Equity and Efficiency Effects from Manpower Programs* (Lexington, D.C. Heath and Co., 1973). For other similar criticisms see the testimony of Greenberg and Bechel in U. S. Senate, Committee on Labor and Public Welfare, *Manpower Development and Training Legislation*, 1970, hearings before the Subcommittee on Employment, Manpower and Poverty, Senate on S 3867, S 2838, 91st Congress, 1st and 2nd Session, 1970.

panies; primary metals; fabricated metal products, and automobile manufacturers.[26]

In recruiting workers, a number of different routes were taken. Ford Motor Co. took its employment office to the ghetto, General Electric used a recruiting trailer, and Pacific Telephone used its present work force to recruit.[27] Television and radio also were used. On selection, an attempt had to be made to screen people in rather than to use the normal technique of screening people out. Some firms, such as General Motors, Ford and Chrysler, had eliminated tests entirely from their selection procedures for unskilled workers. A number of companies have provided counseling services to aid in assimilation into the work force. Remedial education may be provided where necessary. Some companies also provided for special training for their foremen. At General Motors, for example, it was explained to foremen that the new work force had been left out of society and that the company expected foremen to make every effort to bring them into society. Absenteeism and tardiness were common problems in most of the firms hiring the disadvantaged. Various policies were attempted to keep these to a minimum.[28] Some use the "buddy" system whereby regular workers attempt to help the JOBS trainee to better assimilate into the work force.

The JOBS program has been successful in placing people into jobs that formerly were not open for them, but a number of criticisms of the program have been made. In evaluating the JOBS program, both the Government Accounting Office (GAO)[29] and Greenlief Associates[30] were critical of the poor monitoring of the program. In some cases poor statistics or none were collected by the firms involved. The GAO was also critical that about 20 percent of the jobs offered were for positions traditionally held by low skilled and unskilled persons. On this point, Greenlief Associates were even more critical. They held that most JOB trainees were hired either as laborers, machine operators, maintenance helpers, and assemblers, in occupations which traditionally had high turnover rates. Jon Goldstein was critical of the possibilities of subversion of the program by some employers who were interested solely in obtaining

[26]Training and Jobs for the Urban Poor (New York), Committee for Economic Development, 1970).

[27]Lawrence A. Johnson, Employing the Hard-Core Unemployed, (New York: American Management Association, 1969, pp. 55-78.

[28]For a detailed program of working with the disadvantaged, see Elmer H. Burack, Strategies for Manpower Planning and Programming, (Morristown, N.J., General Learning Corporation, 1972), pp. 195-206. For a number of other firms' experiences see Lawrence A. Johnson, op. cit.

[29]Evaluation and Results and Administration of the Job Opportunities in the Business Sector (JOBS) Program in Five Cities (Washington, General Accounting Office, March 24, 1971).

[30]The Job Opportunities in the Business Sector Program, An Evaluation of Impact in Ten Standard Metropolitan Statistical Areas (New York, Greenleigh Associates, June, 1970).

subsidies from the federal government to lower labor costs. He suggested that possible abuse could be avoided by requiring that the employer retain a worker in an acceptable job for a specified period of time following training.[31] Another problem is that in recession years, firms will not hire the disadvantaged. In the 1969-1970 decline, funds originally earmarked for JOBS had to be reallocated to other manpower programs.[32] In a recession, Levitan and Taggart suggested that other programs such as public employment will be needed to supplement the flagging private market. In spite of the criticisms of the JOBS program, we conclude that it has sufficient merit to be continued. At the very least, it insures that those who are at a competitive disadvantage have a better chance for a job.

NEW CAREERS FOR THE POOR

A number of authors have suggested that new careers should be provided for the poor. Pearl and Riesman outlined several types of careers for the poor in the areas of education, health, research, and social work.[33] Those proposing this program go further than merely providing for entry level positions. In education, for example, a person could start as a teaching aide, and then progress to a teaching assistant and then a teacher.

A small beginning of a New Careers for the Poor Program began by an amendment to the Economic Opportunity Act (War on Poverty) in 1966. A year later the program was transferred to the Department of Labor. For several years the program was quite small. Even though the numbers served increased substantially in fiscal 1970 over prior years, the program never served as many as 43,000 (including Public Service Career trainees) and dropped to 21,000 in fiscal year 1972. The goal of providing career ladders never developed, and the workers in the two largest areas of education and health service perform very low-level duties.[34]

In a study of six New Careers programs by the staff of the National League of Cities in the summer of 1968, it was found that the program was too small to reduce significantly municipal manpower shortages.[35] On the

[31]Jon Goldstein, *The Effectiveness of Manpower Training Programs: A Review of Research on the Impact of the Poor*, Paper No. 3 in Studies on Public Welfare, a staff study prepared for the Subcommittee on Fiscal Policy, Joint Economic Committee, 92nd Congress, Nov. 20, 1972.

[32]Sar Levitan and Robert Taggart, III, "Public Employment and Manpower Policy," *Manpower* Vol. 3, No. 3, (March, 1971), p. 19.

[33]Arthur Pearl and Frank Riessman, *New Careers for the Poor: The Non Professional in Human Service* (New York, The Free Press, 1965). See also Frank Riessman and Hermine Popper, *Up From Poverty* (New York, Harper and Row, 1968), and Mark Haskell *The New Careers Concept* (New York, Praeger, 1969).

[34]Sar Levitan, Garth Mangum, and Ray Marshall, *Human Resources and Labor Markets* (New York, Harper and Row, 1972), p. 347.

[35]Lawrence A. Williams, Floyd A. Decker and Andrew B. Horgan, III, *Municipal Government Efforts to Provide Greater Career Employment Opportunities for the Disadvantaged* (Washington, Manpower Administration, 1969).

positive side, it was found that turnover rates were low. Several suggestions were made to improve the program. The program could have been broadened to include jobs in engineering, public works, and water and sewage treatment that were not originally included. More time should have been devoted to preliminary planning and job development, for too few of the programs provided for promotional ladders. In addition, more federal funding was needed to expand the program.

In 1969 a companion program was begun, called the Public Service Careers program. The program follows the philosophy of hiring first and training later.[36] Each trainee is paid the going wage rate for the particular job. Some criticism has been made that Civil Service requirements screen out too many applicants. In 1970 the National Civil Service League recommended not only that written examinations be eliminated, except where validated, but also that arrest records should not be a complete bar to employment. Meaningful training requirements should be established, as should improved supervisory awareness and sensitivity training.[37] This program, like the New Careers, was also criticized for lack of promotional opportunities after hiring. This program also has suffered from a paucity of federal funds.

UPGRADING

Most of the training of the disadvantaged has been for entry level jobs, though some of the job training has been in upgrading. Several experimental upgrading projects have proven successful, but, in general, evaluations have not been optimistic. One of the most detailed upgrading studies was made of five industries in New York City by Charles Brecher.[38] He found that there was a good potential for upgrading only in health services, and in this industry only 15 to 20 percent of employment could be affected.

OVERALL MANPOWER EVALUATION

The most comprehensive evaluation of manpower programs to date was conducted by the Industrial Research Unit of the Wharton School, University of Pennsylvania.[39] This group examined 252 evaluative studies

[36]Grace Aboud, *Hiring and Training the Disadvantaged for Public Employment* (Ithaca, New York State School of Industrial and Labor Relations Key Issues, No. 11, 1973).

[37]Bureau of National Affairs, *Manpower Information Service*, Vol. 2 (October 7, 1970), p. 20.

[38]Charles Brecher, *Upgrading Blue Collar and Service Workers* (Baltimore, Johns Hopkins Press, 1972).

[39]Charles R. Perry, Bernard E. Anderson, Richard L. Rowan, and Herbert R. Northrup, *The Impact of Government Manpower Programs* (Philadelphia, Industrial Research Unit, the Wharton School, University of Pennsylvania, 1975).

of manpower programs. The manpower programs were divided into four groups: skill training, employability development, job development, and work experience. The two programs analyzed under skill training were institutional and on-the-job MDTA training. Under job development programs were the JOBS program, public service careers, the apprenticeship outreach program and the public employment program. Four programs were analyzed under employability development: opportunities industrialization centers (see chapter 23), concentrated employment program, work incentive program (see chapter 7) and the Job Corps (see chapter 27). Lastly two programs were studied under work experience programs, the Neighborhood Youth Corp (see chapter 27) and Operation Mainstream.

A major conclusion of the Industrial Research Unit was that most economic benefit was derived from skill training, followed in order by employability development, job development and lastly work experience. Minority groups were well represented in most manpower programs, and comprised 51 percent of enrollees of all programs. Women comprised 43.4 percent of all enrollees. Operating statistics showed that blacks earned less than whites and women less than men (post-training hourly wages) although both blacks and women experienced larger gains in hourly earnings over pre-training levels than white males. Part of the success of women's training was due to the high and rising demand for services in which most women were trained — the clerical and health service fields. The single most successful minorities program was that of apprentice outreach. Many of the gains of minorities and women were attributed to the higher frequency of employment rather than higher hourly wage rates. Limited data was available to evaluate the non-economic benefits of manpower programs, but the meager evidence available led to the conclusion that manpower programs "undoubtedly generated benefits to trainees in noneconomic well being." An improved management information system was recommended to better evaluate manpower programs.

Bibliography

Azzi, Corry F., *Equity and Efficiency Effects from Manpower Programs* (Lexington, Mass., D. C. Heath, 1973).

Brecher, Charles *Upgrading Blue Collar and Service Workers* (Baltimore, Johns Hopkins Press, 1972).

Burack, Elmer H., *Strategies for Manpower Planning and Programming* (Morristown,,N.J., General Learning Corporation, 1972)

Doeringer, Peter B. and Michael J. Piore, *Internal Labor Markets and Manpower Analysis* (Lexington, D. C. Heath, 1971).

Goodwin, Leonard, *Do the Poor Want to Work* (Washington, Brookings, 1972).

Gordon, David M., *Theories of Poverty and Underemployment* (Lexington, D. C. Heath, 1972).

Johnson, Lawrence A., *Employing the Hard-Core Unemployed* (New York, American Management Association, 1969).

Leacock, Eleanor Burke, ed., *The Culture of Poverty*, (New York, Simon and Schuster, 1971).

Lewis, Oscar, *La Vida* (New York, Random House, 1966).

Mangum, Garth and John Walsh, *A Decade of Manpower Development and Training* (Salt Lake City, Olympus Publishing Co., 1973).

Pearl, Arthur and Frank Riessman *New Careers for the Poor* (New York, The Free Press, 1965).

Reubens, Beatrice, *The Hard to Employ*, European Programs (New York, Columbia University Press, 1970).

Tiffany, Donald W., James R. Cowan, and Phyllis M. Tiffany, *The Unemployed: A Social-Psychological Portrait* (Englewood Cliffs, N.J., Prentice-Hall, 1970).

Valentine, Charles, *Culture and Poverty* (Chicago, University of Chicago Press, 1968).

CHAPTER 16

SEASONAL AND TECHNOLOGICAL UNEMPLOYMENT AND DEPRESSED AREAS

SEASONAL UNEMPLOYMENT

Changes in the seasons have been a cause of unemployment in the United States. When cold weather begins to set in during November, seasonal unemployment increases and reaches a peak in February. In this month, seasonal unemployment is concentrated heavily in outdoor industries and in trade and allied industries. With revival of these industries in the spring, unemployment declines seasonally until June. The end of the school term, with the concomitant increase in job applications, again increases seasonal unemployment. The harvests of August and the return of many to school reduces seasonal unemployment in the fall until it begins to rise again in November. It is expected that the amount of seasonal unemployment will change over the years, for each of the expanding and contracting industries has a seasonal pattern of its own, and the pattern may change within industries.

One yearly study on seasonal unemployment shows that this type of unemployment constituted slightly over 20 percent of all unemployment in 1951 in the United States, but declined to 13 percent of all unemployment in 1962.[1] A more recent figure showed that from June, 1971, through May, 1972, the seasonally adjusted rate of unemployed varied from only 5.2 to 5.5 percent whereas the seasonally unadjusted rate fluctuated from a low of 4.5 to a high of 6.3 percent. If seasonal unemployment could have been entirely eliminated, the unemployment rate would have fallen by more than 0.75 percent.[2]

Entrepreneurs have been aware for many years that the costs of seasonal production are high. Equipment cannot be fully utilized. Many other fixed expenses, such as rent and salaries, continue whether or not sales are made. Labor may become restless when unemployed, and permanent work may be sought elsewhere. Failure to hold a permanent, effi-

---

[1]David C. Smith, "Seasonal Unemployment and Economic Conditions," in A. M. Ross, ed., *Employment Policy and the Labor Market* (Berkeley, University of California Press, 1965), pp. 115-161.

[2]Martin S. Feldstein, "Lowering the Permanent Rate of Unemployment," (Washington, Joint Economic Committee, 93rd Congress, 1st Session, September 18, 1973), p. 31.

cient work force may necessitate expensive training programs for inexperienced workers. Short employment also tends to cause workers to reduce output in order to be paid for more hours than are really necessary. For all of these reasons, many employers have taken definite steps to reduce seasonal unemployment.

Some employers have attempted to push their sales in the off season. At one time, two-thirds of the demand for Sherwin-Williams paint came in the spring of the year. The company put on a "Paint in the Fall" campaign, and was successful in inducing consumers to refinish floors during the winter. A highly seasonal demand was replaced by year-round buying.[3] Not only may sales be pushed in the off season, but also new off-season uses may be made of products. In the food industry, the movement toward frozen foods has aided in increased sales that were formerly not available in the off season.

If the storage costs are not too great, production and employment may be regularized even though demand is highly seasonal. The Gorham Silver Company, producers of wedding silver, found that most of their silverware was sold in June and October. Though they could do little to change the patterns of weddings in the United States, they simply estimated the sales annually, and then manufactured 1/12 of the estimate each month.[4] If storage costs run too high, then perhaps the company may seek to obtain more advance ordering of its product. The Kalamazoo Sled Company, for example, persuaded buyers to order sleds immediately following the Christmas season on the ground that buyers have the best knowledge of requirements at that time.[5]

Products may sometimes be diversified in order to regularize employment. The Dennison Manufacturing Company had formerly made only jewelry boxes, which were sold mainly at Christmas time. The company added other products, such as crepe paper, printed labels, tags, and other types of boxes, and thus was able to provide more stable employment.[6] Sometimes it is possible to sell products in foreign areas where the seasons are the reverse of ours. The Jantzen Knitting Mills Company has been active in developing the sale of bathing suits in the southern hemisphere.[7]

One joint Labor-Commerce Department study on construction seasonality found that in a four northern city survey in 1969, construction

[3]Sam Lewison et al., Can Business Prevent Unemployment_ (New York, Knopf, 1925), pp. 11-12.

[4]Paul Douglas and Aaron Director, The Problem of Unemployment (New York, Macmillan, 1931), pp. 94-95.

[5]Edwin S. Smith, Reducing Seasonal Unemployment (New York, McGraw-Hill, 1931), p. 124.

[6]Ibid., p. 102.

[7]Longshoring and Meatpacking Automation Settlements," Monthly Labor Review, Vol. 82 (1959), pp. 1108-1110.

workers had about 38 weeks of full-time work.[8] Construction during the winter was found to be technically feasible. Recommendations were for the federal government to promote winter-building science and technology, better scheduled buying of construction services, and counseling of private firms. An improved construction employment information program was suggested, along with a subsidy program for winter construction.

In conclusion, it may be stated that there are a number of means available to reduce seasonal unemployment. However, various climatic and other factors present serious obstacles to complete elimination of the problem. It is probable that seasonal unemployment will continue to be experienced in the future.

TECHNOLOGICAL UNEMPLOYMENT

Technology has been defined to include "not only the invention of new types of labor-saving machinery but also simple changes in materials' handling and the flow of work, changes in resource mix used in production, the development of new and substitute products and various managerial efficiencies."[9] In turn, automation has been defined "as the substitution of mechanical and electronic devices for human labor in operating, adjusting, and controlling the production process in general and the machines in particular."[10] There has been some dispute as to whether automation is anything different from the mechanization that has occurred in the past. Mr. Clifton W. Phalen, President of the Michigan Bell Telephone Company, stated as follows: "To me (automation) means general technological progress that has taken place in our industry and in others for many years."[11] On the other hand, others have felt that automation represents something new. Walter Reuther said:

Automation is the second phase of the industrial revolution. . . . Automation makes a completely new development in the technological process because automation, in addition to substituting mechanical judgment for human judgment — the machine begins to substitute the thinking process on a mechanical

---

[8]*Seasonal Unemployment in the Construction Industry* (Washington, U. S. Department of Labor, 1970). See also Joe L. Russell, Daniel Quinn Mills, and Michael J. Pilot, *Seasonality and Manpower in Construction,* (Washington, U. S. Department of Labor, Bureau of Labor Statistics, Bulletin No. 1642, 1970) and Jerome B. Gordon, *Year Round Employment in the Construction Industry* (New York, Praeger Co., 1973).

[9]Garth L. Mangum, ed., *The Manpower Revolution* (Garden City, New York, Doubleday, 1965), p. 237.

[10]Julius Rezler, *Automation and Industrial Labor* (New York, Random House, 1969), pp. 6-7.

[11]*Automation and Technological Change,* Hearings before the Subcommittee on economic Stabilization, the Joint Committee on the Economic Report, 84th Congress (October 1955), p. 516.

basis for the thinking process which heretofore was done exclusively by the human mind.[12]

Julius Rezler concurred with Walter Reuther for two reasons.[13] He quotes Frank Lynn to the effect that the lapsed time between a technical discovery and recognition of its commercial potential has fallen from about 30 years before World War I to sixteen years between the wars, and nine years after World War II.[14] Also individual applications of automated equipment have frequently resulted in from 10 to 50 percent increases in productivity, and a corresponding reduction in the work force.

The term "technological unemployment" was coined many years ago by Karl Marx. Marx contended that the substitution of machines for men would cause mass unemployment if production were controlled by capitalists under a system of private property. The controversy still rages today as to what impact technology and automation will have on employment. A group from the Center for the Study of Democratic Institutions at Santa Barbara contended that: "A quarter of the nation is now dispossessed and soon-to-be dispossessed by the lack of employment."[15] On the other hand, others like Yale Brozen have pointed out that it would take one hundred years of savings to completely automate American industry.[16] Since employment has increased from 28 million in 1900 to 93 million in 1973, during a period of rapid technological progress, it is suggested by some that the fears of unemployment through technological advance are unfounded.

A number of studies have found that many firms which automate experience unemployment.[17] In one such study, E.R.F.W. Crossman concurred with the conclusion of the Ad Hoc Committee for the Triple Revolution that automation would have a serious impact on employment.[18] However, he felt that the process would be much slower than that forecast by the Triple Revolution group. During the long interim, he thought, society might spontaneously adjust to automation's effects.

In spite of the fact that technological improvement has caused a drop in employment in a number of industries, projections from 1972 to 1985

---

[12]*Ibid.*, p. 121.

[13]Julius Rezler, *op. cit.*, pp. 10-12.

[14]Report of the National Commission on Technology, Automation, and Economic Progress on *Technology and the American Economy* (Washington D.C., National Commission on Technology, Automation, and Economic Progress, 1966) I, p. 3.

[15]Ad Hoc Committee for the Triple Revolution, *The Triple Revolution*, (Santa Barbara, California, Center for the Study of Democratic Institutions, 1964).

[16]Yale Brozen, "Putting Economics and Automation in Perspective," *Automation*, Vol. 11, 1964, pp. 14-26.

[17]Richard A. Beaumont and Roy B. Helfgott, *Management, Automation, and People* (New York, Industrial Relations Counsellors, 1964); Julius Rezler, *op. cit.*, pp. 27-31.

[18]E.R.F.W. Crossman, "Automation, Skill and Manpower Predictions," in *Seminar on Manpower Policy and Program* (Washington, D.C., Manpower Administration, 1966).

show an increase in nonagricultural wage and salary workers from 85.5 to 107.6 million.[19] The largest percentage increases are expected in government, followed by finance, insurance, and real estate; other services; contract construction; and durable goods manufacturing. Drops in employment are projected only for mining and agriculture. By occupation, the largest percentage increases are expected for professional workers, followed by service workers, clerical workers, salesmen, craftsmen, managers, operatives.

Increases in unemployment during the 1950's indicated to some that technology was the main problem. However, tax cuts and increased war expenditures during the 1960's demonstrated that high levels of employment could be obtained regardless of technology. The recent energy crises has caused some economists to reassess less optimistically employment projections for the future.

DEPRESSED AREAS

One of the ways technological unemployment has affected America is to cause a decline in certain industries, possibly key ones in particular areas. The loss in employment causes the area to become depressed. Other countries besides the United States have been faced with the problem of depressed areas. In England, six areas were designated for special aid during the 1930's. With the expansion of war industries, government expenditures were channeled into these areas. After World War II, four other regions were added to the list of depressed areas, later called "development areas." The Board of Trade was given authority to pass on the location site of all new factories above a certain minimum size. To this negative control was added the positive authority to construct factories, improve sites, acquire land, and provide financial assistance to local authorities. The program was successful in reducing regional disparities in unemployment.[20]

A number of bills were introduced in the Congress during the 1950's to aid depressed areas. Senator Paul Douglas (Illinois), in sponsoring such bills, pointed out that certain areas in the United States had been depressed for a number of years.[21] The costs of unemployment insurance and welfare payments for those areas were quite high. Money could better be spent in revitalizing these areas than in continuing relief. If industry could be attracted there, higher income for the population could result in improved living for all. Better education could be provided children in

[19]*Manpower Report of the President,* 1974 (Washington, D.C., U. S. Department of Labor), Table E-10, p. 355.

[20]William H. Miernyk, "British and American Approaches to Structural Unemployment," *Industrial and Labor Relations Review,* Vol. 12, No. 1 (1959), pp. 3-19.

[21]*Congressional Record,* Washington, D.C., 85th Congress, 2nd Session, Vol. 104, No. 72 (May 8, 1958), pp. 7435-7538.

these areas, and the children could grow up with the hope of a better life. Senator Douglas estimated that at least 70 of the larger industrial areas in 20 states had large amounts of unemployment and should be aided. These areas included almost five million workers, 7.2 percent of the total national labor force. Rural depressed areas should also be aided, according to Douglas. In the 300 lowest-income rural counties lived seven million persons, most of them in poverty. Senator Douglas contended that the basic problem for these areas was a shortage of capital that could be alleviated by federal loans and grants.

Aid-to-depressed area legislation was not without its critics. President Eisenhower twice vetoed such bills. Although claiming to be sympathetic with the aims of the bills, he maintained that the Douglas bills went too far in diminishing local responsibility for the unemployment problem.[22] President Eisenhower felt that the 40-year loans provided for in the bills were for too long a period. Also, instead of the loans being for 65 percent of the total cost of the project, President Eisenhower favored a lower figure of 35 percent. He also objected to what he considered the artificially low interest rates of the bills that called for one-fourth of one percent above the rate of interest that the government must pay on issues of comparable duration. He also doubted that federal loans for construction of industrial buildings would be an appropriate remedy for the problem of surplus labor in agricultural communities. President Eisenhower stated that he favored an area assistance bill, and hoped that such a bill would be passed by Congress along the lines of his suggestions.

Some groups have entirely opposed aid to depressed areas on the ground that the areas are less amenable to economic growth than other areas. Private entrepreneurs evaluate areas and choose more profitable areas than depressed ones. If a subsidy is granted depressed areas, it will have to be continued indefinitely to keep industry there provided that the more prosperous areas retain their advantage over depressed areas. Proponents of aid to depressed areas counter these arguments by pointing out that entrepreneurs are less that omniscient in their decisions. Perhaps a company had never considered locating on, say, a depressed Indian reservation, but once the feasibility had been pointed out, it may be a better location than others. Also, if the area is depressed solely because of a shortage of capital, the government could overcome this deficiency by loans.

AREA REDEVELOPMENT ACT (1961)

After President Kennedy was elected, the aid-to-depressed areas bill was passed and became law in May of 1961. The act called for 25-year federal

[22]Dwight D. Eisenhower, "Memorandum of Disapproval," *The Labor Market and Employment Security* (September, 1958) pp. 3-4.

loans at one-half percent above what the federal government could borrow money for. The federal government was to lend up to a maximum of 65 percent of the cost of the project. Grants were also provided in case of needed public works in the area. The program was to be administered by the Area Redevelopment Administration, a part of the U. S. Department of Commerce.

In 1965 the name of the agency was changed to Economic Development Administration. In order to encourage planning in the depressed areas before the loan was made, the area was required to draw up an Overall Economic Development Program showing a step-by-step plan which the community felt must be followed to achieve new growth and new jobs. The economy of the area had to be described, and was to include topographic features, climate, land-use patterns, public utility and transportation services, and school and hospital facilities. In addition to facts on population and labor force, information was to be provided on employment by industry, the amount of unemployment and underemployment, the factors contributing to the decline of the area, and the effort which had been made to solve their economic problem. An analysis of the potential of the area was required along with an analysis of the resources, both physical and human, in the area. Deterrent factors were required to be evaluated, such as a lack of venture capital, entrepreneurial initiative, lack of transportation or poor terrain, lack of structures or parking facilities, lack of public utility services, physical deterioration of the area, and weaknesses in local government financial capabilities.

The Aid to Depressed Areas program provided three major programs: public works, loans to private businesses, and technical assistance to entrepreneurs. In Table 16-1 the program in one of the early years, fiscal 1963, is compared with that of one of the later years, fiscal 1974.
The public works program grows in relation to the business and industrial loans when 1974 is compared with 1963. During the past few years, the budget of the EDA has been substantially reduced. The recession of 1974-1975, however, caused Congress to increase the budget.

EVALUATION

The Annual Report of the U. S. Department of Commerce in 1965 indicated that unemployment dropped more in depressed areas than elsewhere in the country when 1964 was compared with 1961.[23] Senator Montoya for the Committee on Public Works reported that since 1966 the Economic Development Administration had created over half a million permanent jobs paying $6,500 a year.[24] Furthermore, each job directly generated cost only $2,200 per job.

[23]Annual Report, 1965, U. S. Department of Commerce, pp. 12-13.
[24]Public Works and Economic Development Act amendments of 1973, Report of the Committee on Public Works on H.R. 2246, United States Senate, Report No. 93-117 (April 12, 1973), p. 5.

TABLE 16-1

ECONOMIC DEVELOPMENT

ADMINISTRATION PROGRAMS — FISCAL YEARS 1963 AND 1974

	Amount of Obligated Federal Expenditures	Number of Projects	Amount of Oblitaged Federal Expenditures	Number of Projects
Public Works	$82,000,000	52	$38,697,119	190
Business Loans	$64,900,00	173	$17,954,000	12
Technical Assistance	$ 3,600,000	111	$ 7,551,609	19

Sources: *Annual Report of the Area Redevelopment Administration,* 1963; and The Economic Development Administration, 1974.

In spite of the merits of the Depressed Area Program, it has met with much opposition. Originally, Senator Douglas had envisaged the program reaching only a relatively small number of severely depressed areas. However, due to the need to get votes for the program, large areas were blanketed in as eligible for loans and grants. About a third of America was made eligible. Even though criticism of covering too many areas came early in the program,[25] 1,729 areas covering 93.4 million of populations were qualified for some type of Economic Development loan or grant as late as July 1, 1972. Obviously with so large an area covered and with relatively small sums allocated, the program does not have a strong enough impact to abolish poverty in all the designated areas.

Another criticism was that some of the areas selected had too few people for adequate growth.[26] Over a third of EDA's funds have gone to towns with less than 2,500 people and over half in towns of less than 5,000 population. Most regional economists consider that the best growth potential is in areas of from 200,000 to 750,000 population. Of 122 development centers in the EDA in 1969, only 18 had populations of 50,000 and over. A criticism made by Niles Hansen was that if areas outside the depressed area, but nearby, had a greater growth potential, resources

[25]Sar Levitan, *Federal Aid to Depressed Areas* (Baltimore, Johns Hopkins, 1964), p. 250.
[26]Sar Levitan, Garth Mangum and Ray Marshall, *Human Resources and Labor Markets* (New York, Harper and Row, 1972), p. 537.

should be channeled to the growth areas.[27] Hansen also contended that money might more effectively be spent for health, education, and training in the depressed areas rather than on public works projects.

Still another criticism of the EDA was that the areas were too small for planning. In recognition of this weakness, the EDA aided in the creation of 116 multi-county agencies (mainly) and 232 growth centers (1972). Some of the districts have too few people to be real growth centers. Recognizing that some of the districts could use even larger area planning, multi-state commissions were created in 1965 and thereafter. An Appalachian Regional Commissions was created in 1965. Thereafter, the following seven commissions were created: Ozarks (1966); New England (1966); Upper Great Lakes (1966); Four Corners (1966); Coastal Plains (1966); Old West (1972); and the Pacific Northwest (1972). The multi-state commissions are state operated with a federal veto power over operations.

Dissatisfaction with various phases of the EDA program resulted in a Nixon administration recommendation that the program be terminated.[28] In its place the federal government would engage in revenue sharing. The Nixon plan called for the states to form their own multi-state agencies if they wished. Under this plan the Economic Development Administration would have been abolished, along with the seven Regional Action Planning Commissions. The Department of Agriculture's Rural Development program would have been continued, as would have been the Appalachian Regional Commissions and the Indian development program. The plan was not implemented.

REGIONAL PLANNING

A major alternative to the Nixon administration's state revenue sharing plan is to have regional planning agencies. Such planning was originally started because of several deficiencies in the grants-in-aids programs that were in existence. By the mid-sixties there were over 1,000 such grants-in-aids programs. Such fragmentation resulted in overlaps, duplications, gaps, lack of coordination, and even direct conflicts.[29] Regional planning is an alternative to the more fragmented grants-in-aids programs and to revenue sharing.

[27]Niles Hansen, "Growth Centers, Human Resources, and Rural Development," a paper written for the Rural Labor Market Strategies Project, The University of Texas, 1971.

[28]Report to the Congress on the Proposal for an Economic Adjustment Program (Washington, D.C., U. S. Department of Commerce and Office of Management and Budget, February 1, 1974).

[29]Monroe Newman, The Political Economy of Appalachia, (Lexington: D.C. Heath and Co., 1972), p. 25.

APPALACHIA

Even with grants-in-aids, certain areas were still deteriorating. The lag of the Appalachian region caused President Kennedy in 1963 to establish the President's Appalachian Regional Commission. The Commission highlighted six major problems of the region: low income, high unemployment, lack of urbanization, deficits in education, deficits in standards of living, and a loss of young working-age adults. To document a few weaknesses of the area, in 1960 several countries in Kentucky and Tennessee had median family incomes below $1,500 annually, compared with a national median of $5,660. (See Table 16-2 for more detail on income). Even as late as 1970, when only 6.9 percent of all U. S. houses lacked some or all plumbing facilities, the corresponding figures for Kentucky, Tennessee, and West Virginia were respectively 20.8, 14.8, and 18.3 percent. The Commission found that the wealth from exploiting natural resources left the region, and investments in the community economy and social system were never made. The Commission suggested that highly interrelated public investment be made in highways, hospitals, schools, and other community facilities.

The President's Commission failed to provide guidelines on how strategy might have to differ in dealing with different sections within Appalachia, for example, that between an emerging Georgia factory community, and an obsolescent West Virginia mining community. Continuing work on a possible program resulted in a strategy favoring concentration of public investment in areas where there was a significant potential for growth and where the return on public dollars would be the greatest. Specific programs were suggested for highways, health, soil and water conservation, eradicating mine scars, and improved sewage treatment. An Appalachian Regional Act was passed in 1965 to aid in these areas.

To administer the Appalachian Regional Act an Appalachian Regional Commission (ARC) was created. The Commission is a nonfederal agency in which the federal government and the 13 Appalachian states participate as equals. Each state has one representative and the federal co-chairman is appointed by the President. A veto is permitted either by the federal co-chairman or a majority of the state representatives. In addition, no action or project can be undertaken in a state without its consent. Staff operations are headed by an executive director, who has a staff of about 100 at his disposal. The Commission requires that each state submit a development plan each year. The states either have their own staff or other state planning units to prepare a plan, or they may use consultants to develop the plans. The Commission staff may provide technical assistance on these plans. To avoid competition between the states in attempting to obtain a larger share of the budget allocation, the Commission uses a state allocation formula for most sections of the act. Once the state plan has been approved, the appropriate federal agency is named as responsible for project administration.

TABLE 16-2

MEDIAN FAMILY INCOME

Selected Appalachian Areas and the United States

	1959		1969	
	Median Family Income	Percent of U.S.	Median Family Income	Percent of U.S.
Three Poorest Counties				
Kentucky	$1,453	26	$2,891	30
Tennessee	$1,610	28	$3,433	36
West Virginia	$2,566	45	$4,431	46
State				
Kentucky	$4,051	72	$7,441	78
Tennessee	$3,949	70	$7,447	78
West Virginia	$4,572	81	$7,415	77
United States	$5,660	—	$9,590	—

Source: U. S. Bureau of the Census, 1970

Note: Data on disposable personal income per capita from 1969 to 1973 show an annual growth rate of 8.1 percent for the United States compared with 9.0 for Kentucky, 9.4 for Tennessee, and 9.6 for West Virginia. Preliminary data for 1974 show respective growth rates of 7.1, 10.0, 7.6, and 10.0 percent. *Survey of Current Business,* April 1975, Table 1, p. 21.

The Commission has identified three (formerly four) sub-regions within Appalachia. The Northern Appalachia area encompasses parts of New York, Pennsylvania, Maryland, southeastern Ohio and northern West Virginia. This area has shifted its dependence on a coal-steel-railroad economy to new types of manufacturing and service firms. Public policy for this area has stressed post-high school and adult occupational training. The Central Appalachian areas covers counties in eastern Kentucky, southern West Virginia, southwestern Virginia and northern Tennessee. Most of the communities in this area are small. In this area, priorities have been designated for transportation, education, health and concerted development of key communities in the area. Southern Appalachia covered parts of Mississippi, Alabama, South Carolina, Georgia, Tennessee, North Carolina, and Virginia. The former agricultural economy is being displaced by apparel, textile and food processing plants. First priority here has been given to improve the educational system. The second priority has been given to the construction of public facilities to aid urbanization.

The largest sums of ARC money have been authorized for a highway system and local access roads. Slightly over $2 billion have been authorized through fiscal 1971. Although the highway program is not sufficiently completed to make a definite evaluation, some scholars have contended that without a significant highway component, no Appalachian program would have been possible. Much smaller amounts of money have gone to supplement grants-in-aids programs, mostly health, education, water and sewer projects, and airports. Over a period of time more emphasis has been placed on human resources as contrasted to physical resource investment. Smaller amounts have also gone to multi-county demonstration health projects, vocational education, mine restoration, and other programs.

In attempting to appraise the Appalachian program, Monroe Newman pointed out that the net out-migration declined from 2.2 million in the 1950's to 1.1 million in the 1960's. The region's per capita income was 75.1 percent of the U. S. average in 1962 and it climbed to 78.8 in 1968. However, the absolute differences in income widened from $577 in 1962 to $727 in 1968. Newman cited data from seven growth centers where relatively large sums of Appalachian money were channeled: Hornell, N.Y.; Gaffney, S.C.; Cookeville and Crossville, Tenn.; Altoona, Pa.; Florence, Ala.; and Carrollton, Ga. All areas except one showed an increase of per capita income from 1959 to 1968 relative to that of the United States. However, population decreased in two of the areas. Newman pointed out that it would be difficult to determine how much of the improvement in Appalachia was due to the Appalachian program and how much due to other factors. One firm conclusion that he arrived at was that there would have to be a long period of rapid change before the Appalachian standard of living approximated that of the nation.

In his final assessment of the Appalachian program, Newman stated that alternative methods of improving the region must be considered. The two major alternatives, grants-in-aids and revenue sharing, both have serious shortcomings, some of which could be remedied by the regional planning approach used in the Appalachian program. On grants-in-aids, Newman was critical of the overlaps, duplications, gaps, lack of coordination, and even direct conflicts in programs. Revenue sharing was criticized because it lacked any federal checks on state and local spending. A federal check might hasten qualitative improvements in state performance. He then concluded that the Appalachian experience has fewer flaws than either grants-in-aids or revenue sharing.

Niles Hansen has noted several weaknesses in the Appalachian program.[30] He contended that too many alleged growth centers have been selected by the ARC. Since some of the areas within Appalachia are not amenable to growth, he suggested that efforts should be made to attract eastern Kentucky Appalachian residents to areas such as Lexington and Louisville, Kentucky lying outside the Appalachian region. Under such a strategy, more emphasis should be placed on developing the human resources of the area for some outward mobility rather than placing money on public work within some areas of Appalachia that have little potential for growth.

Rena Gazaway was critical of the ARC program for not reaching many of the poorest residents.[31] She made a study of 55 families (288 people) living in Kentucky on the edge of the Cumberland plateau. None of the houses had inside toilets and few provided adequate shelter in the winter. Most of the people could not read or write. There was little outward mobility from the community because the people there were laughed at by the outside world. Gazaway suggested that the relevant public policy would have to involve the hollow dwellers in their own habitat. She recommended the construction of a central building that would have water, showers, cooking facilities, refrigeration and dining facilities. Improved education would be necessary to hold youth in schools. Improved housing possibly with a self-help program might help. For employment the men could help level strip mining areas and engage in reforestation. She was not certain that the men would work, but thought her program should be given a try.

The above analysis indicated that there is an Appalachian sub-culture, which may inhibit adaption to modern society. Thomas Ford has listed the principal cultural themes of southern Appalachian society as individualistic and self-reliant, traditionalistic and fatalistic and religiously fundamentalistic.[32] Similarly Jack Weller describes the sub-culture as emphasizing: individualism, traditionalism, fatalism, action seeking, a fear psychology, reference group domination and familism.[33] In attempt-

[30]Niles Hansen, *Rural Poverty and the Urban Crisis* (Bloomington, Indiana University Press, 1970), pp. 59-106.

[31]Rena Gazaway, *The Longest Mile* (New York, Doubleday, 1969).

[32]Thomas R. Ford, "The Passing of Provincialism," in Thomas R. Ford, Ed., *The Southern Appalachian Region: A Survey* (Lexington, Ky., University Press of Kentucky, 1962), pp. 9-34.

[33]Jack E. Weller, *Yesterday's People* (Lexington, The University Press of Kentucky, 1965).

ing to explain the origin and persistence of this subculture Robert A. Ball[34] draws heavily upon the work of Norman R. F. Maier,[35] who makes a distinction between motivation-instigated behavior and frustration-instigated behavior. Motivation-instigated behavior is goal oriented, but frustration-instigated behavior is not because problems become insoluble. In responses, frustration-instigated behavior has no adaptive value in the sense that it is adequate to the situation. Maier claimed that four classes of behavior are induced by extreme frustration: fixation, regression, aggression, and resignation. Ball feels that these four describe well the behavior of many Appalachian residents.

One agency attempting to culturally enrich Appalachia is the Commission on Religion for Appalachia (CORA), organized in 1965 after fourteen religious bodies consulted together.[36] CORA was organized on the premise that the value system traditionally held by mountain churches paralyzed and hindered rather than helped the people of Appalachia to find their creative place in a new age. This group claimed that the church must develop fundamentally new attitudes toward this time and this world if it is going to help the Appalachian people to find their place in a rapidly changing society. CORA has engaged in consultation, research, study, education, coordination of denominational and interdenominational programs, and initiated projects that may be helpful in fulfilling the church's mission in eliminating the hopelessness and escapism of the region.

OUTWARD MOBILITY FROM APPALACHIA

It would be remiss to end a study of Appalachia without discussing the millions who have moved out of the region. The population of the area has decreased more than three million since 1950, although the decrease is slackening. One study of outmigrants dealt with 79 family-households in three neighborhoods in an eastern Kentucky mountain county.[37] Those moving almost quadrupled their family income. Most of those who had moved regarded themselves as very happy in their new locations despite minor problems of adaptation to a new environment and their new occupations. The major reasons for the satisfactory adjustment were higher income, living relatively close to their kinsfolk and many fellow Ken-

[34]Robert A. Ball, "The Southern Appalachian Folk Subculture as a Tension-Reducing Way of Life," in John D. Potiadis and Harry K. Schwarzweller, eds., *Change in Rural Appalachia* (Philadelphia, University of Penna. Press, 1970), pp. 69-79.

[35]Norman R. F. Maier, *Frustration* (New York, McGraw Hill, 1949).

[36]Max E. Glenn, "Cooperative Mission in Appalachia," in Max E. Glenn, ed., *Appalachia in Transition* (St. Louis, the Bethany Press, 1970), pp. 111-121.

[37]Harry K. Schwarzweller, James S. Brown, and J. J. Mangalam, *Transition: A Case Study of Appalachian Migration* (University Park, Pa., The Pennsylvania State University Press, 1971).

tuckians, and visiting back at the family homesteads during a weekend, a summer vacation, or during an extended layoff. The lower the class of the migrant the less satisfactory was the adjustment. This study was much less optimistic about the prospects of those remaining behind.

CONCLUSION: APPALACHIA

Recent data show that per capita income in Appalachia, measured as a percent of United States' income, is increasing. However, if absolute amounts are used, the gap is widening between Appalachia and the rest of the nation. The widening absolute gap indicates that additional steps will be necessary to close the income differential between this region and the rest of the country. A multiplicity of programs need to be expanded to accelerate the growth of the region or facilitate outward mobility.

GEOGRAPHICAL MOBILITY AND DEPRESSED AREAS

In an important study on geographic mobility in the United States, Lansing and Mueller found that there was little difference in the amount of outward mobility from depressed areas than from other parts of the country.[38] Net out-migration from depressed areas, however, does occur because the in-migration to depressed areas is less than to other parts of the country. Although net in-migration to depressed areas was small, it was by no means inconsiderable. The population moving into low income rural or small labor market areas within five years of the survey (1962-1963) was 14 percent, and 22 percent of the population had moved to the area since 1950. Several policy recommendations were made by Lansing and Mueller on depressed areas. Since much depressed area mobility was from one depressed area to another, they suggested better information about job opportunities elsewhere in the country. Secondly, the quality and mobility potential of the labor force in depressed areas should be improved by guidance programs and assistance with special educational and training programs, along with more general support for education in the area. Also, an expanding market was stressed as crucial in affecting the mobility of labor.

RELOCATION ALLOWANCES

Most western European countries provide relocation allowances to speed the mobility of labor. In Sweden, such a program was deemed wise,

[38]John B. Lansing and Eva Mueller, The Geographic Mobility of Labor (Ann Arbor, Survey Research Center, 1967).

because the five northern provinces had over three times the percentage of unemployment as the rest of Sweden. Payment is made not only for personal travel expenses but also for the moving of furniture, subsistence expenses en route, and family allowances if the worker must pay additional rent at the new location before his family moves with him. Also, allowances are paid to cover the worker's living costs until the first pay day. Since the standard of living is much lower in the northern areas, a settlement allowance is paid to enable the family to buy new furniture and clothes. In addition, workers are reimbursed for the decline in their house value in the depressed area. Four factors have aided in the success of the Swedish program. The homogeneity of the population has aided mobility as have high levels of employment, a first-rate employment service, and a training program for those lacking the requisite skills. The ratio of those receiving travel allowances to the unemployed in Sweden is one to three. If such allowances were provided in the United States in relation to the number of unemployed, over one to two million workers would receive relocation allowances.

Relocation allowances have been tried only on an experimental basis in the United States, except for an American Indian relocation program and those displaced due to a lowering of tariffs (Trade Expansion Act of 1962). Amendments to the Manpower Development and Training Act in 1963 provided for a system of loans and grants to unemployed individuals who could not be expected to find full-time employment in the home area and who had bona fide offers of employment elsewhere. Unfavorable experience with loans resulted in most of the program becoming a grant program except for higher paid workers. Moving expenses of both the worker and his family and the cost of moving household goods were provided. Also, a lump-sum allowance was granted for incidental expenses pending receipt of the first paycheck. The program was administered mainly by the U. S. Employment Service along with states' employment services. Relocation projects in 12 of the states were linked together to determine the feasibility of a national relocation program. Under this arrangement an interregional job clearance system was set up. Through 1968, the total of 37 relocation projects were carried out in 28 states. Those relocated with financial assistance numbered 12,234 along with 1,494 who moved without such assistance. Most of those receiving allowances were men who had dependents. About half of the movers were between ages 24 and 44, and a third were under 25. About half had a high school education or better, but one-fourth had no more than an elementary education. The cost of the program came to $9 million.

To evaluate this program, some aimless rural-urban migration was eliminated, since the people had jobs before moving. Another finding was that single persons under 25 were most apt to return home. The inclusion of single youths, thus, would present a problem for a successful national relocation program. Poor housing, particularly in urban slums, also exacerbated the problem of moving, as did discrimination in housing for minority groups. However, most of those moving showed a decided increase in income. Upgrading from unskilled to operative jobs was evident among many workers. The few cost-benefit studies made have been favorable to the program. The most disadvantaged were found to be in need of additional services, such as education and counseling. In spite of the generally favorable evaluation of the program, a national relocation program has yet to be inaugurated in the United States.

Summary

In recent prosperous years seasonal factors account for between a sixth or seventh of our unemployment. The percentage is smaller in recessions, for cyclical factors then account for a larger percentage of unemployment. Since it may be profitable to operate the year around, a number of private companies have engaged in a variety of practices to eradicate seasonal declines. Governments at all levels may aid seasonal adjustment by channeling more orders during the winter. More research on this problem may be worthwhile.

Through most of the history of the United States the number of jobs has increased along with improved technology. Some fear that increased technology may decrease the number of jobs in the long run. Short run forecasts, though, indicate that the number of jobs will increase, particularly in the service and several other industries. Higher skilled occupations should tend to expand rapidly as they have done in the recent past.

Other countries and the United States have experienced the problem of depressed areas. Countries like England and Sweden have directed more programs to solve this problem than has the United States. The major approach in the United States is to direct public works and loans to private business firms to develop these areas. The program has been directed by the Economic Development Administration, but the Nixon Administration has suggested that this agency be dismantled and be replaced by a revenue sharing program.

Regional planning has been engaged in for Appalachia and a number of other depressed areas. Little progress is being made in some of these areas, but others such as Appalachia are showing some improvement in income. Relocation grants may aid in solving the depressed area problem also.

Bibliography

Gazaway, Rena, The Longest Mile (New York, Doubleday, 1969).
Glenn, Max E., ed., Appalachia in Transition (St. Louis, The Bethany Press, 1970).
Gordon, Jerome B., Year Round Employment in the Construction Industry (New York, Praeger Co., 1973).

Hansen, Niles, *Rural Poverty and the Urban Crisis* (Bloomington, Indiana University Press, 1970).

Lansing, John B. and Eva Mueller, *The Geographic Mobility of Labor* (Ann Arbor, Survey Research Center, 1967).

Newman, Monroe, *The Political Economy of Appalachia* (Lexington, Mass., D. C. Heath, 1972).

Photiadis, John D. and Harry K. Schwarzweller, eds., *Change in Rural Appalachia* (Philadelphia, University of Pennsylvania Press, 1970).

Rezler, Julius, *Automation and Industrial Labor* (New York, Random House, 1969).

Schwarzweller, Harry K., James S. Brown, and J. J. Mangalam, *Transition: A Case Study of Appalachian Migration* (University Park, Pa., The Pennsylvania State University Press, 1971).

Weller, Jack E., *Yesterday's People* (Lexington, The University Press of Kentucky, 1965).

CHAPTER 17

CONCLUSION ON UNEMPLOYMENT AND UNDEREMPLOYMENT

FRICTIONAL UNEMPLOYMENT

During World War II, even when there was much excess purchasing power in relation to available goods, the official unemployment statistics recorded more than 670,000 unemployed on an annual basis in 1944. Frictions in the labor market caused that much unemployment. Frictional unemployment is caused by a voluntary shifting of jobs, and changes in the demand for labor by individual companies even when the total number of job opportunities is in the balance with the number of job seekers. The magnitude of job shifting is quite large in the United States. The labor accession rate in 1972 in manufacturing averaged 4.4 percent per month and separations averaged 4.2 percent per month. When multiplied by 12, the yearly rates are quite large. With large numbers entering and leaving the work force each year, some people will not immediately be able to find jobs. Also, each year thousands of firms are discontinued or fail. Although the number of new firms generally exceeds the number going out of business, it takes time before some of the workers get shifted. In the meantime, they are frictionally unemployed. Other frictions may develop in the economy to create unemployment. A strike at one location may cause shortages of materials and unemployment elsewhere. Shortages of energy or other types of materials may cause some frictional unemployment also.

An argument has prevailed for years as to how much unemployment can be considered as frictional. The question is an important one, since at some point corrective measures should be taken to reduce the amount of unemployment. In a study published in 1957, Albert Rees analyzed a number of methods of measuring full employment.[1] He pointed out that probably the most widely used method of measuring full employment was to consider the lowest unemployment previously reached in a peacetime year. From 1946 through April 1954, the minimum unemployment for any 12-month period was 2.3 percent of the civilian work force, for the 12 months ending October, 1953. Some criticism could be made that even

[1]Albert Rees, "The Meaning and Measuring of Full Employment," in National Bureau of Economic Research, *The Measurement and Behavior of Unemployment*, (Princeton, Princeton University Press, 1957), pp. 13-62.

2.3 percent is too high a frictional figure, since part of this percent involved unemployment in depressed areas. Obviously, long run depressed area unemployment should not be computed as a part of frictional unemployment.

The failure to reach such a low figure as 2.3 percent in recent years has caused economists to redefine "full employment" to mean an unemployment rate of four percent. This percentage was first used in 1961 as a target proposed by the Council of Economic Advisors under President Kennedy. In its 1962 annual report, the Council claimed that too high a rate of inflation would be necessary to push the unemployment rate below four percent. More recently, in its Annual Report of the Council of Economic Advisors, released in January of 1973, the figure of 4.5 percent for 1973 was quoted as appropriate, considering other economic goals. This figure was criticized as too high in the 1973 Annual Report of the Joint Economic Committee of Congress, which reflected the views of the Democratic majority members. The Council of Economic Advisors defended itself by pointing out that with more young people and women entering the labor market, the rate of unemployment in November, 1972, would have averaged out as 4.4 percent, given the 1955 age-sex composition. The Joint Economic Committee argued, on the other hand, that improved education over a time should lessen unemployment, since the more highly educated experience less unemployment. Similarly, shifts in industry and occupation make 4.0 rather than 4.5 percent a better target.[2]

Robert E. Hall examined the question of why the unemployment rate was high even during a period of brisk demand.[3] He studied unemployment during April, 1969, when the rate of unemployment was 3.5 percent, lower than most months of unemployment in recent years. He discarded the explanation that the chronically unemployed were causing the relatively high percent of unemployment (at full employment). He found that less than seven percent of the unemployed were out of work for 27 or more weeks. Rather, his explanation was that large fractions of some women and blacks experience abnormally frequent changes of jobs with frequent periods of unemployment between jobs. In support of this explanation Charles Holt found that both the quit and layoff rates for blacks is roughly double that of whites, and explains most of the white-black unemployment differential.[4]

[2]For a fuller discussion of the debate between the Council of Economic advisors and the Joint Economic Council, see Daniel J. Balz, "Economic Report/JEC recommendations refuel debate over appropriate full-employment target," *National Journal*, Vol. 5 (March 31, 1973), pp. 443-449.

[3]Robert E. Hall, "Why is the Unemployment Rate So High at Full Employment," *Brookings Papers on Economic Activity*, Vol. 3 (1970), pp. 369-402.

[4]Charles Holt, "Comments and Discussion," in Robert E. Hall, *Ibid.*, p. 406.

LACK OF AGGREGATE DEMAND

BUILT-IN STABILIZERS

All students of unemployment have concluded that a high aggregate demand is essential for full employment. Whenever a recession occurs, unemployment increases. In order to assure adequate demand, three main techniques are used: built-in stabilizers, monetary, and fiscal policy. Built-in stabilizers are those that automatically take effect to aid the economy without waiting for decision-making of any kind when aggregate demand failure causes recessions. One of the important automatic stabilizers is unemployment insurance. The system is already in existence and total benefits become larger when unemployment increases.

Several studies have been made to determine what percentage of wage loss is compensated for by unemployment insurance. To quote from one, Professor Richard Lester analyzed the data from 1948 to 1959.[5] He found that all public programs for unemployment insurance compensated no more than 23 percent of the wage loss from total unemployment. If total and partial unemployment are combined, no more than 18 percent of the wage loss was compensated for. Over the 12-year period the percentage of wage loss compensated for by unemployment insurance did not rise. Although there were extensions of coverage and increases in the duration of unemployment compensation benefits, these apparently were offset by lags in the weekly benefit amount. Lester also analyzed the protection given in 16 different states. In the 1958-1959 recession, New York provided the best protection, with 23 percent of wage loss compensated for. The poorest record was compiled by South Carolina with only 6 percent of wage loss recovered through unemployment compensation. Where such a small percent of the wage-loss is recovered, unemployment insurance is at best a weak built-in stabilizer. On the other hand, the fact that auto and some other workers have unemployment insurance plus supplemental unemployment insurance plans results in a strong stabilizer for some geographic areas.

Tax reductions also aid as built-in stabilizers. Before the withholding provisions were adopted for the federal personal income tax in 1943, the income tax was paid the year after the income was earned. This meant that in a recession year, relatively high taxes might have to be paid after a down-turn in business. Today the withholding provisions provide for immediate personal tax reductions if income drops. Corporation income taxes also decrease as business declines. OASDHI payments may also be considered a built-in stabilizer since these payments provide a cushion in

[5]Richard A. Lester, "The Economic Significance of Unemployment Compensation," *Review of Economics and Statistics*, Vol. 42 (1960), pp. 349-372.

case older workers are laid off. For the two contraction periods of 1949 and 1953-1954, 14 and 89 percent respectively of the fall in national income was offset by the automatic stabilizers (increases in transfer payments and decreases in taxes). The larger figure of 1953-1954 may be attributed to the large decrease in government revenues during this period.[6]

Although built-in stabilizers aid in recessions, recent findings are that these stabilizers prevent the economy from expanding as rapidly as it otherwise might during an upswing. One analysis showed that in the three expansion periods of 1948, 1949-1953, and 1954-1957, the automatic stabilizers increased government income so much that 28 percent of the increase in national income was absorbed by it.[7] That is, for every increase of $1 billion in national income, increases in the automatic stabilizers absorbed $280 million of the $1 billion increase. In future expansions it may be that the government will be required to direct action to offset the deflationary aspects of the built-in stabilizers. Fortunately, however, the built-in stabilizers provide more beneficial results in recessions, but since they compensate for only a part of the loss of income, other solutions have been advocated to go along with them.

MONETARY REMEDIES

In order to increase the gross national product and provide as large an amount of employment as possible, monetary policies have been used to curb both inflation and contraction. Different monetary weapons are used depending on whether it is inflation or contraction that the authorities are fighting. When the economy is faced with inflation, the monetary authorities may attempt to restrict the use of credit. They are able to restrict credit by a number of methods, such as selling government securities, raising the rediscount rate, raising reserve requirements, and tightening requirements for selective types of loans, such as brokers loans.

During a recesssion period, the monetary authorities reverse the processes described above. The appropriate open market policy is to buy government securities to ease credit along with lowering the rediscount rate. Reserve requirements may be lowered as may margin requirements on brokers' loans. Most economists feel that the monetary weapons are not as powerful in controlling a recession as they are in controlling an expansion. To aid in fighting a recession, about the most the monetary authorities can do is to make credit more available, but they cannot guarantee that use will be made of this credit. In an expansion period, the banking system does have a more powerful weapon in restricting credit.

---

[6]M. O. Clement, "The Quantitative Impact of Automatic Stabilizers," *Review of Economics and Statistics*, Vol. 42 (1960), pp. 56-61.
   [7]*Ibid.*

The use of monetary controls has varied over the years. During the 1920's the Federal Reserve authorities began using the controls outlined above, and monetary controls were held in high regard. The advent of the Great Depression demonstrated that monetary policy alone was insufficient, and it fell into disrepute. After World War II, management of the large federal debt was so new that supporting the price of government securities was given a high priority even though this meant buying securities during an inflationary period. The Treasury-Federal Reserve Accord in 1951 permitted the Federal Reserve to operate more independently. Monetary policy came again into its own, and open market operations and rediscount policy has been used regularly since.

EVALUATION OF MONETARY REMEDIES

Professor Milton Friedman has recommended that the money supply be increased by four or five percent per year as an alternative to Federal Reserve discretionary powers. Friedman favors the abolition of the discretionary powers of the Federal Reserve, and replacing them with an automatic system whereby the supply of money increases by a fixed amount annually. Friedman received some support for his automatic proposal from Professor Martin Bronfenbrenner who tested statistically the performance of the discretionary system over what would have been obtained by an automatic increase in the supply of money from 1901 to 1958. He concluded that the automatic system would have worked better than the discretionary system, although the record of the automatic system was less satisfactory after World War II than before. Ralph Young of the Board of Governors of the Federal Reserve System pointed out, though, that the superiority of the automatic system was mainly due to its superior performance during the credit inflation between 1916 and 1921. If these years had been eliminated, the data would support discretionary monetary policy.[8]

A number of economists have pointed out that Friedman's proposal is particularly weak during a period of recession. At that time, fiscal policy may have to be used to curb the recession and the resultant high unemployment going along with it.

Even after the tight monetary policy of 1969, prices rose 5.9 percent in 1970 and unemployment increased from 3.5 percent in 1969 to 4.9 in 1970 due to the recession of the latter year. In the first eight months of 1971, the consumer price index rose 5.1 percent over the 1970 level and unemployment reached 6.1 percent by August of 1971. Clearly, monetary policy (and fiscal policy) was ineffective during this period in reducing either inflation or unemployment. The result was that in August of 1971, President Nixon inaugurated wage-price controls.

[8]Ralph A. Young, "Report of the Commission on Money and Credit, A Commentary," *American Economic Review*, Vol. 52 (Proc., 1962), p. 314.

FISCAL POLICY

The lack of aggregate demand may also be attacked by government fiscal policy. Once a depression has begun, the government will automatically take in less revenue, even at the same tax rates. Since personal, corporate, and other income will have dropped, lower taxes will be paid on the reduced income. A government budget expected to be in balance will thus incur a deficit because of the drop in revenue. The Committee for Economic Development has suggested that such a deficit will provide sufficient cure for recession. In a severe recession some economists would go further and advocate either reducing taxes or increasing government expenditures, or both. Tax reductions can be either directed at increasing consumption or investment, or both. If additional incentives are desired to increase consumption, the personal income tax can be lowered in such a way as to benefit low-income groups the most. If additional incentives are desired to increase investment, taxes on business groups can be reduced.

If the major problem is inflation rather than unemployment, the appropriate fiscal policy is to raise taxes and cut government spending. It is difficult politically to raise taxes. Most economists have contended that a more restrictive monetary and fiscal policy should have been introduced during the late 1960's, but insufficient restraints were imposed and inflation increased form an average annual rate of 1.3 from 1960 to 1965 to 4.3 percent in 1966 through 1969 and higher thereafter.

The heyday of fiscal policy came with tax reductions in 1964. These were instituted even though that year showed a federal deficit of 8.6 billion in 1964. The reason for introducing the cuts was because the upturn following the recession of 1960 had been sluggish. Even though GNP had increased 68 billion in constant dollars from 1961 through 1964, the rate of unemployment from 1961 through 1964 was reduced only from 6.7 percent to 5.2 percent. After the tax cut, unemployment dropped to 4.1 percent by December, 1965. Rather interestingly with the tax cut business expanded at a fast enough rate that increased federal incomes from taxes resulted in a smaller budget deficit in 1965 than 1964, down from 8.6 billion to 2.7 billion, a much lower deficit than prior to the tax cuts. There was some criticism by Leon Keyserling and others that more appropriate fiscal policy in 1964 would have been to increase government expenditures in such areas as health, education, welfare, and other areas of need. Instead, private individuals and corporations benefitted from personal and corporate tax reductions. This argument aside, it was clear that fiscal policy could reduce the amount of unemployment. However, the problem in the 1970's of trying to reduce both unemployment and inflation at the same time has proven much more difficult for economists to solve.

Even though government fiscal policy was successful in the early 1960's, those on the extreme right have been critical of its use. They have reasoned that since individuals cannot continuously go further into debt year after year without finally having to declare bankruptcy, the same thing is true of government. But what is true of an individual is not necessarily true of a national government. Few economists would argue that the budget should be balanced annually. The reason is that inappropriate fiscal policy would have to be applied that would cause a further drop in GNP. In a recession when income is falling, government revenues fall also. If the budget were to be balanced in a recession, either taxes would have to be raised or government spending reduced. Either of these fiscal policies would worsen the recession. In view of the obvious weaknesses of an annually balanced budget, some economists have advocated that the budget be balanced over a period of years rather than one year. In recessions, a budget deficit could be run but would be offset by budget surpluses in prosperous years.

Even budget balancing over a period of years may be too restrictive. It may be that to achieve full employment continuously, the debt may have to grow over a period of years. From December, 1945 through March, 1975 the Federal debt rose from 259 billion to 510 billion. Only a few would content that the increase in debt over the years has been fiscal lunacy. For one thing, more than a fifth of the debt is held in such trust accounts as social security and others. The government really owes this debt to itself. In addition, large sums are held by the Federal Reserve banks that, although privately owned, are run almost as if they were part of the Federal government. Admittedly, there is some burden on interest charges that must be paid on the debt. However, if the debt is held internally, as most of it is in the United States, there is no net burden from interest charges. There is, though, a redistribution of income from the interest charges in favor of the upper income groups who hold the government bonds. Should such redistribution become too unfavorable, it could, of course, be changed through different taxation policies.

It is doubtful that the government will attempt to raise taxes sufficiently to begin paying off the debt. The debt is simply refunded. Thus no burden is involved here. It should also be pointed out that the burden of the interest charges on the debt are relative to the income of the people. Although interest charges have been rising in recent years and impose a higher fiscal cost on the government, they are still only about three percent of GNP.

The debt may cause some burden on future generations in that money taken by the government might have been spent by private individuals to improve the economy. In wartime there obviously is a burden from deficit spending, but this burden is paid for mainly by the generations living during that time in giving up consumer goods for wartime production. In peace-time recessions when government deficits become larger, there is some doubt that private persons would have invested anyway, so that actually the economy is made stronger by government spending rather than weaker.

Given the possibilities of fiscal policy in reducing unemployment, several problems still remain. Discretionary fiscal policy requires Congressional action, which may be slow in coming. Also after Congressional appropriations have been made, projects must be on hand that can almost immediately use the funds. Good administration is obviously necessary for fiscal policy of a government spending type to work.

Recent experience with a government public works program has been favorable. With unemployment still running 5.9 percent in July, 1971, Congress passed the Emergency Employment Act in that month. Four weeks later money was appropriated and checks were ready within a matter of days for state and local government to hire the unemployed. Within six months all of the billion dollars appropriated had been committed and the target of hiring 140,000 had been reached.[9] States with the most unemployment were given larger sums of money than less disadvantaged states. The unemployed received the higher of the applicable minimum wage for the work they performed or the prevailing wage for similar work at their work place. The largest agencies receiving money were city governments, followed by county governments, other agencies, such as Indian reservations, and state agencies. Rather interestingly, only 37 percent of the unemployed hired were disadvantaged, here defined as a jobseeker who was poor and either a member of a minority group, below 22 or above 44, or had less than a high-school education. In criticism of the program, it could be argued that the disadvantaged were more in need of training than of a temporary government job. Also, even though business improved substantially in 1972, by July of that year only 12,000 of those hired for temporary employment had moved into permanent jobs. In spite of the several shortcomings of the program, it may be concluded that the government can inaugurate a temporary employment program with great speed.

A.W. Phillips, an Australian economist, pointed out when prices are rising in a prosperity period, unemployment tends to be low. Vice versa when unemployment is high, prices tend to fall. Unfortunately during the past few years, high rates of unemployment and inflation have occurred at the same time.

Both monetary and fiscal policy have the disadvantage of promoting inflation when attempts are made to reduce unemployment. Also they tend to increase unemployment when the policies are directed at fighting inflation. In view of the failure of monetary and fiscal policy to adequately reduce either unemployment or inflation in the earlier 1970's, a different approach of wage-price controls was inaugurated by the Nixon administration in August of 1971.

---

[9] Sar Levitan, "The Emergency Employment Act: An Assessment," *Manpower*, Vol. 4, No. 12 (Dec., 1972), pp. 22-27.

WAGE-PRICE CONTROLS

In August of 1971, wage-price controls were introduced by the Nixon administration to curtail inflation. At the same time, tax cuts were granted businessmen to increase investment and hopefully decrease unemployment. The wage-price controls were imposed in the hope that lower price increases would be an inducement to labor unions to reduce wage demands, which in turn would place less pressure for price increases. In 1972, with GNP in constant dollars expanding at an excellent rate of 6.1 percent, unemployment dropped from 5.9 in 1971 to 5.1 by the end of 1972, and the consumer price index for 1972 showed a rise of only 3.3 percent compared with 5.8 percent for 1970. Wage-price controls appeared to be working.

The wage-price controls introduced in 1971 were never intended to be permanent. They have several serious weaknesses. One is that they result in a poor resource allocation. A pure market economy is supposed to guide production into areas of the largest consumer demand. The higher consumer demand makes for higher prices and profits, which are then reinvested in the products demanded. Price controls hold down profits in expanding industries, and, therefore, prices and profits can give no indication of which industries should be expanding. Price controls may even cut into profits so much that production is curtailed rather than expanded. Similarly, wage controls prohibit some rises in wages that may be needed to attract workers into expanding industries. Due to the weaknesses of wage-price controls, the strict controls were removed in early 1973 at a time when business was booming. The results were that although unemployment had been reduced to 4.5 percent in October of 1973, the consumer price index for that year increased 8.8 percent, the largest increase in 27 years. Neither monetary and fiscal policy nor wage-price controls had been able to reduce either prices or unemployment to adequate levels.

Some economists contend that wage-price controls will not work simply because there is too much monopoly in business and labor. If monopoly is the cause of the problem, then the appropriate action may be vigorous antitrust enforcement.

PUBLIC EMPLOYMENT OFFICES

Regardless of the causes of unemployment, improved employment offices may aid in reducing unemployment. Until the 1930's, employment offices in the United States were almost exclusively privately owned and operated. Prior to the depression of the 1930's, Paul Douglas estimated that there were 3,000 to 4,000 private fee-charging employment agencies in the United States, or more than double the number of public offices that existed in 1937, New York City alone had 1,150 fee-charging offices in 1930, and Chicago had approximately 400 offices.[10]

Although private placement offices have provided services to workers in finding jobs, some weaknesses of private agencies were quite apparent in the 1920's and 1930's. In some cases, employment offices had agreements with employers to fire workers regularly so that new employees would have to be hired. Then the fee was split between the employment agency and the employer. High fees were sometimes exacted for finding jobs. In Cincinnati, for example, the average fee of private agencies for higher-paid clerical jobs amounted on the average to 60 percent of the first month's salary. Other abuses were failure to make adequate refunds if jobs were not obtained, rendering of inadequate service, misrepresenting working conditions, and selling jobs to the highest bidder. Since a system of public employment offices might eliminate some if not most of the abuses of private employment agencies, a number of states and municipalities have at one time or another created public employment offices.

At the federal level prior to World War I the federal government had a federal office to provide job information to immigrants arriving in New York City.[11] A limited public employment service was instituted during World War I. In 1919 the Keynon-Nolan bill was introduced for a federal employment service but it did not pass. In criticism of the bill one witness argued that the director of such a service would have so much power that he could elect a President within two years of coming into power. A National Association of Manufacturer's spokesman feared that the agency would not remain neutral, but favor strikers by shutting off the supply of workers and strikebreakers during a strike. The main thrust of the opposition was that the proposal was a guise to operate the labor market differently for the purpose of limiting the freedom of choice of American enterprise and restricting the scope of state governments in relation to the federal government.

The depression of the early 1930's finally brought a public employment service into existence in the United States, many years after that of other industrialized nations. New Zealand had inaugurated its system in 1891, Norway and Sweden in 1906, Great Britain in 1909, the Union of South Africa in 1910, France in 1911, Argentina and Denmark in 1913, Germany in 1914, Hungary and Netherlands in 1916, and Canada in 1918.[12] The implementing legislation in the United States came in 1933 with the passage of the Wagner-Peyser Act. This act provided for a matching of federal with state funds if the states would operate public

---

[10]Paul Douglas and Aaron Director, *The Problem of Unemployment* (New York, Macmillan, 1931), p. 266.

[11]Timothy Larkin, "40 Years of Healing Community Injuries," *Manpower*, Vol. 5 No. 6 (June, 1973), p. 19.

[12]*Ibid.*, p. 18.

employment offices. Later, when the Social Security Act was passed in 1935, it became almost mandatory for the states to create public employment offices, for unemployment insurance could be paid only to those who registered for work at a public employment office. Funds were allocated from Social Security taxes along with Wagner-Peyser matching funds to pay for the costs of the public system. During World War II, the entire system was taken over by the Federal government but was returned again to the states in November of 1946. At the same time, the matching system of the Wagner-Peyser Act came to an end, and the system was financed entirely by federal grants. A United States Employment Service existed within the U. S. Department of Labor to develop and prescribe minimum standards of efficiency for the operation of the state-managed employment offices.

After World War II, the employment service attempted to find jobs for firms who listed openings for them. In many instances during recessions (1954, 1958, 1960), staff had to be diverted from the employment function to that of servicing unemployment insurance claims. The Employment Service over the years began to provide functions other than merely job placement and unemployment insurance administration.[13] Counseling was developed particularly for those about to enter the labor market. Aptitude tests also were given to this group. Special services were provided such groups as veterans, older workers, and professional and technical workers although not much effort was placed on most of these activities. Research was conducted on trends in employment in various industries and occupations. A Dictionary of Occupational Titles was compiled that identifies, describes, and classifies more than 30,000 jobs. Also a small program of aiding employers in solving manpower problems was instituted, along with helping union apprenticeship programs with selection and aptitude tests and aiding other government agencies and community organizations in the area of job information, area redevelopment, and training of workers. Main emphasis, however, was placed on referring clients to employers who listed job openings.

For a decade or so after World War II, the Employment Service became rather stagnant. Not only did placements not keep pace with increases in the labor force, but absolute placements actually declined. The budget for employment services was less in 1960 than it had been in 1948. Under President Kennedy, the scope and functions of the United States Employment Offices were expanded. In his Economic Message to Congress in 1961, President Kennedy suggested that expanded counseling and placement be provided workers in urban depressed areas and rural areas of chronic underemployment. He also suggested more services for those losing jobs through automation, older workers, and recent graduates from colleges and high schools.

[13]William Haber and Daniel H. Kruger, *The Role of the United States Employment Service in a Changing Economy* (Kalamazoo, Upjohn Institute, 1964), pp. 41-58.

Since the early 1960's, an increased effort of the Employment Service was directed at aiding the disadvantaged. Services to these groups increased to such an extent that by fiscal 1972 the disadvantaged constituted nearly half of those counselled and about a fourth of all nonfarm job placements.[14] In 1964, a national network of Youth Opportunity Centers were set up within the employment service to be located near but not in central-city ghettos. These centers not only provided job referral services, but counselled youth, and made referrals to such government programs as training under MDTA and the Job Corps, along with referral for placement in the Neighborhood Youth Corps. In 1965, the employment service inaugurated a Human Resource Development program to aid the disadvantaged. An out-reach program was instituted, along with counselling, job development, and placement geared to serving the needs of this group.

In 1970 an experiment was conducted in Buffalo, New York, to determine what kinds of handicaps existed among potential unemployment insurance exhaustees and what types of special services would prove the most effective in restoring them to the employed work force.[15] The findings of this study were that the unemployed found counselling to be more useful than training.

Concentrating aid on the disadvantaged caused a number of problems. Although federal obligations to state Employment Services increased from $147 million in fiscal 1962 to $379 million in fiscal 1972, nonfarm job placements dropped from a peak of 6.6 million in fiscal 1963 to a low of 3.4 million in fiscal 1971. From 1966 to 1970 when the number of nonfarm jobs rose about 10 percent, Employment Service nonfarm placements dropped about 30 percent. Contacts with employers dropped 20 percent during this period. There was criticism by some employers that the Employment Service was placing so much emphasis on attempting to find lower level jobs for the disadvantaged that the Service was neglecting placement for higher skilled jobs.[16]

Contrary to the above criticism that too much emphasis has been placed on aiding the disadvantaged, a 1971 report prepared by the Lawyers Committee for Civil Rights and the Urban Coalition found that "policy toward the disadvantaged was never really embraced or implemented by tradition-minded state officials who remained strongly oriented toward employers' needs." The findings of a San Francisco area study are pertinent here.[17] A San Francisco poverty area experimental adult opportunity center, opened in May of 1965, was handicapped by

[14]*Manpower Report of the President*, 1973, p. 57.

[15]Murray Dorkin and Herman S. Solomon, *Project Spruce* (Albany, New York, Department of Labor, Division of Research and Statistics, Labor Research Report No. 8, 1973).

[16]Edward J. Giblin and Louis Levine, *Employer Services Activities and Manpower Policy* (Grand Rapids, Michigan Employment Security Commission, 1972), p. 13.

[17]Miriam Johnson, *Counter Point — A Changing Employment Service* (Salt Lake City, Olympus Publishing Co., 1973), pp. 63-90.

lack of job opportunities in the area. This office found that group counselling, group information giving, group selection processes and group
teaching were better tools than one-to-one individual counselling.
Although some job training programs were allocated to this office, one
criticism was that the training programs were for a six-month period, too
short a period to develop usable skills in individuals who had virtually no
skills at all. Remedial education and language training was provided. Unfortunately, the number of training slots reached only 5 to 7 percent of the
applicants. Due to the paucity of job orders, employment service personnel begain using past inactive orders as a guide to where jobs might be
found. A volunteer tutorial program with at least 80 volunteer trainers
aided well over a thousand learners. The office provided a free telephone
message service for those having no telephone. One interviewer provided
an early morning bus service with his car. Although the program was
viewed as innovative and provided new services, Miriam Johnson was
critical because no study was ever made into what was learned from this
program. Furthermore, the program had no significant effect on manpower programs and delivery systems. She was also critical that the office
had few aids for such groups as drug, alcoholic, and gambling addicts. Her
conclusion on the experimental center was that "it could do many
remarkable things, but in the final reckoning it could not change the
world for the disadvantaged, and it could not change the disadvantaged
for the world."[18]

A number of new innovations have been implemented by the
Employment Service in the 1970's. The Employment Service Automatic
Reporting System (ESARS) was installed in 1970 to include a compilation
of more services provided individuals. However, Miriam Johnson has
been critical of ESARS for not making an adequate analysis of the quality
of jobs, the occupational span, or the range of concentrations in which job
orders and placements occur.[19] Furthermore, ESARS did not include a
compilation of many services provided.

Another innovation has been that of the Job Bank, which provides a
day-to-day listing of all job openings. The Job Bank was begun in
Baltimore in 1968 and has expanded rapidly since then, so that by fiscal
1971 it was in existence in over 100 metropolitan areas in 43 states. The
listing of jobs is circulated to such groups as welfare agencies, community
action agencies, high schools, and other public groups. At first the Job
Bank was used only for local jobs, but it has been expanded since then to
several regional and state listings. An interstate program still needs to be
implemented. Due to a lack of interstate information, needed information
from one area to another is not forthcoming. For example, in Barrow,
Alaska, where few jobs are available, Miriam Johnson reported that the

[18]Ibid., p. 90.
[19]Ibid., p. 18.

office did not have a single piece of information about jobs elsewhere.[20] The most recent development is to provide a computerized matching of jobseekers with jobs. This last program is still in an experimental stage.

Joseph C. Ullman and George P. Huber in a study of local Job Banks concluded that the system had not reached the goals of (1) achieving more efficient man-job matching, (2) improving manpower service to the disadvantaged, (3) reducing frictional unemployment, and (4) maintaining or increasing ES volume on overall activity measures.[21] On a fifth goal of "providing more flexible, more rapid and more direct manpower services to the employers and workers," they concluded that the local Job Banks were not providing more rapid service. They could not define "flexibility" to analyze the impact here and they obtained no data on whether the system was more direct. Another criticism of the Job Bank, made by Miriam Johnson, was that the data had not been assembled to clarify or synthesize the local labor market or identify skill shortages.[22]

In analyzing the best practices of the local Job Banks, Ullman and Huber made eight recommendations: (1) both order-taking and referral units should be organized in a specialized fashion, (2) agencies should be encouraged to maintain an adequate employer relations effort; (3) the Employment Service should minimize the involvement of other agencies in Job Banks (including community action agencies); (4) each interviewer should have his or her own Job Bank book or video display device; (5) first-day referrals should be provided to the greatest possible extent; (6) agencies should be encouraged to operate a relatively large number of local offices within each area; (7) procedures for verifying referrals should be reexamined as present telephone verification systems were not working well; and (8) data should be collected and analyzed to determine the effect of the organizational changes recommended by Ullman and Huber.[23]

An Executive Order of the President (No. 11958), effective September, 1971, required a listing of job openings by all private firms receiving federal prime contracts or first-tier subcontracts amounting to $10,000 or more that generate as much as 400 man-days of employment. Some firms have been reluctant to list their job openings with the Employment Service since applications at the plant have provided sufficient manpower. However, awareness of what jobs are available may provide the Employment Service with better information for counselling and training programs.

Recognition of weaknesses in the job placement function in the 1970's resulted in more concentration here so that reports for fiscal 1972

[20]*Ibid.*, p. 169.
[21]Joseph C. Ullman and George P. Huber, *The Local Job Bank Program* (Lexington, Mass., D. C. Heath, 1973), pp. 3-4.
[22]Miriam Johnson, *op. cit.*, pp. 154-161.
[23]Ullman and Huber, *op. cit.*, pp. 20-21.

showed the first increase in a decade in job placements, from 3.4 million in fiscal 1971 to 3.8 million a year later. Whether the improved placement is at the expense of more service to the disadvantaged remains to be seen.

A Special Labor Force Report of 3.3 million unemployed during 1970 indicated that the most frequently used job-seeking method by the unemployed by far was direct application to prospective employers, used by 71 percent of the unemployed.[24] The second most frequent method was the use of public employment offices (39 percent), followed by placed or answered newspaper advertisements (23 percent), aid from friends or relatives (14.3 percent), a private employment agency (10 percent) and other methods (7 percent). Data in 1971 showed about the same picture. Teenagers tended to use public and private employment offices less often and direct application more frequently than those in the prime age groups. Blacks used the public employment offices more than whites, and men used such offices more than women. White-collar workers used public employment offices less frequently than blue-collar workers. Unfortunately, this survey did not indicate the number of times each method was used, so that data could not be assembled on the effectiveness or the cost of each method.

In an analysis of printouts for seven cities in 1971, Miriam Johnson found that placements in all seven were concentrated in a few occupations, mostly in the lowest skill, least stable, and lowest wage secondary labor market. She claimed that it was a safe assumption that the function of the employment service in those seven cities reflected the national picture.[25] Certainly more data on this facet of the employment service is necessary.

CONCLUSION ON PUBLIC EMPLOYMENT OFFICES

Over the years, the public employment service has been faced with severe competition in placement from union hiring halls, federal, state and local civil service commissions, company personnel departments, private employment agencies, temporary employment services, professional and trade associations, high school and college employment services.[26] Given other alternatives to employment, some may conclude that the public employment service could be abolished. On the other hand, the public employment service provides services and placement where other agencies are not deeply involved. More adequate information on labor markets and additional services to the disadvantaged are two functions not

[24]Thomas F. Bradshaw, "Jobseeking Methods Used by Unemployed Workers," *Monthly Labor Review*, Vol. 96, No. 2 (February 1973), pp. 35-40.

[25]Miriam Johnson, *op. cit.*, p. 158.

[26]Garth Mangum, "Afterword," in Miriam Johnson, *op. cit.*, p. 187.

handled well by other agencies, or by the public employment service, for that matter. However, improvements in the public employment service in these areas may be made without too large additional outlays.[27]

COOPERATIVE AREA MANPOWER PLANNING SYSTEM (CAMPS)

The multiplicity of agencies dealing with manpower programs caused seven federal agencies in 1967 to sign an agreement to create a workable and comprehensive manpower planning system. The seven agencies involved were the Department of Labor, Welfare Administration, Vocational Rehabilitation, Vocational Education, the Office of Economic Opportunity, the Economic Development Administration, and the Department of Housing and Urban Development. Within a year, four other Federal agencies had joined the system: Bureau of Indian Affairs, the Water Pollution Control Administration, the Department of Agriculture, and the Civil Service Commission. At the local level, there were local area planning committees which assessed the needs of the area for manpower and supportive services. The local plan was passed on to the state committee, which put the local plans into a workable state plan that was then forwarded to a regional CAMPS committee. There was then a national CAMPS committee to oversee the operations of the entire system.

The CAMPS program never achieved its purpose of creating a coordinated manpower system. Ruttenberg and Gotchess, in 1970, cited four defects in the program.[28] The failure to implement comprehensive planning resulted in a high turn-over of local membership. Secondly, CAMPS had no real authority to allocate resources to manpower programs except for the MDTA institutional program and a part of the OJT program. Since most of the allocations of funds was made to separate agencies from Washington, there was little that local committees could do except decide whether one type of training class or another should be offered. The unwillingness of the various agencies to submit their programs for CAMPS evaluation left little for CAMPS to do. Thirdly, there was little urgency for comprehensive planning because programs were so small in relation to need that all the projects appeared worthwhile. Lastly, CAMPS should have been concerned with a design of programs rather than with operations. Ruttenberg and Gutchess concluded that the CAMPS program was merely a paper conplilation of plans of the various agencies that was read by no one.

Dissatisfaction with CAMPS has led others to suggest that a single manpower agency is needed. Jakubauskas and Palomba have suggested

[27]*Ibid.*, p. 186.

[28]Stanley H. Ruttenberg and Jocelyn Gutchess, *Manpower Challenge of the 1970's: Institutions and Social Change* (Baltimore, Johns Hopkins Press, 1970), pp. 56-63.

that after such a step has been taken, a single formula should be developed for allocating funds based on relative sized of labor forces, unemployment rates, and the proportions of disadvantaged people.[29] The formula should have some flexibility to reflect changes in the national economy. They also recommended that there should be more state and local participation in the key planning and administration of a manpower program.

In order to make CAMPS more than merely an interagency information exchange, funds for governors' and mayors' manpower staffs were almost doubled from fiscal 1970 to 1972. By 1972, the number of state and local manpower staffs came to 1,000, about double that of two years previous. In fiscal 1973, the number of staff increased to 1,200, and a few test areas were selected to develop pilot comprehensive manpower projects under the authority of local elected officials.

COMPREHENSIVE EMPLOYMENT AND TRAINING ACT OF 1973

In 1973, an act was passed to include manpower programs that had formerly operated under authority of the MDTA Act and Economic Opportunity Act and the Emergency Employment Act. Numerous categorical programs were eliminated and in their place a decentralized program was inaugurated. Financial assistance is given to state and local governments for planning and operating comprehensive manpower programs. Direct assistance is given to states, to cities of a certain size, and certain rural areas. Public employment may be provided where unemployment is seven percent or more. The act also established a National Commission for Manpower Policy. Since federal money is involved, the Secretary of Labor may disapprove of a program but only after an opportunity for a hearing is provided. His veto is also subject to judicial review in the appropriate court of appeals.

Summary and Conclusion

Even at full employment, some unemployment exists, called frictional unemployment. This type of unemployment is due to layoffs and job quitting and the time interval it takes to find a new job. The relatively high unemployment in the United States has caused many economists to set four percent as the full employment frictional amount of unemployment,

[29]Edward B. Jakubauskas and Neil A. Palomba, *Manpower Economics* (Reading, Massachusetts, Addison-Wesley Co., 1973), pp. 254-262.

but public policy has been unable to reduce unemployment even to this amount in recent years without causing an unacceptable amount of inflation.

Aggregate demand is obviously important in improving the employment picture. Built-in stabilizers automatically work to brake a recession, but they also tend to inhibit growth during the early phases of a recovery. Monetary policy has been used as a tool for years to control inflations and stimulate business in a recession. The major argument here has been whether to use discretionary monetary policy or simply increase the money supply at a fixed amount each year. Discretionary policy has been used since the introduction of the Federal Reserve system. Monetary policy in fighting inflation has the disadvantage of promoting unemployment.

Fiscal policy has also been used in the past, both to control inflations and reduce unemployment. Monetary policy has an advantage over fiscal policy in that actions can be taken almost at once by the Federal Reserve authorities whereas discretionary fiscal policy depends upon acts of Congress. The Emergency Employment Act of 1971 has demonstrated that employment by the federal government can be increased quite quickly, once the appropriate legislation has been passed. Fiscal policy, though, has the same disadvantage in curtailing employment when inflation is being fought and encouraging inflation whenever unemployment is being fought. The failure of both monetary and fiscal policy to cure either inflation or unemployment during the early 1970's resulted in temporary wage-price controls being imposed. These controls did not work well either.

A federally subsidized Employment Service run by the states was begun in the United States in 1933. The Service was able to find some jobs for people in the 1930's and more during World War II, but in the post-war period placement declined. In the 1960's much effort was placed on providing services for the disadvantaged. A Jobs Bank has aided in placing of workers, but a computerized system of matching jobs with people is still in the experimental stage. Improved evaluation of the various services of the Employment Service is still needed.

An attempt was made to provide for a comprehensive manpower service through CAMPS. Later a decentralized program was inaugurated by the Comprehensive Employment and Training Act of 1973.

Due to the recession of 1974-1975, the unemployment rate has climbed to over eight percent (January, 1975). In early 1975, both President Ford and Congress were busy preparing programs to combat the large amount of unemployment

Bibliography

Giblin, Edward J. and Lewis Levine, *Employer Services Activities and Manpower Policy* (Grand Rapids, Michigan, Michigan Employment Security Commission, 1972).

Haber, William and Daniel H. Kruger, *The Role of the United States Employment Service in a Changing Economy* (Kalamazoo, Upjohn Institute, 1964).

Jakubauskas, Edward B. and Neil A. Palomba, *Manpower Economics* (Reading, Mass., Addison-Wesly, 1973).

Johnson, Miriam, *Counter Point—A Changing Employment Service* (Salt Lake City, Olympus Publishing Co., 1973).

Ruttenberg, Stanley H. and Jocelyn Gutchess, *Manpower Challenge in the 1970's* (Baltimore, Johns Hopkins Press, 1970).

Ullman, Joseph C. and George P. Huber, *The Local Job Bank Program* (Lexington, Massachusetts, D.C. Heath, 1973.).

CHAPTER 18

UNEMPLOYMENT INSURANCE: HISTORY COVERAGE, ELIGIBILITY, AND ADMINISTRATION

Some unemployment probably will remain, even though some of it could be alleviated. Our concern here is what type of programs, if any, should be provided for the unemployed. In past centuries, private or public charitable organizations sometimes looked after those needing care. Unemployment was considered a personal fault, and the doctrine of individualism taught that any person could find a job if enough initiative were used. Consequently, little was done for the unemployed, most of whom were considered shiftless and no better than tramps. Eventually, as more and more social scientists studied the problem of unemployment, it became increasingly clear to them that other causes included economic depressions, secular decline in certain industries, bankruptcies, seasonal declines, and the like. The change in emphasis in the causes of unemployment called for better remedial methods.

Some English trade unions paid unemployment benefits early in their history. In the United States, however, only a few labor unions paid unemployment benefits. It was reported in 1930 that only 13 national or international labor unions ever had a system of unemployment insurance, and that all but four of the plans had been discontinued. The union membership covered by the four plans in the United States was 1,320, and $13,613 was paid in benefits in 1928. Some local unions, as contrasted to nationals formulated systems of unemployment insurance on their own, but in 1928 only about 37 local unions with a membership of 33,400 had such insurance. These locals paid $236,000 in unemployment benefits.[1] Private employers might possibly have solved the problem by voluntarily covering their own employees, but too few employers in the United States provided unemployment benefits. Some 22 plans jointly financed by employers and employees covering 65,000 persons were in existence in 1928, along with 13 plans financed solely by the employer and covering 13,000 employees.[2] Coverage was so small that most of the students of the problem looked elsewhere for a solution. Private unemployment insurance generally has not been advocated as an alternate solution to

[1]Bryce M. Stewart, *Unemployment Benefits in the United States* (New York, Little & Ives Co., 1930), p. 201.
[2]*Ibid.*, pp. 201-202.

government insurance. Although private insurance works well for such types of risks as death, fires, accidents, and the like, the greater risks of insuring against unemployment caused private insurance companies not to handle this type of insurance. It appeared to most students of the problem in the United States that some form of unemployment insurance adopted by the government would be superior to any other method. Experience from abroad tended to support this viewpoint.

Granted that some form of government intervention is necessary to provide unemployment insurance, the question remains whether the federal government should administer the system, or whether it should be the province of state governments. A third alternative is a mixed system of joint federal and state control. Prior to the passage of the Federal Social Security Act of 1935, few states had experimented with unemployment insurance laws. The first law went into effect in Wisconsin in 1932. Other states were reluctant to pass such legislation for fear of putting themselves at a disadvantage taxwise compared with other states. A Washington state law was voided, and a Utah law never went into effect. Four other states had passed unemployment insurance laws prior to the federal act, but these were all passed in anticipation of the federal law. Competition between states to keep taxes low provided too great a hurdle to overcome so far as state legislation of this type was concerned.[3]

At the national level, first notice of unemployment insurance came about when a Socialist representative in Congress in 1916 introduced a resolution for a commission to draft an unemployment insurance bill. At the hearings, several persons testified in favor of such a bill, but Samuel Gompers, president of the American Federation of Labor, argued that the system should be voluntary rather than compulsory. In 1928 another Socialist, Victor Berger, introduced an unemployment insurance bill, but this bill was never reported out of the Committee of the Judiciary. The advent of the Great Depression caused more concern about unemployment, and the 1932 platform of the Democratic Party called for adoption of a compulsory federal law. The American Federation of Labor in 1932 also reversed its position to that of favoring such a law. Finally, in 1935, Congress passed the Social Security Act, which provided for a federal tax on payrolls to finance unemployment insurance but with state administration of the system.

THE SOCIAL SECURITY ACT OF 1935

The Social Security Act provided that a one percent tax be levied on covered employers in 1936, two percent in 1937, and three percent thereafter. In covered employment, the government taxed all employers

[3]Eveline M. Burns, "Unemployment Compensation in the United States," *International Labour Review*, Vol. 37 (1938), p. 585.

who hired eight or more employees on at least one day of 20 weeks per year. An amendment in 1939 made the tax applicable only to the first $3,000 of employee earnings, on the ground that the tax on higher paid employees was too high in relation to possible benefits received.

If the states passed an acceptable unemployment compensation act, employers of the state were permitted to credit against what they owed the federal government any sums they had paid to their state unemployment insurance system up to 90 percent of the federal tax. The federal government receives 0.5 percent (formerly 0.3 percent), and it has used this money partly to reimburse the states for costs arising from administering the system. Since all employers were required to pay the federal tax, all the states found it worthwhile to pass an unemployment insurance law. Otherwise, the federal government would have collected the tax without paying any benefits to the state. In order to build an adequate fund in the states, the federal government required that no payments be made from state funds for two years.

All the funds collected by the state must be sent to the Secretary of the Treasury of the United States, who then deposits this money in the Unemployment Trust Fund. The Secretary keeps as much cash on hand as he thinks necessary to meet the costs of paying unemployment benefits, and the remainder he invests in United States bonds or in obligations which are guaranteed by the United States government. It was thought wiser to have the money invested thus than to permit the states discretion on investments, some of which may have proved to be unsafe.

A further federal requirement is that benefits must be paid through state public employment offices or such other agencies as the Social Security Board may approve. Before the passage of the Social Security Act, many states did not have such offices. The authors of the act felt that an adequate unemployment insurance system should be supplemented by adequate public employment offices, so that those workers applying for unemployment insurance would at the same time be given access to information on where to find another job. In several states, the Social Security Board prevented the payment of unemployment compensation through relief offices,[4] and required that all payments be made through genuine employment offices.

COVERAGE

When the Social Security Act was passed in 1935, many groups were not covered under the act. Major extensions of coverage came in 1954 with

---

[4]Raymond C. Atkinson, *The Federal Role in Unemployment Compensation Administration* (Washington, D.C., Social Science Research Council, Committee on Social Security, 1941), p. 37.

the inclusion of employers having four or more rather than eight or more employees (effective January 1, 1956). Federal civilian employees were covered effective January 1, 1955, as were ex-servicemen in 1958. With later added coverage by a number of individual states, it was estimated that as of January 1, 1965, 15.5 million employees out of 61 million employees were excluded under the unemployment insurance program.[5] Public law 91-373 in 1970, the Unemployment Security Amendments, added coverage of another 4.75 million jobs effective January 1, 1972.[6] The added coverage came in the areas of small firms, non-profit educational, hospital, and other charitable organizations, state hospitals and institutions of higher learning, some outside salesmen, some agricultural procession workers and citizens employed outside the United States by American employers, unless the location of the employment is in Canada or the Virgin Islands.

With the federal expansion to state hospitals and institutions of higher learning, ten states, in amending their law to conform with federal law, added coverage of state employees. As of January, 1975, 28 states cover all their state employees by mandatory coverage. Another 9 states made coverage elective. For local employees, only six states cover all their employees under a mandatory system and 22 other states cover some of their local employees on an elective basis. Statistics from covered states show that while unemployment among such governmental groups is small, it is substantial enough to call for some protection of these employees. Unemployment costs for government employees should be low due to low unemployment. Since state and local groups have to pay only the cost of those becoming unemployed rather than a payroll tax, it has been argued that all government employees should be covered. However, the lack of state and local funds has inhibited adequate coverage of these groups.

Some domestic help is covered in New York, the District of Columbia, and Hawaii. Only 12 states covered domestic servants in college clubs or fraternities as of January, 1973. Effective January 1, 1972 some individuals engaged in agricultural processing activities were covered, but farm labor itself is still generally excluded.[7] Other countries have successfully covered agricultural workers. Great Britain, for example, has included such workers since 1936.[8]

[5]Unemployment Insurance Review, U. S. Department of Labor, Vol. 14, No. 1 (January, 1967), p. 12.

[6]Joseph A. Hickey, "A Report on State Unemployment Insurance Laws," Monthly Labor Review, Vol. 95, No. 1 (January, 1972), p. 40.

[7]For a study of the possibility of covering farm labor, see "Report of the Second Meeting of the Federal Advisory Council on Unemployment Insurance," Washington: U. S. Department of Labor, Manpower Administration, 1972, pp. 25-28.

[8]Comparison of State Unemployment Insurance Laws, No. U-141, Washington, D.C., U. S. Department of Labor, Bureau of Employment Security (January 1, 1966), p. CT-1.

The exclusion of small employers was gradually eliminated until January 1, 1972 when employers of one or more employees were covered provided that the employees worked any 20 days or more in a calendar year, each day being in a different week. An alternative requirement to the 20 days is that the employer pay $1,500 or more in wages. Eight states have more liberal coverage.[9] Originally nonprofit organizations were exempt from coverage, but some of these were covered, effective January 1, 1972.

A particularly knotty problem of coverage arises in the case of seasonal workers. Some seasonal workers are automatically excluded by the exemption on agricultural works, and other are excluded because they have failed to work long enough to qualify to meet the minimum requirements for coverage. Ida C. Merriam felt that exclusions for casual labor may be justified, but she maintained that the arguments for exemptions of seasonal workers are less worthy.[10] One argument for not covering seasonal workers is that they are already compensated for unemployment by reason of higher base rates during the operating season. However, some seasonal workers receive quite low wages. Another argument against coverage is that if seasonal employment is particularly important in a state, heavy drains on the unemployment insurance fund might result. The system might be weakened so much that insufficient money would be available to protect against cyclical unemployment. Since many states limit the benefits and duration to past earnings, there is less drain on the fund from seasonal employment than would occur if benefits and duration were not so limited. The argument that benefit payments to seasonal workers will subsidize and thus encourage seasonal operations may be countered by the argument that with an exemption employers may curtail normal operations in order to be exempt.

In most states no distinction is made in determining an individual's benefit rights between wages received from a covered employer whose operations are seasonal in character and those received in employment not regarded as seasonal. Fourteen states have separate provisions. The most frequent provision, by six of the 14 states, stipulates that wage credits earned in seasonal employment are available for payments of benefits only for weeks of employment in the benefit year that fall within the operating period of the employer or industry where they are earned.

For states having seasonal exclusions, the federal agency administering the federal provisions of the law recommended that seasonal workers who normally and regularly obtain off-season work each year be covered when they fail to obtain their anticipated off-season work. Similarly, they

[9]*Comparison of State Unemployment Insurance Laws,* Washington: Unemployment Insurance Service, U. S. Department of Labor Comparison Revision, No. 1 (August 31, 1972), p. 1-2.

[10]Ida C. Merriam, "Seasonal Workers and Unemployment Compensation," *Social Security,* Vol. 1, No. 9, (September, 1938), pp. 8-15.

recommend that employees who normally are employed the year round in seasonal industries, such as watchmen, clerks, maintenance men, salesmen, and the like, should be covered regardless of the exemption of other workers in the industry.[11] Certain employers favor covering seasonal workers in order to supplement the wages of their workers and provide a stand-by labor force for them.[12]

Miscellaneous exclusions from coverage include insurance agents (45 states), real estate agents (33 states), casual labor not in the course of the employer's business (32 states), part-time service for nonprofit organizations exempt from the federal income tax (34 states), and students working for schools (47 states).[13]

Due to the recession of 1974, a bill was passed, effective after December 31, 1974, that would provide up to 26 weeks of unemployment benefits for about 12 million persons formerly not covered by unemployment insurance — primarily farm workers, domestics, and state and local government employees. Payments are only to be made through March 31, 1976.

SUMMARY ON COVERAGE

In 1935, large numbers of employees were excluded from the unemployment sections of the Social Security Act mainly because of the fear of administrative difficulties in covering small employers and other groups. Since 1935, the trend has been toward more coverage, but in 1973 about one of every six workers was still not covered under unemployment insurance (12.5 million of 79.4 million jobs). The largest exclusions are state and local employees, domestic service, and farm workers. In view of the lack of logical arguments against coverage, it would appear the coverage should be extended to more groups in the future.

ELIGIBILITY

MINIMUM EARNINGS AND EMPLOYMENT

Before workers are eligible for unemployment compensation, some states require that the worker shall have worked a certain length of time and all

[11]*Standards and Procedures for the Compensation of Seasonal Unemployment*, Memorandum No. 11 (Washington, D.C., Federal Security Agency, Social Security Board, Bureau of Employment Security, 1940), pp. 8-9.

[12]*Seasonal Workers in California*, State of California, Department of Employment, Bulletin No. 24 (1947), p. 16.

[13]*Comparison of State Unemployment Insurance Laws* (Washington, D.C., U. S. Department of Labor, Unemployment Insurance Service, Comparison Revision No. 2, January 1973), Table 103, pp. 1-19.

require that a worker shall have earned a certain minimum amount in wages. By such requirements, casual laborers and workers entering the labor market for the first time are eliminated from coverage. The unemployment insurance fund is also protected to the extent that at least a certain amount of money is paid into the fund before it is withdrawn in the form of benefits. Nine states have a flat amount that must be earned, ranging from $300 to $1200. An obvious result of this eligibility requirement is that high wage workers can qualify by working only a few days. Six of the nine states protect against this contingency by requiring work in several quarters. Twenty-eight other states require that some multiple of weekly benefits or wages be earned before benefits are paid. The number of these states are about equally divided between those requiring some multiple of higher quarters wages ranging from 1-3/8 to 1-1/2 and others requiring a certain multiple of the weekly benefit amount, ranging from 21 to 40. Eleven other states require that minimum amounts be earned for a period ranging from 14 to 20 weeks. All but eight states require that the earnings be in at least two different quarters. In addition, 29 states require some employment in the preceeding benefit year. Five other states require certain amounts of work subsequent to the date of the last valid claim, and four other states have additional requirements.

The minimum earning eligibility requirement eliminates a significant number of people from unemployment compensation. California, for example, reported that from 1938 through 1952, 15 percent of all claimants were denied benefits on grounds of insufficient or no earnings.[14] New workers coming into the labor force for the first time are obviously disqualified from unemployment benefits by the earnings requirement. Some scholars have recommended training allowances or government employment for this group.

WAITING PERIOD

Practically all states provide that no unemployment compensation be paid for the first week of unemployment. When the Social Security Act was first passed, a two-week waiting period was common; this figure has gradually been reduced to one. Eight states have no waiting period, and New York has only a four-day waiting period. Eleven states pay for the first week of unemployment provided that the unemployment lasts a certain period of time,[15] but in most states the first week is a "noncompensable" period. This provision has the effect of reducing the cost of the program and reducing the administrative burden of small claims.

[14]*Sourcebook on Unemployment Compensation*, State of California, Department of Employment (1953), p. 68.

[15]*Comparison of State Unemployment Insurance Laws*, Comparison Revision, No. 2, (January, 1973), p. 3-5, and Comparison Revision, No. 1 (August 31, 1972), Table 303, p. 3-33. The prior figure for the states having no waiting period is from Comparison Revision, No. 6, January 6, 1975.

ABILITY AND AVAILABILITY

The eligibility requirement on ability to work concerns physical capability of working. Eleven states protect those who have become ill after they have become unemployed by paying unemployment benefits provided that no suitable work has been offered such claimants. In Massachusetts, one of the 11, the provision is applicable for only three weeks in a benefit year. Generally availability to work means being "ready, willing, and able to work." Time spent by the unemployed in training and retraining programs has been troublesome. Not all the states provide that training will exempt a person from being required to take a job on threat of losing the unemployment insurance benefit. Possible disqualification resulted in the federal government requiring, effective in 1972, that states shall not deny an unemployment insurance benefit to an otherwise eligible individual for any week during which he is attending a training course with the approval of the state agency.

All state laws require registration for employment at a public employment office as a prior condition of eligibility. In theory, the law requires not only registration at the employment office but also that the applicant actively be seeking work on his own. Only Tennessee explicitly states that an individual who is able and available for work, and who has registered and reported, need not actively seek work or make an independent search for it. Maryland exempts those who are 60 years of age or older from actively seeking work or those who will be recalled to their old job within 30 days. Handicapped workers, such as those on crutches, may be treated more leniently than others in their search for work. On the other hand, statements by college students who contend they are looking for work after college begins tend to be suspect.[16]

DISQUALIFICATIONS FROM UNEMPLOYMENT INSURANCE

STRIKES AND LOCKOUTS

Problems of paying or refusing to pay unemployment benefits to strikers must be decided one way or the other. The Federal Emergency Relief Administration in the early 1930's paid strikers on the ground that a denial of relief would be a "particularly cruel method of strike-breaking."[17] However, the position adopted in administering unemployment in-

---

[16]"Recent Appeal Decisions on Unemployment Benefits: Availability of College Students," *The Labor Market and Employment Security* (July 1962), pp. 22-25.

[17]James L. Myers, "Relief for Strikers' Families," *Survey*, Vol. LXX (October, 1934), p. 307.

surance benefits by all states except New York and Rhode Island is the opposite one of denying benefits to strikers. In New York and Rhode Island, benefits are paid only after the waiting period plus seven and six weeks, respectively. The basis of the exclusion is that the strikers are not involuntarily unemployed, but have chosen of their free will to leave work. There is no question that payment of unemployment benefits would provide substantial financial security to workers while striking. Payment of such benefits during a strike could be considered as enlisting governmental aid to finance strikes. It is possible that many more strikes would be called if such governmental financing were available. An added difficulty with compensating strikers is that heavy drains on the unemployment insurance fund would occur in large strikes affecting many thousands of workers.[18]

Many problems have arisen in administering the disqualification for striking. If a strike occurs at one plant of an employer, the states must decide whether the workers at other plants of the employer who are idle because of lack of parts should receive compensation. A strike at the Ford Motor Company at Dearborn, Michigan, idled Ford workers in four other states. Three paid compensation and the other did not. Forty-two of the states require that the workers be directly interested or participating in the dispute to be disqualified. Four states permit unemployment compensation if the employer is failing to conform to labor laws, and four states permit compensation if the employer is failing to conform to the labor contract. Controversy has also arisen over whether workers who are locked out should receive unemployment compensation. In such circumstances, workers do not take the initiative in leaving work, but payment to workers would throw financial support to the workers and militate against the employer. Fifteen states provide payments for lockouts, although one of these provides payments only to establishments functionally integrated with the establishments where the lockout occurs. In some of the states paying benefits during a lockout, problems have arisen in determining whether the dispute was a strike or a lockout.

VOLUNTARILY LEAVING WORK

All states provide some sort of disqualification for workers who voluntarily leave their work without good cause. Good cause has been defined narrowly in 27 states that require that the good cause be connected with the work and attributable to the employer. Personal reasons would thus

---

[18]For example, the West Virginia Board of Review estimated that the coal strike of 1939, which idled over 100,000 miners in West Virginia, would have exhausted the state's unemployment insurance fund in eight weeks even if figured from the highest surplus the fund had accumulated. See K. Pribram, "Compensation for Unemployment During Industrial Disputes," *Monthly Labor Review*, Vol. 51 (1940), p. 1376.

be excluded. If, for example, a woman quit work because of marriage and moved to a new town where she could not find employment, she would be ineligible for unemployment insurance.[19] Pregnancy disqualifications are spelled out specifically in 23 state laws.

Thirty-four states prohibit the payment of any unemployment insurance for the duration of the unemployment to those voluntarily quitting work. Labor unions oppose such a long disqualification on the ground that most workers cannot afford to remain unemployed indefinitely. Unions reason that after a worker has sought employment elsewhere for a certain period, benefits should be paid because the person has been actively seeking work and is no longer voluntarily unemployed. In line with this reasoning, a minority of states limit the disqualification to a fixed or variable number of weeks. If a worker quits a job and finds another one but loses it through no fault of his own, 12 states still consider the first quit when computing benefits. Quite obviously, labor groups oppose this provision and feel that workers quitting should be penalized only to the extent of losing benefits for the job voluntarily left.

MISCONDUCT

All 52 jurisdictions provide for a reduction or cancellation of benefits for those discharged because of misconduct. All states have the problem of defining misconduct, and all must distinguish between misconduct and inefficiency. If a clerk's sales record falls off because he or she has been impolite to customers, should the impoliteness be interpreted as misconduct or simply as a personality failure or inefficiency? Labor groups insist that the misconduct disqualification be used only for genuine cases of misconduct, and they have protested too frequent use of this disqualification by some states in the past. Management, on the other hand, would take fewer exceptions to a broader use of misconduct in disqualification. Normally inadvertent, simple, or ordinary negligence is not considered misconduct.

Twenty states disqualify workers for misconduct for the duration of unemployment. The remaining states postpone the number of weeks of payment on a fixed or variable basis.

REFUSING OTHER SUITABLE WORK

All states provide for some sort of disqualification for refusing other suitable work. A wide difference of opinion separates students of social security on a proper definition of what constitutes other suitable work,

---

[19]For an attack on such stringent disqualifications, see Fred Slavick, *Voluntary Unit Disqualification in Unemployment Insurance, the Iowa Experience*, (Iowa City, Iowa: Bureau of Labor and Management, Research Series, Nov. 20, 1958).

Conservatives hold that almost any type of job should be considered suitable, especially to an unemployed worker. From this viewpoint, many contend that the system of unemployment insurance is subject to a great deal of abuse by persons refusing to take other jobs, even at lower pay and in different localities. Liberals, on the other hand, maintain that wages and other labor standards would be severely threatened if workers are forced to take any job offered upon threat of disqualification for unemployment insurance. Consequently, they hold out for a definition of suitable work that will maintain workers on about the same plane as the one they had before becoming unemployed.

As with the other types of disqualifications, the states are split on whether to disqualify workers completely or simply to postpone benefits after the workers start looking for work again and cannot find any. Sixteen states cancel benefits for the duration of the spell of unemployment. The remaining reduce payments for a fixed or variable number of weeks. Several of these provide additional penalties, such as cancelling wage credits earned for any future unemployment during the benefit year.

DISQUALIFYING INCOME

A number of states reduce or eliminate payment of unemployment benefits if other specific types of income are received. Oregon pays no unemployment insurance benefit for a person drawing OASDI benefits if the worker has voluntarily withdrawn from the work force. Eleven other states reduce the unemployment benefit. Thirty-four states reduce unemployment benefits if the beneficiary draws additional income from a pension plan of an employer. If workmen's compensation is paid, fifteen states reduce unemployment benefits and another nine will pay no unemployment benefits at all. Thirty states either reduce or pay no unemployment payments if wages are paid in lieu of a dismissal pay. Nineteen states either reduce or pay no unemployment benefits if dismissal pay is provided.

DISQUALIFICATIONS — CONCLUSIONS

Over the years, administrators have been disqualifying more and more unemployment insurance claimants. In 1949, the number of disqualified per 1,000 claimants was 15.9; this figure increased to 23.5 by 1964.[20] The laws have also been amended to provide for longer periods of disqualification. In 1937, only one state disqualified for the duration of unemployment for voluntarily quitting, two states for engaging in mis-

---

[20]William Haber and Merrill Murray, *Unemployment Insurance in the American Economy* (Homewood, Ill., Irwin, 1966), Table 15-1, p. 283.

conduct, and six for refusing suitable work. By 1966, the respective number of states were 26, 24, and 23.[21] The purpose of the tighter administration and stricter laws is, of course, to prevent abuse of the system. As
would be expected, management and labor have split over this issue, with
management favoring more disqualification and labor less. Neutral observers have split over this issue, also. At the very least, the cancellation of
benefit rights for future spells of unemployment should be abolished,
since such provisions obviously are punitive in nature and as such have
no place in an insurance system.[22]

ADMINISTRATION OF
UNEMPLOYMENT INSURANCE

FEDERAL ADMINISTRATION

At the present time, the Unemployment Insurance Service of the U. S.
Department of Labor administers the unemployment insurance sections
of the Social Security Act, as amended. The Unemployment Insurance
Service has the function of reviewing requests for funds to administer the
program by state agencies. It also administers the sections of the law requiring state compliance on such matters as not denying compensation if
work is less favorable, if a strike is in existence, or if the individual is required to join a company union, or refrain from joining or remaining a
member of a bona fide labor union. Federal control of unemployment insurance is limited to the federal tax on payrolls, control over administrative expenses of state agencies, and several restrictions on administering
the law.

STATE ADMINISTRATION

Most of the administration of unemployment insurance laws in the
United States is under control of state governments, and practically all
personnel hired for both unemployment and employment services are
state employees. At the state level, a frequent type of administration is
that of an independent state agency (11 states). Fourteen other states provide for an independent department that reports directly to the governor
of the state. In 25 states, unemployment insurance is administered under
the state Department of Labor or other state agency.[23] The trend in the

---

[21]*Ibid.*, p. 302.
[22]*Ibid.*, pp. 304-305.
[23]*Comparison of State Unemployment Insurance Laws*, January, 1975, Table 500, pp.
5-12-14.

past few years has been toward a state Department of Labor or other state agency.

All but two states have advisory councils to assist in recommending improvements in the program. The members of the advisory council are appointed either by the governor (26 states) or by the agency administering the program. The purpose of the advisory councils is to study the unemployment insurance program and the administration of it. Recommendations are made either to the governor or to the legislature. Professor Joseph Becker made an intensive study of 15 state advisory councils plus the Federal Advisory Council. He found that the prospects of effective councils varied greatly from state to state and even within states over a period of time. He felt that the one necessary condition for success was the factor of personalities. He suggested that the most successful types of councils were those in which labor and management representatives hammered out amendments to the law by the process of bargaining and compromise.[24] A different view is that council members should think of themselves as a part of government, and give serious attention to the general public interest. Richard Lester was critical of "agreed bills," that is, agreement by the labor and management members of an advisory council, on the ground that such bills lack any evaluation of contents of the law.[25]

All states have had the problem of determining how many of its functions can best be handled in the central office and how many should be handled locally. Some states have found that delegation of functions to the local offices has not only saved the state money, but also speeded payment of benefits.[26] Since both the state employment offices and unemployment benefits are administered by the same agency, the question arises as to whether the same personnel should perform both functions, or whether more specialization should occur. No hard and fast rules can be made. In a local office containing only one or two workers, these employees will of necessity have to perform both functions. As the offices grow larger, more specialization may be permitted. A problem has arisen in most offices, at one time or another, of having to transfer personnel away from the employment function in order to handle an unusually large number of applications for unemployment insurance. One suggestion here is to hire temporary claims takers so that the work of the employment service will not be neglected at that time.[27]

[24]Joseph M. Becker, *Shared Government in Employment Security* (New York, Columbia, 1959), pp. 472-474.

[25]Richard L. Lester, *The Economics of Unemployment Compensation* (Princeton, Princeton, 1962), p. 107.

[26]Hendrick G. Nobel, "Decentralization of Benefit Claims Operations," *Employment Security Review*, Vol. 18, No. 3 (March 1951), pp. 27-29.

[27]Robert C. Goodwin, "The Administrator's Responsibility for a Balanced Employment Security Program," *Labor Law Journal*, Vol. 1 (November 1950), p. 1111.

The states are required by the federal provisions of the act to provide an appeal on those claims for which the state refuses payment. All except three states provide for two appeal stages before cases can be appealed to state courts. The initial appeals authority is generally one person, called either an examiner, or referee. For the final appeal, either a one-man referee or a three-man appeal board is used.

ABUSE OF UNEMPLOYMENT INSURANCE

Fulton Lewis, Jr., asked a number of young male unemployment insurance claimants whether they would accept jobs on his Maryland farm. When they refused such work, he classified them as illegitimate claimants. Of those interviewed, he found that 96 percent should have been disqualified from receiving benefits since they refused work on his farm.[28] Those who feel that the unemployed should be required to accept only work suitable to their training and skills justify the refusal of farm work and would find no abuse. Other violations of the law are more clear cut. Sometimes persons fail to report finding a new job, and illegally draw unemployment compensation at the same time that they are working. Others permanently withdraw from the work force but draw benefits by falsely claiming that they are looking for work.

Investigations have been made on the number of people drawing benefits illegally. The number of working violators in three states varied from 1 to 12 percent, and the percent of nonworking violators was even higher.[29] A comprehensive study of abuse of unemployment compensation was made by Joseph Becker after World War II. He concluded that if the whole program is viewed from the perspective of how many persons filed claims in relation to all those covered under the system, there was little evidence to support the view that unemployment insurance promoted widespread malingering and substantially reduced potential employment. Only 13 percent of those covered under the program received any unemployment benefits at all in 1946, and only 5.9 percent of potential claimants exhausted all their benefits.[30] Furthermore, unemployment did not climb to a particularly high figure even at the peak of the reconversion period. More recent statistics show that in fiscal 1964, only 12 out of every 1,000 beneficiaries were found to have made fraudulent claims that resulted in overpayment of benefits. Of every $100 paid out in benefits, only 31 cents was an overpayment resulting in fraud, and 64 percent of the overpayments due to fraud were recovered from the claimants.[31]

[28]Joseph M. Becker, The Problem of Abuse in Unemployment Benefits (New York, Columbia, 1953), p. 57.

[29]Ibid., pp. 169-239.

[30]Ibid., p. 358.

[31]William Haber and Merrill G. Murray, op. cit., p. 137.

Fortunately, good administration can reduce the amount of abuse of unemployment insurance. Audits on wages can be taken to apprehend working violators. Frequent interviews and field investigations can also be used to reduce abuse. Fraud detection is made somewhat easier from findings that fraud tends to be concentrated among those drawing unemployment benefits for extended periods of time. In Florida, for example, of all fraud detected, 77 percent involved claimants receiving five or more payments in a calendar quarter.[32] We may conclude, then, that fraud does exist in the unemployment program, but that it is only practiced by a small minority of recipients. It is detectable by efficient administration. Good administration can remove most of the complaints about abuse of the program.

PROBLEMS OF THE JOINT FEDERAL-STATE SYSTEM

Although the Social Security Act left formulation of the program and administration of it to the states, several federal requirements are written into the law and must be observed by the states before money is released to the states either for administration or unemployment benefits. The law reads as follows:

> Compensation shall not be denied in such State to any otherwise eligible individual for refusing to accept new work under any of the following conditions:
> a. If the position offered is vacant due directly to a strike, lock-out or other labor dispute;
> b. If the wages, hours or other conditions of work offered are substantially less favorable to the individual than those prevailing for similar work in the locality;
> c. If as a condition of being employed the individual would be required to join a company union or to resign from or refrain from joining any bona fide labor organization.

In addition, the states must meet certain administrative requirements in order to be entitled to a grant for administration. These include (1) adequate methods of administration and personnel standards; (2) payment through public employment offices or such agencies as the Secretary of Labor may approve; (3) opportunity for a fair hearing before an impartial tribunal for all individuals whose claims for benefits are denied; and (4) submission of such reports as are required by the Secretary of Labor.

Due to an overruling of a California decision by the federal government, requests were made to Senator Knowland to introduce legislation

[32]William U. Norwood, "Matching Wage Records and Benefit Payment Records," *Employment Security Review*, Vol. 19, No. 2 (June, 1952), p. 11.

amending the controls section of the act. Such an amendment passed in 1950, providing that the Secretary of Labor may not make a finding of noncompliance until the question shall have been decided by the highest judicial authority given jurisdiction under the state law. Management favored the amendment, as did the legislative committee of the Interstate Conference of Employment Security Agencies, a group of state officials who have been fearful of undue federal interference. Labor unions, on the other hand, strongly opposed this amendment. They feared that the states could unduly prolong the appeals procedure and thus hamstring proper enforcement of the law. In California, for example, in a case that had gone to the State Supreme Court from the appeals board, 29 months elapsed before the final decision.[33]

In view of the number of federal-state controversies,[34] the Secretary of Labor asked the Bureau of Employment Security to study the possibility of providing sanctions that stopped short of withholding funds. The Bureau was unable to suggest effective sanctions that would be less sweeping.

FEDERAL FUNDS FOR ADMINISTRATION

The problem of the joint federal-state system is that ever since the beginning of the Social Security system and at the present time, the federal government pays 100 percent of the money for administration of the system; yet it is the states that do the administering. One possible objection to this system is that the states may become wasteful in operating the system, since it is the federal government rather than the states which must pay the bills. The federal government, however, has kept a close rein on expenditures, and therefore waste has been kept to a minimum. Many states maintain that so little money is appropriated to them that they cannot do an adequate job of administering the system.

When the Social Security system was first inaugurated, and at the present time, the federal government had obtained funds needed for administration from an earmarked part (now 0.5 percent) of the payroll tax used to finance the system. The money collected by the earmarked tax has been used not only for administration but also for loans to states with heavy unemployment and for paying extended benefits (to be discussed below). Several alternatives to the present 100 percent administrative grant to the states suggest themselves. One is that the federal government simply return to the states the exact amount collected from it for administration. Naturally, the states with high administrative costs would not like this system for their administrative tax might have to be raised. Another suggestion is to abolish the federal collection for administration and have the states raise their own money. Both of the above suggestions have the

[33]Arthur P. Allen, "The Knowland Amendment to the Social Security Act," *Labor Law Journal*, Vol. 2 (1951), p. 425.

[34]For a summary of these, see Haber and Murray, *op. cit.*, pp. 448-450.

weakness that they might eliminate some of the federal standards which now exist in the program. In view of this weakness, it is likely that the present system of 100 percent federal grants for administration will continue.

INTERSTATE WORKERS

Another problem created by the joint federal-state system is that of interstate workers. Obviously with a purely federal system, all workers would be treated uniformly, regardless of whether they crossed state boundaries. Under the present system, in which the various states have many different requirements, a number of problems arise with interstate workers. Satisfactory adaptations have been made to some of these problems. For example, if a worker qualifies for unemployment insurance in one state but then moves to another state and becomes unemployed, the state to which he has moved agrees to act as an agent in processing the claim of the worker, and then forwards it to the first state for payment. Reciprocal arrangements also have been worked out in most states on the problem of the worker having insufficient eligibility in one state but would have sufficient eligibility if employment in a previous state had been counted.

ADVANTAGES OF A PURELY FEDERAL SYSTEM

The advantages of a purely federal unemployment insurance system are substantial. All of the other countries of the world, with two exceptions, have adopted a nationwide system (Switzerland and Norway).[35] The reason for predominantly national systems is that such systems have marked advantages. In the United States, many of the states are quite small. In New England, for example, six separate systems had to be created with a director and an administrative system for each state. Had the federal government administered the program, it would have streamlined the system more in accordance with actual need for personnel. Furthermore, personnel could more readily be transferred from place to place. The smallness of some states also militates against sound insurance principles, for a small state probably will have little diversification of industry. If industry becomes depressed, heavy drains are made on the unemployment insurance fund.

The records and tax system could be simplified if only one federal levy were provided. Furthermore, inequities in dealing with interstate workers would not arise. In addition, more uniform benefits would be

[35]Atkinson, *op. cit.*, p. 3.

provided throughout the country. Tax rates would be uniform also, so that the purely federal system would eliminate the present competition among states to reduce the unemployment insurance tax through experience rating. All states are trying to attract more industry or to hold what industry they already have. Such action creates pressure to reduce or hold down benefits, and to make eligibility and disqualifications more severe in order to hold down the tax rate. Such competitive pressure would be eliminated if there were a purely federal system. Also, bearing the cost of unemployment nationally would place less burden on the states experiencing heavy unemployment. Solvency of 52 systems combined into one would be greater than for any one separate system. The fact heavy payments are concentrated in several of the states means that these states cannot afford to pay as high benefits as could the federal government, which would have an average burden that was less than that in the heavy-unemployment states. Finally, the present system of requiring the federal government to estimate needed administrative expenses in states in which coverage, benefits, disqualifications and administrative organization differ is more difficult than if the federal government were administering a uniform system throughout the country.

ADVANTAGES OF A MIXED FEDERAL-STATE SYSTEM

The unemployment insurance system actually adopted in this country has been one of joint federal and state control. The federal government provided for a 3 percent tax (in 1938 and thereafter, but now 3.2 percent) on all covered employers in the country. The states were practically forced to adopt the program unless they wanted to lose the tax money collected. Although the federal government appropriates money to administer the program and requires that certain minimum standards be met, actual administration of unemployment insurance is carried out by the states. One argument in favor of the mixed system, of major importance when the Social Security Act was passed, was that having many different jurisdictions would enable the states to experiment with various types of programs. With the passage of time, though, it could be argued that the best methods in each of the states should now be recognizable, and that one system including all the best methods should now be adopted. When the Social Security Act was first passed in 1935, there was some question whether a completely federal system would be constitutional, but at the present writing there is no question that it would be. Another argument in favor of the present mixed system is that the cost of living is higher in certain parts of the country than in others and that benefits should vary accordingly. Another advantage of decentralized administration is that the program is operated by those who are more fully aware of local conditions, although offsetting this factor is the possible broader experience of federal administrators. Finally, an argument in favor of the present system is that local administration is probably more sensitive toward pressure for faster service than a purely federal system would be. The fact that there is some anti-federal bias in the United States, and that there is a great deal of state pride, will probably result in keeping the present mixed system intact.

Summary

The failure of private enterprise, labor unions, and state governments to provide unemployment insurance in the United States resulted in the federal government providing for such a program under the Social Security Act of 1935. The United States adopted such legislation later than Western Europe.

Although coverage has been expanded since the original act of 1935, large groups are still excluded from the law (about one-sixth of all employees). Before workers become eligible for unemployment compensation, they must have earned a minimum of wages or have been employed for a minimum period of time. A waiting period of one week is required in most of the laws, but a few have reduced the waiting period below this length of time to qualify for benefits. Workers must be able and available for work. Several disqualifications are provided for striking, voluntarily leaving work, misconduct, or refusing other suitable work.

Administration of the laws is primarily the responsibility of the several states. Some states have administered the law well and others have not. Weaknesses have been noted in preventing abuse of the program. Several problems arose with federal controls, one serious enough to result in the Knowland Amendment, which provides that the Secretary of Labor may not make findings of state noncompliance of the law until the question is decided by the highest judicial authority of the states. Although the mixed system has resulted in a number of deficiencies, there is at present little support for a completely federal system.

CHAPTER 19

UNEMPLOYMENT INSURANCE: BENEFITS AND TAXATION

BENEFITS

In formulating a program of unemployment benefits, either all workers could be paid an equal amount, or benefits could be graduated according to past wages. Most countries graduate benefits. There are several reasons for gradation of benefits. One is that higher-paid workers are used to a larger amount of income; therefore they should receive larger benefits. Higher benefits enable them to maintain a standard of living approximating their normal status. Also, in countries where a payroll tax is used, the higher the wages, the more taxes are collected. The larger tax collections from higher-paid workers may justify larger benefits to them.[1]

In the United States, all states vary benefits according to past wages. Of necessity, then, some record of past wages must be kept, and some formula must be devised to correlate benefits with past wages. In most states (37), a record of quarterly earnings rather than weekly or annual wages is kept. The benefit is then paid as a fraction of the highest quarterly earnings in the base period.

The definition of base period is spelled out in all the laws. The base period is most frequently defined as the first four of the last five quarters preceding the benefit year (35 states). The benefit year, in turn, is defined most frequently as the one year, or 52-week period, in which unemployment first begins (46 states). An alternate definition of the base year is the last four quarters preceding the benefit period (4 states). Since wage rates generally rise rather than fall, the use of the latter formula tends to provide a higher weekly benefit than the more common formula of the first four of the last five quarter.

Choosing the highest quarter on which to base benefits was done primarily to gear benefits to full weekly wages rather than to a quarter when less than full employment is experienced. With 13 weeks in a quarter, the payment of 1/13 of the highest quarter's wages would provide the worker with 100 percent of his previous wages. Since such benefits would reduce the incentive to seek work, no state pays as high a fraction as 1/13 of the high quarter wage. The use of 1/26 theoretically would provide for 50 per-

---

[1]Joseph M. Becker, *The Adequacy of the Benefit Amount in Unemployment Insurance* (Kalamazoo, Upjohn Institute, 1961), pp. 13-18.

cent compensation, but even in the high quarter some part-time work may be experienced. Thus, use of the fraction 1/26 would probably not compensate the workers for 50 percent of the loss of a full week's pay. On the other hand, there is a possibility that paying benefits based on high quarters earnings may overstate earnings, particularly if much overtime had been worked in that quarter. Most states basing wages on the highest quarterly earnings pay either 1/25 or 1/26 although a few pay more. Most states use the same fraction for all workers, but seven states vary the fraction according to the wages earned. In these seven states, the fraction is adjusted so that lower-paid workers will receive a larger percentage of benefit than higher paid workers.

Four states base benefits on annual rather than quarterly or weekly earnings. Annual earnings, compared to quarterly earnings, tends to hurt the irregularly employed. A third option, used by 9 states, is to base wages on average weekly earnings. Weeks in which pay was low are excluded. The weekly method has the advantage of using a base period immediately prior to the beginning of unemployment, but if the worker had a long spell of underemployment, his benefit is correspondingly reduced. After weighing the advantages and disadvantages of the three types of wages upon which benefits are based, quarterly, annual, and weekly, Haber and Murray concluded that using weekly wages is the best.[2] However, there has been no trend toward the use of weekly wages over the past few years.

TABLE 19-1

MINIMUM WEEKLY INSURANCE BENEFITS

(January 1975)

Minimum Weekly Benefit	Number of States
$ 5-$ 9	2
$10-$14	20
$15-$19	29
$20-$24	8
$25-$29	2
$30	1

Source: *Comparisons of State Unemployment Insurance Laws,* 1 Comparison Revision No. 6, Table 304, pp. 3-36.

[2]William Haber and Merrill G. Murray. *Unemployment Insurance in the American Economy,* (Homewood. Illinois. Irwin. 1966), pp. 175-178.

TABLE 19-2

MAXIMUM WEEKLY INSURANCE BENEFITS
(January 1975)

Maximum Weekly Benefit	Number of States
$50-$59	1
$60-$69	6
$70-$79	12
$80-$89	14
$90-$99	5
$100 and above	14

Source: *Comparison of State Unemployment Insurance Laws,*
Comparison Revision No. 6, 1975, Table 309, pp. 3-45 to 3-47.

MINIMUM AND MAXIMUM BENEFITS

In order to provide a minimum of subsistence to unemployed workers, all states designate that regardless of full-time wages earned a worker will receive at least a minimum weekly benefit. Eleven states add dependent's allowances. The amounts must of necessity be low so as not to encourage workers to draw benefits rather than work. The minimum, including dependent's benefit, are shown in Table 19-1.

The states with the lowest minimums pay half or less than the highest paying states. In general, the lower-paying states are the lower income states of the South. Several of the low-paying states, however, have relatively high per capita incomes. It is true that certain areas have lower costs of living than others that might possibly justify lower benefits, but differences in the cost of living are not nearly so great as the differences in minimum benefits.

Although the fraction of wages paid provides workers at least 50 percent of their full-time weekly wage loss, 20 jurisdictions have a flat maximum weekly benefit amount. Thirty-two other jurisdictions have a flexible maximum, with the maximum rising as wages rise in the state. Flat maximums are obviously more restrictive than maximums based on state wage averages. Ohio adjusts its maximum to the consumer price index. The maximum amounts are shown in Table 19-2. As with the minimum benefits, the range in maximum, from $50 to $156, is great.

ADEQUACY OF BENEFITS

Adequacy of unemployment benefits has been analyzed in a variety of ways. One way is to compare benefits today with those in the past. Table 19-3 traces unemployment benefits from 1930 to the present, and compares benefits with the consumer's price index and average weekly earnings.

Table 19-3 shows clearly that average weekly benefits have outstripped the cost of living. The real income of unemployment benefit recipients has therefore increased. On the other hand, benefits as a percentage of average weekly wages tended to drop for a number of years after the inauguration of unemployment insurance, but more recently have tended to increase (except for 1974).

ARGUMENT FOR HIGHER BENEFITS

Some of the unemployed are precluded from drawing higher benefits because of the maximum amounts established by state law. In 1939, for example, only 26 percent of all benefits were at the maximum ceiling, whereas by 1954, 62 percent were at the ceiling. Some improvement has been made in raising maximums since 1954, but in 1961, 46 percent of all the unemployed were obtaining the same maximum benefit. In fifteen states, in 1961, the percent of claimants eligible for maximum benefits varied from over 60 to 81 percent.[3] The fact that average benefits are only 40.8 percent of wages (Table 19-3) has caused many to press for higher benefits. A Federal Advisory Council recommended that the maximums be raised to not less than three-fifths to two-thirds of average weekly earnings. The vote, however, was not unanimous. The recommendation passed by a 12-5 vote, with all the negative votes being cast by employer members. Also, three of the public members who cast an affirmative vote stated that they would have preferred the maximum to be set at 50 percent.[4]

Some have argued for higher benefits on the basis of need. A number of studies have shown that unemployment benefits do not pay the costs of food and shelter, let alone other amenities of life.[5] Furthermore, a number of studies have found that single workers' benefits are more adequate

---

[3]*Evaluation of Coverage and Benefit Provisions of State Unemployment Insurance Laws, as of December 31, 1961* (Washington, D.C., U. S. Department of Labor, Bureau of Employment Security) Table 6.

[4]Miriam Civic, "Height and Width of Unemployment Benefits," *Conference Board Business Record*, Vol. 11 (1954), p. 311. For a recent, detailed analysis of maximum benefits, see William Papier, "Standards for Improving Maximum Unemployment Insurance Benefits," *Industrial and Labor Relations Review*, Vol. 27 (1974), p. 376-390.

[5]Joseph Schachter, "Unemployment Benefits, Wages and Living Costs," *Social Security Bulletin*, Vol. 11 (May, 1948), p. 8.

TABLE 19-3

UNEMPLOYMENT BENEFITS, CONSUMER
PRICES, AND WEEKLY WAGES

Year	Average Weekly Benefits	Index of Benefits[1]	Consumer Price Index[1]	Average Weekly Wages	Index of Average Weekly Wages[2]	Benefits as Percentage of Wages
1939	$10.66	100	100	$ 23.86	100	40.4
1951	21.08	198	187	64.71	271	32.6
1957	28.21	265	202	82.39	341	34.2
1965[3]	38.81	364	226	110.92	464	35.0
1972	58.10	545	305	139.13	583	43.2
1974[4]	65.19	612	372	159.94	670	40.8

[1]1939 = 100
[2]For production workers in manufacturing
[3]December
[4]October

Sources: *Adequacy of Benefits Under Unemployment Insurance*, U. S. Department of Labor, Bureau of Employment
Security (Sept. 1952), Table B-13. *Monthly Labor Review*, various issues. *Social Security Bulletin*, various issues.

than married workers'. For one thing, single workers need less income. For another, married workers earn about 50 percent more than single workers so that their benefits are curtailed more by weekly benefit ceilings. One study found in Michigan that a single person was receiving more than needed to provide for food and shelter, whereas larger families were not receiving enough to pay for these necessities. In a sample study from six states it was found that weekly benefits for single persons equaled or exceeded nondeferable expenditures, defined as cash outlays for food, shelter, utilities, and medical care. However, for four-person households, benefits fell short in all six states, ranging from 12 to 40 percent less than nondeferable expenditures.[6]

One method of overcoming the loss to families is to provide dependency benefits. In 1973, 11 states had dependents' benefits. Nine of the 11 cover older children not able to work. Seven of the 11 cover a non-working wife or husband, and two cover a nonworking dependent parent or brother and sister. Nine of the 11 limit the number of dependents who may be compensated, the limits ranging from two to five. The 11 states pay allowances that range from $1 to $22 additional per dependent, but for 6 of the 11 the range was from $1 to $6 per dependent. Seven of the 11 pay a flat amount per dependent, but four vary the amount either according to the amount of earnings or the amount of earnings and the number of dependents. All 11 place a limitation on the weekly allowances paid for dependent benefits, either a fixed amount that ranges from $3 to $25 weekly in five states or other types of formulas. All 11 states also have a fixed amount that maximum weekly benefits may be raised by dependents' benefits. These range from $8 to $52 in nine of the states. The other two states permit no increase in the maximum weekly benefit at all so that dependents' benefits in these two states go only to workers drawing less than the maximum benefit.

Another argument for higher benefits is that they would aid in alleviating recessions. Professor Richard Lester has estimated that unemployment compensation made up about 18 percent of wage and salary loss caused by unemployment from 1948 to 1961. The percentage remained about the same over the years. Increases in coverage and duration of benefits were offset by lagging benefits. A larger percentage of wages is paid in the early stages of the recession before the limit on the duration of benefits is reached. Even with a relatively small percentage of wages being compensated, in the aftermath of the 1969-70 recession unemployment benefits rose to almost $6 billion in 1971, an increase of almost $4 billion from the previous prosperity. Increases in benefits, however, can have only a limited countercyclical effect during recessions, since such

[6]Senator James M. Teahen, "Michigan's New Approach to Maximum Benefit Rates in Unemployment Compensation," American Economic Security, Vol. 11, No. 3 (June-July, 1954), p. 26; Richard A. Lester, The Economics of Unemployment Compensation (Princeton, Industrial Relations Section, 1962), pp. 32-33; Haber and Murray, op. cit., pp. 186-192.

benefits amount to less than 2 percent of labor income or total consumption expenditures.[7]

In a study of four cycles from the first quarter, 1948, to the fourth quarter, 1964, Neil Palomba found that unemployment insurnace taxes were stabilizing in their effect. He found that unemployment benefits, as contrasted to taxes, were stabilizing during the first and fourth cycles but destabilizing during the second and third. The high unemployment during 1950's caused benefits to be paid regularly, regardless of the cycle.[8]

ARGUMENTS AGAINST HIGHER BENEFITS

Those opposed to higher benefits point out that benefits have risen faster than the cost of living (see Table 19-3). Frank Cliffe, a vice-president of the H. J. Heinz Company, who represented the United States Chamber of Commerce in a Congressional hearing on Social Security, stated that by 1954 maximum benefits had about tripled over 1937, whereas the cost of living had not even doubled.[9] The cost of living argument has not been without its critics. Professor Richard Lester pointed out that the earlier period was one of less than full employment when industrial product and income were quite low. Benefits in such a period, according to Lester, should not be compared with the economy of today with its much larger production and income.[10]

Income taxes are much higher today than they were during the beginnings of social security. The suggestion has therefore been made that maximum benefits be compared with wages after taxes rather than before taxes. On the other hand, it should be pointed out that workers today receive much larger fringe benefits than during the 1930's. The fringe benefits are not included in the statistics on average weekly wages. It may well be, then, that the additional fringe benefits tend to offset the additional income taxes they must pay.

Some contend that benefits are now so high that the incentive to work is being impaired. For lower-paid workers drawing minimum payments, benefits come close to matching wages, particularly if carfare and other incidental expenses are considered. On the other hand, certain fringe benefits are lost by not working, which should be considered as in-

---

[7]Lester, op. cit., pp. 8-24, 35-39.

[8]Neil Palomba, "Unemployment Insurance: Stabilizing or Destabilizing," Journal of Political Economy, Vol. 76 (1968), pp. 91-100. For a citation of other studies on this problem, see p. 92 of this article.

[9]Testimony of Frank Cliffe, vice president of the H. J. Heinz Co., representing the U. S. Chamber of Commerce, Unemployment Insurance, Hearings before the Committee on Ways and Means, House of Representatives, 83rd Congress, 2nd Session on HR 6546, 7054, 8857 and 8585, p. 132.

[10]Testimony of Richard Lester, Idem., p. 231.

come also. Furthermore, the higher the wage, the less the possibility that benefits will approach wages.

ADEQUACY OF BENEFITS—CONCLUSION

When all the arguments for and against benefit increases are analyzed, several conclusions can be made. First, the fact that benefits are so low that many workers cannot pay nondeferrable expenses would indicate that benefits need to be raised. Second, the fact that such large proportions of workers receive the maximum benefit, which in many instances is far below 50 percent of wages, would call for a raising of maximum benefits. The use of 66-2/3 percent of average state wages would provide a great majority of claimants with at least 50 percent of wages. Last, dependents' benefits are necessary in order to provide for the greater need of the unemployed who must support a family. In line with some of this thinking, President Nixon in 1973 recommended that every eligible insured worker when unemployed be paid a benefit equal to at least 50 percent of his average weekly wage, up to a state maximum which should be at least two-thirds of the average weekly wage of covered workers in the state. Estimates were that costs would have to be increased 15 percent to pay for the larger benefits.

DURATION OF BENEFITS

All states limit the duration of benefits by specifying a maximum number of weeks of payment which may be made during a benefit period. In addition, all but nine also restrict duration by limiting the total dollar amount of benefits that may be received during the benefit period. This is done by various devices. The most frequent method is to specify that total benefits may not exceed some fraction, such as 1/3, of wage credits in the base period. That is, if a claimant had earned $300 in base-period wages, his maximum benefit would be $100. If his benefits amounted to $25 per week, then he would be eligible for unemployment benefits for only four weeks.

Most states have 26 as the maximum number of weeks of benefit. For the lengthening of this number of weeks over time, see Table 19-4. When the unemployment insurance system was first started, most states had a payment period of less than 17 weeks. After this relatively short period, workers were expected to go on to such work relief programs as WPA and others. The abolition of the work relief programs meant that unemployment insurance had to bear a larger share of unemployment costs, and, accordingly, the duration of benefits was lengthened.

TABLE 19-4

DISTRIBUTION OF STATE MAXIMUM LENGTHS OF DURATION
OF UNEMPLOYMENT INSURANCE, ON SPECIFIED DATES

Distribution in Weeks	Number of States									
	Dec. 1, 1937[1]	Aug. 1, 1941[1]	June 30, 1945	Sept. 1, 1949	Dec. 1, 1953	Oct. 1, 1957	Jan. 1, 1962[2]	Jan. 1, 1964[3]	Jan. 1, 1966[3]	Jan. 1, 1975[4]
12-14	12	9	2	1	0	0	0	0	0	0
15-17	33	29	14	5	4	1	0	0	0	0
18-20	4	12	23	23	18	13	1	0	0	0
21-23	0	0	6	5	2	3	2	1	1	0
24-26	0	0	5	17	27	33	39	40	41	43
27 and over	0	0	1	0	0	1	9	10	9	9
Total Number of States	49[1]	50[1]	51	51	51	51	51	51	51	52

[1]In 1937, two states based maximum duration in terms of money rather than weeks; in 1941, one state did so.
[2]Seven states provided for a longer benefit when unemployment in the state reached a specified level.
[3]Eight states provided for a longer benefit when unemployment in the state reached a specified level.
[4]Four states provided for a longer benefit when unemployment in the state reached a specified level.

Source: Comparison of State Unemployment Insurance Laws, U. S. Department of Labor, Bureau of Employment Security, various issues.

LIMITATIONS ON DURATION BY PAST
WAGES OR EMPLOYMENT

When limits on duration of benefits were first placed in the state laws, experts were convinced that avoidance of heavy drains on unemployment insurance necessitated tying duration of benefits to past wages, or periods of employment. Such methods of limiting duration have tended to discriminate against the worker who has been employed only a short time or earned low wages. A number of studies showed that higher-paid workers, who were entitled to more weeks of benefit payments than lower-paid workers, tended to exhaust benefits less frequently than the lower-paid worker. From these studies, conclusions were drawn that those who needed unemployment insurance least (the highest-paid workers) were receiving the most protection. Conversely, tying duration of benefits to past wages or employment tended to reduce the number of weeks of benefit for those least able to finance periods of unemployment.[11]

Administrative simplicity would favor a uniform number of weeks' benefits for all workers. Furthermore, payments tied to past wages are not really necessary for actuarial soundness. otherwise, life insurance benefits would have to be geared to the number of payments made. Actuarial soundness requires only that benefits paid to the whole group be, at most, equal to or less than the amounts collected in the system. Since adequate amounts have been collected over the years, including those states which provide for a uniform duration, there appears to be no necessary reason why duration of benefits should be tied to past wages or employment. Sound administration should be able to overcome the objection that workers would abuse the system if duration of benefits were not directly related to past earnings.

ADEQUACY OF DURATION

Several different conclusions on duration of benefits have been drawn. Some have reasoned that those drawing benefits for the longest periods are in need of help other than unemployment insurance, and thus they argue for a relatively short duration of unemployment benefits. They would place more emphasis on retraining programs and moving people from depressed areas to places where jobs are available. Long-term unemployment benefits may merely tie workers to a depressed area when they should be seeking work elsewhere. All the experts are in agreement that unemployment benefits should not be continued indefinitely, but if they are not, how long should benefits be paid? Twenty-six weeks is now

---

[11]*Duration of Benefits Under Unemployment Insurance*, Program Letter No. 175. (Washington. D.C.. Federal Security Agency. Bureau of Employment Security. 1949). p. 13.

paid by most states. Eveline Burns felt that a normal benefit duration of 40 weeks may be too long, both because payments may be made to those who do not want year round employment, and because an effort should be made to train workers for a different type of work after they have been unemployed for so long a period of time.[12]

Even though it is agreed that unemployment benefits should not be paid indefinitely, a case can be made for extending benefits beyond 26 weeks in recession years. The federal government passed the Temporary Unemployment Compensation Act of 1958 (TCU) to provide for 50 percent longer individual benefit payments due to the recession of that year. Money was loaned from the Federal government to make the payments. High unemployment states later had difficulty in repaying the loans. A grant rather than loan program was instituted in 1961.

The recession of 1969-70 called forth legislation to extend benefits in 1970 (Public Law 91-373). If a state enters into an agreement with the Secretary of Labor, the federal government will pay an additional sum amounting to the lesser of (a) 50 percent of the total amount of regular compensation, or (b) 13 times the average weekly benefit amount of unemployment insurance provided that a recession exists. There is an overall limitation of 39 weeks on regular and extended benefits. The program starts operation during periods of high unemployment at either the State or national level. Nationally, the "on" indicator is reached when the seasonally adjusted rate of insured unemployment equals or exceeds 4.5 percent in each of three consecutive months. The State indicator originally was considered "on" if the state's insured unemployment rate averaged four percent for any period of 13 consecutive weeks and was 20 percent higher than the average rate for the corresponding 13 week period in each of two preceding years. The 20 percent trigger was eliminated in 1972 when it was found that extended benefits had to be discontinued even though unemployment was still large but not sufficiently high to be 20 percent above past unemployment.

Extended benefits begin with the third week after a week for which there is a national or state "on" indicator, whichever occurs first. The period ends with the third week after the first week for which there are both national and state "off" indicators. This program is financed equally from Federal and state funds.

The recessions of 1969-71 and 1974 both resulted in legislation extending benefits up to 52 weeks. The latest 1974 legislation calls for the last 13 week payments to be made out of general Treasury revenues without any additional payroll taxes.

Recessions have made the 26-week limit inadequate. Even when there are no recessions, tying duration to past wages resulted in as many

[12]Eveline Burns. "New Guidelines for Unemployment Insurance." *Employment Security Review*, Vol. 29. No. 8 (August 1962). p. 8.

as one-third of the beneficiaries' exhausting benefits in some states during the prosperity of the late 1960's. Overall benefit duration was long enough, however, to protect 80 percent of the beneficiaries during this prosperous period.

PARTIAL UNEMPLOYMENT BENEFITS

When the Social Security Act was first passed and states began formulating their own laws, the states had to decide what to do about the problem of partial unemployment. If a worker were totally unemployed, benefits would be paid. But what about the worker who worked one day each week and received only 20 percent of his regular pay? By not working at all, he could possibly draw as much as 50 percent of his wages in unemployment insurance. In order to give workers an incentive to work part time, all states now provide for some form of partial benefits.

Partial unemployment insurance can be especially justified whenever states adopt experience rating, as all the states have now done. Experience rating provides for a lowered unemployment insurance tax rate if few workers are laid off. Since reporting little unemployment provides tax advantages, an employer might cut the hours of work of his employees rather than lay them off. The payment of partial benefits would tend to forestall excessive cutting of hours.

Most of the states (29) classify a worker as partially unemployed if he earns less in industry than he would draw in unemployment benefits. Twenty-one other states favor the unemployed somewhat more by providing that compensation may be received if earning are less than weekly benefits plus certain amounts. Most states provide that the partial benefit shall be the normal weekly benefit amount minus earnings, with certain amounts of earning disregarded in the deduction. To cite an example, if $10 in earning is disregarded in computing partial benefits, a worker who normally would draw $25 in benefits, but who earned $20 by working a few days, would obtain $15 in unemployment benefits.

UNEMPLOYMENT INSURANCE TAXATION

Any tax might possibly have been chosen to finance unemployment insurance. We have already discussed why a payroll tax on both the employer and employees was chosen as the most appropriate tax to finance old-age pensions. Even though our system of unemployment insurance was created by the same act as our old-age pension plan, the Social Security Act of 1935, the tax programs to finance both systems were not identical. To finance unemployment benefits, a 3 percent tax (after the first several years) was placed on payrolls of employers only. A 1939 amendment provided that the 3 percent tax shall apply only to the first $3,000 of each employee's earnings. The tax rate was raised to 3.1 percent effective January 1, 1961, and to 3.2 percent on the first $4,200 of employees' earnings effective January 1, 1970.

In requiring that both employer and employee contribute to finance old-age pensions, it was felt that employee contributions would give workers the feeling that they were earning and thus deserving their pensions. On the other hand, it was concluded that unemployment was more the responsibility of the employer. In view of the fact that the unemployment insurance program was to take care of only a minimum amount of unemployment, it was felt that the employer could finance this part himself. Public works and other governmental aid would be used for longer periods of unemployment.

SHOULD EMPLOYEES BE TAXED?

Since the passage of the Social Security Act, some have advocated that the system of taxation be changed to include the taxing of employees also.[13] Nine states, at one time or another, have taxed employees in addition to employers, but today only three states tax both employees and employers. Alabama has a 0.25 to 0.50 percent tax on the first $3,000, Alaska has a 0.3 to 0.9 percent tax on annual wages up to $7,000, and New Jersey has a tax of 0.25 percent on annual wages up to $3,000. An Advisory Council on Social Security once recommended the taxing of employees on grounds that it would demonstrate more clearly the right of the worker to obtain unemployment benefits. It would also convey more of an impression that the program was an insurance program rather than relief or public assistance. In addition, most other countries provide for contributions by both employers and employees. It was felt also that worker participation would arouse more interest in the program among workers. Lastly, since part of the tax on employers is shifted to consumers in the form of higher prices or back to workers in smaller pay increases, the tax on employees would simply give more recognition to the fact that the workers pay for the unemployment insurance program.

An analysis by Richard Lester challenges the viewpoint that most of the employer's payroll tax is shifted. He points out that the differential tax rate between states makes it difficult for some employers to pass on the tax to consumers. The same reasoning applies for the differential rates within states. For these and other reasons, Lester estimated that perhaps no more than a third of the unemployment compensation tax burden is

---

[13]*Unemployment Insurance — A Report to the Senate Committee on Finance*, Senate Document No. 206 (Washington, D.C., 80th Congress, 2nd Session, Advisory Council on Social Security, 1948), pp. 27-29.

shifted to consumers in the form of higher prices.[14] He agreed that an additional amount, unspecified by him, would be shifted backward to workers in the form of smaller wage increases.

In opposing a payroll tax on employees, spokesman for laboring groups point out that the present taxes are already high enough to pay for the program, and that the workers should not be burdened with another direct and regressive tax. This group would rather have the government bear part of the costs of the program out of general revenue, as is done in Great Britain and elsewhere. More reliance would thus be placed on the personal and corporate income taxes, which are more progressive than payroll taxes. Eveline Burns once pointed out that relatively little attention has been given to using more progressive taxes, and she suggested that if the unemployment insurance program is expanded to bear most of the brunt of unemployment, more attention might possibly be paid to it.[15]

ADEQUACY OF THE PAYROLL TAX

When the Social Security Act was passed, so little experience with unemployment insurance had been accumulated that it was not known exactly how high a tax should be levied. In view of the fact that many millions were unemployed during the 1930's, a relatively high tax of 2.7 percent on payrolls, plus 0.3 percent for administration, was assessed. In order to build the fund, it was also provided that collections should be made for two years before any payments were made. Experience over the years has shown that even with increased benefits and duration of payments, many states did not need a tax of 2.7 percent. Table 19-5 shows the income and disbursements for the unemployment insurance program since its inceptions. Beginning in 1940, the balance in the fund began to grow by leaps and bounds. Payrolls increased to enlarge contributions while at the same time unemployment was being cut to such low levels that benefits were dropping. By 1945, the surplus had reached over $7 billion. Then it rose more slowly until it reached $9.6 billion in 1953. The recessions of 1954, 1958, 1960, 1970, and 1974 caused decreases in the fund. Prosperity in the other years caused the fund to grow to $12.6 billion in 1969, but it dropped to $9.4 billion in 1972 and to $7.4 billion in 1975.

The adequacy of unemployment insurance reserves varies state by state. Congress has permitted the states to vary their tax rate by experience rating. Under this system, an employer with a record of stable employment may qualify for lower tax rates. In 1938 only one state was experimenting with such a system, and by 1940 only four varied the payroll tax according to employment experience. However, the failure of

[14]Lester, The Economics of Unemployment Compensation, op. cit., pp. 60-67.
[15]Eveline M. Burns, The American Social Security System (Boston, Houghton-Mifflin, 1949), p. 155.

TABLE 19-5

THE UNEMPLOYMENT INSURANCE TRUST FUND
(in millions)

Year	Receipts	Interest Earned in Fund	Expenditures	Total Assets at End of Year
1937	$ 567	$ 8	$ 2	$ 638
1940	861	59	615	1,958
1945	1,161	118	462	7,537
1950	1,190	146	1,342	7,721
1955	1,215	185	1,352	8,764
1960	2,300	195	2,748	6,653
1965	2,973	266	2,165	8,568
1970	2,508	610	3,848	11,897
1971	2,637	527	4,957	9,703
1972	3,899	442	4,471	9,423

Source: *Annual Statistical Supplements to the Social Security Bulletin.*

Congress to permit a lowering of the tax rate except through experience rating caused state after state to adopt the system in order to keep reserves from growing too large. In 1941, 17 had adopted experience rating, which number grew to 34 in 1942 and 45 in 1945. Finally, by 1948, all the states had inaugurated experience rating into their laws. Puerto Rico does not have experience rating in its law; Alaska repealed its experience rating in 1955, but reinstituted it in 1960.

Some of the states have cut their payroll taxes quite low, and so threatened the safety of their unemployment insurance system. Several other states have had a high incidence of unemployment in depressed industries and have been unable to accumulate adequate reserves even though their tax rate is 2.7 percent or higher. In the recession of 1958, Alaska, Michigan, and Pennsylvania had such heavy expenditures that they had to receive federal money to stabilize their dwindling reserves.

Serious criticism has been raised against the financial methods used by some of the states. Professor Orme Phelps has gone so far as to contend that the tax and benefit formulas have been formulated in such a haphazard manner that only a pretense of an insurance system remains.[16] Others have also pointed out the poor coordination between taxes and costs.[17] To cite an example, both Iowa and Massachusetts from 1946 to

[16]Orme W. Phelps, *Introduction to Labor Economics* (New York, McGraw-Hill, 1950), p. 175.

[17]E. J. Eberling, "Financial Policy in a Period of Low Unemployment Insurance Disbursements," *Employment Security Review*, Vol. 18, No. 12 (December 1951), p. 7.

1950 were using the same tax rate of 1.3 percent. Iowa had the highest reserves of any of the states, and was paying out relatively small benefits. Massachusetts, on the other hand, had the lowest reserves of any of the states at the end of 1950, and was faced with high costs due to the large amount of unemployment in the state. An analysis of other states shows the same lack of balance between taxes, benefits, and reserve.

To determine the safety of a state reserve, the Bureau of Employment Security used a criterion of 1-1/2 times the highest 12-month benefit cost rate during the preceding ten years. On this basis, the reserves of 20 states were inadeqaute in 1964.[18] In 1970, all the states had over twice the amount in the fund that they paid out in that year, a depression one, but reserves have dwindled since then.

The longest post World War II recession, 1974-1975, has placed serious strain on many of the state reserve funds. Recently, the five states of Connecticut, Washington, Vermont, New Jersey, and Rhode Island have been forced to borrow a total of $301 million from the federal Unemployment Loan Fund, and two additional states, Massachusetts and Michigan, as well as Puerto Rico, are expected to borrow in April, 1975. By the end of fiscal 1976, one Department of Labor estimate shows that 30 states will exhaust their reserves. If they do so, estimates show borrowing of up to $6.8 billion. The federal Unemployment Loan Fund, as of February, 1975, had only $348 million in reserve so that the Fund may have to borrow from the general treasury to provide unemployment insurance payments in some states.

EXPERIENCE RATING

When unemployment insurance was first inaugurated in the United States, a majority of states had what might be called a "pooled" fund. That is, all the funds collected from each employer went into a common or pooled fund, and benefits were paid from this fund. Seven states, on the other hand, followed the system first introduced in Wisconsin of having individual reserve funds. Instead of the tax money flowing into a pooled fund, the amounts collected from each employer were duly recorded and credited to the account of each employer. When a benefit was paid, the amount then was deducted from the reserve of the employer who laid off the worker. Professor John R. Commons of the University of Wisconsin was a leading advocate of the individual reserve fund. Prior to formulating plans for unemployment insurance, he had worked with problems of workmen's compensation. In this field, he was quite impressed with the fact that possible reductions in rates greatly influenced employers to install safety programs and reduce the number of accidents. He then concluded that if each employer were held accountable and had to pay higher

[18]Haber and Murray, op. cit., p. 323.

taxes for each employee that he laid off, unemployment might be considerably reduced. He, therefore, advocated the individual reserve fund in preference to the pooled fund. Unfortunately, however, the individual reserve fund has the fundamental weakness that when unemployment strikes, the individual employer may not have accumulated sufficient reserves to pay adequate benefits. Pooling all the money into one state fund, and spreading the risks among all employers, enables the fund to be more adequate. Consequently, over the years all of the states that began with the individual reserve fund, including Wisconsin, have changed over to the pooled fund.

Even though the pooled fund has become the sole method of handling funds, the states have attempted to exert some influence on employers to stabilize and regularize employment by offering them the possibility of a reduced tax if few employees are laid off. The Social Security Act permits a reduction in the 3.2 percent tax for one reason only—a good record of maintaining employment. A record is kept on each employer, and if it is found that he has stabilized employment, his tax rate may be cut below 3.2 percent. The system of reducing taxes is known as experience rating, for the reduction is contingent on the employment experience of individual employers. As was stated above, all the states now use one type or another of experience rating.

RESERVE—RATIO SYSTEM

Four major types of experience rating have been developed in the United States, each type being used by three or more states. The purpose of each type is to stimulate the employer to regularize his employment so that a tax reduction may be obtained. The earliest and most popular system, the reserve-ratio system, is now used by 32 states. Under this system, a record is kept of all the money paid into the unemployment insurance fund from each employer. A reserve is then computed for each employer by subtracting benefits paid from the contributions made. The reserve is then computed as a percentage of taxable wages in order that the ratio will be a meaningful one. A $100,000 reserve may appear quite large to an employer who has only $10,000 in taxable wages each year, but it would be much smaller for a firm having a payroll of four million dollars. To cite a hypothetical example, if an employer had contributed $40,000 to the unemployment insurance fund, and had paid out $6,000 in benefits, his reserve would be $34,000. If his annual payroll was $340,000, his reserve ratio would be 10 percent. A tax on a 10 percent reserve might be one percent. If the reserve percent were higher, the tax would be less, and if the reserve percent were lower, the tax would be higher.

Several criticisms have been leveled at the reserve-ratio system. For one thing, the actual number of weeks of unemployment benefits drawn is not subject to control by the employer, yet is is a vital factor in computing his tax. If an employer happens to be located in a small town with few opportunities for employment, his employees may draw benefits for the maximum number of weeks. Thus the benefits paid out will be large, and the reserve of the employer low. On the other hand, an employer in a large metropolitan area may experience the happy result of having his employees find jobs elsewhere almost immediately. There will be little drain on his reserve, and thus he will qualify for a lower tax rate. The rural employer might have attempted to regularize employment on a much broader scale than the metropolitan employer; yet he will pay a higher unemployment insurance tax.[19] Another criticism of the reserve-ratio plan is that when payrolls are reduced, the tax rate automatically drops.[20] Since the ratio is that of reserves to payrolls, the lower the payroll becomes, the higher the ratio, and the higher the ratio the lower the tax. Some states use different systems of experience rating, but all of these have weaknesses also.

EXPERIENCE RATING—EVALUATION

Proponents of experience rating have advanced a number of arguments in favor of it. First, it may provide a stimulus to regularize employment. Three empirical studies have been made to test the possible benefits of reduced taxes on employment regularization. The results of the three were generally similar. About one-quarter of the firms surveyed, employing about one-third of the covered employees, were influenced to an appreciable degree. The remaining three-fourths of the firms were affected very little or not at all.[21] Most unemployment insurance costs are beyond the control of the individual employer, but some firms may be influenced by experience rating to regularize seasonal unemployment and to avoid any unnecessary costs by regularizing employment as much as they can.

Another argument of experience rating is that such a system allocates costs where they belong. If unstable employers are the cause of heavy unemployment benefit costs, then they or the consumers of their products should pay for the higher costs of doing business. Joseph Becker uses this argument as the major one in favor of experience rating. Second to it, according to Becker, is the advantage of increasing employer participation in administration of the program to reduce unjustified benefits.[22]

One criticism of experience rating is that it tends to lower taxes in good times and raise them in periods of depression. However, five studies

---

[19]Almon R. Arnold, "Experience Rating," Yale Law Review, Vol. 55 (1945-1946). p. 232.

[20]Harry Weiss. "Unemployment Prevention Through Unemployment Compensation." Political Science Quarterly, Vol. 58 (1938). p. 18.

[21]Joseph M. Becker. Experience Rating in Unemployment Insurance, (Baltimore: The Johns Hopkins Press. 1972). p. 316.

[22]Idem., p. 320.

showed that experience rating did not have this impact.[23] The reason was that the downturns were of a short duration, and the tax rate did not begin to increase until business was in an upturn. For a longer recession, experience rating might have a harmful effect, but the tax itself is a small one. Furthermore, under the reserve-ratio systems as payrolls drop, the tax rate drops also.

Another criticism of experience rating is that it has lowered tax rates too low. This argument is really not applicable to experience rating per se, since unemployment taxes may be raised or lowered regardless of whether there is experience rating. The question is whether given a certain average tax rate there should be experience rating or not. The Social Security Act has permitted a reduction of the tax rate for one reason only, experience rating, and since an average tax rate of 2.7 percent was not needed, almost all of the states proceeded to lower the tax rate below that amount through experience rating. Some states have lowered the tax rate to extremely low levels. In general, the states that have the lowest tax rate pay the lowest benefits. The problem of too low tax rates could possibly be solved by having a federal minimum tax rate. Thereafter, experience rating could be used to obtain the advantages of allocating resources more efficiently, providing better administration of the program through influencing employers to reduce unjustified benefits, and aiding in a minor way in regularizing employment.

RAISING THE TAX BASE

An argument has ensued in the program as to whether it would be best to obtain more revenue by raising the tax base or raising the tax rates. When the $3,000 limit originated in 1939, this figure included 98 percent of the total wages paid in covered employment. By 1963, the figure had dropped to 58 percent. Professor Lester has cited a number of reasons in support of raising the tax base rather than raising tax rates.[24] First, failure to raise the tax base results in a lower percentage of wages being taxed in good times than during recessions. Second, a tax on the first $3,000 results in a highly seasonal tax during the first part of the year. Third, the financial soundness of the program is weakened when maximum benefits are raised without providing additional tax revenue. In 1961, 15 states had a maximum benefit of $45 or more per week. Assuming that 50 percent of wages should be paid in benefits, the recipient's earnings would have to be $4,680 to qualify for the maximum yet the tax base was only $3,000. Clearly the maintenance of the $3,000 tax base both undermined the financial soundness of the program and kept benefits low. In addition, the $3,000 tax base placed a relatively larger tax burden on low wage, highly

[23]*Idem*, pp. 266-271.
[24]Lester. *The Economics of Unemployment Compensation, op. cit.*, pp. 72-83.

competitive industries than higher wage industries. In Mississippi, where low wage industries exist, 76 percent of all wages were taxed for unemployment insurance, whereas in Michigan, which has higher-paid industries, only 56 percent of total wages were taxed. In view of these arguments it would appear that raising the tax base would be one of the most equitable means of raising additional revenue. The logic of raising the tax base was pervasive enough to cause Congress to raise the base from $3,000 to $4,200, effective January 1, 1970.

RECENT CONTROVERSY

Recently, Martin Feldstein suggested that the current unemployment compensation disincentives increased the 1972 unemployment rate by at least 1.25 percent.[25] He cited an example of a Massachusetts worker with a wife and two children who earned $500 a month. If the worker became unemployed, his net loss would be less than $100 a month, since he saves on the federal income tax, the federal social security tax, the state income tax, and retrieves 50 percent of the loss of wages by unemployment benefits, plus additional dependents' allowances. Costs of transportation to and from work are saved, plus other expenses associated with work. Feldstein concluded that the overall effect of small loss in net pay from unemployment is almost certain to increase the duration of unemployment and increase the frequency with which individuals lose jobs and become unemployed. Unemployment insurance also makes for hiring more workers in seasonal and cyclical industries, since employers pay lower wages than they would have to in the absence of unemployment insurance. Workers are willing to take less because they then recoup some losses in unemployment insurance. More workers are hired in seasonal and cyclical industries than would be the case in the absence of unemployment insurance, and thus more seasonal and cyclical unemployment results.

To reduce the disincentive effects of unemployment compensation, Feldstein suggested that the unemployment insurance tax ceiling be removed on the employer's rate of contribution, and that the minimum rate of taxation be lowered to zero. Also, unemployment insurance benefits should be taxed in the same way as other earnings. He stated that a much more important reform would be to shift the basis of experience rating from the firm to the individual. Under his plan, an individual experiencing heavy unemployment would pay higher unemployment insurance taxes.

Several comments on Feldstein's paper are in order. He claims that unemployment insurance will induce more quitting of work, but workers

[25]Martin Feldstein, "Lowering the Permanent Rate of Unemployment," (Washington, Joint Economic Committee, 93rd Congress, 1st Session, 1973).

are disqualified from unemployment insurance for quitting, and over half the states make this an outright disqualification. Other states pay after a time period has elapsed, but only if the claimant begins looking for work. Also, Feldstein claims that unemployment insurance promotes casual labor even though the states require that minimum earnings be earned before unemployment insurance is paid. Even if the minimum earnings are earned and then the worker quits, he is subject both to the disqualification for quitting and later limited to benefits due to small earnings. Possible loss of fringe benefits should also be calculated in estimating what workers lose by not working. Also, individual experience rating would tend to widen the income gap between the underprivileged who experience heavier amounts of unemployment and higher earners who have less unemployment.

In a careful survey of a number of studies of the work disincentive effects of unemployment insurance, Munts and Garfinkel concluded that the weight of evidence suggests that there were some work disincentive effects of unemployment insurance.[26] However, they found also that there may be some economic benefits which arise from some of the disincentive effects, such as enabling some workers to obtain better jobs by looking longer. Also, the unemployment insurance system provides some work incentive effects by inducing some marginal workers who would otherwise withdraw to remain in the labor force. Given these contrary forces, Munts and Garfinkel were unable to ascertain the magnitude of the overall work disincentive effects of the unemployment insurance system. Even if answers were available here, they added that value judgments are involved in determining whether obtaining a higher replacement income by unemployment insurance is more important than the work disincentives caused by it.

Summary

In almost all countries, higher unemployment benefits are granted to higher paid employees. Basing benefits on past wages results in the inconvenience of collecting past wage data, but most countries feel that benefits should vary according to the past earnings of the worker. In the United States, minimum weekly benefits vary from $3 to $25 per week, and maximum benefits vary from $50 to $156 weekly. Recently, average unemployment benefits have been rising faster than average wages, although for a number of years they did not do so. Arguments for higher

[26]Raymond Munts and Irwin Garfinkel. *The Work Disincentive Effects of Unemployment Insurance* (Kalamazoo. W. E. Upjohn Institute for Employment Research. 1974). (For a bibliography on unemployment insurance. see *Selected Bibliography of Unemployment Insurance Program Research Studies: 1951-1970*, U. S. Department of Labor. Manpower Administration (August 1971).

benefits have stressed the needs of beneficiaries and the inadequcy of dependents' allowances. Those opposed to increasing benefits fear that too high benefits may curtail the incentive of the unemployed to find regular jobs. The duration of benefits has been extended over the years primarily because work relief projects were no longer available as a second line of relief. Most states now provide for 26 weeks of benefits, but due to recent federal legislation the period is extended if a recession exists.

Unemployment insurance in the United States is financed by a payroll tax on employers. The tax has proved adequate to finance unemployment benefits, but the reserves in many of the states in 1975 are so low as to invite worry. The states have been permitted to lower the federal tax by experience rating. A major argument for experience rating is that it places the costs of unemployment on those who are causing the costs. Experience rating has been abused by a number of states, which have reduced the tax rate so low as to preclude adequate benefits. Because of this abuse, some have advocated a completely federal unemployment insurance system. Others have suggested that the federal government at least impose a minimum tax rate on all employers above the tax it collects for administrative purposes.

CHAPTER 20

PRIVATE METHODS OF ALLEVIATING UNEMPLOYMENT

THE GUARANTEED ANNUAL WAGE (GAW)

As the name inplies, guaranteed annual wage plans attempt to guarantee the wage of the worker for one year. Such plans may be used as an alternate system to unemployment insurance. Perhaps little unemployment insurance would be needed if workers were guaranteed a wage for at least one year. Guaranteed wages have been motivated by the quest for more security. Since some salaried employees and farm employees are guaranteed wages the year around, some wage earners feel that they should obtain similar guarantees. One of the first such plans was put into operation in 1894 in the wallpaper industry. A newly formed amalgamation of wallpaper producers controlled from 50 to 75 percent of the business in the industry. In 1894, as a result of economies effected by the amalgamation, the plants were closed down for a longer period than usual. Before the members of the National Association of Machine Printers and Color Mixers labor union would agree to a new contract, they demanded and won a guarantee of 11 months' employment. In 1896, the guarantee was extended to 12 months. The plan was continued in existence until 1930, when a dispute over administration of the plan, the Depression, and the rise of substitute materials all helped to cause its abandonment.[1]

The most comprehensive study of guaranteed annual wage plans was made by the Bureau of Labor Statistics from 1944 to 1947. Ninety-thousand employers were contacted to determine the extent to which guarantee plans had been adopted in the United States. In their sample, the bureau found that 347 plans had been instituted from before 1900 through 1945. Only three were started prior to 1900, and only 55 had been begun before 1934.[2] Three of the largest companies initiating successful plans were the Procter & Gamble Company (started in 1923), the Geo. A. Hormel and Co., meatpackers (begun in 1931), and the Nunn-Bush Shoe Company, which put its plan into operation in 1935. The plans of these three companies will be described briefly.[3]

---

[1]*Guaranteed Wage or Employment Plans*, (Washington, D.C., U. S. Department of Labor, Bureau of Labor Statistics, Bulletin No. 906, 1947), pp. 4-6.

[2]*Ibid.*, pp. 1-5.

[3]Jack Chernick and George Hellickson, *Guarenteed Annual Wages* (Minneapolis, Minn., University of Minnesota Press, 1945); see also: *The Guaranteed Annual Wage* (Washington, D.C., Bureau of National Affairs, 1955).

PROCTOR & GAMBLE PLAN

The Procter & Gamble Guarantee of Regular Employment plan originated in 1923 with William Cooper Procter, whose grandfather had started the business many years before. William Cooper Procter is also credited with introducing a half-day off on Saturday in 1886, even before he became the chief officer of the company. Other enlightened policies followed, such as profit-sharing, old-age pensions, and death and disability allowances. Mr. Procter's attitude toward employees was one of kindness tempered with firmness. One of the major reasons for instituting the guarantee was his concern for the unemployed worker who wanted and needed to work.

Procter & Gamble produces such well-known items as Ivory Soap and Crisco, along with other household products. While the purchase of such products by consumers was fairly regular, the sales of the company fluctuated widely and made for irregularity of employment. The fluctuations were caused by speculative buying of soaps and shortenings by wholesalers. This alternately slowed or speeded production and resulted in peaks and valleys in factory output.

Since final consumption of the products was relatively stable over the year, Mr. Procter sought to stabilize product sales. He instituted in 1920 a practice of selling products directly to retailers. New district sales offices were created by P & G, these offices making estimates of yearly sales in advance. Then, a production schedule was developed by the P & G manufacturing department. By 1923, the attempt to regularize sales was so successful that Mr. Procter could put the Guarantee of Regular Employment in effect. It provided a guarantee of at least 48 weeks of employment in each calendar year for eligible employees. During 1933, the company reduced the work week as permitted by the plan to 75 percent of the established amount at three factories because of the Depression. However, by the end of that year the situation had righted itself, and all employees had worked their full 48 weeks or its time equivalent.

Successive revisions of the plan have increased the length-of-service eligibility requirement from one-half to two years of continuous service, and limited the guarantee to hourly-rated employees. These employees are the ones primarily affected by ups and downs in business conditions. It appears that these changes, most of which were made in 1932, 1933, and 1936, were due mainly to the depressed and uncertain business conditions existing during the thirties. The guarantee has remained much the same since then, except that employees of several plants who entered the plan on a 32-hours-a-week basis later were raised to a 40 hours-a-week basis.

The Guarantee of Regular Employment Plan was proposed and inaugurated by the company when no labor unions existed at Procter & Gamble. Although at the present time labor unions bargain with Procter & Gamble, the guarantee has not been altered in collective negotiations. The company may transfer workers to lower-paid jobs on the ground that it is employment rather than wages that are guaranteed. Workers may also be discharged at any time, and the entire plan may be cancelled upon due notice by the company. The company has never set aside special funds to finance the plan, and it maintains that even during the poorest business years the plan did not cost more than 3 percent of its payroll.

GEO. A. HORMEL AND CO. PLAN

Although Geo. A. Hormel and Co. is not one of the largest "Big Four" meat packers, it is one of the largest family-operated organizations in the meat-packing business. When the plan was put into effect, Jay Hormel, the son of George Hormel, was managing its operations. In 1929, he was accosted by one of his laid-off employees, who informed Hormel that horses were treated better than men, that at least they were not turned out on the street by the company. This statement started Jay Hormel to thinking. A few years later (1931), a guaranteed wage plan was inaugurated in several departments on an experimental basis. Although Mr. Hormel talked to the employees about the plan and tried to enlist their support, they remained cool to the whole idea. In 1933, they organized an independent union, later affiliated with Packinghouse Workers (AFL-CIO). One of the demands they attempted to enforce by a strike was that the guaranteed annual wage be dropped for fear that it would cause a speed-up. Later, however, when the union had to deal with layoff of workers, it suggested that the guaranteed annual wage be reconsidered. Mr. Hormel has felt that a union is indispensable to such a plan in order that the workers can more adequately express themselves about the various problems involved. Mr. Hormel contended that the hourly wage must have been started by some employer who was trying to chisel an advantage from workers. He added that even if this were not true, the hourly wage system makes the worker carry the burden of declines in business.

The Hormel Company was faced with receiving an uneven supply of livestock during different periods of the year. In some months the number of livestock received were more than two and a half times that received at other times. Under such circumstances, employment by the month was quite irregular, although on an annual basis it was much more stable. Under the Hormel guaranteed annual wage, 52 weekly paychecks are guaranteed each year at the employee's hourly rate times the number of hours in the standard work week. The Hormel plan is one of the few that takes advantage of a Fair Labor Standards Act provision that waives overtime pay up to 56 hours a week if an annual wage guarantee is given. In actual practice, the company and union have agreed to pay for overtime in excess of 50 hours unless 10 hours are exceeded in any one day whereupon the penalties become effective but only after 48 hours in that week. Either side may terminate the guarantee upon 90 days' notice. In addition to the guarantee, workers may participate in both a profit-sharing and incentive wage plan.

Most students consider that the Hormel plan has been quite successful. One estimate showed that Hormel's workers were 50 percent more productive than others in the meat-packing industry. Cost of the plan from 1939 to 1945 was estimated at about 3 percent of payrolls. In the recession of 1954, the company had to pay out $650,000 for 400,000 hours of unworked time, or 1.5 percent of total wages. However, Hormel has benefited from higher productivity, from lower unemployment insurance taxes, and from the savings in not having to pay time and a half for overtime. Roughly $350,000 was saved on lowered unemployment insurances taxes alone in 1954.

NUNN-BUSH SHOE COMPANY

The Nunn-Bush Shoe Company adopted its annual wage plan in 1935 as a result of the depression. In 1932, the company's shoe sales fell off 30 percent, and 20 percent of the regular work force were laid off. The company was unable to cut prices because of inflexible wage rates. A plan was then evolved with employee participation to tie wage payments to the price of shoes. Employees were rewarded for possible cuts in wages by guaranteeing them 52 paychecks per year. At first a certain percentage of the wholesale value of the company's products went into wage payments. Later, the system was changed to provide that 36 percent of the value added to raw material costs would be set aside for payments to labor. The new system proved more accurate, because raw material costs fluctuated and labor's participation was wholly in connection with added values. Conservative estimates were made on the amounts to be paid in weekly earnings. Any surplus that accrued from the money allocated from the 36 percent of the value added was placed into a reserve fund. At the end of each 30-day period, the money from the surplus fund was paid to the workers over and above any reserve which the employees decided to maintain. If the reserve became depleted during the course of a year, the weekly draw of the workers was cut.

The plan was jointly administered by both management and an independent labor union. Workers were divided into three classes. Only class A employees participated in the 52-paycheck guarantee and the flexible wage plan. Class B employees did not have a 52-paycheck guarantee, but did participate in the flexible wage plan. Class C employees, those with fewer than two years of service, operated under neither the guarantee nor the flexible wage plan. At the end of 1954, class A and B employees comprised 70 percent of all the workers. No one in these groups had ever been laid off, so that the class B employees had experienced regular employment even though not under the 52-paycheck guarantee.

As to the effectiveness of the plan, demand was not more stable in this shoe company, but management made a conscious effort to stabilize production, and succeeded to an appreciable extent. Thus, employment was appreciably stabilized also. Statistics from 1950 to 1953 showed that Nunn-Bush employees had been enlarging the spread between their earnings and that of the leather and leather products industry in general. As of February, 1963, the Nunn-Bush Company had issued 1,440 consecutive weekly paychecks without missing a payment to workers.[4]

In 1965, the Nunn-Bush Company discontinued its guaranteed annual wage plan in favor of a wage incentive plan. In 1967, the Nunn-Bush Shoe Company was purchased by the Weyenberg Shoe Manufacturing Company. Due to the obsolescence of the Milwaukee plant, where the GAW had existed, production operations were discontinued there in 1972.

SUPPORT FOR GAW PLANS

Guaranteed annual wage plans before the 1930's were fostered and supported mainly by businessmen.[5] Then, during the 1930's, government attempted to encourage such plans by providing for tax exemption or reduction from the unemployment insurance tax. In Wisconsin, a complete exemption from unemployment taxation was provided under state law. Ninety-six of the 347 plans studied by the Bureau of Labor Statistics were Wisconsin firms who introduced plans to obtain tax benefits. When the Federal Social Security Act was passed, Wisconsin elected to be covered by it, and so the tax exemption was lost. Although the Federal Social Security Act provided tax reduction for those guaranteeing employment, no firms took advantage of this provision. All 96 Wisconsin firms abandoned their plans at this time.

Federal government encouragement of guaranteed plans has been more successful under the Fair Labor Standards Act. The 1938 provisions of this act stated that firms that guaranteed 2,000 hours of employment per year, no more nor less, were permitted to hire workers for 12 hours a day or 56 per week without paying overtime rates. Some of the rigidity of the exemption was removed in the 1949 amendments of the act, which permitted the overtime exemption for as little as 46 weeks a year and 30 hours per week. Firms can employ workers for as many as 2,240 hours per year, although all employment over 2,180 hours must be paid at one and a half times the regular rate of pay. A few firms have taken advantage of waiving overtime pay by guaranteeing wages.

---

[4]Letter from Walter Fanning, Vice President, Nunn-Bush Shoe Company (February 19, 1963).

[5]For a brief history of guaranteed annual wage plans, see Don Seastone, "The History of Guaranteed Wages and Employment," *Journal of Economic History*, Vol. 15 (1955), pp. 134-150.

The main impetus in favor of such plans since 1940 has come from labor unions. Philip Murray, Walter Reuther, and others from the Congress of Industrial Organizations came out strongly for such plans. Reuther, for example, stated at the 1953 convention of the Congress of Industrial Organizations that the labor union movement would mobilize its resources in a major effort to obtain the guaranteed annual wage for workers.[6] Although the United Automobile Workers, United Steel Workers, the International Union of Electrical Workers — the "Big Three" of the Congress of Industrial Organizations — and other unions proposed plans to be worked out by collective bargaining, few such plans were sold to management. A sample study by the Bureau of Labor Statistics in 1952 found only 20 plans which guaranteed wages or employment for a substantial part of the year. Beginning in 1952 through 1955, local 688 of the Teamsters Union was able to negotiate such plans with 75 firms in the St. Louis area. The Packinghouse Workers and east-coast Longshoremen have also signed several annual wage contracts. However, as of March, 1955, only about 15,000 to 18,000 workers were covered by guaranteed annual wage plans.[7] A later Bureau of Labor Statistics study of 1,773 labor contracts under which about 7-1/2 million workers were covered in 1962-63 found that 139 contracts covering about 600,000 workers guaranteed employment or wages for at least a week to some or all the workers. Of these contracts, only six provided for the annual guarantee.[8]

Partisan supporters of the guaranteed annual wage picture substantial advantages arising from such plans. For one thing, the security of the worker is greatly strengthened. No longer do workers have to worry as much about being laid off, for they have a 52-week guarantee of either wages or employment. Consumption expenditures of groups assured a stable income should be expected to increase, and this trend has been verified statistically at Austin, Minnesota, the headquarters of the Hormel Packing Co. From 1932 to 1940, the time deposits of the two banks in Austin dropped from almost $2-1/2 million to $2 million, even though population increased 50 percent and average weekly earnings increased by the same percentage. However, some increase in building and loan savings and savings in the Hormel Company credit union was noted.[9]

A major advantage of annual-wage schemes is that they tend to regularize seasonal unemployment. An American Legion study of 12 firms that adopted the annual wage showed that prior to the plan, 58 percent of their workers were fully employed, compared with 91 percent

---

[6]"Guaranteed Annual Wages," *Economic Outlook*, Vol. 14, No. 10 (October 1953), p. 75.
[7]*The Guaranteed Annual Wage, op. cit.*, p. 8.
[8]*Major Collective Bargaining Agreements: Supplemental Unemployment Benefit Plans and Wage-Employment Guarantees*, Bulletin No. 1425-3, Washington, D.C., U. S. Department of Labor, Bureau of Labor Statistics (1965), p. 2.
[9]Chernick and Hellickson, *op. cit.*, p. 122.

after the plan had been adopted.[10] Lessened turnover of workers, higher morale, and steadier production all should make for lowered costs for companies.[11] Although such plans are not a cure-all for the business cycle, they may contribute toward cyclical stability by collecting funds to pay for the guarantee during prosperity and then help to maintain consumption by paying out such funds during the recession.

WEAKNESSES OF THE GAW

Critics of the guaranteed annual wage have vigorously protested against such plans. The redistribution of income to potentially unemployed workers obviously must be paid by someone, and the critics fear that the increased costs to the businessman will deter investment. One of the more detailed estimates of costs of a plan was presented by Murray Latimer in the Steelworkers brief in 1952 before the Wage Stabilization Board.[12] On the assumption that unemployment would not be heavy in the steel industry because of large defense orders and a sizable civilian demand for steel products, Latimer estimated that gross costs would be 8.4 cents per hour.[13] Payment of part of this cost would be paid through the already existent unemployment insurance system. Subtracting this cost, the net cost would be 6.5 cents an hour. The guarantee would have gone only to those with three or more years' seniority with the company, and the guarantee would be for 30 hours for 52 weeks. Costs were figured if the guarantee were for either 20, 30, or 32 hours per week. For 30 hours, the gross cost was 8.4 cents per hour, or 6.5 per hour net. Of course, costs would be substantially higher if heavy unemployment occurred, or if all workers were covered 40 hours a week for the 52 weeks.

Professor Wayne Leeman felt that the adding of such costs to the employer and forcing employers to carry the added risks of possible unemployment might seriously deter business investment. Less investment would be undertaken, because any expansion of plant and work force would call for additional wage guarantees.[14] Wages change from variable to fixed costs, and this change adds to the employer's risks, because fixed costs cannot be cut when business drops off. Other authors concur on the deleterious effects on investment. A. D. H. Kaplan, for example, doubted whether the Ford Company could have shut down to

[10]*Ibid.*, p. 106.

[11]"Guaranteed Employment in 1955," *Economic Outlook*, Vol. 16, No. 4 (April 1955), p. 29.

[12]Don Seastone, "The Status of Guaranteed Wages and Employment in Collective Bargaining," *American Economic Review*, Vol. 44 (1954), pp. 911-913.

[13]"Guaranteed Wages and Unemployment Insurance," *Business Record*, Vol. 11 (1954), p. 26.

[14]Wayne Leeman, "The Guaranteed Annual Wage, Employment, and Economic Progress," *Industrial and Labor Relations Review*, Vol. 8 (1955), pp. 565-571.

change from the Model T to new models in 1927 had it been forced to pay wages to the workers while unemployed.[15]

Management's extreme reluctance to make guarantees of a nature that may possibly bankrupt companies, especially during a serious depression, has caused labor unions to formulate guaranteed plans with limited liability. The 1953 Steelworkers plan not only limited the number of workers covered (those with three years or more seniority), but also limited the number of hours guaranteed from 28 to 32 per week. The Steelworkers went one step further, and agreed that whenever the fund was exhausted, the companies would not be required to continue the guarantee. The company guarantee was to be limited to the cents-per-hour figure set aside to pay the 28-32 hour guarantee. Labor groups and others thought that by limiting the liability, corporations would be much more receptive to the guarantee plan. However, few corporations agreed to introduce the plans even with the limited liability.

Frank Cassell, manager of Industrial Relations for the Inland Steel Company, pointed out that once the fund money was exhausted, labor would clamor for the companies to continue paying the guarantee. He cited the case of the United Mine Workers, who originally negotiated a five cents per ton welfare fund for coal miners in 1946, and then because of the inadequacy of the fund kept renegotiating until by 1954 the charges were 40 cents per ton on bituminous and 50 cents per ton on anthracite.[16]

Emerson Schmidt, economist for the United States Chamber of Commerce, and others also contend that limited liability is only a snare to employers, and that they would be under extreme pressure to make good the guarantee.[17] However, it is true that the guarantee plans in existence during the great depression of the 1930's managed to continue without the pressure to hold fast to the 100 percent guarantee. For example, seven substantial revisions downward in the guarantee were made by Procter & Gamble in 1932-1933. Other plans were modified in a similar manner.[18] On the other hand, management spokesmen are correct in maintaining that only if the 52 weeks guarantee is to be maintained should the plans be called guaranteed annual wages.[19] The proposed Steelworkers plan for 30 hours guarantee for 52 weeks really only guarantees 75 percent of pay, and perhaps not even that much if the fund becomes exhausted. With

---

[15]A.D.H. Kaplan, *The Guarantee of Annual Wages* (Washington, D.C., Brookings Institution, 1947), p. 185.

[16]Frank H. Cassell, "Where Do We Stand with the Guaranteed Annual Wage_" *Personnel*, Vol. 30, No. 5 (March 1954), p. 351.

[17]Emerson Schmidt, "The Guaranteed Wage — Super Unemployment Compensation," *American Economic Security*, Vol. 12 (1955), p. 14.

[18]S. Herbert Unterberger, "How the New Guaranteed Annual Wage Proposals Meet Employer Objections," *Labor Law Journal*, Vol. 6, No. 5 (May, 1955), p. 315.

[19]Thomas F. Johnson and Leonard J. Calhoun, "The Guaranteed Annual Wage in Collective Bargaining," *American Economic Security*, Vol. 11 (1954), p. 27.

such limitations of liability, the guaranteed plans are more similar to supplemental unemployment benefit plans than they are to 100 percent guaranteed wages.

Another criticism of the guaranteed annual wage is that it will tend to keep workers from attempting to find jobs elsewhere. This may be true even though the plan requires that the employees enroll at the government employment office for work. For example, the Federal unemployment insurance program for World War II veterans called for payment of $20 per week for 52 weeks. In Puerto Rico, the $20 a week was as high or higher than average wages for those working. Consequently, 62 percent of the veterans of Puerto Rico who started to draw compensation obtained payments for 52 weeks. On the other hand, in Wisconsin, where the $20 a week was below the regular rate of pay, only 2.4 percent who drew benefits did so for 52 weeks.[20]

Still another criticism revolves around the problem of who should receive the guaranteed payments. Older workers with the most seniority would retain their jobs, and be paid their regular wages for working, while the men with the least seniority would be drawing their pay for not working. Furthermore, even though wages are maintained, consumption may still drop because laid-off workers may be reluctant to buy such durable goods as cars, houses, and the like.[21]

SUPPLEMENTAL UNEMPLOYMENT BENEFITS

As early as 1937, at the first convention of the Steelworkers union, Philip Murray had voiced a demand for the guaranteed annual wage.[22] The union, during World War II, was able to get the War Labor Board to consider the proposal. The Board did not implement the plan because it was contrary to the Board's policy to introduce major innovations in collective bargaining, but it recommended to President Roosevelt that such plans be comprehensively studied on a national scale. Later, in 1947, a report was produced by the Advisory Board of the Office of War Mobilization and Reconversion, with Murray W. Latimer as research director. The Advisory Board suggested that the guaranteed annual wage would not be feasible for such industries as steel, which experience wide and unpredictable fluctuations in employment. Instead, the Advisory Board recommended that unemployment insurance be supplemented by benefits paid from a

[20]"Jobs or Jobless Pay — The Real Issue Behind the New Guaranteed Wage Proposals," (Washington, D.C., U. S. Chamber of Commerce, 1954), p. 12.

[21]Johnson and Calhoun, op. cit., pp. 20-26.

[22]For a history of SUB plans, see Joseph M. Becker, Guaranteed Income For the Unemployed: The Story of SUB (Baltimore: Johns Hopkins Press, 1968), Chapter 1.

fund built by employment contributions. Limiting benefits to the amount in the fund would greatly ease the burden of unlimited liability called for in the guaranteed annual wage.

The United Automobile Workers Union (UAW) was interested in such plans, and made a detailed study of them from 1953 to 1955. The UAW normally would have started negotiations in 1955 with General Motors, but upon learning of an adamant position against such a plan by General Motors, the UAW settled on Ford as the target company. Prior to the negotiations, Ford had made a long and intensive study of such plans. The UAW-Ford contract in 1955 was the first SUB plan adopted. With the breakthrough at Ford, the UAW was able to get a supplemental unemployment benefit (SUB) plan at all the other auto companies in 1955, but American Motors was given a year within which to commence the plan. The Steelworkers negotiated such plans with the major basic steel companies in 1956, the United Rubber Companies obtained such plans with the major rubber companies in the same year, and beginning in 1959 the Cement Workers obtained contracts covering most workers in cement. Multi-employer contracts have been negotiated by the Garment Workers (ILGWU), the National Maritime Union, and by some of the construction unions. By 1960, 1.7 million workers were covered, and by 1970, a total of 2.5 million workers had the protection of SUB plans.[23] Such plans have been heavily concentrated in the auto, steel, apparel, rubber, and cement industries.

SUB plans have been dovetailed with unemployment insurance, although the eligibility and disqualification provisions of SUB plans are stricter than the requirement for unemployment insurance.[24] For example, SUB plans in the steel industry required two years of seniority, and those in the auto industry require one. The trend over the years has been to liberalize the eligibility requirement of SUB plans.

In a study of SUB plans from 1955 to 1965, Joseph Becker found that all of the core plans showed some increase in benefit-wage ratios. As of 1965, the take home pay of workers from supplemental unemployment benfits varied from 72 to 84 percent. This figure included both UI and SUB. Some workers may not receive this large amount because the SUB plan places a maximum dollar limit that may be received, or their UI may expire. Both of these limitations have been lessened during the life of such plans. Some of SUB plans pick up the slack when UI benefits are exhausted (steel, can, and rubber industries), but others do not have this provision (auto, cement or agricultural implements).

One of the significant additions to benefits has been that of providing payments when employees are working a short week. Thus, according to

---

[23]*Handbook of Labor Statistics*, 1974, Washington, D.C., U. S. Department of Labor, Bureau of Labor Statistics, 1974, Table 118, p. 298.

[24]For a more detailed analysis of eligibility requirements, see Joseph M. Becker, *op. cit.*, Chapter IV.

Becker, unions have been approaching "one of their long cherished goals, a guaranteed weekly income." The duration of benefits has also been extended since the beginnings of SUB. The first plans by the Steelworkers only called for 26 weeks benefits, but all the core plans now provide for at least 52 weeks of benefits. Some of the plans provide for up to five years of benefits, and the Alan Wood Steel Company in 1965 introduced an unlimited duration plan for all those with ten years or more of seniority. The UAW made an important breakthrough in 1967, when a contract was negotiated with Ford that provided 95 percent pay.[25] In order to provide for this increase, Christmas bonuses were waived. Most other firms, however, have not followed suit with such large benefits.

In a study of 14 plans, Joseph Becker found that as of March, 1966, eight were financed by a six cents an hour or less maximum cost, which included any maximum addition to contingent liability if the plan carried such a liability. The most expensive plan called for a 42 cents per hour charge on employers, and was negotiated by the Carpenter's union in Buffalo. The trend from the beginning of the plans has been to increase the contribution rate. Also, there has been more use of contingent liability over the years that provided for increased payments to the plan whenever the fund dropped below a certain level. Originally, a good experience rating called for lower payments into the fund, but such rating had been abandoned or severely restricted by 1965. In almost every year in the 1960's the funds accumulated more from employers than were paid out in benefits. Most plans appear to be adequately financed.[26] In most of the original plans, only unemployment insurance supplements were paid, but over the years different types of benefits were added. In Becker's study of 14 plans as of March, 1966, six of the SUB plans provided for severance pay, five each for sickness and disability pay, and supplements to workmen's compensation, and two each for health insurance and relocation allowances.

A different type of SUB plan was negotiated by the flat glass unions and others. At the Pittsburgh Plate Glass Co. (now PPG Industries), the money was contributed into an individual savings plan for the individual worker. He may draw out the money for such emergencies as unemployment, illness, or even a transfer to another company. At death, the money credited to the worker goes to the widow, or nearest beneficiary. In the PPG Industries contract, the company agrees to contribute 10 cents an hour into a trust fund, which must keep the money in cash or in United States government obligations. After the fund reaches $600 per worker, the company still pays 10 cents per hour, but it then goes to the worker as additional vacation pay. If a worker becomes injured, ill, or unemployed

[25]Norma Pope and Paul A. Brinker, "Recent Developments with the Guaranteed Annual Wage," *Labor Law Journal*, Vol. 19, No. 9, September, 1968, pp. 555-562.

[26]Emerson H. Beier, "Financing Supplemental Unemployment Benefit Plans," *Monthly Labor Review*, Vol. 92, No. 11, November, 1969, p. 35.

for more than two pay periods, he may draw a maximum of $30 per week from the fund or 10 percent of the money he has in the fund, whichever is less. The minimum payments are $15 per week, or the balance in the fund, whichever is less.

In the individual savings plan (PPG Industries), there is no redistribution of income from employed workers to the unemployed. The individual savings plan calls for a continuous payment of 10 cents per hour, whereas some of the other SUB plans provide for no further contributions after the fund has reached a certain level. Under this type of financing, the individual savings plan is more expensive than other SUB plans although additional types of benefits have been added to SUB plans.

In administration of SUB plans, all provide for a trustee, usually a bank or other judiciary institution, to receive the employer's contribution.[27] The immediate administrator is the employer, who receives the applications, determines the applicant's eligibility and amount of the benefit, and prepares the check. The determination by the employer may be appealed. Single arbitrators, or a panel of them, hand down the final decision. Over the years, administration has been simplified. Other types of proof of eligibility are accepted other than eligibility for UI. In some plans, the claimant may mail in his claim rather than appearing in person.

In appraising SUB plans, Joseph Becker noted an effect on the demand for labor due to added labor costs. Also, there was a tendency to work a smaller labor force for longer hours. On the supply side, SUB plans have helped to maintain the employer's work force intact during temporary layoffs. Also, some workers have chosen a layoff to working, particularly if they know that the layoff is temporary. SUB plans have not influenced unions to stop working for UI improvements. Internally, SUB plans have supplemented the UI amount by at least 50 percent, and very few SUB claimants have exhausted their benefits. Becker doubts that improvements in UI will make SUB plans unnecessary. An educated guess on his part was that UI costs would have to double to provide SUB type benefits to all workers. His final conclusion was that the first decade of experience under SUB plans must be judged a success.

Several explanations may be made as to why SUB plans do not cover more workers. In stable industries, the problem of unemployment is not that great to call forth bargaining on SUB plans. In other industries with heavy unemployment, the costs may be so great as to preclude introducing a SUB plan. Only wealthier firms that experience heavy amounts of unemployment are prime targets by labor unions to negotiate such plans. The limited liability of SUB plans and their lower benefits have provided an advantage of SUB over GAW plans, so that many more workers have been covered under the former than the latter.

---

[27]For a more detailed analysis of administration, see Joseph M. Becker, *op. cit.*, Chapter VII.

SEVERANCE PAY AND LAYOFF BENEFIT PLANS

Severance Pay and Layoff Benefit Plans have grown rapidly since World War II. A study in 1965 was made of almost 2,000 major agreements in which almost 7-1/2 million workers were employed. Such plans appeared in 30 percent of the agreements and covered about 40 percent of workers under all agreements.[28] The plans were concentrated in manufacturing, and five labor unions were parties to almost half of the plans: Steelworkers, Auto Workers, Communication Workers, Ladies Garment Workers, and Electrical Workers (IBEW). A number of plans provided for severance pay upon termination of employment (rather than layoff).

The same study found that most of the plans were unfunded, but the funded plans have continued to grow and in 1973 constituted one-fourth of all plans. The amount of benefit was generally based on the length of service, with one week's pay for one year of service being typical for short-service employees. For those employed for a number of years, more weeks pay was granted for each year of service, sometimes as high as four weeks' pay for each year of service.

A later study of 620 agreements in existence in 1971, in which 2,000 or more workers were covered per contract, 136 contracts covering 1.5 million workers had severance pay plans.[29] A year earlier, for 252 agreements with coverage of 5,000 or more workers per contract, 106 had severance pay plans covering 1.5 million workers.[30] The reason why smaller unions and firms prefer severance to SUB plans is that they are simpler to administer and thus easier to negotiate. Too, they use less money in administration. They also have the advantage of promoting labor mobility. For this reason, Joseph Becker suggested that severance pay and SUB plans operate concurrently.

It is interesting to compare private plans in the United States and other countries. In Japan, for example, workers receive full pay when laid off. Lifetime guarantees of employment are granted. Such a guarantee aids workers because it provides social stability and inspires deep loyalty. However, it should be noted that there was a shortage of labor in Japan. Under these circumstances, the guarantee aids management in an assurance of an available labor supply. Under conditions of less than full employment, the economic costs of such a program would be quite high.

[28]Leon Lunden and Ernestine Moore, "Severance Pay and Layoff Benefit Plans," *Monthly Labor Review*, Vol. 88, No. 1 (January, 1965), pp. 27-34.
[29]*Characteristics of Agreements Covering 2,000 Workers or More* Washington, D.C., U. S. Department of Labor, Bureau of Labor Statistics, Bulletin No. 1729, 1972), Table 66, p. 67.
[30]*Characteristics of Agreements Covering 5,000 Workers or More*, Washington, D.C., U. S. Department of Labor, Bureau of Labor Statistics, Bulletin No. 1686,(1970),Table 62, p. 63.

Summary

Guaranteed Annual Wage plans have been in existence for many years. A few were inaugurated before the turn of the century. Several large companies, such as Procter & Gamble and the Hormel Co., have successfully operated such plans for a number of years. Since 1940, the main impetus in support of such plans has come from labor unions. In general, management has not been enthusiastic about such plans, due to the potentially high costs involved. Labor unions have been more successful in negotiating SUB plans, which generally provide from 70 to 85 percent of take-home pay for a period of 52 weeks. If employers had to choose between the GAW or SUB plans, they would choose the latter, due to the lower costs involved. In recent years, there has been a rapid growth of severance pay plans for workers who are terminated or, sometimes, merely laid off.

PART V

PROBLEMS OF LOW INCOME AND SPECIAL GROUPS

CHAPTER 21

RURAL POVERTY

Rural areas (less than 2,500 population) are poorer than urban areas. Within rural areas, larger percentages of those with a farm residence are poorer than the rural nonfarm people. However, since the rural nonfarm population is so much larger than the farm population, about 2-1/2 times the number of rural poor have a nonfarm residence than live on farms.

Rural areas are in short supply of medical personnel. There are almost five times as many physicians per person in cities with over 5 million people than in rural areas.[1] There are also fewer pharmacists, nurses, and dentists per person in rural areas. One suggested solution here is that grants and loans should be made to those specializing in medicine only on condition that several years be spent in a rural areas after graduation.

Housing is also less adequate in rural areas.[2] In order to promote rural home ownership, the Farmers Home Administration (FmHA) now makes low interest loans to buyers. Over $1 billion will be loaned in fiscal 1974 to aid 51,000 families purchase new homes. Smaller amounts have been appropriated to about the same number of families to repair or rehabilitate their homes. There has been some criticism that there is no program for areas with 10,000 to 25,000 since the FmHA may only service areas with less than 10,000 population and the Federal Housing Administration may loan only to areas with 25,000 population and over. Also, there has been some criticism of housing loans in rural areas on the ground that such loans tend to keep people there even though adequate job opportunities are scarce or nonexistent. Rural education is deficient also mainly due to lack of financial resources.

FARM POVERTY

Thanks to a rising GNP and outmigration, the numbers in poverty with a farm residence declined from 2.7 million in 1967 to 1.4 million in 1972. However, farm families still showed a larger percentage living in poverty than non-farm families—12.8 and 9.2 percent respectively.[3] Per capita dis-

[1]Tresa H. Mathew, "Health Service in Rural America," (U. S. Department of Agriculture, Rural Development Service, *Agriculture Information Bulletin*, No. 362, July 1973), Table 6, p. 8.

[2]The 1970 Census showed that whereas 96.5 percent of all occupied houses within standard metropolitan statistical areas had all plumbing, the corresponding figure for rural areas was 83.1. See *General Housing Characteristics*, *U. S. Summary*, U. S. Bureau of the Census, 1970, Table 10, p. 1-53.

[3]*Characteristics of the Low-Income Population: 1972* (Washington, Bureau of the Census, Series P-60, No. 88, June 1973), p. 60.

posable income of the farm population has been rising as a percent of non-farm income. In 1934, farm per capita income was only 33 percent of non-farm income. It rose to 49 percent in 1942, 50 percent in 1952, 62 percent in 1962, and 83 percent in 1972. Farm income per capita surpassed nonfarm income in 1973, and was about the same in 1974.[4]

Theoretically, a market economy should not have any industry that is poorer than others in the long run. Mobility out of the industry should make one as profitable as another industry. A number of agricultural economists have suggested reasons for lower returns in agriculture over a long period of time. Luther Tweeten developed a general theory of economic stagnation that he applied to rural areas.[5] His theory contains three basic elements. First, areas require adjustments to changing resources, products, and technology. Secondly, there are identifiable characteristics which give rise in the ability of areas to adjust to change. The capacity to adjust is highest when (a) birthrates are low, (b) educational levels are high, (c) transportation and communication are adequate, (d) people have a "mobility" ethic, (e) the rural culture is malleable and compatible with that of growth areas to which people must migrate, (f) there are no institutional barriers such as racial discrimination to preclude mobility, and (g) the area is in reasonable proximity to an urban-industrial complex.

The third segment of Tweeten's theory holds that when the forces requiring adjustment are large in relation to the ability to adjust, the environment develops anomie (social alienation) and other disfunctional syndromes inimical to rapid change. Due to a lack of potential of some farm areas to develop economically, outward mobility is needed. In some serious problem areas, only one in sixteen farm youths will find adequate opportunities in farming. However, mobility from these areas has been insufficient to equalize resource returns in all U.S. areas. Some poverty areas have been handicapped by high birthrates, low educational levels, and inadequate transportation and communication. Consequently, their culture has developed those anomic traits that reduce mobility.

Rural farm poverty is particularly concentrated where farms are small and technology is so deficient that little is produced. Table 21-1 shows that over the years the number of farms producing small amounts have been decreasing in number. Several studies have indicated that the net income on many small farms is a negative figure.[6] For all farms below $2,500 sales, the realized net income was $1,100 in 1972.[7] Fortunately,

[4]*Farm Income Situation* (Washington, U. S. Dept. of Agriculture, Economic Research Service, FIS-225, February 1975, p. 5.

[5]Luther Tweeten, *Foundations of Farm Policy* (Lincoln, University of Nebraska Press, 1970), pp. 375-394.

[6]Luther Tweeten, "Low Returns in a Growing Farm Economy, *American Journal of Agricultural Economics*, Vol. 51, No. 4 (Nov., 1969), pp. 798-817; Frank Orazem, "Economic Status of Income Groups by Farm Size," in A. Gordon Ball and Earl O. Heady, eds., *Size, Structure and Future of Farms, (Ames, Iowa State University Press, 1972), Table 4.11, p. 73*.

[7]*Farm Income Situation*, U. S. Department of Agriculture, Economics Research Service, FIS-222 (July 1973), Table 2d, p. 69.

TABLE 21-1

NUMBER OF FARMS BY VALUE OF SALES CLASSES, 1960-72

Year	$40,000 and over	$20,000 to $39,999	$10,000 to $19,999	$5,000 to $9,999	$2,500 to $4,999	Less than $2,500	All Farms
			Thousands of Farms				
1960	113	227	497	660	617	1,849	3,963
1965	161	280	463	509	459	1,484	3,356
1970	235	343	382	404	420	1,170	2,954
1972	297	404	353	359	420	1,037	2,870
			Percentage distribution				
1960	2.9	5.7	12.5	16.7	15.6	46.6	100.0
1965	4.8	8.3	13.8	15.2	13.7	44.2	100.0
1970	8.0	11.6	12.9	13.7	14.2	39.6	100.0
1972	10.3	14.1	12.3	12.5	14.6	36.2	100.0

Source: *Farm Income Situation,* U. S. Dept. of Agriculture. Economic Research Service. FIS-222 (July 1973) Table 1d. p. 68.

sufficient off-farm income is made to provide an adequate income for many small farmers. In 1972, off-farm annual income of the median farm operator producing less than $2,500 was $9,496.[8] It was the small farmers without adequate off-farm income who were living in poverty.

SOLUTIONS TO FARM POVERTY

PARITY PRICING

In the Great Depression of the 1930's, farm income supports were basically a relief measure designed to prevent the collapse of our farm economy. During World War II, and to a lesser extent in the Korean War, farm income supports were used to stimulate farm production. Thereafter, income supports have been used primarily to counteract falling prices caused by increased productivity.[9] In the past few years, the major program to maintain farm prices has been payments to farmers not to produce. Also, the federal government has taken surplus commodities off the market.

Over the years it was recognized that attempting to help farmers through higher prices tended to benefit those farmers who produced most. Thus, the larger farmers obtained the lion's share of government price support programs. In 1972, the largest farmers with gross income of $40,000 and more received an average government payment of $5,138 per farm, whereas the farmers selling less than $2,500 obtained $225 per farm. Of a total of almost $4 billion distributed in direct government payments in 1972, farms selling over $20,000 (24 percent of our farms) received 64 percent of all direct government payments.[10]

Criticism of the largest farmers receiving the largest subsidies and the disappearance of farm surpluses in the early 1970's resulted in 1973 in eliminating payments on 40 million acres. As of 1975, government aid will only be forthcoming if prices drop drastically.

OUTMIGRATION

Millions of people in the United States have migrated from farms for many years. The annual average net outmigration is shown in Table 21-2. This table shows that the net outmigration during the depression decade of the thirties was nil. Fewer jobs were available during the depression decade, and many farm people had no alternative but to stay on farms. These statistics demonstrate that one solution to the surplus farm popula-

[8]*Ibid.*, Table 5d. p. 72.

[9]Kermit Gordon, "How Much Should Government Do," in Vernon W. Ruttan, Arley D. Waldo, and James P. Houck, eds., *Agricultural Policy in an Affluent Society*, (New York, W. W. Norton, 1969). p. 132.

[10]*Farm Income Situation, op. cit.*, Table 6d. p. 73.

TABLE 21-2

CHANGES IN U. S. FARM POPULATION, 1920-73,
WITH EFFECTS OF NATURAL INCREASE AND OFF-FARM MIGRATION

| Time Period | Average Farm Population for Period 1 | Average Natural Increase per Year 2 (thousands) | Average Net Off-Farm Migration per Year 3 | Average Population for Period | | |
				Natural Increase 4 (%)	Net off-farm migration 5 (%)	Net off-farm migration minus natural increase 6[1] (%)
1920-29	31,270	485	630	1.6	2.0	0.5
1930-39	31,444	385	383	1.2	1.2	0.0
1940-49	26,481	390	1,139	1.5	4.3	2.8
1950 59	19,475	271	1,013	1.4	5.2	3.8
1960-61	15,219	162	823	1.1	5.4	4.3
1962-63	13,840	140	1.086	1.0	7.8	6.2
1965-66	11,979	90	858	0.7	7.2	6.4
1967-68	10,664	60	481	0.6	4.5	3.6
1972-73(Apr.)	9,541	26	164	0.3	1.7	1.4

[1]Column 3 minus column 2 divided by column 1.

Source: U. S. Department of Agriculture. Farm Population Estimates for 1910-62. p. 23. ERS-130. and subsequent annual issues.

tion lies in expanding production in areas other than agriculture. The faster the non-agricultural sector expands, the more our surplus farm population can be absorbed into it. Evidence exists, from Table 21-2, that our smaller farms have been decreasing in number. One projection for the year 2000 shows that the number of farms will decline to about 1 million from 2.9 million in 1972, with over two-thirds of the decrease coming on farms with sales under $2,500.[11]

In spite of the large migration from farms, it has not been sufficient to eliminate rural poverty. Part of the problem is that there has been some return migration. One study of those returning showed that the returnees were young married persons, over half of whom took farm jobs. They had a low level of education. From these data, Professor D. Gale Johnson inferred that the low educational achievement of this group may have given them insufficient training for urban life.[12] Another study in Indianapolis found that southern white migrants' propensity to return home after a brief period resulted in employers regarding them as poor employment risks for jobs requiring any substantial training, and they were considered as inferior workers even at unskilled jobs.[13]

Several studies show that rural persons tend to take low level jobs when they migrate.[14] Some of the problem is their low level of education. They also tend to move into poverty areas of cities more than non-migrants or urban migrants. This was particularly true of blacks.[15] Only a few governmental experimental programs have attempted to facilitate movement to tight labor market areas where the pay is better.[16]

FARM TENANCY LOANS

Another proposal to improve farm income is to reduce farm tenancy. Farm tenancy increased from 1880 until 1930 when more than 50 percent

[11]Rex F. Daly, J. A. Dempsey, and C. W. Cobb. "Farm Number and Sizes in the Future," in A. Gordon Ball and Earl O. Heady, eds., *Size, Structure and Future of Farms*, (Ames, Iowa State University Press, 1972), Table 17.3, p. 321.

[12]D. Gale Johnson, "Policies to Improve the Labor Transfer Process," *American Economic Review*, Vol. 50, No. 2 (May 1960), p. 407.

[13]Eldon D. Smith, "Non-farm Employment Information for Rural People," *Journal of Farm Economics* (August, 1956), pp. 813-37.

[14]Ronald Freedman and Deborah Freedman, "Farm-Reared Elements in the Non-farm Population," *Rural Sociology*, Vol. XXI, No. 1, (March 1966), pp. 50-61. Calvin L. Beale, John C. Hudson, and Vera J. Banks. *Characteristics of the U. S. Population by Farm and Non-farm Origin*, U. S. Department of Agriculture, Economic Report No. 66 (1964). For analysis of a number of rural to urban mobility studies, see Varden Fuller, *Rural Worker Adjustment to Urban Life: An Assessment of the Research*, (Ann Arbor, Institute of Labor and Industrial Relations, The University of Michigan, Wayne State University and the National Manpower Policy Task Force, 1970).

[15]*The Economic and Social Condition of Rural America in the 1970's*, U. S. Department of Agriculture, Economic Research Service, prepared for the Senate Committee on Government Operations, 92nd Congress, 1st Session, May 1971.

[16]Donald Schon. "Assimilation of Migrants into Urban Centers," in President's National Advisory Commission of Rural Poverty, *Rural Poverty in the United States*, op. cit., p. 280.

of all farms were operated by tenants.[17] The causes of the increased tenancy were that there was a shortage of capital to buy farms, recurring depressions that depleted farm resources, and a high human fertility rate in farm area. During the 1930's the trend toward increasing farm tenancy was reversed, and in 1969 only 13 percent of farms were operated by tenants (20 percent for minority groups). Better transportation aided outward mobility of tenants, as did World War II and the post World War II prosperity. Also, both public and private credit facilities have improved. Although most of the credit facilities have been used by higher-income commercial farmers, the Bankhead-Jones Act of 1937 specifically provided for loans to tenants to buy farms. This program has been continued under the Farmers Home Administration (FmHA) today, and provides for 100 percent no down-payment loans. Also, the Farmers Home Administrator may insure the mortgages of private lenders. A low default rate enabled the FmHA to expand the program until at the end of fiscal 1972 there were 111,016 mortgages either owned and/or insured by it. The increase in the number of loans in the first six months of 1972 was 5,566. The average mortgage was $27,880. Questions have been raised as to whether the farms bought are large enough to provide an adequate living for those becoming owners. The average value of all farm land and buildings in the United States is about three times the average of the amounts loaned by FmHA to purchase farms.

PRODUCTION LOANS

After experimenting with production loans to those farmers who could not obtain credit from regular sources, the FmHA concluded that loans of a "seed, feed, and fertilizer" nature should not be made. For a farmer who earned only $600 annual income and received a "seed, feed, and fertilizer" loan to obtain the same income the next year, a government loan program merely perpetuated rural poverty. Capital loans have not been made to the poorest farmers with the smallest acreages, but to intermediate-sized farmers who might use their capital to increase income. The latest innovation in the program is to have the FmHA insure loans of private creditors rather than make direct loans; thus, government expenditures are saved through insuring rather than through making direct loans. The program was cut back from 50,980 borrowers in 1973 to an estimated 39,000 in 1974. Expenditures also were cut from $455 million to $350 million.

Data from the FmHA has indicated that farm income of those receiving production loans has increased considerably. Furthermore, the loss ratio on such loans has been small. When the United States was burdened with farm surpluses, there was some criticism of production loans that the

[17]The Tenure Status of Farmworkers in the United States (Washinton, U. S. Department of Agriculture, Agricultural Research Service and Agricultural Marketing Service, Technical Bulletin No. 1217, 1960, p. 1.

Figure 21-2

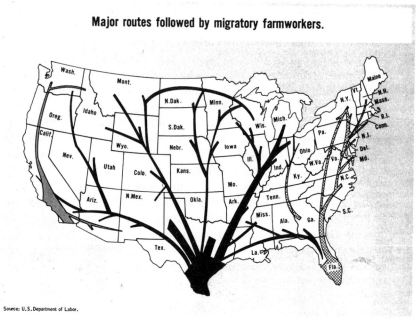

Major routes followed by migratory farmworkers.

Source: U.S. Department of Labor.

government was paying to increase farm production on the one hand and to restrict acreage on the other. In 1975, with high food prices and a decrease in the carryover of farm products, this criticism, of course, carries less weight. The FmHA program has been successful on a relatively small budget of enabling some farmers to increase earnings enough to climb out of poverty. Although such loans tend to keep resources in agriculture the fact that some of the borrowers have used the funds to buy others out has blunted the criticism that the program inhibits outward mobility.

HIRED FARM LABOR

Many hired farm workers are poor. Crop restriction programs have tended to hurt farm laborers by taking land out of production and thus decreasing the demand for labor. Technology has displaced farm labor, also. Figure 21-1 shows that the number of hired farmworkers has dropped from over 4 million before 1960 to less than 3 million in 1973. Even though year round workers constitute a minority of all hired farm laborers, they put in many more days of work in total than seasonal or casual labor.

EARNINGS OF HIRED FARM LABOR

Underemployment constitutes one of the major problems of hired farm labor. A total of 351,000 farm workers worked only 161 days in 1973, almost two-thirds of which was farm work. Their annual earning came to only $2,542. For the 247,000 farm workers who averaged 226 days, their annual earnings were $3,926, and for the 421,000 persons averaging 320 days, the pay was $4,499.[18]

Not only are some hired farm workers handicapped by underemployment, but their wage rates while working are substantially below most other industries. Farm wage rates in January of 1975 were $2.53 an hour for those receiving cash only compared with $4.40 an hour for private nonagricultural payrolls. In some areas of the United States, farm wage rates are far lower than in other states. In California on April 1, 1974, farm wage rates without board or room averaged $2.46 per hour, compared with $1.71 in Alabama and $1.80 in Mississippi.[19]

SOCIAL LEGISLATION FOR FARM LABORERS

Agricultural labor has been exempt from most of the labor and social legislation passed to aid practically all other segments of our society. Farm laborers are not covered under the National Labor Relations Act, which guarantees labor the right to organize free from employer interference and to bargain collectively. The failure to cover agricultural workers has made organization of farm workers exceptionally difficult. The International Longshoremen and Warehousemen's Union has successfully represented Hawaiian farm workers for a number of years, but all attempts to organize mainland farm workers had failed until Cesar Chavez used the technique of enlisting the aid of consumers to boycott grapes in the early 1970's. This union, however, is still quite small, and has become involved in jurisdictional disputes with the Teamsters. For a number of years, employer groups had opposed coverage of farm workers under the National Labor Relations Act on the ground that their crops must be harvested during a relatively short period of several weeks at which time a strike would be economically disastrous. Recently, however, the American Farm Bureau reversed itself and recommended a law covering farm

[18]The Hired Farm Working Force of 1972, U. S. Department of Agriculture, Economic Research Service, Agricultural Economic Report No. 239, 1973, Table 7, p. 17.
[19]Farm Labor, U. S. Department of Agriculture, Crop Reporting Board, February, 1975, p. 28.

workers provided that there were such safeguards as exempting small farms, outlawing secondary boycotts, and others.[20]

In most states, agricultural workers are not covered under workmen's compensation laws. They were covered, but only temporarily, under our unemployment insurance laws in 1974. Farmers who use 500 man-days of labor in any calendar quarter of the previous year must pay a minimum wage of $1.80 (1975), a figure below the $2.10 minimum paid by most industrial employers. Farm workers are now covered under the old age insurance program, but sometimes lack of information about the program has precluded their applying for insurance.

MIGRATORY FARM WORKERS

As part of the hired farm labor force, migratory workers are exempt from labor and social legislation, the same as the nonmigratory hired farm labor force. Inclusion of farm laborers under these laws would aid both groups. When comparing wages of migratory and nonmigratory farm labor, for those engaging in farm wage work only (over half of both groups), the migratory workers earned more than nonmigratory farm laborers—$2,457 and $1,805 respectively in 1973. However, when the wages of those doing both farm and non-farm work are compared, migratory workers earned only $2,610 compared with $3,131 for nonmigratory farm workers. The number of migratory workers is much fewer than that of nonmigratory farm workers—203,000 and 2,467,000 in 1973. Only 52,000 of the migratory workers were employed 150 days or more in that year. The U.S. Employment Service has helped here by contacting 49,200 migrants (1972) about an Annual Worker Plan whereby the whole season's itinerary may be planned in advance.[21] The program however, has been noticeably lacking in the California area. The major routes that migratory workers follow are shown in Figure 21-2.

Some of the problems of migratory workers are described by a migrant worker's housewife written from La Belle, Florida:

> Hundreds of us that are out of work have tried every way we know to get help . . . I'm about to lose my trailer and have my electricity turned off because I can't pay the bills. This is the rainy season here so my husband

[20]Testimony of Matt Triggs, American Farm Bureau Federation, Agricultural Labor-Management Relations, *Hearings before the Subcommittee on Agricultural Labor of the Committee on Education and Labor*, House of Representatives, 92nd Congress, 2nd Session on H.R. 5010 and related bills, March 23, April 27, 1972, pp. 80-82. For a discussion of the issues involved in covering farm workers, see Karen S. Koziara, "Collective Bargaining in Agriculture: The Policy Alternative," *Labor Law Journal*, Vol. 24, No. 7, July 1973, pp. 424-426.

[21]"Annual Worker Plan in 1972," *Rural Manpower Developments* (Washington, D.C., U. S. Department of Labor, Manpower Administration, Fall 1973), pp. 25-26.

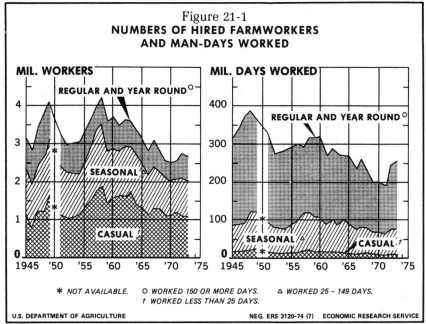

Figure 21-1
**NUMBERS OF HIRED FARMWORKERS
AND MAN-DAYS WORKED**

* NOT AVAILABLE.   O WORKED 150 OR MORE DAYS.   △ WORKED 25 - 149 DAYS.
† WORKED LESS THAN 25 DAYS.

U.S. DEPARTMENT OF AGRICULTURE   NEG. ERS 3120-74 (7)   ECONOMIC RESEARCH SERVICE

doesn't get much work either . . . Now if any of us old migrants gets bad sick, we must hunt up one of our commissioners to get his approval to go to a doctor and you might as well forget it, for the county don't want to pay and to them we are just dirty old farm workers and not human. . . . We are not asking for a handout but just some program that will let us work and earn our own living, for there are a great many people that are still hungry.[22]

HOUSING

Housing presents a particularly difficult program for migratory workers. Since migratory workers need shelter for only a short time, employers are reluctant to spend much money on housing facilities. It is possible at a relatively low cost to provide for barracks-type facilities with indoor plumbing and a minimum of conveniences. Most migratory workers do not have these, and are forced in many instances to live in barns, shacks, tents, or any makeshift type of arrangements.

In 1936, the Federal Resettlement Administration began the operation of two emergency housing camps, which had been constructed by the California State Relief Administration. Later, the program consisted of 95 camps serving 121 cities in 16 states. At first tents were used. These were later replaced by small wooden or metal shelters that had a minimum of

[22]*New York Times*, November 1, 1971, p. 41.

furniture, a stove, and bed frames. Community comfort stations contained toilets, showers, and laundry facilities. Community centers were added for recreational, governing, and nursery activities. Also the camps had health clinics. Along with federal supervision, the camps had democratically elected camp councils. The standard camp was constructed at a cost of from $200,000 to $250,000. Some mobile units were added to provide housing for migrants after they had left their home base. The American Farm Bureau Federation, the National Grange, and other employer groups were instrumental in forcing the sale of these camps in 1943. The major fear was that a concentration of laborers in one place might lead to unionization of farm workers.[23] Although suggestions have been made since World War II to improve migrant housing, little has been done. In 1974, the estimated federal expenditures to aid the building of low rent domestic housing for farm labor came to $3 million.

HEALTH

The income of most migratory families is so low that vitamin and other dietary deficiencies result. Their health problems are further complicated by poor housing and a lack of sanitary facilities. Couple the above deficiencies with insufficient income to purchase adequate medical treatment, and the result is serious health problems for many migratory workers. Their problems were vividly described by Dr. Hector Garcia, a physician from Corpus Christi, Texas, in testimony before the National Advisory Council on Farm Labor:

> The children of migrant parents are born into a world completely of their own. An anemic mother, and possibly a tubercular father—a life that will take him into his world where he may possibly die within one year, either from diarrhea, tuberculosis or malnutrition. His infancy would be a very close association with his brothers and sisters. Their home would be (a) one- or two-room shack, with no inside running water and no flushing toilet facilities. If he lives to be of school age, he could possibly go to many schools on different occasions at different places, but will never average more than three years of schooling in his life time . . . His future life will be one of wandering, poverty and more sickness.
>
> As a migrant, his world will be from the Atlantic to the Pacific—from the Great Lakes to the Rio Grande. It will be his world, however, only in that the only piece of property that he will own will be his grave.
>
> I may be here because I am still haunted by that remembrance of a day ten years ago when the little boy came to my office to ask me to go and see

[23]Clay L. Cochrán, *Hired Farm Labor and the Federal Government*, unpublished Ph.D. Dissertation, University of North Carolina, (1950), pp. 118-131.

his mother who was sick. I went to his home—a one-room shack. I found a dead mother with six children laying in the same bed, all covered with blood from the hemorrhage of a dying tubercular mother.[24]

The above conditions existed years ago, but some of the same problems still remain. For example, a typhoid epidemic occurred at the South Dade Labor Camp of Homestead, Florida, in February of 1973. The Senate Committee on Labor and Public Welfare, in 1972, listed the following shortcomings in health care of migrants:

Migrants births occur outside of hospitals at nine times the national rate (18.1% to 2.4%).

Infant Mortality for migrants is 25% higher than the national average (30.1 to 24.4 per 1,000 live births).

Mortality rates for TB and other infectious diseases among migrants are two and one-half times the national rate; for influenza and pneumonia, it is 20% greater than the national rate . . .

The average American has seven times the number of medical visits per year than the average migrant (4.3 vs. 0.61 visits).

In 1968, $12 per capita was spent for health services for migrants; more than $250 per capita was spent nationally.[25]

Using emergency relief funds, the Federal Farm Security Administration in 1938 began operation of a number of health clinics in various parts of the United States. Nurses were employed to operate camp clinics to dispense simple medical care. Physicians were hired either by the hour or were paid a set fee per patient for visits to the doctor's offices. Operations, child deliveries, and other major operations were paid for on a fee-for-service basis. By March, 1943, the medical program in the California-Arizona area alone included 16 clinics, two mobile medical units, and three referral offices. Clinics were operated in other parts of the country, and two hospitals were opened. In 1943, with the widespread opposition to the work of the Farm Security Administration, the program was abolished.[26] With a more liberal Congress in 1962, a Migrant Health Act reinstituted the program. However, the program is on such a small scale

[24]Testimony of Dr. Hector Garcia, *Report on Farm Labor*, before the National Advisory Committee on Farm Labor, Washington, D.C. (1959), pp. 5-6.

[25]*The Domestic and Seasonal Farm Work Health Act of 1972*, Report to Accompany S.3762, Committee on Labor and Public Welfare, U. S. Senate, 92nd Congress, 2nd Session, Report No. 92-1063, p. 3.

[26]Clay L. Cochran, *op. cit.*, pp. 128-131.

that the above noted deficiencies continue to exist. In fiscal 1973, about $22 million was appropriated for the program. At the present time, such limited funds deny most migrants access to hospital care. The Department of Health, Education, and Welfare has estimated that comprehensive care and hospital services to farm workers would cost $600 million. Of the almost 900 countries that have a seasonal migrant impact, some 700 are not covered by the current program.[27]

EDUCATION

Migratory worker children must suffer not only from the weaknesses of rural schools, but they face additional education problems as well. In moving about, their education is interrupted, and they are not welcome in many areas of their temporary residence. Some of those with a Spanish background have language handicaps as well. That migrant children do not fare well may be shown by a study of Idaho migrant children, where it was found that their drop-out rate was four times greater than that of the Idaho state-wide average.[28]

A FIELD STUDY

In 1971, the General Accounting Office (GAO) conducted fieldwork to evaluate the federal migrant effort in six major agricultural areas of the United states: Hidalgo County, Texas; Kern County, California; Benton and Yakima Counties (Yakima Valley), Washington; Palm Beach County, Florida; Wayne County, New York; and Berrien County, Michigan.[29] The GAO found only limited efforts to meet the manpower training needs of the migrant workers. Systematic and coordinated plans were lacking. In educational experimental programs, objective measurement data was generally not available for proper evaluation. In all six areas there was a shortage of low cost, safe, decent and sanitary housing. In the area of health care, policies had not been established to provide continuity of services to migrants. Insufficient day-care center facilities were available. The Federal Department of Labor, HEW, Agriculture, and OEO were all involved in programs that were not coordinated. The GAO recommended that the Office of Management and Budget either create a farmworker council to coordinate overall policies and determine priorities, or involve the Domestic Council in this effort.

[27]The Domestic and Seasonal Farm Work Health Act of 1972, op. cit., p. 3.

[28]Everett D. Eddington, Disadvantaged Rural Youth, paper prepared for the Select Committee on Equal Educational Opportunity, United States Senate, 92nd Congress, lst Session (Sept. 1-3, 1971), p. 6492.

[29]Impact of Federal Programs to Improve the Living Conditions of Migrant and Other Seasonal Farmworkers, (General Accounting Office, Report No. B-177486, February 1973).

RURAL NON-FARM POVERTY

The Census of 1970 showed that 54 million people in the United States lived in rural areas, defined as places of less than 2,500 population. This group constituted slightly over a fourth of our population. Of this group, 44 million had a nonfarm residence, while 9.7 million had a farm residence. It is an interesting fact that, although farm population has declined for years, the rural non-farm population has not done so. In 1920, the rural nonfarm population was 19.6 million (18.5 percent of our population) and both the numbers and percent have increased regularly since then until by 1970 there were 44 million non-farm residents that constituted 21.7 percent of our population.

A number of polls have consistently indicated a preference for rural living. A Gallup poll of February, 1970, revealed that 24 percent preferred a farm residence, and another 31 percent a small-town residence other than a suburb of a city. One of the factors helping to maintain rural population is that nonfarm employment grew faster in rural areas during the 1960's than it did in metropolitan areas. However, this study did not indicate whether the growth was within the orbit of a metropolitan area or not.[30] Unfortunately, farm outmigration has tended to lessen the income of some nonfarm rural population, since rural merchants have fewer people to sell to.

As has been indicated above, there are about 2-1/2 times the number of rural nonfarm poor as farm poor, but the latter do show a higher percentage in poverty. Table 21-3 shows that certain rural areas such as the Mississippi Delta, the Ozarks, and the Southeast Coastal Plains have a high degree of poverty. In the latter two regions, Commissions have been created to attempt to alleviate poverty.

Niles Hansen concedes that depressed rural areas have some advantages, such as a stable labor force that is relatively cheap and plentiful, adequate and relatively cheap land, and easy access to work and recreation areas.[31] However, he cites a number of disadvantages these areas must overcome. Cheap land and low tax rates may be more than offset by low levels of services. There is little entrepreneurial talent there. Labor may be costly to train. Transportation costs may be high. Cultural and educational services may be lacking. Finally, there is a mistrust of industrialization in many rural areas. Hansen quotes with approval the conclusions of Brian Berry that towns of less than 50,000 have too small an

---

[30]F. Ray Marshall, "Obstacles to a Public Employment Program in the South," in Harold L. Sheppard, Bennett Harrison, and William J. Spring, *The Political Economy of Public Service Employment* (Lexington, D.C. Heath, 1972), p. 353.

[31]Niles Hansen, *Rural Poverty and the Urban Crises*, (Bloomington, Indiana University Press, 1970); Niles Hansen, *Intermediate-Size Cities as Growth Centers* (New York, Praeger Co., 1971); Niles Hansen, *Location Preferences, Migration, and Regional Growth*, (New York, Praeger Co., 1973).

TABLE 21-3

INCIDENCE OF OPEN COUNTRY POVERTY BY AGE OF HEAD AND PERCENTAGE OF POOR HEADS UNDER 65 YEARS OF AGE, SELECTED AREAS

Study Area	Age of Head	
	Under 65	65 and over
		Percent
Incidence of poverty: Open Country		
East North Central States	7	29
Mississippi Delta	53	65
Ozarks	19	37
Southeast Coastal Plain	47	56
Proportion of poor heads in age group specified: Open Country		
East North Central States	46	54
Mississippi Delta	67	23
Ozarks	49	51
Southeast Coastal Plain	79	21

Source: *Open Country Poverty in a Relatively Affluent Area — The East North Central States*, U. S. Department of Agriculture, Economic Research Service, Agricultural Economic Report No. 208, 1971, Table 3, p. 7.

impact on surrounding areas to justify putting public resources into them.[32]

Hansen is also critical of efforts to further develop our large metropolitan centers. Here, he contends, traffic congestion, social discord, the city-suburb conflict, fiscal crises in central cities, inadequate parks and recreation facilities, natural beauty marred by building and billboards, and air pollution outweigh such external economies as relative abundance of public overhead capital, proximity to buyers and sellers, the presence of numerous auxiliary business services (banking brokerage, insurance), educational facilities, and a welltrained labor force.

[32]Brian J. L. Berry, "A Summary — Spatial Organization and Levels of Welfare: Degree of Metropolitan Labor Market Participation as a Variable in Economic Development," *Research Review* June. 1968). pp. 1-6.

Hansen favors growth in intermediate sized cities. He quotes Wilbur Thompson to the effect that once urban areas reach a critical size of around 250,000 population, further economic growth is ensured because of such advantages as industrial diversification, political power, huge fixed investments, rich local market, and a steady supply of industrial leadership.[33] In Hansen's own study of 100 cities that reached a population of 250,000 during the period from 1900 to 1965, he found that 88 of the 100 experienced a growth spurt as the cities approached the 200,000 population level. His policy recommendations were that migration should be encouraged from lagging areas, and growth should be encouraged for intermediate sized cities, in the population range of 250,000 to 750,000 or perhaps even from 50,000 to 1 million.

Hansen has been critical of some of the Appalachian program for not attempting to channel people to growing areas outside the region, such as Lexington, and Louisville, Kentucky and the Piedmont Crescent. Similarly, he suggests that the Southern Coastal Plains Commission could aid poverty in their area by directing some of the surplus population to the nearby Piedmont region outside the Southern Coastal Plains Region. Similarly, for the Ozarks Region, some of the surplus population might well be induced to go to growth centers of Tulsa and Oklahoma City, which are nearby, but outside the Ozarks. One other important point is made by Hansen. From the fact that return migration exists, he concludes that the real problem of lagging regions is underinvestment in human resources rather than migration as such.

In implementing a growth center strategy, Hansen recommends that more emphasis be placed on measures that will appeal to growth industries and less on subsidies needed by small firms in slow-growing, low-wage industries. More efforts should be devoted to equipping relatively sophisticated industrial sites, and less to building water and sewer lines that may be sorely needed in rural areas, but which would not aid industrial growth much. The programs recommended in intermediate areas would depend upon the specific needs in the area. Alternatives depending on need are investment in amenities, investment in more directly productive infrastructure, and possibly labor training, or a combination of these.

RURAL DEVELOPMENT ACT

As early as 1955, pilot projects were begun by the Department of Agriculture in an attempt to eradicate rural poverty. A now defunct Rural Communities Development Service was created in 1957. This agency emphasized improved farming and marketing along with attempts to stimulate industrial growth and aid youth in educational and training pro-

[33]Wilbur R. Thompson, *A Preface to Urban Economics* (Baltimore, The Johns Hopkins Press, 1965), p. 24.

grams, stay-in-school campaigns and vocational guidance. Lack of funding caused this agency's demise, but the Department of Agriculture, through the Rural Development Act of 1972, was given further opportunity to develop rural areas. Under this program in fiscal 1974, it is estimated that $470 million will be spent for water and waste disposal systems, and $50 million for community facilities such as fire protection, ambulances, community centers, libraries, public buildings, airstrips, industrial parks, street improvement, roads, and recreational facilities. Such facilities are only for towns of less than 10,000 population, with a priority going to towns of less than 5,500. In addition, an estimated $200 million will be expended to guarantee and insure loans to private entrepreneurs and corporations who plan to locate in towns not having over 25,000 population. Most of this money is distributed through the FmHA, but there is a staff of about 100 in or loaned to the Rural Development Service to engage in research and coordinate work with state and local rural development committees.

The size of the communities to be helped under the Redevelopment Act are obviously smaller than those suggested by Niles Hansen. There has been good growth in some small towns, and there are some such towns that can profit from additional industries or community facilities. Hansen has pointed out that, in the 1960's, there were 200 nonmetropolitan areas towns with populations of between 10,000 and 50,000 that grew by 15 percent or more, while the corresponding rate for the country as a whole was 13%. He conceded that some smaller towns may become useful service centers, but he still favored channeling most development funds to larger intermediate cities.

A RECENT ANALYSIS

In a comprehensive study of the rural problem, Professor Ray Marshall pointed out that although manufacturing jobs were increasing faster in rural than urban areas, some agricultural workers would still need to find nonfarm jobs.[34] Industrialization has brought limited benefits to rural residents because firms bring workers with them or attract them from other areas, "skim" local labor supplies, and pay low wages. The Rural Manpower Service has been criticized in the past for aiding mostly farm employers, but it is changing to meet more of the needs of the workers themselves. Rural manpower programs in the past have not obtained their share of programs in relation to the amount of poverty nor even population.

Marshall suggests that improvements are needed in both the quality and quantity of rural education through more Federal financing. Also,

[34]Ray Marshall, *Rural Workers in Rural Labor Markets*, (Salt Lake City, Olympus Publishing Co., 1974).

more and better rural manpower programs are needed. He suggests six remedies for the above problems: (1) allocating manpower programs on the basis of poverty rather than the unemployment rate, (2) attaching rural manpower agencies to such existing entities as farmers' organizations, chambers of commerce, local governments, cooperatives, and labor unions, (3) gearing training to the development of the area and providing public employment from those not likely to benefit from industrialization or relocation, (4) promoting organizations like unions, cooperatives, and community development agencies, and providing the same protection to them as nonfarm workers, (5) providing public development coordinators in predominantly rural counties, and (6) providing more technical and credit assistance to such areas.

Summary

Farm areas have been poorer than urban areas for many years. Although outmigration has occurred in line with economic theory, it has been insufficient to eradicate rural poverty. A number of government programs have addressed themselves to the rural poverty issue, but in the past the largest farm program of price supports has tended to benefit the largest farmers. Some smaller farmers have been helped by Farmers Home Administration loans. Hired farm labor has been particularly handicapped by not being covered under such legislation as the National Labor Relations Act, and workmen's compensation and unemployment insurance laws.

Attempts have been made for a number of years to attract industry through loans and grants. However, there is insufficient industry to provide employment for all rural residents. Some outmigration is still needed. To facilitate outmigration, employment services for rural areas still need to be developed. Migration grants might also be helpful particularly if they are tied to migration to areas where more workers are needed.

To facilitate integration into urban areas, the rural school systems need upgrading. Improved education has been stressed by almost all students of rural poverty. Also public policy should encourage the growth of intermediate cities that have the best potential for growth. Smaller towns should receive smaller amounts to become useful service centers for rural people.

Bibliography

Ball, A. Gordon and Earl O. Heady, ed's. *Size, Structure, and Future of Farms* (Ames, Iowa State University Press, 1972).

Capstick, Margaret, *The Economics of Agriculture* (New York, St. Martins Press, 1970).

Hansen, Niles, *Rural Poverty and the Urban Crises* (Bloomington, Ind., Indiana University Press, 1970).

Roy Ewell Paul, *Contract Farming and Economic Integration* (Danville, the Interstate Printers and Publishers 1972).

Johnson, Glenn L. and C. Leroy Quance, ed's., *The Overproduction Trap in U.S. Agriculture* (Baltimore, Johns Hopkins Press, 1972).

Leagans, J. Paul and Charles P. Loomis, ed's. *Behavioral Change in Agriculture* (Ithaca, Cornell Univ. Press, 1971).

Marshall, Ray, *Rural Workers in Rural Markets* (Salt Lake City, Olympus Publishing Co., 1974).

Ruttan, Vernon W., Arley D. Waldo, and James P. Houck, Ed's. *Agricultural Policy in an Affluent Society* (New York, Norton, 1969).

Taylor, Ronald B., *Sweatshops in the Sun: Child Labor on the Farm* (Boston, Beacon Press, 1973).

Tomek, William G. and Kenneth L. Robinson, *Agricultural Product Prices* (Ithaca, Cornell Univ. Press, 1972).

Tweeten, Luther *Foundations of Farm Policy* (Lincoln, University of Nebraska Press, 1970).

CHAPTER 22

URBAN POVERTY, HOUSING, AND OTHER PROBLEMS

In the United States, there has been a trend toward more urban living for many years. In 1790, about seven percent of our population lived in urban places (having 2,500 or more people).[1] By 1900 in coterminous United States, almost 40 percent of the population lived in urban places, and by 1970 the figure climbed to 73.5 percent.[2] By March of 1972, of 53.3 million families in the United States, 36.5 million lived in metropolitan areas (see footnote for definition).[3] Of those living in metropolitan areas, 16.1 million families resided in central cities, and 20.4 million families lived in the ring outside the central cities.[4] Much larger percentages of white families than Negroes live in the suburbs rather than the central cities.

From 1960 to 1970, although central cities as a whole showed a gain of 3.8 million persons, almost half of our 50 largest cities lost population. The very large cities of the Northeast and the North Central regions showed the large population declines whereas many central cities grew in the South and West. St. Louis' central city recorded a 17 percent drop in population and the central cities of Cleveland, Buffalo, Cincinnati, Minneapolis, and Pittsburgh all lost more than 10 percent of their population. The suburbs of SMSA's on the other hand, gained almost 16 million in population and areas outside SMSA's grew by about 4 million people. Both improved transportation and location of industry in suburbs have stimulated the population moves to suburbs. A better place to raise children is the most frequently cited reason for moving to the suburbs.[5]

[1]*Our Cities and Suburbs*, Bureau of the Census, Reports from the 1970 Census, No. 7 (1973), p. 1.

[2]*Population, Distribution and Policy* (Washington, The Commission of Population Growth and The American Future), Vol. 5, 1972, Table 12, p. 61.

[3]Those having a metropolitan residence live in standard metropolitan statistical areas (SMSA's), which is a county or contiguous counties, except for New England, that contains at least one city of 50,000 inhabitants or more, or "twin cities with a combination of 50,000 inhabitants or more." In addition to the county, or counties, containing such a city or cities, contiguous counties are included in an SMSA if, according to certain criteria, they are essentially metropolitan in character and are socially and economically integrated with the central city. In New England SMSA's consist of towns and cities, rather than counties.

[4]*Population Characteristics*, U. S. Bureau of the Census, Series P-20, No. 246, February 1973, Table 1, p. 13.

[5]Timothy Schiltz and William Moffitt, "Inner-City/Outer-City Relationships in Metropolitan Areas: A Bibliographic Essay," *Urban Affairs Quarterly*, Vol. 7 (1971-72), pp. 75-108. See also Richard Muth, "The Urban Economy and Public Problems," in John P. Crecine, ed., *Financing the Metropolis* (Beverly Hills, California, Sage Publications, Urban Affairs Annual Reviews, Vol. 4, 1970), pp. 435-456.

Whites have been leaving the central city, and minority groups have been increasing in numbers there, although after the riots of the 1960's the rate of increase of blacks in central cities has decreased. By 1968, blacks accounted for one-fourth of the population in central cities of over one million population, compared with 18 percent in 1960. For smaller metropolitan areas the respective figures were 16 and 14 percent.[6] Central cities also tend to be overrepresented by the aged. In 14 out of the 16 largest central cities, the proportion of the population 65 and older was as high or higher than the national average.[7]

POVERTY

In 1972, about 59 percent of our poor lived in metropolitan areas. In percentage terms, nonmetropolitan residents are more apt to be poor, but the larger metropolitan population results in over half of the poor residing there. The suburbs house less poor than the central cities. Of the 14.5 million poor residing in metropolitan areas, 9.2 million lived in the central cities. Census data for 1970 indicated that 55 per cent of the central city poor were members of minority groups; although a majority were white, some were Mexican-Americans.

The suburbs of metropolitan areas housed 5.3 million poor. Not all suburbs are inhabited by white professionals. A number are working-class suburbs, some are industrial suburbs, and others may be populated entirely by blacks.[8] Data show that income is higher in suburbia than in central cities — $11,210 and $9,510 respectively. Nevertheless, suburbs house 22 percent of all poor families in the United States.[9]

Some interesting contrasts have been made on poverty between larger and smaller metropolitan areas.[10] There is proportionally less poverty in the smaller metropolitan areas than larger ones. However, the fact that the larger central cities have considerable higher median income than the smaller central cities indicates that there is a much more unequal income distribution in the larger central cities.

In an earlier chapter it was pointed out that over a period of time the number of those living in poverty has declined substantially, thanks to a rising GNP and improved social security. The same picture is evident for central cities. In 1959, 20 percent of all central city residents were living in poverty. By 1967, the percentage had declined to 14 percent and to 11 per-

[6]Roger Noll, "Metropolitan Employment and Population Distribution and the Conditions of the Urban Poor," in John C. Crecine, ed., op. cit., pp. 484-489.

[7]Oscar A. Ornati, "The Spatial Distribution of Urban Poverty," in Warner Blomberg, Jr., and Herman J. Schmandt, eds., Urban Poverty: Its Social and Political Dimensions (Beverly Hills, California, Sage Publications, 1968), p. 71.

[8]Timothy Schiltz and William Moffitt, op. cit., p. 86.

[9]Our Cities and Suburbs, op. cit., pp. 11, 14.

[10]Roger Noll, op. cit., p. 491.

cent in 1969, but the recession of 1969-70 caused the figure to rise, so that it stood at 14.7 in 1972. The decline in poverty was particularly good for both white and Negro families headed by a male. From 1959 to 1967, both groups recorded a drop in poverty of 41 percent in central cities. The percentage drop for families headed by white women was much less — 14 percent, and for families headed by black women, the figures showed an increase of 25 percent.

EMPLOYMENT

When 1970 is compared with 1960, central city employment dropped by 280,000 for males, whereas suburban male employment increased by 4.7 million. The respective figures for females showed increases of 1.5 million and 4.4 million. Male jobs in clerical, sales and manufacturing were particularly lacking in the central cities. These statistics tend to underestimate the drop in central city employment, since some annexations occurred during this period.

There have been a number of reasons for the better employment record of suburbs. The larger population growth there has opened a number of service and trade jobs. Transportation congestion has caused some firms to move to outlying areas. Recent technological changes have aided in the attraction of industry to the suburbs. Some of these technological changes have been: "containerization, the jet age, telecommunications, mechanized methods of materials handling, continuous processing, do-it-yourself deliveries, and automation."[11]

In the chapters on unemployment, statistics were cited showing that within certain portions of central cities, the average annual earnings were quite low. Many of the working poor are employed full time throughout the year. Thus, the problem of this group is low wages. In December, 1974, at a time when weekly earnings for private firms averaged $159 per week, many industries had average weekly earnings ranging from about $90 to $125 per week, such as box furniture, games, costume jewelry, cigar, hosiery, shirts, and underwear manufacturing, all industries typically located in or near the central city. Incomes in retailing averaged $104 weekly.[12] The above figures are only averages, so that obviously many firms were paying below those wages. The problem of poverty here is one of a poor secondary labor market, as outlined by Doeringer and Piore in Chapter 15. The problem is exacerbated by ghetto residents holding the lowest paid

[11]John R. Meyer, John F. Kain, and Martin Wohl, "Economic Change and the City: A Qualitative Evaluation and Some Hypotheses," in Ronald E. Grieson, ed., Urban Economics: Readings and Analysis (Boston, Little, Brown and Co., 1973), p. 70.

[12]Employment and Earnings, U. S. Department of Labor, Vol. 20, No. 7, February 1975, Table C-2, pp. 89-103.

occupations within these industries.[13] With the labor market not providing good jobs for most ghetto residents, many of the people there rely on welfare for support.[14]

Daniel Fusfeld, following L. A. Ferman,[15], has characterized the urban poverty economy as an irregular economy.[16] It is exemplified by informal work patterns often invisible to outside observers, a network of occupational skills unique to ghetto life without significance outside the ghetto and of little use there. Several occupational types are artists, such as entertainers and painters; hustlers; fixers; and producers of specialty foods. Most of the activities are legal, but there is a substantial amount of illegal activity carried out by fences, thieves, bookies, narcotics pushers, pimps, and prostitutes. An outstanding disadvantage of such occupations is that it accustoms persons to work laxly and to have high rates of turnover.

Although both private and public groups have attempted to increase employment in central cities,[17] such efforts have been insufficient to eradicate the high unemployment and subemployment there. A number of obstacles inhibit industrial growth in central cities.[18] Land costs are high, and in many central cities land is not available. Considerable displacement of central city residents would be necessary to provide industrial locations there. Severe housing shortages would be caused by such displacement. High crime rates and social disorganization may also prevent location of industry there.

---

[13]A survey in 1968-69 of occupations in selected poverty areas within six large central cities found that from 82 to 86 percent of the males in 5 of the 6 cities were employed either as blue collar or service as contrasted with white-collar, professional, technical, and managerial workers. See *Handbook of Labor Statistics, 1970*, U. S. Bureau of Labor Statistics, 1971, pp. 108-110. Also a study of 51 selected central-city neighborhoods during 1970 found that 30.5 percent of the employees there earned less than $2.00 per hour. See *Census Employment Survey*, U. S. Bureau of the Census, 1970.

[14]A survey of slum areas in major U. S. cities in 1966 showed that 47 percent of the occupants surveyed were receiving welfare or other non-employment income. In all the areas surveyed a very large proportion of the city's welfare cases were slum residents. See Daniel R. Fusfeld, "The Economy of the Urban Ghetto," in John P. Crecine, ed., *op. cit.*, p. 374.

[15]L. A. Ferman, "The Irregular Economy: Informal Work Patterns in the Urban Ghetto," (Mimeo), (n.d.).

[16]Daniel R. Fusfeld, *op. cit.*, pp. 372-373.

[17]Senator Fred R. Harris and Mayor John V. Lindsay, *The State of the Cities* (New York, Praeger Publishers, 1972) pp. 13-14; William E. Zisch, "The Role of Business and the Profit Criterion," in Charles C. Moskowitz lectures, *The Urban Environment* (New York, New York University Press, 1969), p. 26; *Industrial Location Policy*, Hearings before the Ad Hoc Subcommittee on Urban Growth of the Committee on Banking and Currency, House of Representatives, 91st Congress, 2nd Session, (July-Dec., 1970), p. 132; National Industrial Conference Board, *The Urban Dilemma: Seven Steps toward Resolution* (New York, National Industrial Conference Board, 1969), pp. 3-12.

[18]Neil N. Gold, "The Mismatch of Jobs and Low-Income People in Metropolitan Areas and Its Implications for the Central-City Poor," *Population, Distribution and Policy* (Washington, U. S. Commission of Population Growth and the American Future, 1972), pp. 480-481.

There are relatively few cities with really serious central-core decline, about 15 in number. Federal policy could be concentrated on these areas, but the political process has fragmented aid so widely into so many other additional areas that the 15 central city ghetto areas remain severely depressed.

TRANSPORTATION

Since most of the new jobs in metropolitan cities are located in the suburbs, some thought has been directed toward providing transportation of central-city residents to the suburbs. Suburban residents who have jobs in the central-cities also have transportation problems in getting to and from the central-city. More thought and effort have been spent on the transportation problems of suburban residents than those of the central-city.

The rise of the automobile has resulted in less use of urban mass transit facilities. Deficits of all such systems came to $680 million in 1973. Raising fares has not solved the problem because then fewer persons ride the rapid transits. One result has been more public ownership of such facilities. In 1964, a Federal Urban Mass Transportation Act was passed to improve urban transportation. Federal money has been expended to purchase buses for urban areas and to provide rail rapid transit in a few cities. In spite of the relatively large expenditures for city transportation recently, the problem of providing access to suburban plants has still not been solved for central city residents. Without automobiles, some urban workers are stranded at the end of suburban transportation facilities.

Furthermore, a comprehensive study of commuting patterns of American workers concluded that most American workers will not commute more than one hour each way.[19] In view of the fact that many suburban jobs are located farther than an hour's trip from ghettos precludes solving much of the ghetto employment problems through improved transporation.

HOUSING

From 1959 to 1967, New York City lost 47,110 manufacturing jobs, whereas its suburbs gained 138,440. These were the jobs most suited for low-skilled workers with little education. The National Committee Against Discrimination in Housing concluded that improved transportation was not the answer to the problem.[20] Instead, this group recom-

[19]John B. Lansing, *Residential Location and Urban Mobility: The Second Wave of Interviews* (Ann Arbor, Survey Research Center, University of Michigan, 1966), pp. 73-105.

[20]Ernest Erber, "Jobs Go Where the Poor Can't," *Manpower*, (Vol. 2, No. 9, September 1970), pp. 3-7.

mended that housing be made available in the suburbs. Since the New York City ghetto residents are mainly members of minority groups, the National Committee recognized that it would not be easy to open housing to these groups. Zoning ordinances and the high prices of homes in many of the suburbs keep out all but the most prosperous of those who want to buy or build. In 1969, the average New York City area factory worker earned only $129.23 weekly; service workers earned even less. People with this income were not able to buy new single-family homes or rent new apartments, the cost of which then was $180 for a four-room apartment. The National Committee suggested that public and private housing be made available for 700,000 nonwhites in suburbs.[21]

HOUSING ABROAD

In many of the Western European countries, it has been recognized that lower-income groups have insufficient funds to purchase or pay rent for adequate housing. In England, both the Conservative and the Labor Party have supported public housing, which has been constructed on a large scale. In the past years, cooperatives or nonprofit organizations have been responsible for one-fifth of all housing in Norway, about one-third in Iceland, and almost half in Denmark, Finland, and Sweden.[22] In the latter country, government capital has been responsible for the construction of over 90 percent of all dwellings produced. In addition, state subsidies have been paid on the construction of housing for large families, for invalids, and for old persons living on government pension.[23]

PUBLIC HOUSING (U.S.)

For many years in America an argument has ensued whether private housing could provide all of the needs of residents here. One argument was that if there was sufficient upper- and middle-class housing built, the lower classes could move into that vacated by the upper classes. Unfortunately even though in some areas adequate housing was available, in many instances the poor often did not have the income to pay the rent or buy an adequate house. Also some landlords may make a higher return by not investing provided that other landlords invest. Under such circumstances, there is a tendency for many landlords to underinvest, and thus the area deteriorates.[24]

[21]For arguments in favor of opening the suburbs, see Anthony Downs, *Opening Up the Suburbs*, (New Haven, Yale University Press, 1973).

[22]George R. Nelson, ed., *Freedom and Welfare* (Denmark, Krohns Bogtrykkeri, 1953), p. 286.

[23]Leonard Silk, *Sweden Plans for Better Housing* (Durham, Duke, 1948), pp. 105-106.

[24]Otto A. Davis and Andrew B. Whinston, "Economic Elements in Municipal Zoning Decision," in Ronald E. Grieson, *op. cit.*, pp. 150-151.

As early as 1908, President Theodore Roosevelt appointed an advisory committee to study slum problems. Public housing on a small scale was constructed during World War I, the Great Depression, and World War II. The Housing Act of 1949 set as its goal a decent house for every family, but the act began public housing on such a small scale that it was unable to reach the goal. The Housing Act of 1968 set a ten-year deadline to meet the goal. Six million subsidized units were to be built during this period. Although public housing starts expanded, the Nixon Administration in 1973 called a moratorium on further expenditures until an improved program could be worked out.

Census housing data (1970) indicated that there were 4.7 million year-round houses in the United States that lacked some or all plumbing facilities out of a total of 67.7 million units. Over a fifth of these were located in central cities. In addition there were 1.8 million units with all plumbing facilities that were classified as dilapidated. Overcrowding has caused problems also. Eight percent of the houses were overcrowded in 1970, down from almost 16 percent in 1950. However, in 1970, 19 percent of blacks and other minority races were living in overcrowded housing.

POLICIES UNDER PUBLIC HOUSING

The guiding policy under the federal public housing acts has been for the federal government to approve projects owned and administered by local public authorities. To obtain capital, the local authorities usually sell bonds and temporary notes to private investors. The federal government agrees to pay a maximum amount equivalent to the debt-service requirements over four (originally six) decades. The annual federal contributions are reduced by the income received from the local authorities.

A number of innovations have been made to the public housing program. Under the Turnkey I program, instead of relying on the standard method of competitive bids for the housing, local housing authorities were permitted to deal directly with any local builder, whose housing plan appeared acceptable to them. Under Turnkey II, the management of public housing was turned over the private management firms, but this program was not successful.[25]

Integration of projects has caused problems. Although no discrimination is permitted in admittance policies, the fact that most of the projects have been located in central cities has fostered segregation. Once a large percentage of the inhabitants are members of a minority group, the project then tends to become populated 100 percent by the minority group.

Another problem with some of the public housing projects has been vandalism. Deterioration of some projects became so great that some,

[25]Henry Aaron, "Low Rent Public Housing," in Donald J. Reeb and James T. Kirk, Jr., *Housing the Poor* (New York, Praeger, 1973), p. 202.

such as Pruitt-Igoe in St. Louis, had to be abandonead altogether. In analyzing the failures, some was attributed to poor architecture. Others looked to the people themselves.[26] Obviously such a multiplicity of problems necessarily call for a multiplicity of solutions.[27]

RENT SUPPLEMENTS

A program simply to pay to poor additional money to rent adequate housing has been experimented with on a small scale in the United States. Such payments enable some poor families to move to better neighborhoods. The program also has the advantage of not congregating large numbers of poor in one location, as so much of public housing does. On the other hand, a major weakness of such a program is that with increasing demand and no increased supply, rents tend to rise. Thus it is possible that the only beneficiary of such a program would be landlords who are enabled to raise rents. It is obvious that such a program will not work in the short run in a tight housing market, but it may work where the vacancy rate it high. In order to encourage construction under a rent supplement program, some housing experts have recommended that the supplements be paid only on newly constructed buildings.

Under the Housing and Community Development Act of 1974, federal policy on housing for the poor has shifted from construction to subsidizing rents. Once a poor family has put up to 25 percent of its annual income in rent, HUD pays the difference between that amount and a fair market rent. Leasing subsidies are provided only for 20 years, a period that some contend is too short. The act limits subsidized families in any one project to 20 percent of all families in order to encourage racial and economic diversity. However, this rule does not apply to elderly tenants, or buildings of 50 units or less. Some authorities have suggested that the exemption will result in most subsidies going to the elderly and to small apartment projects.

It is too early to evaluate the new rent supplement program. As of early 1975 the program had not even been implemented because of the criticism that the supplement was not tied to new construction.

REHABILIATION

Some scholars have suggested that rehabilitation be undertaken instead of construction of new houses for the poor. If housing has not seriously

[26]J. Jack Fasteau and A. D. Silverman, *Progress Report, Joint Task Force on Health, Education and Welfare Services and Housing*, (Washington, D.C., U. S. Department of Health, Education and Welfare, October 1964).

[27]For a study of an attack on these problems in New Haven, see Bernard A. Stotsky and Joseph N. Marci, *Psychodynamics and Enablement in the Rehabilitation of the Poverty-Bound Client* (Lexington, D. C. Heath, 1970).

deteriorated, rehabilitation can be undertaken more cheaply than building entirely new houses.

URBAN RENEWAL

The Urban Renewal Administration was created under the Housing Act of 1949. It was felt that something more than public housing was needed for proper community development. The entire needs of the city must be analyzed before any program is adopted. When certain slums are cleared, for instance, other facilities may be more needed than low-rent public housing.

Planning advances are granted local authorities to make the necessary surveys and plans for their community. Capital grants are then made available by the federal government up to two-thirds of the new project cost. About $1 billion per year has been spent on this program. Relocations grants are given to individuals up to $300 for families and individuals, and up to $10,000 for businesses. As of June, 1972, there were 1,931 urban renewal projects and 584 Neighborhood Development Programs either completed or under development.

One criticism of Urban Renewal is that it has channeled so much money into areas other than housing that the supply of housing for the poor has decreased. At the end of June, 1971, about 600,000 had been demolished, whereas 200,687 had been constructed. However, a decade earlier, the ratio of demolitions to replacements had been much higher — 5 to 1. A 1969 amendment now requires that for every low income unit eliminated a new low-cost unit must be constructed to take its place.

Another of the main criticisms of Urban Renewal has been the long delay for development after clearance. By 1971, about 24 percent of the land obtained was not ready for disposition, although this was a lower percentage than in 1963 (27 percent).

Another negative finding on Urban Renewal was that in 20 of the most active renewal cities, abandonment of housing and deep citizen unrest still exist. Of these cities in the middle and late sixties, five of the group had major disorders and eight had minor disorders.

MODEL CITIES

In view of the fact that neither the public housing program nor Urban Renewal obliterated slums in most cities, a Demonstration Cities and Metropolitan Development Act was passed in 1966. Originally, it was planned that 60 to 70 cities in America would be able to obtain up to 80 percent in grants to rebuild entire slum neighborhoods. An innovation of the program was that it was to combine physical rehabilitation of areas with social rehabilitation of the people who live in them. Almost two-thirds of Model Cities money went for four programs: education, 20 percent; environmental protection and development, 17 percent; housing, 16 percent; and health, 11 percent. Smaller amounts went to manpower and job development, business development, recreation, crime control, transportation, and other programs.

In evaluating the Model Cities program, Booz, Allen and Hamilton were critical in that insufficient purchases of goods and services for the program were made within the central city.[28] They also found that the program did not make ghetto residents more upwardly mobile. A Library of Congress study concurred on this finding.[29] A GAO study was critical of the lack of monitoring and evaluation. Also, the program had little communication with Community Development Agencies. HUD, itself, found little participation by the poor.[30] A four-year study by Kaplan, Gans, and Kahn concluded that the program had not achieved the legislative objectives of improving the quality of life in the disadvantaged areas of our cities. Minimal staffing and money precluded success.[31]

NIXON ADMINISTRATION PROPOSALS

Several suggestions were made by the Nixon administration to improve urban living. The fragmentation of programs resulted in a suggestion that a number of these be consolidated, but this suggestion never came to fruition. Another suggestion was that these programs be scuttled in favor of revenue sharing. The Housing and Community Development Act of 1974 implemented such a suggestion, and directed that $11.5 billion be allocated for state and local housing and urban development projects. The federal government obviously will have less monitoring functions under the new programs. State and local governments will have more control over deciding which programs to continue, discontinue, or expand.

EDUCATION OF THE URBAN POOR

The average number of years of schooling in the United States has increased significantly over the years. Unfortunately, the highest dropout

---

[28]Booz, Allen and Hamilton, *Study of the Concentration and Dispersion Impact of the Model Cities Program* (Washington, D.C., U. S. Department of Housing and Urban Development, June 1971), 2 Vol's.

[29]*The Central City Problem and Urban Renewal Policy,* (Congressional Research Service, Library of Congress, for the Subcommittee on Housing and Urban Affairs, Committee on Banking, Housing and Urban Affairs, U. S. Senate, 1973), pp. 9-10.

[30]*Citizen Participation in the Model Cities Program* (Washington, D.C., Department of Housing and Urban Development, Community Development Evaluation Series, No. 2, Jan. 1972).

[31]*The Model Cities Program* (Washington, D.C., U. S. Department of Housing and Urban Development, Office of Community Development Evaluation Division, 1973).

rates are among the rural and urban poor. Minority groups have less education than whites. Their record of attendance is improving, but additional schooling is still needed by these groups if equality with Anglos is to be reached. Not only do central-city youth receive less education than youths elsewhere, but their performance in school has been below average.

A number of explanations have been propounded to explain the poorer performance of central city youths. Some stress family and community disorganization as greatly inhibiting school performance. Others place much emphasis on the fact that teachers in lower income neighborhoods feel students are inferior. A number of studies have indicated that where teachers think that their students are inferior, these students do poorly on examinations. On the other hand, students will perform better in school if teachers think they are bright, regardless of whether or not they are.[32] Not only the individual teachers, but the schools themselves, can communicate higher expectations to students. Various street academies and the Upward Bound program (discussed in Chapter 27) have motivated numbers of youth to enroll in colleges who otherwise may not have done so.[33]

Still others stress a meaningless curriculum as the cause of the low performance of ghetto youth.[34] A too-demanding curriculum may result in frustration, confusion, demoralization, resentment and impaired self-confidence. Scholars citing a poor curriculum recommend materials more pertinent to ghetto living, and more stress on business and vocational training.

Some have pointed to the seniority system in education as causing poor performance. Senior teachers choose higher income schools, and thus ghetto schools are left with inexperienced teachers. One study of nine larger cities schools showed that not only were the teachers less experienced but were less verbal as well. Informal pressure to keep black teachers in predominately black schools may be the explanation for the lower verbal ability, since a number of black teachers have themselves gone to inferior public schools and colleges.[35]

Inadequate financing of central-city schools has also been cited as a cause of poorer performance in the ghettos. The wealthy suburbs have more money to spend on education than the central cities.[36] The city

[32]R. Rosenthal and L. Jacobson, Pygmalion in the Classroom (New York, Holt, Rinehart and Winston, 1968).

[33]Michael Lipsky, "Street-Level Bureaucracy and the Analysis of Urban Reform," Urban Affairs Quarterly, Vol. 6, No. 4 (June 1971), p. 398.

[34]Daniel P. Ausubel, "A Teaching Strategy for Culturally Deprived Pupils," in Harry L. Miller and Marjorie B. Smiley, eds., Education in the Metropolis, (New York, The Free Press, 1967), pp. 284-295.

[35]John D. Owen, "Distribution of Educational Resources in Large American Cities," Journal of Human Resources, Vol. 7 (1972), pp. 26-28.

[36]Wilson C. Riles, Chairman, The Urban Education Task Force Report (New York, Praeger Publishers, 1970), Table 15, p. 48.

schools also have larger enrollments per class than the suburbs. Low expenditures are particularly harmful for ghetto children, since there are many more problem children there who need additional costly services to provide them an adequate education. The obvious financial weakness of central-city schools has resulted in some aid being channeled from the federal government. Programs to improve education of the poor are discussed in detail in Chapter 25.

CRIME

The total number of arrests in the U.S. in 1971 was 6.6 million compared with 3.5 million in 1960. The numbers arrested have increased much more rapidly than the population has increased. The number of serious crimes has been increasing faster than less serious crimes. Part of the explanation for the increasing crime rate is that the younger aged groups who commit most of the crimes have been increasing faster than the rest of the population. Also, the widespread use of drugs has caused an increase in crime. One estimate for Washington, D.C., indicated that some 85 percent of serious crime against property was committed by drug users.[37]

Increasing sums are now being spent on the crime problem. Government expenditures have increased from $3.3 billion in 1960 to $10.5 billion in 1971. About 60 percent of this money goes for police protection, 20 percent for the judicial system, and 20 percent for corrections. In recent years, it has been recognized that a better trained and educated police force is necessary. From 1970 to 1973, expenditures in the training area have almost tripled to a figure of $141 million. One suggestion here is that a National Police Academy be formed so that improved and uniform police training could be provided throughout the country. Also, the United States has been slow in reforming its correctional institutions. Large percentages of those going into correctional institutions return there again. More and better probational services along with more occupational training and psychiatric services have been recommended for such institutions.

CITY FINANCING

The expenditures of cities has increased significantly for a number of years. In 1966-1967, cities spent a total of $24.3 billion and by 1971-1972 this figure had reached $42 billion. The largest single cost is for education, 16 percent, followed by police protection, 11 percent, public welfare and highways, 8 percent each, and hospitals and health, 8 percent.[38] Other

[37]Senator Fred Harris and Mayor John V. Lindsay, op. cit., pp. 86-87.
[38]The Municipal Year Book, 1973 (Washington, International City Management Association, 1973) Tables 1/1 and 1/2, pp. 92-93.

lesser services provided in decreasing order of importance are fire protection, sewerage, parks and recreation, housing and urban renewal, and others. Central-cities have larger expenditures than suburbs since most must aid in financing public welfare. Wealthier suburbs with fewer poor have much smaller welfare costs. Although both the federal and state governments pay well over half of all welfare expenditures, in all except six of the metropolitan areas with a population of over one million, there are significant locally financed outlays for public assistance.[39] If welfare costs were shifted from cities, the disparity in fiscal effort (local taxes as a proportion of income) would be decreased from 33 to 18 percent for the country's 22 largest metropolitan areas.[40] Costs for police and fire protections are higher in the central-cities also. Suburbanites reap the advantages of a high quality central-city police force, where they exist, without having to pay for the costs of them.[41] In addition, central-cities provide a number of services that suburbanites use but pay little for, such as the use of city streets, buildings, shopping services, museums, libraries, orchestras, and public television.[42] With higher costs and additional services provided, the results are that per capita general expenditures of local governments in central-cities are higher than for their suburbs, even though larger amounts are spent for education in the suburbs.[43]

Taxation in the cities has been insufficient to finance city expenditures. One result has been that municipal debt has soard from $35 billion in fiscal 1967 to $53 billion in fiscal 1972. Originally, local property taxes had been used almost exclusively to finance city government. A number of weaknesses have been found with this tax such as being a tax on a necessity, hurting the aged with small income, impeding improvements and encouraging mediocrity in building due to higher taxes, and being a poor revenue producer due to depreciation of property.

With all the weaknesses of property taxes, cities have had to look elsewhere for additional revenue. Property taxes were 31 percent of total city revenues in 1971-72 (including intergovernmental transfers).[44] Sales taxes and local income taxes have increased in proportion the past few years, as have transfers from state and the federal government.

In spite of increased revenue, cities still lack funds to provide adequate services. A number of suggestions have been made to improve the fis-

[39]Dick Netzer, "Financing Urban Government," in Ronald E. Grieson, ed., *Urban Economics: Readings and Analysis, op. cit.*, p. 436.

[40]Alan K. Campbell, "Metropolitan Organization, Politics and Taxation," in *Municipal Income Taxes, Proceedings of the Academy of Political Science, 1968*, Vol. 28, No. 4, 1968, p. 567.

[41]Harvey E. Brazer, "Some Fiscal Implications of Metropolinism," in Ronald E. Grieson, *op. cit.*, p. 409.

[42]Ronald E. Grieson, *op. cit.*, p. 377.

[43]For statistical comparisons on this point, see Harvey E. Brazer, *op. cit.*, Table 2, p. 404.

[44]*City Government Finances in 1971-72* (Washington, Bureau of the Census, Social and Economics Statistics Administration, GF 72, No. 4, 1973).

cal position of cities. One is that other levels of government should bear a larger share. Care of the poor should not be the responsibility of city government, since problems of the poor are national in scope. More federal and state financing of welfare, health, housing, and education would ease the local burden. User taxes for streets might aid in obtaining revenue from suburbanites who come to the city to work. Local income and sales taxes could be used to a larger extent, although the latter tax is a particularly regressive one.

CITY GOVERNMENT

Over the past several decades, criticisms have been numerous that local governments were to small and fragmented. If the central cities could annex the suburbs, then more revenue would be available to finance the needs of the central city more adequately. Also, suburban governments quite frequently have used their zoning powers to require such expensive lots and expensive housing that the lower income groups have been kept out. Thus, fragmented government has tended to perpetuate a segregated society.

Certain problems spill over from the central cities to the suburbs and cannot be handled by small, decentralized governments. Such problems as transportation, pollution control, housing, poverty programs and anti-discrimination efforts need to be solved on a broader scope than that of a central-city. Larger scale local government has also been advocated to obtain the advantages of the economies of scale. The Committee for Economic Development (CED) quoted a minimum size of 50,000 in order to achieve economies of scale.[45] Yet, in a later study, the CED found that two-thirds of the municipalities have less than 5,000 population.[46]

The proponents of larger local government have not been without their critics. An obvious weakness of larger local government is that it will be unable to reflect the needs of its constituents. Suburban dwellers tend to vote against the proposal.[47] Blacks and other minority groups are placed in an anomalous position in that political control of their own area may have to be sacrificed for what may be only illusory gains. Decentralized government may give the citizen more control over the government bureaucracy, and may give a more important role in decision making to its citizens.

In order to obtain the advantages of both centralization and decentralization, the Committee for Economic Development has recom-

[45]Committee for Economic Development, *Modernizing Local Government* (New York, CED, 1966), p. 35.

[46]Committee for Economic Development, *Reshaping Government in Metropolitan Areas* (New York: CED, 1970), p. 13.

[47]For a voting analysis on consolidation, see Bert E. Swanson, *The Concern for Community in Urban America* (New York, Odyssey Press, 1970), pp. 141-155.

mended a two-tier form of government.[48] The larger government could administer some functions and the smaller government others. Smaller areas would still have some authority, but they may not be willing to delegate other functions to the larger organization.

In the past few years there has been a rapid growth of councils of government (COGs), which are voluntary associations of municipalities and counties to attack area-wide problems. They have received some financial support from the federal government, and have been given some function to serve as clearinghouse evaluators of federally sponsored projects and regional planning. One analyst of COG's pictured them as "a beleaguered organization, surrounded by unsure federal partners, unwilling local members and a barely awakening state government."[49] Another student of the subject saw them as having many of the basic flaws inherent in the United Nations, namely: "The problem of representation, membership, the lack of legislative powers, and the lack of enforcement."[50]

OMBUDSMEN

Some authorities have recommended making city government more responsive by following a system originating in Sweden in 1809, that of creating an office of ombudsman. Ombudsmen process complaints about alleged maladministration from government agencies. Their function is to investigate cases of citizens who feel that they have not received justice. They make a determination on each case brought to them. Although they have no legal power to change administrative decisions, ombudsmen do negotiate with administrative officials. Their power lies in the possible threat of reporting publicly their findings and recommendations.

The most urgent categories of grievances in the ghetto involve social welfare services, public health, public housing, relationships with law enforcement officials, unkeep of streets and alleys, and prices in neighborhood stores.[51]

In spite of the rapid expansion of the office of ombudsman, several weaknesses of the system may be noted. The services of an ombudsman may be more frequently used by the middle rather than lower classes simply because they have superior access to the media of communication through which his services are publicized. Furthermore, Cloward and

[48]Committee for Economic Development, *Reshaping Government in Metropolitan Areas* (New York, CED, 1970).

[49]Melvin B. Mogulof, "Metropolitan Councils of Government and the Federal Government," *Urban Affairs Quarterly*, Vol. 7 (1971-72), p. 496.

[50]Joseph F. Zimmerman, "Metropolitan Ecumenicism: The Road to the Promised Land," *Journal of Urban Law*, XLIV (1966-67), pp. 433-457.

[51]Larry B. Hill, *Ombudsmen, Bureaucracy and Democracy*, forthcoming book to be published by Oxford University Press.

Elman maintain that discrimination by race and class are so ingrained in American society that ombudsmen have little power to remedy injustices.[52] They also may tend to represent the establishment rather than the poor.[53] John E. Moore contends that the most urgent problems of the poor are clearly beyond the reach of ombudsmen.[54] Such factors as an inadequate income, employment and education, are barely affected by the work of ombudsmen. A professional legal staff for the poor might be, according to Moore, more useful than an ombudsman who may be incapable of challenging the law as well as the correctness of its administration. Nevertheless, Moore still favored the use of ombudsmen on the ground that some complaints can be handled successfully. In some instances, the settling of such cases without going to a court of law may ease tensions in the ghetto.

One study attempted to analyze statistically whether inter-city variance of urban policy outputs could be explained in terms of political structure and region.[55] The city manager-commission form of government, a reform type, had less percentage of municipal employees covered by civil service and fewer urban renewal requests than the mayor-council form of government. The city manager-commission type, however, did have more per capita city planning expenditures, but type of government accounted for only three percent of the variance. Thus the reform of local government is only one small facet of urban problems.

CONCLUSIONS

Edward Banfield denies that there is such a thing as an urban crisis.[56] He points out that most urban dwellers live in comfortable housing and in pleasant neighborhoods. Low status groups constitute only slightly less than nine million persons in the largest 20 cities and their suburbs. Furthermore, in metropolitan areas, poverty decreased during the 1960's for this group. Three-fourths of the blacks in these areas were not poor. The median income of intact black families in this area was 99 percent of whites in the same areas, although more black wives worked. The percentages of housing occupied by Negroes in central cities "not meeting specified criteria" dropped from 25 percent in 1960 to 9 percent in 1968. Finally, in the last 20 years the schooling of the average black parent increased from 7 years to 11 years.

[52]Richard A. Cloward and Richard M. Elman, "Poverty, Injustice and the Welfare State — Part 1: An Ombudsman for the Poor_" Nation, Vol. 202 (1966), pp. 230-235.

[53]Victor G. Rosenblum, "Controlling the Bureaucracy of the Anti-Poverty Program," Law and Contemporary Problems, Vol. 31 (1966), pp. 191-195.

[54]John E. Moore, Ombudsmen and the Ghetto," Connecticut Law Review, Vol. 1, No. 2 (December, 1966), p. 261.

[55]Richard L. Cole, "The Urban Policy Process," Social Science Quarterly, Vol. 52, No. 3 (Dec. 1971), pp. 646-655.

[56]Edward C. Banfield, "The Urban Crises — Reality or Myth_" Manpower, Vol. 4, No. 5 (May 1972), pp. 9-13. See also a more recent book of his cited in the bibliography.

The Commission of the Cities in the 70's came to quite different conclusions. The Commission visited four cities and its staff two, in addition, in 1971. The Kerner Commission had visited the same six cities in 1968. The conclusions of the Commission of the Cities in the 70's for the cities they visited were that conditions since 1968 had worsened:[57]

Housing is still the national scandal it was then . . ..
Schools are more tedious and turbulent.
The rates of crime and unemployment and disease and heroin addiction are higher.
Welfare rolls are larger.
And with few exceptions, the relations between minority communities and the police are just as hostile.

The recessions of 1969-1970 worsened conditions. We agree with Banfield that in the long run a rising GNP should reduce the numbers in poverty. At the present, however, millions of people in the ghettos are living in such dire conditions that immediate improvement is needed. A short description of one section of Harlem follows:

Somebody had gotten cut the night before, and blood was still in the hall. And somebody had pissed on the stairs, and it was still there, just like it should have been . . .. On the landing just before ours, somebody had vomited. Pimp stepped in it and started to cuss . . ..[58]

A major need for ghetto improvement lies in the job market, both in higher pay and more jobs. A large percentage of the working poor work full time. The poor secondary labor market where most of these people work needs either to be converted into a better market, or subsidies need to be paid. Open housing in the suburbs would help tap the suburban labor market. Those who cannot work and are poor need subsidies also. Significant improvement in education and housing are still needed in the ghettos. Lastly, some psychiatric and social work services are necessary for those caught in the culture of poverty. Remedies on all fronts must be made to eradicate both ghetto poverty and alienation there.[59]

[57]Senator Fred R. Harris and Mayor John V. Lindsay, op. cit., p. 5.
[58]Claude Brown, Manchild in the Promised Land (New York, The Macmillan Co., 1965), p. 52.
[59]Several facets of urban problems have been omitted from this chapter. Ethnic and racial problems in the ghetto are discussed in the next two chapters. Educational problems are discussed in more detail in chapter 25. The War on Poverty program created Community Action agencies, many of which exist in the ghettos. This program is discussed in chapter 27.

APPENDIX A—NEW YORK CITY

Although the core area of New York City lost 177,000 people from 1950 to 1960, and had a minute increase, 10,800 from 1960 to 1970, the inner and outer ring outside the core area expanded by 1.4 million from 1950 to 1960, and by 1.7 million from 1960 to 1970.[60] By 1970, about 19 million people lived within the area that included New York City and nearby vicinities in New York state, New Jersey, and Connecticut. Minority groups have been moving into the area heavily, so that by 1970, 20 percent of the city's population was black, 10 percent were Puerto Rican, and another two percent were nonwhite other than black. Minority groups constitute 70 percent of those living in poverty in New York City.

The following are negative factors in New York City: loss of manufacturing jobs, the slow growth of total employment, the relocation of some corporate headquarters out of the city, the continued substantial rate of in-migration, the marked rise in welfare rolls, the shortcomings of the educational system, and violence on the streets. On the other hand, New York City is a thriving economic center. It has repeatedly demonstrated the capacity to expand in such areas as air transportation and financial activities.

The following are several of many suggestions made by Ginzberg and the Conservation of Human Resource staff to improve life in New York City.[61] The city needs to improve its intraurban public transportation system. The growth of illicit and illegal operations within the city needs to be controlled better. More efforts to rehabilitate drug addicts would be helpful, also. Career guidance in the city needs improving, along with education in general. More labor market information is needed to better match available workers and available jobs. The city's 62 Community Planning Boards need additional resources for staff and technical assistance. Given such aid, they could become spokesmen for broader segments of the population. More persons on welfare should be employed in public service jobs, even if only while they are acquiring training, skill, and orientation to the world of work. Lastly, more efforts are needed to prevent neighborhood deterioration and to facilitate housing rehabilitation. In the area of city financing, Dick Netzer pointed out[62] that city governments cannot conceivably finance massive income-redistributive services. Thus, outside aid is needed for the poor in housing, education, income, and health. Higher public education also should be financed mainly at the state level. By taking on fewer tasks, quality of the local government could be improved.[63]

[60]Richard Knight, "The Growth Pale," in Eli Ginzberg, ed., *New York is Very Much Alive* (New York, McGraw-Hill, 1973), pp. 1-19.

[61]Eli Ginzberg, *op. cit.*, pp. 285-296.

[62]Dick Netzer, "The Budget: Trends and Prospects," in Lyle C. Fitch and Annmarie Hauck Walsh, eds., *Agenda for a City* (Beverly Hills, Sage Publications, 1972), pp. 651-714.

[63]For a recent study of the Lower East Side, see Harry Schwartz, *Planning for the Lower East Side* (New York, Praeger Publishers, 1973).

Bibliography

Banfield, Edward C., *The Unheavenly City Revisited*, (Boston, Little, Brown, and Co., 1974).

Blomberg, Warner, Jr. and Herman J. Schmandt, ed's, *Urban Poverty: Its Social and Political Dimensions* (Beverly Hills, Cal., Sage Publications, 1968).

Committee for Economic Development, *Reshaping Government in Metropolitan Areas* (New York, CED, 1970 .

John P. Crecine, ed., *Financing the Metropolis* (Beverly Hills, Sage Publications, Urban Affairs Annual Reviews, Vol. 4, 1970).

Downs, Anthony, *Opening Up the Suburbs* (New Haven, Yale University Press, 1973).

Grieson, Ronald E., ed., *Urban Economics: Readings and Analysis* (Boston, Little, Brown and Co., 1973).

Harris, Fred R. and John V. Lindsay, *The State of the Cities* (New York, Praeger Publishers, 1972).

Reeb, Donald J. and James T. Kirk, Jr. *Housing the Poor* (New York, Praeger, 1973).

Riles, Wilson C., Chairman, *The Urban Education Task Force Report* (New York, Praeger Publishers, 1970).

Rosenthal, Robert and Lenore Jacobson, *Pygmalion in the Classroom* (New York, Holt, Rinehart, and Winston, 1968).

CHAPTER 23

BLACKS IN POVERTY

Racism has been a factor in perpetuating poverty in the United States. Psychologists, social psychologists, and sociologists have tended to develop alternative theories of racism.[1] Some psychologists have based their theories on a negative family environment, which tends to frustrate personality needs. A frustrated personality develops, authoritarian and prejudiced by nature. The frustrated person may then attempt to satisfy his needs by becoming aggressive against minorities, who in turn may become frustrated themselves and develop self-hatred toward themselves.

Purely psychological theories have been heavily criticized on the ground that prejudice may be learned through in-group socialization. Individuals experiencing a negative family environment may become highly prejudiced, but societal factors may have an effect, also. In highly racist societies, most dominant group individuals reflect prejudice regardless of personality, whereas in societies with a low degree of racism, personality factors may be more important.

Some social psychologists have stressed reference group norms as a cause of prejudice. If most members of a group to which an individual wishes to relate have highly prejudiced views toward a minority group, then the individual himself will subscribe to such ideas. The position of an individual within the social structure also affects the degree of prejudice. Those with more education, a higher income, and better occupations tend to be less prejudiced. Also, the extent and quality of contacts with minority groups tend to affect the degree of racial prejudice.

Sociologists writing on racism have tended to stress the historical and present societal setting in which relations between groups have developed. Some sociologists have placed much emphasis on the original contacts between groups. The initial superiority of one group over another will tend to mold future relations, which, however, will tend to change over time. The change will be affected by the upward mobility of the lower racial group who deny that they are inferior. Pressure from the allegedly inferior group will tend to modify the original superior-inferior position. Racial conflict will ensue, due to the refusal of the originally inferior group to accept continuing inferiority. As a result, some new form of accommodation will occur.

---

[1]Gordon C. Kinloch, *The Dynamics of Race Relations* (New York, McGraw-Hill, 1974), pp. 58-116.

HISTORICAL PERSPECTIVES

SLAVERY

After the Portuguese explorations of the African west coast in the 15th century, African slaves were imported to work in both Spain and Portugal, and later in the Western Hemisphere. The growth of cotton production in the early 19th century resulted in large importation of slaves. The slave codes adopted by the Southern colonies were similar to old Roman slave law, which provided that slaves were a thing, whose person and labor was owned by a master. Slaves could be freely bought and sold, they had no civil rights, and were denied the rights of property or contract or the right of marriage. They had no political rights, nor was common law protection granted to them. Such codes also prohibited their education and right of assembly.

The result of slavery was the dehumanizing of blacks. The most fanatical of white racists held that blacks were another species altogether, more a kin to ape than man. Most whites in the South held blacks to be irresponsible and stupid. Even many of the antislavery leaders of the North held that the blacks were inherently inferior.[2] A few years before the Lincoln-Douglas debates in 1858, Abraham Lincoln had held that he was not in favor of the social and political equality of the white and black races. He opposed black suffrage, and held that physical differences would forever forbid their living together in terms of social and political equality.[3] A survey of the antislavery literature during the antebellum period found the same negative stereotypes of blacks.[4]

THE 1865-1900 PERIOD

It had been the intention of President Lincoln and his successor, Andrew Johnson, that self-government be restored to the former Confederate states as soon as possible after the war. In line with this thinking, by the end of 1866 President Johnson had recognized the reconstituted governments in all of the southern states except Texas. Black codes were created to regulate the former slaves. Although blacks were given some rights, such as those to marry, to own personal property and to sue, many codes denied blacks the right to vote, to serve on juries, to hold office, or to testify in cases among whites. Black children without support could be

[2]Eugene H. Berwinger. "Negrophobia in Northern Proslavery and Antislavery Thought." *Phyion*, Vol. 33 (1972). pp. 266-275.

[3]Dan Lacy. *The White Use of Blacks in America*, (New York. McGraw-Hill. 1972). p. 49.

[4]David W. Levy. "Racial Stereotypes in Antislavery Fiction." *Phylon*, Vol. 31 (1970). pp. 265-279.

sold into an apprenticeship, with the former masters being given the first choice as buyers.[5]

Due to northern reaction against the Black Codes, Congress refused to seat the Congressional delegations sent from the South, and by a series of acts in the spring of 1867 restored military governments in the South. Political control passed into the hands of Republicans, composed of blacks, Northern whites (carpetbaggers), and native whites. Only in South Carolina did blacks constitute a majority of the state legislators. Voting rights were granted blacks, but black voters were intimidated by the Klu Klux Klan, an organization founded by a former Confederate general in 1867. Its temporary demise occurred in 1877 after segregated government had been restored in the South.[6]

Free public schools were called for, but the later program was not implemented even for whites, let alone blacks. What education the blacks received was mainly through churches. Although illiteracy was reduced, grave weaknesses remained in the educational system.

A system of sharecropping developed in agriculture in the South. Although there had been some talk of providing blacks with 40 acres and a mule, this program was never inaugurated. Since the white farmers had little or no cash to pay for wage labor but did own the land, a system developed whereby the blacks worked the land and shared the income with the owners after harvest. At its best, the sharecropping system provided only a meager living for blacks. Some blacks were able to save enough money to buy farms, but in general these farms had inferior soils and were located in areas difficult to reach. In 1920, when black farm ownership reached a peak, there were 180,000 black owners compared with 704,000 sharecroppers.

At its worst, the sharecropping system degenerated into a system of peonage.[7] Advances to blacks before the harvest carried high interest rates that averaged 37 percent on an annual basis. Those owing money were not permitted to leave. One estimate showed that about a third of the larger farmers held workers in peonage, and cases reported in Alabama from 1903 to 1905 showed that peonage existed in almost every county. In 1911, the U.S. Supreme Court struck down an Alabama peonage statute,[8] and again in 1942 a Georgia peonage statute was declared unconstitutional.[9] Even after these decisions, peonage complaints continued to be received. From 1961 to 1963, the Justice Department received 104 such complaints, and other complaints were made in later years.

[5]Dan Lacy, op. cit., pp. 73-82.

[6]Richard Schaefer, "The Ku Klux Klan: Continuity and Change," Phylon, Vol. 32 (1971), pp. 143-157.

[7]Peter Daniel, The Shadow of Slavery: Peonage in the South: 1901-1969 (Urbana, University of Illinois Press, 1972), p. 22.

[8]219 U.S. 23.

[9]315 U.S. 29.

The fact that most blacks remained in agriculture as sharecroppers after 1865 resulted in an extremely low income for them. Segregated schooling resulted in inferior schools for those of the blacks who went to school. Then, in 1896, the Supreme Court added its blessing to segregation by declaring in *Plessy v. Ferguson* that a separate but equal school system was permissible. Clearly, blacks made few advances from 1865 to 1900.

THE TWENTIETH CENTURY

Several agencies to aid blacks were organized early in the twentieth century. In 1909, the National Association for the Advancement of Colored People was organized to combat segregation. It concentrated on civil rights in the belief that race problems would dissolve when blacks obtained full status as citizens. One year later, the National Urban League was founded as a social work agency to help blacks in the area of jobs, housing, and education. World War I opened jobs to many blacks that had formerly gone to European immigrants, who could no longer migrate due to the War. Boll weevil infestation in 1915 and 1916 stimulated out-migration of blacks also. Although blacks obtained voting and some other rights in the North that they did not have in the South, the movement northward resulted in numerous problems which led to the bombing of 24 black homes.[10] Also, in a seven months period in 1919, race riots occurred in 25 towns and cities.[11]

In 1941, with many workers drafted into our armed forces and many new war jobs becoming available, it was still the practice of many employers to refuse to hire Negroes. President Randolph of the Railway Porters Union threatened to march on Washington to protest discrimination in the employment of Negroes. Although no fair employment legislation would have been possible at that time because of filibuster privileges in the U.S. Senate, President Roosevelt issued an executive order outlawing discrimination in the government and on war orders. Improvement in black employment was immediate, but the final report of the Commission stated that only about 30 percent of the cases not dismissed for lack of jurisdiction or other reasons were settled to the satisfaction of complainants in the South.[12]

Rumblings of protest against discrimination and poor economic conditions accelerated after World War II. In 1954, upon a suit filed by the National Association for the Advancement of Colored People, the Supreme Court unanimously ruled that *de jure* segregated schools were

[10]Dan Lacy. *op. cit.*, p. 154.
[11]William M. Tuttle, Jr., "Violence in a 'Heathen' Land: The Longview Race Riot of 1919," *Phylon*, Vol. 33, 1972, p. 324.
[12]Fair Employment Practice Committee. *Final Report*, (Washington. D.C., Government Printing Office. 1946).

illegal.[13] Implementation of this decision has been slow, but some progress has been made in integrating schools. HEW reported that whereas 68 percent of blacks had been attending 80-100% minority schools in 1968, the figure dropped to 49% in 1970. The drop in 11 southern states was particularly sharp — from 79 to 39 percent.[14] However, even as late as 1975 it is still unclear how much of de facto segregation is illegal, and how much bussing may be ordered by the courts, if any. After 1955, bus strikes against segregated seating on buses were successful as were sit-ins to protest segregation in lunch counters and restaurants.

After a black march on Washington in 1963, a comprehensive Civil Rights Act was passed in 1964. This act provided more voting privileges for minorities, outlawed discrimination or refusal of service on the basis of race in hotels, motels, restaurants, gasoline station, places of amusement and public facilities. Also, discrimination in employment was outlawed for both labor unions and employers with 100 or more employees, later reduced to 15.

Even though the economy was improving throughout the 1960's, and civil rights legislation had conferred additional rights to minority groups, in 1967 the United States was rocked by riots that occurred in at least 75 towns and cities. Eighty-three deaths were reported, 82 percent of which were in Newark and Detroit. The Kerner Commission appointed to study these riots found that the basic cause of the riots was white racism.[15] Among the major complaints received from blacks were those of police intimidation; unemployment and underemployment; poor housing, education, and recreation facilities; and the ineffectiveness of the political structure and grievance mechanisms. The Kerner Commission suggested a number of recommendations to improve employment, housing, education, and welfare, among others.

POPULATION

The number of blacks in the United States in 1900 was a little less than 9 million, or 12 percent of our population. By 1950, the number of blacks had grown to 15 million, but the white population had grown faster, so that the black population was only 10 percent of the population. By 1972, the black population had climbed to a total of 23.4 million out of almost 208 million persons, or 11 percent of the U.S. population.[16] Although the

[13]Brown et. al. v. Board of Education of Topeka, 347 U.S. 483 (1954).

[14]National Survey of Racial and Ethnic Enrollment in Public Schools (Washington, HEW Press Release, Table 2A, June 18, 1971).

[15]Report of the National Advisory Commission on Civil Disorders (New York, Bantam Books, 1968). For a completely different interpretation of the riots, see Edward C. Banfield, The Unheavenly City Revisited (Boston, Little, Brown and Co., 1974). pp. 211-233.

[16]The Social and Economic Status of the Black Population in the United States, 1972, U.S. Bureau of the Census, Series P-23, No. 46 (1973). pp. 9-14.

blacks have a higher death rate than whites, the excess in the birthrate of blacks has enable the nonwhite population to grow at a faster rate than the white population since 1950. Movement out of the South by blacks has resulted in the percentage of blacks living in the South to drop from 68 in 1950 to 52 percent in 1972. About a fifth of all blacks live in the Northeast, another fifth live in the North Central states and 8 percent live in the West.

Census data for 1970 indicate that about 71 percent of blacks lived in metropolitan areas, and of these almost 80 percent lived inside central cities. Later data, from March, 1970 to March, 1973 indicate that there was a net movement of blacks to metropolitan areas of 97,000. Newcomers from outside metropolitan areas moved mainly to areas inside central-cities, but for blacks already living in metropolitan areas, there was a net migration of 63,000 from the central-cities to the suburbs. The net increase of blacks moving to central-cities during this period was only 26,000 (3-year-olds and over). However, with larger numbers of whites still moving out (almost 2 million during 1970-73), percentages of blacks living in central-cities is still increasing.[17]

In an interesting analysis of black migration, one study showed that if blacks had moved into states with the lowest average unemployment, the 418,000 migrants from 1955 to 1960 would have moved into substantially different states than they actually moved to.[18] The largest gainers of population in a more rational move would have been Ohio, followed by Iowa, Wisconsin, and Minnesota. Fewer persons would have migrated to New York, California, Pennsylvania, and New Jersey.

INCOME

Family income of blacks rose substantially from the migration out of farming to urban areas. In 1959, median black income was $3,047, and by 1972 had risen $6,864, a rise substantially faster than the rise in the cost of living.[19] Median black family income rose as a percent of white family income from 52 percent in 1959 to 61 percent in 1969 and 1970. The percentage then declined in 1971 and 1972 to 59 percent (the data for the latter two years was not strictly comparable to earlier data). When broken down regionally for 1972, median black family income in the South was only 55

[17]*Mobility of the Population of the United States: March 1970 to March 1973*, U. S. Bureau of the Census. P-20. No. 256. (November 1973). Table 1. p. 3.

[18]David E. Kaun. "Negro Migration and Unemployment." *Journal of Human Resources*, Vol. 5 (1970). pp. 191-207.

[19]For an article contending that the official statistics seriously underestimate the disparity of black-white family income. see Henry S. Terrell. "The Data on Relative White-Nonwhite Incomes and Earnings Re-Examined." *Journal of Human Resources*, Vol. 6 (1971). pp. 384-391.

percent of white income, whereas it was 64 percent in the Northeast, 70 percent in the North Central states and 71 percent in the West.

When absolute differences in incomes since 1959 between whites and blacks are compared, the relative position of blacks has worsened. In 1959, the median black family had $2,846 less annually than the median white family. By 1972, the differential was $4,685. Black income must grow much faster percentage-wise so that absolute differences between races will not widen.

The number of blacks in poverty in 1959 was 9.9 million, or 55 percent of all blacks. By 1973, this figure had dropped to 7.4 million, or 32 percent of all blacks. However, the data for the past few years has not been reassuring. By 1969, the number of blacks in poverty had been reduced to 7.1 million. With the recession of that year, the number in poverty increased to 7.7 million from 1970 to 1972, but some progress was made in 1973 in reducing the number to 7.4 million. Almost all of the retrogression from 1969 to 1972 was in female-headed family. In 1973, of the 1.5 million black families in poverty, 974,000 or 64 percent were headed by women.

EDUCATION AND TRAINING

The level of black education has improved markedly in the last decade.[20] For persons aged 20 to 29, only 38 percent of the blacks had completed high school in 1960 compared with 64 percent in 1972. However, the respective white percentages increased from 64 to 84 percent. The dropout rate of blacks has been improving, but in 1972 it was 9.4 percent for 16- and 17-year-olds compared with 7.8 percent for whites. College graduation for blacks 25 to 34 years of age increased from 4.1 percent in 1960 to 7.9 percent in 1972, but during the same period the respective figures for whites was 11.9 and 18.8 percent. In 1972, whereas 18 percent of blacks aged 18 to 24 were enrolled in college, the corresponding figure for whites was 26 percent. In order to improve the college record even more, William F. Brazziel has offered several suggestions: provide better guidance to encourage more black enrollment, grant more scholarships, build more colleges in black communities, expand and strengthen black colleges, and permit qualifiable (instead of qualified) blacks in Caucasian colleges.[21]

In the middle 1960's, a comprehensive study, The Coleman Report, was made to determine the equality of educational opportunity in the United States.[22] This study shows that the original deficiencies of blacks worsened as they progressed through school. At grade six the average

[20]The Social and Economic Status of the Black Population in the United States, 1972, op. cit., pp. 58-65.
[21]William F. Brazziel, "Black-White Comparability in College Enrollment," Journal of Human Resources, Vol. 5, 1970, pp. 106-116.
[22]James Coleman et. al, Equality of Educational Opportunity (Washington, D.C., U. S. Department of Health, Education and Welfare, Office of Education, 1966).

Negro was 1.6 years behind whites, but by the twelfth grade they were 3.3 years behind. Blacks were particularly disadvantaged in the South, where they scored further below southern whites than northern blacks scored below northern whites.

An important part of the study was the analysis of the factors affecting the achievement of the students. One finding was that facilities and curricula of the schools account for little variation in pupil achievement. Students achieved more when their teachers scored higher on the verbal skills and tests, had a high level of education, and had parents who had a high level of education. Also, and quite important, students did better if the aspirations of the other students in the school were high. This finding has important implications for the integration of schools. Lower-class students can be helped by associating with middle- or upper-class students of either race.

The Coleman Report has been subject to much review.[23] Some of the statistical techniques proved deficient and need refinement. Although several recent studies have shown little improvement through integration of schools, an analysis of all the most recent studies still support the Coleman finding of improvement by integration.[24]

A number of studies in the past show that income of blacks increased little with increased education.[25] However, the most recent data indicate that those blacks recently coming into the labor market earned substantially larger amounts the more schooling they had.[26]

TRAINING

We have already commented on the manpower programs in earlier chapters that have enrolled a number of blacks to improve their work skills. The blacks themselves under the leadership of the Rev. Leon Sullivan founded the Opportunities Industrailization Center (OIC) in Philadelphia in 1964 to aid in the training for those willing to enroll without subsidies of any kind. Since that time, a large number of centers throughout the country have been placed into operation. About 27,000 disadvantaged people are being trained annually in over 200 occupations. Incomes before training were $2,094, and rose to $4,277 immediately after training.[27] One

[23]Frederick Mosteller and Daniel P. Moynihan, eds., On Equality of Educational Opportunity, (New York. Random House, 1972).

[24]Gary Orfield, "School Integration and Its Academic Critics," Civil Rights Digest, Vol. 5, No.5 (Summer, 1973), pp. 2-10.

[25]Bennett Harrison, "Education and Underemployment in the Urban Ghetto," American Economic Review, Vol. 62 (Dec. 1972), pp. 796-812; and Barbara O. Bergmann and Jeolyn R. Lyle, "The OccupationaL Standing of Negroes by Areas and Industries," Journal of Human Resources, Vol. 6 (1971), pp. 411-433.

[26]Finis Welch, "Black-White Differences in Returns to Schooling," American Economic Review, Vol. 63, 1973, pp. 893-907. See also James N. Morgan, et al., Five Thousand American Families (Ann Arbor, Institute for Social Research, University of Michigan, 1974), pp. 335-336.

[27]"Ham and Eggs on Earth," Manpower, Vol. 3, No. 6. (June 1971), p. 2.

of the major weaknesses of OIC has been that it has been heavily over-represented by females, since the lack of cash grants while in training precludes many male blacks with a family from using its services.

EMPLOYMENT

Table 23-1 traces occupational changes from 1950 to January of 1974. Vast numbers of blacks have moved out of agriculture, but by 1974 black males were still underrepresented in professional, managerial, and sales work, and as craftsmen.[28]

Nonwhite women have made considerable progress in moving out of private household work into clerical jobs, but the percentages employed in clerical work is still far below that of whites. Much of the relative gain in black-white family income quoted above has come because of improvement in incomes of black females. In 1950, black female income was only 40 percent of white female income, but by 1970 it had climbed to 79 percent. The respective figures for black males showed much less gain — from 61 to 66 percent.

UNEMPLOYMENT AND UNDEREMPLOYMENT

In 1961, the non-white male unemployment rate was 12.4 percent compared with 6 percent for whites. The unemployment of blacks steadily decreased to 6.4 percent in 1969, because of the prosperity of the 1960's, but recessions in 1969-1970 and 1974 caused the male rate to rise to 14.0 percent compared with 7.9 percent for white males in January of 1975. The respective figures of the latter date for females were 13.7 and 9.1 percent. The figures for young male blacks is particularly high, 42.7 percent in January of 1975 for youths 16 to 19, compared with 18.2 percent for the corresponding white group. The respective figures for females were 34.9 and 15.7 percent. Youthful blacks are handicapped by not being near suburban jobs, nor having as much access to job information. They are also refusing to take menial jobs. Lastly, a high birth rate has resulted in a large number of black youth coming into the labor market.

In the prime ages of 25 to 54, only 89 percent of nonwhites were in the civilian labor force compared with 95 percent for white males (January, 1975). Part of the explanation for the lower participation rate is that some males have become so alienated from the secondary job market that

[28]For a study on blacks and labor unions, see F. Ray Marshall, *The Negro and Organized Labor* (New York, Wiley, 1965). For a discussion of blacks and apprentices, see F. Ray Marshall and Vernon M. Briggs, Jr., *The Negro and Apprenticeship* (Baltimore, Johns Hopkins Press, 1967).

TABLE 23-1

OCCUPATION GROUP OF EMPLOYED PERSONS, BY SEX, FOR THE UNITES STATES
1940 to January, 1974 (in percentages)

| | Male | | | | | | Female | | | | | |
| | White | | | Non-White | | | White | | | Non-White | | |
	1940	1966	1974	1940	1966	1974	1940	1966	1974	1940	1966	1974
Professional	6.6	13.0	14.7	1.9	5.7	9.2	14.8	13.8	15.7	4.3	8.6	11.2
Farmers and farm managers	14.2	4.3	3.3	21.1	2.4	0.9	1.1	0.5	0.3	3.0	0.5	0.2
Managers, officials, and proprietors	10.6	14.2	15.3	1.6	3.4	4.6	4.3	4.8	5.4	0.8	1.5	2.5
Clerical and kindred	6.5	7.1	6.3	1.2	6.6	7.3	24.5	34.8	36.6	1.0	13.4	24.6
Sales workers	6.8	6.5	6.5	1.0	1.9	2.0	8.1	7.9	7.3	0.6	1.9	2.7
Craftsmen, foremen and kindred	15.9	20.4	21.2	4.4	12.4	14.7	1.1	1.0	1.6	0.2	0.7	1.0
Operatives and kindred workers	18.7	19.9	17.7	12.4	27.2	17.4	20.3	15.4	12.6	6.6	15.8	16.9
Private household workers	0.1	0.1	(2)	2.3	0.3	2.7	10.9	5.5	2.7	58.6	28.6	12.0
Service workers	5.2	6.2	7.0	12.3	15.3	15.4	11.5	14.0	16.0	10.4	25.5	26.5
Farm laborers	7.0	2.2	1.6	20.0	5.2	2.5	1.2	2.0	0.9	12.9	3.5	0.6
Laborers	7.6	6.2	6.4	21.3	19.6	16.5	1.2	2.0	0.9	12.9	3.5	0.6
Occupation not reported	0.7	0.0	—	0.6	0.0	—	1.3	0.0	—	0.7	0.0	—
Total[1]	100.0	100.0	100.0	100.0	100.0	100.0	100.0	100.0	100.0	100.0	100.0	100.0

[1]May not add to total due to rounding.
[2]Less than 0.5%.

Sources: *Monthly Labor Review*, U. S. Department of Labor, Vol. 76 (1953), p. 599; *Employment & Earnings*, Vol. 20, No. 8 (February 1974) Table A-21, p. 44.

they simply drop out of the work force entirely, or else engage in illegal activities. Participation rates are also lower due to poor health. One study of National Alliance of Businessmen's training projects for blacks in Chicago found that their staying power was much greater if higher wages were paid than in earlier jobs.[29]

DISCRIMINATION[30]

The 1964 Civil Rights Act created an Equal Employment Opportunity Commission (EEOC) at the federal level to attempt to eradicate discrimination in employment. In the first year of the act, the number of charges filed with the agency was almost 6,000, and grew each year to 32,840 in fiscal 1972. In an important Supreme Court case in 1971,[31] a unanimous Court ruled that the respondent's requirement of a high school diploma and passing of intelligence tests violated the Civil Rights Act, since these requirements were not directed at or intended to measure the ability to learn to perform a particular job or jobs.

Important amendments on employment were made to the Civil Rights Act in 1972. For the first time, the EEOC was given the power to enforce its orders by going to the courts in civil actions. Also, for the first time, organizations rather than merely individuals may file charges on behalf of an aggrieved person. Some have suggested improving enforcement even more by granting the EEOC power to issue cease and desist orders. The 1972 amendments also added coverage under the law by eliminating the exemption of employees of state and local governments and employees of educational institutions. In that year, the law applied to all employers and labor unions with 15 or more full-time employees.

EMPLOYMENT — CONCLUSION

Occupationally, the employment picture of blacks has been improving. However, so many blacks are employed in low-wage firms and industries that they are precluded from climbing out of poverty.[32] Multifaceted approaches are necessary to improve the economic position of blacks. The secondary labor market needs to be transformed into a primary labor

[29]Theodore V. Purcell and Gerald F. Cavanaugh, *Blacks in the Industrial World* (New York, The Free Press, 1972), pp. 242-246.

[30]For an excellent discussion of several economic theories explaining racial discrimination, see Daniel R. Fusfeld, *The Basic Economics of the Urban Racial Crisis* (New York, Holt, Rinehart and Winston, 1973), pp. 60-74. See also Ray Marshall, "The Economics of Racial Discrimination," *Journal of Economic Literature*, Vol. 12, No. 3 (Sept. 1974), pp. 849-871.

[31]*Griggs v. Duke Power*, 401 U.S. 424 (1971).

[32]For excellent field studies of this problem see Eliot Liebow, *Talley's Corner* (Boston, Little, Brown and Co., 1967); and Ulf Hannerz, *Soulside* (New York, Columbia University Press, 1969).

market. Since private enterprise will not be able to solve the secondary labor market problem immediately, wage supplements and the government as employer-of-last-resort are new programs that could be inaugurated. Black youth is particularly in need of a better start in the labor market. More education and training are needed along with an elimination of discrimination. A full-employment economy is necessary to keep the black unemployment rate as low as possible. Lastly, social work and psychiatric services should be provided for those who have fallen into an alienated life style.

NEGRO BUSINESS

Although the percentages of blacks who are managers and proprietors are growing (see Table 23-1), there are only about one-third as many black males in these occupations as whites, in proportion to their population. In the past, the types of businesses most frequently established by blacks were small-scale stores, such as eating and drinking establishments, grocery stores, barbershops, cleaning and pressing establishments, taverns, and filling stations.[33] Several reasons have been suggested as to why black business remains a small percentage of total business.[34] First, the black is at a competitive disadvantage because of the small-scale nature of his business. Second, credit is not as available to blacks as it is to whites. Third, black consumers are poorer than white consumers. Fourth, some discrimination is involved in not renting choice real estate sites to blacks. Last, blacks lack a business tradition. It has only been recently that Howard University opened a School of Business Administration.

The American Negro Reference Book recorded a decline of 20 percent in the total number of black businesses between 1950 and 1960. The decline continued into the 1960's. However, recently the National Business League, a black organization, has been pushing for more entrepreneurship among blacks. This group has developed a revitalization program for blighted urban areas, but the program has not been funded on any large scale. Blacks have been helped on a small scale by loans from the Small Business Administration, which has organized a Minority Enterprise Program to promote black entrepreneurship. Business loans to blacks should aid in improved economic conditions for blacks, but it is our view that the economic betterment that possibly can be generated by black entrepreneurship is limited. We have already cited a trend toward location of firms outside the inner-city due to cost factors. People will have to go where the jobs are, although it is realized that inadequate

[33]E. Franklin Frazier. The Negro Family in the United States (New York. The Dryden Press. 1951). p. 402.

[34]Ibid., pp. 409-413.

transportation and housing discrimination make accessibility of many suburban jobs difficult for blacks.[35]

FAMILY PROBLEMS

Family separations, female-headed households, and shifting unions have been not only more common among blacks in the American ghetto, but in other black communities elsewhere on the American continent. Explanations have revolved around a West African polygamy background,[36] slavery,[37] and the present ungenerous social structure.[38]

Once the black family has been weakened, Daniel P. Moynihan suggests that the weak family itself becomes an independent factor causing further deterioration. He pointed to increasead welfare rolls that were occurring simultaneously with decreased unemployment. In his own words, "at the heart of the deterioration of the fabric of Negro society is the deterioration of the Negro family." In order to improve conditions for blacks, emphasis should be placed on strengthening the black family.

Moynihan's analysis has met with a number of criticisms. Herbert Gans points out that it would be much more difficult to attack the problems of family instability than provide more employment and improved schools.[39] Gans cites studies showing that there is no relationship between school performance and broken families. Also, growing up in a broken family does not increase the likelihood of mental illness as much as did poverty and being of low status. Others have pointed out that in the vast majority of cases, a male is the head of the black family. Thus, the matriarchal family itself cannot be cited as the heart of black problems. Furthermore, the statistics on the drop in husband-wife black families from 80 percent in 1930 to 69 percent in 1969 tend to be misleading.[40] Actually, males as heads of husband-wife families increased (62 to 66 percent) from 1950 to 1960. The explanation for the supposed contradiction in the two sets of statistics is that many females who formerly lived with others as children, sisters, or other relatives of family heads are now heading families of their own. In addition, data are available showing that the proportion of husband-wife black families increase as income, educational attainment, and occupation improves, and all of these have shown improvement.

[35]For a more optimistic viewpoint of the potential for ghetto industry, see Geoffrey Faux, CDC's: New Hope for the Inner City (New York, Twentieth Century Fund, 1971); and Howard Hallman, Neighborhood Control of Public Programs: Community Corporations and Neighborhood Boards (New York, Praeger, 1970).

[36]Melville Herskovitz, The Myth of the Negro Past (New York, Harper, 1941).

[37]E. Franklin Frazier, The Negro Family in the United States (Chicago, University of Chicago Press, 1939).

[38]R. T. Smith, The Negro Family in British Guiana (London, Routledge and Paul, 1956).

[39]Herbert Gans, "The Negro Family: Reflections on the Moynihan Report," Commonweal, Vol. 88, No. 2 (Oct. 15, 1965), pp. 47-51.

[40]Reynolds Farley, "Family Types and Family Headship: A Comparison of Trends among Blacks & Whites," Journal of Human Resources, Vol. 6 (1971), pp. 275-296.

HOUSING

Due to lower income and renting more, the percentages of blacks living in housing with all plumbing facilities was 83 percent in 1970, but the white rate was 95 percent. Both groups showed improvement from 1960, when the respective figures were 59 and 88 percent.

Although the overall statistics show improvement over the years, some areas, particularly ghettoes, have retrogressed. To cite one example, Newark, in the core area vacant housing units doubled during the 1960's. In 1960, about one-fourth of the vacant units had been rated unusable, and by 1967 an estimated half of the vacant units were beyond repair, and two-thirds of the remainder were in poor condition.[41] In a detailed study of the Newark housing market, George Sternlieb suggested that code enforcement, improved financing, and tax relief all would help housing there, although the demand for housing was weak. He found that the prime generator of good maintenance was having the owner live in the area. More financial aid to this group might aid in improved housing in the area.

Blacks have been one of the prime beneficiaries of public housing. Less beneficial to blacks has been Urban Renewal, because in some areas more housing has been destroyed than built. Some scholars have been critical of programs to revitalize badly deteriorated areas. For example, Kain and Persky note that the continued growth of central-city ghettos has expanded de facto segregation and thus has limited economic and educational opportunities for blacks.[42] According to them, a better program than beautifying the fundamentally ugly structure of the current metropolis would be to provide the individuals there the tools to break out of the structure. They favor a ghetto dispersal strategy rather than a ghetto gilding one.

A number of studies have found highly segregated living patterns in the United States.[43] Title VIII of the Civil Rights Act of 1968 outlawed discrimination in the sale, rental, or financing of housing, although the act exempts (1) single-family houses sold by the owner without the help of a real estate broker or the use of discriminatory advertising; (2) small apartment houses occupied by the owner; and (3) noncommerical units connected with private clubs or nonprofit organizations.

Minor aid to blacks has been given by enforcement of the above Title by HUD. In 1971, HUD concluded an area-wide fair housing marketing plan with a group representing all the major homebuilders in the Dallas

[41]George Sternlieb, *The Tenement Landlord*, (New Brunswick, N.J., Rutgers University Press, 1966).

[42]John F. Kain and Joseph J. Persky, "Alternatives to the Gilded Ghetto," *The Public Interest*, No. 14 (Winter, 1969), pp. 74-87.

[43]Karl and Alma Taeuber, *Negroes in Cities* (Chicago, Aldine Publishing Co., 1965).

metropolitan area. This plan has been copied elsewhere. Recently, court decisions on zoning have helped also in a minor way.[44]

In 1970, the United States Commission on Civil Rights made a study to determine whether the federal 235 ownership housing program for low-income people was enabling minority families to move into suburbs. Their finding was that minority families were still being excluded from the suburbs, and that the 235 program for minority groups was being confined to the central-city.

Weaknesses of the exemptions in Title VIII of the Civil Rights Act, and less than rigorous enforcement against housing discrimination, has resulted in the United States still having predominately segregated housing patterns.

HEALTH

Nonwhites live about seven years less than whites. Part of the problem is that the infant mortality rate of nonwhites is over twice that of white infants. The lack of medical care at child birth is an important cause of the higher death rates. Also nonwhites tend to see a physician less frequently than whites, and fewer nonwhites have hospital insurance. Both Medicaid and Medicare have brought more medical care to minority groups, but these programs have not achieved parity in health care between whites and nonwhites.

WELFARE

The facts that blacks have a lower income than whites, and have more families headed by women, have resulted in disproportionate percentages of blacks being on welfare. All the weaknesses of our welfare program discussed in Chapter 7 bear heavily upon blacks. Black desertion is at a premium because of the much higher amounts paid under AFDC than GA. If intact families are a goal of American public policy, then some form of guaranteed annual income will have to supercede welfare.

In child welfare, the professional view geared to white society has suggested that adoptive homes should have two parents who are married to each other, have never been married before, and have been married for a certain length of time. The wife must not work, there must not be other children, and housing should be adequate. A substantial fee should also be paid for adoption. Billingsly and Giovannoni contend that such standards are not conducive to adoption in the black society.[45] They recom-

---

[44]See *Dailey v. City of Lawton, Oklahoma*, 425 F2d 1037 (1970); *Kennedy Park Homes, Inc., v. City of Lackawanna, N.Y.*, 436 F2d (1970); and *SASSO v. City of Union City, California*, 424 F2d 291 (1970).

[45]Andrew Billingsley and Jeanne M. Giovannoni, *Children of the Storm: Black Children and American Child Welfare*, (New York, Harcourt, Brace, Jovanovich, 1972).

mend a system of subsidization so that more black children could be adopted. They further suggest that agencies controlled and administered by blacks could better serve black communities.

VOTING

The Voting Rights Act of 1965 has aided in the registration of many more black voters. In 1962, in the 11 southern states, only 1.5 million black voters were registered, but by 1970 the number had climbed to 3.3 million persons. The percentages of registered blacks, however, still lags behind that of whites — 66 and 83 percent respectively. Also, the percentage of those registered who vote is less for blacks than whites.

The increased voting of blacks has aided in more blacks being elected to office, although in 1972 of 522,000 elected officials, only 2,264 were blacks, or 0.4 percent of the total.[46] The United States Commission on Civil Rights has made a number of recommendations to improve voting of minority groups. Some of their recommendations have been implemented, but others have not.[47]

CONCLUSION

Urban migration has resulted in a substantial increase in income of blacks. Median family income of urban blacks has doubled that of rural farm blacks, $6,578 compared with $3,197.[48] The above figures are medians only, however, and hide the disorganization of the lowest-income city dwellers. It has been pointed out that three-quarters of the persons living in inner-city poverty areas are not poor, but nevertheless considerable disorganization exists for those who are poor.[49]

Of the 1.5 million black families in poverty, 974,000 or 64 percent are headed by women. Data for one year indicated that of all poor families headed by black women 62 percent of the women did not work. For this group, a larger government subsidy, or work, is necessary if they are to be released from poverty.

[46]Vernon E. Jordon, Jr., "Barriers to Black Political Participation," *Civil Rights Digest*, Vol. 5, Oct. 1972, p. 3.

[47]"Implementation of Commission Recommendations," *Civil Rights Digest*, Vol. 4, No. 4, (Dec. 1971), p. 46.

[48]*Negro Population*, U. S. Bureau of the Census, 1969, Census of Population, PC (2)-1B, Table 9, p. 143.

[49]For various portrayals of ghetto life, see Claude Brown, *Manchild in the Promised Land*, (New York, The Macmillan Co., 1965), p. 52; Christopher Lasch, *The Agony of the American Left* (New York, Alfred Knopf, 1969); Kenneth B. Clark, *Dark Ghetto* (New York, Harper and Row, 1965); Angus Campbell and Howard Schuman, *Racial Attitudes in Fifteen American Cities* (Ann Arbor, Survey Research Center, Institute for Social Research, June 1969); Richard J. Hill and Calvin J. Larson, "Differential Ghetto Organization," *Phylon*, Vol. 32, 1971), pp. 302-311.

For the poor families headed by a male, 29 percent work full time 50 to 52 weeks a year. Obviously, higher pay is necessary for this group to climb from poverty. The alternatives here are a higher minimum wage, wage subsidies, and the government as employer of last resort, all to be discussed in the last chapters. Over a third of the poor black families headed by a male recorded some work for the male head, but less than full time. Here, part of the problem may be lack of work, or discrimination, or the pay and conditions of the secondary labor market may be so unattractive that excessive turnover results. A full employment policy, better enforcement of our anti-discrimination laws, and a transformation from a secondary to a primary labor market would help this group.

For those poverty families headed by a male who did not work at all (about a third of male headed poor black families), the single most frequent reason for not working, affecting about half of this group, was either illness or disability. Subsidies for the ill and disabled were insufficient to provide a sufficient income for this group to climb from poverty.

Additional government programs for both the working and nonworking poor blacks are necessary if poverty is to be eliminated among this group.

Bibliography

Billingsley, Andrew and Jeanne M. Giovannoni, Children of the Storm: Black Children and American Child Welfare (New York, Harcourt, Brace, Jovanovich, 1972).

Clark, Kenneth B., Dark Ghetto (New York, Harper and Row, 1965).

Daniel, Peter, The Shadow of Slavery: Peonage in the South; 1901-1969 (Urbana, University of Illinois Press, 1972).

Hannerz, Ulf, Soulside (New York, Columbia University Press, 1969).

Kinloch, Gordon C., The Dynamics of Race Relations (New York, McGraw-Hill, 1974).

Lacy, Dan, The White Use of Blacks in America (New York, McGraw-Hill, 1972).

Liebow, Eliot, Talley's Corner (Boston, Little, Brown, and Co., 1967).

Purcell, Thoedore V. and Gerald F. Cavanaugh, Blacks in the Industrial World (New York, The Free Press, 1972).

Marshall, F. Ray, The Negro and Organized Labor (New York, Wiley, 1965).

Rutledge, Aaron L. and Getrude Z. Goss, Nineteen Negro Men (San Francisco, Jossey-Bass, 1967).

CHAPTER 24

MEXICAN AMERICANS AND AMERICAN INDIANS

MEXICAN AMERICANS

HISTORICAL PERSPECTIVES

The Mayans developed an advanced civilization that reached its peak at about 700 AD in the area of the Yucatan and Guatemala. Corn was the principal crop, and sufficient surpluses were produced to enable the Mayans to build great cities and develop astronomy, mathematics, and other sciences. Centuries later, by the time of the arrival of the Spanish in 1519, the Aztecs had developed a flourishing civilization centered at the present Mexico City. A number of their cities had a population of more than 100,000 people. The Aztecs produced such crops as corn, cotton, tobacco, beans, squashes, and maguey. They had a highly organized class system headed by an emperor, followed by priests, nobles, merchants, free peasants, and slaves. They also had a system of schools that included insitutes of higher learning and libraries.

After the Spanish conquered Mexico and intermarried with the natives, they expanded northward and established settlements at Durango in 1563, Saltillo in 1586, Sante Fe in 1609, and El Paso in 1659. Later, towns were established in San Diego in 1769, San Francisco in 1776, and Los Angeles in 1781. Mexican independence was declared in 1821.

Many more Anglos than Mexicans settled in Texas so that in 1836, Texas declared its independence from Mexico. A later annexation of Texas to the United States, and a boundary dispute between Texas and Mexico, resulted in the Mexican-American War, which began in 1846. The United States was victorious, and for a $15 million payment annexed about half the land of Mexico in the treaty of Guadelupe-Hidalgo of 1848. This territory included California, Texas, Colorado, and parts of Utah, Nevada, Arizona and New Mexico. Additional territory in the south of what are now the states of Arizona and New Mexico was obtained through the Gadsden Purchase of 1853.

Although the treaty of Guadalupe-Hidalgo guaranteed citizenship to Mexicans residing in the acquired territory and no expropriation of property, differences in Mexican and Anglo law caused heavy property losses for Mexicans. Land titles generally had been unregistered, and no property taxes had been assessed under Mexican law. Instead, revenue was obtained by taxes upon harvest and livestock increases. Anglo law required registration of property with precise delineation of boundaries and the payment of property taxes. Many Mexicans lost their land during the 1870's and 1880's. Many swindles were perpetuated through collusion of lawyers. Some lawyers filed suit for the land, while others, supposedly defending the Mexican property, obtained the land by charging fees for their services. Bribes were also resorted to. The "Santa Fe Ring" was particularly adept at fleecing Mexican sheepherders of their land. One ring leader obtained 2 million acres outright and was part owner, or lawyer for, 4 million more acres.[1] Within a few years over 80 percent of the Spanish and Mexican grants in New Mexico were lost by their owners.[2] One response by some Mexican Americans was to form such vigilante groups as La Mano Negra and Las Gorras Blancas. Railroad ties were destroyed and barbed wire of Anglo ranchers was cut. The governor issued a proclamation for the Las Gorras Blancas to disband, and threatened to call out the militia and obtain Federal troops if necessary. Reaction of both Anglos and Mexicans to excesses of this group caused its decline and eventual demise.[3]

Belatedly, in 1891, a Court of Private Land Claims was established to rule on the conflicts over the land. Although land grants with over 35-1/2 million acres were brought to the court, title to less than 2 million acres was validated. Ninety-four percent of the claims of the villagers were dismissed. Thus court rulings were used to justify and legalize the theft of Mexican-American land.[4] A Congressional Act of 1891 also set aside large tracts of land in New Mexico as national forests. Over half the land in New Mexico is not federal or state controlled. The refusal to permit grazing in the forests forced many Mexican Americans to reduce their sheep and goat herds, and has caused controversy to the present time.

Both in the nineteenth and twentieth centuries many Mexican-Americans lost land because of a failure to pay property taxes. Some of this land was lost because Mexican-American land was assessed at higher valuations than Anglo land. The result of all these land policies was that, by 1939, Mexican Americans owned only 85,000 of the original 275,000 acres, and about a fourth of the owned land was under lease.[5]

POPULATION

In the first decade of the 20th century, about 24,000 Mexicans emigrated to the United States. After the 1910 revolution, emigration speeded ap-

[1]Stan Steiner, La Raza: The Mexican Americans (New York, Harper and Row, 1969), p. 58.

[2]Victor Westphall, The Public Domain in New Mexico: 1854-1891 (Albuquerque, The University of New Mexico Press, 1965), p. 49.

[3]Matt S. Meier and Feliciano Rivera, The Chicanos: A History of Mexican Americans (New York, Hill and Wang, 1972), p. 105.

[4]Stan Steiner, op. cit., p. 60.

[5]Carey McWilliams, North from Mexico (Philadelphia, Lippincott, 1949), p. 78.

preciably to 225,000 in the second decade. Even more came in the 1920's (437,000), when the Immigration Acts of 1921 and 1924 greatly reduced the numbers coming from Europe. During consideration of the immigration laws, some Congressmen suggested that Mexicans be included in the quotas, but the only legislation affecting them merely established a $10 visa fee in 1924.

By March, 1973, 5.9 million Mexican-Americans were living in the United States. Census data for 1970 showed that the largest concentration of Mexican Americans lived in California (1.9 million) followed by 1.6 million in Texas, and over 462,000 in the three states of Colorado, New Mexico and Arizona combined. There has been a definite trend toward movement to California cities and out of agriculture. The four cities with the largest Mexican American populations are Los Angeles, 822,000; San Antonio, 296,000; El Paso, 176,000; and Houston, 139,000.

INCOME

In 1971, the median family income of Mexican Americans was $7,539. During that year, 28 percent of all Mexican American persons were living in poverty. Family income varied considerably in a five state southwestern area from a low of $5,439 in Texas to a high of $8,050 in California (1969). Within Texas, in 1969 median family income was particularly low in the Brownsville-Harlingen-San Benito area ($4,077) and Laredo ($4,396). Over 50 percent of persons of Mexican origin were living in poverty in both areas. On the brighter side, both male and female Mexican-American income as a percentage of U.S. male and female income grew from 1960 to 1970. Male Mexican income was 75 percent of total male income in 1969 compared with 68 percent a decade earlier.

EDUCATION

The number of years education of Mexican-Americans has gradually increased. In Texas, Mexican-American males who were 20 to 24 years of age in 1970 had completed 11.4 years of schooling, and 46 percent were high school graduates. The corresponding figures for females was 11.6 years and 47 percent. In 1960, Mexican-American males 20 to 24 years of age in Texas had completed only 5.5 years of schooling and females 8.6. Using data for the five southwestern states combined, for those 25 years of age and older in 1970, Mexican-Americans born in Mexico had only 5.4 years of schooling. Those born in the United States of Mexican parents had completed 8.7 years of education, and those born of native Mexican-Americans had 9.9 years.

In spite of the improvement in years of schooling, Mexican-Americans still drop out of school in far larger percentages than Anglos. Fewer attend college although here, too, the record is improving. Almost all tests have found that Mexican-Americans read below their grade level. Many Mexican-American children have a language problem, and a number of educators have cited this problem as a leading cause of school dropout. In 1968, a strike among Mexican Americans in Los Angeles high schools resulted in some attempts to improve education after 38 demands had been aired. Remedies suggested have been to provide a full year of education for children five years of age, with a gradual transition from speaking Spanish to English, and an emphasis on preparation for reading English.[6] Others have suggested that teachers' attitudes of the inferiority of Mexican American children have precluded educating them to their potential. Also Mexican culture and history have been lacking from curricula.

EMPLOYMENT

Data for Texas from the 1960 and 1970 census show only slight occupational improvement for Mexican Americans. In 1960, only seven percent of Mexican Americans males were professionals, or managers, and by 1970 the respective figure was 10 percent. There was no increase in the percentages of males in sales and clerical work, but the percentage of craftsmen increased from 17 to 22 percent. The percentages employed as laborers and farm laborers decreased from 29 percent to 23 percent. Employment for women increased slightly in the professional category from 6 to 7 percent and those in clerical work from 18 to 24 percent. Those employed as farm laborers or private household workers decreased from 19 percent to 11 percent. In spite of these improvements by March of 1972, only 23 percent of Mexican American people were employed as white-collar workers compared with 40 percent for the total population in the United States. Mexican Americans were overrepresented in blue-collar, farm and service work. Mexican Americans also have the added handicap of having higher unemployment rates than the rest of the population. In March of 1972, 7.4 percent of Mexican Americans males aged 16 to 64 were unemployed compared with 6 percent for the entire population. This ethnic discrepancy was even greater for women, 10.0 and 6.6 percent respectively.

Part of the employment problem of Mexican Americans has stemmed from differentials in wages paid Mexican-American workers for the same work. Organization of Mexican-American workers into union helped to alleviate this problem, but as late as 1944 it took a National War Labor Board order to outlaw wage differentials among copper mining companies, and a strike two years later by the Mine Mill and Smelter Workers to hasten compliance with the order.[7] Several decades later, the

---

[6]Herschel T. Manuel, *Spanish-Speaking Children of the Southwest: Their Education and the Public Welfare* (Austin, University of Texas Press, 1965), p. 122.

[7]Meier and Rivera, *op. cit.*, pp. 182-184.

U.S. Civil Rights Commission found that the El Paso Natural Gas Permian division hired no Mexican-American workers even as unskilled workers, although a large percentage of the population it served were Mexican-Americans. Mexican-American workers were seriously underrepresented in the telephone, banking, and other industries. It is hoped that work of the Equal Employment Opportunity Commission will be able to eliminate discrimination in employment.

ETHNIC CONFLICT

Conflict began centuries ago between the English and Spanish in their competition for colonies. After the Mexican-American War, Mexicans lost much of their land. When many thousands rushed to California in the gold rush of 1849, a law was quickly passed in 1859, called the foreign Miners Tax Law, that taxed all foreigners who worked at gold digging. Mexican nationals were forced to leave the area. Further injury was added in 1855 with a California law prohibiting vagrance. The law was called the "Greaser Law" because the word "greaser" appeared in the text of the law. In Texas, in the 1850's, a number of Mexican men led raids to obtain the return of their lands. The most successful was Juan Cortina, a wealthy ranchers and landowner who liberated the entire valley from Brownsville to Rio Grande City from 1868 to 1875. However, the Mexicans were later pushed back by the United States Army and the Texas Rangers. Anglo vigilante groups were organized, and lynchings, murders, and border warfare became common.

Ethnic conflict has continued into the 20th century. In the 1920's and 1930's, Rubel reports, in south Texas there was "open tension and hostility between members of the Anglo-American and Mexican-American groups."[8] To keep Mexican-American workers out of Colorado when the Great Depression of the 1930's caused a loss of jobs, the governor there called out National Guard troops to patrol the borders between Colorado and New Mexico. The order was rescinded several days later, and the action was later declared unconstitutional. Minor clashes between American soldiers and Mexican-American youth in Los Angeles eventually led to serious rioting in 1943. Fleets of sailors hired taxicabs to attack zoot-suit Mexican-Americans wherever they could be found. Similar outbreaks spread to Pasadena, Long Beach, and San Diego. Several decades later during the 1970-71 period, East Los Angeles became the most riotous area in the nation. Extensive damage and destruction occurred in the central business district there. In 1972, similar rioting existed at Santa Paula, California.

In a recent study of attitudes of Mexican-Americans and Anglos toward each other in a border city in South Texas, it was found that

[8]Arthur J. Rubel, *Across the Tracks: Mexican-Americans in a Texas City*, (Austin, University of Texas Press, 1966), p. 47.

typically Anglos held the Mexican-Americans to be an inferior group.[9] Mexican Americans were stereotyped as unclean, drunken, deceitful, unpredictable and immoral. Mexican-Americans themselves defined Mexican ways as undesirable, inferior, and disreputable, although racial pride set the tone of their demands and striving for equal status. Their images of Anglos tended to be both favorable and unfavorable. They identified Anglos as being ambitious and industrious, although they were also held to be unkind, mercenary, exploitive, stolid, phlematic, cold-hearted, distant, conceited, inconstant, and insincere. Mutual stereotyping, exclusion practiced by Anglos, and isolation practiced by Mexican Americans, have resulted in separateness of the two groups. Such separateness has been a massive barrier to realization of expectations.

THE TRADITIONAL CULTURE CONTROVERSY

A number of anthropologists, including William Madsen,[10] have maintained that different cultural values of Mexican-Americans have made adaptation to Anglo society difficult. Madsen points out that La Raza (literally, the race) has a strong belief in fatalism which produces an attitude of resignation. Misfortune is viewed as an act of fate rather than something which must be overcome. From such behaviour, Anglos concludes that Latins lack drive and determination. Latins also lack a future orientation and the Anglo passion for planning ahead. So as not to belittle others, personal gains or advancement are concealed. Thus Mexican-Americans engage in inconspicuous consumption rather than conspicuous consumption, as Anglos do. Such behavior may cause passivity.

The view that Mexican-Americans are excessively passive has been criticized by Octavio L. Romano.[11] He points out that several hundred Mexican-American cowboys went out on strike in the Texas Panhandle in 1883. In 1903, over 1,000 Mexicans, Mexican-Americans, and Japanese went on strike in California. In 1922, Mexican field workers attempted to organize in Fresno, and in 1927 formed a large union. Strikes by Mexicans occurred in the Imperial Valley in 1927 and 1930, and in both Los Angeles County and the San Joaquin Valley in 1933. Both celery and citrus crop workers struck in 1936. During the 1930's agricultural strikes by Mexicans occurred in eight other states. Sheepherders struck in west Texas, as did pecan shellers in San Antonio and Mexican coal miners in New Mexico.

---

[9]Ozzie G. Simmons, "The Mutual Images and Expectations of Anglo-Americans and Mexican-Americans, in Edward Simmen, ed., *Pain and Promise: The Chicano Today* (New York, New American Library, 1972), pp. 106-118.

[10]William Madsen, *The Mexican-Americans of South Texas* (New York, Holt, Rinehart and Winston, 1964).

[11]Octavio I. Romano, V, "The Anthropology and Sociology of Mexican-Americans: A Distortion of Mexican-American History," in Octavio I. Romano, V, ed., *Voices* (Berkeley, Cal., Quinto Sol Publications, 1971) pp. 26-39.

Grebler, et al., also criticize the passivity theory about Mexican-Americans. His group polled a number of Mexican-Americans in both Los Angeles and San Antonio, and found that a majority had a more active than passive orientation toward life.[12]

Salvador Alverez has taken issue with the prevalent idea that traditional culturalism has kept Mexican-Americans divided and unorganized.[13] He cites a listing of 800 organizations in the Directory of Spanish-Speaking Community Organizations, most of which are Mexican-American. If these groups had all been failures he doubts that they would still be in existence today. Some Mexican-American groups have disbanded simply because of the overwhelming superiority of Anglo force.

Recent history has witnessed substantial organization among Mexican Americans. In New Mexico, Reies Tijerina, a former circuit preacher for the Assembly of God, founded the Alianza Federal de Mercedes in 1962 in an attempt to recover the land formerly lost by Mexican-Americans. Ranch burnings, cut fences, and warnings have been issued to Anglo owners. Also, forest fires have been set. The National Guard was called to quell a riot after the Alianza attacked a county courthouse in retribution for having a permit to assemble revoked.

In 1970, La Raza Unida party was organized after a number of students had walked out of school in Crystal City, Texas, in 1969 for poor conditions there. The party has not only participated in voter registration, but also provides draft counseling and supplies economic expertise and support to Chicano Chambers of Commerce. Branches have been organized not only in many Texas counties but also in Colorado, New Mexico, Arizona, and California. Some elections have been won by this group.

ASSIMILATION

Mixed marriages between Anglos and Mexican-Americans were reported to have declined at the turn of this century, if not before.[14] As late as the 1930's, one study shows that mixed marriages were rare both in Taos and Las Cruces, New Mexico. Even later, in 1948, in the Albuquerque area, Anglos were not considered to be suitable marriage partners. There was no trend toward mixed marriages from 1930 to 1947, but a definite movement toward more mixed marriages developed from 1957 to 1964. In 1947, only seven percent of Mexican-American marriages in the Albuquerque area were mixed marriages, whereas, by 1964, the percentage had become

[12]Leo Grebler, Joan Moore, and Ralph Guzman, The Mexican-American People (New York, The Free Press, 1970), pp. 432-439.

[13]Salvadore Alvarez, "Mexican-American Community Organization," in Octavio I. Romano, V, op. cit., pp. 91-100.

[14]Nancy Gonzalez, The Spanish-Americans of New Mexico (Albuquerque, University of New Mexico Press, 1969), p. 165.

32 percent.[15] In the mixed marriages, it was more typical for the Anglo male to marry a Mexican-American female than vice versa. A study in Los Angeles found in 1963 that 40 percent of the marriages were mixed, whereas, from 1924-1933 the figure had been only 17 percent.[16]

Grebler, et al., analyzed differences between Mexican-Americans in Los Angeles and San Antonio. A much larger percentage of Mexican-Americans in Los Angeles than San Antonio worked as factory operatives, whereas in the latter town much larger percentages worked as laborers and service workers, including private household workers. Income was substantially higher for Mexican-Americans living in Los Angeles than in San Antonio, as was their educational level. Second generation Mexican-Americans were able to increase their earnings over first generation Mexican immigrants in Los Angeles, but not in San Antonio. Many more Los Angeles Mexican-Americans lived in mixed neighborhoods than those in San Antonio. There was more social distance felt by San Antonio Mexican-Americans than those in Los Angeles. In Los Angeles, many more Mexican-Americans had Anglos as classmates, friends, and fellow workers. In short, more integration was found in Los Angeles than in San Antonio.

CONCLUSION

Income of Mexican-Americans has been aided by their massive move from rural to urban areas, particularly to cities in California. Income for Mexican-Americans has increased relative to Anglos, although it is still far below that of Anglos. Income is particularly low in Texas, and Mexican-Americans have not made as much advance there as elsewhere. Grebler, et al., found that although educational levels were improving, they have been too slow in San Antonio to permit the massive changes necessary in movement from manual to nonmanual occupations that are required for substantial improvement in income and social status. Grebler, et al., viewed the responses of the larger society to aid Mexican Americans as being too little as well as too late. Although the bracero program was terminated, they felt that it is highly inequitable to permit commuters to cross the border and lower the wages of those living on the American side. In education, they recommended a major experimental effort extending throughout the entire system, ranging from teacher training to administration. Since local variations in all areas of activity are great, they stress that concerted efforts must be made in each local area.

In summarizing the findings of the Committee Hearings on Mexican American Affairs (1967), Grebler, et al., cite three major themes in the

[15]*Ibid.*, Table 4, p. 167.
[16]Leo Grebler, *et al., op. cit.*, p. 406.

testimony. One is that most social institutions and governmental programs do not operate in accordance with their mission. Mexican Americans are distrustful of the inertness of social institutions and the inefficacy of action programs. Secondly, social institutions and government programs fail to reach Mexican-Americans because of insufficient funding, or gross neglect. Lastly, Mexican-Americans are discriminated against in employment, administration of justice, social security, and welfare. They conclude their study with the observation that our institutions will need to change now far more rapidly than in the past in order to better cope with the Mexican American problems of today.

AMERICAN INDIANS

HISTORICAL PERSPECTIVES

British policy toward the Indians in the seventeenth century had two basic principles.[17] One was that Indians had a compensable interest in the lands they occupied and used. The other was that Indians required the protection of the colonial governments. Although laws were passed by the colonies to protect Indians, much abuse of the latter occurred. Later when the United States became independent, the Constitution gave the United States power to regulate commerce with foreign nations, between the states and "with the Indian Tribes."

Since many of the Indian tribes lived in a hunting and fishing culture, it was felt by many that Indians could live as well farther west. Even permanently settled agricultural tribes were displaced, mainly by treaties. In 1835, for example, the Cherokees were forced into a treaty removing them from Georgia, and other areas of the South to Oklahoma. Those refusing to leave were forced by military intervention. One group forceably removed in the winter of 1838-1839 experienced severe problems of hunger and cold, so that one-fourth of the group died en route to their new location, in what has become well known today as the "Trail of Tears."

TREATIES

From 1789 until 1850, the United States negotiated and ratified 245 treaties with the Indians. During this period the United States government secured more than 450 million acres of land for less than $90 million, or 20

---

[17]James E. Officer, "The American Indian and Federal Policy," in Jack O. Waddell and O. Michael Watson, eds., *The American Indian in Urban Society* (Boston, Little, Brown and Co., 1971), pp. 8-10.

cents an acre.[18] The consensus is that wholesale fraud was perpetrated upon the Indians in acquiring the land. Land-hungry speculators, military defeats, and plain dishonesty robbed the Indians of much of their land. Sitting Bull, for example, stated that he would be glad to make a treaty with white men if the government would send him a white man who would tell the truth. The Cherokee tribe took a voluntary vow of poverty, because they believed that as long as they possessed anything worth taking, white men would keep after them until they got it.

Until the Civil War, the national policy in dealing with Indian tribes was based on treaty, with the tribes considered as independent nations. During and after the Civil War it was reasoned that Indian tribes had none of the elements of nationality. Rather, they were wards of the country. Beginning in 1867, Indians were placed on reservations in the West regardless of the wishes of the Indians. An act of 1871 specifically denied independent nations status to Indian tribes. Although most Indians had little concept of property rights, the Dawes Act of 1887 authorized the President of the United States to divide Indian reservations into individual holdings of 160 acres per family. Any Indian who received an allotment was granted full citizenship rights. The lands were to remain in trust for 25 years or longer if the President deemed an extension desirable. Thereafter the Indian could do with the land as he wished, subject to the laws of the state or territory in which he lived. In 1906, the Burke Act gave Indians the right to sell their land immediately if they were shown to be competent. More than half of the landholders sold their land, spent the proceeds, and then became destitute.

In 1924, all Indians were granted citizenship. The next significant Indian legislation came in 1934, when allotting of tribal land to individuals was abolished by the Indian Reorganization Act. Two million dollars a year were appropriated for the purchase of land for tribes. The act called for the establishment of tribal governments, tribal corporations to aid in resource development, tribal courts to deal with Indian offenses, and reservation day schools to replace boarding schools. In 1946, an Indian Claims Commission Act created a separate commission to hear claims arising from past frauds perpetuated on Indians. Prior to that time, a special act of Congress had to be passed before a tribe was permitted to file a lawsuit with the U.S. Court of Claims. Since that date, through December 31, 1973, 611 cases were docketed. Awards have been made in 231 cases, for a total of $469 million.

The Bureau of Indian Affairs had been created in 1834 under the War Department to administer Indian Affairs. In 1849, the Bureau was transferred to the Department of Interior at a time when Indian removal from the eastern half of the continent had been largely completed. A cen-

[18]Stanley Vestal, *Southwesterners Write* (Albuquerque, N.M., University of New Mexico Press, 1946), p. 337. For a different viewpoint, see Bernard W. Sheehan, "Indian-White Relations in Early America," *William and Mary Quarterly*, Vol. 26 (April, 1969), pp. 267-287.

tury later, after the Claims Commission Act of 1946, suggestions were made that federal services should be withdrawn from Indians. In 1953, Congress passed House Concurrent Resolution 108 that declared that as rapidly as possible federal services should be withdrawn. At that time two large tribes, the Menominees of Wisconsin and the Klamaths of Oregon, along with a number of smaller tribes, underwent termination. A study of the Menominees after termination found that the tribe had to close its hospital and sell its utilities. By 1961, the tribal treasury was virtually depleted, and later its lumbering operations teetered on insolvency.[19] The richly-forested Klamath reservation was sold after termination, and over $40,000 per person was paid out. However, a few years after termination many of the Klamaths were destitute and on welfare. They were described as having "no land left, no money and no future."[20] The failure of the compulsory termination policy has resulted in its now becoming a voluntary program.

Two new important programs were inaugurated in the 1950's. A relocation program was inaugurated in 1952, and an industrial development program in 1955. Both of these programs are discussed in detail below. Although both programs have aided in raising the income of some American Indians, they have not been on a large enough scale to remove American Indians from the unenviable position of having the lowest income of any minority group.

Some American Indians have become alienated by the slow rise in the status of their group. Some have turned to activism. When the state Supreme Court of Washington ruled in 1963 that Indians could not fish in several of the rivers in the state, in spite of a treaty in 1854 guaranteeing them such rights, fish-ins were engaged in by the Indians. The Supreme Court granted the right of Indians in 1968 to fish in several of the rivers, but it also ruled that the state may rule on the issue, provided there is no discrimination against Indians. Controversy continued after the decision. In 1969, the deserted island of Alcatraz was temporarily taken over by Indians. One study, 1961 to 1970, indicated that obstructive tactics of Indians, contrasted to facilitative tactics, have increased from zero to 42 percent of all collective actions.[21] In the early 1970's, the BIA office in Washington, D. C., was ransacked, and militants occupied Wounded Knee, South Dakota, for 71 days.

POPULATION

One estimate of Indian population before the arrival of the white man is from 800,000 to 1 million. By 1850, the Indian population had dwindled to

[19]Nancy Oestreich Lurie, "Menominee Termination: From Reservation to Colony," *Human Organization*, Vol. 31 (1972), pp. 257-270.

[20]Peter Collier, "The Red Man's Burden," *Ramparts*, Vol. 8, (February 1970), pp. 26-38.

[21]Robert C. Day, "The Emergence of Activism as a Social Movement," in Howard M. Bahr, Bruce A. Chadwick, and Robert C. Day, eds., *Native Americans Today: Sociological Perspectives*, (New York, Harper and Row, 1972), Table 1, p. 516.

250,000. The reduction in population was due to disease, whiskey, and attendant dissipation, removal, starvation, massacres, and adverse effects of unaccustomed conditions.[22] From 1850 to 1900, the Indian population remained about the same, and since that time has climbed. The 1970 Census recorded 792,730 American Indians, over half of whom live in the five states of Oklahoma (96,803), Arizona (94,310), California (88,263), New Mexico (71,582), and North Carolina (44,195). There has been a trend toward moving to cities. The 1960 census reported that about 30 percent of American Indians lived in cities, and by 1970, this figure had climbed to 45 percent. The largest concentration of urban Indians are found in Los Angeles (23,908), Tulsa (15,183), Oklahoma City (12,951), and San Francisco (12,041). In 1960, slightly over half of all American Indians lived on reservations, but by 1970 the percentage had dropped to 28 percent (213,770 of 763,594). By far the largest reservation is that of the Navajos in Arizona, New Mexico, and Utah, with 56,949 people. The next largest is the Pine Ridge reservation in South Dakota, with 8,280 persons.

INCOME

The median family income of American Indians in 1969 was $5,832, the lowest of any of the minority groups. A total of 38 percent of all American Indians were living in poverty in that year. In urban areas, income was substantially higher than in rural or reservation areas. Median Indian family income for the four towns with the largest Indian population was as follows: Los Angeles, $8,342; Tulsa, $8,058; Oklahoma City, $7,857; and San Francisco, $8,790. Of the 30 SMSA's with more than 2,500 Indian population, only the following had income below $6,498: Fayetteville, North Carolina, $5,806; Ft. Smith, Arkansas area, $3,893; Lawton, Oklahoma, $4,110; Phoenix, $5,442; and Tuscon, $3,389.

The largest reservation family income was $6,115, at Laguna, New Mexico, but of 24 reservations, nine had income below $4,000.[23] Of these, the Papago of Arizona, and the Navajos and Hopis on the Joint Use Area in Arizona, had particularly low incomes, $2,500 and $2,052, respectively.

That Indians have made some progress relative to the rest of the nation from 1960 to 1970 may be shown from the figures that Indian male income of those 14 years of age and older was 39 percent of all male income in 1960, and 51 percent in 1970. Yet in absolute amounts, the differential in income between Indian males and all males has widened slightly in 1970 over 1960.

[22]J. Mixon Radley, "The Demography of Indians," *Annals of the Academy of Political and Social Science*, Vol. 311 (May 1957), p. 27.
[23]*1970 Census of Population: American Indians* (U. S. Bureau of the Census, PC(2)-1F 1973), Table 14, pp. 168-173.

EDUCATION

Education of American Indians will have to improve considerably if their income is to increase. The original United States policy, beginning with a treaty in 1860, was to educate Indians in boarding schools so that the children would be freed from the language and habits of their untutored, and as considered then, savage parents.[24] The few that were educated were under a boarding-school system. According to the 1950 census, 21 percent of American Indians over 5 years of age had no formal education. As late as 1953, half of the Navajo children were not in school, mostly due to lack of facilities. Since that time, a more determined effort has been made to increase the education of American Indians. It was decided that as many as possible should attend public schools near their homes rather than attend far-removed boarding schools. By 1970, 93 percent of all Navajo reservation children aged 7 to 13 were attending school, but for those aged 14 to 17 the figure dropped to 86 percent. In that year, 10 percent of all Navajos 25 years of age and older had completed high school, the lowest percentage of any reservation.

Data for all American Indians over 25 years of age and older show that the median school years completed increased from 7.9 years in 1960 to 9.8 years in 1970. Education for those 25 years of age and older was substantially more in urban areas, 11.2 years compared with 8.4 years in rural farm areas. The comparable figure for urban areas from the 1960 census was about 9-1/2 years of schooling. Exactly a third of all American Indians 25 years of age and older were high school graduates in 1970, but in the four cities cited above with the largest American-Indian population the figure had reached about 50 percent.

In spite of improvements in the amount of American Indian education, serious weaknesses still exist in both the quality and quantity of education. On the quality side, studies show that American Indians score much lower on various educational tests than whites. Also the dropout rate is much higher for American Indians than for whites. Poor education prevails and scandals because of mistreatment have arisen at some of the Indian boarding schools.[25] After holding hearings for several years, the Senate Subcommittee on Indian Education concluded in 1969 that Indian education, both public and at boarding schools, was "a national tragedy."[26] Among the reasons for the failure is the fact that many teachers are inexperienced and some lack formal certification. Some have been in-

[24]Annual Report of the Indian Commissioner to the Secretary of the Interior, 1885, p. 23.

[25]For a summary of a few of these, see Peter Collier, "The Red Man's Burden," in Bahr, Chadwick and Day, eds., op. cit., p. 58.

[26]Hearings, Senate Subcommittee on Indian Education (Washington, D.C., Government Printing Office, 1967-1968, 5 Vols.); Field Investigation and Research Reports, Senate Subcommittee on Indian Education (Washington, D.C., Government Printing Office, 1969); Indian Education, A National Tragedy (Washington, D.C., Government Printing Office, 1969).

sensitive to the cultural differences between American Indians and whites. An impoverished home environment along with undernourishment and poor health contributed to the problem. Children of families with a traditional culture have been handicapped because of the Anglo emphasis on punctuality, competition, and individual achievement, all of which are lacking in traditional Indian cultures. Some American Indian children have a language handicap, and many have a low self-esteem and alienation caused by 300 years of disastrous culture contact. Finally, the orientation, programs, and quality of Indian schools have been weak.[27] Over the past several decades there has been a trend toward educating Indian children more frequently in public schools.[28] There has been some consolidation of Indian boarding schools, but the number of enrollees has not diminished. A recent innovation has been to turn over some of the boarding schools from the Bureau of Indian Affairs to the tribes to administer.

EMPLOYMENT

In 1960, only 11 percent of American Indian males aged 14 and over were engaged in white-collar work, but by 1970, the figure had climbed to 22 percent. The respective figures for females were 23 and 42 percent. During the decade of the 1960's, the percentages of all American Indians aged 14 and over engaged in agriculture, forestry, and fisheries dropped from 18 percent to 2 percent. During that same period, the percentages employed in manufacturing increased from 16 to 24 percent. The American Indian males aged 14 years of age and older cut their unemployment rate from 15.6 percent in 1960 to 11.7 percent in 1970.

RELOCATION PROGRAM

Income on most reservations has fallen far short of the needs for a decent livelihood for American Indians. Among the Navajos, for example, it has been estimated that 45,000 people could earn an adequate living on the reservation; yet the population in 1956 was 78,000. In 1959 it was reported that on at least 8 of the 17 Land Management Districts, the ranges were seriously overgrazed, and the number of livestock exceeded the total estimated range capacity by nearly 33 percent.[29]

One of the programs designed to aid in employment of American Indians was the Relocation Program, now called the Economic Assistance

[27]Brewton Berry, The Education of American Indians: A Survey of the Literature (Washington, Senate Subcommittee on Indian Education, 1969).

[28]Theodore Fischbacher, A Study of the Role of the Federal Government in the Education of the American Indian (San Francisco, R and E Research Associates, 1974).

[29]The Navajo Yearbook, 1961, Washington, D.C., U. S. Department of the Interior, Bureau of Indian Affairs, p. 164.

Program. Under this program, which began in 1952, the Bureau of Indian Affairs offers financial assistance and limited social services to place American Indians in full-time employment. The Bureau of Indian Affairs will pay transportation costs from the reservation to the city of employment and subsistence expenses en route. A small amount is provided for the shipment of household goods. Up to four weeks of subsistence allowances are provided after arrival at the new destination. A supplemental subsistence allowance is also made available for those who become unemployed through no fault of their own, and who are not eligible for unemployment compensation. Tools and equipment for apprentices, also, may be provided.

A number of relocation offices have been opened in such places as Los Angeles, Oakland, San Jose, Chicago, Cleveland, Denver, Dallas, Oklahoma City, Tulsa, and Minneapolis. A few offices have been closed (Waukegan and Joliet, Illinois; Cincinnati; San Francisco; and St. Louis) because of their comparative unpopularity as a destination of reservation Indians. At the reservation end, services are provided to process clients. In 1956, an important improvement was made in the program by providing additional training assistance for those interested in moving into industrial jobs.

The Economic Assistance Program has been criticized because of the large numbers of relocated American Indians who move back to the reservation. A Denver study indicated that about half of the Navajos moved back to the reservation within a three months period.[30] The Navajos had averaged only 8-1/2 years of education. The disorganization and alcoholism experienced in Denver, along with the failure to find jobs with earnings considered adequate, influenced one researcher to conclude that less money should be spent on relocation and more on industrial development on reservations.[31] In the study centering on Denver, the BIA was criticized for overselling the relocation program.[32] It was alleged that merely because Federal monies were allocated for relocation, the Bureau of Indian Affairs made every effort to spend the money irrespective of prospects of success. Other studies elsewhere show that at the Fort Fall reservation in Idaho (Shoshone-Bannock Indians) 80 percent of the relocatees returned to the reservation.[33] A record of all Navajos from 1952-1961 found the 37 percent had returned to the reservation.[34] A record of all tribes from 1953 to 1957 indicated a return rate varying from

[30]R. S. Weppner, "Urban Economic Opportunities: The Example of Denver," in Jack O. Waddell and O. Michael Watson, op. cit., p. 254.

[31]Theodore D. Graves, "Drinking and Drunkenness Among Urban Indians," in Jack O. Waddell and O. Michael Watson, op. cit., p. 309.

[32]Peter Z. Snyder, "The Social Environment of the Urban Indians," in Jack O. Waddell and O. Michael Watson, op. cit., pp. 220-221.

[33]Peter Colline, "The Red Man's Burden," in Bahr, Chadwick, and Day, op. cit., p. 55.

[34]Navajo Agency, Navajo Yearbook (Window Rock, Arizona, 1962).

24 to 32 percent.[35] The Bureau of Indian Affairs eliminated this statistical series in 1959, allegedly because too much ammunition was being provided for critics of the program.[36]

Due to criticisms of the Economic Assistance Program, its orientation in the 1970's has been revamped considerably. Now the program emphasizes job development on or near the reservations. Contracts for job training will be let by Indian tribes. On-the-job training will also be stressed along with labor union contracts to train craftsmen for reservation or near reservation work. Wherever possible, Indian tribes rather than the Bureau of Indian Affairs will administer the Economic Assistance Program.

The curtailment of mobility grants throughout the country may not be in the best interests of American Indians, particularly where industry cannot be attracted to the reservations. For example, there are little employment opportunities as yet in western Oklahoma. The relocation program there was quite successful.[37] Only 15 percent of the relocated Southern Plains Indians, from 1968 to 1972, left their relocation city within a year. Most of the relocatees not only had a high school education, but vocational training as well. In areas where outward mobility has proven successful, it should be continued.

INDUSTRIAL DEVELOPMENT PROGRAM

The program being stressed today is attracting industries to reservation areas. The Bureau of Indian Affairs began an Industrial Development Program in 1955. The Bureau has worked with tribal leaders for industrial development. Industrial development foundations have been formed to attract industry. In fiscal 1973, $3.4 million had been expended for 225 new businesses, and an expansion of 144 old businesses. Several thousand new employees were hired by these firms. A variety of types of businesses have been aided, including such industries as metal plating, leather garment manufacturing, meat processing, pottery manufacturing, trucking, and tourism. However, the income data for reservations cited above indicates that an insufficient number of firms have been attracted so that income on American Indian reservations is still far below that of the rest of the nation.

[35]*Indian Relocation and Industrial Development Program,* Report of a Special Committee on Interior and Insular Affairs, House of Representatives, 85th Congress, 1st Session (1957), p. 3.

[36]Alan L. Sorkin, "Some Aspects of American Indian Migration," in Bahr, Chadwick and Day, *op. cit.,* p. 470.

[37]Paul A. Brinker and Benjamin J. Taylor, "Southern Plains Indians Relocation Returnees," *Human Organization,* Vol. 33, 1974, pp. 139-146.

HEALTH

All studies of American Indians show that their economic resources have been so poor that they have experienced serious health problems. In 1950, the average life span for Indians was 36 years, compared with 61 years for non-Indians. Some of the poorer tribes averaged substantially less than the average. For Papagos it was 17 years and for Navajos 20 years.[38] Since that time the number of medical personnel in the Division of Indian Health of the Public Health Service has increased considerably. Progress has been made. During the 1955-1971 period, the infant death rate of Indians in the Aberdeen, South Dakota, area dropped 60 percent. However, the death rate for infants aged 28 days to 11 months was still almost 3 times as high in the Indian Aberdeen area as for all races in the United States. The death rate for tuberculosis is also quite high.[39] In fiscal 1974, there were almost 500 physicians attending American Indians, but another 169 are needed, based on an estimate of one physician for 750 people (the overall U.S. average is one physician for every 600 people). About a third more registered nurses are needed, and other medical personnel are in short supply also. The result of the shortages is that patients are going untreated. To cite the problem at one Indian hospital at Rosebud, South Dakota, there was an identifiable backlog of 558 surgical cases. Estimates of the unidentified backlog are much larger. In short, although medical facilities for American Indians have improved, this group receives less medical care than the average American.

URBAN ADAPTATION

In a study of American Indians in Los Angeles, John Price found that about one-third of the married American Indians had white spouses.[40] Only 20 percent of those with children said that their children spoke an Indian language. The same percentage reported that their usual associations were with Indians only. By tribe, it was found that members of the Five Civilized Tribes had a relatively full adaptation to Los Angeles society, the Navajos had made only a weak adaptation, and Sioux fell in between. Although only one-fifth of the group were socially active in

[38]James R. Show, "Guarding the Health of Our American Indians," *Journal of the American Hospital Association* (April 16, 1957).

[39]*Indian Health Service Recruitment Problems*, Hearings before the Subcommittee on Indian Affairs of the Committee on Interior and Insular Affairs, 93rd Congress, 1st Session, Nov. 19-20, 1973. For statistics showing a higher death rate of American Indians nationwide, see Monthly Vital Statistics, published by the Health Services and Mental Health Administration, HEW.

[40]John A. Price, "The Migration and Adaptation of American Indians to Los Angeles," *Human Organization*, Vol. 27, 1968, pp. 168-175. A Study of Papagos found 84 percent of unmixed Papago ancestry even though 55 percent lived off the reservation. David G. Smith, "Modernization, Population Dispersion and Papago Genetic Integrity," *Human Organization*, Vol. 31 (1972), p. 188.

pan-Indian associations in Los Angeles, Price concluded that pan-Indian-
ism seemed to be emerging as a stabilizing element and a significant facet
of ethnic diversity in the urban adaptation of the Indian migrant.

A study of American Indians locating in San Francisco shows that of
34 families migrating in 1954-55, 25 of them associated mostly or only
with other Indians.[41] The corresponding figure for 19 families coming
later was 16. Again, less association was found among the Navajos than
the Sioux. The Indians place themselves in a unique Indian social niche
which was alien to the Anglo values of planning and the amassing of personal wealth. There was little evidence of attempting upward mobility.
This study concludes with the observation that the need of Indians to be
with others of their group is a cohesive force for the development of pan-
Indianism.

All of the studies of the urban Indian show serious problems of
alcoholism. Price found that in Los Angeles 32 percent of his respondents
listed drunkenness as their major problem. Throughout the entire country, in 1968 the arrest rate for drinking-related offenses was over 20 times
as high for Indians as for whites, and was nine times higher for American
Indians than for blacks.[42] One group of authors maintained that the most
fundamental problem causing alcoholism was the Indian's "economic
marginality; more than anything else, the migrant needs better jobs."[43]

After collecting and editing a series of articles, in a book on Indian urban adaptation, Waddell and Watson attempted to synthesize the articles.[44] A major question was whether difficulties in urban adaptation
were primarily due to the Indian's cultural values on the one hand, or
social structure and social organizaton of the dominant society on the
other. Although none of the authors denied the significance of cultural
factors, most emphasis was placed on such structural factors as Federal
Indian policy, Anglo attitudes, and institutions.

CONCLUSION

Both minority groups studied in this chapter have had less economic
wealth than whites for centuries. Both in the last several decades have
moved to higher occupational levels. Mexican-American median annual
family income of $6,962 in 1969 was substantially below that of whites
($9,961), but was above that of mainland Puerto Ricans ($6,115), blacks
($6,067), and American Indians ($5,832). Both Mexican-Americans and

---

[41]Joan Ablon, "Relocated American Indians in the San Francisco Bay Area: Social Interaction and Indian Identity," *Human Organization*, Vol. 23, 1964, pp. 296-304.

[42]Charles Reasons, "Crime and the American Indian," in Bahr, Chadwick and Day, *op.
cit.*, Table 2, p. 321.

[43]Bahr, Chadwick and Day, *op. cit.*, p. 403.

[44]Waddell and Watson, *op. cit.*, pp. 393-397.

American Indians have shown percentage increases in income relative to whites. Yet the percentage increases have been so small that absolute differentials between whites and the minority groups have widened. Both have over a fourth of their populations living in poverty. With such large numbers still poor, additional policy needs to be implemented to reduce such poverty as quickly as possible.

APPENDIX A
MAINLAND PUERTO RICANS

In an autobiography of growing up in New York City, Piri Thomas, a Puerto Rican, states that most of his friends ended up in crime, or on drugs, and some in prostitution.[45] On the other hand, a study of the worst block in El Barrio shows that a majority of youth had gone straight.[46] Housing was considered the worst problem, and drugs and bookmaking existed in the area. A voluntary neighborhood group was able to help some of the people there by organizing the tenants, relocating families and renovating 17 tenements. It also persuaded the city to build a vest-pocket park in the block.

Census data indicated that Puerto Ricans improve their income by coming to the United States. Puerto Rican islanders' median family income was $3,063 compared with $6,115 for mainland Puerto Ricans (1970 Census data). In 1971, of 1.5 million mainland Puerto Ricans, 489,000 were living in poverty (32 percent compared with 12.5 percent of the entire U.S. population). However, census data from 1960 and 1970 show that male Puerto Rican mainland income has increased from 71 to 76 percent of male income throughout the United States, although the absolute differential has widened.

Mainland Puerto Ricans have been aided by improved education. Second generation mainlanders aged 25 and over have improved their years of schooling (11.5 years) over that of the first generation mainlanders (8.4) years, but they are still behind the average of the New York-Northeastern New Jersey area (12.1 years). The larger amount of education has enabled more of the second generation to move into white collar work (42 percent) compared with the mainlanders born in Puerto Rico (23 percent).

One study on assimilation shows that the rate of out-group marriage between the first and second generation Puerto Ricans from 1949 to 1959 was as great as the increase for all immigrants in New York City in the

---

[45]Piri Thomas, *Down These Mean Streets* (New York, Alfred A. Knopf, 1967), p. x.
[46]David and Sopluy Burnham, "El Barrio's Worst Block is Not All Bad," *New York Times Magazine*, January 5, 1969, pp. 24-25.

years 1908 to 1912.[47] There was a significant increase in the rate of out-group marriage of the second generation over the first.

A study of adaptation to the mainland in one middle-sized eastern seacoast city reveals that a majority of residents preferred the mainland for better working conditions, opportunities for children, health care, and improved schooling. On the other hand, a majority felt that Puerto Rico was better for entertainment, weather, and neighborhood relations.[48]

Puerto Rican riots occurred in the sixties in such cities as Chicago, New York, Newark, Jersey City, Paterson, Passaic, Perth Amboy, Trenton, and others. Demonstrations of Puerto Rican college youth occurred at Queens, Brooklyn, and Lehman Colleges, and the City College of New York was temporarily shut-down by Puerto Rican youth. The Young Lords Party, organized in New York City in 1969, engaged in militant action at several hospitals, and occupied a church in East Harlem in the Spring of 1970.

Improvements in education, occupation and income have not come as fast as some had hoped.

Bibliography

Bahr, Howard M. Bruce A. Chadick and Robert C. Day, ed's, *Native Americans Today: Sociological Perspectives* (New York, Harper and Row, 1972).

Briggs, Vernon M., *Chicanos and Rural Poverty* (Baltimore, Johns Hopkins Pres, 1973).

Gonzalez, *The Spanish American of New Mexico* (Albuquerque, University of New Mexico Press, 1970).

Grebler, Leo, Joan W. Moore and Ralph C. Guzman, *The Mexican-American People* (New York, The Free Press, 1970).

Meier, Matt S. and Feliciano Rivera, *The Chicanos: A History of Mexican Americans* (New York, Hill and Wang, 1972).

Romano, Octavio I, *Voices* (Berkeley, Cal., Quinto Sol Publications, 1971).

Rubel, Arthur J. *Across the Tracks: The Mexican-Americans in a Texas City* (Austin, University of Texas Press, 1966).

Simmen, Edward, ed., *Pain and Promise: The Chicano Today* (New York, New American Library, 1972).

Steiner, Stan, *La Raza: The Mexican-Americans* (New York, Harper and Row, 1969).

Waddell, Jack O. and O. Michael Watson, ed's *The American Indian in Urban Society* (Boston, Little, Brown, and Co., 1971).

[47]Joseph P. Fitzpatrick, "Intermarriage of Puerto Ricans in New York City," *American Journal of Sociology*, Vol. 71, No. 4, 1966, p. 398.

[48]Lloyd H. Rogler, *Migrant in the City: The Life of a Puerto Rican Action Group* (New York, Basic Books, 1972), Table 13-6, p. 206.

CHAPTER 25

WOMEN AND CHILDREN

WOMEN

INCREASING EMPLOYMENT OF WOMEN

Over the years the number and percentage of women employed outside the home has been increasing. As early as 1870, the census of that year listed 7 million women in the work force, or one out of every eight women over 10 years of age. Since that time there has been an increasing participation of women in the work force. The trend was accelerated during World War II when manpower was scarce, and women by the millions moved into industry. After the war, many decided that they preferred working to remaining at home. From 1960 to 1970, an additional million entered the work force. By 1973, 34.6 million women were in the labor force, or about 39 percent of the work force.

The age and marital status of women in the work force has changed considerably since 1920. Then the typical working woman was single, about 28 years old, and from the working class. Even in 1940 70% of working women were single. By 1970, 59% of working women were married, and husband present, and another 19% were either widowed, divorced, or their husband was absent. Only 22% of working women were never married.[1] Labor force participation of women by groupings has changed noticeably. In 1940 the highest labor force participation was by women aged 20 to 24. By the 1960's and 1970's labor force participation had become bi-modal, that is, two age groups, 20 to 24 and 45 to 54 had the highest participation rates.

Single and young married women to about 25 are heavily represented in the labor force. When children are born many leave the labor force until their homemaking responsibilities lessen. From about 35 on, they return to the labor force in large numbers and many then work until retirement age. A further change occurring is that more and more women with pre-school children are working. The labor force participation rate of this group has risen from 18 percent in 1960 to 33 percent in 1973.[2]

[1]Elizabeth Waldman, "Changes in Labor Force Activity of Women," *Monthly Labor Review*, Vol. 93, (June 1970), pp. 10-18. See also Howard Hayghe, "Labor Force Activity of Married Women," *Monthly Labor Review*, Vol. 96 (April 1973), pp. 31-36.

[2]"For Women: More Jobs, But Low Pay," *U. S. News and World Report*, Vol. 75 (October 8, 1973), pp. 41-42.

WOMEN'S OCCUPATIONS AND EARNINGS

Although the census of 1870 listed some women working in all 338 oc-cupations, domestic service accounted for almost half of all women employed. By adding six other occupations, agricultural laborers, seamstresses, milliners, teachers, textile mill workers, and laundresses, 93 percent of all paid work of women was accounted for. Although women have entered many more types of work since 1870, they are still concentrated in domestic service, teaching, clerical work, nursing, and retail sales. Out of over 250 distinct occupations listed in the 1970 census, half of all women workers were employed in 21 of them. Male workers are much more widely dispersed than women, with 50 percent of them in 65 oc-cupations.[3] The limited kinds of jobs in which women are employed have been often simply extensions of work women have done in the home. These include the care of the sick, the instruction of children, food preparation and serving, textile weaving and sewing, and correspondence and clerical work.

At the same time, certain factors discourage women from entry into other occupations. Jobs requiring lifting of heavy weights and other jobs requiring brawn may be beyond the capability of most women, although various mechanical devices now do much of the hard and heavy work. Other jobs may require longer periods of preparation than many women are willing to undertake, for instance, jobs requiring advanced degrees. But discrimination and widely held prejudices that some jobs are feminine while others are masculine have artificially restricted women's jobs beyond the limits set by job requirements or working conditions.[4]

Whatever the cause, it is a well-known fact that women workers on the average earn considerably less than men. In March, 1973, census data showed that families with a male head had a medium income of $10,305, while families with a female head had $5,341.[5] Part of the difference in annual income is explained by the fact that men are more apt to work fulltime. Women, because of homemaking responsibilities, pregnancy, and care of children are more apt to work at part-time jobs and to work fewer weeks per year than men. The 1970 census showed that 80 percent of employed male heads of families worked 50 to 52 weeks per year, while only 62 percent of employed female heads of families did. Also, higher income in male headed families is partially due to the fact that in families

    [3]Janice Neipert Hedges. "Women Workers and Manpower Demands in the 1970's." *Monthly Labor Review*, Vol. 93 (June 1970), pp. 19-29. This article explores at considerable length the various professions and skilled trades where there are manpower shortages which women may be able to fill.
    [4]*Ibid.*, p. 19.
    [5]*Current Population Reports*, Consumer Income. U. S. Department of Commerce. Bureau of the Census. Series P-60. No. 90. December 1973. Table 21. p. 60.

headed by a male there is a greater probability of having more than one wage earner.[6]

The root question is whether or not there are pay differences in hourly earnings between men and women in the same job. John Buckley addressed himself to this question in a study of ten occupations which employed large numbers of both men and women.[7] Men's earnings exceeded those of women by an average of 18 percent. He further found that the differential was somewhat greater, 22 percent, when establishments hiring only men were compared to establishments hiring only women. He noted, however, that men often had longer job tenure than women, which may account for some of the difference. Also, where both men and women are listed in the same job category, such as janitor, the man may be doing the heavier and the women the lighter janitorial duties.

Victor Fuchs in a different study which dealt with the causes of the overall difference in annual income between men and women workers found little reason to believe that the differential was due to overt discrimination by employers. Instead, he concluded that most of the differential could be explained by the different roles assigned to men and women by society: "Role differentiation, which begins in the cradle, affects the choice of occupation, labor force attachment, location of work, post-school investment, hours of work, and other variables that influence earnings."[8] He went on to say that role differentiation can result from discrimination, but he had found little evidence that deliberate employer discrimination is a direct influence on male-female differentials in average hourly earnings. If role differentiation, which is deeply rooted in the folkways and mores of society, is the cause of the pay differential, it will be difficult to eliminate by state or federal legislation. But society is changing, as may be seen in the changes occurring in women's education.

Formal schooling of any kind for girls was not generally accepted prior to the nineteenth century.[9] College education for women came even later. It was not until 201 years after Harvard College opened its doors that the first woman was admitted to an American college—Oberlin in 1837. The arguments made for depriving women of higher education were that women were mentally inferior, that they were too frail to stand the rigors of a college education, and that education of women would reduce the birthrate. These arguments no longer carry any weight.

Table 25-1 shows the dramatic changes which have taken place in enrollments in institutions of higher learning. Since 1950, the percentages of women enrolled have been increasing. Women, however, still lag

[6]1970 U. S. Census, Detailed Characteristics, Table 262, p. 998.

[7]John E. Buckley, "Pay Differences Between Men and Women in the Same Job," Monthly Labor Review, Vol. 94 (November 1971), pp. 36-39.

[8]Victor R. Fuchs, "Differences in Hourly Earnings Between Men and Women," Monthly Labor Review, Vol. 94 (May 1971), pp. 9-15.

[9]Mabel Newcomer, A Century of Higher Education for American Women (New York, Harper & Row, 1959), pp. 5-32.

behind in graduate degrees and thus in the professions. A Carnegie Commission study found that women make up the following percentages of all people in each respective group: high school graduates, 50.4 percent; bachelor's degrees, 43.1 percent; graduate degrees, 36.5 percent; faculty members, 24 percent; and full professors, 8.6 percent.[10] Similarly a study by the Council of Economic Advisors found very light participation by women in many professions, as follows: physicians, 9 percent; lawyers and judges, 5 percent; architects, 4 percent; clergy, 3 percent, and engineers, 2 percent.[11] Women participate heavily in such occupations as registered nurses, dietitians, elementary school teachers, librarians, social workers and others, but these are often relatively low-paying pursuits. Role differentiation, as noted above, tends to direct women into certain occupations, but this may become a less important factor in the future.

TABLE 25-1

WOMEN ENROLLED IN INSTITUTIONS OF HIGHER LEARNING, 70-1973

Year	Number	As Percent of All Women Aged 18 to 21	As Percent of All Students Enrolled
1870	11,000	0.7	21.0
1880	40,000	1.9	33.4
1890	56,000	2.2	35.9
1900	85,000	2.8	36.8
1910	140,000	3.8	39.6
1920	283,000	7.6	47.3
1930	481,000	10.5	43.7
1940	601,000	12.2	40.2
1950	806,000	17.9	30.2
1960	1,231,000	26.4	34.5
1970	3,013,000	41.7	40.0
1973	3,502,000	—[a]	42.8

a   Not available.

Sources: Mable Newcomer, *A Century of Higher Education for American Women* (New York, Harper & Row, 1959), p. 46; *Statistical Abstract of the United States, 1972*, Table No. 159, p. 108; and *U. S. News and World Report*, Vol. 76 (May 27, 1974), p. 42.

[10]"For Women: More Jobs. But Low Pay," *op. cit.*, p. 42.
[11]*Ibid.*

WOMEN'S PROTECTIVE LEGISLATION

As early as the 1870's protective legislation was passed on the state level to protect women workers. Most frequently such laws dealt with minimum wages, maximum hours, meals and rest periods, and night work. Other laws forbade the employment of women in the mines, as bartenders, and in various other occupations. Ostensibly the motive behind such legislation was to protect the health and welfare of women and their children, although some women's groups have charged that the real motive was to reduce competition by women for men's jobs. Male-dominated labor unions have often supported such legislation, and correspondingly have often opposed the Equal Rights Amendment. In any case the legislation was often weak and poorly enforced, so it is doubtful that either women or labor unions received much benefit.

The enactment of Title VII of the Civil Rights Act of 1964, discussed below, nullified most state legislation designed to protect women, or has extended its protection to men. The federal courts have tended toward a strict interpretation of the law and have ruled that state laws embodying different treatment for women than men are overridden by the federal legislation.[12] Typically, it is held that the employer must extend the benefits or restrictions of the state laws to both sexes. Hence, invalidation of the state law is not necessary, but equal application of the state law is necessary. Some states have in fact acted to extend the legislation to both sexes, while in other cases the women's protective legislation has simply been inoperative.

EQUAL PAY FOR EQUAL WORK

As early as 1868 the Knights of Labor made equal pay for both sexes one of their major objectives. During World Wars I and II the War Labor Boards adopted equal pay as a guiding policy. In 1920 the Women's Bureau was established in the U. S. Labor Department and it has consistently promoted the idea that there should be a rate of pay for the job, not pay based on sex. In 1923 the Classification Act established the principle of equal pay for all federal government employees. Michigan and Montana enacted legislation in 1919, but not many other states passed bills until during and after World War II. On the federal level, equal pay bills were introduced in each Congress beginning in 1945, but success was not achieved until 1963 when the Equal Pay Act of that year was enacted and made a part of the Fair Labor Standards Act (FLSA).[13]

[12]Barbara A. Brown, Thomas I. Ferguson, Gail Falk and Ann E. Freedman, "The Equal Rights Amendment: A Constitutional Basis for Equal Rights for Women," *Yale Law Journal*, Vol. 80 (April 1971), p. 926. This article, 114 pages in length, is a very comprehensive and well-documented discussion of the economic, social and legal implications of the Equal Rights Amendment.

[13]This section is based primarily on Robert D. Moran, "Reducing Discrimination: Role of the Equal Pay Act," *Monthly Labor Review*, Vol. 93 (June 1970), pp. 30-34.

The fact that the act was made a part of the Fair Labor Standards Act was a disadvantage, since the latter act covered only about 60 percent of the jobs in the United States. Recent amendments to the FLSA have extended coverage somewhat. Another problem is that "equal work" is difficult to define and enforce; "comparable work" would have been preferable language. Courts, however, have not insisted that the work be identical. One advantage of being part of FLSA is that that act has strong administrative and enforcement procedures. By June 1972, over $50 million in underpayments had been found owed to more than 100,000 employees. Employer violations can be very costly. In the Wheaton Glass case in New Jersey the employer was assessed over $900,000 in back pay and other costs. In that case the judge of the apellate court laid down the principle that jobs need be only "substantially equal", not identical. The Supreme Court in May 1970 denied *certiorari*, in effect upholding the decision of the appellate court.[14]

Statistically the Equal Pay Act cannot be shown to have made much difference in the overall disparity in pay. In the Buckley study referred to above, men's earnings exceeded those of women's by 19 percent in 1960, by 18 percent in 1965, and still 18 percent in 1970.[15] This seems consistent with Victor Fuchs observation that "role differentiation," not overt discrimination, is the main source of income inequality between the sexes. This appears to justify much of the activity of the Women's Liberation Movement which is endeavoring to change the roles played by women in our society.

TITLE VII OF THE CIVIL RIGHTS ACT OF 1964, AS AMENDED IN 1972

As amended in 1972, Title VII of the Civil Rights Act of 1974 provides that it shall be unlawful practice for an employer, who has 15 or more employees, to discriminate against any individual with respect to his compensation, terms, conditions, or privileges of employment, because of such individual's race, color, religion, sex, or national origin. Generally, the same provisions apply to unions with 15 or more members, and to employment agencies. The 1972 amendments extended coverage to federal, state, and local employees, and to employees of educational institutions. Enforcement provisions of the law, previously weak, were strengthened somewhat by giving the Equal Employment Opportunity Commission (EEOC) power to file suit in court to gain compliance. After a two-year period in which it shares authority to bring pattern or practice suits with the Department of Justice, EEOC has sole authority to bring

[14]Irene L. Murphy, *Public Policy on the Status of Women* (Lexington, Mass., D. C. Heath and Co., 1973), pp. 25-27.
[15]John E. Buckley, *op. cit.*, p. 38.

such action. These provisions are stronger than those existing before 1972, but fall short of the power to issue cease and desist orders as had been desired by proponents of the legislation.

EEOC has been and continues to be the primary enforcement agency directed toward reducing discrimination based on sex or other reasons. It has been handicapped by a lack of enforcement authority and by a shortage of funds and personnel. In 1972 EEOC had a backlog of complaints approaching 70,000, nearly 30 percent of which concerned sex discrimination.[16] The expanded jurisdiction of the EEOC may add to its backlog of cases, but the stronger enforcement powers should make it a more effective agency in the future. A Congressional grant of authority to issue its own cease and desist orders would make it even more effective.

EQUAL RIGHTS AMENDMENT

In March, 1972, Congress approved and submitted for ratification by the states a proposed amendment to the Constitution, guaranteeing equal rights to women. In the hearings to this amendment, it had been documented that women had been discriminated against in a number of areas. In a few states women had been denied rights to a college education; differential rights existed on signing contracts and leases; dual pay schedules existed for men and women teachers; other state laws had barred women from certain occupations or professions. The amendment has not been without its critics. Some fear that women may lose on alimony arrangements and custody of children in divorce cases. In case of a military draft, both sexes would be subject to call. Some fear the losses on women's protective legislation although, as we commented above, the losses here should be minimal.

CHILDREN

The income statistics of 1972 show that about 10 million children out of a total number of 69 million in the United States under 18 years of age were living in families whose income was below the poverty level. Thus, 14.5 percent of the children in the United States are being raised in families with extremely meager economic resources.[17] These are often families with a female head and frequently nonwhite. Thirty-five percent of children in a family with a white female head and 61 percent of children in a family with a black female head were in poverty. Also, the larger the family the higher the percentage of the families below the corresponding

16Irene L. Murphy, op. cit., pp. 39-42; 51-53.
17Characteristics of the Low Income Population, 1972, Bureau of the Census, Current Population Reports, Series P-60, No. 91, December, 1973, Table K, p. 12.

poverty threshold. Thus, only 7.5 percent of all four-person families are in poverty but 22 percent of families with seven or more are.[18]

CHILD WELFARE SERVICES

Over the centures, civilized societies have been concerned about the welfare of their children. Most children are adequately cared for, loved and nurtured, in their own homes. But a minority are not. Society has endeavored to take measures to come to the rescue of children in trouble. This includes children who are orphans; children born to unwed mothers; children subjected to cruelty and abuse; children whose parents have emotional or behavioral problems or are chronically ill; children of migratory workers; children in families with dire economic need; children born with malformations; children who are mentally retarded or who develop catastrophic illness; and children who are delinquents or drug addicts. For centuries most child welfare activities were private, including care by friends or relatives, nonprofit organizations, or proprietary arrangements. In recent decades, local, state, and federal governments have supplemented or taken over previously private child welfare activities, mainly because private activities were grossly inadequate.

Child Welfare might be said to include several of the programs discussed in previous chapters, but more commonly child welfare is confined to the classification given by Lela Costin:

1. Services designed to support or reinforce the ability of parents to meet the child's needs, such as
   (a) casework services in their own homes, . . . ;
   (b) protective services . . . ; and
   (c) services to unmarried parents . . .
2. Services designed to supplement parental care, or to compensate for certain inadequacies in such care, such as
   (a) homemaker services, and
   (b) day care services . . .
3. Services designed to substitute for parental care . . . such as
   (a) foster family care services;
   (b) group care services . . . ; and
   (c) adoption services.[19]

[18]*Ibid.*, Table 21, p. 87.
[19]Lela B. Costin, *Child Welfare: Policies and Practice* (New York, McGraw-Hill, 1972), p. 21.

MATERNAL AND CHILD HEALTH SERVICES

Under Title V of the Social Security Act the federal government appropriates fixed annual grants to states ($350 million in fiscal 1972) to assist with four major programs: maternal and child health services, a crippled children's program, a mental retardation program and a health program for preschool and school age children. A large variety of services are provided mainly to poor families and their children such as public health nursing, medical clinic service, hospital in-patient care and others. Unfortunately the programs vary widely in coverage from state to state. In 1971, 10 states provided no maternity clinic services, 14 states provided no family planning services, 11 states reported no dental services, and only 20 states reported general pediatric clinic services.

FOSTER CARE AND ADOPTIONS

Since ancient times, civilized societies have made arrangements to provide for children without homes or whose homes are unsatisfactory. Foster care refers to foster family homes, group homes, and child welfare institutions for neglected, dependent, emotionally disturbed, mentally retarded or delinquent children. About 75 percent of all children under foster care are in foster homes, about 1 percent in group homes, and 24 percent in institutions. Public agencies provide for about 65 percent of such children, while voluntary agencies, often church related, provide for the other 35 percent. In 1971 somewhat over 300,000 children were receiving such care in the Untied States.[20]

The problems which lead to placement in foster care concern both the parents and the children. Usually the need arises from deviant parent behavior (abandonment, neglect, abuse, etc.), psychosocial stress (separation, divorce and mental illness), children born out of wedlock, physical illness of the parent, or financial incapacity of the parent or parents.[21] In about one-fifth of the cases the child's own behavior (emotionally disturbed or social deviant) or the child's physical or mental incapacity, leads to the need for foster care arrangements. Where possible, the child welfare agencies endeavor to place the children in suitable private foster homes, but reality is typically short of the ideal. Most studies indicate that care in foster homes leaves much to be desired. When necessary, children are placed in institutions. These include correctional institutions for delinquents, institutions for the mentally retarded, the emotionally disturbed, and the physically handicapped. Where possible, the children are given training, depending on their needs and capacities.

[20]This section is based primarily on Lela B. Costin. *op. cit.*, Chapters 11 and 12. pp. 321-399.

[21]*Ibid.*, p. 329.

Part of the funds for foster care comes from the state Child Welfare Service, part from the AFDC program. The 1962 Social Security Amendments required that state child welfare plans be coordinated with services provided under AFDC, and such state plans were required to work toward a goal of providing child welfare services to all children in the state who need them by July 1, 1975. The Social Security Amendments of 1967 liberalized the eligibility rules for making AFDC payments to children in foster homes, and the existence of an AFDC-Foster Care program became mandatory in each state as of July, 1969.

In contrast to foster care, which is often a temporary arrangement, adoption tends to be permanent. The child is transferred to a new home and when legally adopted has all the rights, privileges and obligations of a biological child. In 1971, there were 169,000 adoptions, about 86,000 by petitioners related to the child, the rest by unrelated petitioners.[22] About 87 percent of the children adopted are white. Of all children adopted, about 60 percent are born out of wedlock. Such children are usually adopted by unrelated petitioners. Two-thirds of adoptions by related petitioners are of children born in wedlock.

The severest criticism of our child welfare services comes from those who charge that the system still operates to discriminate against the black child.[23] It is charged that the system is manned by whites and mainly benefits white children, and that many of the personnel in the various agencies operate on the basis of racist assumptions. One of the suggestions made by Billingsley and Giovannoni is that separate private child welfare agencies staffed by blacks, and operated for the benefit of black children be instituted.[24]

WIN AND DAY CARE FACILITIES

The growth of the Work Incentive Program (WIN) has accelerated the need for day-care centers. Under WIN the local welfare departments screen and refer welfare mothers to Department of Labor agencies for possible work or for training leading to work. The high costs of training and providing day-care for children of those on welfare has resulted in little saving to the tax payer. Whether WIN will be implemented on a larger scale still remains to be decided. If WIN is expanded, then more day-care facilities will be necessary. The costs here are quite high — around $3,200 per child, or almost half of what the average female head earns. Clearly subsidies will be necessary to implement such a program on a large scale.

---

[22]*Adoptions in 1971*, U. S. Department of Health, Education and Welfare, Social and Rehabilitation Service, NCASS Report E-10, May 1973, Table 1.

[23]See Andrew Billingsley and Jeanne M. Giovannoni, *Children of the Storm: Black Children and American Child Welfare* (New York, Harcourt, Brace, Javanovich, 1972).

[24]*Ibid.*, pp. 221-239.

CHILD LABOR LEGISLATION

A hundred or more years ago in the United States, when our economy was not nearly so productive as it is today, much more poverty existed than now. The only alternative most families thought they had was to put their children to work. As time passed it was realized that putting children to work without educating them was self-defeating. Children who received an education were often able to climb out of poverty; those with little education often lived in poverty for life. In addition, many children were killed or disabled while at work.

As early as 1813 in Connecticut, legislation was passed to regulate child labor. In that year, Connecticut required that mill owners teach the children in their mills to read, write and do arithmetic. Massachusetts in 1836 required employed children under 15 to attend school at least three months a year. Six years later, the same state limited hours for children under 12 years of age to 10 hours of work a day. The first state to ban child labor for those under 12 was Pennsylvania in 1848.[25] The law applied to employment in cotton, woolen and silk factories. In 1906, a federal law to curb child labor was first introduced into Congress. The bill was not passed at that time, but finally was approved in 1916, only to be declared unconstitutional. Twenty-eight states then approved an amendment to the constitution to outlaw child labor, but an amendment became unnecessary when Congress again passed a bill outlawing child labor as part of the Fair Labor Standards Act of 1938. The Supreme Court then ruled that the law was constitutional.[26]

CHILD LABOR PROVISIONS OF THE FAIR LABOR STANDARDS ACT

Under the Fair Labor Standards Act the employment of "oppressive child labor" in the production, shipment or delivery of goods in interstate commerce is prohibited. Oppressive child labor is defined as:

1. The employment of minors under 18 in any occupation found to be particularly hazardous by the Secretary of Labor. Some 17 occupations, such as coal mining, logging, wood working and many others, have been declared hazardous.

2. The employment of minors under 16 for most other occupations, except that minors between 14 and 16 may be employed in nonmanufacturing and nonmining occupations, subject to regulation by the Secretary of Labor. Such minors may not work more than 18 hours in any week that school is in session; more than 40 hours in any week that school is not in

[25]*Self-Training Unit on Child Labor Laws for Youth*, Bulletin No. 202. Washington. D.C., U. S. Department of Labor. Bureau of Labor Standards (1959). p. 2.
[26]*Ibid.*, p. 3.

session; more than 3 hours in any day that school is in session; or more than 8 hours in any day that school is not in session.

3. The employment of a minor under 14 in any occupation unless specifically exempt.

Exemptions from the above requirements are granted for: children under 16 years of age employed by their parents in occupations other than manufacturing or mining or occupations declared hazardous for minors under 18; children under 16 employed by other than their parents in agriculture if the operation has not been declared hazardous; children employed as actors or performers; newspaper delivery; and certain other homework such as wreath making. The enforcement of the law may be by injunction, by criminal prosecution of willful violators, or by a civil penalty of up to $1,000, added by the 1974 amendments.[27]

Violations of the child labor laws continue to occur, and the recent expansion of the coverage of the act to certain retail and service establishments not previously covered has added to the number of violations found. In fical year 1973, 12,461 minors were found employed in violation of one or more child labor standards. About one-fifth of these were minors aged 16 and 17 employed contrary to hazardous occupations orders , and about one-half of other violations involved the employment of minors under 14.[28] Undoubtedly many violations go undetected.

STATE CHILD LABOR LAWS

All states have laws regulating child labor, and whenever the state law sets a higher minimum age than the Fair Labor Standards Act, the state requirement must be followed. About 20 states set the minimum age at 16 for employment in manufacturing both during and after school hours. The majority of the remaining states set the minimum at 14 or at 15. Most states exempt agriculture and domestic service from these minimums. On the other hand, many states set higher minimum ages in hazardous industries.[29] Each year many states amend their legislation. In 1973, several states enacted legislation which made their laws apply in an equal manner to boys and girls. In some cases where employment in certain occupations had been prohibited below age 21, the state lowered the permissible age to 18, consistent with the establishment of 18 as the legal age of majority.[30]

[27]For greater detail see the *Labor Relations Reporter, Wage and Hour Manual*, Bureau of National Affairs, pp. 99: 1-76; see also *Federal Labor Laws and Programs*, U. S. Department of Labor. Employment Standards Administration. Bulletin 262. September 1971. pp. 87-90.

[28]*Minimum Wage and Maximum Hours Standards Under the Fair Labor Standards Act*, U. S. Department of Labor. Employment Standards Administration. 1974. p. 16.

[29]*State Child Labor Standards*, U. S. Department of Labor. Bureau of Labor Standards. Bulletin No. 158 (1966). pp. vii-ix. For current detail on each state see *Labor Relations Reporter, State Labor Laws*, Bureau of National Affairs.

[30]David A. Levy. "State Labor Legislation Enacted in 1973." *Monthly Labor Review*, Vol. 97 (January 1974). pp. 28-29.

EDUCATION AND POVERTY

It is obvious that education occupies a valued place in the American scheme of things. Legions of the poor in the past have seen in education a chance for their children to lift themselves up and out of poverty. Much of the movement to restrict or eliminate child labor was motivated by a belief that children should be in school rather than at work. Common observation told them that those who were better educated got the better jobs, and such statistics as were available tended to bear out their observation.

Census data today show a correlation between education and size of family income. In 1972, the median school years completed for families earning less than $4,000 per year was nine; for families earning $6,000 to $9,999 per year, 12; and for families earning $25,000 to $49,999, it was 15. Similarly, only 11 percent of those with less than eight years of education had such income, compared to 33 percent of those who had completed high school, 59 percent of those who had completed college, and 67 percent of those with five or more years of college.[31] It should, however, be noted that some people without much education do achieve above average incomes. Native ability, personality characteristics and environmental conditions of all sorts are also factors in the achievement of above average incomes. The above publication also tells us that 41 percent of those who had completed college and 33 percent of those with five or more years of college had annual incomes of less than $15,000. So high educational attainment is not a guarantee of high income,[32] but should instead be regarded as an essential aid in the long run effort to climb out of poverty.

INVESTMENT OF HUMAN CAPITAL (EDUCATION)

Over the past twenty years a number of studies were made and articles and books written purporting to show that we were underinvesting in human capital, especially education, and overinvesting (relatively) in real capital.[33] It was commonly found that the rate of return on investment in

[31]*Money Income of Families and Persons in the United States*, Bureau of the Census, Series P-60, No. 90, December 1973, Table 30, p. 79.

[32]For an extensive discussion of these issues see Ivar Berg, *Education and Jobs; The Great Training Robbery* (New York, Praeger, 1970); and Thomas I. Ribich, *Education and Poverty* (Washington, D.C., The Brookings Institute, 1968).

[33]See for instance, Theodore W. Schultz, "Reflections on Investment in Man," Supplement, October 1962, "Investment in Human Beings," *Journal of Political Economy*, Vol. LXX, Part 2 (1962), pp. 1-8. Edward F. Denison, *The Sources of Economic Growth in the United States and the Alternatives Before Us* (New York, Committee on Economic Development, 1962); Gary Becker, *Human Capital* (New York, Columbia University Press, 1964); Fritz Machlup, *The Production and Distribution of Knowledge in the United States* (Princeton, Princeton University Press, 1962); and Mary Jean Bowman, "The Human Investment Revolution in Economic Thought," *Sociology of Education*, Vol. 39 (1966), pp. 111-137.

education was perhaps 9 or 10 percent while investment in corporations was on the average somewhat less. The difference found depended considerably on what costs and benefits were included. If nonmonetary matters, such as the effects on democratic government, equality of opportunity, culture and the like were excluded, the rate of return to investment in education was only slightly greater. On the other hand, if these nonmonetary matters are included as benefits, and somehow given a value, the return on human capital greatly exceeded the return on real investment. In more recent years, other studies such as those by Berg and Ribich, cited above, have tended to deflate the idea that there is extensive underinvestment in education.

Berg, Ribich and others have pointed out that high educational attainment may not necessarily lead to high income. People with ability normally are directed into higher education, and as a rule they do have higher incomes later in life, but this may be due to their native ability, not purely to their education. Also, high school education and a college degree provide credentials for hiring and for promotion. Rightly or wrongly, personnel directors, when confronted with applicants with and without a degree, tend to hire and promote those with the degree. Thus, native ability, personnel practices in industry, and other factors, such as inherited wealth, may explain much of the correlation between income and education, rather than educational attainment itself.

THE QUALITY AND QUANTITY OF EDUCATION

The quality of education in the United States has long been under attack. Recent data published by the National Assessment of Educational Progress points to some of the difficulties.[34] Data show student achievement in writing, citizenship, science, reading and literature. The data are classified by region, sex, color, parent's education and size and type of community. By region, student achievement is consistently lower in the southeastern states than in the rest of the nation, while the northeastern states usually, but not always, rank the highest. Female students rank above male in reading, writing and literature, while males score better in citizenship and in science. Whether this reflects differences in natural ability, or role differentiation or some other cause, is not known.

Black and other minority races consistently score lower than whites, but again the causes are not precisely known. Parent's education, however, provides a clue. The higher the educational attainment of the parents, the higher the score of the child. It is likely that past discrimination and lack of education and health of black parents are being reflected in current test scores of black children. Children in the inner city consis-

[34]*Digest of Educational Statistics, 1973, op. cit.,* Tables 179-183, pp. 155-159.

tently scored the lowest of all the seven types of communities, while children in the suburbs scored the highest. Remote rural areas and the inner-city fringe were also below the national median.

The quantity of education each person receives is also a problem. Too many students drop out for one reason or another. For every ten pupils in the fifth grade in 1964, 7.5 graduated from high school in 1972. Of these 4.3 entered college that fall, and only about 2.3 will receive bachelor's degrees in 1976.[35] Again there are differences by race and six. *sex*

Although enrollment in college has increased greatly in recent years, large additional groups not now going to college could profit from higher education. Of those who finish in the upper one-fourth of their class, about one out of three does not go to college. College attendance is closely correlated with income of the parents. The data are shown in Table 25.2. Students from low-income families are underrepresented in the college population; those from upper-income families are overrepresented.

TABLE 25-2

DISTRIBUTION OF INCOME IN THE UNITED STATES, 1972, COMPARED
TO PARENTAL INCOME OF COLLEGE FRESHMEN, 1972

	Percent of Population with such Income	Percent of College Freshmen with such Parental Income
Less than $4,000	21.8	8.0
$4,000 to 6,999	11.1	6.1
6,000 to 7,999	10.7	8.2
8,000 to 9,999	10.4	10.4
10,000 to 14,999	21.9	30.3
15,000 to 24,999	18.2	23.7
25,000 and over	5.9	13.4

Sources: *Money Income in 1972 of Families and Persons in the United States*, Bureau of the Census, Current Population Reports, Series P-60, No. 90, December 1973, Table 7, p. 31; and *Digest of Educational Statistics*, 1973, U. S. Department of Health, Education and Welfare, Office of Education, Table 92, p. 78.

[35]*Ibid.*, p. 13.

One hopeful note in regard to the quality of education is the long run decline in illiteracy. Of the population aged 14 and over, in 1870 about 80 percent of the nonwhite population and 11.5 percent of the whites were illiterate. By 1900, the percentages were 44.5 and 6.2, respectively, and in 1969, 3.6 percent and 0.7 percent. The difference between the sexes was negligible: 1.1 percent of the men and 1.0 percent of the women.[36]

FEDERAL AID TO EDUCATION

Since many of the suggestions for improving the school system involve increased expenditures of funds, one of the public policy questions is the degree to which the federal government should aid education. Opponents of federal aid have agreed that the states and localities are not doing as much as they could to support education, but they further argue that the federal government already has too large a deficit. One of their major arguments has been a fear of federal control of education.

Proponents of federal aid on the other hand point out that certain regions of the country have more resources with which to finance education than do others. The highest income states have about twice the per-capita personal income of the low income states, and the difference is much more severe if the wealthiest counties are compared to the poorest counties.[37] Many rural people leave their poorer states to reside in wealthier states. Local financing simply means that the poorer states have to bear a heavy burden of educating their youth, only to see them leave. Also the progressive income tax used by the federal government is a more equitable tax than the regressive taxes used by state and local governments.

Federal aid to education of one sort or another has been present since the founding of the country. Under the Northwest Ordinance of 1787 land grants to the states for the establishment of educational institutions were authorized. In 1862, the first Morrill Act authorized land grants to the states for the establishment and maintenance of agricultural and mechanical colleges. The second Morrill Act, in 1890, authorized money grants for support of instruction in such colleges. In 1917, the Smith-Hughes Act provided for grants to states to support vocational education, and the Smith-Bankhead Act of 1920 authorized grants for vocational rehabilitation. A long list of other legislation has followed including such as the school lunch program, the school milk program, many acts aiding health research, veterans education, a Library Services Act, and many others. Since 1953, about 45 different federal laws have been enacted aiding or affecting education. The more important legislation in recent years has been the National Defense Education Act of 1958, the Vocational

---

[36]*Ibid.*, p. 17.

[37]Paul A. Brinker, "County Income and Federal Aid to Education," *Southwestern Social Science Quarterly*, Vol. 42 (1962), pp. 390-391.

Education Act of 1963, the Higher Education Facilities Act of 1963, the Elementary and Secondary Education Act of 1965, and the Higher Education Act of 1965, with amendments.

The Elementary and Secondary School Act of 1965 was designed specifically to aid children of the poor. Almost all the money in this act went to Title I, programs for the educationally deprived. Much smaller amounts provided for improved library resources, supplementary education centers, strengthening state departments of education, a bilingual program and a dropout prevention program. Expenditures under this act reached a peak of $1.8 billion in 1972 but dropped to $614 million two years later.

There has been covert disagreement over the relative importance of Title I's several purposes, which have been listed as breaking the federal aid barrier, raising achievement, pacifying the ghetto, building bridges to private schools, and providing fiscal relief to school districts.[38] If the program is viewed as a vehicle to provide fiscal relief, it may be viewed as successful if fiscal collapse is avoided. Emphasis on achievement would result in a different evaluation.

A number of criticisms have been leveled at administration of the act.[39] One is that there has been poor monitoring of the program from the Federal Office of Education. Secondly, parents have not been involved nearly as much as was originally planned. Thirdly, some 30 percent of the children receiving aid were not disadvantaged, whereas at the same time millions of disadvantaged children were not being reached at all. Lastly, most state departments of education were so weak as to preclude adequate monitoring of the program.

In a comprehensive review of many studies on the effects of varying school expenditure, Christopher Jencks, et al., concluded that equalizing the quality of elementary schools would reduce cognitive inequality only by three percent or less. In high school, the corresponding figure would be 1 percent or less. Also, additional school expenditures are unlikely to increase achievement and redistributing resources will not reduce test score inequality. More positively his group found that eliminating racial and socioeconomic segregation in the schools might reduce the score gap between black and white children and between rich and poor children by 10 to 20 percent.[40] On the assumption that more equalitarianism is desirable, they concluded that progress will remain glacial if public policy must depend on ingenious manipulations of marginal institutions like schools. His group suggested that political control over economic institutions (socialism) would be required for more equalitarianism.[41]

[38]Jerome T. Murphy, "Title I of ESEA: The Politics of Implementing Federal Education Reform," *Harvard Educational Review*, Vol. 40 (1971), p. 43.

[39]*Idem.*, pp. 35-63.

[40]Christopher Jencks, *Inequality: A Reassessment of the Effect of Family and Schooling in America* (New York, Basic Books, 1972), p. 109.

[41]*Idem.*, p. 265.

A Rand Corporation study found through large surveys of compensatory education that both the ESEA and Head Start with Follow Through have no beneficial results on the average. But two or three smaller surveys tended to show modest and positive effects in the short run.[42]

Edward Banfield noted the same lack of improvement with increased expenditures.[43] He claims that lower-class persons cannot be given much training, because they will not accept it. He maintains that class-cultural factors largely account for the conspicuous difference between the slum and suburban school, and he doubts that schools can change the child's class culture. His major policy recommendation is to lower the normal school leaving age to 14 and get the nonlearners out of school.

A contrary viewpoint was expressed by James N. Morgan, et al., who found that more education does break the cycle of poverty. Their views are as follows:

Several chapters in this volume have documented the pervasive importance of education for various components of economic well-being. Chapter 1 showed that a family's chances of being in the target population or being persistently poor are strongly related to the educational attainment of that family's head. Chapter 3 found that education was the single most powerful predictor of wage rates; Chapter 4 showed that education is strongly associated with unemployment experience, even after occupational and wage differences are taken into account. Finally, Chapter 6, Volume II, provides evidence that when non-pecuniary aspects of jobs (such as flexibility of work hours and choice in work) are added to the wage rate to get a more general measure of work payment, the importance of education increases.[44]

In conclusion, equity would call for equalized expenditures per child. Improved experimentation should result in methods by which more children can be taught to the limit of their potential. Additional aid is needed to enable more of the poor to obtain a higher education. But limited success in educational programs so far is apt to keep federal budgets for education lower than otherwise until more results can be shown.

[42]Harvey A. Averch, Stephen J. Carroll, Theodore S. Donaldson, Herbert J. Keserling and John Pincus, How Effective is Schooling_ A Critical Review and Synthesis of Research Findings (Santa Monica, California, The Rand Corporation, R-956-PCSF-RV, March 1972). Multilithes, p. 125.

[43]Edward C. Banfield, The Unheavenly City Revisited, (Boston, Little, Brown and Co., 1974), pp. 148-178.

[44]Greg Duncan, "Educational Attainment," in James N. Morgan, et al., Five Thousand American Families: Patterns of Economic Progress, Vol. I (Ann Arbor, Institute for Social Research, University of Michigan, 1974), p. 271.

Summary

Women are increasingly entering the labor force in the United States. Some do so because their family income is particularly low. Employment of women is bimodal as to age. Large numbers work before their first child is born, then they leave the labor force for a period of years and reenter when there are no longer children at home. But increasing numbers of women with school age and preschool age children are now working, and more would do so if better day-care facilities were available. Even with increased employment of women, income of many families remains low. This is particularly so if women are the major breadwinner in the family. Part of the poverty of families headed by women may be explained by the fact that the employment of women tends to be concentrated in lower paying occupations. In other cases there is discrimination in pay to women. Legislative efforts to improve the status of women include the Equal Pay Act of 1963 and the Civil Rights Act of 1964. Recent efforts have been directed toward the approval of the Equal Rights Amendment to the constitution.

Many children are handicapped because they are reared in families with extremely low income, or in families which are broken or disruptive. Child Welfare activities are directed toward mending the family, if possible, and toward foster care and adoption, if necessary. Day-care facilities are slowly expanding, enabling more mothers to work. Child labor laws restrict the employment of children, especially in hazardous occupations and during school hours. More equity is needed in our educational programs.

Bibliography

Becker, Gary S., Human Capital (New York, National Bureau of Economic Research, 1964).

Berg, Ivar, Education and Jobs: The Great Training Robbery (New York, Praeger, 1970).

Berg, Ivar (ed.), Human Resources and Economic Welfare: Essays in Honor of Eli Ginzberg (New York, Columbia University Press, 1972).

Billingsley, Andrew and Giovannoni, Jeanne M., Children of the Storm: Black Children and American Child Welfare (New York, Harcourt Brace Javanovich, 1972).

Costin, Lela B., Child Welfare: Policies and Practice (New York, McGraw-Hill, 1972).

Kreps, Juanita, Sex in the Marketplace: American Women at Work (Baltimore, Johns Hopkins Press, 1971).

Levitan, Sar A., Mangum, Garth L., and Marshall, Ray, Human Resources and Labor Markets (New York, Harper and Row, 1972).

Murphy, Irene L., Public Policy on the Status of Women (Lexington, Mass., D. C. Heath, 1973).

Ribich, Thomas I., Education and Poverty (Washington, D.C., The Brookings Institute, 1968).

PART VI

SOLUTIONS TO POVERTY

CHAPTER 26

WAGE AND HOUR LEGISLATION

MINIMUM WAGES

A number of countries have passed minimum wage laws for the purpose of raising the income of low-wage earners. In the United States prior to 1974 the minimum wage was $1.60 per hour. This provided a worker an annual income of $3,200 per year if the worker was fortunate enough to work 40 hours a week for 50 weeks. Such an income was substantially below the poverty level of $4,540 for a four-person nonfarm family in 1973. Under the 1974 amendments the minimum was raised to $2.00 an hour in 1974, to $2.10 an hour in 1975, and to $2.30 an hour in 1976. At $2.30 per hour, annual income is $4,600, or barely above the 1973 poverty level. This chapter raises the question as to whether or not minimum wage legislation is a viable method of dealing with the problem of poverty.

HISTORICAL DEVELOPMENT

Federal government activities to improve wages, hours and child laboring conditions have existed for many years. As early as 1840, President Martin Van Buren by executive order established a ten-hour day for workers in the federal navy yards. Congress in 1868 reduced the hours for the same group to eight. By 1892 all federal employees and all workers employed under contracts to which the federal government was a party enjoyed the benefits of an eight-hour day. Under the commerce clause of the constitution, the Adamson Act of 1916 granted railroad employees the eight-hour day, with time-and-a-half for overtime. The passage of child labor legislation has already been discussed in chapter 25.

The first minimum wage laws on the state level were enacted in the second decade of the 20th century, beginning with Massachusetts in 1912.[1] Eight additional states enacted such laws in 1913, but progress thereafter was slow, and by 1923 only 17 states had laws. Most laws were limited in coverage and poorly enforced. Typically, the state established a

[1]*Growth of Labor Law in the United States*, U. S. Department of Labor, 1962, pp. 107-122. In colonial times Massachusetts enacted a law in 1633 setting maximum wage rates at two shillings a day, and imposing fines on employers who paid more than that amount. Other colonies also enacted similar maximums. Generally, such laws could not be enforced and were eventually repealed.

wage board composed of representatives of employers and employees in a particular industry, and if and when agreement could be reached, a state authority would order the agreed-upon minimum wage to go into effect in that industry. In 1923, the U. S. Supreme Court declared the District of Columbia legislation unconstitutional on the grounds that it violated the principle of liberty of contract. Thereafter, most such legislation fell inoperative until the 1930's.

Early in the 1930's, several states enacted "fair value" minimum wage laws in the hope that they would be found constitutional. But in June, 1936, the Supreme Court struck down the New York law, holding that its effect was the same as earlier minimum wage legislation. Meantime, however, a shift was occurring in the membership of the Supreme Court, so that less than a year later, in March, 1937 the Supreme Court reversed itself and declared the Washington State minimum wage valid. Minimum wage laws were soon enacted in a few other states, but the center of attention now shifted to the national stage.

At the outset of Franklin Roosevelt's administration in 1933, Congress enacted the National Industrial Recovery Act (NIRA), which contained several of the provisions later included in the Fair Labor Standards Act.[2] The NIRA required that employers comply with the maximum hours of labor and minimum wages approved or prescribed by the President, as "NRA codes of fair competition." Most of the NRA codes called for a 40-hour week with overtime above 40 hours, and a minimum wage of 40 cents in most industries, with a lower figure of 30 cents for a minority. After the National Industrial Recovery Act was declared unconstitutional in 1935, the Democratic Party in the presidential election year of 1936 endorsed the enactment of a federal wage-and-hours law as an important plank in its platform. Such a law, called the Fair Labor Standards Act, was passed in 1938.

COVERAGE OF THE FAIR LABOR STANDARDS ACT

At first, coverage under the Fair Labor Standards Act was rather narrowly defined. To be covered the individual employee had to be in interstate commerce. Within any one plant, some workers might be covered, others not. If the worker worked on a product which went into interstate commerce he would be covered; those working on products sold only in intrastate commerce were not. In addition, many businesses, industries and occupational groups were specifically exempted or excluded. Since then,

---

[2]Orme W. Phelps, *The Legislative Background of the Fair Labor Standards Act*, Studies in Business Administration, Vol. IX, No. 1 (Chicago, The University of Chicago Press, 1939), pp. 5-8.

coverage has been broadened by amendments enacted in 1949, 1955, 1961, 1966 and 1974.[3]

Generally, the law covers employees individually engaged in interstate or foreign commerce, or in the production of goods for such commerce, and all employees of certain large enterprises. Thus, employees in transportation and communications are obviously covered, and those engaged in the direct or indirect production of goods which will cross state lines are covered. Employees are covered if their firm sells to another firm which then ships the goods across state lines, or if their firm buys materials or component parts from another firm which brings the materials in across state lines. The 1974 amendments significantly extended coverage by including government activities, some domestic workers, more chain stores, more conglomerate business and additional agricultural labor.[4]

CURRENT LEGAL MINIMUMS

Over the years, the legal minimum wage has been gradually raised, from the 25 cents per hour effective in 1938 to the $2.30 per hour effective in 1976. Actually, different minimums currently exist for different categories of workers, depending on when they were first covered. For all workers covered prior to 1966, the minimum is $2.10 per hour in 1975 and $2.30 in 1976. For workers first covered by the amendments of 1966 and of 1974, the minimum is $2.00 in 1975, $2.20 in 1976, and $2.30 in 1977. For farm workers, regardless of when they were first covered, the minimum is $1.80 in 1975, gradually increasing to $2.30 in 1978. For workers in Puerto Rico and the Virgin Islands, the minimum wage will increase by 15 cents an hour each year if their 1974 wages are more than $1.40 per hour, or by 12 cents an hour each year if 1974 wages are below $1.40 an hour, until all workers reach $2.30 an hour. Eventually, the minimum wage will be the same, $2.30 an hour, for all workers in the 50 states and in Puerto Rico, unless again changed by new amendments in some future year.

STATE MINIMUM WAGE LEGISLATION

Forty-three jurisdictions have minimum wage laws and minimum wage rates in effect. Two states have wage board rates on their statute books, but no minimum wage rates are in force in these states. Eight states, mainly southern, have no minimum wage laws.[5] In 1973, twenty jurisdic-

[3]Specific detailed provisions may be found in the publications of the Bureau of National Affairs. Commerce Clearing House, Inc., and in the Prentice-Hall Reports.

[4]See *How the 1974 Amendments Changed the Law*, Bureau of National Affairs, 1974, pp. 1-15.

[5]*State Minimum Wage Laws, A Chartbook of Basic Provisions*, U. S. Department of Labor. Employment Standards Administration. Labor Law Series No. 4. May 1972.

tions raised their minimums, and in January 1974 eleven states and Guam had higher statuatory minimums than the federal rate of $1.60 then in effect.[6] Several states have amended their laws to provide that the state minimum will be automatically raised to match increases in the federal rate. Coverage of state legislation is quite spotty, ranging from virtually all employers to none. Twelve states cover only employers who have more than some number of employees, such as the Arkansas law which is applicable to employers of five or more. Various industries or occupations are exempted from coverage, and there is limited coverage of agricultural employees in only 12 states.

MINIMUM WAGE RELATIVE TO AVERAGE HOURLY EARNINGS

Table 26-1 shows federal minimum wage rates relative to average hourly earnings for private nonfarm employment for selected years. The years selected, with some exceptions, show pairs of years, one in which a minimum went into effect and the last year before a new minimum was imposed. In the last column may be seen the minimum wage as a percent of average hourly earnings. When a new minimum is first enacted it has tended to be from 50 to 56 percent of average hourly earnings. After a few years with rising hourly earnings but a constant minimum wage, the percentage has drifted downward to a range of 44 to 48 percent. Congress has then tended to put a new higher minimum into effect. The rates effective for 1974, 1975 and 1976 thus appear to be consistent with past experience.

ARE MINIMUM WAGE LAWS HARMFUL?

Controversy has raged within the field of economics as to the merits of minimum wage legislation. The marginal productivity theory tends to show that minimum wage laws are harmful. The theory holds that under competitive conditions workers are paid the value of their marginal product. Converted to dollars, this is known as the "marginal revenue product," or MRP, and is taken as the firm's demand curve for labor. (See Figure 26-1.) Given the assumptions of this theory, a raise in wages would cause unemployment, for if wages equaled the value of a marginal product before the wage increase, they would exceed it after the increase. In terms of supply and demand for labor in an entire competitive market, the same would be true. At the new higher wage, some employees would have to be discharged. In Figure 26-1 (a) the firm's demand for labor is shown by the MRP curve. In Figure 26-1 (b) the corresponding effect is

[6]David A. Levy, "State Labor Legislation Enacted in 1973," *Monthly Labor Review*, Vol. 97 (January 1974), pp. 22-31.

TABLE 26-1

MINIMUM WAGE RATES RELATIVE TO AVERAGE HOURLY EARNINGS IN PRIVATE NONFARM EMPLOYMENT, SELECTED YEARS, 1947-1976

Year	Minimum Wage	Average Hourly Earnings, Private Nonfarm Employment	Minimum Wage as Percent of Average Hourly Earnings
1947	$0.40	$1.13	35.4%
1949	0.40	1.28	31.3
1950	0.75	1.34	56.0
1955	0.75	1.71	43.9
1956	1.00	1.80	55.6
1960	1.00	2.09	47.8
1961	1.15	2.14	53.7
1962	1.15	2.22	51.8
1963	1.25	2.28	54.8
1966	1.25	2.56	48.8
1967	1.40	2.68	52.2
1968	1.60	2.85	56.1
1972	1.60	3.65	43.8
1974	2.00	4.05(est)	49.4
1975	2.10	4.25(est)	49.4
1976	2.30	4.45(est)	51.7

Source: *Monthly Labor Review*, January 1974, Table 18, p. 106; and Thomas W. Gavett, "Youth Unemployment and Minimum Wages," *Ibid.*, March 1970, p. 5.

shown for the entire market. If the wage level is at W_1, E_1 men are employed. If the wage is raised to W_2, employment shrinks to E_2.

Professor George Stigler, among others, concludes that "the legal minimum wage will reduce aggregate output, and . . . direct unemploy-

Figure 26-1

Employment effects of a wage increase in one firm
and in the entire labor market

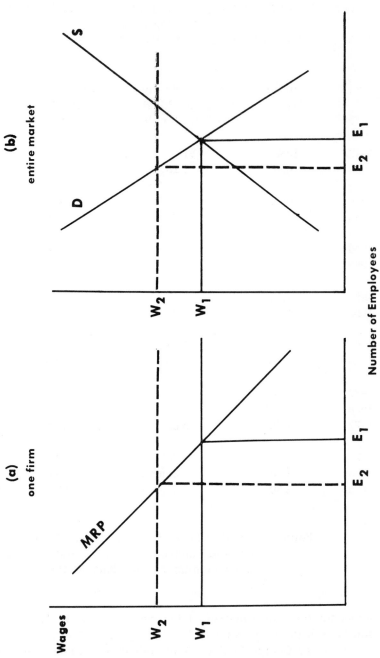

ment is substantial and certain."[7] Professor Milton Friedman adds that a minimum wage law is apt to have harmful effects on some of the very people it is supposed to help, that is, low-income people, blacks and other minorities, and teenagers:

I am convinced that the minimum wage law is the most anti-Negro law on our statute books — in its effect, not its intent. It is a tragic but undoubted legacy of the past — and one we must try to correct — that on average, Negroes have lower skills than whites. Similarly, teen-agers are less skilled than older workers. Both Negroes and teen-agers are only made worse off by discouraging employers from hiring them. On-the-job training — the main route whereby the unskilled have become skilled — is thus denied them.[8]

Other economists have pointed out that a nationwide minimum wage may discourage the flow of capital from high wage to low wage areas. Generally, wages have been higher in the North and West and lower in the South, so these economists have feared that the minimum wage might cause the South to stagnate.[9] Fortunately this has not been the case. The South has in recent years been able to advance at a more rapid rate than the rest of the nation. Excess labor has continued to flow to the North and West, and capital has flowed into the South. The basic reason for this is that labor costs on the average are still higher in the North and West than in the South. As long as the minimum wage is set at a relatively low level the possible harmful effects on the South are mitigated.

ECONOMIC ARGUMENTS IN DEFENSE OF THE MINIMUM WAGE

Some economists see at least some justification for minimum wage legislation. They argue that the labor market is not perfectly competitive in the

[7]George J. Stigler, "The Economics of Minimum Wage Legislation," *American Economic Review*, Vol. 36 (1946), p. 361. See also: George Macesich and Charles T. Stewart, Jr., "Recent Department of Labor Studies of Minimum Wage Effects," *Southern Economic Journal*, Vol. XXVI (April 1960), pp. 281-290; H. M. Douty, "Some Effects of the $1.00 Minimum Wage in the United States," *Economica*, Vol. 27 (May 1960), pp. 137-147; John M. Peterson, "Research Needs in Minimum Wage Theory," *Southern Economic Journal*, Vol. XXIX (July 1962), pp. 1-9; Yale Brozen, "Minimum Wage Rates and Household Workers," *Journal of Law and Economics*, Vol. 5 (October 1962), pp. 104-109; David E. Kaum, Minimum Wages, Factor Substitution, and the Marginal Producer," *Quarterly Journal of Economics*, Vol. 79 (August 1965), pp. 478-486; William J. Shkurti and Belton M. Fleisher, "Employment and Wage Rates in Retail Trade Subsequent to the 1961 Amendments to the Fair Labor Standards Act," *Southern Economic Journal*, Vol. XXXV (July 1968), pp. 37-48; and Yale Brozen, "The Effects of Statutory Minimum Wage Increases on Teen-Age Employment," *Journal of Law and Economics*, Vol. 12 (April 1969), pp. 109-122.

[8]Milton Friedman, *Newsweek*, Vol. 68 (September 16, 1966), p. 96.

[9]See, for instance, John V. Van Sickle, "Geographical Aspects of a Minimum Wage," *Harvard Business Review* Vol. 24 (1946), pp. 277-294.

first place. Various kinds of monopoly and imperfect competition exist in both product and resource markets. In some cases, the employer may not be paying labor its value of marginal product, and a minimum wage law may compel him to do so without necessarily causing unemployment. In cases where there is monopsonistic hiring of labor, a minimum wage law can be shown, in theory at least, to cause the employer to hire more labor, not less. Figure 26-2 illustrates such a possibility. In monopsonistic hiring, the supply curve of labor to the one employer is upsloping. Therefore, the marginal cost of labor will be above the supply curve. The employer will hire only to the point where the MRP equals the marginal cost of labor and will pay wage W_1. If a minimum wage is now imposed at level W_2, the W_2 level now becomes the marginal cost of labor out to the point of intersection with MRP. The employer will now have incentive to expand employment out of E_2.[10]

Figure 26-2

Employment effects of a wage increase in the monopsonistic hiring of labor

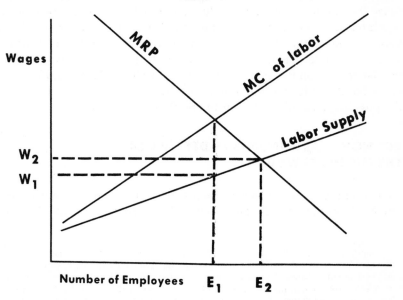

Other circumstances may occur where the minimum wage will have little or no effect on employment. If the industry is one of oligopoly and if the demand for the product is "kinked," the MRP curve will have a "discontinuity" as shown in Figure 26-3. If the minimum wage is raised in the area of the discontinuity, the employer will have no incentive to change the volume of employment. Employment will remain at E_1 even if the

[10]Allan M. Cartter and F. Ray Marshall. *Labor Economics* (Homewood. Ill.. Irwin. 1972). p. 424.

Figure 26-3

Employment effects of a wage increase with a discontinuous MRP

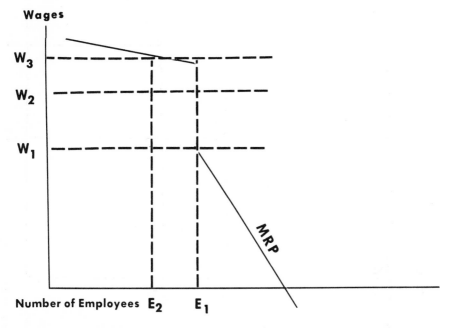

Number of Employees

wage is raised from W_1 to W_2. Obviously, however, if the wage is raised high enough to say W_3, employment will then be reduced to E_2.[11]

Yet another circumstance in which an increase in the minimum wage will have little effect on employment occurs when the MRP curve is quite inelastic, as shown in Figure 26-4 (a). If, however, the MRP curve is relatively elastic as in Figure 26-4 (b), there will be substantial reductions in employment.[12]

Others have also argued that the minimum wage will not necessarily cause unemployment because employers may be able to offset the effects of the wage increase by operating more efficiently.[13] Others point out that labor morale, and thus labor productivity, may be increased by raising the minimum wage. Still others have contended that higher incomes for labor in general will increase the demand for goods and services. This, in turn, will increase the demand for labor so that a cut in employment may not occur. Higher prices of finished products might, however, accompany

[11]*Ibid.*, p. 218.
[12]*Ibid.*, p. 226.
[13]Paul A. Brinker, "The $1 Minimum Wage Impact on 15 Oklahoma Industries," *Monthly Labor Review*, Vol. 80 (1957), pp. 1092-1095.

Figure 26-4

Employment effects of a wage increase if MRP is (a) Inelastic or if MRP is (b) Elastic

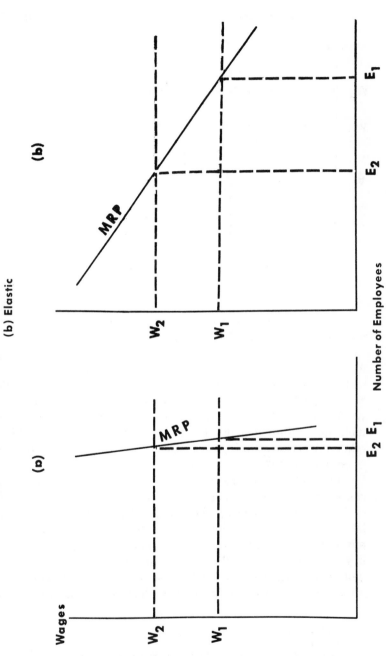

such a process, so that the worker's real wage might be almost unchanged. Some also hold that low-paid workers in the secondary labor market will be taken advantage of by unscrupulous employers. The minimum wage protects the weak against this type of exploitation.

EVALUATION OF FOREGOING ARGUMENTS

The foregoing conflicting theories raise a root question: Which is the more nearly valid in the real world? Granted that all of the above circumstances may exist at certain times and palces, which most accurately describes the situation in industries where the minimum wage law has it impact? The monopsonistic hiring of labor, the situation shown in Figure 26-2, is probably relatively rare. It is difficult to find many real world examples of this situation. Even if such do exist, the minimum wage must be raised by just the right amount, and it is very unlikely that a nationwide statutory minimum would fit every circumstance. If raised too much, the minimum will cause unemployment even in the monopsonistic illustration.[14]

The kinked oligopoly demand curve, as shown in Figure 26-3, is most likely to occur in our giant industries, such as automobiles, steel, home appliances, and others. In these industries the prevailing wages for most skills are already considerably above the statutory minimums. If some low level skills in these industries are affected by the legal minimum, unemployment effects will be avoided only if the wage change falls within the discontinuity. It is difficult to prove that this is the case, although it could be. In any case this situation could not cause an increase in employment.[15]

The case of the highly inelastic marginal revenue product curve as shown in Figure 26-4 (a) is also of doubtful application to the minimum wage question. Such a MRP curve is apt to occur only in capital-intensive industries, such as oil refining. In most such industries the prevailing wages are again already above the statutory minimums. The foregoing cases raised in defense of the minimum wage thus appear to have only very limited applicability.

On the other hand, the competitive model appears to have wide applicability. A long list of the industries which are affected by the minimum wage include many that approximate competitive conditions.

[14]Frank Falero, Jr., "A Note on Monopsony, Minimum Wages and Employment, *American Economist*, Fall 1966. See also comment by Ralph Gray and John E. Morril, "A Note on Monopsony, Minimum Wages and Employment: Extended," *American Economist*, Spring 1968.

[15]John M. Peterson and Charles T. Stewart, Jr., *Employment Effects of Minimum Wage Rates* (Washington, American Enterprise Institute, 1969), pp. 28-36.

While almost no industries can be said to be "perfectly competitive," a large number of industries, such as retail stores, the garment trades, laundries and dry cleaning establishments, restaurants, hotels and motels, and farming, affected by the minimum wage law are at least "imperfectly competitive," and the competitive model provides a first approximation of their behavior. Thus economic analysis appears to indicate that the minimum wage may be damaging to the level of employment, and especially to the employment of marginal workers.

EMPIRICAL STUDIES OF THE EFFECTS OF MINIMUM WAGE RATES

In view of the allegation that minimum wage laws will cause unemployment, a number of studies have been made to measure the impact of such legislation. Some of these have been conducted by the Department of Labor, others by independent researchers often using Department of Labor data. Department of Labor studies have generally concluded that the effects of the minimum wage on the volume of employment have been minimal. But several critics have questioned the research techniques used by the department, and have tended to find an adverse impact.

Most observers agree that the effects of increases in the minimum wage have frequently been obscured by other developments in the economy. Thus, the first increases required by the Fair Labor Standard Act in the years 1938 to 1945 were obviously overwhelmed by the great expansion of demand occasioned by World War II, so that the 40-cent minimum was largely meaningless by 1945. To a lesser degree this has been true of other increases. A 75-cent minimum went into effect in 1950, but the Korean War also began in that year. The minimum of $1.40 in 1967 and the $1.60 minimum in 1968 obviously coincided with the inflation associated with the Vietnam War. On the other hand, the increases to $1.00 in 1956, to $1.15 in 1961, and to $1.25 in 1963 mainly occurred in peacetime years, although the effects of the 1963 increase may have been partly obscured by the Vietnam War also. The inreases in the minimum wage thus did not appear to have caused a large amount of unemployment, but neither does the foregoing show that there was no effect.

Labor Department studies and other studies supporting the minimum wage have often found that after a period of time employment in an industry is as great or is greater than it was at the time of the increase in the minimum wage. But such data do not prove much; too many factors will also have changed in the meantime. Certain Labor Department studies did, however, show adverse effects. Following the increase to $1.00 in 1956, the Department reported in March 1957 that 17 or 23 low-wage industries showed absolute declines in employment between August 1955 and August 1956. On the other hand, only three of 13 high wage industries, who would not be much affected by the minimum wage, showed declines. Generally, however, the department leans toward the position that its studies do not show significant harmful effects on employment.[16]

THE PETERSON-STEWART STUDIES

Peterson and Stewart[17] have criticized Labor Department and other studies on the grounds that their research methods are flawed. Instead of asking whether or not employment increased or decreased, they should ask what have been the relative changes in employment in industries or businesses much affected by the minimum wage, compared to industries or businesses little affected. Both sets of industries might show increases, or both might show decreases. But the relative amount of increase or decrease may be different, and thus be indicative of employment effects of the minimum wage. Peterson and Stewart surveyed the literature and reworked the various studies that have been made, including comparisons between manufacturing industries, comparisons within manufacturing industries such as hosiery, cotton garments, furniture and sawmills, and comparisons within nonmanufacturing industries, such as retail stores, laundries and dry cleaning. While the results were not uniform, and they saw a need for yet more research, some of their more significant findings were that the competitive model in economics. . .

(a) most nearly corresponds to the observed results of statutory minimums, whereas the alternative models used to support minimum wage advocacy have been shown to be nonpredictive in theory and in fact.

(b) the impression created in most government studies that no significant adverse employment effects occur is erroneous.

(c) The weight of evidence in academic literature is that adverse relative employment effects are related to the relative wage impacts of legal minimums.

(d)Both theory and fact suggest that minimum wage rates produce gains for some groups of workers at the expense of those that are least favorably situated in terms of marketable skills or location.[18]

Peterson and Stewart then go on to say that "Given these findings, the unqualified claim that statutory minimums aid the poor must be

[16]Numerous articles have appeared in the *Monthly Labor Review* reporting on various studies of effects of raising the minimum wage. These include Vol. 80 (1957). pp. 323-328; pp. 441-446; pp. 1087-1091; pp. 1092-1095; pp. 1339-1343; Vol. 81 (1958). pp. 492-501; 737-743; 1137-1142; Vol. 83 (1960). pp. 238-242; pp. 677-685; Vol. 84 (1961). pp. 839-845; Vol. 88 (1965). pp. 541-543; Vol. 89 (1966). pp. 1378-1384; Vol. 90. (June 1967). pp. 21-25; September (1967). pp. 26-29; and Vol. 93 (March 1970). pp. 3-12.

[17]*op. cit.*

[18]*Ibid.*, pp. 153-156.

denied. The evidence provides more basis for the claim that while they help some workers they harm those who are least well off."[19] As to policy implications, they call for further study of minimum wage effects, caution in raising minimum wage rates and extending coverage, and advise that policymakers "look to means other than statutory minimum wages for dealing with the problems of low wage rates and poverty."[20]

A LOWER MINIMUM WAGE FOR TEENAGERS?

Prior to the enactment of the 1974 amendments, the Nixon Administration proposed that lower minimum wages be established for teenagers on the grounds that the minimum wage was one of the causes of a high rate of unemployment among such age groups. While the unemployment rate of the entire work force in the post-World War II period has tended to range from 3 to 8 percent, white teenage unemployment has often ranged from 8 to 18 percent, and the rate for nonwhite teenagers has ranged from 10 to a catastrophic 41 percent in 1975. (See Table 26-2.) Sar Levitan states that:

It is probable that the rising minimum wage has contributed to this unfortunate trend as low-wage employers have opted for more mature and experienced workers, adjusted working schedules, increased their use of capital investment, eliminated low paying jobs, or gone out of business. Evidence that the minimum has been a major factor is especially persuasive for black teenagers whose incidence of unemployment is more than twice that of whites. In mid-1971, one of every six white teenagers was employed; among ghetto black teenagers two of every five were unemployed. Many more who are not counted among the unemployed would take jobs if work were available. But there are simply not enough jobs for youths even at present minimum rates. . . . A lower minimum for youth could compensate for a decline in employment resulting from extensions of coverage to sectors employing many young workers.[21]

There are no doubt other reasons besides the minimum wage for the high unemployment rate among teenagers, including a lack of education and experience, reluctance on the part of employers to hire teenagers because of dissatisfaction with their absenteeism and unreliability, uncertainty about their military status, laws limiting the employment of

---

[19]Ibid., p. 155.

[20]Ibid., pp. 155-156.

[21]Statement of Sar A. Levitan, Hearings before the Subcommittee on Labor, Senate Committee on Labor and Public Welfare, Part 5, 92d Congress, 1st Session, September 30, 1971, pp. 1786-1791.

TABLE 26-2

TEENAGE UNEMPLOYMENT, 1948-1975

Year	Total Labor Force, Aged 16 and Over	Unemployment Rate (Percent)	
		Whites Ages 16-19	All Others Ages 16-19
1948	3.8%	8.9%	11.2%
1950	5.3	11.8	15.3
1952	3.0	8.3	10.5
1954	5.5	12.1	16.6
1956	4.1	10.1	18.1
1958	6.8	14.4	27.4
1960	5.5	13.5	24.3
1962	5.5	13.3	25.3
1964	5.2	14.8	27.3
1966	3.8	11.2	25.4
1968	3.6	11.0	24.9
1970	4.9	13.5	29.1
1972	5.6	14.2	33.5
1975 (Jan)	8.2	18.4	41.1

Source: *Monthly Labor Review*, various issues.

teenagers on hazardous jobs, racial discrimination, and other reasons.[22] But a Bureau of Labor Statistics study indicated at least some negative effect. The study also stated that "minimum wage legislation may have had greater adverse effects upon 16- and 17-year old youths," and the "extensions of coverage of the minimum wage had more of effect than changes in the relative level of the minimum wage."[23]

Under the Fair Labor Standards Act, employers holding full-time student certificates already have authority to employ youth at 85 percent of the minimum wage. But employers make very little use of such certificates. In 1969, only about 4,615 employers held certificates, and of these only 452 in the whole United States made full use of this authority. Many employers are apparently not aware of student certificates, others complain of certificate restrictions and of the problems of record-keeping, and

[22]Thomas W. Gavett, "Youth Unemployment and Minimum Wages," *Monthly Labor Review*, Vol. 93 (March 1970), pp. 3-12. This article is the summary chapter of a Bureau of Labor Statistics study of the same title, published as BLS Bulletin 1657.
[23]*Ibid.*, p. 5.

still others appear to believe that a 15 percent "discount" is not enough to offset the poorer quality of student help.[24] In any event, student certificates have been used little, and unemployment of teenagers has mounted.

Accordingly, Secretary of Labor Hodgson in 1971 and Secretary Brennan in 1973 proposed that the act be amended to establish lower nationwide minimum wage for teenagers.[25] Generally, most business and industry lobbyists supported the proposal, while organized labor argued against it. Andrew Biemiller of the AFL-CIO argues that the minimum wage should be a floor under wages and that "no one — young or old, black or white, male or female — should be asked to work for less than the wage floor." He also argued that a lower minimum wage for teenagers "would actually mean the displacement of working heads of families, discrimination based solely on age, and higher profits for employers at the expense of young mothers."[26] In any event, Congress in enacting the 1974 FLSA amendments, did not provide a lower minimum wage for teenagers. Some in Congress argued that there should be intensified work and training programs for unemployed people.

In Western Europe, Canada and Japan there are youth differentials by law, contract or custom. In the United Kingdom, the Netherlands and Japan, young workers start at about one-third the adult rate. In some countries such as Britain, Germany and the Netherlands, there are extensive apprenticeship programs which channel children from school to work. Rates of unemployment for both youth and adults, are generally lower in Europe than in the United States. In Germany, the unemployment rate during most of the 1960's was one percent or less, and youth unemployment was no higher than that for adults. In the Netherlands, Britain and Japan the youth rate was only slightly higher than that for adults. On the other hand, experience in Canada, Italy and France was not greatly different from that in the United States.[27] Overall, however, foreign experience seems to indicate that a youth differential might be helpful in reducing the high unemployment rate of teenagers, and also that intensive programs to channel youth into gainful employment, as in England and Germany, are of value.

EVALUATION OF MINIMUM WAGE LEGISLATION

On the theoretical level, where competitive conditions do not prevail, the minimum wage may sometimes be raised without decreasing employ-

---

[24]Ibid., p. 7.

[25]Statement of Peter J. Brennan, Secretary of Labor, Hearings before the General Subcommittee on Labor of the Committee on Education and Labor, House of Representatives. 93rd Congress, 1st Session, April 10, 1973, pp. 259-264.

[26]Statement of Andrew Biemiller, Director, Department of Legislation, AFL-CIO, Ibid., pp. 88-92.

[27]Youth Unemployment and Minimum Wages, U. S. Department of Labor, Bureau of Labor Statistics, Bulletin 1657, 1970. See especially Chapter X.

ment. But the minimum wage more commonly applies to situations where the labor market approximates competitive conditions, and harmful effects on the employment of marginal workers are apt to occur, particularly if business is not expanding. Minority groups and teenagers are apt to bear the brunt of such effects.

Unfortunately, the abolition of the minimum wage would not solve the poverty problem for low-income workers. Even at the present minimum, insufficient income is earned to lift a family of four out of poverty. Abolishing the minimum would likely result in lower wages being paid to many low income workers. If such workers are to climb out of poverty, either minimum wages will have to be raised, causing some unemployment, or some other program, such as a government wage supplement, will have to be adopted. The latter programs appear to hold more promise than raising minimum wages.

HOURS LEGISLATION

HISTORICAL DEVELOPMENT

Legislation restricting the number of hours of work per day or per week preceded minimum wage legislation. The first recorded effort to restrict the hours of work was in the 1830's, and the first legislation in the United States was a New Hampshire law enacted in 1847 which established a maximum of 10 hours per day. After this date, a number of other eastern states enacted similar legislation over the next few decades, but progress was slow until the 20th century. Most early legislation applied to women and children only, but men were eventually covered in several states. More rapid change occurred in the second decade of the century: in 1913, 27 states had maximum hours legislation of some sort, and by 1920, 42 states had laws. The 10-hour day and the 60-hour week were gradually supplanted by the 9-hour day, and eventually, in most states, by the 8-hour day and the 40-hour week. The state legislation, however, was often restricted to only a few industries, often did not cover men at all, and in many cases was poorly enforced.[28]

In 1938, when the Fair Labor Standards Act was first passed, large numbers of people were unemployed. At the same time, other people were working overtime. In an attempt to spread employment, it was provided that wages would have to be paid at a rate of not less than time and a half for any hours worked over 44. These were gradually reduced, so that today, time and a half must be paid for all hours worked over 40 in any workweek. Most states which have minimum wage laws also now re-

[28]*Growth of Labor Law in the United States, op. cit.,* pp. 73-84.

quire time and a half pay for overtime work. Many collective bargaining contracts require double time for work on holidays or on Sundays, but such arrangements are over and above statutory requirements.

"PORTAL-TO-PORTAL" PAY AND "OVERTIME-ON-OVERTIME"

In general, the overtime provisions of the law have been less controversial than the minimum wage provision. However, there were two early disputes which caused raging controversies. These were the "portal-to-portal" pay issue and the question of "overtime-on-overtime."

The basic question in the portal pay case was how to define "hours worked." Should a coal miner be considered to have begun work as soon as he checked in at the employer's premises or only when he was ready to begin digging coal? The United States Supreme Court ruled in 1944 and 1945 that hours worked must be counted from portal to portal, that is, from the time employees reached the employer's premises until they leave, in coal and iron mines.[29]

The same interpretation was applied to a manufacturing case in 1946 in the celebrated Anderson v. Mt. Clemens Pottery Case.[30] In that case, the company had not paid for the time spent putting on aprons, turning on lights, sharpening tools and other tasks prior to their work. Many other suits were instituted for back pay, and the total of such claims reached $6 billion.[31] In order to ease the burden on employers, Congress in 1947 passed the Portal Pay Act. This act outlawed all claims prior to May, 1947, unless such activities were compensable by contract, custom or practice. Today, the employer does not ordinarily pay for activities preliminary to work or subsequent to work. Collective bargaining contracts, however, may lawfully provide for such pay.

Another question which arose was whether premium pay, such as extra pay for the night shift, should be considered as part of regular pay upon which time and a half would be paid or whether the premium pay itself could be considered as part of the time and a half. The Wages and Hours Administrator had ruled in 1938 that premium pay could be counted by the employer as the required overtime payment. In 1948, however, the Supreme Court overruled the administrator, and held that the premium rates should be considered as regular pay upon which time and a half was to be computed and paid.[32] Numerous lawsuits were again

---

[29]*Tennessee Coal, Iron and Railroad Co. v. Muscoda Local No. 123* (1944), 321 U.S. 590; *Jewel Ridge Coal Corp. v. Local No. 6167 United Mine Workers of America* (1945), 325 U.S. 161.

[30]*Anderson v. Mt. Clemens Pottery Co. (1946), 328 U.S. 630.*

[31]*Prentice-Hall Labor Course, 1958* (Englewood Cliffs, N.J., Prentice-Hall, 1958), p. 7058.

[32]*Bay Ridge Operating Co. v. Aaron* (1948), 334 U.S. 446.

filed by employees to recover past wages. To forestall such suits, Congress passed the "Overtime-on-Overtime" law (1949), which provided that premium pay, such as time and a half for work on Saturday or Sunday, could be excluded from the computation of overtime.

EVALUATION OF OVERTIME PROVISIONS

Generally, the overtime provisions of the law have worked satisfactorily, partly because the employer is permitted an option. If a company needs extra production, it can require overtime work, provided it is willing to pay time and a half. Premium pay sometimes causes the employer to hire more workers rather than pay for overtime work. For this reason, especially during periods of recession, the AFL-CIO has pushed for a law requiring the payment of overtime after 35 hours of work per week. Most post-war recessions, however, have been relatively mild, so that there has not been much support outside the ranks of organized labor for this proposal.

ADMINISTRATION

In administering the Fair Labor Standards Act, a Wage and Hour Division was created within the Department of Labor. This division is headed by an administrator appointed by the President. The administrator has authority to issue binding regulations concerning specific provisions of the act. Regulations have been issued concerning such matters as record-keeping, apprentices, and many other facets of the law. In addition, interpretative bulletins are issued. These are not official but serve as guides to those who are covered by the act.

Records are required of covered employers, although the administrator has not prescribed any particular form in which they must be kept. Data on payrolls must be kept for three years and supplementary basic records must be kept for two years. The Wage and Hour Division has authority to inspect employers' records, and has subpoena power to require them. The Wage and Hour Division does make regular inspections of covered firms, but relatively few firms are visited. The failure to inspect more firms annually has resulted in much violation of the law, although often it is unintentional. In fiscal year 1973, 39,000 complaints were received, and the majority of these were investigated under the agency's "worst first" policy. About 151,000 employees were found to have been illegally paid less than the minimum, and about 200,000 workers were not fully paid for overtime work.[33]

[33]*Minimum Wage and Maximum Hours Standards Under the Fair Labor Standards Act,* U. S. Department of Labor, Employment Standards Administration, January 1974, pp. 15-16.

Back pay payments agreed to by the employer were often much less than that due employees. Prior to the 1961 amendments, employees were requred to authorize a court proceeding to enforce restitution. In many instances, employees were reluctant to bring suit for fear that they would lose their jobs. The 1961 amendments provided that the Department of Labor may bring suit, and this has tended to result in larger amounts of back pay being awarded to employees. The Department of Labor attempts first to informally aid the worker to collect back pay in order to avoid court litigation. Injunctive and criminal actions may also be brought against employers.

WAGE STANDARDS ON FEDERAL CONSTRUCTION PROJECTS

The Davis-Bacon Act, passed in 1931 and amended and extended on many occasions since, provides that all employers having contracts of more than $2,000 on federal construction, alteration, or repair projects must pay at least the minimum wage prevailing in the community as determined by the Secretary of Labor. The Secretary also specifies the prevailing fringe benefits, such as medical care, pensions, vacations and the like. The purpose of the act is to prevent contractors from receiving the low bid on government contracts by paying substandard wages. The determination of the minimum wage and fringe benefits is made in advance of the release of the request for bids. The wage standards are based on the prevailing wages paid in the area for the same types of workers on similar projects. The act covers only mechanics and laborers.[34]

The law requries that employees must be paid in full at least once a week, and certain penalties exist under the act. If the contractor fails to live up to any provisions of the contract, he is deemed to have broken it, and the government may cancel his contract and give the work to another contractor for completion. Also, contractors who violate this law may be barred for three years from receiving further federal contracts. In case of violation the Comptroller General is authorized to withhold sums due to the contractor and to pay the amounts due the workers. If there is insufficient money with which to reimburse the workers, they may sue the contractor and his surety. To guarantee that payment will be made, the Miller Act, passed in 1935 and amended in 1959, requires that all contractors with contracts over $2,000 post surety bonds.

The Davis-Bacon Act says nothing about paying time and a half for overtime. But the Work Hours Act of 1962, which consolidated previous "Eight Hour Laws" into a single statute, provides for an 8-hour day, a 40-hour work week, and time and a half for all hours in excess of those stan-

[34]Ibid., pp. 96-98.

dards. The law applied to laborers, mechanics, watchmen and guards working under any contract with the federal government. It also applies to any contract financed in whole or in part by loans and grants from the federal government. The contractor is liable to employees for unpaid overtime compensation, and there are criminal penalties for intentional violaters.[35] Other laws dealing with public work construction projects include the Copeland Act of 1934 and the "Anti-Kickback" law of 1948. These laws regulate the lawful deductions which an employer may make from an employee's pay, and more importantly outlaw kickbacks to employers from employees on such projects.[36] Prior investigation by the Senate Committee on Commerce had revealed that as much as 25 percent of the money supposed to be paid out of federal funds to employees was actually repaid to employers in an improper manner.

PUBLIC CONTRACT REQUIREMENTS

The Walsh-Healey Act of 1936, as amended, provides for the regulation of wages, hours and working conditions on public contracts, especially purchase contracts (as contrasted to public construction under the Davis-Bacon Act). The Walsh-Healey Act applies to contracts in excess of $10,000. The Secretary of Labor determines the prevailing minimum wage for similar work in the industry, either on the basis of geographic area or industry-wide. The minimum set may not be less than that prevailing in the Fair Labor Standards Act. Time and a half must be paid for all work in excess of 8 hours in one day or 40 in one week. Convict and child labor are prohibited on such contracts, and work performed must conform to state and federal safety and health regulations.

Coverage of the law extends to all persons engaged in the fabrication, assembly, handling, or shipping of the contracted items, but does not extend to executive, administrative or professional positions nor to those engaged in office, custodial or maintenance work. Under specified conditions the contract may permit the payment of less than the established minimum to beginners, apprentices, student-learners, and handicapped workers.[37] Penalties for violation of the act are similar to those under the Davis Bacon Act.

In evaluating the act, Herbert Morton pointed out that the act had weaknesses in coverage of small firms, agriculture, subcontractors and office workers.[38] Delays of two and a half to three years between the wage surveys and the effective date of determination of the wage have blunted

[35]*Ibid.*, pp. 100-101.
[36]*Ibid.*, pp. 99-100.
[37]*Ibid.*, pp. 94-96.
[38]Herbert C. Morton. *Public Contracts and Private Wages (Washington, Brookings Institute, 1965).*

the effects of the designated wages. Also the cents-per-hour increases are smaller under Walsh-Healey than under the FLSA since firms need not bid on government contracts. Morton concluded that the Walsh-Healey Act had little impact on employment, wage rates, prices or output. The act did not attempt to raise wages since it merely requires that a rate equaling the prevailing minimum rate be paid. Likewise, Carroll Christenson and Richard A. Myren found that the law had little impact on the actual preexisting wage structure. However, setting a relatively high rate in bituminous coal contributed to the growth of mechanical underground and increased strip and auger mining.[39]

Summary

Many countries of the world, including the United States, have enacted minimum wage legislation, the main U. S. legislation being the Fair Labor Standards Act of 1938, as amended. This act had three main parts: minimum wages, penalties for overtime work, and limitation of child labor. Economists disagree as to the desirability of minimum wage legislation. Some defend it on grounds that it tends to raise the income of low income workers. Others criticize it sharply, arguing that it tends to cause unemployment, and especially unemployment of the very people it is supposed to help — low-income people generally, minority groups and teenagers.

A number of empirical studies have been made to test the merits of minimum wage legislation, especially at times following increases in the minimum. Labor Department studies tend to show that the unemployment effects are not large; studies by independent investigators have tended to be more critical. Over the years the effects of raising the minimum have often been concealed by wage and price inflation associated with various wars.

The extent of coverage of the law has also been the source of much argument and lobbying in Congress. Various amendments have expanded coverage. Some have argued that all workers of any age on any job should be covered; others have held that recent extensions of coverage may add to the unemployment effects on teenagers and others. For this reason, an effort was made to establish a lower minimum for teenagers than for the rest of the population, but Congress has kept the minimum wage the same for all age groups.

Due to the large scale unemployment of the 1930's, the Fair Labor Standards Act required that time and a half be paid for overtime work. When a dispute arose over whether overtime should be paid when the

[39]Carroll L. Christenson and Richard A. Myren, *Wage Policy Under the Walsh-Healey Public Contracts Act* (Bloomington, Indiana, Indiana University Press, 1966).

worker clocked in, or sometime later when he began work, Congress, in 1947, passed the Portal Pay Act which outlawed all portal-to-portal claims prior to May 14, 1947, unless such activities were compensable by contract, custom or practice. In 1949, the Overtime-on-Overtime law was passed to provide that certain premium pay could be excluded from regular rates of pay when computing overtime rates of pay. During the past few years there has been little demand to change the overtime provisions of the Fair Labor Standards Act.

The Davis-Bacon Act, dealing with federal construction projects, and the Walsh-Healey Act, dealing especially with purchase and service contracts, authorize the Secretary of Labor to establish wage, hour and other regulations on contracted work.

Bibliography

Barton, H. D., Jr., and Solo, Robert A., *The Effect of Minimum Wage Laws on the Economic Growth of Puerto Rico*, Center for International Affairs (boston, Harvard University, 1959).

Brozen, Yale, and Friedman, Milton, *The Minimum Wage — Who Really Pays?* An Interview (Washington, The Free Press Association, 1966).

Cartter, Allan M., and Marshall, F. Ray, *Labor Economics* (Homewood, Illinois, Irwin, 1972).

Cullen, Donald E., *Minimum Wage Laws*, Bulletin 43 (Ithaca, New York, State School of Industrial and Labor RElations, 1961).

Levitan, Sar, Cohen, Wilbur J., and Lampman, Robert (eds.), *Towards Freedom from Want* (Madison, Industrial Research Association, 1968).

Peterson, John M., and Stewart, Charles T., Jr., *Employment Effects of Minimum Wage Rates* (Washington, American Enterprise Institute, 1969).

Thiebolt, Armand J., Jr., *The Davis-Bacon Act*, Labor Relations and Public Policy Series, Report No. 10 (Philadelphia, University of Pennsylvania Press, 1975).

Youth, Unemployment and Minimum Wages, Bureau of Labor Statistics, Bulletin 1657 (Washington, D.C., U. S. Government Printing Office, 1970).

Chapter 27:

CHAPTER 27

THE WAR ON POVERTY

In the 1930's domestic policy necessarily had to deal with poverty. President Franklin D. Roosevelt's classic statement that one-third of our population was "ill housed, ill clad and ill nourished" spelled out the problem. Solutions at that time revolved around the Social Security Act to provide income to the aged, the unemployed and those on welfare. Various public works also were implemented. The working poor were covered by the minimum wage law of 1938. The involvement of the United States in World War II resulted in our energies being directed toward winning the war. World War II provided a bonus in full employment and a substantially improved per capita income. After the war and throughout the 1950's, little policy was implemented to aid the poor.

Impetus toward helping the poor in the 1960's came from a number of sources. One was John F. Kennedy's campaigning for the presidency in poor areas of West Virginia in 1960. There he found much more poverty than he had seen in the wooden tenements of Charlestown, Massachusetts in earlier campaigns.[1] Later in December, 1962, when President Kennedy was reviewing year-end economic conditions, he remarked to Walter Heller, the chairman of the Council of Economic Advisors, that: "Now, look! I want to go beyond the things that have already been accomplished. Give me facts and figures on the things we still have to do. For example, what about the poverty problem in the United States."[2] That comment set in motion staff work that eventually culminated in the War on Poverty program.[3]

In 1963, a task force of the Council of Economic Advisors, the Bureau of the Budget, and the White House staff began working on a poverty program. They were in the midst of a review of various federal department responses for specific anti-poverty proposals when they were informed that President Kennedy had been shot. Shortly thereafter, President Johnson advised Walter Heller to go "full speed ahead" with the program. In his State of the Union Message, in January of 1964, President Johnson declared "unconditional war on poverty." The next month he appointed Sargent Shriver, director of the Peace Corps, as chairman of a Task Force to design a poverty program.

[1]Robert A. Levine, *The Poor Ye Need Not Have With You* (Cambridge, Mass., The M.I.T. Press, 1970, p. 32.

[2]Quoted by Walter Heller in a speech at Indiana State College, Indiana, Pa., March 25, 1965.

[3]Robert Coles, "Rural Upheavel: Confrontation and Accomodation in James L. Sundquist," ed., *Politics and Policy: The Eisenhower, Kennedy and Johnson Years*, (Washington, The Brookings Institute, 1968), p. 112.

The Task Force developed a program that was basically community action oriented. It drew upon a Ford Foundation "gray areas" program that had attempted to rejuvenate slum areas of 14 large cities. It also received direction from the President's Committee on Juvenile Delinquency and Youth Crime that had been created by an executive order of President Kennedy in 1961. Theoretical underpinnings of the group had come from a work by Cloward and Ohlin, who contended that the origins of delinquency among lower-class youth were less a failure of their personalities than a failure of the opportunity structure.[4] The Task Force downplayed a large employment program on the ground that a tax cut would improve employment.

A decision also had to be made whether to administer the poverty program through old line agencies such as the Department of Health, Education and Welfare, the Department of Labor, or a new agency. The decision was made that a new agency be created within the Office of the President and be called the Office of Economic Opportunity (OEO). This agency was to coordinate the War on Poverty and directly run three of the main programs. These three were the Job Corps, Community Action and Vista. Other programs were to be included in the budget of the OEO but delegated to other agencies for implementation.

The annual budget of the OEO never rose to more than slightly over $2 billion. Income supplements had been rejected as a part of the program on the ground that they were too expensive. It is easy to see now that the OEO program could not immediately, or in the near future, abolish poverty when many more times that amount of money was needed in income supplements alone to remove everyone from poverty. It had been hoped that expenditures would be expanded as the program became functional, but expenditures for the Vietnam War were escalated much faster than for the War on Poverty. From fiscal 1965 through 1973, a total of $15.5 billion was spent for the War on Poverty compared with some $120 billion for the Vietnam War.[5]

COMMUNITY ACTION PROGRAMS

Originally any local group could propose programs to be funded by the OEO. The only guideline was that there should be "maximum feasible participation" of the poor. Over 1,000 such agencies have been created in the United States, about a third as many as the number of counties. Many of the agencies created Neighborhood Service Centers as headquarters from which a number of services could be dispensed. A study in 1970 in-

[4]Richard A. Cloward and Lloyd E. Ohlin, *Delinquency and Opportunity* (Glencoe, Illinois, The Free Press, 1960).
[5]John C. Donovan, *The Politics of Poverty* (Indianapolis, Pegasus, 2nd ed., 1973), p. 178.

dicated that 2,518 multiservice agencies were operating in the United States, but these include both OEO and non-OEO centers.[6] About 62 percent of all centers had been established after 1964. Most of the centers were located in cities of over 100,000 people. About 38 percent exist where over half or more of the population is black. In a breakdown of 51 OEO Community Action programs scattered throughout the entire country,[7] there were 116 educational programs in all, mainly Head Start. These were compensatory or enrichment programs. The second largest group of programs, 103 in all, involved such social services as recreation programs, homemaker services and day care centers. The third most frequent service program was job training (52 programs), followed by health services (23 programs). Fifty-five programs involved community action, with a primary objective of involving and training indigenous staff for such action. Thirty-four of the programs were concerned primarily with community organization among the poor that either involved the creation of new neighborhood centers or activating more program involvement in existing centers. Of all the programs in the 51 agencies, roughly three out of four were concerned with traditional services and only a minority involved community action or community organization.

HEAD START

Summer preschool programs became an early favorite of Community Action agencies. Later, a 9-months program was added. The original popularity of Head Start in the first few years resulted in more money being appropriated for it than any other one program. The program was designed to prepare poor preschool children for primary school experience, although it added a health and nutrition component as well. As late as 1966, only three of every ten preschoolers attended nursery school or kindergarten, and children of the poor had only about half the opportunity of attending than higher income families had.

One criticism of Head Start was that little training was given teachers. Although a third of the staff had no prior experience and almost half had not worked with the poor before, many staff received no training at all.[9] Another criticism was that Head Start has been more traditional and has not assimilated the methods of successful programs that have heavily stressed more instruction.[10] The effects of even instructional

[6]Edward J. O'Donnell and Otto R. Reid. "The Multiservice Neighborhood Center. *Welfare in Review*, Vol. 9, No. 3 (May-June 1971), pp. 1-8.

[7]Kenneth B. Clark and Jeanette Hopkins. *A Relevant War Against Poverty* (New York. Harper & Row. 1968), pp. 64-65.

[8]Sar Levitan. *The Great Society's Poor Law* (Baltimore. Johns Hopkins Press. 1969), pp. 133-134.

[9]*Idem.*, pp. 148-149.

[10]Marshall S. Smith and Joan S. Bissell. "Report Analysis: The Impact of Head Start," *Harvard Educational Review*, February 1970. p. 59.

preschool programs tend to wash out particularly if adequate regular school programs exist. On the basis of these findings, one expert in the field concluded that the wisdom of concentrating compensatory education in a preschool period was questionable.[11]

Evaluations that showed only limited Head Start success[12] resulted in President Nixon's declaring in 1969 that he would treat the program as experimental rather than operational. In that year the Head Start program was transferred from OEO to HEW. Criticisms of the Head Start program resulted in grafting a Follow-Through program to it whereby poor children also receive help during the first few years of school. Arguments still exist as to whether an adequate program could be inaugurated to begin with so that remedial work would not be necessary.

UPWARD BOUND

Attempts have been made to motivate poor youth to go to college by providing summer programs on college campuses while the youth are still in high school. Many of the students attend 6- to 8-week summer sessions for several years. Tutorial and other instructional aid is also given during the regular school period. This program, too, was separated from the Community Action program and since 1969 has been administered by the U. S. Department of Education.

A study by the General Accounting Office of the program[13] indicated that the Upward Bound students had a lower high school dropout rate than other students in low income areas and that they had a higher rate of college admissions than their older siblings and the national average of all high school graduates. They also remained in college in larger percentages than the average college student although their test scores measuring college potential were below average.

One criticism leveled at the program by the Educational Associates, Inc., was that some projects sought out students who were already getting good grades and were likely to go to college without benefit of the program.[14] Only twenty-odd thousand are enrolled in this program per year,

[11]Carl Bereiter, "An Academic Preschool for Disadvantaged Children: Conclusions from Evaluation Studies," in Julian C. Stanley, Preschool Programs for the Disadvantaged (Baltimore, Johns Hopkins Press, 1972), p. 15.

[12]Victor C. Cicirelli, et al., The Impact of Head Start: An Evaluation of the Effects of Head Start on Children's Cognitive and Affective Development, Washington, D.C., Office of Economic Opportunity, June 12, 1969. For a statistical critique of the Westinghouse-Ohio report and a rejoinder, see Marshall Smith and Joan S. Bissell, op. cit., pp. 51-104; and Victor G. Cicirelli, John W. Evans and Jeffry S. Schiller, "A Reply to the Report Analysis," Harvard Educational Review, Vol. 40 (1970), pp. 105-125.

[13]Comptroller General of the United States, Review of Economic Opportunity Programs (Washington, D.C., Government Printing Office, 1969).

[14]Educational Associates, Inc., "Financial Assistance to Upward Bound Students," (June 1968) (mimeographed).

a figure indicating that only about seven percent of those eligible are reached. Levitan concluded that small appropriations preclude the program from having a major impact on the educational industry.[15] The costs in 1972 were $1,072 per pupil. Levitan points out that remedial costs are much higher than providing the correct kind of education to begin with. The program, however, has been successful, according to Levitan, in demonstrating that motivational and educational obstacles to higher education can be overcome.[16]

ADULT BASIC EDUCATION

In order to provide literacy and basic educational training to the poor, Community Action agencies funded a number of such programs. In 1966, this program was transferred to the U. S. Department of Education. Most of the classes meet in school buildings two evenings a week for three hours each session from September through May (about 190 hours of instruction). Thirty-two percent of the enrollees are black and another twenty percent are either Mexican Americans, Cubans or Puerto Rican. The law was amended in 1970 to enable adult basic education students to work toward high school diplomas or equivalency certificates. In fiscal 1974 state allotments from the federal government were over $53 million (up from $29 million in fiscal 1968), and about 1 million persons were reached. Among the suggestions for improvements of the program, the National Advisory Council on Adult Education has recommended planning a full range of adult education services beyond reading, writing and computational skill training and increased learning opportunities for institutionalized adults.[17]

NEIGHBORHOOD HEALTH CENTERS

The first neighborhood health centers in the United States were developed in the early 1900's. Some were financed publicly and others through private philanthropy. Mainly, they provided services to the poor in combatting infectious desease and infant malnutrition.[18] The health center movement declined during the 1930's and was not revived until the early 1960's.

Community Action agencies fostered a total of 49 centers. The agencies generally delegated the running of such centers to such groups as hos-

---

[15]Levitan, *op. cit.*, p. 175.

[16]Sar Levitan, *Programs in Aid of the Poor for the 1970's* (Baltimore, Johns Hopkins Press, 1973), p. 98.

[17]National Advisory Council on Adult Education, *Annual Report, 1974* (Washington, D.C., Government Printing Office, March 1974).

[18]J. D. Stoeckle and L. M. Candid, "Reform Ideas of Yesterday and Today," *New England Journal of Medicine*, Vol. 280(25), June 1969, pp. 1385-1391.

pitals, medical schools, health department and others. Most of the centers, depending on size, provided medical and dental services, laboratory, X-ray and pharmacy centers and other support services needed for providing comprehensive care.

Much larger sums for medical care for the poor were allocated through Medicaid (Social Security Act) than through OEO neighborhood health centers. In 1966, the House of Delegates of the American Medical Association recommended that funds for medical care for the poor be channeled through Medicaid rather than OEO nieghborhood centers. Later, the Nixon Administration transferred administration of this program to HEW. In 1971 it was estimated that 2,000 neighborhood health centers existed in the United States, although little data is available on the services provided by such centers. Statistical studies are needed to determine whether such neighborhood centers can provide quality care at costs as low as other methods of medical delivery.

FAMILY PLANNING

The OEO spent about $16 million on family planning in the first four years of its existence. Information and supplies were distributed mainly through the Planned Parenthood — World Population organization or through Community Action agencies themselves, with a few also being administered by health departments. The program has been criticized by some religious groups, although Gallup polls show increasing numbers favoring the distribution of birth control information. In 1971, for example, 86 percent of Protestants, 83 percent of Catholics and over 95 percent of all others favored the dissemination of information. There was some controversy over whether unmarried persons should be given information and supplies, but this dispute was settled by Congress, which made all persons eligible for the program.

A number of arguments have been cited in favor of a family planning program. It is indicated in chapter 3 that larger families are more apt to experience poverty than small ones. Furthermore, many of the poor do not want more children. The 1972 Report of the Presidential Commission on Population Growth and the American Future indicated that from 1966 to 1970 there were 2.7 million unwanted births in the United States, concentrated most heavily among the less educated and those with a lower income. Additionally, a mother can give more attention to each child if she has fewer of them to care for. She also may have better health if she has had fewer pregnancies. The costs of providing information and supplies is obviously much smaller than providing additional welfare payments for each child. If the program will reduce the number of births it would have an exceptionally high benefit-cost ratio, but data still needs to be gathered for proof of its effectiveness in reducing population.

Under the Family Planning Services and Population Research Act of 1970, the program is now administered by HEW. In November of 1972, there were 3,602 registered family clinics within the 50 states. About 1.5 million patients accounted for the approximately 2.0 million patient visits in the program. It has been estimated that about 30 percent of all eligible low income women of childbearing age currently receive subsidized medical contraceptive services. The budget for the program in fiscal 1975 was almost $101 million.

LEGAL SERVICES

The poor are in need of many legal services. A private organization, the National Legal Aid and Defender Association (NLADA), had been providing some services for the poor, but within a few years the budget of the OEO for legal services became much larger than that of the NLADA. A question that had to be faced originally was whether to provide direct legal services through staff hired by community action agencies or to delegate money to the NLADA. The OEO solved this problem by allowing Community Action agencies to do as they wished. About 40 percent of the Community Action agencies permitted existing legal aid societies to administer the funds.[19] In five states an experimental "Judicare" program was funded similar to that used by the British. In this system the poor receive services from regular private attorneys, who are then reimbursed by the government. After evaluation of Judicare, the OEO decided not to adopt the system mainly because it negated the concept of a coordinated attack on the legal problems of the poor. Also, the costs were about three times as high as under the standard OEO program — $139 per case compared with $48.

Legal aid groups within OEO have made significant contributions in rendering services to the poor. They successfully challenged state residence requirements for eligibility for welfare. A California group brought a class action suit that was able to restore $210,000 for medical care for the poor in that state. In addition, legal aid has been provided in such areas as family problems, housing, sales contracts, garnishments, bankruptcy, and problems with workmen's compensation and unemployment insurance.[20]

Interference in legal aid by several governors resulted in bills being introduced in Congress to create a Legal Services Corporation separate from OEO. On threat of a veto by President Nixon, this bill did not pass. Currently, legal services is one of the few programs still administered by the OEO, but its budget has been cut substantially, from $74.6 million in fiscal 1973 to an estimated $33.1 million in fiscal 1975.

[19]Levitan, *The Great Society's Poor Law, op. cit.*, p. 180.
[20]For a breakdown of the percentage of cases spent in each area, see *Idem.*, Table 6-1, p. 184.

MAXIMUM FEASIBLE PARTICIPATION OF
THE POOR

Several arguments have been advanced extolling the advantages of having the poor participate in poverty programs.[21] First, citizen participation
provides a means of mobilizing unutilized resources that are not otherwise tapped. Secondly, the poor are a source of knowledge, since they
know the full dimensions of poverty. Just as the patient aids the physician
in diagnosis by describing the illness, so, too, the poor may aid by outlin-
ing the dimensions of poverty. The poor can also aid in providing information as to how well programs are working. Thirdly, participation by the
poor is an end in itself, an affirmation of democracy and hopefully an
elimination of alienation.

In view of the advantages of enlisting the participation of the poor,
the Economic Opportunity Act of 1964 included in it a provision that
there must be "maximum feasible participation of the poor." In order to
insure more participation, an amendment to the Economic Opportunity
Act was passed in 1966 that required that at least one-third of the members of Community Action agencies were to be representatives of the
poor. There was no requirement, however, that those representatives be
poor themselves. In order to promote more participation by the poor
themselves, some areas required elections be held in which only the poor
could vote. In general, there was a small turnout for these elections. In
two Los Angeles elections one percent of the poor voted in the first election and two percent in the second. In Philadelphia the percentage was
two percent, and in Hartford six percent. Low participation by the poor
led Ralph Kramer to conclude that "a second government," in the sense of
a parallel electoral process, did not develop.[22] Even when the poor themselves were elected to office, Karmer found that there was no constituency organization to which they were accountable. Most Community Action agencies did not bother with a direct election process. Instead, members were self-selected, and represented various community agencies or
the local government.

Studies of CAA's found that most of the poor members were controlled by other members of the agency,[23] or played only a small role in
the operations.[24] Several studies found those representing the poor were

---

[21]Edgar S. Cahn and Jean Camper Cahn, "Maximum Feasible Participation: A General
Overview," in Edgar S. Cahn and Barry A. Passett, eds., Citizen Participation: Effecting
Community Change (New York, Praeger Publishers, 1971), pp. 16-39.

[22]Ralph M. Kramer, Participation of the Poor (Englewood Cliffs, Prentice-Hall, 1969),
p. 226.

[23]Kenneth B. Clark, Statement in Senate Subcommittee, Examination of the War on
Poverty, Hearings 1967, Part 1, p. 290.

[24]Dale R. Marshall, The Politics of Participation in Poverty (Berkeley, University of
California Press, 1970), p. 194.

not poor themselves.[25] In one of these studies, Irving Lazar maintained that it is unrealistic to expect much participation from the poor until their basic economic and health needs were provided for. In the Los Angeles CAA study, Dale Marshall concluded that it was unrealistic to assume that poor members of the agency can represent the poor.[26] However, they can become ombudsmen for poverty programs and be spokesmen for aggrieved clients or staff members of the poverty program. In a Pittsburgh study, Neil Gilbert concluded that unless a base of supportive membership is developed to whom the representatives of the poor are formally accountable, citizen participation would not provide a sufficient impulse for the democratization and reform of social welfare.[27] His findings were substantiated by Howard Hallman's study of 35 poverty agencies for the Senate Committee on Manpower, in which he found that no indigenous group of poor had initiated a program at all, although eight civil rights groups had done so.[28]

In a study of a number of programs centering around the San Francisco area, Ralph Kramer found that local neighborhood groups continually were in conflict with the central CAA board for the city.[29] The neighborhood groups were not generally conceived of or controlled by the poor, but at least the programs were for the poor. Regardless of the sources of control, the programs in all the agencies were quite similar. Most of the programs involved such social service amenities as day care centers, language training, youth employment, and remedial education. Kramer attributed the sameness of the programs to the OEO funding policy of quickly approving the funding of well-known types of programs.

CONFLICT WITH CITY HALLS

Some community action agencies spent part of their funds to organize the poor. Voter registration activities were engaged in by some agencies. Whenever city hall was threatened by local groups, action was taken by city government to control the agencies. In Syracuse, San Francisco and the MFY program in New York City, where the political structure felt threatened by the poverty program, the city had sufficient power either to stalemate or defeat the program. Protests poured into Washington from the big city mayors about some agencies. The result was the Green amendment to the Economic Opportunity Act (EOA) in 1967, which pro-

[25]Ralph M. Kramer, op. cit., pp. 191-199; and Irving Lazar, "Which Citizens Participate in What?" in Cahn and Passett, op. cit., p. 99.

[26]Dale R. Marshall, op. cit., p. 55.

[27]Neil Gilbert, Clients or Constituents (San Francisco, Jossey-Bass, 1970).

[28]Howard Hallman, Examination of the War on Poverty, Staff and Consultants' Reports for the Subcommittee on Employment, Manpower and Poverty of the Committee on Labor and Public Welfare IV (Washington, D.C., Government Printing Office, September, 1967).

[29]Ralph M. Kramer, op. cit., pp. 210-215.

vided that a Community Action agency must be a state agency or political subdivision thereof, or have been designated by the political subdivision. It also required that no more than one-third of agency board members be representatives of the poor. The other two-thirds were equally divided between government officials and representatives of other community groups. Actually, the Green amendment had only a little effect upon most Community Action agencies. Most such agencies had implemented programs to improve services to the poor that did not threaten local government. In less than five percent of CAA's did government institute action to take over control. A number of authors have pointed to the incongruity of a federal funding program to change local power relations. Although challenge to vested interests and the status quo are necessary, it has become obvious that the technique of independent CAA's was not the vehicle through which such change would come about.

EVALUATION OF THE COMMUNITY ACTION PROGRAM

One of the most severe critics of community action has been Daniel P. Moynihan, who helped draft the bill as a U. S. Department of Labor representative. He had recommended employment and training rather than community action. In a book on the community action program he concluded that in this phase of the program, "the government did not know what it was doing."[30] He also labeled the program "a sell out."[31] Most critics of community action are more charitable. Donovan points out that even Moynihan, in the same book in which he criticized the program, admitted that significant changes were made in the lives of the poor that the program reached. Moynihan cited such benefits as "new jobs, special training, more earnings, education stretching available dollars further, improvement of neighborhoods, and increased hope, self-respect and confidence in the future. . . ."[32]

A number of advantages of community action programs have been cited. Some conventional services not formerly available to the poor have now been provided for them. In many cities, public employment facilities were moved to the ghetto for the first time. More education and training were made available, as were health, family planning, legal and other counselling services. Some students of community action programs have pointed to the aid given ethnic groups for political action. Alan A. Altshuler, in a study of black demands for participation in larger cities, concluded that the current movement for neighborhood control was

[30]Daniel P. Moynihan, *Maximum Feasible Misunderstanding* (New York, The Free Press, 1969), p. 170.

[31]*Idem.*, p. 203.

[32]*Idem.*, pp. 196-197.

largely set in motion by the "maximum feasible participation" provision.[33] Marshall also argued that board membership influenced community representatives to become more active in the community.[34] Board membership made a change in the self-image of the persons involved in that they then saw themselves as potential leaders in the community and activated themselves to further participation. Ralph Kramer concluded in the same vein: "It (resident participation) contributed to some new hopes, provided opportunities for minority groups to obtain control over additional resources, and made it possible for a top stratum of persons to obtain jobs and to participate in decision making in the community."[35] Marris and Rein concur: "Of all the innovations of community action, this may prove the most important: it created the professional reformer, and invented an organizational framework appropriate to his function."[36]

An evaluation study of community action programs by Barss, Reitzel, and Company analyzed whether any significant changes had been made in a major private welfare agency, the public welfare program, the Employment Service, and the school system. They found that in about two-thirds of the sample, CAA's played a vital part in significant changes in at least one of the four institutions.[37] On the other hand, and most important, neither sufficient jobs nor income have been provided by Community Action agencies to enable many of the poor to climb from poverty.

YOUTH PROGRAMS

Title II (Community Action Programs) and Title I (Youth Programs) took most of the money allocated to the OEO program.

NEIGHBORHOOD YOUTH CORPS (NYC)

The largest youth program has been the Neighborhood Youth Corps, administered by the U.S. Department of Labor. In this program, youths aged 14 and above may work mainly at public service jobs at from $1.25 an hour and higher. The program is divided into three parts: a summer program for youth, an in-school program during the school year, and a program for out-of-school youth. In fiscal year 1972, a peak enrollment of over 1 million youths was recorded, with about three-fourths being summer workers. In fiscal 1973 the budget was cut from $517 million to $417

[33]Alan A. Altshuler, *Community Control* (New York, Pegasus, 1970), p. 184.
[34]Dale R. Marshall, *op. cit.*, p. 134.
[35]Ralph M. Kramer, *op. cit.*, p. 257.
[36]Peter Marris and Martin Rein, *Dilemmas of Social Reform* (Chicago, Aldine, 1973), p. 222.
[37]Robert Levine, *op. cit.*, p. 166.

million, with the result that only 628,000 were enrolled that year. Most of the cut came in summer enrollment.

Since this program has been one mainly of work rather than training, little increase in earnings were reported from participation in the program. Also, the program has not been able to lower the school dropout rate.[38] Neither did many enrollees enter formal training programs.[39] One favorable aspect was reported by Levine, who stated that the program may have increased the return to school of younger dropouts.[40] Most of the advantage of the program has been to keep youths off the streets and provide them with a little work experience. The program has been criticized for providing little training, but Congress until recently has not honored requests to provide additional money in the program for training. The program was redesigned in 1970 to provide more training. It is hoped that the training component will provide more useful future jobs for youths.

THE JOB CORPS

Another youth program provided residential training for 16- and 17-year old school dropouts who came from disadvantaged neighborhoods. It was thought that removing them to residential centers might improve their chances of success. To some degree the program was patterned after the Civilian Conservation Corps of the 1930's, which provided conservation work for enlistees. The Job Corps, though, was a more complex agency, since it attempted to provide training along with conservation work. The Job Corps had two kinds of centers. For the more disadvantaged, rural centers, run mainly by the government, provided literacy and other basic training, along with conservation work. Urban centers were operated mainly by private corporations—such as Litton Industries, I.B.M., Philco, and many others. The urban centers took enlistees who had more education, and who could absorb more advanced training. The urban centers were larger and had more enrollees, but numerically rural centers predominated. Originally, the program was administered by the OEO itself, but later the U.S. Department of Labor took over. Criticism from Congressmen that too few women were being trained resulted in an OEO 1966 amendment, which provided that by July 1, 1967 at least 25 percent of the enrollees be women. A later amendment in 1967 required that as soon as feasible, half the trainees would be women.

Some of the camps had difficulty beginning operations. Some recruits arrived before blankets and other equipment, and in some instances they had to be bedded in high school gymnasiums. Almost immediately

[38]Sar Levitan, *Programs in Aid of the Poor, op. cit.*, p. 112.
[39]Donovan, *op. cit.*, p. 136.
[40]Levine, *op. cit.*, p. 129.

thereafter newspapers reported a high dropout rate, which was particularly high during the first few weeks and months. A requirement was added that the enlistee remain for at least 90 days, but dropouts were not significantly reduced. About one out of six left the center within one month, but the Job Corps also pointed out that for those remaining past a month only one out of eight failed to finish the course.[41] However, a poll by Louis Harris and Associates showed a much smaller completion rate—six dropouts or kickouts for every Job Corps graduate.[42]

One of the major problems with the Job Corps has been its high cost per student. As late as 1972 it was reported that the cost was $8,400 per man per year. The high costs are due to expenses related to maintaining residency for the participants, plus training expenses and living allowances. When high cost is combined with the Louis Harris finding that unemployment was higher among Job Corps dropouts than before they enrolled, some pessimism must be expressed about the program. Due to its high cost, the numbers in the program have never been large, and have been reduced slightly the past few years to 43,400 in fiscal 1973. A review of 26 benefit-cost studies of the program showing the benefit-cost ration to vary from .2 to 1 to 32 to 1, with the mean of 1.7 to 1.[43] No definitive study has been made as to whether the disadvantaged can profit as much or more from residential training as from remaining at home. Some have concluded that the especially disadvantaged particularly need high quality education and resource aids. Perhaps by placing emphasis on quality, the program may be justified on a small scale.[44]

WORK STUDY PROGRAM

Under the work-study program, college students from low income families were provided 15 hours of work a week during the regular school year and up to 40 hours a week during the summer. This program was spun off early from OEO and transferred to the U.S. Office of Education in 1965. Recently, eligibility requirements have been relaxed so that only one of every three is from a poor family. In fiscal 1974 about 560,000 students were aided by this program at a cost of $271 million. Another program to aid disadvantaged college youth has now become much larger than the work-study program. Under this program, in fiscal 1974, basic opportunities grants were given to 594,000 students at a cost of $1.3 billion. In addition, supplemental opportunity grants went to 304,000 at the cost of an additional $211 million. Under this program, grants from $200 to $1,400

[41]Christopher Weeks, Job Corps (Boston, Little, Brown and Co., 1967), p. 209.
[42]Idem., p. 239.
[43]Levine, op. cit., Table 9, p. 124.
[44]Christopher Weeks, op. cit., p. 241.

are given to needy students. The amount is based on need of the student determined by estimated amounts he or his parents are expected to contribute. The grant may not exceed one-half the cost of the education. An additional program provides loans to needy students and benefitted 682,000 students in fiscal 1974.

TITLE III RURAL POVERTY PROGRAM

Money appropriated for the remaining War on Poverty programs has been so little that no major impact could be expected from these programs. When originally proposed, it was suggested that grants should be given to low income farmers to help them to get back on their feet. However, even grants of as low as $1,500 were deleted from the EOA on the ground that no grants were provided for the urban poor. The program, then, became one of loans to low income farmers administered by the Farmers Home Administration. In the agriculture chapter, we have already pointed out that loans to the lowest income farmers were not successful, and the small EOA loans of up to $3,500 (1966) were no exception. However, Kershaw defended the small program of some $30 million annually on the ground that the loans were going to older people who would not move in any case.[45] A part of the original bill was deleted which provided that the federal government purchase large tracts of land for resale to tenants and sharecroppers.[46]

Another rural program was aid to migratory workers, but this program, too, was so small ($4 per migrant) that it accomplished little. What little money that was allocated in this section went for providing child care, education, sanitary facilities in migrants camps, housing, health, and legal services.

TITLE IV SMALL BUSINESS ADMINISTRATION LOANS

Small funding was provided through the EOA to the Small Business Administration (SBA) to make loans to low income entrepreneurs either to enter or expand their businesses. Loans originally were set at $25,000, but were later reduced to $15,000. Few loans were made to those below the poverty line mainly because of lack of entrepreneurial ability. The OEO concluded that the program was not worth the effort as part of the poverty

[45]Joseph A. Kershaw, *Government Against Poverty* (Washington, D.C., Brookings Institute, 1970).

[46]Adam Yarmolinsky, "The Beginnings of OEO," in Sundquist, *op. cit.*, p. 46.

program, and it was transferred entirely to the SBA without objection from the OEO. The SBA then provided loans without reference to income of the borrower, mainly to black entrepreneurs.

VISTA

Patterned somewhat after the Peace Corps, a Volunteers in Service to America (VISTA) was organized as part of the poverty program. Most of the recruits for the program have been college students, although others, such as retired teachers and senior citizens have been tapped. VISTA workers are paid a small stipend plus expenses. Most of them have been assigned to community action agencies or programs funded by such agencies, although a few have been placed on Indian reservations, in migratory labor camps, and at the Job Corps.[47] They have engaged in such programs as literacy training, preschool programs, self-help housing projects, recreation programs, and many others. Most volunteers have stayed for one year only. The cost of VISTA has been about $6,850 per full-time volunteer. The total budget has been a small one of $30 million, and many applicants had to be turned away due to insufficient funds.

Some have criticized the program because of the inexperienced help it used. Others point out that the poor themselves, rather than college students, should be hired as aides. Levitan and Kershaw both concluded that the best work by VISTA workers was in rural areas that lack many services. Here VISTA workers may improve communication with the outside world. In 1971, VISTA was merged with other volunteer efforts to from the ACTION program,[48] but most of the volunteers remained active on CAA sponsored projects. In 1972, regular VISTA volunteers accounted for 4,300 man-years of service, and another 600 man-years were contributed by 1,200 students in exchange for academic credit in the University Year for Action program.[49]

WAR ON POVERTY—CONCLUSION

The fact that many millions in the United States are still in poverty in the 1970's indicates that the War on Poverty did not eradicate poverty.

[47]For a more complete analysis of VISTA, see William H. Crook and Ross Thomas, *Warriors for the Poor* (New York, William Morrow and Co., 1969).

[48]ACTION was created as an independent agency under the provisions of Reorganization Plan 1 of 1971 and Executive Order 11603 of June 30, 1971. Besides VISTA, it includes the Peace Corps, a foster grandparents program, a retired senior volunteer program, a service corps of retired executives, an active corps of executives to aid small business, a university year for action to permit college students to spend a year off campus working on anti-poverty programs, and a national student volunteer program.

[49]Sar Levitan, *Programs in Aid of the Poor for the 1970's, op. cit.,* p. 81

Whereas expenditures for the War in Viet Nam were escalated, priorities there precluded an escalation of the War on Poverty. It is obvious that expenditures of several billion on the War on Poverty could not eliminate a problem that would cost many times that amount to eradicate—estimates showed around $10 billion is needed in income maintenance, plus at least another 10 billion in other services.

When a separate agency was instituted to fight the War on Poverty, it was reasoned that some coordinated body was needed to finally eradicate poverty. However, each of the many agencies administering War on Poverty programs jealously guarded their own programs. Budgets of each of the groups were not subject to over-all evaluation and control by the OEO. Recognition that the OEO was not succeeding as a coordinating agency resulted in the Nixon Administration revamping the organization to be primarily one of research and experimentation. Successful programs were spun off to the regular agencies of government who operated in a particular field. For example, education programs were delegated to the U.S. Department of Education. Due to the spinning off of programs, the budget of the OEO is much smaller now than in former years. In fiscal 1974, it was slightly over one-half billion, almost half of which went into community action programs, followed by legal services, research, development and evaluation, and health and nutrition. Further and deeper cuts were expected in fiscal 1975.

A basic weakness of the War on Poverty program was that no income maintenance scheme was included in it. When the program was being organized, income maintenance was dismissed as being too costly. The result was that although needed services were provided by the EOA, many of the poor remained without income. An agency which could not provide income or jobs, important requirements for many of the poor, simply could not eradicate poverty.

The War on Poverty was successful in providing some services to the poor that had not been reaching them. Legal services aided many poor as did health clinics. Public employment services were provided in some low-income areas for the first time. Additional education and counselling aided both youth and adults. The War on Poverty was also successful in providing upward mobility and more community participation by some of the poor, particularly in energizing minority groups to more action.

In the area of institutional change, the analysis above shows that some changes were made, but not enough to eliminate poverty. The OEO was not sufficiently powerful to radically change the status quo at the local level. It is doubtful that a federal agency would be permitted to create such a powerful political force at the local level. However, even if such political groups had been formed there, aid from the majority at the national level would still be required before some local problems are solved.

To place the War on Poverty in proper perspective, it should be remembered that the program provided much smaller sums of money for the poor than social insurance, welfare, health care, and other federal programs. However, it would have been possible with a larger War on Poverty expenditure to adequately supplement the larger programs to eliminate poverty, but this it never did.

Bibliography

Altshuler, Alan, Community Control (New York, Pegasus, 1970).

Cahn, Edgar S. and Barry A. Passett, ed's, Citizen Participation Effecting Community Change (New York, Praeger, 1971).

Clark, Kenneth B., and Jeanette Hopkins, A Relevant War Against Poverty (New York, Harper and Row, 1968).

Donovan, John C., The Politics of Poverty (Indianapolis, Pegasus, 2nd ed., 1973)

Kramer, Ralph M., Participation of the Poor (Englewood Cliffs, Prentice-Hall, 1969).

Levine, Robert A., The Poor Ye Need Not Have With You (Cambridge, Mass., The M.I.T. Press, 1970).

Levitan, Sar, The Great Society's Poor Law, (Baltimore, Johns Hopkins Press, 1969).

_____, Programs in Aid of the Poor for the 1970's (Baltimore, Johns Hopkins Press, 1973).

Marshall, Dale Rogers, The Politics of Participation in Poverty (Berkeley, University of California Press, 1970).

Moynihan, Daniel P., Maximum Feasible Misunderstanding (New York, The Free Press, 1969).

CHAPTER 28

RECENT PROGRAMS AND TRENDS—CONCLUSION

Even though the numbers in poverty have been reduced in recent years, the fact that many millions still remain in poverty has resulted in a number of suggestions of various new programs that might successfully eliminate all poverty. These programs are discussed below.

NEGATIVE INCOME TAX

Under the "negative income tax," the Bureau of Internal Revenue would send checks to all those families below a certain income, depending on family size. Professor Milton Friedman, an early proponent of the negative income tax, suggested that all other social insurance and public assistance programs be abolished and be replaced by a negative income tax scheme. In his original proposal, a family of four would be guaranteed an annual income of $1,500. In order to provide incentive to work, the government subsidy would be reduced by $1 for each $2 increase in income from work. Thus, his proposal provided for a 50% negative income tax. When work income reached $3,000, there would be no further government payment. Above $3,000 the worker would begin paying the regular "positive" income tax.

Many variations of the negative income tax are possible. The minimum income guarantee could be increased above $1,500, as would be necessary if the proposal is to substantially eliminate poverty. The tax rate might also be some other percentage, such as 30 or 40 percent. As a consequence, a wide variety of proposals exist. The higher the minimum income guarantee and the lower the negative income tax rate, the greater would be the reduction of poverty. But such changes would also greatly increase the expense of the proposals.

Since many of the poor do not and cannot work (old age, disability and other reasons), an argument can be made for a relatively high minimum income guarantee — perhaps set at or near the poverty line as currently determined by the Social Security Administration. To do otherwise would leave many of our most helpless citizens in poverty, especially if other welfare programs were abolished.

An important advantage of the negative income tax proposal is the possible elimination of the "notch" problems discussed in Chapter 8. The notch problem occurs when the poor are eligible for several types of benefits. But if their income rises above a certain level they may lose eligibility to several types of benefits at once. If this is so, the working poor who are receiving various benefits are subjected to a "notch." That is, their total well-being is reduced if they earn more than the critical amount. If the negative income tax scheme replaced public assistance, food stamps, housing benefits, free tuition, etc., few if any notches would exist. An associated advantage of one program instead of many would be simplified administration.

Another possible advantage of the negative income tax would be to reduce equity problems. These occur under present programs where non-working low-income people are eligible for several types of benefits and may be able to achieve a higher standard of living than a working person who is above the poverty line and eligible for few if any such benefits. Such a situation inevitably generates resentment against welfare recipients by those who are working.

One of the major objections to the negative income tax is that it might reduce the incentive to work. This criticism is not relevant to those who are unable to work, but might be relevant if applied to the working poor. Supporters of the plan argue that incentives to work would exist, since a worker could always add to his income by working. A number of federal negative income experiments have been inaugurated in New Jersey, Pennsylvania, Iowa, North Carolina, Seattle, Gary and Denver. New Jersey-Pennsylvania experiments have been analyzed to determine the effect of such plans on the incentive to work.[1] Slightly more husbands participated in the work force after receiving the bonus than did a control group not in the program. For wives, it was found that the temporary negative income tax caused a substantial percentage reduction in the proportion of working wives in large, low-income families, at least among white wives. The above results must be interpreted with caution, since labor force participation rates may vary differently in a temporary program than one in which the negative income tax becomes permanent.

An interesting study was made in the negative income tax experiments to determine their impact on consumption, health, and social behavior.[2] Four hypotheses were tested. One was that the additional money received would be wasted either on drugs, drinking and gambling, or dissipated in increased leisure time unproductively used. A second hypothesis was that the assurance of financial support would lead to adoption of middle-class values and would result in increased political activity, lower crime rates and reduced neurosis and psychosis. An intermediate hypothesis was that the program simply would not interfere materially with the recipients' life styles, aside from augmenting spending power.

---

[1] For an analysis of the New Jersey-Pennsylvania experiments, see a series of seven articles in the Spring, 1974 issue of The Journal of Human Resources.

[2] William J. Baumol, "An Overview of the Results on Consumption, Health and Social Behavior," Journal of Human Resources, Vol. 9, No. 2, Spring 1974, pp. 253-264.

The second intermediate hypothesis was that a social experiment limited in number of participants and duration, where the range of alternative states is chosen to be rather narrow, would be unlikely to show striking effects. The findings in New Jersey and Pennsylvania were that, by and large, the program left their living patterns undisturbed and did not affect their health, their social activities or the number of their children. The major change that the support program apparently produced was an improvement in housing standards and an increase in home ownership.

A major difficulty with the negative income tax is that it is not yet politically feasible in the United States to guarantee income payments regardless of whether people work or not. The Protestant work ethic might not tolerate a program without requiring a work test of some sort. But with the passage of time it may be that the electorate will come to favor such a program.

Some versions of the negative income tax suggest abolition of welfare services entirely. If the Bureau of Internal Revenue administered the program, welfare departments could be abolished throughout the country. On the other hand, if certain welfare services were considered worthwhile, they could be continued even though the income payments were made through the Bureau of Internal Revenue.

Another major objection would be the cost of the program particularly if the minimum was set at the poverty level. Most of the income of the program would go to those above the poverty level so that those having an increase above that level would remain ahead of the poor. Estimates range from four to six times the cost of bringing all persons to the poverty minimum.

One Senate Finance Committee proposal recommended a minimum of $2,400 for all four-person families, and a subsidy of three-fourths of the difference between the actual wage and the minimum wage. If, for example, a person was earning $1.20 per hour, the federal government would contribute an additional 60 cents per hour (three-fourths of the difference between $1.20 and a minimum wage of, say, $2.00). Under this arrangement the working poor would be paid a total of $1.80 per hour. A wage subsidy has the advantage of encouraging work, whereas it is contended that an income subsidy may tend to discourage work.

FAMILY ALLOWANCES

Under the family allowance program the government would pay each family according to the number of children. Such payments would aid in eradicating poverty, particularly in larger families, if the payments were large enough. Today, the United States is the only Western industrialized nation without such a system. Alvin Schorr estimated that if payments of $50 per month were paid for each child, poverty would be eliminated for about three-fourths of the poor children.[3] This would mean, of course, that poverty would still exist for a fourth of the children living in poor families. The subsidies granted abroad typically have been small. In England they have been less than $100 per year for a family of four, and in France, which provides the most generous subsidy, the amount has been only $182 annually for a family of four.[4]

Several criticisms of family allowances may be noted. If subsidies are granted to all children, then much of the subsidy would go to nonpoor families. Three-fourths of the payments would be made to nonpoor families. This problem can be solved, as Denmark has done, by varying the family allowance payments with income, and discontinuing them altogether after a certain level of income is reached. It has been contended, also, that family allowances would tend to increase the birth rate, but there is little statistical evidence to support this contention. Higher incomes in the past have tended to curtail family size and may continue to do so even with a family allowance. One last and important criticism of family allowances as a poverty solution is that they do not reach certain groups. They do not reach single individuals nor childless couples, many of whom are aged. The aged and the others could, of course, be subsidized under some other program.

GOVERNMENT AS EMPLOYER OF LAST RESORT

On June 16, 1968, a Gallup poll showed that the public opposed a guaranteed income minimum, but that a large 78 percent majority favored guaranteed work. All the working poor could be guaranteed that they would earn a certain minimum provided that they worked for the government. In view of the strong resentment against public works during the Great Depression, there is some question whether such a program is politically feasible, even though most would prefer that the poor work rather than receive an income subsidy without working. A number of students contend that many needed projects could be carried out under this plan. The plan itself would need to be supplemented by some other program to care for those not able to work.

Low wage employers would much prefer that they be permitted to keep their workers and have the government subsidize them for remain-

---

[3]Alvin L. Schorr, "A Family Allowance Program for Preschool Children," in Theodore M. Marinor, ed., *Poverty Policy* (Chicago, Aldine Atherton, 1969), p. 123.

[4]Melville J. Ulmer, *The Welfare State: USA* (Houghton-Mifflin, 1969), pp. 100-101.

ing in private enterprise. This group would certainly oppose the government as employer of last resort, and would favor a wage supplement program instead. Also, it is true that if the government paid the entire cost of employment, the cost would be much larger than if the state merely supplemented the private wage bill. A counter argument is that under the wage supplement program collusion may tend to occur between workers and employers, since the government would be required to pay the difference between the private hourly earning and the minimum government guarantee. On the other hand, since some workers are unemployed and not working in private enterprise, some economists have argued that at least a minimum number of unemployed should be provided work by the government.

RECENT TRENDS IN SOCIAL WELFARE

A TEN-COUNTRY SURVEY

A study of social security in ten countries was recently published.[5] The ten countries were Austria, West Germany, Ireland, the United Kingdom, Denmark, the Netherlands, Canada, U. S. A., New Zealand and Australia. Without exception, all ten countries expanded their social security programs as a per-cent of gross national product from 1952 to 1966. In the latter year, the top country, Austria, was spending 18.5 percent of its GNP on social security, compared with the lowest of 7.2 percent for the U. S. A. Six of the ten spent 11.8 percent or more on social security. Left-of-center governments tended to expand social security, but not invariably; and right-of-center governments tended to be more "moderate." The fact that 8 of the 10 had left-of-center governments in 1972 indicated a trend toward more social security. The fact that inflation was occurring also tended to expand social security. On the other hand, two forces were at work to curtail expansion of social security. One was the revolution of rising expectations that put much emphasis on immediate consumption. The other was the slowing in the growth of the GNP.

In the ten-country study, seven programs were analyzed in detail: employment injury; temporary disability; invalidity; old age; unemployment; family endowment; and health service. When the countries were arranged in order of high standards, the United States placed at the bottom in six of the seven. Only for old age was it not at the bottom, and even in this program it was not one of the top countries.[6]

In a review of the ten-country study, Wilbur Cohen was critical of the underestimation of U. S. support for the poor.[7] The official data used

[5]P. R. Kaim-Caudle, *Comparative Social Policy and Social Security* (New York, The Dunellen Co., 1973).

[6]*Ibid.*, Table 9-1, p. 301.

[7]*Journal of Economic Literature*, Vol. 12, No. 4 (December, 1974), pp. 1375-1376.

in the study do not include estimates of amounts spent privately under sick leave and annual leave provisions. More attention by the author to Medicaid, survivors' benefits and health care benefits would have placed United States programs in a more favorable light. Furthermore, it should be noted that the cutoff date for this study was 1966, and since that year U. S. programs have expanded.

ECONOMIC INSECURITY: 1910-1960

Professor John Turnbull has made a valuable contribution in tracing the changing causes in economic insecurity from 1910 to 1960.[8] He pointed out that fewer people are dying prematurely today. Furthermore, the OASDHI program plus private insurance is much more adequately taking care of the problems caused by premature death in 1960 than in 1910. Although more people are living longer and retiring more frequently today than in 1910, Turnbull felt that the problem of the aged should be lessened in the future due to the OASDHI program. He also pointed out that the aggregate risk of unemployment is less today than 25 years ago and about the same as in 1910, although special risks, such as loss of skills, may be greater. Measured by the extent of coverage and the level of income restoration, society has taken care of the risk of unemployment much less successfully than for the risks of premature death and old age. Turnbull states that between 1955 and 1960 illness decreased by one-half to two-thirds in the aggregate. Fewer public programs exist to protect against illness, but private insurance is providing about as much protection for this risk as our public programs for unemployment insurance and workmen's compensation.

In 1910, Turnbull estimated that two-thirds of our poverty was due to the four causes: premature death, old age, economic unemployment and illness. In 1960, he estimated that these four accounted for about 50 percent of poverty. In the future the reduction in the risks of premature death, unemployment and illness should more than balance the increasing risks of old age. He concluded that improvements are still necessary in fighting the four risks. Since the risks in three of the four are declining, attention will have to be directed to other causes of poverty, which are becoming more important.

A 5,000 FAMILY STUDY

The Institute of Social Research (ISR) of the University of Michigan in 1974 published a two-volume work on a nationwide sample of over 5,000

---

[8]John G. Turnbull, *The Changing Faces of Economic Insecurity*, (Minneapolis, Minn., University of Minnesota Press, 1966).

families in tracing their economic well-being from 1968 to 1972.[9] The ISR found that for families with the same head in all five years, the correlation between income or well-being measured the first year compared with the last year was high, around .64. On the other hand, for families with a different head, the correlation drops to .29. Education was found to have a pervasive effect on the level of earnings of both men and women. However, there was almost no evidence that education explained *changes* in the components of family well-being. Family composition change was the most important variable in explaining changed well-being.

The ISR attempted to measure the impact of such variables as time horizon, planning ahead, risk avoidance, connectedness to sources of information and help, economizing the use of resources, and behavior, such as home production, which would increase real incomes. They found "very little evidence" that these variables had consistent effects on changes in well-being. Self-rated attitudes, such as aspiration, ambition, trust-hostility, sense of personal efficacy and perceived propensity to plan ahead affected almost none of the components of economic status and their changeover time. What seemed to matter were the backgrounds and unchanging characteristics of individuals, such as age, sex, education, race and family background.

The ISR concluded that if these findings are confirmed by additional years of data, they may have dramatic implications for the way the poor are viewed in society. If the poor cannot control their own fates, then it seems unfair to do what society now does in distinguishing between the old and disabled as deserving poor, and the rest as undeserving and in need of persuasion to change. The ISR groups concluded that society may have been oversold on the Protestant ethic, and has refused to see the extent to which people are the victims of their past, their environment, of luck, and of chance. They doubted that spending public money to change the behavior and attitude of dependent members would make much difference in income levels.

FUNCTIONS AND DYSFUNCTIONS OF THE POOR

Herbert J. Gans cites fifteen functions that poverty serves for affluent groups today: (1) providing the dirty or dangerous, temporary, dead-end and underpaid, undignified and menial jobs; (2) subsidizing investments (via low wages) and other activities of the affluent, such as domestic service, which frees affluent women for a variety of professional, cultural, civic, or social activities; (3) providing jobs to serve the poor in such areas

---

[9]James M. Morgan, *et al., Five Thousand American Families: Patterns of Economic Progress* (Ann Arbor, Institute of Social Research, University of Michigan, 1974).

as social work and penology, the latter of which would be miniscule without the poor; (4) buying goods that others do not want, such as secondhand clothes, old houses and the like, along with providing employment for poorly-trained and incompetents to serve the poor since they cannot attract more affluent clients; (5) upholding the legitimacy of dominant norms, because many of the poor are identified and punished as alleged or real deviants; (6) evoking compassion, pity, and charity for the deserving poor to help those practicing the Judeo-Christian ethic to feel altruistic and moral; (7) offering affluent people vicarious participation in the uninhibited sexual, alcoholic and narcotic behavior in which many poor people are alleged to indulge; (8) guaranteeing the status of those who are not poor in a stratified society; (9) providing upward mobility for the nonpoor by enabling others with more education and less negative stereotyping to obtain better jobs; (10) keeping the affluent busy by practicing social-mindedness toward the poor; (11) helping to create surplus capital that frees the affluent for "high" culture; (12) adopting the low culture of the poor by some of the more affluent; (13) providing symbolic constituency for the radical left and opposition to "welfare chiselers" by conservatives, whose views of the alleged moral inferiority of the poor reduce the moral pressure to eliminate poverty; (14) absorbing the costs of change and growth in American society, by providing land for urban renewal and urban universities, hospitals and civic centers, and providing the foot soldiers for Viet Nam and other wars; and (15) shaping a more centrist political arena, since the poor participate less in politics.[10]

Gans points out that whether poverty should exist or not or whether it must exist or not depends in part on whether dysfunctions of poverty outweigh the functions. Obviously, poverty has many dysfunctions, mainly to the poor themselves, but also to the affluent. He commented that whether the dysfunctions outweigh the functions is a question that clearly deserves more study. He maintained also that poverty persists not only because it is functional but because its elimination would be quite dysfunctional for the more affluent members of society. Since the poor and blacks are minority groups, Gans cites them as "permanently outvoted minorities." Without some political change, the demands of these two groups will never be approved by a majority.

Gans suggests improvements in the political system that fall into two main categories. One category would be to make government more responsive. Here he suggests adequate voter registration, elimination of gerrymandering, election of party leaders by party members, and nomination of party candidates by primaries or democratically chosen conventions. He also recommends the abolition of the seniority system in legislative bodies, more accountability of administrative agencies, funding of all election campaigns by government, requiring all citizens to vote, as

[10]Herbert J. Gans, *More Equality* (New York, Pantheon Books, 1973), pp. 106-114.

some European countries do, and improved communication systems between citizens and elected representatives.

Gans' second major category involves increased minority power. Here he suggests constitutional amendments to establish an economic and racial bill of rights that would guarantee every American citizen the right to a job and an income above the poverty line. Cabinet departments could be created representing minority interests. The income tax could be made more progressive and school-equalization payments could be made. Proportional representation could be adopted. Minorities could rule in their own section of town. Lastly the "one person, one vote" rule could be applied to corporations.

MINORITY GROUP POVERTY

A recent study was published by Thomas Sowell on both earlier and latter minority immigrants.[11] A massive influx of eastern European Jews came to the United States in the last quarter of the 19th century, so that by 1910 more than a million Jews lived in New York City alone. The Jewish people passed the earlier Irish immigrants in income, and today have higher incomes than the average American, as well as more education and higher IQ's. They were aided in the United States by having had an urban, commercial and marketing background, and had a reverence for learning. The rise of the Irish was slower. As late as 1890, 42 percent of Irish-Americans were working in personal and domestic service. Although the Italians came to America several generations later than the Irish, they too passed the Irish in income by 1968. Sowell explains the faster rise of the Italians as the result of their attitude that work at any wage was better than charity. Also, Italians were sent out to work earlier and were less dependent on their families than the Irish. The Japanese-Americans were another minority group who put much emphasis on getting ahead. Sowell's major conclusion on minority groups is that their success has dependent mainly on attitudes of self-reliance. Such factors as self-reliance, work skills, education and business experience are slow to develop but the results are more direct and immediate than job quotas, charity, subsidies and preferential treatment, which undermine self-reliance and pride of achievement in the long run. An implication of Sowell's study is that the newer poor minority groups today could best improve their status by more self-reliance.

The Kerner Commission reported cited in the chapter on blacks came to conclusions diametrically opposite to those of Sowell.[12] The Kerner Commission pointed out that prior immigrants were favored over the pre-

---

[11]Thomas Sowell, *Race and Economics* (New York, David McKay, 1975).

[12]*Report of the National Advisory Commission on Civil Disorders* (New York, Bantam Books, 1968).

sent blacks in that the former immigrants had available to them many unskilled jobs that are no longer present. Secondly, discrimination is much more pervasive toward blacks today than it was toward former immigrant groups. Thirdly, some of the earlier immigrant groups were able to use city political machines for aid, and these no longer exist. Also, ability to open businesses was less available to blacks, since stores and other businesses already existed in the ghetto. The Kerner Commission maintained that white racism was at the root of most of the problems of blacks.

POVERTY IN THE SEVENTIES

In an attempt to project the poverty rate in the future, Robert J. Lampman isolates six groups prone to poverty: those with low education; the aged; the female-headed family or single individual; the disabled; the large family; and the non-white.[13] He projected that only the last group would tend to increase as a percentage of our population, whereas the first two groups would decrease and the remaining three stay the same. Although the first four groups had a high immunity to improving their condition through economic growth, he pointed out, economic growth is necessary to eradicate poverty. He cited statistics to the effect that a one-point reduction in unemployment brings a reduction in poverty of about 1.5 million persons and increases the national product by over $30 billion. He recommended a $2 billion subsidy to raise public assistance minimums in low-income states. He would also provide an income supplement for the working poor at $4 billion. Although neither of the two programs would take anyone out of poverty, they would reduce the poverty gap from $10 billion to $4 billion. Lastly he would allocate $4 billion to increasing job-related education and training and to create jobs for the poor. He expected the latter program to reduce the number of persons in poverty by 2 million and to interact with the income supplement in reducing the poverty income gap.

Conclusion

The Great Depression of the 1930's forced attention to the problem of poverty. Besides temporary work relief, the New Deal inaugurated comprehensive social insurance and welfare programs for the nonworking poor and a minimum wage for the working poor. Although the two programs of social insurance and welfare programs totalled $132 billion in 1974, the payments were still not large enough nor coverage broad enough

[13]Robert J. Lampman, *Ends and Means of Reducing Income Poverty* (Chicago, Markham Publishing Co., 1971).

to solve the poverty problem. After World War II, the threat of possible unemployment resulted in passage of the Employment Act of 1946. Although this act did not go as far as some had wished in guaranteeing a job for all who desired one, it did create a Council of Economic Advisors to analyze the economy and offer suggestions for improvement. The Truman Administration, also, began a small, almost token, public housing program and covered the disabled under welfare. In the Eisenhower Administration, the disabled were covered for the first time under the social insurance program.

The 1960's saw a proliferation of programs to aid the poor. An aid to depressed areas program began in 1961. Training of the poor began on a small scale with this act and was later enlarged by many other programs. Vocational education was strengthened by the Vocational Education Act of 1963, and educational aid to the poor was enacted in the Elementary and Secondary School Act of 1965. The year 1964 saw both a new War on Poverty and civil rights legislation. In 1965, Medicare and Medicaid were adopted, and the 1968 Housing Act promised to eliminate all substandard housing in 10 years. Expenditures for all social welfare skyrocketed from $77 billion in 1965 to $242 billion in 1974. Part of the increases did not go to the poor. Lampman estimated that of the 1972 total public social welfare expenditures of $193 billion, only $25 billion was income-tested in a way so as to be confined to the poor. However, he cited an additional $35 billion of $80 billion cash transfers as going to the pre-transfer poor along with $32 billion of such non-cash services as education, health, veterans' services, housing, social services and food stamps.[14].

Although the official poverty statistics do not consider in-kind contributions, we concur with the view that the 23 million officially recorded as poor in 1973 lack substantially, some absolutely in lack of food and other necessities, and others relative to most of the rest of America.

Several problems still remain before poverty is solved in America. Clearly, those poor not able to work will need additional aid to bring them to poverty minimums. Similarly, the working poor, many of whom work full time, need a subsidy also if they are to climb from poverty. Improved income maintenance is required for both the nonworking and working poor.

In a Brookings Institute staff paper, Henry Aaron points out that a major problem with income maintenance programs is the notch problem.[15] If working incentives are written into the program, then the poor may receive larger incomes than the nonpoor. In order to provide equity for the nonpoor, subsidies will also have to be provided them. Such sub-

[14]Robert J. Lampman, "What Does It Do for the Poor? — A New Test for National Policy," *Public Interest*, No. 34 (Winter 1974), p. 70.
[15]Henry J. Aaron. *Why is Welfare So Hard to Reform?* (Washington, D.C., Brookings Institute, 1973).

sidies make maintenance programs exorbitantly expensive. On the other hand, wage subsidies approaching the minimum wage will still leave many with a below-poverty income.

Both Henry Aaron and Robert Lampman point out the problems associated with the multiplicity of programs now in existence. Lampman points out that a more adequate funding of in-kind benefits would be quite costly.[16] He cites possible benefits of $1,000 as the insurance value of Medicaid, a housing allowance of $1,000, a food stamp bonus of $1,300, a college scholarship worth $1,400, and a family assistance of $2,400 (under the Nixon Family Allowance Plan). The total comes to $7,100. A working man would have to earn substantially more than this amount to have an after-tax income of $7,100. He states that there are only a few ways out of this dilemma. Either the in-kind programs should be curtailed or be made applicable to more people. For example, under broadened applicability, medical care could be provided for all under a universal health insurance program.

During the past few years the rate of inflation has increased over that of most years previously. Those opposed to the welfare state lay a large share of the blame of the inflation on increased social welfare expenditures. Their prescription is to reduce social welfare expenditures so that inflation will be abated. Writing from a different viewpoint, liberal Swedish economist Gunnar Myrdal contends that the fundamental cause of the inflation is that people are not prepared to make sacrifices in their private consumption large enough to pay for the public expenditures they want made.[17] Instead of curtailing social welfare expenditures, Myrdal would prefer to curtail private consumption expenditures. Regardless of whether either or neither of the above viewpoints are espoused, there is no question that the present problem of inflation has made more difficult the solving of the poverty problem in the United States.

In spite of the difficult problems associated with eradicating poverty, the official statistics record a decided drop in the numbers living in poverty over the years. Whether further reduction in numbers will occur remains for determination in the future. Even if an income poverty level is reached, as measured by absolute minimum figures, the problem of gross inequalities in wealth and income may remain, along with possible racial discrimination and weaknesses in housing, health and education. All of these areas bear further study, action and improvement.

[16]Robert J. Lampman, *op. cit.*, pp. 66-82.

Bibliography

Gans, Herbert J., *More Equality* (New York, Pantheon Books, 1973).

Green, Christopher, *Negative Taxes and the Poverty Problem* (Washington, D.C., Brookings Institute, 1967).

Kaim-Caudle, P. R., *Comparative Social Policy and Social Security* (New York, The Dunellen Co., 1973).

Lampman, Robert J., *Ends and Means of Reducing Income Poverty* (Chicago, Markham Publishing Co., 1971).

Morgan, James N., *et al.*, *Five Thousand American Families* (Ann Arbor, University of Michigan, Survey Research Center, Institute for Social Research, 1974).

Theobald, Robert., ed., *The Guaranteed Income* (New York, Doubleday, 1966).

Turnbull, John G., *The Changing Faces of Economic Insecurity* (Minneapolis, University of Minnesota Press, 1966).

Bibliography

[References, faded and illegible]

GENERAL INDEX